GLOBAL BANKING

GLOBAL BANKING

Roy C. Smith
Ingo Walter

New York   Oxford
OXFORD UNIVERSITY PRESS
1997

Oxford University Press

Oxford   New York
Athens   Auckland   Bangkok   Bogota   Bombay
Buenos Aires   Calcutta   Cape Town   Dar es Salaam
Delhi   Florence   Hong Kong   Istanbul   Karachi
Kuala Lumpur   Madras   Madrid   Melbourne
Mexico City   Nairobi   Paris   Singapore
Taipei   Tokyo   Toronto

and associated companies in
Berlin   Ibadan

Library of Congress Cataloging-in-Publication Data
Smith, Roy C., 1938–
Global banking / Roy C. Smith and Ingo Walter.
p. cm.
Includes bibliographical references and index.
ISBN 0-19-509038-1
1. Banks and banking, International. 2. Capital market.
3. Competition, International. I. Walter, Ingo. II Title.
HG3881.S5434   1996
332.1′5—dc20   95-13440

2 4 6 8 9 7 5 3

Printed in the United States of America
on acid-free paper

Preface

Few sectors of the global economy equal banking and financial services in dynamism or structural change. When we began work on this project in the mid-1980s, transformation of the industry was already under way. Regulatory and technological changes were the main catalysts, making entrenched competitive structures obsolete and mandating the development of new products, new processes, new strategies, and new public policies toward the industry. This rapid evolution in one of the most important yet least understood international industries gave rise to our 1990 book on this subject.

Since that time developments have, if anything, accelerated. Financial centers, in vigorous competition with each other, have undergone further regulatory change in their efforts to capture a greater share of international trade in financial services, even as common efforts at the regional and global level have tried to support safety and soundness and a reasonably level competitive playing field. Banks and securities firms have had to devise and implement new strategies—sometimes leading events or (perhaps more often) responding to them—and the financial services industry has seen a wave of mergers, acquisitions, and strategic alliances in virtually all parts of the world. Severe recession in the early 1990s battered the industry in Europe and Japan, and to a lesser extent in the United States, even as cycles in interest rates, volatile exchange rates, and economic transformation in emerging markets contributed to a boom in capital markets and trading activity. Much of the conventional wisdom of the late 1980s, such as the dominance of Japanese banks in the global financial system, proved to be wrong just as, no doubt, much of today's conventional wisdom will lose meaning in an industry whose reconfiguration has some way to go.

In this book we attempt to assess this transformation process—its causes, its course, and its consequences. We begin with an overview of recent developments. We then consider in some detail the major dimensions of international commercial banking, including the issue of cross-border risk evaluation and exposure management and the creation of a viable regulatory framework in a global competitive context. We undertake a parallel assessment of international investment banking, linking the two by means of a "bridge" (chapter 7) consisting of the roots and branches of global financial intermediation. With respect to each area of global banking activity, whether loan syndication or merger and acquisition advisory work, we make an effort to identify the factors that appear to distinguish the winners from the losers. This is brought together in the final section of the book, which deals with problems of strategic positioning and execution.

The book is intended for two more or less distinct audiences. The first comprises banking and finance professionals and executives in nonfinancial firms who would like a "helicopter" view of developments in this industry that affect their vital interests either because they are in it or because they want to understand patterns of competition among vendors of financial services. The second comprises university courses, either at the advanced undergraduate or graduate level, and executive development programs in international banking and financial markets. Participants in such courses usually find it very helpful to understand both the structure and the dynamics of the global banking and securities industry as they prepare for or develop their professional careers.

We are grateful to colleagues at The Stern School of Business, New York University, and the Institut Superieur Européen d'Administration (INSEAD) who have provided valuable feedback on our 1990 book, *Global Financial Services*, and on various drafts of the manuscript for this book. The subject is complex and requires some slogging. This is certainly not a novel that's impossible to put down. But we think the reader will be well rewarded for the effort required to work through the discussion.

Finally, we are especially grateful to Ms. Gayle DeLong and Ms. Ann Rusolo at New York University and Ms. Isabel Schirmer at INSEAD, who helped immeasurably in preparing the manuscript for publication.

New York   R.C.S.
February 1996   I.W.

Contents

GLOBAL BANKING

1

The Continuous Restructuring of Global Financial Services

Financial people know in their bones that their profession goes back a long way. Its frequent association with "the oldest profession" may occur simply because it is almost as old. After all, the technology of finance is very basic, requiring little more than simple arithmetic and minimal literacy, and the environment in which it applies is universal—that is, any situation that involves money, property, or credit, all of which are commodities that have been in demand since humankind's earliest days.

These financial commodities have been put to use to facilitate trade, commerce, and business investment and to accommodate the accumulation, preservation, and distribution of wealth by states, corporations, and individuals. Financial transactions can occur in an almost infinite variety, yet they always require the services of banks, whether acting as principal or as agent, and financial markets in which they may operate.

Banks, too, therefore have a long history—a history rich in product diversity, international scope, and, above all, continuous change and adaptation. Generally, the latter have been required to adjust to changed economic and regulatory conditions, which have on many occasions been drastic. On such occasions banks have collapsed, only to be replaced by others eager to enter this traditionally dangerous but profitable business. New competitors have continually appeared on the scene, especially during periods of rapid economic growth, opportunity, and comparatively light governmental interference. Competitive changes have forced adaptations too, and in general have improved the level and efficiency of services banks offer to clients, thereby increasing transactional volume. The one constant in the long history of banking is, perhaps, the sight of new stars rising and old ones setting. Some of the older ones have been able to transform themselves into players capable of competing with the newly power-

3

ful houses, but many have not. Thus the banking industry has much natural familiarity with economic restructuring.

It is doubtful, however, that there has ever been a time in the long history of banking that the pace of restructuring has been greater than the present. Banking and securities markets during the 1980s and 1990s in particular have been affected by a convergence of several exceptionally powerful forces—deregulation and reregulation, rapidly increasing competition and disintermediation, product innovation and technology—all of which have occurred in a spiraling expansion of demand for financial services across the globe. Bankers today live in interesting, if exhausting and hazardous, times.

Before these are examined in detail in the body of this book, a brief look at where we have come from should be useful in orienting ourselves to the present.

The Legacies of Global Banking

History reveals that both bankers and credit were plentiful and active in the ancient world. The recorded legal history of several great civilizations started with elaborate regulation of credit, such as the Code of Hammurabi, about 1800 B.C.E., where the famous Babylonian set forth, among other laws, the maximum rate of interest for loans of grain ($33\frac{1}{3}$ percent) and of silver (20 percent).[1]

In the Ancient World

Maritime trade abounded in the Mediterranean, and was already highly developed by the Greeks and the Phoenicians in 1000 B.C.E. Such trade involved long-distance shipment of commodities that were not locally available. Wherever trade occurred there had to be a means of payment acceptable to both sides, often obtained only through the good offices of a bank represented in both countries acting as a foreign exchange or bill broker.

Banks also helped the merchants, shipowners, and, later, public officials manage their money—sometimes by accepting it on deposit, sometimes by investing it for them in precious metals, stones, or the financial assets of the day. One could make money on money long before Alexander the Great.

By the time of the second century C.E., the Romans, then at their peak, had reorganized everything. Their power in the Mediterranean was absolute, peace reigned along its shores, piracy had been eliminated, trade flourished, and coinage was available throughout the Empire. Bankers and financiers prospered. Will Durant described them as follows:

> One of the streets adjoining the forum became a banker's row, crowded with the shops of the moneylenders and money-changers. Money could

be borrowed on land, crops, securities, or government contracts, and for financing commercial enterprises or voyages. Cooperative lending took the place of [commercial] insurance; instead of one banker completely underwriting a venture, several joined in providing the funds. Joint-stock companies existed chiefly for the performance of government contracts . . . they raised their capital by selling their stocks or bonds to the public in the form of *partes* or *particulae*, i.e. "little parts," or "shares."[2]

Under other circumstances this financial and commercial infrastructure might have grown to produce large international banking and trading companies of the kind that exist today. However, this didn't happen in the Roman period, largely, it seems, because the state, focused as it was on conquest and strict control of its empire through efficient administration, reserved for itself the principal financial powers in the society. As the state was the principal holder of capital, it became the principal dispenser of it too, lending large sums to the public, no doubt accompanied by some degree of corruption. Perhaps to preserve this convenient arrangement the Roman senate did not permit limited liability companies to be formed, thus keeping the private wealth of the Empire where it could best be controlled, among individuals.

In any case, large banks and commercial houses never emerged in the Roman days, though banking transactions themselves were plentiful on a small scale. This may have proved to be a contributing cause in the decline of the Empire, which along with political deterioration suffered acute economic decay. In the third century much economic difficulty was experienced, including the "great crash" of 259—after the Emperor Valerian had been taken captive—when markets collapsed and there were runs on banks in various parts of the empire.[3]

During the following century Roman economic decline was irreversible. Money and gold bullion were leaving the Empire in a great payments drain (they ended up in the Near East and in India). The population was declining and barbarians had to be brought in to replenish the dwindling supply of workers. Wealth had become highly concentrated at the top, and the nouveau riche had been suppressed. Society's savings were dissipated in consumption, military conquests were no longer being undertaken to resupply the state with plunder and slaves, and the Empire itself was breaking into two parts, with most of the action taking place in the eastern capital, Constantinople. What was left of the smart money moved there.

After the Romans

The rest, sadly, we know, though one historian of the period, Harold Mattingly, a distinguished Cambridge University scholar and expert on Roman finance, makes a curious observation:

> The possibilities at the disposal of an all-powerful state are enormous, if it can [utilize] its resources in money, natural wealth and man-power. If the Roman State could have been administered by a syndicate of men of

modern capacity in banking and industry, there might have been rationalization on a magnificent scale. The State might have been able to meet all demands upon it and still have left its subjects to enjoy a very fair measure of prosperity. If it failed to realize all these possibilities, that will have been due to lack of knowledge as well as lack of interest.[4]

This thought brings to mind the Communist "empire" of our century, the collapse of which in the late 1980s might equally have been avoided if its rulers (like the Chinese) had understood free-market capitalism just a little bit better.

The Roman Empire collapsed in the fifth century. It was succeeded by the Byzantine Empire, which ruled in the eastern Mediterranean until the Arab conquests of the seventh century, which in turn diminished its scope and power.

In the western Mediterranean, absent the Romans, trade between the great ports and up the rivers leading into them was sporadic, again interrupted by pirates, and almost totally lacking in finance. After the Arab conquests, trade flourished but European trade did not. For all practical purposes it was in limbo for several hundred years. From the point of view of European bankers and financiers, these truly were the Dark Ages.

Where there was no trade, economic life collapsed back upon villages or counties. People consumed what they grew or raised or made, and no more. There were no surpluses beyond local needs, as there were neither markets to send them to nor any way to send them. No trade, no money, no finance—there was nothing to buy with money anyway. From this stagnant, landlocked condition the feudal system emerged, digging its roots deeply into European life.

Christian Capitalism

The Catholic Church appeared as a major social and economic force in Europe around this time. Founded when the brutality of the all-conquering Romans was at its peak, as an institution devoted to Christ's teaching of brotherly love and human equality before a single, caring, and redemptive God, the Church had profound influence in establishing the way people should live and treat each other. Naturally, people behaved much as before, but now they were told what was right and what was wrong according to a supreme being, and what would happen to them if they offended God and were not subsequently forgiven.

Christ was not just a prophet, the Church declared, he was the son of God, and therefore an extremely authoritative source for these new teachings, which instructed humankind in God's will. According to the teachings, everyone was a sinner, but sinners could be forgiven. People were supposed to treat their neighbors kindly, not to take advantage of them or climb over them on their way up. These teachings, as further interpreted by holy men over the years, came to establish the standards of Christian morality, of good and evil, of right and wrong in everyday life. How one had lived one's life would be judged at its end, and rewarded either in heaven or in hell. It was a powerful notion because of the hope it contained, especially for a future life better than the miserable one that most people then lived, and it spread throughout Europe.

The teachings of the medieval Church began with the idea that everyone should know his or her place and not unduly strive to improve it at the expense of others. Peasants should be happy enough as peasants. Upward mobility was not encouraged. One's future would be secure in the next life if one served God and trusted completely in Him. Kings, and their associated nobles, were those designated by God (through divine right) to rule. They should be obeyed and not interfered with (or revolted against).

The late Barbara Tuchman, in her fascinating report on the catastrophic fourteenth century—when a great famine, the Black Death, and the Hundred Years' War all fell in one century—notes that the Christian attitude toward commerce during the Middle Ages was "actively antagonistic":

> It held that money was evil, business was evil, that profit beyond a minimum necessary to keep the dealer alive was avarice (a sin), that to make money from the lending of money was usury (also a sin), and buying at wholesale and selling at retail was immoral and condemned by canon law. In short, as St. Jerome said: "A man who is a merchant can seldom, if ever, please God." [5]

Thus business people, merchants, and bankers were not only conceived in original sin, they were made to live in it daily, or otherwise be prohibited from just about everything that an ambitious person trying to get ahead might think to do.

However, as Tuchman also points out: "As restraint of initiative, this was the direct opposite of capitalist enterprise. It was the denial of economic man, and consequently even more routinely violated than the denial of sensual man.

The ways of humans, and those of heaven, were in stark opposition to one another. Violations would occur, naturally, but these would have to be atoned for, thus resulting in the enormous accumulation of wealth and financial power in the Church itself.

This took some time to happen, however. While Western Europe suffered the dismal period in the years from 500 to 1000 the conflict was moot, there being very little commerce to tempt people into sin. However, the Vikings began voyages in the eighth century, and for two hundred or three hundred years sailed and rowed their way up the rivers and into the lakes and seas of Europe, replanting the seeds of commerce and trade in their fearsome wake. After a while it became easier and much more profitable to trade with their counterparts than to slaughter them, and economic life in the north and west of Europe was reborn. At about the same time, Venice emerged as a principal entrepôt of trade and finance within southern Europe and between Europe and the Arab and Asian worlds.

By the beginning of the twelfth century the Crusades had begun; these military-religious expeditions were sent into the Holy Land of Palestine to reclaim Jerusalem for Christian society. Although they were never successful, these expeditions lasted two hundred years. They were guided by the religious order of the Knights of the Holy Temple of Jerusalem (called Knights Templar), which collected vast sums of money and property from well-to-do supporters in Europe. The Knights invested the money, making loans and buying and selling property throughout the Middle East. They evolved into possibly the first full-fledged modern bankers through careful development of their unique franchise.

Upward Mobility in the Middle Ages

With the rekindling of trade, of course, came opportunity for those seeking it—often, no doubt, those on the bottom rungs of society as it was then inflexibly cast.

A French historian of the Middle Ages, Henri Pirenne, repeats the story of one St. Godric of Finchale as an example of the way the nouveau riche were formed in the latter part of the eleventh century. Godric was born of poor peasant stock in Lincolnshire, and was forced, no doubt, to leave his parents' meager holdings to make his own way. He became a beachcomber, looking for wrecks, which were numerous at the time. Finding one, he put together a peddler's pack and set out on the road, where in due course he fell in with a band of "merchants" (possibly bandits). In time he amassed enough money to form a partnership with others, owning a ship engaged in coastal trade, which subsequently branched out into long-distance trade, merchanting, and banking. He became very rich, subsequently made his peace with God, and became a saint, no doubt leaving much of his fortune to the Church. Pirenne is emphatic that there were many Godrics operating at the time in Europe, though few among them were saints. They emerged as the bourgeoisie, and the commercial rebirth of Europe was soon an accomplished fact.

By the late twelfth century, business schools were in operation for those seeking a career in commerce to learn basic reading, bookkeeping, and arithmetic. By the thirteenth century, banking and finance had become quite sophisticated. Great textile factories were established in Flanders, furnished with wool from Britain and flax from Egypt, and the cloth was sold all over Europe with financing provided by expatriate Italian bankers speaking French. By the fourteenth century long-term credits were available, offered by merchants seeking to place their excess cash, or by bankers acting on their behalf.

Public authorities and noblemen were also borrowers as, for example, when they needed to buy grain during a famine or to outfit a regiment to be sent off to the Crusades. It became easier to borrow from moneylenders than to send one's plate to the mint.

The Italian Era

By the fifteenth century the mighty house of Medici reigned supreme in Italy, with its various branches throughout Europe acting as bankers, merchants in wool and cloth, dealers in spices and silks, goldsmiths, shipowners, deposit takers, and foreign exchange brokers. The influence of the Medicis and other houses like them reached into the papacy and the Church, and to princes and noble families all over the continent.

By this time the modus operandi of relations between merchants and the Church was reasonably well fixed, if complicated. To redeem his soul, the merchant would make contributions to the Church and its charitable works and alms houses, perhaps leaving a substantial part of his fortune to the Church upon his death. He would also suffer, as an ordinary cost of doing business, numerous fines and other charges for violating religious laws restricting commerce. He could purchase benefices or indulgences from the Church to expunge his guilt; before long literally hundreds of such benefices were offered for sale by the Church. He might also, as a lowly member of the bourgeoisie, have to renounce high social position in his community, though it is unlikely that Lorenzo de Medici ever did so.

On the other hand, having done these things to the extent required, he would be left alone to grow as rich as he was able, to likewise ascend in society and to leave most of his fortune to his heirs. It was a delicate balance perhaps, but one that was efficient for both the Church and the emerging middle classes. Each became mutually supportive of the other, despite the unbridgeable chasm of their intellectual and spiritual positions, and each prospered.[6]

The more developed Italian banking became during the Renaissance, the more it was exposed to the great risks of the times, mainly shifts in political and religious power and influence. These were in constant turmoil during the sixteenth century, and even the Medicis couldn't last. They were succeeded in the world of merchants, after the Reformation, by German and Swiss protestant bankers, many of whom developed ties in Britain, Holland, and France. The modern era developed in which commercialism and finance were substantially freed of the stern admonitions of the Church.

Financial Markets Appear

The Dutch moved especially quickly, and had set up organized markets for trading in financial instruments by 1602. The Amsterdam Stock Exchange followed in 1611, on which trading and speculation in securities of all types developed rapidly. The "tulip mania," in which the prices of bulbs temporarily reached extraordinary levels (one traded as high as £20,000), came in 1636. The Amsterdam market permitted various forms of short selling, puts and calls, and futures transactions in many different commodities (tulip bulbs being one) and securities, including shares of the dominant and prosperous Dutch East India Company. Insider trading was first made an illegal practice in Amsterdam in the seventeenth century. The shrewd and profit-minded Dutch traders knew that insider trading was not in fact a victimless crime.[7]

By the beginning of the eighteenth century trading in bills of exchange and other financial instruments, including shares of a limited number of corporations, took place daily in the City of London in an area called Exchange Alley. This was the scene in 1720 of the "Great South Sea Bubble," in which thousands of British investors developed a mania for shares of a new company that would have monopoly rights to trade off the east coast of South America, the prospects for which were never much better than dim. Many people bought their shares on margin, an early example of financial leverage at work. The bubble burst, of course.

British Capitalism

During the latter part of the eighteenth century the American and the French revolutions had occurred, changing forever the way ordinary people would think about their lives, and how much they would come to value the freedom to take one's own chances and venture one's own capital on a better, more prosperous future. Also at this time Adam Smith's influential work, *The Wealth of Nations,* appeared and helped to ensure nearly a hundred years of prosperous laissez-faire economic policy in Great Britain.

Britain's defeat of Napoleon at the battle of Waterloo in 1814 set the stage for nearly a century of economic dominance. It also was the occasion for the House of Rothschild to rise from obscurity to supreme prominence from the great killing it made in the market by getting the jump on the outcome of the battle and the defeat of Napoleon, and then wrong-footing everybody else on the Exchange by at first selling, then buying large amounts of British paper. The Rothschilds had earlier amassed a smaller fortune in buying and selling commercial bills from both sides during the war. Neither of their activities was illegal or considered improper at the time, though both would be condemned today.

With the end of the Napoleonic era came a great era of capitalism, nourished by the industrial revolution and the ascendancy of "the people" in Europe and America. The result has been that since 1800, the general growth in the economic well-being of those people affected has been several times that which had been experienced over the entire four thousand years that preceded it. Indeed, in those areas of the world still ruled by conquerors or by religious groups, not much general improvement has been experienced. And in those areas where old regimes have been toppled by peoples' (i.e., communist) revolutions and capitalism was stamped out, some, but far less, growth has occurred, a fact that has become painfully obvious in recent years.

The Roots of Modern Banking

Our modern economic and financial heritage, then, begins with the coming of democratic capitalism, around the time of Adam Smith. Under this system the state does not prevent or discourage anyone willing to work hard enough, and who also has access to capital, from becoming a capitalist himself.

A hundred years after Adam Smith, England was at the peak of its power. Politically, it ruled 25 percent of the Earth's surface and people. The British economy was by far the strongest and most developed in the world. Its competitors were still partly asleep. France was still sorting itself out after a century of political chaos and a war with Prussia that had gone wrong. Germany was just starting to come together politically, but still had quite a way to go to catch up with the British in industrial terms. The rest of Europe was not all that important. There was a potentially serious problem, however, from reckless, often irresponsible, competition from America, which fancied itself a rising economic power, but otherwise the horizon was comparatively free of competitors. British industry and British finance were very secure in their respective positions of world leadership.

English financial markets had made it all possible, according to Walter Bagehot, the editor at the time of *The Economist*, who published a small book in 1873 called *Lombard Street* that described these markets and what made them tick. England's economic glory, he suggested, was based on the supply and accessibility of capital. After all, he pointed out, what would have been the good of inventing a railroad back in Elizabethan times if there was no way to raise the capital to build it? In poor countries there were no financial resources anyway, and in most European countries money stuck to the aristocrats and the landowners and was unavailable to the market. But in England, Bagehot boasted, there was a place in the City of London—called Lombard Street—where "in all but the rarest of times, money can be always obtained upon good security, or upon decent prospects of probable gain." Such a market, Bagehot continued, is a "luxury which no country has ever enjoyed with even comparable equality before."

However, the real power in the market, Bagehot went on to suggest, is its ability to offer the benefits of leverage to those working their way up in the system, whose goal is to displace those at the top. "In every district," Bagehot explained, "small traders have arisen who discount their bills largely, and with the capital so borrowed, harass and press upon, if they do not eradicate, the old capitalist." The new trader has "obviously an immense advantage in the struggle of trade:"

> If a merchant have £50,000 all his own, to gain 10 percent on it he must make £5,000 a year, and must charge for his goods accordingly; but if another has only £10,000 and borrows £40,000 by discounts (no extreme instance in our modern trade), he has the same capital of £50,000 to use, and can sell much cheaper. If the rate at which he borrows be 5 percent,

he will have to pay £2,000 a year [in interest]; and if, like the old trader he makes £5,000 a year, he will still, after paying his interest, obtain £3,000 a year, or 30 percent on his own £10,000. As most merchants are content with much less than 30 percent, he will be able, if he wishes, to forego some of that profit, lower the price of the commodity, and drive the old-fashioned trader—the man who trades on his own capital—out of the market.

Thus, the ambitious "new man," with little to lose and access to credit through the market, can earn a greater return on his money than a risk-averse capitalist who borrows little or nothing. The higher return enables the new man to undercut the other man's prices and take business from him. True, the new man may lose on the venture and be taken out of the game, but there is always another new man on his way up who is eager to replace him. As the richer man has a lot to lose, he risks it less, and thus is always in the game, continually defending himself against one newcomer or another until finally he packs it in, retires to the country, and invests in government securities instead.

"This increasingly democratic structure of English commerce," Bage-hot continued, "is very unpopular in many quarters." On one hand, he says, "it prevents the long duration of great families of merchant princes . . . who are pushed out by the dirty crowd of little men."

> On the other hand, these unattractive democratic defects are compensated for by one great excellence: no other country was ever so little "sleepy", no other was ever so prompt to seize new advantages. A country depen-dent mainly on great "merchant princes" will never be so prompt; there commerce perpetually slips more and more into a commerce of routine. A man of large wealth, however intelligent, always thinks, "I have a great income, and I want to keep it. If things go on as they are, I shall keep it, but if they change I *may* not keep it." Consequently he considers every change of circumstance a bore, and thinks of such changes as little as he can. But a new man, who has his way to make in the world, knows that such changes are his opportunities; he is always on the lookout for them, and always heeds them when he finds them. The rough and vulgar struc-ture of English commerce is the secret of its life. . . .[8]

In 1902, a young American new man named Bernard Baruch took Bagehot's essay to heart and made himself the first of many millions in a Wall Street investment pool, buying control of a railroad on borrowed money.[9] The United States had come of age financially around the turn of the century, and Wall Street would soon displace Lombard Street as the world's center of finance.

The Rise of the Americans

Early in the century, J. P. Morgan organized United States Steel Corpora-tion, having acquired Carnegie Steel and other companies in a transaction valued at $1.5 billion, an amount worth perhaps $20 billion today. This was the largest financial deal ever done (until the RJR-Nabisco transaction in 1989) and it occurred in 1902 during the first of four merger booms to take place in the United States. Each of these booms was powered by different factors, but in each, rising stock markets and easy access to credit were major contributors.

By the early 1900s New York was beginning to emerge as the world's leading financial center. True, many American companies still raised capital by selling their securities to investors in Europe, but they also sold them to American investors. These investors, looking for places to put their newly acquired wealth, also bought European securities, perhaps thinking they were safer and more reliable investments than those of American companies. By the early years of the twentieth century European issues in the New York market were commonplace. This activity proved especially beneficial when World War I came—both sides in the conflict sought funds from the United States, although the Allied Powers raised by far the larger amounts.

After the war, American prosperity continued while Europe's did not. Banks had a busy time, raising money for corporations, foreign governments, and investment companies and making large loans to investors buying securities. Banks were by then "universal," that is, they were free to participate in commercial banking (lending) and investment banking, which at the time meant the underwriting, distribution, and trading of securities in financial markets. Many of the larger banks were also involved in a substantial amount of international business. There was trade to finance all over the world, especially in such mineral-rich areas as Latin America and Australia. There were securities new issues (underwritings) to perform for foreign clients, which in the years before the 1929 crash aggregated around 25 percent of all business done. There were correspondent banking and custodial (safekeeping) relationships with overseas counterparts, and a variety of financial services to perform for individuals, with respect to both foreigners doing business in the United States and the activities of Americans abroad.

The stock market crash in 1929 was a global event—markets crashed everywhere all at the same time, and the volume of foreign selling orders was high. The Great Depression followed, and the banks were blamed for it, although the evidence has never been strong to connect the speculative activities of the banks during the 1920s with either the crash or the subsequent depression of the 1930s. Nonetheless there were three prominent results from these events that had great effect on American banking. The first was the passage of the Banking Act of 1933 that provided for the Federal Deposit Insurance system and the Glass–Steagall provisions of the Banking Act, which completely separated commercial banking and securities activities. Second was the depression itself, which led in the end to World War II and a 30-year period of banking being confined to basic, slow-growing deposit taking and loan making within a limited local market. And third was the rising importance of the government in deciding financial matters, especially during the postwar recovery period. There was little for banks or securities firms to do until the late 1950s and early 1960s.

By then, international business had resumed its rigorous expansion and U.S. banks, following the lead of First National City Bank (now Citicorp), resumed their activities abroad. The successful recovery of the economies of Western Europe and Japan led to pressures on the fixed-rate foreign exchange system set up after the war. The Eurodollar market followed, then the Eurobond market and the reattraction of banks and investment banks to international capital market transactions.

Global Banking Emerges

Next came the 1971 collapse of the fixed exchange rate system in which the dollar was tied to gold. Floating exchange rates set by the market replaced this system, obviating the need for government capital controls. In turn this led to widespread removal of restrictions on capital flows between countries, and the beginnings of the global financial system that we have today.

This system, which is based on markets setting prices and determining the flow of capital around the world, has drawn in many new players—both users and providers of banking and capital market services. Competition among these players for funds, and the business of providing them, has greatly increased the stakes of individual institutions and indeed the risks of the banking and securities businesses.

The effects of competitive capitalism have been seen and appreciated during the past decade as they have not been since 1929. The 1980s witnessed further rounds of deregulation and privatization of government-owned enterprises, indicating that governments of the industrial countries around the world have found private-sector solutions to problems of economic growth and development preferable to state-operated socialist programs. Thus there have been radical changes in Europe, where massive deregulation of financial markets in the United Kingdom and several other countries has occurred, and where the Single-Market and Economic and Monetary Union initiatives of the European Union (EU) promise similar effects on European business and finance. Deregulation in Japan has freed vast sums of capital to seek investment overseas and to create an active global securities market in Tokyo.

Most financial businesses are now effectively global. Banking and capital market services have proliferated, and numerous new competitors have emerged on the scene—many of which are not banks at all. Indeed some, like General Electric Capital Services (GECS), are customers of banks. New regulations are constantly being introduced and old ones changed. Telecommunications provides an ease of access to information that separated banks from their clients, pushing much of today's business into trading markets in which advice and service are less valuable than the latest quotation posted by securities and foreign exchange traders. It is a time of great and widespread change, affecting everyone. It is a time of massive restructuring for all financial service firms.

This book attempts to wade into the chaos and confusion of today's global banking and capital market environment and strip out the central parts of it, so that each can be examined separately. The purpose is to gain a better understanding of the evolution of international banking and finance, the services represented in today's market, the competitive processes involved, and the impact these have on prominent public policy issues. By treating the services of commercial banks and investment banks separately we are not acknowledging that these are or should be separated—we are simply using a traditional distinction for examining what these services are and how competition works in each.

Evolving Competitive Strategies

Our main emphasis is on the issues of formulation, implementation, and evaluation of competitive strategies (that is, strategies that succeed because they are ultimately shown to be competitive) of banks and capital market institutions. Each financial services business will have to reformulate its own global competitive strategy over the coming years. There is no single strategy that will work for all. Indeed, there are so many different types of firms, from different countries and possessing different strengths and weaknesses, that an enormous variety of different strategies is likely to result. Our effort in this book is aimed at making clear the process of strategic determination in this period of enormous change, with its inescapable requirement for rethinking how individual business fits into the totality of global finance—rending that process more understandable to students of the subject and to practitioners.

Notes

1. Sidney Homer, *A History of Interest Rates,* 2 ed. New Brunswick, N.J.: Rutgers University Press, 1977, p. 5.

2. Will Durant, *Caesar and Christ.* New York: Simon & Schuster, 1948, pp. 79–80.

3. Harold Mattingly, *Roman Imperial Civilization.* Garden City, N.Y.: Doubleday Anchor Books, 1957, pp. 225–47.

4. Ibid., p. 241.

5. Barbara W. Tuchman, *A Distant Mirror.* New York: Alfred A. Knopf, 1978, pp. 37–38.

6. Henry Pirenne, *Economic and Social History of Medieval Europe.* London: Routledge & Kegan Paul, 1936, pp. 47–168.

7. Joseph de la Vega, *Confusions de Confusiones* (1688), reprinted in *Publications Number 13* of the Kress Library of Business and Economics, Harvard Business School, 1957; from E. C. Bursk et al. (eds.), *The World of Business*, Vol. 2. New York: Simon & Schuster, 1962, pp. 794–97.

8. Walter Bagehot, *Lombard Street, A Description of the Money Market*. London: Henry S. King, 1873, pp. 1–20.

9. Bernard M. Baruch, *Baruch: My Own Story*. New York: Henry Holt, 1957, pp. 165–76.

I

INTERNATIONAL COMMERCIAL BANKING

2

International Commercial Lending

International lending has changed dramatically over the years. Major, highly rated corporations, public-sector enterprises, and governments have largely migrated to the capital markets, where their own securities command terms that are competitive (and often superior) to those banks can provide. This has largely supplanted straight bank-to-client lending, and even smaller and less highly rated borrowers have found it possible to tap the capital markets using various kinds of credit and liquidity backstops and asset-backed structures. And as a result of the less-developed country (LDC) debt crisis of the 1980s, a major class of sovereign borrowers disappeared—borrowers for whom the capital markets have traditionally been closed—with the exception of forced loan rescheduling and new-money packages in the 1980s as the debt crisis wore on, and some renewed interest in banking lending to LDCs (emerging market borrowers) more recently.

Nevertheless, international bank lending continues as an important part of global financial markets. In times of financial instability, the capital markets tend to shrink and in some cases even disappear as viable sources of finance, and borrowers flock back to the banks. Many creditworthy corporate borrowers, for example, maintain sizable bank lines even in the best of times, partly to make sure the banks are there when and if they are needed. And for certain kinds of financings, such as short-term lending to finance merger, acquisition, and leveraged buyout transactions, as well as longer-term lending on project financings, there are no good substitutes for traditional bank loans. This may be because the borrower cannot be sure precisely when the funds will be required or when they can be repaid out of the proceeds of stock or bond issues or asset sales, or because the transaction is likely to encounter significant and unanticipated developments over its life that requires a form of financing where the added flexibility is worth more than the added cost. Bank lending provides one of the few alternatives for close borrower-lender contact and monitoring, and therefore maintains significant advantages in contracting and information costs.

Commercial Lending Facilities

There are various ways to classify international bank lending to corporate, government, and other types of borrowers.

First, a bank may *lend to local clients out of branches or affiliates* in foreign countries in which it operates, funded by local-currency deposits or by local money-market borrowings. This is purely local business, competing mainly with local banks. Foreign-based banks normally have to compete purely on price or by focusing on a specific market niche—special industry expertise, for example. Foreign banks lending in local markets may also focus on affiliates of multinational companies based in their own home countries, or on financing international trade transactions. It nevertheless remains essentially "domestic lending abroad," and the only thing international about it is the transfer of product or credit know-how, or client relationships, from the parent organization or from affiliates in third countries.

Second, a bank may undertake *direct cross-border lending to clients located in another country.* Such loans appear to be relatively minor in importance. They focus on special kinds of transactions as part of close bank relationships to particular clients, including foreign affiliates of multinationals; as part of workouts of earlier troubled loans; or as part of international private banking relationships (see chapter 7). In many cases such loans take the form of syndicated Eurocurrency facilities (discussed below).

Lending facilities, whether direct or syndicated, can take a number of forms. There are "revolving credit agreements" (called "revolvers"), which permit clients to borrow, on demand, up to a certain maximum amount over an agreed period under an agreed interest formula. In return the bank earns a commitment fee for standing ready to lend, whether or not such lending actually occurs. These are usually "committed facilities," and the commitment is legally enforceable and covered by appropriate legal documentation. Committed facilities require the same kind of careful credit analysis as actual loans, especially since, for some clients, committed facilities will be taken down only when capital market financing is unavailable or more expensive. Such facilities often take the form of "backstop lines," which rating agencies like Moody's and Standard & Poor's require issuers of commercial paper to have in place in order to assure investors that the liquidity will be there when the paper matures. Borrowers may also arrange for "uncommitted facilities," which are not legally enforceable and hence involve lower fees. Clients may find these attractive because of the lower cost if they believe there is little likelihood of difficulty in accessing financial markets in the foreseeable future.

In the course of ordinary credit relationships with clients, banks will have in place limits on the amount of lending exposure they are willing to incur, sometimes called "undisclosed, unadvised guidance lines," which may be increased or decreased at the bank's own discretion on the basis of changing circumstances.

Whether committed or uncommitted, international commercial lending facilities may be associated with a range of other banking products, especially those involving interest-rate or exchange-rate protection. Examples include "forward-rate agreements" (FRAs), which permit a client to lock in an interest rate today for a loan to be taken at some future date; interest-rate caps or collars; and currency swaps, as discussed in chapter 10. The bank, in turn, will hedge these transactions in the market and keep whatever spreads or fees it is able to earn on these collateral services.

Bank Financing of Foreign Governments and Government Entities

Lending to units of foreign governments took on major importance in the 1970s. The reasons include:

- The rapid growth of balance-of-payments financing needs on the part of national governments, particularly after 1973
- The use of government agencies as intermediaries to secure external financing for a wide variety of borrowers domestically
- Major borrowing needs on the part of governmental and quasi-governmental entities like power authorities, sewage systems, trading companies, airlines, and shipping companies and the like, both at the national and state-local level
- Active participation of governments as owners of manufacturing and trading companies, as well as financial houses and banks
- The growing use of government guarantees to facilitate foreign borrowing on behalf of private ventures

Sovereign lending collapsed after the debt crisis in the early 1980s and the migration of Organization for Economic Cooperation and Development (OECD) government entities to the global bond markets, but has revived gradually in the 1990s.

Government borrowing abroad may be undertaken by a national entity charged with managing the country's external finance, for example, its central bank, monetary authority, ministry of finance, or similar institution. It may also be undertaken by other government-owned authorities or corporations, often called *parastatals*, although such external borrowing usually must have the approval of a coordinating agency such as the central bank.

Balance-of-payments borrowing is undertaken by countries with current-account payments deficits that are not offset by private capital inflows, resulting in a balance-of-payments deficit. The proceeds of external borrowing by the country's monetary agency are often used to intervene in foreign exchange markets to support the external value of the national currency, the exchange rate. Balance-of-payments borrowings may be *seasonal* or *cyclical,* in response to periodic underlying variations in export receipts and import disbursements or capital flows, or they may be *structural* due to an essentially permanent shock (e.g., a major drop in export prices) to which it will take time to adjust. Such borrowings may also be *chronic* as a result of a more or less permanent excess of domestic absorption over production, capital flight due to lack of confidence in the country's future, and similar factors.

Seasonal and cyclical balance-of-payments borrowing is essentially self-correcting and finds its everyday parallels in corporate working-capital borrowing and personal finance. To the extent that such needs cannot be handled from a country's own reserves, short-term borrowings under bank credit lines, reviewed periodically, may be an alternative method of handling. Structural balance-of-payments borrowing is designed to ease the pain of adjustment to new economic realities and can also be fully justified provided the necessary adjustment actually comes about within an acceptable time frame. This is not the case with a country essentially living beyond its means and engaging in chronic external borrowing, its government unable or unwilling to take the steps needed to restore balance via domestic macroeconomic or exchange rate policies, ultimately heading for a rough landing for debtors and creditors alike.

Fiscal borrowing concerns external financing to cover budgetary deficits, and is linked directly to the balance of payments and its financing. In many cases fiscal borrowing involves short-term loans made in anticipation of government receipts, and therefore it tends to be self-liquidating.

Development borrowing involves the financing of infrastructure projects—schools, hospitals, roads, railways, airports, port facilities, communication networks, power grids, sewer systems, public housing, and a variety of others. Some projects are direct producers of foreign exchange (generating exports or saving on imports), while others are not, as discussed in chapter 3. As distinct from development *project* lending, *program* lending may involve literacy training or vocational education, for example, with potentially far-reaching domestic and international consequences that are usually extremely difficult to forecast.

Loan Syndication

As noted, most major international lending facilities are *syndicated.* In simple form, a syndicated credit facility involves the combined activities of a number of banks in the assembly of a relatively large loan to a single borrower under the direction of one or several banks serving as lead managers.

The borrower has the advantage, under such an arrangement, of being able to raise a larger sum than any single bank would be willing to lend, at substantially lower cost and more efficiently than the same amount of borrowing from multiple sources on its own. Moreover, the borrower enters the market fewer times and thus may improve its future access to financing in less jeopardy. Borrower "visibility" is enhanced by major syndications involving a large group of banks, possibly making future financings easier.

The lenders have the advantage of:

• Better diversification of their asset portfolios
• Participation in lending they might not otherwise have access to
• Cooperation with multiple banks (often home based in a number of different countries) having greater collective expertise and information than any single bank
• Reduced risk of borrower default due to the enhanced penalties of such action in terms of limited future access of the borrower to financial markets
• Certain legal protection inherent in syndicated loan agreements

Banks also find participation in a variety of syndicated loans an efficient way to obtain necessary expertise, market exposure, and visibility without incurring unacceptable financial exposure.

Essentially, international syndicated loan facilities represent a cross between debt underwriting and traditional commercial bank lending. They open medium-term financing opportunities to many borrowers who might not otherwise be able to obtain credit on comparable terms through the international or domestic securities markets, private placements, and other financial vehicles.

Historically, international syndications of medium-term credit facilities began in the late 1960s, when changes in interest-rate levels and volatility increased the attractiveness of major financings on floating-rate terms, as opposed to fixed-rate bond issues, and borrowers' needs outstripped the lending capabilities of individual banks. Their antecedents include the long-standing practice of multibank term lending to corporate customers in the United States, priced at or above the domestic prime lending rate. During the 1970s and 1980s, somewhat over half of all medium- and long-term borrowings in international capital markets, well over 80 percent of such borrowings by developing countries, and almost all such borrowings by centrally planned economies were in the form of syndicated loans. While LDC lending and project financings took up the bulk of syndications in the 1970s, mergers and acquisitions (M&A) and leveraged buyout (LBO) syndications took their place in the latter part of the 1980s. Both continue at far lower levels in the 1990s.

The geographic center for syndicated lending has always been the City of London. Much smaller centers have developed to service the Asian markets in Hong Kong and Singapore. New York has played a relatively minor role. The actual booking of syndicated loan participations is done as well in the various offshore banking centers like Luxembourg.

The Syndication Process

Borrower contact—with a national government agency, an electric power authority seeking to finance a significant capacity expansion, a corporation seeking a standby facility for a major acquisition, perhaps a national development bank intending to take up a large sum internationally which it will then on-lend in smaller amounts to domestic enterprises, or anyone else—is maintained routinely by lending officers of major international banks. The better the "relationship" between the bank and the potential borrower, the better the bank's information about the client's evolving financing needs and the greater its chances of playing a significant role in meeting those needs.

In seeking syndication business, banks rely on:

- their own branches, representative offices, or other affiliates maintaining contact with the prospective borrower
- referrals from other units of the bank, or referrals through established corporate and other client relationships
- referrals from other banks anxious to render a service to their own clients, yet not in a position to take leadership position themselves, with whom good relations have been maintained
- direct solicitations from potential borrowers or, in the event of joint lead-managed syndications, other banks
- approaches by investment banks acting as advisers to borrowers, one of whose functions is to facilitate capital-market access through introductions to a competent bank active in loan syndication

Knowing the borrower and conditions in international lending markets, a prospective *lead bank* will carefully draw up a proposal to arrange the loan, thereby seeking a *syndication mandate*. The proposal will specify pricing, terms, fees, and other pertinent aspects of the loan and will indicate whether the syndication will be *fully committed*. If so, the bank will undertake to provide the full amount of the loan to the borrower according to the terms of the mandate, whether or not it is successful in its efforts to interest other banks in participating in the loan. If the syndication is *partially committed*, the bank will guarantee to deliver part of the loan, with the remainder contingent on market reaction to the loan. In a *best-efforts syndication* the borrower will obtain the funds needed only if sufficient interest and participation can be generated among potential participating lenders by the good-faith efforts of the bank seeking the mandate.

By this time, or shortly thereafter, the bank may have brought in one or more co-lead managers to help with the syndication and share in the underwriting commitment, especially if the amount to be raised is very large or the deal is rather complex. Generally, the larger the loan, the larger tends to be the management group involved, including several *lead managers, managers,* and *co-managers,* each group accepting a different share of the underwriting responsibility, and several "brackets" of *participants,* whose role is usually confined to supplying funds.

The terms of the formal letter seeking the mandate will follow extensive discussions with the borrower and will be carefully tailored to its needs as well as market conditions. It will have to be fully competitive with other banks going after the same mandate. The mandate letter will also specify *exclusivity* of the mandate, and repeatedly note the leading roles the mandated bank is to perform in the syndication.

There are a variety of negotiable trade-offs, as between the tenor and size of the loan, drawdown schedule, grace period, amortization schedule, spread, fees, tax issues, borrower information, and legal covenants. In seeking a mandate, the prospective lead bank must strike a balance between what the borrower wants and what the market can live with, that is, what will result in a successful syndication—always keeping a watchful eye on what competitors may propose. Sophisticated borrowers will often accept "second best" proposals from highly responsible and prestigious lead banks over more "imaginative" or lower-cost proposals from aggressive competitors if they feel that this will better serve their long-term standing in the market. Still, the tolerance for less than fully competitive bids is generally very low.

If the borrower decides to go ahead with the syndication, the mandate will be awarded to one of the competing banks or to joint bidders, who then become lead manager(s) of the syndicate. Suppose a single bank has won a mandate on a $100 million fully committed syndication, and the lead bank wishes to keep $15 million of this in its own portfolio—its *target take*. It will then have to find a way to *sell down* the remaining $85 million to other banks. To do so it will have to develop a *syndication strategy* that will successfully raise the required sum yet call for minimum sharing of the management fee that will be paid or of the visibility the bank attracts for putting the loan together. Several other banks may have to be asked to manage or co-manage the loan jointly, however, and thus be allocated a portion of the total funds to be raised. Part of these funds they will take into their own portfolios in turn and the rest they will sell down to other syndicate participants, in return for a share of the management fee.

The lead bank is generally expected to take a share in the loan that is at least as large as that of any other lender. The management group (lead manager(s), managers, and co-managers) may retain as much as 50 to 70 percent of the total loan for their own portfolios.

The syndicate will be put together by the lead manager and the management group who will send offering faxes to banks around the world followed up quickly with elaborate written documentation and personal discussions.

Deciding which banks to invite into the syndicate is a major part of a lead bank's task and will help determine its strategy. It must be able to judge the invitees' country and industry exposures, past client relationships, degree of sophistication in syndicated lending (especially in complex deals), its own relationships with invitees, and similar factors that will determine individual banks' receptivity to the deal. In some cases the borrower will express a preference as to which banks should (and should not) be invited to participate. Contacting 200 or 300 banks to obtain twenty or thirty ultimate participants is not unusual. Banks invited to participate will usually decline, accept, or request further information on the basis of the offering fax, and careful track will be kept of the responses by the lead manager or management group.

If there are several lead managers, one of them is assigned to keep track of responses from each of the banks that have been approached. This can be rather complex when several hundred banks in a variety of countries are involved, with responsibility for contacting them divided among members of the management team.

Meanwhile, the lead manager will work on preparation of an *information memorandum*, in which the borrower will disclose financial and economic—and sometimes historical and political—facts pertinent to current and projected creditworthiness. This, together with a *term sheet* restating the conditions of the loan, will be sent to interested banks and carefully prefaced by an emphatic disclaimer of all responsibility for its content on the part of the lead manager. A disclaimer is necessary to avoid possible legal liability in case of default or other problems with the loan that may arise later. The information memorandum, although prepared by the borrower, will be carefully checked for accuracy and completeness by the lead bank(s).

If things go well, the loan will be fully subscribed. If it is oversubscribed, participations will either be *prorated* among the interested banks, or occasionally the total amount of the loan will be increased at the option of the borrower. In the latter case, however, prospective syndicate members may wish to consider whether they are comfortable with a larger loan to the borrower concerned. An oversubscribed syndication may well result in an unhappy borrower (who thinks the interest rate or fees are too high) or unhappy banks (who are unable to get as much of the loan as they were initially offered). The competence of the lead manager is called into question by both sides.

If insufficient funds are raised, the borrower will have to make do with less if the syndication is on a best-efforts basis, or the banks in the management group will have to book the balance themselves and thereby exceed their target take if the syndication is fully committed. In such a case the syndication is considered "unsuccessful," with potentially serious adverse consequences for the future prospects of the borrower as well as the lead manager(s) in the market. Again, the competence of the lead manager will be called into question.

Both undersubscribed and oversubscribed deals must be avoided, and this is why tailoring the terms of the loan to perceived market receptivity—accuracy in pricing—is such an important determinant of competence in loan syndication leadership. Particularly desirable participations are those that present a favorable risk/return profile, both in comparison with other loans available in the market and with those offered in the months immediately ahead. Lead banks with a track record of completing such deals are rewarded by further leadership roles and, obviously, adding attractive paper to their own portfolios.

Along the way, a *loan agreement* will be drawn up; this spells out the rights and obligations of all parties to the deal, governing law, and related matters. Drafting of the loan agreement, especially in complex deals, may be initiated during the syndication process, and various possible points of contention will be discussed with the borrower. Even after the successful completion of syndication, work on the loan agreement may continue until all points are agreeable to both sides. No bank is finally committed in a loan syndication until it has agreed to the terms of the loan agreement. If no consensus can be reached on a point a bank has identified as being vital, that bank can gracefully withdraw from the syndicate. However, most of the time the loan documentation seems to be sufficiently standard that preparation time and acceptability questions are relatively minor problems. Selection of competent legal counsel in syndicated loans is of great importance in this regard.

Definition of the purpose of a loan in the loan agreement may or may not be helpful. On the one hand, it is the creditworthiness of the borrower as a whole that matters, not what it intends to do with a specific block of funding. Excessive specificity in a loan agreement may unintentionally throw the loan into default, to the chagrin of borrower and lender alike. On the other hand, the purpose of a loan may be a good tip-off as to how the borrower is likely to conduct its affairs in the future, or to its current financial condition, and could therefore figure prominently in an overall creditworthiness assessment.

Publicity will eventually have to be arranged and a signing ceremony held (and arrangements made for signing of the loan agreement for those banks not present), usually including formal lunches and dinners. Finally, an *agent bank* will be appointed early in the game, whose job it will be to run the books on the loan—a critical and influential role that the lead manager will usually want to keep for itself.

Where multiple banks form the lead management group, they will split the main jobs between them: (1) preparation and distribution of the information memorandum, (2) keeping track of syndication responses from potential participants, (3) negotiation of the loan agreement, (4) arranging for the signing, (5) handling of publicity, and (6) taking on the agency function. Those tasks providing the closest contact with the borrower or the greatest visibility in the market are most sought after, and will generally go to the dominant members of the syndication group.

Figure 2-1 depicts two *tombstones,* announcements of typical full syndications that represent a standard aspect of publicity on a deal. Note the

HFC

B A N K

guaranteed by

Household International, Inc

£236,000,000

Revolving Credit Facility

arranged by

The First National Bank of Chicago   Lloyds Bank Capital Markets Group

Lead Managers

Commerzbank Aktiengesellschaft
London Branch

The First National Bank of Chicago

Lloyds Bank Plc

Royal Bank of Canada

The Royal Bank of Scotland plc

Managers

ABN AMRO Bank N.V.

The Bank of Nova Scotia

Banque Nationale de Paris p.l.c.

Bayerische Landesbank Girozentrale
London Branch

The Fuji Bank, Limited

The Mitsubishi Trust and Banking Corporation

N M Rothschild & Sons Limited

The Sakura Bank Limited

The Tokai Bank, Limited

Union Bank of Switzerland

Co Managers

Bank of Ireland International Finance Ltd

Brown, Shipley & Co Limited

The Chuo Trust and Banking Company, Limited

Dresdner Bank AG
London Branch

Mellon Bank, N.A.

The Sumitomo Bank, Limited

Yamaichi Bank (U.K.) Plc

Facility Agent
Royal Bank of Canada Europe Limited

FIRST CHICAGO
The First National Bank of Chicago

Lloyds Bank
Capital Markets
Group

Figure 2-1. Sample tombstones.

The Dow Chemical Company
$3,000,000,000
Revolving Credit Facility

Agent:
Citibank, N.A.

Co-Agents:
ABN AMRO
Bank of America NT&SA
The Dai-Ichi Kangyo Bank, Ltd.
Union Bank of Switzerland

Lead Managers:
Barclays Bank PLC
Credit Lyonnais
Royal Bank of Canada

Provided By:

Banque Nationale de Paris • Morgan Guaranty Trust Co.
Societe Generale • The Sumitomo Bank Limited
Swiss Bank Corporation • The Toronto Dominion Bank

Bank Brussels Lambert • The Bank of Nova Scotia
The Bank of Tokyo Trust Company • Bankers Trust Company
Berliner Handels–Und Frankfurter Bank • Canadian Imperial Bank of Commerce
Credit Suisse • Dresdner Bank AG • The First National Bank of Chicago
The Fuji Bank Limited • Generale Bank N.V. • Kredietbank N.V.
Mellon Bank, N.A. • NBD Bank, N.A. • Security Pacific National Bank
Westpac Banking Corporation

Banca Commerciale Italiana • Banco Bilbao Vizcaya • The Bank of New York
Bayerische Landesbank Girozentrale • Bayerische Vereinsbank AG • Cariplo
Chase Manhattan Bank, N.A. • Continental Bank N.A. • Credito Italiano
The Daiwa Bank, Limited • Deutsche Bank AG
The Hong Kong and Shanghai Banking Corporation Limited
The Industrial Bank of Japan, Ltd.
Istituto Bancario San Paolo di Torino • Lloyds Bank PLC
The Mitsubishi Bank, Limited • National Westminster Bank PLC
NCNB Texas National Bank • Northern Trust Co.
The Sanwa Bank Limited • The Sumitomo Trust and Banking Company Ltd.
Wachovia Bank of Georgia, N.A. • Westdeutsche Landesbank Girozentrale

This transaction was arranged and syndicated by Citicorp Securities Markets, Inc.

JULY 1991

Citicorp Securities Markets, Inc. is a wholly owned subsidiary of Citicorp.

29

prominence of the lead manager and the balance of the management group at the top, the agent bank (usually the lead manager that put the deal together) at the bottom, and the several *brackets* of participants between the upper-bracket banks that have committed more funds and hence play a more important role in the deal, and the lower-bracket ones.

There are a number of variants of this general *full syndication* pattern. If market conditions are not receptive to a full syndication, or if a borrower is regularly in the market for funds, a *club loan* may be arranged, wherein a separate information memorandum is not necessary and the lead bank together with the rest of the management group provide the entire amount of the loan themselves. In a *semisyndication,* an unusually large share of the funds is provided by the managers themselves and the balance by a relatively small number of participants who generally know the borrower or its industry well and hence get involved on a more exclusive basis. Figures 2-2 and 2-3 give examples of club loans and semisyndications, respectively.

In *participation loans,* one or more banks will underwrite the entire financing and execute the loan agreement, later individually selling down participations to a small number of other banks without the formal structure of a full syndication. Also called a *pre-advanced syndicate,* the borrower actually gets its money from the lead bank(s) before part of the loan is sold down on the basis of a participation certificate only and no borrower contact whatsoever. The same is true of *loan notes,* which are sold freely among any banks interested in booking participations in a particular transaction employing a loan note structure.

The entire syndication process normally takes anywhere from two weeks to three months, depending on the borrower, the complexity of the deal, market conditions, competence of the managers, size of the loan, and similar factors. All out-of-pocket costs involved in the syndication, including legal fees, advertising, travel, and communications charges, are for the account of the borrower.

Maturities and Structure

Syndicated lending is often medium term in nature, and the banks involved may have to take a relatively long view of the borrower's ability and willingness to service the loan. This has been one reason for the importance of government and government-guaranteed borrowing in this market. Many private-sector syndications (such as acquisitions financings) are much shorter in maturity and are designed to be eliminated by lower-cost bond or stock issues later.

Given borrower needs, maturities tend to follow market conditions and borrower creditworthiness. Syndicated loans usually involve a *drawdown schedule,* according to which the borrower will acquire the principal of the loan, generally related to the date on which the loan is signed. Repayment of principal may be over a 5- to 10-year period, and there may

L A U R A A S H L E Y G R O U P

£50,000,000

5 Year Revolving Credit Facility

Arranged by:

Citicorp Investment Bank Limited

Participants:

The Bank of Tokyo, Ltd.

Citibank, N.A.

Den Danske Bank

Midland Bank plc

The Dai-Ichi Kangyo Bank, Limited

Banca Popolare di Novara
London Branch

Bank Mees & Hope NV

Facility Agent:

Citicorp Investment Bank Limited

Financial Advisors to Laura Ashley Group

Lazard Brothers & Co., Limited

CITIBANK

24 January 1992

Figure 2-2. Example of a club loan.

31

Mobil Exploration Norway Inc.,
Norwegian Branch

U.S.$ 300,000,000
Revolving Credit Facility

Underwriters and Senior Lead Managers:

Citibank, N.A.   National Westminster Bank Plc

Lead Managers:

ABN AMRO Bank N.V.   Banque Nationale de Paris   Banque Paribas
Belgian Branch

Bayerische Landesbank Girozentrale   Canadian Imperial Bank of Commerce
London Branch

Crédit Lyonnais   The Dai-Ichi Kangyo Bank, Limited   Den Danske Bank
London Branch

The Hongkong and Shanghai Banking Corporation Limited   NMB Bank

Rabobank Nederland   Scotiabank (Ireland) Limited
London Branch

Svenska Handelsbanken   WestLB Group

Managers:

Bank of America NT&SA   Banque Indosuez Norge A/S

Société Générale   The Sumitomo Bank, Limited
London Branch

Co-Arranger and Facility Agent: Co-Arranger:

Citicorp Investment Bank Limited   NatWest Capital Markets Limited

February 3, 1992

Figure 2-3. Example of a semisyndication.

32

be a grace period of as much as 4 or 5 years during which no repayment of principal is due. Principal repayment may then be made on an amortization basis over the rest of the life of the loan, all at once at the end (a *bullet loan*), or on some other mutually agreed schedule.

Clearly, maturity and loan structure considerations must meet both borrower and market requirements. In devising an appropriate structure the lead bank must use its expertise, market positioning, influence with the borrower, and creativity in bringing the two sides together. And, unlike ordinary loans between a borrower and a lender, the terms of syndicated loans generally become publicly known. It is difficult to keep pricing, fees, maturity information, legal covenants, and borrower information confidential if it has to be fully disseminated among 20, 50, or more banks in a major syndicated loan.

Borrowers and lenders constantly compare terms of syndications, both over time for individual borrowers and among borrowers, so that precedent plays an important role in the market. A borrower will compare the terms offered with those it faced the last time it entered the market and those apparently being offered to others. If the borrower shows up too frequently, if its credit-worthiness is perceived to have deteriorated, if the purpose of the loan is questioned either in its own right or as an indication of its overall competence, or if others enter the market who are deemed to have better standing, it may have to live with higher costs or shorter maturities, or both. And what happens today will help set the stage for the borrower's next foray into the market.

Pricing

Syndicated loans in international banking are generally priced on an agreed upon *floating base* rate of interest, in most cases the London Interbank Offered Rate (LIBOR), as a proxy for the banks' own cost of funds. To this floating base is added a *contractual spread,* which may be fixed for the entire life of the loan or may be *split,* that is, fixed at one spread for the first several years and another spread for part or all of the remainder. For example, the rate on a typical eight-year syndicated credit to a major borrower may be set at LIBOR + ¾ percent for the first five years and LIBOR + ⅞ percent for the rest of the period.

Interest payable by the borrower is adjusted on a *rollover date* usually every three or six months, at the borrower's option, with the new period's base rate being specified in the typical loan agreement as the average LIBOR quoted two days earlier by selected *reference banks* that are members of the syndicate. The strongest of these banks can often attract three- or six-month deposits at a cost below LIBOR or may fund the loan in other maturities, depending on relative interest rates, to secure funding profits in addition to the contractual spread.

This may be combined with a cap, floor, or collar option defining maximum allowable deviations from the interest-rate benchmark to protect borrowers and lenders from interest rate risk. Note that floating-rate pricing in syndications places the basic interest-rate risk, except that between rollover dates, on the borrower. Banks nevertheless retain credit risk and country risk as well as funding risk, that is, the risk that funds in the needed currency may not be available when present funding has to be rolled over. The possibility of widening or narrowing future spreads does leave banks with some residual interest-rate risk even on floating-rate loans. For example, a bank may participate in a very finely priced syndication today, and market conditions dictate substantially wider spreads for the same borrower a year or two later.

All payments of principal and interest in syndicated loans are specified *net to the lender,* that is, free and clear of all taxes levied by the borrower's taxes or fully creditable against the taxes levied in the bank's home country. Liability for taxes levied where the loan is booked is often a point to be negotiated. Participants in syndicated loans tend to be comparatively detached in evaluating loan pricing, since they, unlike the banks in the management group, have little or nothing to gain in terms of a relationship with the borrower. What's good for the lead managers is not necessarily good for the participants.

In the past, however, banks have participated in syndications on the thinnest of spreads in order to compensate for slack loan demand elsewhere, to secure access to the market or client, or to generate opportunities for funding profit, or due to sloppy risk assessment and loan portfolio management. Such banks became known in the trade as "stuffees."

Fees

Of particular interest in evaluating the returns to banks from loan syndication are the fees paid by the borrower to the participants. These take several forms.

First, managers will have to be compensated for arranging and underwriting the loan, including assumption of the risks involved. This usually takes the form of a front-end *management fee* as a flat percentage of the total loan (e.g., 1 percent) payable at or shortly after the signing. The size and complexity of the loan, the nature of the borrower, competition among banks for the borrower's business, and similar factors figure into the negotiated size of the front-end fee.

A part of the management fee will usually have to be shared by the syndicate manager(s) with other participants to successfully sell down a loan, especially a very large one. This *participation fee* takes the form of a flat percentage of each bank's final amount lent. It is often divided into size categories based on the level of participation by groups of banks.

Second, since a particular loan may not be drawn down immediately but has to be made available to the borrower over time as specified in the loan agreement, a separate *commitment fee* is often provided, generally a flat percentage (e.g., ½ percent) on the undrawn portion of the loan, starting on the day of the signing and prorated among the participating banks.

Finally, the bank acting as agent in a syndication will normally negotiate an *agent's fee,* usually a fixed sum (e.g., $50,000 per year for the life of the loan) payable by the borrower up front or annually in recognition of that bank's responsibilities in running the books on the loan.

While the agent's fee and the commitment fee are clearly set in the deal terms, the division of the management fee among syndicate participants is a matter for negotiation and may in the end be quite complex. On a $100 million fully committed loan lead-managed by a single bank that has negotiated a 1-percent management fee, or $1 million, the bank may decide that it has to distribute $750,000 to all banks in the "co-lead" category to ensure a successful syndication, but it can withhold ¼ percent ($250,000) for itself as compensation for serving as "manager of the managers." This ¼ percent portion is called a *praecipium* and represents the unique return to lead manager(s) for arranging the deal.

It may now decide to offer a participation fee of ¾ percent of final participation to banks (including itself) that lend at least $10 million each (co-lead managers), ½ percent to banks participating at a level of $5 million or more, and ¼ percent to banks that take under $5 million. Suppose, of the $100 million total loan, the lead manager takes $15 million into its own portfolio, four co-managers are in at $10 million, plus 6 banks are in at $5 million and 15 banks at $1 million. Of the available $750,000 in participation fees, the lead manager thus gets $112,500 (¾ percent on its $15 million participation, or *final take*), co-managers get $300,000 (¾ percent on $10 million × 4 banks), first-level participants get $150,000 (½ percent on $5 million × 6 banks), and second-level participants get $37,500 (¼ percent on $1 million × 15 banks). Under these conditions, a total of $600,000 in participation fees have been allocated, leaving $150,000 unallocated, called the *pool.* This pool is normally distributed to the management group in proportion to their individual underwriting commitments.

In this example, the fee earnings by the lead manager out of the $1 million management fee are:

Praecipium	$250,000
Participation	112,500
Pool share	40,909
	$403,409 (1 bank)

Each of the co-managers gets:

Participation	$ 75,000
Pool share	27,273
Total	$102,273 (4 banks)

Each of the first-level participants gets:

> Participation $ 25,000   (6 banks)

Each of the second-level participants gets:

> Participation $ 1,500   (15 banks)

All of this adds to $1 million: $403,409 + $102,373 (4) + $25,000 (6) + $2,500 (15) = $1 million (rounded-off).

For the lead manager this means an immediate return of 2.69 percent of its final take ($15 million), for co-managers 1.02 percent, for first-level participants 0.5 percent, and for second-level participants 0.25 percent. But because these fees are immediate, the interest equivalents based on the average life of the loan are proportionally higher in comparison to the contractual spread. This illustrates the importance that credit-related fees tend to assume in evaluating a bank's overall return on syndication activity. The objective for lead banks is to maximize fee income per dollar actually lent, and this obviously means commanding a position in the upper tiers of syndications where the bulk of the fee income (as well as the risks and the required skills) are lodged. It also means, for the lead managers, trying to maintain confidentiality about the overall size of the fee—and sharing that fee only to the extent necessary to ensure a successful syndication.

As components of returns to the participating banks (and costs to the borrower), spreads and fees are obviously related. Because higher contractual spreads may carry negative connotations about the borrower's creditworthiness, it may agree to fatter fees to compensate the lenders for finer spreads in order to improve its market positioning in future borrowings. Similarly, borrowers will sometimes undertake *benchmark financings*—syndicated loans with extremely fine pricing even if there is no real need for funds (with the borrower viewed by the market as particularly creditworthy) just to "show the flag" and try to improve future borrowing conditions. A borrower's "name" in the market evolves over a period of time, as does a bank's competitive performance, and both have a great deal to do with the structure of pricing and fees.

The Agency Function

The task of servicing a syndicated loan falls on the agent bank, usually the lead bank or one of the lead managers assigned the job. In one respect, the agency function is purely a mechanical one, involving running the books on the loan. There are at least seven functions:

- Seeing that the terms of the loan agreement are complied with regarding drawdown, rollover, interest payments, grace period, and repayment of principal

- Collecting funds from participants as per the drawdown provisions and disbursement to the borrower
- Fixing the interest rate peridically against the floating-rate base (such as LIBOR) as per the contractual spread
- Computing interest and principal due, collecting from the borrower, and distributing to the lenders (not such a simple task when funds are due in one place and time and payable in another)
- Monitoring loan supports, such as collateral valuation, guarantees, and insurance
- Evaluating and ensuring compliance with covenants in the loan agreement and informing participants, as necessary
- Collecting periodic reports from the borrower, independent auditors, or other information and distributing them to participants

Such tasks have to be done reliably, efficiently, and promptly, yet they are little more than clerical in nature.

It is when trouble brews that the agency function takes on a far more complex and different character. The loan documentation will obviously specify under what conditions default occurs, but this may involve zero, partial, or full agent discretion. A capable agent bank that has attained this role by virtue of a superior track record in this function, participation in syndicate leadership, and a sizable loan commitment for its own book is likely to have sufficient familiarity with the borrower and large enough stakes in the outcome to be trusted with some measure of discretion and forbearance in problem situations, unless such decisions can only be made by a stipulated voting procedure among syndicate participants.

If a borrower does encounter difficulties, the syndicate leadership and/or the agent bank performs a critical role in explaining the problem to loan participants and creating a climate within which a workout can be accomplished—one that is obviously in the fundamental interest of both sides. The role of agent took on enormous importance during the sovereign debt renegotiations throughout the 1980s.

Defining the agent's proper role is not easy. What is the agent's legal responsibility to the borrower and to lenders? If the agent bank is also lead manager, it may well have long-standing ties to the borrower, and potentially divided loyalties. What information obtained by the agent about the borrower's financial condition should be kept in confidence, and what should be passed on to participants? Discretion also carries with it potential liability, which an agent bank may wish to avoid. Yet a continuing and digestible flow of information to syndicate participants may form the basis for smoothing adjustments to problem situations, sound advice to the borrower, avoidance of crises where everyone loses, and preparing the way for possible infusions of additional funds by syndicate members where workout situations are encountered. Day-to-day borrower contact is critical, and this cannot possibly be provided by the whole syndicate. A certain degree of agent discretion—perhaps backed up by a small committee of syndicate members—and flexible interpretation of the terms of the legal documentation may lead to a far better outcome than applying no flexibility at all. There must be mutual trust and commonality of interest, coupled with adequate flow of information, for which no amount of legal language can effectively substitute.

The agency function is enhanced by the fact that full borrower due diligence can be inadequate in the case of some syndicate participants. They may be too small and have inadequate staff capabilities or the cost may be excessive. Or the time available before a decision has to be made may be too short. Yet the lead banks' own assessments cannot be made available because of the implied liability involved. Apart from the lead banks' efforts to ensure an accurate and complete information memorandum, there is no good solution to this problem.

Competitive Performance

Relatively few banks dominate international loan syndication activities. Table 2-1 gives the 1994 rankings for lead banks on publicized Eurosyndications, while Figure 2-4 provides market-share information by home country of lending banks. The name of the game is obviously syndicate leadership, and in a market where news travels fast and is rife with scuttlebutt, a strong position may be difficult to attain and to hold.

Table 2-1 Top 50 Arrangers of Syndicated Loans and Note Issuance Facilities, 1994 (proportionate credit)

Rank	Bank	Dollar Volume	Rank	Bank	Number of Deals
1	Chemical Bank	211,576.90	1	Chemical Bank	385
2	J.P. Morgan	85,297.22	2	Citicorp	70
3	Citicorp	47,373.68	3	J.P. Morgan	152
4	Bank of America	42,372.22	4	Chase Manhattan	143
5	First Chicago	41,022.70	5	Bank of America	138
6	Chase Manhattan	39,553.85	6	ABN AMRO	135
7	NationsBank	24,211.76	7	First Chicago	129
8	Crédit Suisse	22,783.74	8	NatWest	121
9	Bankers Trust	20,432.98	9	Barclays	115
10	UBS	19,528.24	10	UBS	108
11	Barclays	17,914,48	11	Crédit Suisse	99
12	NatWest	17,168.18	12	DKB	79
13	SBC	16,725.55	13	Fuji	78
14	ABN AMRO	13,517.55	14	Bankers Trust	76
15	Toronto Dominion	12,958.15	15	Sumitomo	72
16	BNS	12,865.43	16	BNS	68
17	RBC	9,559.88	17	Société Generale	66
18	Société Generale	7,370.75		Toronto Dominion	66
19	Bank of New York	7,216.57	19	Nations Bank	64
20	HSBC	6,922.73	20	Deutsche Bank	62
21	Deutsche Bank	6,846.73	21	HSBC	60

continued

Table 2-1 (continued)

Rank	Bank	Dollar Volume	Rank	Bank	Number of Deals
22	Lloyds	6,647.05		Sanwa	60
23	Bank of Boston	6,273.20	23	WestLB	59
24	DKB	5,638.83	24	Bank of Tokyo	52
25	CIBC	5,584.86	25	Bank of Boston	49
26	Banque Indosuez	5,274.98	26	Standard Chartered	46
27	Chiao Tung	5,000.00	27	LICB	45
28	Continental	4,858.92	28	CIBC	38
29	Fuji	4,373.19		RBC	38
30	Sumitomo	4,143.17		SBC	38
31	Crédit Lyonnais	3,819.28	31	Sakura	36
32	WestLB	3,779.65	32	Bank of New York	35
33	Bank of Montreal	3,738.63	33	Banque Indosuez	34
34	Bank of Tokyo	3,722.72		Crédit Lyonnais	34
35	Ensklida	3,057.09		Mitsubishi	34
36	Banque Paribas	2,625.61	36	IBJ	33
37	IBJ	2,523.89	37	Continental	32
38	EXIM Japan	2,493.57	38	Banque Paribas	31
39	Sanwa	2,219.16	39	KDB	29
40	LTCB	2,166.14		Lloyds	29
41	Dresdner Bank	2,156.04	41	KEB	28
42	Standard Chartered	2,067.37	42	Dresdner Bank	26
43	Mellon	1,988.10	43	Bank of Montreal	24
44	Kleinwort Benson	1,840.38		Commerzbank	24
45	Commerzbank	1,792.05	45	CBK	23
46	CBA	1,688.25	46	ANZ	19
47	Svenska	1,672.63		Bayerische Landesbank	19
48	Pittsburgh National	1,595.15		Enskilda	19
49	ANZ	1,495.89		Schroders	19
50	Westpac	1,482.94	50	AFC	18
				BNP	18

Data: International Financing review, Securities Data Corporation, OmniBase.

Lead managers in syndications carry heavy responsibilities to both borrowers and lenders. They must be absolutely forthright and reliable in their dealings with participants. They must stay away from substandard deals and develop a pattern of offering participations that have attractive risk/return profiles. They must avoid the "hard sell," a difficult thing to do when things are not going well, and retain participant respect even in the heat of the syndication process. They must be thoroughly familiar with market conditions and individual banks' attitudes toward particular borrowers, and develop a good overall working relationship with a broad array of banks—including participations and possible management roles in syndications led by others. And they must have a major presence in syndication centers staffed by specialized groups that can effectively back up the lending officers at the customer end to win mandates and at the same time be capable of structuring a syndicate and successfully getting the deal. Such individuals are generally bright, tactful, resourceful, and tough bargainers.

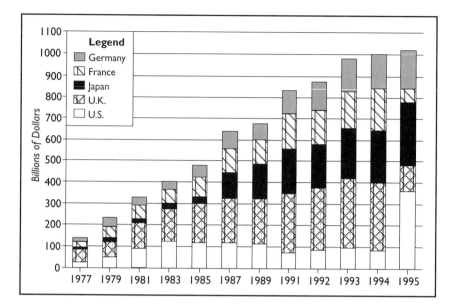

Figure 2-4. Cross-border bank credit to nonbanks by residence of lending bank, 1977–95. Source: IMF, International Financial Statistics Yearbook, 1995, p. 67.

At the other end of the deal, successful lead banks must have established sound working relationships with (and reputation among) potential borrowers, often covering the gamut of banking services (possibly a local presence), and a track record of commitment in good times and bad. They must be a steady source of sound advice, even if this runs counter to the current desires of the borrower. They must be able to convince the borrower of their strong position in the syndications market, and the ability to bring off a syndication on the most competitive terms possible. Their image of competence must be unquestioned, and they must be seen as an important player in the market. Above all, lead managers must avoid errors. Misestimating market conditions or borrower acceptability may produce a "failed" syndication or an embarrassing return to the borrower for sweeter terms. Best-efforts syndications can obviously fail outright, leading to red faces all around, a loss of fees, or a humiliating return to the market with sweetened terms. Renegotiated fully committed syndications have similar consequences. Both can strain relationships between the syndicate leadership, the borrower, and participating banks. If repeated too often, they can severely erode the ability of those responsible to compete for syndications in the future. Likewise, mishandling the job of agent, which is always possible in problem situations, can cause serious difficulties to borrower and syndicate participants alike. They can produce "black marks" which, when cumulated and amplified by market gossip, can seriously erode a bank's competitive position for the most lucrative aspects of the business.

Since loan syndication is rather similar to the underwriting function for debt securities (discussed in chapter 9), one might expect investment banks to play a much stronger competitive role in loan syndication than appears in Table 2-1. However, borrowers like banks awarded syndication mandates to take a substantial share of the loan themselves, and in a fully committed deal they *must* be in a position to do so if necessary. This investment banks are generally unable or unwilling to do. Similarly, syndicate participants like to see lead managers and agents with sizable stakes in the game, whereas investment banks may be viewed as working primarily for the borrower's interests. To fully serve their clients, some investment banking firms, notably Merrill Lynch and CS First Boston, have created a syndicated lending capability.

In the early days of international loan syndication the status of the lead bank played a dominant role in determining the success of the deal. But the LDC debt crisis and highly leveraged M&A and real estate loans of the 1980s, together with pressure by bank regulators, have tilted the balance toward a much more careful and detailed examination of borrowers by participating banks.

Commercial Paper and Note Issuance Facilities

Commercial paper has existed for more than 100 years in the United States (USCP)—short-term promissory notes sold without documentation by high-grade issuers to sophisticated investors (such as mutual funds, corporations, banks, and pension funds) who use the market to invest at short-term interest rates that exceed those available from the treasury bill market. Most paper is issued in very short maturities, sold at a discount, and rolled over at maturity. Commercial paper is usually rated, and many CP investors are restricted from purchasing unrated paper. Issuers of commercial paper normally must also provide committed bank loan "back-up" facilities to ensure the availability of cash to redeem maturing paper in the event of a market disturbance that might restrict rollovers. Figure 2-5 illustrates the dramatic rise in USCP's market share against bank lending.

To meet the quality standards of the market, many issuers sell paper accompanied by a letter of credit (see chapter 3) of a major bank. International corporations as well as governments and agencies issue commercial paper in the U.S. market—virtually all of it is placed with U.S. institutional investors. A Eurocommercial paper (ECP) market exists in London and operates very much like the USCP market, except that it is much smaller and the maturities are longer, thus allowing secondary-market trading. As indicated in Figures 2-5 and 2-6, CP markets have developed in other countries as well. Over the years, the commercial paper markets have attracted most U.S. and many large foreign corporate borrowers to issue paper at rates substantially below bank lending rates.

Some ECP programs are created as part of a Euro *note issuance facil-*

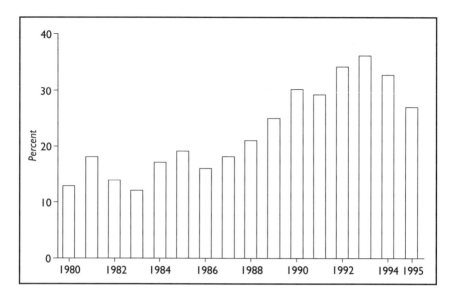

Figure 2-5. Nonfinancial commercial paper to C & I loans. Source: Federal Reserve Bulletin, February 1994.

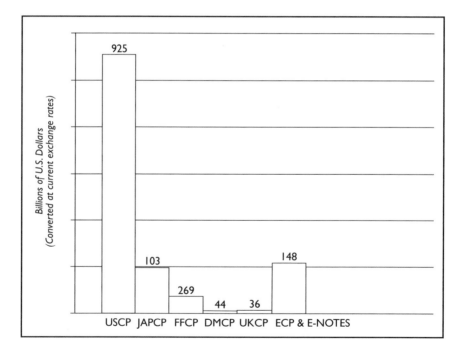

Figure 2-6. Domestic and international markets for commercial paper (CP) and medium-term notes (amounts outstanding at year-end 1993). Source: BIS 64th Annual Report, June 1995.

ity (NIF), which provides a borrower with an assurance of a medium-term financing facility (provided by a syndicate of banks) under which the borrower may either sell notes (i.e., ECP) to the market at a money-market rate set by auction at the time of sale, or sell the notes at a rate reflecting an agreed maximum spread over a base rate, either LIBOR or the "bid" side of the London Interbank market rate for deposits (LIBID).

NIFs can provide a structure that permits auctioning off the Euronotes at the time of their sale through a *tender panel*—a designated group of banks (possibly including some other than the NIF providing banks) and dealers who agree to tender, or bid, for notes when they are offered. The tender panel members may bid any rate they choose, so that their participation is in effect on a best-efforts basis. If the bids are not competitive with the maximum agreed spread over the base rate, none is accepted and the notes are instead purchased by the NIF-providing banks. Another version of this structure is *revolving underwriting facility* (RUF), under which a designated sole placing agent—not necessarily a backstop-providing bank—uses its best efforts to place the notes at rates below the agreed maximum rate. If it is not successful, the RUF-providing banks either purchase the notes or offer a loan at the agreed maximum spread instead.

The issuer pays arrangement and underwriting fees for a NIF or RUF. The tender panel banks are not paid fees—their compensation comes from the spread earned by reselling notes to the market at a slightly higher price than they paid for them. The NIF or RUF structure is designed to give the borrower guaranteed rollover at an agreed spread for several years, and the opportunity to sell paper at rates lower than the agreed rates when the conditions permit. Figure 2-7 maps out the structure of underwritten Euronote facilities.

Figures 2-8 and 2-9 present tombstones on typical ECP and RUF structures, respectively, in which the roles of arranger, underwriters, tender panel, and sole placing agent are clearly identifiable.

The borrower may also add a provision to the NIF or RUF agreement to permit the use of the facility for backstopping the issuance of U.S. commercial paper. In such cases an undrawn portion of the facility is set aside for this purpose. The commercial paper will be sold and rolled over by a dealer in the United States, but only a portion of the facility will actually have to be made available in New York (in overnight funds)—an amount adequate to cover single-day rollovers. This portion of the facility is called a *swingline*.

A variation is a NIF or RUF with a built-in provision for a letter of credit from a bank (usually with the lead bank in the facility) under which the notes (or U.S. commercial paper) are issued. This arrangement enables issuers of lesser credit standing to use the ECP or the U.S. commercial paper market, or to borrow directly from the banks, whichever is cheaper. A *prime issuance facility* is similar to the NIF except that the maximum interest spread is expressed in terms of the U.S. prime interest rate instead of LIBOR or LIBID. In the *transferable revolving underwriting facility*

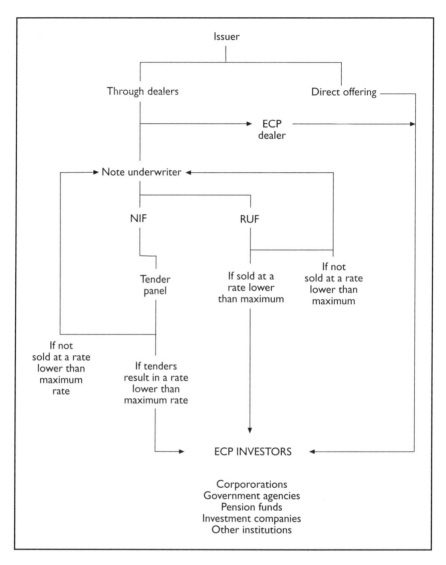

Figure 2-7. The Euronote and ECP issuing process. NIF = Note issuance facility; RUF = revolving underwriting facility.

(TRUF), the underwriting bank's contingent liability to purchase notes in the event of nonplacement is totally transferable (i.e., sellable) to other banks. Finally, there is the *multioption financing facility* (MOFF), whereby the banks' medium-term underwriting commitment consists not only of Euronotes, but extends to a wider range of instruments such as bankers' acceptances and short-term advances, possibly in a number of different currencies. Figure 2-10 presents a typical MOFF tombstone with the respective roles of the various participants clearly identified.

10th March, 1992

Renault Crédit International S.A.
Banque

Renault Acceptance B.V.

with the guarantee of

Renault Crédit International S.A.
Banque

U.S. $500,000,000

Euro-Commercial Paper Programme

Rated: A1-P1

Arranger

UBS Phillips & Drew Securities Limited

Dealers

Crédit Lyonnais

NatWest Capital Markets Limited

UBS Phillips & Drew Securities Limited

Issuing and Paying Agent

Citibank, N.A.

Figure 2-8. Sample tombstone for a typical Eurocommercial paper structure.

45

Victorian Public Authorities Finance Agency
U.S. $100,000,000

Revolving Underwriting Facility

Guaranteed by

The Government of Victoria

Arranged by

Citicorp Investment Bank Limited

Underwriters

Algemene Bank Nerderland N.V. • BankAmerica Capital Markets

Bank of Montreal Asia Limited • The Bank of Tokyo (Holland) N.V. • Banque Nationale de Paris

Barclays Bank PLC • CIBC Capital Markets • Citibank (Channel Islands) Limited

Commonwealth Bank of Australia • Crédit Lyonnais, Singapore Branch • Crédit Suisse

Duetsche Bank Luxembourg S.A. • DKB International Limited

Fuji International Finance Limited • The Industrial Bank of Japan (Luxembourg) S.A.

International Westminster Bank PLC • Mitsui Finance Asia Limited

Nomura Europe N.V. • Sanwa International Finance Limited

Security Pacific Hoare Govett Asia Limited • Société Générale • State Bank Victoria

Sumitomo Finance (Asia) Limited • Swiss Bank Corporation • Westpac Banking Corporation

Facility Agent

Citicorp Investment Bank Limited

Issuing and Paying Agent

Westpac Banking Corporation

December 21, 1987

CITICORP⊕INVESTMENT BANK

Figure 2-9. Sample tombstone for a typical revolving underwriting facility.

BRITISH AEROSPACE

British Aerospace Public Limited Company
U.S. $825,000,000
Multiple Option Facility

Arranger

Citicorp Investment Bank Limited

Lead Managers

The First National Bank of Chicago • Banca Nazionale del Lavoro, London Branch

Bank of America NT&SA • The Bank of New York • Bankers Trust Company

Bayerische Landesbank Girozentrale, London Branch • The Chase Manhattan Bank, N.A.

Citibank, N.A. • Credit Suisse • Daiwa Europe Bank plc

Gulf International Bank B.S.C. • The Long-Term Credit Bank of Japan, Ltd.

The Mitsubishi Bank, Limited • The Mitsui Bank, Limited

The National Bank of Kuwait SAK, London Branch • Rabobank Nederland, London Branch

Riyad Bank, London Branch • Security Pacific National Bank

Société Générale, London Branch

Managers

Credito Italiano, London Branch • The Royal Bank of Canada

Co-Managers

Amsterdam-Rotterdam Bank N.V. • Arab Bank Limited • The Bank of Nova Scotia

The Bank of Tokyo, Ltd. • Chemical Bank • Clydesdale Bank PLC

The Dai-Ichi Kangyo Bank, Limited • The Fuji Bank, Limited • Grindlays Bank p.l.c.

The Hongkong and Shanghai Banking Corporation • The Industrial Bank of Japan, Limited

Manufacturers Hanover Trust Company • The Mitsubishi Trust and Banking Corporation

The Sanwa Bank, Limited • Saudi American Bank, London Branch

Seattle-First National Bank • The Sumitomo Bank, Limited (London Branch)

Westdeutsche Landesbank Girozentrale, London Branch • Westpac Banking Corporation

Agent and Tender Panel Agent

Citicorp Investment Bank Limited

June 28, 1989

CITICORP

Figure 2-10. Typical multioption financing facility tombstone.

47

The Principal Players

Investors in the Euronote/ECP market include: (1) banks and other financial institutions looking for spreads over LIBOR or their own cost of
funds, and (2) nonbank investors whose short-term assets include bank
deposits, CDs, short-term government securities, and commercial paper.

Borrowers in the market include sovereign and corporate issuers. The
latter can be subdivided between companies viewed as high-quality credits,
which tend to use uncommitted CP programs, and those of lesser credit
standing, which require committed, underwritten facilities.

Commercial paper and Euronote facilities are extremely flexible. Borrowers are not locked into any one interest-fixing date as they are, for
example, in syndicated Euroloans or floating-rate notes in the Eurobond
market (see chapter 9). So they have more opportunities to take advantage
of interest-rate windows as they occur—clearly of great interest in volatile
market conditions. This speed of response may be especially valuable in
multioption facilities, which allow the borrower access to a range of currencies and credit forms. They can play the yield curve and respond to
particular openings of investor interest. One large program can serve both
to retire outstanding, more expensive debt and to rationalize debt management requirements. For a competitive commitment fee, the borrower using
Euronotes can access cheap funds as and when needed, expanding or contracting the level of debt at will, safe in the knowledge that if market
conditions are not receptive to the notes, funds are nevertheless assured.
The broken or odd-dated maturities, which are a common feature of many
CP programs, also provide a great deal of flexibility, allowing issuers to
tailor the period of their financings precisely to their specific funding requirements.

Although the ECP market still has nowhere near the depth of its U.S.
counterpart, it nevertheless has certain distinct advantages that have contributed to its growth. It offers longer maturities at competitive rates and
caters to a global investor base, whereas demand in the U.S. market is
almost wholly domestic. Investors from Australia, continental Europe, the
Far East, and the Middle East (corporate treasurers as well as central and
commercial banks and other institutions) constitute an investor base that
allows a broad range of maturities, while the speed with which the leading
ECP houses are able to arrange and distribute deals is greatly helped by
limited regulation.

Summary

Figure 2-11 summarizes how capital is raised on the international debt
market. Note the dominance of capital market instruments, notably the
international bond market, in terms of new issues. Nevertheless, international syndicated lending and related activities such as underwritten Euro-

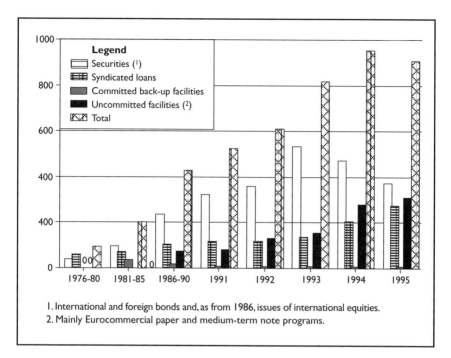

Figure 2-11. Borrowing on the international capital markets ($ billion, annual averages). Source: Organization for Economic Cooperation and Development, *Financial Market Trends,* February 1995.

note facilities continue to have a place. Each has its specific uses, and particularly in the case of syndicated lending there are no good substitutes for purposes such as short-term M&A financing or project finance (see chapter 3).

Few banks that purport to provide a full range of services to their global client base are not actively involved in syndicated lending. We have seen that it has advantages for borrowers and lenders alike. We have spelled out the characteristics of success in syndicate leadership, which is where the real competitive game is played and where the real profits are lodged.

The story of Euronote programs and Eurocommercial paper is one of rapid change at all levels. The competitive structure of the market has undergone substantial modification with bargaining power tending to shift away from borrowers to investors. In the early days top and lesser-quality names alike benefited from the intense competition among banks resulting from deregulation and disintermediation. They profited as well from a lack of investor sophistication. Today, most corporate and institutional investors have a full understanding of the workings of the market and what is available to them. And distributive power has been concentrated in the hands of a few houses, which are more interested in volume and profitability than the number of dealerships they hold. Gone are the days of loss-leading for a place in the market. Attention is on courting the investor base in search of greater diversification of funding.

Other changes have occurred as well. Distribution methods have been modified to suit new conditions and demands. The use of ratings has increased in the ECP market, with the need for investors to react quickly in fast-moving markets. The very nature of the instrument has evolved, with the nonunderwritten ECP now predominating over Euronote programs. These changes will continue as new economic conditions give rise to new requirements and new responses. The Euronote grew as a substitute for syndicated loans, floating rate notes in the Eurobond market, and Eurocertificates of deposit issues by banks. Its success came in part from the events shaping the financial world at the time. As increasing globalization brought increasing competition, so the pace of product innovation has quickened.

As the Euronote market deepened, it became obvious that prime borrowers could dispense with underwritten facilities altogether, thus reducing costs. ECP provided greater flexibility for borrowers and investors alike. It offered a faster and more efficient method of placement. These advantages led to a widening of the investor base and consequently further reduced costs and increased flexibility. Euronote programs and subsequently ECP have had substantial success. They are perhaps best viewed as a complement to rather than a replacement for more traditional forms of bank finance, an additional financial string to the borrower's bow, offered as part of an increasingly efficient international money market.

3

Asset-Related and Project Financing

The previous chapter discussed international commercial lending and related activities in terms of general obligations of borrowers. There are, in addition, several specialized forms of lending that have limited recourse to ultimate borrowers and their balance sheets, or sometimes none at all. These can provide attractive lending opportunities but also can expose banks to significant risks. Some such transactions, in which the asset is a major basis for the financing, also lend themselves to securitization, selling to other financial institutions, and repackaging. This chapter discusses the various types of lending that are based on the value of assets underlying trade financing, ship financing, commodities financing, international leasing, and project financing. Each has its own unique characteristics and poses unique challenges to banks hoping to compete effectively. Loan securitization, involving the issuance of securities against various types of bank loans, will be considered in chapter 7.

Financing International Trade

Banks have been involved in the financing of international trade and effecting payments for international trade transactions since at least medieval times. The basic *transactions* services involve circumventing information and transactions costs for importers and exporters, making payment for international transactions as expeditiously and cheaply as possible, and providing associated foreign exchange and risk-shifting services. The basic *credit* services involve the direct extension of credit from the time merchandise leaves the factory door (and sometimes before that) to the time the buyer completes payment or, alternatively, making possible credit extension for this purpose by the financial market in terms of providing backstops for the risk involved, again in the most cost-effective available form.

Forms of International Payment

Probably the easiest and cheapest forms of payments for international trade transactions of sales from an exporter to an importer are made on an open-account or consignment basis, or against payment in advance. Both are possible only if the two parties know each other well and trust each other.

If a transaction is done on a consignment basis, the exporter ships the merchandise and sends the shipping documents to the importer, which is then able to claim the goods when they arrive. When the importer sells the merchandise, it sends the proceeds minus its markup to the exporter. The same thing happens when the transaction is done on an open-account basis, except that the importer remits payment to the exporter on arrival of the goods or within an agreed period thereafter. Selling on consignment loads the entire risk (that the merchandise will actually be sold and that the importer will actually pay), as well as the financing of the goods while in shipment and in the importer's inventory, on the exporter. Selling on open account loads the credit risk on the exporter as well, and also part or all of the financing. Nevertheless, the exporter may be willing to accept the risks involved in selling on consignment depending on its underlying competitive position. Selling on open account is normally done when there is a close connection between importer and exporter, as when the importer is an affiliate of the exporting company. Serious collection problems arise in the event of default, in part because all claims must be filed under the laws of the importer's country.

Payment in advance may be specified in certain cases where the exporter is able to load onto the importer all of the risk and credit costs— the risk that the goods will actually be shipped and will arrive as specified and the cost of credit during the time the goods are in transit, and sometimes even as the goods go through the production process. This form of payment is sometimes specified for custom-made products that cannot be sold to anyone else, or when the exporter has very substantial bargaining leverage.

In all three cases (payment in advance, consignment, and open account), banks get involved only in the payment function itself, and receive customary fees for this service as well as for the spot or forward exchange transactions involved.

International Collections. Perhaps the most straightforward, direct involvement of banks in international trade is collection of amounts due on arm's-length transactions between importers and exporters. Suppose the two parties do not know each other well. The exporter would not want to ship merchandise on a straightforward basis, because he could not be sure of getting paid. The importer could take care of this problem by simply paying in advance, but then could not be sure the merchandise actually got shipped. This calls for an intermediary who takes care of the risk exposure on both sides.

The exporter prepares a "trade bill," or draft, which the importer is supposed to pay either when it takes possession of the merchandise (*documents against payment,* or D/P draft) or when it accepts the draft (D/A draft) for payment at some specified future date, such as 30 or 90 days down the road. The exporter prepares the merchandise for shipment and obtains a *bill of lading* (B/L) from a common carrier such as an airline or shipping company attesting to the fact that the goods are as specified and that they were shipped on a given date and along a specified route. The B/L and the D/P or D/A draft is sent to the exporter's bank, which in turn sends the draft and documents to its correspondent bank in the importer's country with instructions to hand over the documents (permitting the importer to claim the merchandise) against payment or against acceptance of the draft, as the case may be.

If it is a D/P draft, sometimes called a *sight draft,* the payment is collected by the bank in the importer's country, transferred to the bank in the exporter's country, and credited to his account. No credit is extended, and the collection process is compensated by fees—plus a spread and fees on a foreign exchange transaction in the middle. The same thing happens if it is a D/A draft, a *time draft,* except that the payment is collected for the account of the exporter on the specified date 30, 60, or more days in the future, after shipment has been accepted by the importer. In the meantime, the time draft may be held to maturity by the exporter, or it may be accepted by the importer's bank and either held to maturity or sold in the local banker's acceptance market, with the discounted proceeds collected for the exporter immediately. In this case, credit is extended by the holder of the time draft, who collects interest in the form of the discount.

Letters of Credit.   Documentary time drafts for collection provide one vehicle for access to credit to finance international trade transactions, other than straightforward bank loans to the exporter or the importer. An alternative is the *letter of credit* (L/C), which efficiently takes care of properly allocating the credit risks to those best able to carry them and at the same time greatly facilitates access to financing at the best available terms.

Assume the exporter and importer do not wish to extend credit to each other or to take payment risk. The exporter asks the importer to request his bank (the *opening bank*) to issue an irrevocable letter of credit for the transaction amount in the exporter's favor. By doing so, the bank commits itself to paying the specified amount if the importer is unwilling or unable to pay—assuming the merchandise has been shipped precisely as specified in the terms of the L/C. The opening bank will then send the

L/C to its correspondent bank in the exporter's country (the *advising bank*) which will forward it to the exporter. The transaction will subsequently take place using a sight or time draft, as discussed earlier, with the credit risk covered by the opening bank. An L/C of this type will cover only a single transaction, with tight specification of what will be shipped and how it will be shipped.

It may also be, of course, that the exporter is unfamiliar or uncomfortable with the importer's bank. In that case it may request that the opening bank's L/C be confirmed by the advising bank in its own country—a "confirmed, irrevocable letter of credit." Should the importer default, the importer's bank will pay. Should both be unwilling or unable to pay, the exporter's advising bank will pay. Of course, the advising bank must be comfortable with the credit standing of the opening bank and with the country-risk involved (e.g., the risk that exchange controls may be imposed that prevent the necessary currency from being made available to the importer or his bank). Again, the transaction will take place as specified earlier, and in the case of a time draft the acceptance can take place in the exporter's country and be discounted in the local banker's acceptance market at money-market rates. Figure 3-1 shows how the process works.

In addition to unconfirmed and confirmed irrevocable letters of credit, there are other variants. Revocable letters of credit may be amended or canceled by the opening bank at any point, and will therefore offer the exporter less protection and a lower price. Revolving letters of credit will cover multiple or continuous shipments of merchandise. If a revolving L/C is cumulative, any amounts used become reavailable once the transaction has been consummated, which is not the case in a noncumulative revolving L/C unless specifically amended. A "transferable L/C" permits the exporter to assign the proceeds to one or more secondary beneficiaries (e.g., subcontractors), while in a back-to-back L/C the exporter uses the first L/C (opened by the importer in his favor) as the basis for requesting his bank to open a second L/C in favor of his own supplier(s). This would tend to be used by exporters who are middlemen between domestic manufacturers and foreign buyers and do not have acceptable credit standing of their own.

In the case of international trade transactions covered by L/Cs, banks have a number of opportunities to earn fee and interest income. Fees go to banks for issuing (opening) L/Cs and for advising and confirming them, for collections, for foreign exchange transactions, for accepting time drafts, and (when the draft is held on the bank's own books) for extending credit—with the rate of interest reflected in the associated discount. Obviously, this is a highly competitive, transactions-intensive business. Banks that are best at it have strong client bases involved in international trade; procedures that are convenient to use, efficient, and error free; and substantial networks of correspondent banks.

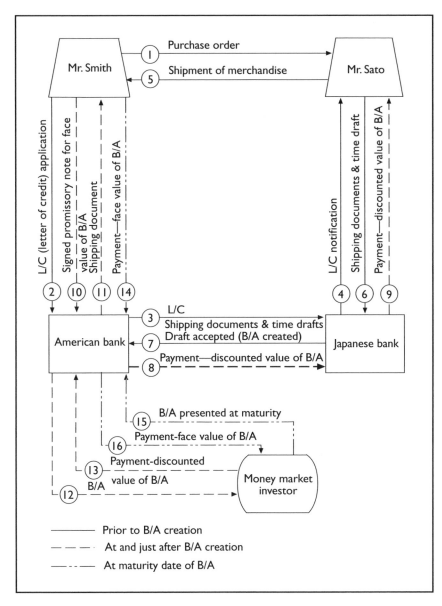

Figure 3-1. Trade financing via letter of credit (L/C) and banker's acceptance (B/A).

Forfaiting and International Factoring

Another form of international trade financing, particularly common in Europe, is *forfait financing*. Under this structure, a bank (forfaiting house) will buy from the exporter the obligations due it on the part of importers in various countries without recourse to the exporter itself. The exporter will receive the discounted proceeds immediately, against evidence covering the quality, quantity, and shipment of the merchandise. The discount reflects both the interest charge and the credit risk (commercial as well as country) the forfaiter is assuming. The promissory notes involved are usually endorsed by the importer's bank. The notes, now endorsed by both the importer's bank and the forfaiting house, can be held to maturity or resold in the market.

To some extent, a forfait transaction is similar to *factoring,* which is familiar in the United States and certain other domestic markets. Factoring involves a bank that believes it is sufficiently familiar with the customers of a particular client to buy the client's accounts receivable on a nonrecourse basis at a discount. The goods have already been shipped and the bills sent out, and it is up to the bank to collect. Factoring is common in the garment industry. It is a specialized business in which risk must be carefully managed through intimate knowledge of the industry and creditworthiness of customers as well as diversification. It can be highly profitable for banks that know how to manage the risks involved. Internationally, factoring is more difficult because risk management is problematic— a domestic bank having the basis to understand the risks associated with a client's foreign customers is difficult to imagine, unless two or more banks (or branches of a single bank) work together, swapping factored receivables involving customers in each bank's home country.

Government Export Financing, Backstops, and Countertrade

Governments in most industrial and many developing countries provide export assistance of various kinds to stimulate foreign sales of domestic companies. These involve guarantees covering commercial risks as well as political and economic risks associated with the importing country, as well as concessionary financing of various types. For example, in the United States the Export-Import Bank (Eximbank) provides direct loans to exporters and importers, export credit insurance and guarantees, and backstops for banks involved in international trade financing. Short-term credit support, up to 180 days, is run through the Foreign Credit Insurance Association (FICA) run by Eximbank and private insurance companies. Export financing of commodity transactions is handled by the Commodity Credit Corporation (CCC). There are similar agencies in other countries, such as Hermes in Germany and COFACE in France. All permit the lodging of certain risks with the government at concessionary prices, thereby taking them out of the commercial market. Often these can result in very attractive profits for the banks involved, in light of the limited foreign risks they have to assume.

Banks in several countries have become very active in arranging and facilitating "countertrade," "barter," "buybacks," "switchtrade," "offset," and other transactions with countries experiencing foreign exchange problems. For example, a company may ship a piece of capital equipment to a particular country in return for which it is obligated to take back (or buy for cash) certain other commodities or arrange their sale to third parties. Or it may build a plant on a turnkey basis, for which it gets paid in a stream of production from that plant. This business is highly specialized and risky. Normally the companies involved are in the best position to price countertrade services and to manage the risks. Banks in some countries get involved in facilitating such transactions, and in a few cases in taking on the role of principal as well, but in general they are in a poor position to carry the risks.

Ship Financing

One of the most risky sectors of international lending involves ship financing. Shipping is a cyclical business, shipowners often put up very little equity, and the value of used ships that are attached in cases of default may be little more than scrap value.

Ships are generally financed with a first mortgage, covering perhaps 70 or 80 percent of the construction cost. The remainder may be financed by the shipyard or the export finance agency of the exporting country, with the shipowner often putting up only a small amount of equity. Since the secondary ship market is so uncertain and becomes critical at precisely the time conditions in the industry are likely to be at their worst, other sources of comfort must be sought by lenders. Shipowners usually "charter," or lease, the ships they own to operating companies, which range from major oil companies, grain transporters, and container ship operators to cruise lines, under one of two basic types of charters. The first is a "bare boat charter," in which the operator is responsible for all operating charges and risks of the vessel and the costs of labor, fuel, insurance, maintenance, and repairs. The second is a "time charter," in which the operator rents the ship from the owner for a specified time but the owner bears the costs and risks. Charters may range from a comparatively short-term leasing arrangement to 10 years or more. If a vessel is to be operated under a succession of short-term charters, but seeks financing of a longer term, then the banks carry the risk that successive "charter hire payments" will be sufficient to cover the required amounts of debt service on their ship loans. In such cases the credit standing of the shipowner is of principal importance. On the other hand, in cases where a shipowner has arranged an adequate long-term bare boat charter with a major oil company, the shipowner's own creditworthiness is of lesser importance.

History is littered with cases of bank-owned ships sold at great losses or scrapped. To be in this business a bank has to develop not only a firm understanding of the shipping business and the reputation of shipowners (and their ability to comply with the terms of charters as well as their ability to operate ships profitably), but a sixth sense as well. To the extent that financial projections are reliable, they will cover the ship operator's cash flows, cost structures, competition, demand conditions, and related variables. Banks will also have to be familiar with admiralty law and the laws of countries like Panama, Greece, and Liberia that are the countries of registry for much of the world's shipping tonnage. In case of difficulties leading to a ship having to be "arrested," or seized by its creditors, the bank must be fast on its feet to prevent the values underlying its claim from slipping away.

With the high risks can come high returns, and the spreads on shipping loans are commensurately high. This has from time to time attracted inexperienced banks into shipping loans, often to their great distress. The risks also prevent shipping loans from being easily syndicated, sold, or participated-out. Nor do ships lend themselves to financing via securities issues, for risk-related reasons and because of the need for flexibility in the case of restructuring.

Commodities Financing

A further aspect of international asset-based bank financing involves commodities—grains, timber, oil, pulp, natural fibers—with traders heavily financed with short-term bank debt. The traders' profit margins are small and turnover is rapid, with the liquidation of assets expected to provide fully for debt service. There is generally little sense in looking for recourse to the commodity trading company, which frequently takes speculative positions that could wipe it out, so financing has to be structured fully along asset-based lines. Commodity traders, as opposed to dealers, often match buy and sell orders so that the commodities are presold and therefore the final customer's ability to pay becomes critical.

Banks in the business of financing commodities must assure themselves of the credit quality of the ultimate buyers, the diversification of the commodity firm's exposure to buyers, and the volume of business. Critical are the firm's own financial controls, its credit standing, and its ability to hedge its exposure. Like much of asset-based financing, this is a specialized activity that requires banks to have equally specialized knowledge. At times it can be quite lucrative, especially when the bank gets paid handsome spreads for effectively taking risks associated with top-quality customers such as the multinational oil or grain companies.

International Lease Financing

Another important form of asset-based financing involves leasing of mobile capital goods. These can include aircraft, barges, containers, drilling rigs, pallets, power generation equipment, computers, production machinery, medical equipment, materials handling equipment, and the like.

In leasing, the lessor owns the equipment and leases it to an operator, receiving the lease payments and the residual value, which cover the equipment's acquisition cost plus profit. Lessors may or may not have the option to acquire the equipment during or at the end of its useful life. Such *financial leasing* is distinguished from *operating leasing*, where the lessor is responsible for maintaining and insuring the equipment and covering any applicable taxes. Financial leases are noncancelable, whereas operating leases are often used by customers to cover their short-term equipment needs and can be canceled at any time. Operating leases tend to be the province of specialized leasing firms that finance themselves with bank loans or in the capital markets, with full recourse to the lessor, on the basis of their own credit standing.

There are two types of financial leases. Straight bank leasing involves 100-percent bank financing on equipment procured according to the customer's specifications, with the asset acquired by the bank and delivered to the customer against assignment of the leasing documentation. Lessor and lessee may get together on the basis of a long-standing banking relationship, or they may be brought together by a broker. Alternatively, the lease may be structured through a leasing company, which pledges the equipment as well as lease revenues, with full recourse. Leveraged leasing is generally done through a separate leasing affiliate of a bank or its holding company and an ownership trust, which owns the equipment. The bank contributes a part of the required funds in the form of equity (generally at least 20 percent), and the leasing affiliate borrows the remainder on a long-term basis from banks or institutional lenders such as insurance companies that have recourse to lease payments and to the equipment.

Leasing tends to be heavily tax driven. Lessees are able to deduct lease payments as part of the cost of doing business, while the lessor deducts both interest costs and depreciation on the asset. Internationally there are instances of "double dip" tax-driven leases, due to the chance to deduct interest and depreciation expenses in two tax jurisdictions because of the structure of the lessor arrangements for the lease.

International leasing once again is a specialized business, and is often dominated by specialized firms such as the major aircraft leasing companies—Guinness Peat Aviation (GPA) of Ireland (controlled by General Electric) and International Lease Finance Company (ILFC) of the United States (controlled by American International Group)—which provide operating and financial leases to airlines that cannot afford to purchase their aircraft outright or have temporary capacity needs, or for tax reasons. By careful diversification across customers, these lessors attempt to limit their exposure to risk, although the fact remains that they are often heavily exposed to the risk embedded in the industry of the lessees (such as airlines), and the opportunities for hedging their assets or equipment orders are relatively narrow. Other nonfinancial companies, such as General Electric Capital Services (GECS), engage in a broad array of leasing activities. They in turn finance themselves with bank debt, commercial paper, and capital market instruments.

Project Financing

The financing of large-scale projects such as pipelines, oil and gas production, tunnels and bridges, energy plants, major office buildings, and similar long-gestation, highly capital-intensive ventures has evolved into a major competitive arena for international financial services firms. The sheer size of the financing needs that are frequently encountered, and the complex financial-structuring and specialized risk-evaluation requirements have concentrated leadership in this business in the relatively few banks that developed the financial resources and technical skills needed.

Driven by increased competition and growing pressure on the profitability of conventional international lending, a number of commercial and investment banks have succeeded in developing capabilities in a broad range of banking functions, enabling them to offer comprehensive financial support and advice through the life of a major project.

Background

Modern project financing appears to be largely an American invention. It can be traced to bank financing of independent oil companies during the 1930s, particularly in Oklahoma and Texas. Few of the "wildcatters" who dominated the oil business at the time had the financial resources to bring new discoveries into production, or strong enough balance sheets for ordinary unsecured bank borrowing on anything but a very limited scale. Secured borrowing was likewise precluded, since the principal "assets" to be financed were usually a hole in the ground and some associated equipment and supplies with questionable resale value. Yet it was clear that the resources in the ground themselves represented a prospective value as a future revenue stream that could become the basis for attractive lending opportunities. Bank loans could be serviced from the proceeds of the future sale of the resource without necessarily looking exclusively to either the operating company's balance sheet or to production assets for credit support.

Called *production payment financing,* this early approach in effect mortgaged the resource in the ground, with financial institutions betting that it was actually present in sufficient quantity, that it could be lifted economically, and that it could be sold at a price that lived up to a set of initial expectations, all within reasonable margins for error. Given the nature of large-scale energy projects such as offshore oil and natural gas ventures as well as terminals, pipelines, and other facilities relying for cash flows on throughput charges, "project financing" eventually grew in volume and international scale. The concepts underlying project financing were later extended from energy to other ventures such as power plants and cogeneration facilities, tunnels, bridges, pipelines, office buildings, and telecommunications facilities. Here, the loan is based on the future receipts of the project.

Structural Aspects of Project Financing

A fairly standard approach to structuring a project's financing, for example, in the petroleum industry, is for the sponsors (e.g., BP, Shell, Exxon) to establish a vehicle company in which they are principal shareholders. The vehicle company tends to have relatively thin capitalization in relation to the financial needs of the project. Each sponsor holds a sufficiently small share of the equity in the joint venture that the vehicle company cannot be construed for legal and accounting purposes as a subsidiary. Funding of the project is then routed through the vehicle company. Ideally, a record of such financing does not appear on the sponsors' balance sheets at all. If it does, it is only as a footnoted contingent liability. Similarly, the assets acquired in the course of undertaking the project appear on the financial statements of the vehicle company alone. One purpose of project financing is thus to preserve the sponsors' own credit standing and future access to financial markets. A typical alternative-cash-flow profile is depicted in Figure 3-2.

Vehicle companies may take a variety of forms, particularly if the project involves multiple sponsors whose presence might be appropriate if:

- The project exceeds the financial, technical, or human resources of a single company.
- The need for risk sharing clearly exists.

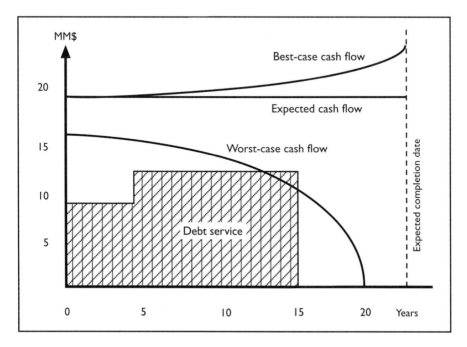

Figure 3-2. Projected project cash-flow profile.

- The project is so large that it yields significantly greater economies of scale than several smaller ones.
- The resource itself is jointly owned.
- The sponsors are complementary in terms of their capabilities.
- The country where the project is located mandates a joint venture with local interests.

In the case of multiple sponsors, either a separate corporate entity, partnership construction trust, or contractual joint venture may be created. Each entity may have a number of subforms and different managerial, legal, tax, and credit implications. Each may exist through the life of the project or for specific shorter time periods. Figure 3-3 depicts a tombstone for a typical vehicle company formation in the Republic of Kazakhstan.

Financial Design

Once the vehicle company has been established, the financing of a project must be "engineered." The financial design process must take into account the risks involved; the various prospective sources of financing, accounting, and tax regulations; the possibility of recourse to the various parties; the different entities having an interest in the project; and similar factors. Financial design may be assigned to a financial adviser—possibly an investment or merchant bank. The adviser must have the technical expertise, contacts, track record, and innovative thinking necessary to help stitch together the highly complex financial undertakings required, each of which may have one or more unique characteristics.

Working closely with sponsors' financial staffs, the adviser must pay careful attention to potential sources of finance worldwide, understand opportunities for laying off risks and achieving leverage targets, and be able to aid in identifying project risks and support arrangements, contingencies, foreign-exchange aspects, and related facets of the deal. The objective is to minimize the cost and exposure to risk of the sponsor, while making the loan attractive to prospective lenders and investors. Individual lenders, including local banks in host countries and smaller banks in third countries, may be receptive to particular deals at various times. Attractive "windows" for parts of a financing package are often open only for brief periods. Supplementary financial advisers may be brought in for their special expertise and contacts to help arrange official export credits and legal and tax issues involved in accessing national capital markets, and to help with coordination with multilateral development agencies.

Financing Components

The principal components of project financing differ considerably from one project to the next, but generally comprise multiple sources of funds. These include short-term and long-term debt, with medium-term lenders

The Republic of Kazakhstan
through its affiliates Kazakhstanmunaigaz and Tengizneftegaz Production Association

and

Chevron Corporation
through its wholly owned subsidiary Chevron Overseas Company

have formed

Tengizchevroil
a limited liability partnership registered in the Republic of Kazakhstan

to develop the Tengiz and Korolev oil fields

J. P. Morgan Securities Inc. acted as financial advisor to the Government of the Republic of Kazakhstan, Kazakhstanmunaigaz, and Tengizneftegaz

JP Morgan

April 1993

Figure 3-3. Tombstone for a typical vehicle company formation.

often replacing short-term lenders on completion of the project. Repayment schedules may be quite flexible, including some automatic resetting of debt service under various conditions (such as delays and cost overruns). This permits sponsors to develop financial strategy in other parts of their business with less concern for possible unanticipated project cash needs. To obtain the most favorable financial arrangements for projects, all conceivable sources of funds must be tapped.

Sponsor loans are advances made by the sponsor-owners of the vehicle company. Such loans would appear on the sponsors' balance sheets, compromising the off-balance-sheet intent of project financing. Sponsor-owned captive finance companies can be used to achieve the same objective. The captive finance company, with limited equity investment by the sponsor, can borrow and lend on its own account without altering the financial profile of the parent corporation, thus permiting greater financial leveraging.

Supplier credits are granted by manufacturers who can provide the needed equipment on competitive terms and whose governments may vigorously promote such exports. Energy projects in particular are highly capital intensive, and much of the total capital outlay involves machinery and equipment—drilling platforms, steel pipe, draglines, pumps, engines and compressors, communications equipment, and so on. Concessionary terms include long maturities, fixed interest rates well below market levels, and attractive insurance cover for lenders. It is advantageous to shop for the most attractive (subsidized) supplier credit arrangements—financing provided either directly by governmental export credit agencies or by banks benefiting from government credit subsidies and guarantees.

Such loans can be quite lucrative for commercial banks, and banks may provide related loans to the same project at preferential rates if they are guaranteed a piece of the export credit package. In addition to the benefits of below-market fixed-interest rates and longer maturities, such credits sometimes are linked to government grants, soft loans, and similar forms of foreign aid to the country where the project is situated. This component of project financing thus takes advantage of intense export competition among supplier countries. A number of potential sources of supplier credits may be approached by project sponsors and their advisors to secure the best possible financing terms for equipment of engineering services.

Large-scale projects will obviously vary widely in terms of the percentage of total cost accounted for by capital equipment and services eligible for supplier credits. If capital equipment and construction services are to be provided domestically by vendors in the country where the project is located, the prospects for financing through supplier credits will naturally be correspondingly less.

Customer credits can also be an attractive source of financing, especially when a project is specifically designed to provide raw materials or energy to a particular buyer (for example, an electric utility, steel company, trading house, government procurement agency). For example, the Overseas Mineral Resources Corporation in Japan has provided equity capital for joint ventures abroad. United States utilities have sometimes subsidized exploration and development of energy resources through advance payments, and private German and Japanese buyers of metals have been willing either to provide direct financing or to help secure support from government sources. Individual firms, trading companies, and minerals

consortia have made sizable loans against future resource deliveries to ensure themselves of reliable supplies.

Advance payments by sponsors may also be used for this purpose, in
effect loans to the vehicle company to be repaid in the form of shipments
after the facility comes on-stream. The absence of customer credits—perhaps due to financial limitations or lack of agreement on price concessions—may sometimes be partially offset by loans from indigenous sources
in the country where the project is located, giving other prospective lenders an indication of the project's importance.

Insurance companies and pension funds, traditional sources of long-
term financing in many countries, would appear to be ideal participants in
project financing packages, because the gestation periods on large-scale
ventures are often very long. The relatively stable and predictable cash
flows of such nonbank institutions would seem to allow them to finance
at much longer maturities than, for example, commercial banks. However,
insurance companies and pension funds generally demand commensurately
higher interest rates, as well as strict security arrangements or guarantees.
And in many countries, including the United States, they are restricted in
their lending abroad. This could require a supplementary guarantee from
their home government, or it may negate their participation altogether.
Lack of investor interest in anything but conventional government and
corporate debt limits the international bond markets as a source of financing for projects until they are up and running with a proven track record.

Lease financing represents another potentially useful source of project
financing, which may have important legal, tax, and accounting advantages. As discussed earlier, a leasing company (perhaps bank owned) typically holds title to mobile equipment used on a project, claims depreciation
for tax purposes, and leases the equipment to the project operator, who in
turn may be able to claim lease payments as an expense for tax purposes.
The leasing company may also pass some of its tax benefits on to the
operator in the form of lower equipment rentals. The lessor, in turn, may
finance the equipment through long-term borrowing secured by the equipment itself, often at relatively favorable rates of interest.

Commercial bank loans usually form a major part of the typical project financing package, generally in the short- and medium-term maturities
priced on a floating-rate basis. Bank loans normally cover the critical earlier years of a project, and traditionally involve full recourse to sponsors
or third-party guarantors. They may also be serviced by production payments on a nonrecourse basis if appropriate guarantees can be provided,
and if the issue of legal claim to the source of the underlying cash flows
can be satisfactorily resolved. Bank loans are often arranged on a syndicated basis, which means that multiple banks have to be convinced of the
soundness of the loan and the project. Successful bank financing depends
in part on the "fit" between the term over which a loan is needed and the
repayment requirements specified by lenders. For many projects, financial
needs may extend well beyond conventional bank lending terms, some-

times limiting this form of financing to shorter periods in the construction or initial operating stages.

Equity capital can nevertheless cover a significant part of total project cost. Sponsors may inject cash into the project, particularly in the very early planning and start-up stages, or they may contribute to engineering staff, know-how, or administration. In addition, third parties, particularly potential customers, may be prepared to provide equity capital to a project on a minority participation basis. In a few cases, such as Eurotunnel, major public equity offerings may be undertaken to form the basis for large-scale debt financing.

Other potential sources of project funds may thus include wealthy individuals (domestic and foreign), central banks or monetary authorities, and investment management firms. Participation forms may include common or preferred stock, notes and debentures, convertible debentures, trade credit, and commercial paper. Straight or unsecured loans are often enhanced by warrants, conversion rights, or rights to other securities. Local-currency financing may be secured from indigenous banks, particularly for working capital purposes, or possibly on a longer-term basis from local insurance companies or other sources of term financing. Often one form of financing, such as subordinated loans, will make participation more attractive to one or more other sources of funding.

Standby Letters of Credit and Guarantee Facilities

Project financings often involve guarantee instruments that cover the performance of contractors involved in construction and related services. These can provide an important source of security for project participants, since sizable progress payments are sometimes made to contractors. Contractor default could place a project's vehicle company and its sponsors in financial jeopardy.

Under a standby letter of credit, a contractor asks a bank to open a letter of credit in behalf of the entity that has awarded the contract, which may be "called" by the beneficiary under certain, specified conditions of nonperformance contained in the guarantee instrument. If a "call" occurs, the bank will make payment and the contractor in turn is obligated to make prompt reimbursement to the bank. The bank's obligation is limited to paying the amounts specified to the beneficiary; it does not include direct intervention to assure completion of the work involved. Standby L/Cs include:

- Advance payment guarantees, posted against up to 100 percent of advance or progress payments to a contractor
- Bid guarantees, to ensure that a bidder will actually accept the award if made or that he will subsequently post required performance guarantees, usually 1 to 2 percent but sometimes 5 to 10 percent of the bid price
- Performance guarantees, often valued at 5 to 10 percent of the contract

price, stating that the contractor will actually perform in accordance with the agreement
- Maintenance or retention guarantees, used to cover contractor warranties after full payment has been made, perhaps 10 percent of the contract price

Under a standby L/C the contractor signs an indemnity agreement outlining its obligation to the bank, which in turn is triggered by an incurrence of liability on the part of the bank to the beneficiary under terms and conditions carefully specified by the contractor and agreed to by the beneficiary. The two represent separate sets of legal obligations. If the beneficiary calls the standby L/C for whatever reason, the bank must pay, although it will not incur a loss unless indemnification by the contractor is refused. For this reason, and because contractor losses in the event of a call may vastly exceed the value of the standby L/C, careful credit assessment of the contractor on the part of the issuing bank is essential. Calls may occur because of a contractor's financial difficulties preventing completion, technical or operating problems, or even arbitrary or fraudulent action on the part of the beneficiary. The latter possibility reinforces the need to specify conditions of default, possibly including independent certification, since the bank's obligation is unconditional.

To backstop its position, a bank issuing a standby L/C or other type of guarantee may require a lien on the contractor's assets, other security interest, cash margins, or certain covenants related to debt and coverage tests. The guarantee instrument may also be structured to diminish over time, while the project draws to completion and the risks involved decrease commensurately. Fees for standby L/Cs or other guarantee instruments can be substantial, and are paid by the contractor, presumably to be passed forward to the extent possible in the contract price.

Foreign Exchange Considerations

Foreign exchange aspects can assume a major dimension of project financings since cash needs, financial obligations, and resource sales will often be denominated in different currencies. The risks involved may be addressed in the short term by means of currency swaps or borrowings in the currencies needed and, in the long term, by financing in the appropriate currencies, swaps, long-dated forward contracts, and local-currency financings. Because of the extended duration of project financing, the foreign exchange aspects can be exceedingly complex and test the ingenuity of the financial advisors and banks involved.

Co-financing

The World Bank, regional development banks in Asia, Latin America, and Africa, and other intergovernmental institutions have traditionally been in the business of project financing. They are often able to provide attractive terms because of direct agency financing by participating national governments, or because the agency is able to fund itself long-term on domestic or international markets on a favorable basis. Particularly large projects in developing countries that exceed conventional financing capabilities may be able to proceed under a co-financing arrangement with international institutions, based on agreements with the host-country government.

Co-financing can take the form of *joint financing*, where all lenders share in responsibility for the entire project, or *parallel financing,* where each lender finances a separate part of the project. The World Bank has a long history of bringing other lenders and investors in on large-scale natural resources ventures where it has taken a leadership role.

Co-financing is clearly desirable for projects where the resources of the borrower, the World Bank, and other immediately related sources of finance are insufficient to cover necessary outlays. It "stretches" World Bank resources over a broader portfolio of projects without significantly diluting its degree of responsibility or the care taken in project appraisal. At the same time it gives co-lenders additional assurances of the quality of projects and the prospect of reduced sovereign risk attributable to the World Bank's presence.

In evaluating the financial requirements of a project likely to require co-financing, the World Bank looks first to prospective sources of long-term, fixed-rate financing, most often found among official bilateral or multilateral institutions or official export credit agencies and generally tied to purchases in a particular country. Funding is then sought from commercial sources to fill remaining gaps. In the case of a typical electric power project, for example, the Bank reviews a specific portion of the borrower's investment program and agrees to finance certain subprojects within it. Funds from private lenders are then sought to help finance other subprojects closely related to those financed by the Bank.

Generally, the Bank's resources can only be used to finance the foreign exchange costs of goods and services identified in advance, and only those expenditures that are made after approval of the loan by the Bank's executive directors. Hence, borrowers often find that commercial financing is required to cover expenditures that may not qualify for World Bank assistance, such as start-up costs, other imported goods and services, local procurement, and working capital needs. In addition to the use of private co-financing to complete the financing plan of a project as defined by the Bank, there have been cases in which co-financing was sought to help fund investment programs that were complementary to, but not included in, Bank-assisted projects.

Under the World Bank's co-financing program, borrowers are ultimately responsible for selecting the private lenders brought into a deal. However, the Bank does provide assistance by making co-financing opportunities widely known to potential lenders, and often provides borrowers with names of banks in the major capital markets that have in the past shown an interest in co-financing. At the request of borrowers, the Bank also takes the initiative in establishing contacts with prospective private lenders to ensure that borrowers make a reasonable effort to explore the prospects for commercial financing with a representative sample of banks before reaching a decision. The Bank encourages private lenders and borrowers to establish early and direct contact whenever a co-financing opportunity has been identified.

The terms and conditions of the commercial loans under co-financing are negotiated directly between the private lender and the borrower, just as the World Bank negotiates, independently of co-lenders, the terms and conditions of its own commitments directly with the borrower. Once drafts of the loan documentation pertaining to each lender become available, the World Bank and the private lenders agree on any cross-reference clauses to be included, as well as provisions to be incorporated in the text of the memorandum of agreement. The Bank reserves the right to approve clauses in the loan agreement between the private bank and the borrower that affect its own rights, such as the cross-default clause.

World Bank borrowers securing co-financing from private sources generally choose syndicated lending. The lead banks, acting on the borrower's mandate, assume full responsibility for arranging and managing the loans, although, at the request of the borrower, the World Bank's co-financing staff has occasionally helped to identify potential syndicate participants. The applicable loan agreements have followed established Euroloan precedents with respect to terms and conditions, again negotiated directly between the private lenders and the borrower. Since the disbursement procedures of private banks differ substantially from those of the World Bank, they are handled separately and independently. Although it is common practice to agree upon periodic staged disbursements over a fixed period, loans are frequently drawn down in a lump sum soon after signing. Similarly, payment of interest and principal to co-lenders is set independently of the World Bank loan.

A longer-term benefit related to World Bank co-financing activities involves introducing borrowers in developing countries to new commercial bank lenders, and thus assisting them in securing continued access to international capital markets. At the same time, commercial banks emphasizing the financing of specific projects, as opposed to country lending, have found new clients in developing countries. World Bank projects for which private co-financing has been arranged have historically been concentrated in the industrial and utility sectors. Figure 3-4 depicts a project financing by the International Finance Corporation (IFC), The European Bank for Reconstruction and Development, and the U.S. Overseas Private Investment Corporation in Russia. Figure 3-5 shows an agricultural project financing in Turkey involving IFC equity and lending participation, lending by Dutch and German aid agencies, and a private-sector project loan by the Rabobank of the Netherlands.

Figure 3-6 provides a summary overview of a complex project struc-

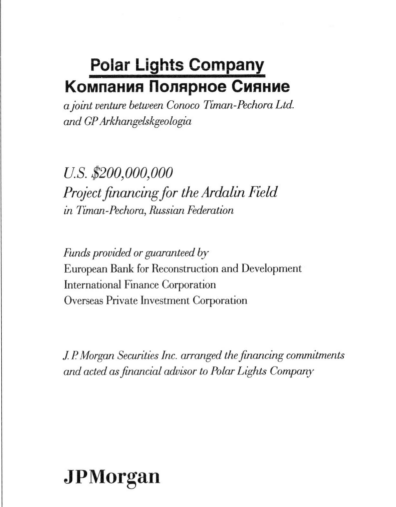

Figure 3-4. Example of a project financing.

ture. Linked to the project is the sponsor, working with the agent bank on the financial structure, injecting equity and receiving profits. Also identified are the contractors undertaking the construction work, which may also be involved as equity investors and possibly take product in partial or full payment for their services. Then there are suppliers (possibly working under a supply-or-pay agreement), the project operator working under an operating and management (O&M) agreement, and the customers, possibly involving a take-or-pay agreement. Also identified in Figure 3-6 are the project lenders, international institutions and the possibility of co-financing, and the government of the host country possibly providing guarantees or allowing the project to proceed under a build, operate, transfer (BOT) agreement.

Risk Assessment and Risk Management in Project Finance

Project financing is intended to design financial structures to be serviced from future cash flows, often with limited recourse to the project's sponsors. Financing that is structured in this way limits the burden placed on sponsors' balance sheets and diminishes future borrowing capacity and credit-worthiness less than other modes of financing. Lenders and investors rely on the project's expected revenue stream, and often carry a share

This announcement appears as a matter of record only.

aytaç
DIŞ TİCARET
YATIRIM SANAYI A.Ş.

Istanbul, Turkey

US$34,000,000

Financing for the construction of an integrated
meat and dairy plant at Çerkeş, Province of Çankiri

US$6,700,000
Common Equity
Provided by
International Finance Corporation
ifu-Industrialiseringsfonden For Udviklingslandene

US$18,000,000
Senior Term Loan
Provided by
International Finance Corporation
and through participations
in the IFC Loan by

FMO - Nederlandse Financierings   RABOBANK Nederland
Maatschappij voor Ontwikkelings Landen n.v.   Agri-Project Finance Team

DM 15,000,000
Senior Term Loan
Provided by
DEG - Deutsche Investitions-und Entwicklungsgesellschaft mbH

June 1994

Figure 3-5. Example of an agricultural project financing.

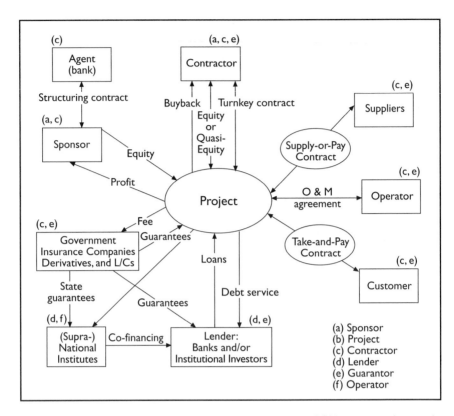

Figure 3-6. Complexity of project finance relationships. O&M = operating and management; L/C = letter of credit; BOT = build, operate, transfer.

of the technical, commercial, and political risks. Evaluation of risk and the application of risk-limiting techniques thus is critical in project financing because of the heavy reliance on the project itself to provide effective debt service. There are at least nine distinct types of risks lenders face in project financing (see Table 3-1).

Resource risk involves the possibility that the oil, gas, or minerals in the ground, which represent the basis for debt service in natural resource and energy projects, are not, in fact, present in the required quality or quantity.

Input or *throughput* risk concerns nonextractive projects such as power plants or pipelines where the basic viability of the project depends on the availability and price of energy, raw materials, or other resources under the original terms. In the case of tunnels, bridges, and similar projects, the risk is that supply or demand factors may result in a traffic shortfall, leading to a revenue deficiency.

Technical risk relates to the engineering characteristics of the project itself. A project may turn into an outright failure for technical reasons, or may result in substantial cost overruns requiring significant additional capital infusions.

Timing risk focuses on the possibility that delays, from whatever source, will stretch out the period of construction before the cash flows that support the financing actually begin. Such delays (especially in an inflationary period) can be the source of substantial cost overruns, and raise interest charges considerably. Even relatively short delays may lead to extensive escalation of construction costs.

Completion risk combines technical and timing risks. Completion problems include errors in engineering and design; construction delays due to strikes, weather, or late delivery of equipment and supplies; unanticipated topological problems; new and untested construction techniques under prevailing conditions; cost escalation due to a serious lack of skilled labor, and similar factors. In practice, the lenders have traditionally been willing to rely on cash flows from projects only after they have become operational, requiring the sponsors to provide financial supports and guarantees before loans become strictly nonrecourse. More recently there has been a greater willingness on the part of lenders to accept, under appropriate circumstances, a range of precompletion risks that previously the sponsors alone had to carry.

Market risk concerns future demand for the product or service supplied by a given project. Prices for many raw materials are naturally volatile, and they also may be subject to significant long-term (secular) shifts over the extensive period of time that faces the financing. What happens, for example, when demand for the customer's own output undergoes a severe and prolonged recession? In addition, some products and services such as natural gas, transportation, and electric power are highly dependent on local or regional market developments, and may easily encounter a demand shortfall. This problem may be complicated by difficulties in storing or finding alternative uses for certain resources (e.g., natural gas). In assessing market risk, demand forecasts clearly hinge on such factors as

Table 3-1 Types of Risk Encountered in
Project Financing

Resource risk
Completion risk
  Technical problems
  Timing problems
  Cost overruns
Market risk
  Demand shortfalls for resource or service
  Throughput shortfalls in infrastructure projects
Country risk
  Political issues
  Economic performance
Force majeure risk

---

price and income elasticities, competition, exchange rates, availability of substitutes, government policies, political developments, and environmental concerns.

Operating risk focuses on the long period of time that projects and their financing generally involves, over which costs may change or labor, transportation, or other critical elements may be disrupted by external sources or management incompetence. Operating problems also include inability to meet output targets or quality specifications, poor engineering or design work, unexpectedly high maintenance costs due to corrosion or wear, price increases on energy equipment and materials, exchange-rate movements, and other factors.

An important source of operating risk is the quality and stability of the local labor pool, particularly in developing countries. This risk often can be reduced by training programs, astute labor relations, and tapping of external labor sources. Prospective operating expenses and their variability, project location, complexity of environmental problems, and similar factors may also influence perceived operating risks. The best assurance to lenders is a proven track record under similar circumstances on the part of the project operator. Management-related sources of operating risk are of direct concern to sponsors and operators if the project is to be completed and operated as planned. Project logistics, subcontractor reliability, labor relations, and environmental conflicts are often of major concern here.

Force majeure risk involves acts of God, such as earthquakes, hurricanes, or other weather-related calamities; warfare; and other uncontrollable events that may lead to failure, escalate costs, delay completion, or disrupt operations. Provisions to take on force majeure risk are usually accepted by lenders in project financings, generally for a limited duration only.

Political risk involves the political conditions that surround a project during the period covered by a financing. Terrorist acts, labor disruptions, tax changes, newly imposed pollution controls, invasions from abroad, and similar events arising from the political environment fall under this general heading. So do expropriation or nationalization, imposition of exchange controls, changes in royalties or depletion allowances, and pressures for indigenization of equity or human resources—some of which may be imposed retroactively.

Issues related to country problems are supposed to be covered in standard country-risk assessments carried out independently by project lenders and investors (see chapter 5). However, a given project may have a risk profile that is quite different from that of the country as a whole. A project may be politically sensitive in a country that is otherwise characterized by a very low degree of assessed risk. The specific kind of natural resource involved, project location, employment of nationals, nature of the target markets and downstream uses, and shifting government and interest group priorities may dictate a project risk profile that may be a cause for lender concern. This deviation of "project-specific risk" from conventional country risk often requires complex analysis.

As with any type of business risks, those related to project financing hinge on the variance in the expected returns to lenders and investors. Some of these risks are related to short-term exposures and will be liquidated early in the life of the project, or are incurred and eliminated during comparatively brief periods as the project moves ahead. Others involve relatively long-term exposures where the expected returns are characterized by a rather high degree of variance. Moreover, for some lenders, variance in expected returns is not symmetrical (they can only lose, never gain), while for investors, variance in expected returns describes the chance of gain as well as loss that may be attributed to some of the sources of project risk. Finally, it is important to note that, within the framework of a given project, exposure to risk does not lend itself to diversification, unlike cross-border lending to countries, where some local borrowers may fare quite differently from others in response to changed country conditions.

In essence, lenders have to decide which of these risks are "bankable" and which must be covered by any of the available contractual arrangements involving either project sponsors or third parties such as customers, governments, or international organizations. This decision depends on experience, technical expertise, financial innovation, and the perceived degree of control over a wide range of variables. Such perspectives, of course, differ among participants in project financings—a complex deal can yield several different views on who is really carrying the risks involved. Banks' willingness to assume project risks remains very much project or sponsor specific. For example, lenders might be fairly comfortable evaluating the risks associated with a new production platform in the South China Sea or offshore Nigeria if they have done a number of similar deals in the past.

Evaluation and Mitigation of Project-Related Risks

Sources of risk to lenders and investors in project financing sometimes relate only to completion of a project, or they may be longer term and concern the project's operation over many years. Evaluating and reducing both completion and operating risk requires expertise and ingenuity. Financial management of these risks generally relies on various guarantees. These may be *direct* (full and unqualified commitment on the part of the guarantor), *limited* in terms of amount or duration, or *contingent* involving relatively unlikely events that lenders may feel the need to be covered for to secure their participation. Guarantees may be *implied* as an obligation of the guarantor, or *indirect* via performance of some related activities which will, in effect, make the lender whole in the event of problems.

Resource risk facing lenders is often evaluated by independent technical studies. The sponsoring firm or consortium will have made its own evaluation of the available quantity and quality of the resources to be recovered. This information will be carefully assessed by the major lenders' in-house technical experts and confirmed by outside consultants, with cost of any further independent evaluation of natural resource reserves borne by the vehicle company or its sponsors. Project financings will almost always involve multiple financial institutions. The technical assessment of available resources must be convincing to the lead institutions and to the other participants. This procedure has the added advantage of independent verification of the viability of the project.

Similarly, the sponsor's own evaluation of the technical problems involved in *completing* a project needs to be assessed in-house and possibly by engineering consultants or other outside experts. The track record of the sponsors in successfully undertaking comparable projects elsewhere is of great importance. Projects involving new technologies or particularly adverse conditions (climatic, topological) tend to multiply the risks incurred.

Lenders often require completion guarantees from project sponsors, who unconditionally warrant that performance will be as specified (quantity, quality, timing, and minimum period of operation) and that they will cover any and all cost overruns. Sponsors are typically asked, in advance, to agree to specific tests of physical and/or economic completion, with lender recourse lapsing only after these tests have been satisfactorily met. Cost-sharing arrangements may oblige sponsors to carry a specific pro-rata share of all project outlays, including debt service payments.

Other ways of reducing completion risk include penalty clauses, performance bonds, and guarantees such as standby L/Cs covering contractors on the project and completion guarantees issued by the sponsors themselves or other banks. These warrant that construction will be finished on schedule and that there will be no cost overruns. Technical criteria relating to performance of the facility on completion are often employed to ensure that things work as they should. The guarantor, in turn, may syndicate the guarantee or protect himself by means of bonds or insurance covering individual contractors and others involved in the construction phase of a project.

Sponsors may also provide *comfort letters*, sometimes called "letters of moral intent" or "keepwells," promising to supervise and maintain an active interest in the vehicle company throughout the precompletion and operating phases of the project without issuing a formal guarantee. Such documents, even when tightly worded, cannot be viewed as de facto guarantees by project lenders.

Supply or throughput risk on major resource-related projects such as pipelines can, where applicable, be handled by obtaining guarantees from the suppliers of raw materials or energy sources, specifying the required throughput amounts and prices to be charged. In payments for the use of such facilities, there often is a "hell-or-high-water" clause that anchors the absolute, unconditional nature of the obligation irrespective of nonperformance by the other party.

Market risk in project financings is often met by "take-or-pay" contracts, whereby the ultimate buyers of the output unconditionally commit themselves to make specific payments for a given period, whether or not they actually take delivery. One problem with take-or-pay contracts is that the sponsor, in effect, sacrifices a certain degree of control over the facility. Since the guarantor may be a third party, this can involve somewhat higher borrowing costs. Such issues have to be weighed against the drawbacks of an explicit sponsor guarantee for the life of the loans involved. A "take *and* pay" obligation is a somewhat softer version that depends on actual delivery of the resource. Naturally, the credit standing of the purchasers must be carefully reviewed, as must a variety of market-related elements. Market risk can sometimes be reduced by direct customer equity participation in projects, debt participation, floor prices, and price-escalation arrangements.

It may also be possible in project financings to obtain "deficiency guarantees" covering an entire venture, either from the sponsors or from the government of the country where the project is located—or perhaps the home-country governments of the sponsors. Some guarantees cover losses of principal and interest suffered by lenders after any collateral has been liquidated in the event of default. In the case of a government's sovereign guarantee, country-risk assessment will determine its true value. Collateral in offshore project financings can take many forms:

- A lender's mortgage over the borrower's interest in the license or project facilities
- Assignment of the lender's interests in the various agreements and contracts
- Assignment of insurance proceeds
- Assignment of revenues received, such as liens on accounts receivable; liens on petroleum inventories
- Contingent claims on related bank accounts; a pledge of shares of the borrower

In addition, sponsors may be required to not reduce their financial interest in a venture below a specified level. Sellers of equipment to the project may also be willing to provide certain guarantees, or this function may be taken up by exporting-country government agencies. The existence of a complex of guarantees, of course, provides support for project financing only to the extent that the guarantors are able and willing to meet their obligations, and hence each guarantor has to be subjected to careful credit analysis. Even after all guarantees are taken into account, the underlying soundness of the project itself still tends to be the determining factor.

Political risks in project financing can be dealt with in a variety of ways, including purchase of political risk insurance and participation of influential banks from a number of different countries (particularly from major trading partners or creditors of the host country), of regional development banks, or of the World Bank. Sometimes the country's needs for continued balance-of-payments loans, including rollovers of maturing debt, may give banks sufficient implied leverage to constrain adverse political moves.

A central function in project financing is thus to identify and quantify the various categories of risks and to structure the deal to allocate these risks acceptably among the various participants. As financial institutions develop a better understanding of the risks in particular types of projects, they seem increasingly prepared to accept a larger share of total project risks. That means less onerous covenants and guarantees for project sponsors. A reputable sponsor with a good record should be able to negotiate over a range of risks that bankers would not have accepted early in the history of project finance. The fundamental challenge facing financial advisers on major projects is to put together a financing package that will align the interests of all parties, given (1) the financing sources available, (2) the risks, and (3) the options available for reducing these risks.

Build, Operate, Transfer

Given the scarcity of public financings for infrastructure projects in many countries, the build, operate, transfer (BOT) model has made its appearance. Essentially, BOT takes what is conventionally defined as a public-sector infrastructure project under a concession granted by the government; applies private capital to develop the project and operate it for a certain period at a profit to give the investors an acceptable return, and then transfers the facility to the government. The technique actually originated with the development and financing of rail systems in various parts of the British Empire in the nineteenth century.

BOT equity is raised from private sources or through a public share offering by a sponsorship consortium for a special-purpose vehicle company. The sponsors may be contractors seeking engineering and construction work, operating companies, equipment manufacturers, suppliers, or customers, usually with the active support (but not direct participation) of the public sector. The equity serves as an incentive for the contractor and operator to perform on time and within budget, since each has a significant stake in the venture, and provides cushioning and comfort to lenders in terms of the project's economic viability. A pure BOT project would raise debt financing purely on its own merits, although in many cases government guarantees are in fact involved. Eurotunnel between France and Great Britain is an exception in this regard. Designing BOT structures is not cheap, and the higher the risk assessment, the higher the costs incurred by the sponsors who have no guarantee that the project will in fact go ahead.

Advantages and Costs of Project Financing

The growth of project financing is obviously linked to material advantages over other, more traditional, forms of lending to accomplish the same objectives. First, to be economically viable projects often have to be so large that they outstrip the financial capabilities of the firms involved, even in the joint ventures. North Sea oil development, the Alaska pipeline, and the Eurotunnel are perhaps the most well-known examples of project financings. With all possible supports for the loan captured in the financing package, the project itself must in the end be capable of justifying a significant share of the debt incurred.

Second, project financings are largely off balance sheet as far as the sponsoring companies are concerned, except perhaps as footnotes related to long-term debt. Full guarantees, nevertheless, have to be captured in financial statements as contingent liabilities, although completion guarantees might be omitted on the grounds that they are merely normal parts of doing business. Project financing enhances sponsors' borrowing capacity in the view of prospective lenders. This permits a far higher degree of de facto leveraging of their capital than would otherwise be possible without incurring commensurate risks. If successful, ventures structured along project-financing lines can have very positive effects on sponsors' profitability.

Third, project financing may permit a greater degree of bank risk reduction through loan-portfolio diversification than alternative forms of financing. In some ways, project financing may indeed be superior to sovereign lending. The project itself may generate independent export revenues or reduce import expenditures, or may have broad-gauge favorable effects on the external debt-servicing capacity of the host economy. Projects may also provide a good indication of a country's long-range economic outlook and the quality of its economic management.

Project financing costs can be expected to exceed the costs of comparable financings undertaken directly by project sponsors. Involvement of multiple lenders and other parties tied together by a complex structure of undertakings absorbs a substantial amount of time and effort that can translate into equally substantial legal, management, and financing fees, and interest spreads on for the most part nonrecourse financings will tend to reflect the incremental risks accepted by lenders—with borrowing costs potentially well above the sponsors' corporate borrowing rates. Where such risks are shifted through insurance, the associated premiums will add to overall financing costs, while other forms of risk transfer such as offtake contracts or consumer financing may involve substantial price concessions. It is also to be expected that state-owned energy and resources companies will sometimes shun project financing, since government-guaranteed or imputed government-backed financing is less costly for them.

Competition among Financial Institutions

From a profitability point of view, project financing offers potentially attractive opportunities to certain financial institutions. The global presence of large international banks provides an important information advantage in obtaining leadership positions in project financings and in evaluating risks and assembling the financial resources necessary to carry them out.

Financial "packaging" is the essence of project financing, and economic returns to advisors and others that can be attributed to this function—actually returns on proprietary information and financial innovation—can be very substantial. However, project sponsors and their advisers sometimes find it possible to "unbundle" the project financing package to secure different services—loans, foreign exchange contracts, standby L/Cs, lease financing—from a variety of different competitive suppliers.

An institution serving as financial adviser on a project can work closely with sponsors, governments, international agencies, suppliers, customers, other advisors, and guarantors to establish contracts that may prove useful in generating future business. This is a high-profile activity, where the adviser is called on to use a great deal of ingenuity. It must be able both to satisfy borrower needs for suitably structured financing at lowest possible cost and to satisfy prospective lenders, who often have quite distinct interests and objectives, of the inherent soundness of the project. Usually advisers must design a financial plan that can be presented to lenders as a unified, consistent whole to minimize disagreements, negotiations, and delays.

Success in project financing gets around quickly—but so does failure. The most lucrative part of project financing clearly is fee income, which on a complex financing arrangement can be sizable. Since to some extent fee income is unrelated to lending, it can have a very positive impact on overall returns on assets. A lead institution in a project financing will generally participate directly in a financial package. It may also be called on to lead-manage one or more syndicated loans or bond or equity issues, thereby tapping into profits from that source as well. Additional returns may come from funding profits, foreign exchange business, interest-rate swaps, and other activities.

The profitability of project financing to international commercial or investment banks, and to the limited number of other banks able to participate effectively, is tied to its complexity and its risks and returns. Relatively few financial institutions seem to have the necessary legal, accounting, tax, financial, and technical skills, either at their head offices or at strategically located regional offices, to become major players. When this constraint is combined with the need for large-scale financing power in various maturities, the capability of effective syndicate leadership, and close sponsor contact, it is not surprising that the number of major participants is limited. As a result of the high barriers to entry, project financing has emerged as something of an oligopolistic market, in that it is dominated by those few major banks with financial and technical resources and the experience and expertise to evaluate the risks and devise suitable financing packages. Because of their reputation and power in the market, the leadership in most project financings is likely to involve at least one of these major players. Other banks may rely on the 10 to 12 international banks that constitute the top tier in project financing, in the same way that smaller banks may look first to the lead manager and then to the borrower in making a decision to participate in a loan syndication or in lending to a sovereign borrower. Such reliance, without adequate recourse, is clearly unhealthy and may well lead to a suboptimal allocation of financial resources in project financings worldwide.

Project financing techniques and large-scale capital-intensive ventures are clearly inseparable. The latter could not be carried out with any degree of effectiveness and efficiency without access to global financial markets and the economic discipline imposed on the ventures by the funding approaches developed in project financing. Lending techniques are brought to bear that ensure that all risks and returns are carefully weighed by a large number of parties, and that the risks are borne by participants best able to cope with them in the light of perceived returns.

4

International Retail and Private Banking

A notable characteristic of banking for individual clients in the 1990s is the unprecedented level of competition facing all players in the market. This competition has forced many institutions into a reappraisal of their existing client bases and an attempt to penetrate new and attractive markets. We discuss two segments of this market here. One comprises wealthy or *high-net-worth* (HNW) individuals and families requiring so-called private banking services, which are often international in nature. The second is *mass-market retail banking,* which is basically a local business but can be penetrated by foreign-based financial firms as well.

The Nature of Private Banking

Since the late eighteenth century, international private banking has been the particular domain of Swiss, British, and other banks engaged in fiduciary activities. Examples include Coutts & Co. in the United Kingdom and Lombard Odier & Cie. and Bank Julius Baer in Switzerland. Competition has increased considerably. In the late 1970s a number of American banks, in particular, established "private banking" departments to cater specifically to the needs of wealthy clientele, whose requirements had been served on a more ad hoc basis. Private banking strategies were developed by banks such as J.P. Morgan, U.S. Trust Company, Chase Manhattan, and Citicorp, and rapidly became a focus for targeting HNW financial services clients. It turned into the first real attempt to segment the consumer market. The term has come to mean different things in different banks, but a general definition would include all mainstream services a bank can legally provide specifically for high-net-worth individuals.

Why has international private banking enjoyed such interest and credibility, and why have the HNW clients become so valuable? With competition reducing the margins on lending and regulatory concerns about capital adequacy, banks have had to review carefully all new on-balance-sheet activity, with many deciding to emphasize off-balance-sheet and other fee-generating services. Simultaneously, there has been an attempt to reduce dependence on commoditylike bank-lending as against higher value-added financial services. This has involved a reappraisal of the profitability of retail and in particular private banking as banks have been focused increasingly on the profit potential of individual clients.

The HNW client base offered a number of attractions. In terms of competitive analysis, it appeared underbanked. This was especially so in view of the increasing demographic importance of the wealthy in the main industrialized countries. The baby boomers of the 1960s were entering the 30 to 40-year-old age group, a time when income level and wealth base tends to increase significantly. It was also a time when national income had been growing at between 1 percent and 3 percent for several years in real terms and falling inflation had stimulated equity markets throughout the world, increasing both individuals' wealth and their awareness of financial assets. Notwithstanding the rapid rise in HNW-individual banking competition, bankers considered the market as one retaining attractive potential.

Due to the highly personal nature of private banking, HNW clients generally prefer to "stay with" a particular bank, if possible. This results in lower price elasticity of demand, facilitating product cross-selling and enabling institutions to compete on qualitative variables instead of pricing alone. In addition, the cost structures of many banking activities allows significant economies of scale in transactions processing and portfolio-management activities.

The range of private banking services is extraordinarily broad, from deposit, payments, and investment advisory services all the way to having meals arranged for clients in prison or hospitals (as some Swiss banks have been said to do), from traditional fiduciary activities to arranging personal lines of credit, secured loans on yacht purchases, leveraged buyouts, and tax shelter financing. The essential factor is to offer a truly personal service. Private banking services ultimately affect the HNW client's net worth. This may involve a focus on either the asset or liability side of the client's balance sheet, or a combination of both. But the common factor is that the services affect the structure of that balance sheet and its composition over time.

Wealth and the Wealthy

For a financial institution developing its private banking business, an understanding of the nature of wealth and of the HNW client characteristics is important in deciding which specific segment of the potential client base to target and what services to offer.

Wealth can be discussed in terms of command over economic resources. It may be either financial (currency, bank balances, stocks, bonds) or real (commodities, precious stones, objets d'art, real estate). It may be considered on a liquidity/yield continuum ranging from highly liquid but low-yielding assets (e.g., currency or gold) to higher yielding but low-liquidity assets (e.g., real estate, antiques.) Command over economic resources depends on an individual's claim on risk-adjusted expected future returns. The market value of a portfolio of assets will depend on the expected returns and risks associated with that portfolio. The risk of an asset derives from the variance of its expected returns and that of a portfolio from the covariance in the returns of all the assets contained in it. The ability to measure wealth at any given time will depend on the existence of a market for the particular asset and the ability to "mark to market."

Such a definition of wealth is a purely economic measure. It does not necessarily equate to an individual's own assessment of his or her personal worth in a broader context, which is affected by many other factors. People vary, for example, in the satisfaction they gain from higher wealth levels. They differ in their reaction to risk. They are influenced by social, political, religious, and philosophical attitudes to wealth. All of these factors color their vision of the value of what they have, and are highly relevant for the private banker seeking to understand the client and the marketplace.

Wealth can be generated legitimately or illegitimately. Legitimate wealth is the product of economic returns in the provision of goods and services to society—returns to labor and capital above the normal returns that would be earned in a competitive marketplace. In that sense, the individual wealth accumulated, from the provision of superior products or services or superior cost effectiveness can be considered strong evidence of economic contribution in a market-oriented system.

Wealth can, however, also be amassed at the expense of the rest of society through such illegitimate means as extortion, prostitution, racketeering, insider trading, gun running, and drug trafficking. Such activities cost society twice over, both by noncontribution and social damage and by causing otherwise productive resources to be diverted to anticrime measures.

A further subdivision can be made according to the specific income-generating activities involved, and provides a useful method of categorizing the wealthy according to the source of their assets—which in turn affects their attitudes and banking requirements. We distinguish five main groups: corporate, entrepreneurial, and family (socially legitimate); political and criminal (socially illegitimate).

> *Corporate wealth.* Wealth generated through service within a corporation in the form of salaries, bonuses, stock options, severance payments. This form of wealth is increasingly common, particularly in the United States and Western Europe where the corporate culture is strong.

Entrepreneurial wealth. Wealth that an individual has accumulated over his or her lifetime either as sole or co-owner of a business enterprise. It is particularly pervasive in the United States and Asia due to their respective patterns of economic development. To a large extent, entrepreneurial wealth is paper wealth; in the case of private companies it may be realized only when the enterprise is sold or goes public.

Family (inherited) wealth. This involves the transfer of wealth from one generation to another and is therefore highly dependent on national fiscal and economic policies. "Old" wealth is probably more pervasive in Europe than elsewhere. It can arise from any of the other sources of wealth specified here.

Political wealth. Wealth that can usually be attributed to corruption in political office at varying levels within national or regional governing administrations. The sources include misappropriation of public funds, bribery, extortion, political contributions, kickbacks, and financial holdings benefiting from government contracts. Although functionaries within government usually receive limited official compensation, the power residing in their hands often makes siphoning off funds relatively easy. This form of wealth may be more pervasive in some emerging-market countries than in the United States, Japan, and Western Europe, although scandals and corruption afflict virtually all countries from time to time.

Criminal wealth. This represents wealth deriving from organized crime and other illegal activities. Criminal organizations thrive on every continent, ranging from the Italian, American, or Russian mafias through Chinese tongs and Japanese yakuza to the Latin American drug syndicates. This type of wealth can be expected to occur in most societies, but there is reason to believe that it is more pervasive in developed countries due to greater scope for illegal activities and greater organizational abilities of criminals.

While it is dangerous to generalize, it may be reasonable to argue that the more reliance societies place on the operation of free markets and transparent, rule-based democratic politics and administration, the more important will be entrepreneurial and corporate wealth and the less important political and criminal wealth. This is because fewer distortions tend to exist in free and open systems. Political corruption and criminal activities arise in part from market distortions.

Determinants of Wealth Distribution

The matter of wealth distribution, both on a national and international scale, is of basic importance for private banking. Wealth distribution is primarily a factual question, although certain conceptual factors are of interest as well:

Per capita income. Wealth is a "stock" measure and income is a "flow" measure. Since wealth is based on past or current resources used in an economy—and since capital, along with labor, natural resources, and productivity determines national income and output—higher-income countries should harbor greater wealth concentrations than poorer ones.

Market distribution mechanisms. The distribution of property rights as well as those of capital ownership, education levels, and other sources of earning power differ significantly from one country to another. In these circumstances, markets for goods and services, capital, and natural and human resources may generate quite different distributions of wealth and income between countries, even when economic size and per capita income are comparable.

Government policies. These tend to result from a confluence of historical, religious, cultural, and sociological factors that generate a political concept of a "fair" distribution of income and wealth—and more important, the extent to which free markets are permitted to determine that distribution. This political concept will, in turn, determine national policy with respect to taxation, wealth and income transfers, nationalization, expropriation, and other policy measures affecting the wealthy and how they react to them.

These three factors, analyzed together, explain to a large extent the geographic distribution of wealth within different countries—not only where wealth may be found, but also where it is privately held rather than institutionalized.

There are plenty of "wealthy" societies in which wealthy individuals are few and far between, and others that have the wealthy in abundance—Sweden versus Switzerland, to cite one comparison. This is of great importance to the private banker. If wealth accumulation is heavily taxed or heavily institutionalized, in the form of pension funds or union assets, for example, it is of little interest for private banking. Rather, it is the disposable (discretionary) element of wealth and income that matters. It is where markets are allowed to determine income and wealth levels that high net worth individuals and families can emerge.

Also relevant is the social and political "climate" of wealth. We noted earlier that legitimate wealth accumulation is evidence of economic contribution. But this is in a capitalist context. There are societies where wealth may instead be considered evidence of exploitation and economic parasitism. Even without going that far, views on the "worth" of wealth vary widely. What does it bring in terms of kudos, power, and worry? These variables will affect an individual's attitude to wealth accumulation, which in turn is likely to influence his or her economic performance.

While factors such as these will be among the principal determinants of the geographic distribution of wealth, supply-side developments also drive world wealth allocation. One notable case involved the oil shocks of the 1970s. This was particularly important because people in the Middle East at the time had little experience in managing wealth and national economic infrastructures initially had difficulty absorbing the volume of funds generated. Middle Easterners were besieged by offers of help from private bankers especially from the United States, Switzerland, and the United Kingdom, with the latter's merchant banks succeeding in attracting a significant share of the net investible funds.

Wealth Allocation

What does the HNW client look for in private banking services? He or she is faced with the question of how to manage wealth effectively. At its broadest level this is an exercise in balance-sheet management, where the overall objective is maximizing net expected returns subject to a risk constraint (or minimizing risk subject to a total return target) together with a desired level of confidentiality, tax minimization, estate allocation, and possibly other objectives. This will involve a number of critical decisions on asset allocation. Especially where the objectives are mutually inconsistent, the client essentially needs help to make and execute those decisions. The basic choices may be divided into six main categories:

1. *Investment or consumption.* In what proportion should the client's wealth be divided between current consumption and asset accumulation? This will obviously depend on individual time preferences and the opportunity cost of consumption. The higher the expected real after-tax return on assets, the higher the opportunity cost of consumption. So that an optimum consumption/investment pattern can be achieved, the fact that a measure of consumption can take place simultaneously with real investment also must be taken into account. The German Expressionist painting hanging in the dining room, for example, provides the owner with both intrinsic and status benefits even as it may make good sense from an investment perspective.

2. *Domestic or international investments.* How much wealth should be committed to home-country interests and how much to investments in political jurisdictions abroad? This will depend on the relative attractions and risks associated with various asset markets and the value of confidentiality.

3. *Onshore or offshore investments.* How much wealth should be allocated within domestic or foreign national jurisdictions, and how much to "offshore" havens? Tax considerations as well as questions of security and secrecy will again play a role here, as will national economic and financial policies.

4. *Real or financial assets.* This choice will be influenced by macroeconomic environments. The expected level of domestic inflation is one determinant. In periods when inflation exceeds the rate of interest, individuals tend to leverage themselves as much as possible, since funds borrowed today are repaid deeply discounted in real terms at the end of the infla-

tionary period. Preservation of the real value of wealth is of paramount importance. Real assets and financial assets denominated in stable currencies will tend to be favored over domestic financial assets in such circumstances, and there is typically a rise in demand for gold, property, and objets d'art. Some of these assets are notable for their lack of liquidity and imperfect markets. If they have to be sold quickly, substantial discounts may have to be accepted. The investor's attitude toward liquidity, therefore, plus his or her likely future cash-flow requirements and need for "precautionary funds," are important factors in determining any real/financial asset split.

5. *The political environment.* Political stability has an important bearing on this particular choice. Preferential taxation for individuals investing in private enterprise, for example, may encourage wider stock ownership. Tax relief on mortgage interest may increase investment in real property. Governments in many countries have from time to time offered preferential treatment to public rather than private investment in order to fund fiscal deficits. Sometimes the incentives are reversed, with governments encouraging privatization or attempting to improve the attractiveness of venture capital.

6. *The economics of financial intermediation.* How much wealth should the HNW client place with financial intermediaries, and on what terms? At one extreme such clients may seek minimum involvement from a financial institution. At the other, they may entrust a large share of assets to an individual agent such as a bank's trust department, acting in a fiduciary capacity. This may give rise to principal-agent problems, including the adviser's incorrect interpretation of the client's wishes, and dangers of the adviser's self-enrichment at the expense of the principal. Alternatively, HNW clients may commit their wealth to multiple investment managers in order to impose the discipline of competition.

Financial intermediation and related private banking services provide four principal advantages to a wealthy individual:

1. *Risk-shifting.* There are two categories of risk-shifting, depending on the nature of risk-pooling involved. One alternative is for the investor to place funds at the disposal of the financial institution, which then invests them. The individual has no control over the allocation of the funds or the levels of risk borne by the bank, and is thus exposed to the risk of the bank itself (bank intermediation). The alternative is for funds to be directed to specific investments, with the financial institution reacting to the individual's own risk preferences in the allocation process. In this case the HNW client bears the risk of the investment (investment intermediation). Bank intermediation may be considered as a lower value-added, commodity-type service to private clients, while investment intermediation represents a higher-value, interactive and personal service. In general, the former will be characterized by interest-margin income to the financial institution, and the latter by fee income.

2. *Information.* To optimize (within a cost constraint) often complex

personal objectives, most people need expert advice and help. Banks provide expertise in two key areas—products and markets—for clients who frequently have little interest or effort to spare for such things. The proliferation and increasing complexity of new financial instruments makes it ever more difficult for an individual to stay abreast of developments. At the same time, given its broad network of daily market contacts resulting from a broad range of trading functions, a financial institution is likely to have a more comprehensive knowledge of market sentiment and a more soundly based view of future market developments than most individuals. It will also receive critical new information more quickly than an outsider.

3. *Market power.* The larger the financial institution and the greater the volume of transactions it carries out in a particular market, the greater its firepower to obtain better prices. The rationale for grouping together small securities deals into block orders has been exemplified by the rapid growth in recent years of mutual funds and unit trusts. The net price achieved will also be affected by the commission structure of the markets. Where commissions are negotiated, larger dealers benefit, since they have the market power to achieve more advantageous rates. The extent to which a financial institution will in turn pass on any benefits to the client will naturally depend on how important that client is and how much leverage he or she has.

4. *Time considerations.* The effective management of wealth is exceedingly time consuming. Individuals in the wealth-building phase of their lives, in particular, typically work under severe time constraints. They therefore expect a prompt response to their banking needs, and will want to deal with someone with the authority and ability to make quick decisions. Other private banking clients devoting time to charitable or other pursuits have similarly limited time for investment decisions. This may require decentralization of private banking decision-making, with the allocation of more authority to officers. Clients with significant time constraints also tend to be less price sensitive.

Individual Objectives

We have considered the main decisions required for private wealth allocation as separate and distinct. They are, of course, highly interrelated and tend to be resolved intuitively and simultaneously—aimed at satisfying the individual's objectives, which are themselves an amalgam of preferences across a number of variables among which time, yield, security, confidentiality, and service level are paramount. Each of these plays a distinctive role.

> *Yield.* The traditional European private banking client was concerned with wealth preservation in the face of antagonistic government policies and fickle markets. These clients demanded the utmost in dis-

cretion from their private bankers, with whom they maintained life-long relationships initiated by personal recommendations. Such HNW clients have given way to more active and sophisticated customers. Aware of opportunity costs and often exposed to high marginal tax rates, they consider net after-tax yield to be far more relevant than the security traditionally sought by HNW clients. They may prefer gains to accrue in capital appreciation rather than interest or dividend income, and can be expected to have a much more active response to changes in total rate of return.

Security. The world today is arguably a more stable place than it has ever been. The probability of revolution, war, and gross confiscatory taxation has dropped in Europe, North America, the Far East, and Latin America. Nevertheless, a large segment of the private banking market remains highly security conscious. Such clients are generally prepared to trade off yield for stability and safety.

Confidentiality. Secrecy is a major factor differentiating international from domestic private banking. Clearly, with every government in the world subject to international pressure, "secure" funds against which another country makes legal claim can rapidly become insecure if their presence is advertised to those who have leverage over the authority regulating the custodian private banker. We shall return to this issue below.

Service level. While some of the tales of personal services provided for private banking clients are undoubtedly apocryphal, the "fringe benefits" offered to a HNW client may well influence his or her choice of and loyalty to a particular financial institution. Such benefits may save time, reduce anxiety, increase efficiency, and make the whole wealth management process more convenient. Personal service is a way for banks to show full commitment to clients accustomed to high levels of personal services in their daily lives.

The essence of private banking is to have the flexibility and expertise to satisfy each client's unique objectives as fully as possible in a highly competitive marketplace.

Private Banking in National Financial Systems

Domestic private banking consists of all banking services provided within a country explicitly for wealthy residents. It should be viewed as an extension of the concept of "personal banking" or a broadening of the concept of "trust banking." It is primarily concerned with credit extension, tax minimization, and investment management.

The concept of domestic private banking is well developed in countries such as the United States, which has large amounts of private wealth and social attitudes that tend to be highly positive, with social success generally accompanying economic success. In recent years nearly all major banks have committed themselves to compete in the market in one form or another. The prime difference between financial institutions competing for this business is the wealth cut-off point for private banking clients. For example, a bank may require a minimum of $10,000 in balances for checking accounts and $5 million for custodial and/or investment management accounts. Another may be more flexible—a minimum requirement of $500,000 in investible assets may be dropped if an individual appears to have "potential," or exceptions from a $1 million net worth rule may be made for the "right" clients. Or a bank may require that each HNW customer generate a certain amount of fees annually. Other financial institutions have positioned themselves at the not-so-wealthy end of the market. There are also many small niche players in the field that focus on fee-generating private banking business. All of this is indicative of the general move in U.S. banking away from typical commercial lending and the growing awareness of the need for meaningful market segmentation into distinct client categories. Private banking is one aspect of this transition.

The Client Base

The client base for domestic private banking services consists of resident wealthy individuals. Again, they may be divided into two groups with differing risk, liquidity, and credit needs—the passive and the active investors.

Passive investors are traditional risk-averse individuals whose predominant use of financial resources is for consumption purposes. Taxes are paid mainly on income and real property. Bank performance is primarily measured against rates of return on assets under management and the deposit rates.

Active investors, on the other hand, represent a less traditional customer base for the larger banks, their needs having in the past been served by specialized institutions. Some do not maintain bank accounts at all, and those that do may use them primarily for transactions purposes. They tend to be more risk oriented than the passive client, and are much more financially sophisticated. They are profit rather than income motivated, and generally use their financial assets to increase their wealth.

Banks compete aggressively in their home markets for private banking customers and are particularly eager to attract the active investor, in whom they perceive useful lending possibilities as well as asset management. They are also interested in individuals in the wealth-building phase of their lives, the so called "seed-corn" client; by helping them in the early stages of wealth building, a bank may keep them later on. And there is a move to look beyond the high-net-worth to the high-income individual, high current income being strongly related to future wealth accumulation. The large U.S. banks were at first slow to exploit the active investor, losing ground to many small independent banks and investment banks, but they have firmly reentered the battle, often with client segmentation focused on professionals.

Private Banking Services

Many banks are attempting to become one-stop financial supermarkets for the wealthy, offering the entire gamut of financial services from loans and deposits on the banking side to investment management on the trust side.

Deposit-Related Activities. A proliferation of deposit and checking account services have become available to wealthy individuals—money-market accounts, savings accounts and checking accounts, certificates of deposit (CDs), commercial paper, bankers acceptances, Treasury bills, and a variety of "checkable," taxable, and nontaxable mutual funds. They vary in yield and liquidity characteristics and in flexibility, with short-term accounts particularly attractive to the passive investor concerned about combining liquidity with yield.

Credit Extension and Personal Lending Activities. The need to borrow is particularly prevalent among entrepreneurial HNW individuals. This client is in the wealth-creating phase of life, and will tend to be illiquid. He or she will rely on the private banker to find a way to structure a deal around an existing asset base. The skills necessary for this function fall into three main categories:

- Creativity in constructing a nontraditional deal, combined with the ability to analyze a loan request and understand the reality of personal financial statements by identifying outside sources of repayment and collateral beyond the assets financed by the loan
- Valuation skills, to accurately appraise and evaluate the market for a range of assets from fine art to thoroughbred horses
- Organizational and administrative skills, to give the client quick responses to loan requests

Corporate Lending Activities. The overlap between the personal and corporate needs of HNW clients is particularly interesting for banks. It allows them to penetrate more deeply into the individual's finances and to provide a range of corporate banking activities in addition to personal financial services. These include bankers' acceptances, letters of credit, revolving lines of credit, and term loans. In many cases the lending activities will be undertaken as an adjunct to the financial advisory service provided by the banker. Due to the links between the corporate and personal sides, familiarity with the individual's attitudes to risk, currency, maturity, and liquidity requirements gives a significant advantage to an institution already servicing banking needs. In addition, the closeness of the relationship can provide bankers with a good feel for the client's business, and the chance to observe the evolution of the company's earnings and risk profile over time. This can substantially reduce the risk associated with bank financing. The bank will advise on the acceptable level of personal leverage and the most prudent structure for borrowings.

Investment Management.   Services provided to HNW clients vary between and within institutions, depending on the type of client served and the size of funds available for investment. Due to economies of scale in portfolio management, smaller accounts will often be pooled, with many banks offering a variety of funds across a broad range of investments. The bank may also provide real estate services, custodian accounts, investments in precious metals, currencies, commodities, art work, and advice on the establishment of estates, trusts, and corporations. Tax advice is another key private banking function, where financial advice can have real value. Changes in the tax structure as well as changes in the client's circumstances will mean that the optimal structure of an individual's balance sheet will also have to change. For many banks, investment management activities were originally handled in trust departments, and later taken into the mainstream, enabling the bank to tailor investment vehicles to clients in a more comprehensive and personal way.

Specific Personal Services.   In a business where quality of service is of paramount importance and where the fiduciary nature of the relationship is critical, private bankers provide a range of activities atypical to mainstream banking.

Strategic Considerations and Competitive Dynamics

The relatively small numerical size and the attractiveness of the HNW market has resulted in fierce competition in private banking. Institutions compete in different ways. There are advertising campaigns, toll-free numbers, attempts to influence intermediaries such as attorneys and accountants, and referrals from other sections of a bank. Whatever the "surface" tactics for attracting clients, the key to profitable private banking is relationship with a client, which banks try to maximize across all product offerings.

Packaging of HNW services can make sense strategically for several reasons. When functions are bundled it is much more difficult to evaluate the price/return relationship of each one, allowing the bank to extract higher fee income. It is also possible that the client may be less price-sensitive with respect to the purchase of bundled services than with respect to each of the services separately. While other parts of banking have been subject to a general unbundling of services as a result of a proliferation of new financial products and techniques, this has been less true of private banking.

Due to the existence of economies of scope, a bank can often provide two services more economically than can two banks each providing a single service. This represents an important rationale for cross-selling of banking products. Since the fiduciary nature of the relationship gives the bank access to client-specific information, it has a competitive advantage in servicing the client and will not face the same search costs as other banks.

To perform effectively, private bankers in competitive markets thus have to engage in more meaningful market segmentation. The simplistic distinction between "haves" and "have nots" must be developed into a far more sophisticated analysis that incorporates the differing characteristics, needs, and financial sourcing habits of specific customer groups. This can help an organization focus its resources more accurately in order to target its product line, its distribution system, and its promotional efforts to particular market segments more successfully than its competitors.

Marketing is vital to persuade customers to stay with a given bank even when their wealth and portfolio preferences change. However, the most important component of any private banking effort is the quality of the bankers. It is not easy for a private client to share confidences with his banker, so that a low turnover rate in staff is particularly important. This provides the bank with an opportunity to compete on more qualitative variables than on yield or pricing.

Given the tendency for HNW clients to prefer to stay with the private banker they know, it is not surprising that the predominant competitive focus is to find new clients rather than to poach existing ones from other financial institutions. The objective is to acquire seed-corn clients. Nevertheless, there are some client segments that appear to be more yield conscious and therefore more mobile, and success depends on what the client's yield elasticity really is and whether he or she can be persuaded through quality service to stay.

International Private Banking

International private banking (IPB) is distinct from its purely domestic counterpart in that it consists of banking services provided primarily for wealthy nonresidents. It also differs in the priorities of clients—safety and secrecy have often outweighed investment performance as criteria. In general, the main objective of international private banking clients is to maintain and increase their wealth in an environment safe from the potential scrutiny of certain third parties. Figure 4-1 presents a typical IPB "pitch" to attract a certain type of client, although such open solicitation is relatively new to the business.

Figure 4-1. Typical international private banking presentation.

Secrecy

For some people, just having assets offshore is satisfactory. For others, the guarantee of banking secrecy is a prerequisite. There are a number of locales throughout the world specializing in the provision of confidentiality. A country provides the ability to sell secrecy to a bank through an appropriately structured regulatory system and/or built-in secrecy protection. Success depends on domestic banking laws. Although Switzerland automatically comes to mind in this context, it is hardly unique. Luxembourg, Austria, Panama, and the Cayman Islands are among many countries that have strict secrecy provisions embedded in their banking statutes. Switzerland is nevertheless quite different in that not only is breach of banking secrecy a criminal offense, but there is a two hundred-year tradition of conservative and reliable asset management and quality personal service to back it up.

There are indications, however, that the quality of secrecy may be on the decline as a private banking criterion. It is not only national secrecy provisions that count, but also international attitudes toward financial secrecy and the kinds of pressure that national tax and criminal authorities bring to bear on foreign jurisdictions. Due to the pervasive powers of national authorities in the United States and elsewhere, their growing determination to use them to combat criminal uses of secrecy as well as tax evasion, and their increasing willingness to share information, it is becoming more difficult to guarantee total secrecy. The primary driving force is governments' appreciation that financial secrecy facilitates criminal activities and that one of the best ways to attack these is to increase the cost and reduce the opportunities to launder money.

Moreover, there seems to be a growing disparity between the degree of financial secrecy offered in the up-market or value-added offshore centers like Switzerland and those of lesser standing. This is probably because high-quality financial centers have more to lose from being "tainted," and are at the same time more vulnerable to outside pressure due to their own banks' large presence internationally.

The IPB Client Base

The core client base for international private banking is the security-seeking HNW individual or family that wishes to hold funds offshore in a form that will maintain its value but will also be protected from exposure to national regulatory and political authorities. They may have a variety of reasons for the need for offshore banking, most of which, it has been suggested, can be traced to either fear or greed. A primary concern is to have funds in a safe haven in case of emergency—to facilitate temporary residence abroad, for example, or even permanent emigration. People wish to protect their wealth from political uncertainty, taxation, expropriation, arbitrary exchange controls, adverse inheritance laws, and the like.

The needs and attitudes of clients affect the range of services offered by private bankers. While the European or American client, for example, may well be happy to leave money with professional money managers, the generally less sophisticated Latin American client may be hesitant to grant anyone discretion over his or her funds and will consequently be unimpressed by banks' trust activities, usually preferring deposit and fiduciary accounts and avoiding gold and commodities whose prices can fluctuate dramatically. Even given the common secrecy component, HNW clients using IPB services have varying risk/return attitudes with respect to different elements of their portfolio.

For schematic purposes, one can split an IPB portfolio into three notional categories: *sacred, safe,* and *speculative.* These are terms that are obviously subjective—an acceptably safe portfolio for one individual may for another be entirely speculative. Wealth can thus be arranged across a risk continuum ranging from perceived total security—where the client will be effectively yield inelastic, the primary objective being to maintain the real or nominal value of wealth—to the other extreme targeting on high yields and with little exposure to risk. In essence this suggests two main categories—yield-seeking and stability-seeking money. Institutions that attempt to service both IPB client groups may encounter delivery problems in attempting to supply them simultaneously.

Products and Services

Essentially four types of services that comprise the international private banking business: transactions activities, credit extension, asset or portfolio management, and personal services.

Transactions Activities. A major role for the financial institution serving the IPB client with a significant component of his or her wealth offshore is to ensure that funds are where they are needed when they are needed. This is all the more difficult since in some cases IPB clients are not permitted to hold foreign currency under exchange-control regimes imposed by their national authorities, and any transactions involving offshore currency will, of necessity, have to be done abroad. In many countries foreign mail can be opened randomly by the authorities, and great care must be taken by private bankers to ensure total efficiency and discretion. One bank error could cost a client a fortune, a career, or worse. This exposure to risk, combined with the personal nature of many of the transactions (e.g., mortgage and credit card payments), render the IPB client highly service oriented. The IPB business, even more perhaps than its domestic counterpart, is closed linked to personalities. When top names leave a bank, they usually take a number of important clients with them.

Credit Extension. Although few banks actually extend credit to IPB clients in the traditional sense of the term, some institutions will lend clients certain small amounts that are backed by assets, typically no more than 40 percent of the value of the portfolio under management, and generally for short time periods. Banks generally will not provide unsecured loans as part of their IPB business, although some institutions will provide trade financing and other forms of transactional or corporate lending activities. These include:

- Lending against promissory notes. The client may request a personal loan backed by deposits or other assets.
- Letters of credit. IPB clients often need to import goods in the course of the business. This type of service is provided by many banks when backed by deposits.
- Overdrafts. Overdraft facilities usually involve less documentation than promissory notes, but are again only given when backed by deposits.
- Credit card loans. Many banks offer their own credit card services, while others act as references for their clients. Worldwide the most popular cards remain the American Express Gold Card and the corresponding credit-linked Visa and MasterCard products.

Asset or Portfolio Management.   Fiduciary activities for IPB clients dominate the product range. As noted, the objective is to build a portfolio appropriate to each client's needs, which manages effectively the interrelationship between risk, return, liquidity, and confidentially, all of which are interdependent, and among which difficult trade-offs often have to be made. IPB provides clients with access to financial, real, and speculative assets, given that their clients have complex financial objective functions encompassing a variety of financial products, in a number of currencies, across a range of locations. A broad range of portfolios may thus be available to satisfy a given individual's specific requirements.

Personal Services.   The personal services provided for IPB clients are as wide ranging, if not more so, than those provided to clients of domestic private banking operations. A key difference between these and transactions-related activities is that they are typically paid for explicitly, while the former are part of the "extended product" of an IPB relationship.

Location Criteria

IPB clients from certain geographic areas tend to use particular IPB arenas. Three main factors affect the attraction of specific locales.

First, geographic location will determine the convenience of managing transactions. Communications and transportation are important, as are time zones that can limit the amount of time available each day to control an account. A balance will also have to be struck between the HNW client's residence and the location of his or her business interests. There is sometimes a cycle where the client places funds offshore, then sets up business abroad, and finally emigrates.

A second issue involves matters related to country risk. An individual will have less real control over assets when they are offshore, a problem compounded by the fact that such locales may be associated with unstable governments. The IPB client may well thus be paying for secrecy in part by accepting higher levels of country risk. There also exists information risk. The IPB client is buying confidentiality, but there is always the possibility that his or her affairs will not remain totally secret—that third parties, be they national authorities or unscrupulous bank employees, will somehow gain access to the details of financial affairs. At the other end of the scale, it may be that the IPB client is denied full information on his or her own assets, due to the need for total discretion in such matters to avoid the prying eyes of home-country authorities.

Third are financial and yield concerns. Although the client's primary motivation may be security, many IPB customers are becoming increasingly yield conscious. Therefore, the net yield characteristics of a location, the overall level of financial sophistication, and the integrity and efficiency of the local banking sector and of the individual banks themselves will all be of relevance in the client's decision. The main arenas for international private banking are Switzerland, the United States, the United Kingdom, Luxembourg, Hong Kong, and Singapore. The institutions providing IPB services differ in each case.

IPB clients pay for services in two ways—through real costs and opportunity costs. The former relate to the explicit fees paid, the latter to yields foregone by having money managed in a particular arena with a particular level of service and degree of confidentiality. Since the primary concern for many IPB clients remains security, they tend to be willing to incur greater opportunity costs than other clients, and each location varies in the costs its institutions tend to exact. Banks charge a variety of fees. These consist of government charges as well as bank charges, and fees for brokerage, custody, dividend collection, and asset management. The client may also be charged market rates even though banks themselves may have executed deals at substantially lower prices.

Sellers of IPB services, no less than of other banking services, must work within the complex and diverse regulatory structure that characterizes the international banking arena. Each private banking vehicle will be constrained by a set of regulations specifically relevant to its location and organizational form. One must therefore view the regulatory structure in terms of the financial institution itself as well as the arena in which it operates. The obvious approach for individual institutions is to specialize in the IPB services that each does best, especially given the cultural and other difficulties of attempting to manage both yield-seeking and stability-seeking funds within the same institution.

The major question involves the extent to which an individual institution can succeed in broadening its private banking services range to attract—and, more important, to keep—the existing clients of other players. "Attracting" has traditionally been the more difficult part, due to HNW client preference for a personal and long-term relationship. But with the growing breed of performance-oriented HNW clients, "keeping" them poses problems as well. There is evidence of an increasing incidence of both intrasectoral private banking competition, where rivalry takes place in the same product segment, and intersectoral private banking competition, where it takes place between product segments. In the case of the intrasectoral competition, there may be an increasing focus on price and performance due to the difficulty of qualitatively differentiating between the same product offered by different financial institutions. The intersectoral competitive dynamics depend on the perceived level of product and institutional substitutability—for some IPB clients, London merchant banks and U.S. commercial banks may be interchangeable, for others they may not.

An alternative second strategy for developing a strong IPB base involves attracting new HNW clients rather than clients already being served by other financial institutions, particularly in view of the fact that the distribution of wealthy individuals can change rapidly. The specific services offered in each IPB market depend not only on the chosen target segment, but also on an institution's inherent strengths.

Retail Financial Services Abroad

The competitive changes that have taken place in the banking environment have forced many banks to reconsider various areas of commercial banking, none more so than retail banking. Technological development has been very influential because it has changed dramatically the economics of retail banking. Its primary effect has been to drive down the high costs associated with dealing with billions of individual transactions and to offer faster, more accurate, and more responsive information and processing systems. These have allowed banks to become more aware of developments in the retail market, and enabled them to identify various subsegments that make up that market, improve their marketing skills, and assess more clearly the profitability and risks associated with different retail products and various segments of the market. At the same time, the pace of deregulation—while clearly more rapid in some markets than in others—is allowing banks to widen the range of services they offer their customers, price them according to their costs and market demand, and in particular open up new possibilities for cross-selling products to customers (see Table 4-1). And in many areas there has been a general increase in retail banking clients' income and assets. The objective for many banks has become to capture fiduciary control of as much of this increased income and wealth as possible, as well as to maximize fee income associated with various financial products and services.

All in all, banks and other financial firms have increasingly come to realize that retail clients provide both unusually low-cost and reliable sources of funds for asset management and good opportunities for retail securities placement and funds management. On top of this, spreads on retail lending—including credit-card loans—are wide, and comparatively provide good opportunities for portfolio diversification and securitization. Many banks have thus made a strategic reassessment of the economics of

Table 4-1 Inventory of Retail Financial Services

Liability-side services	Insurance
Current account	Whole life
Savings account	Term life
Money-market account	Auto
Asset-side services	Home
Auto loans	Health
Mortgage lending	Casualty
Big-ticket consumer-durables lending	Other consumer services
Credit card loans	Travelers checks
Bank	Retail forex
Travel and entertainment	Travel agency
Personal loans	Real estate brokerage
Investment management	Estate agency
Mutual funds/unit trusts	T&E cards
Pension plans	Debit cards
Individual portfolio management	Money transfer
Stockbrokerage	Mortgage servicing
Fixed-income securities saless	Custody/lock-box
Personal financial risk management	Tax planning
	Estate planning

certain aspects of retail, mass-market banking, especially as rapid advances in transactions processing and information technologies has reduced the costs and improved the achievable quality of retail transactions.

Retail and Branch Banking

Retail banking is that part of commercial banking concerned with the activities of individual customers, generally in large numbers. While branch banking was at one time seen mainly as a source of cheap deposits, it increasingly became a valuable source of high-margin lending as well as fee and commission income. The high levels of cash left on deposit free of interest or in low-interest saving accounts in the past were typically sufficient to cover the cost of running branch systems and money transfer networks. This has become less important as market-related interest began to be paid on deposits. So the economics of running large branch networks became less attractive, and this put more pressure on banks to reduce their operating costs or increase revenues, or both.

Demographics.   The age profiles of the major economies have been subject to significant changes, and an accurate demographic breakdown of the consumer banking client base is important due to the different spending and saving characteristics of each age segment. Financial behavior has also been influenced by family structure. The most significant changes are the rise of two-income households, as well as the single-parent family structure. Two-income households tend to have more money and less time and are thus less interest sensitive and more convenience sensitive.

Household Wealth and Debt.   Real incomes have increased in most countries, and have been accompanied by an increase in the wealth of consumers as well as an increase in household debt obligations, especially in the United States.

Financial Preferences.   Consumers today tend to be more active in managing assets, liabilities, and liquidity than in the past. Many can even be classified as aggressive financial planners, and in many countries there has been a significant change in attitudes toward household debt.

While the predominant trend in wholesale banking in some countries has been toward disintermediation, the trend in retail banking in others has been toward increasing financial intermediation, sometimes linked to securitization. Credit cards, debit cards and automated teller machine (ATM) cards have become ubiquitous in many countries, providing growing opportunities for lending as well as fee income. And, although consumers have become more interest-rate sensitive, they are not especially so.

Regulation.   The banking industry has been one of the most protected industries in the world. Due to the negative externalities associated with banking failures, the importance of the stability of the monetary system, and the fiduciary nature of many banking activities, banks' activities have received three main types of protection—on price, product, and the market. Their costs of funds have often been kept artificially low through deposit rate ceilings. Their product scope has often been narrowly defined, with nonbank competitors denied access. In some countries they were often constrained on a regional basis. All such restrictions had repercussions on the development of the market. Interest-rate regulations motivated consumers to find higher yielding assets elsewhere. Regulations on nonbanks providing banking services also restricted banks from providing nonbank services, and geographic constraints stifled the natural spread and development of the industry. Most regulations have now been significantly liberalized.

Competitive Dynamics

The competitive posture of banks for retail business has changed considerably. Higher levels of competition, both from banks and from nonbanks, drove down returns on consumer lending, which caused some banks to take on marginal credits with a resulting higher level of write-offs and movement of consumers into higher-yielding financial assets such as mutual funds. The continuing rapid pace of technological innovation has entailed significant front-end investment requirements, and competition from outsiders for the payment function traditionally controlled by the banks has intensified. And there have been increasing levels of financial sophistication among clients. As in most aspects of the banking industry, buyers of retail banking services face a wide array of institutions trying to service their financial needs. These include retailers, manufacturers, security houses, life insurance companies, and savings institutions.

Barriers to Entry

With increasing levels of deregulation in the market, banks are losing their monopoly position over retail banking activities as barriers to entry fall. It is widely felt that the payments system is the heart of the financial system, so that it will be important for banks to retain control of access to the payments system to impede nonbanks from mounting an even greater challenge. The term *retail banking* is no longer homogeneous with respect to market definition. Instead, it is composed of a large number of smaller strategic businesses, each with a distinct competitive structure requiring distinct strategies.

Automation and Electronic Banking

Automation has revolutionized transactions processing as well as the customer interface. Automating the processing of payments has accelerated transactions and reduced costs. Automation has also brought advantages directly to the client. With the proliferation of ATMs, customers no longer require face-to-face interaction for routine transactions. It has also enabled a much wider range of products and services to be made available to the consumer. Many observers believe that computer-based interactive video communication will totally transform retail banking, to the point of making classic branch banking obsolete.

Automation has additionally allowed far more efficient transfer of information within the organization, enabling the bank to market more selectively and profitably. The advancement of technology has permitted banks to generate the information necessary to work out the profitability of different products and market segments. Banks today increasingly need large-scale, flexible, on-line systems to generate the necessary information—appropriately broken down for management use—and to reduce operating costs.

Global Retail Financial Services

First are services that appear on the liability side of the bank's balance sheet—demand and savings accounts as well as customer balances linked to money-market interest rates such as certificates of deposit. These services, from the point of view of the customer, are valued in terms of quality (convenience, timeliness, and accuracy of account statements, and transaction efficiency) as well as cost—the latter reflected in fees charges on deposit and payments services as well as interest paid in comparison with market rates that represent potential alternatives to the customer. Liability-related and transactions services are handled in widely divergent ways internationally, ranging from countries in which most consumer transactions are conducted in cash, to those that are highly check oriented, to still others that rely heavily on bank transfers. For banks, liability-related consumer services are the source of potentially significant fee income as well as relatively low-cost, stable funding. Foreign-based banks find this attractive for doing local-currency lending—the alternative being to borrow in the local money market, which is generally dominated by indigenous bank competitors.

On the other hand, consumer deposits are also high cost in nature. Thousands of transactions, many of them very small, have to be processed. Contact points with the customer have to be numerous and convenient, often involving high real estate expenses. Deposit and transactions services are labor intensive as well. Fortunately, technology has taken the cost out of much transactions processing via ATMs, credit and debit cards, computer banking, and point-of-sale terminals (POSTs), as well as electronic funds transmission for both payments and customer deposits. The effort to get the transactions costs out of liability-related consumer services is likely to continue to grow, with further improvements in information and processing technologies. The hardware can be bought. It is in the applications software that the product differentiation and the barriers to entry are created, as well as the scope for technology transfer internationally among markets where a bank wants to be active in local-currency retail funding.

Second are consumer transactions that appear on the asset side of the bank's balance sheet. In the absence of interest-rate ceilings and usury laws, the spreads between interest-rate charges on consumer transactions and funding costs can be very wide in many markets. Such transactions include loans to finance big-ticket consumer items such as automobiles, boats, and other consumer durables, as well as secured and unsecured personal loans and credit card overdrafts, some of which lend themselves to securitization. They also include first and second mortgage lending and home-equity transactions. This business lends itself to differentiation in terms of product quality and is extremely cost sensitive in some environments, requiring direct contact with large numbers of customers and heavy transactions processing. Consequently, the establishment of retail outlets and their associated costs have often been unavoidable, more so than in the case of deposit and transactions services since the scope for automation has been more limited. Nevertheless, automated lending is possible to some extent on a preapproved or revolving basis, as in the case of credit cards.

Consumer lending is also sensitive to credit risks, and default rates tend to differ substantially across countries. However, since there are large numbers of relatively small transactions it is possible to develop an actuarial fix on credit risk.

Again, it is possible to transfer marketing, risk assessment, account management, and processing technologies internationally at relatively low cost in consumer lending, and this has made it possible for some banks to gain a strong consumer franchise in foreign markets—Citibank, Hong Kong & Shanghai, and Standard Chartered in particular.

Third is investment management services marketed to consumers abroad. This includes mutual funds (called unit trusts in some countries), pension plans, and portfolio management for individuals. It also includes stockbrokerage and sales of fixed-income securities to individuals and families, and helping them to manage risks related to interest rates, inflation, recession, and other economic shocks. Attractive opportunities in this area exist among wealthy clients, as discussed earlier. But mass-market clients are also buyers of money management services, a fiduciary business that can be highly profitable.

Portfolio management for the mass market is not a very labor-intensive business, although, because customers can relatively easily determine performance, funds under management can be quite volatile. Such management can also be highly automated, with telephone and computer links to the customer being used to handle a significant share of routine account inquiries, funds transfers among accounts, and the like. Besides portfolio performance and charges, the quality and timeliness of statements and transactions accuracy are important qualitative variables.

The fact that such services are relatively new in some markets makes it possible for foreign-based players to gain a viable foothold, as Fidelity Investor Services of the United States has shown in the United Kingdom, and other European markets. Product technologies, such as financial planning using notebook computers in the home of the client by agents for companies like Allied Dunbar in the United Kingdom, can be highly innovative. It also lends itself to abuse by charlatans—as Investor Overseas Services (IOS), operating at the retail level throughout Europe from a base in Geneva, demonstrated during the 1960s.

Fourth is insurance, generally categorized into mass life and property and casualty (P&C). Whereas a full discussion of the retail insurance market is beyond the scope of this chapter, it has become clear in some markets that insurance and retail banking services can be effectively cross-marketed, a practice termed *Allfinanz* in Germany and *bancassurance* in France. Many banks in these countries and many others have either gone directly into the insurance business or affiliated themselves with local insurance companies.

Insurance is attractive to banks because, in addition to direct profits from underwriting, it provides a relatively predictable set of fund flows that can be used to complement normal banking liabilities to structure more efficient asset portfolios. On the other hand, the insurance business requires quite different actuarial and sales skills and is often compensated by means of commission structures. These differences have sometimes made it hard for banks to compete effectively with insurance companies. Only banks that solve these problems effectively at home have any prospects of competing in this segment of retail financial services in foreign markets—often against extremely stiff and entrenched competition.

Fifth is an amalgam of other consumer financial and related services, such as travelers checks; travel and entertainment cards; bank credit and debit cards; retail foreign exchange at airports and retail bank outlets; domestic and international money transfer; safekeeping and lock-box services; real estate, tax, and estate planning; and even travel services. It is unlikely that many of these would serve as a viable business base in their home countries, much less abroad, given the nature of competition from existing players in those businesses. Exceptions are services that can easily be grafted onto a general retail banking business—such as foreign exchange and lock-box services—and two major exceptions, credit cards and travelers checks. Foreign-based issuers of travelers checks, most notably American Express but also including Citibank, Fuji, Barclays, and a few others, have taken a large share of the global market. The same is true of credit card networks, notably American Express, Diners Club (Citibank), MasterCard, and Visa.

In all such cases, prompt replacement in case of loss as well as widespread acceptance at point of sale must be assured—near-universal acceptability of travelers checks and broad acceptance of travel and entertainment (T&E) credit cards for example. This implies the creation of global networks to provide servicing on the ground locally and therefore sharing of returns with these institutions. For example, travelers checks are sold locally through franchised outlets, for which the customer will normally pay a 1 percent selling commission, while interest-free balances (float) accrue to the issuing institution. T&E cards, with debit balances payable monthly, are issued on a proprietary basis by individual institutions such as American Express, normally against an annual fee paid by the client as well as commissions paid by the establishments accepting the card for payment. Credit cards work the same way, often with lower fees and commissions, except that balances do not have to be settled monthly—if the client fails to pay in full, a revolving credit line is automatically activated and the client has the option to pay in monthly installments. Debit cards may be issued either by a single bank or by a bank consortium (such as Carte Bleue in France), and any charges are automatically debited to the account of the cardholder. Finally, there are check cards and ATM cards (e.g., Eurocard) that permit the client to pay by check for merchandise or services abroad, or obtain cash at banks in various countries.

Cards thus have five basic functions—payment convenience, passive extension of credit (as when credit card balances are settled monthly), active extension of credit (as when the customer activates his or her credit line by not paying monthly balances in full), access to cash, and protection from loss and theft. These functions can be added or subtracted from a card product. The American Express T&E green card has all these features except active credit extension, while its gold card includes a revolving personal credit line. A variety of additional features can be added, for example enhanced loss protection and card registration, "smart" features such as ATM refills using a microchip embedded in the card, availability of cash machines at airports and rail terminals to dispense currency notes and travelers checks, and the like.

The key in the card business is networking globally, due to the critical importance of widespread acceptability. With the introduction of micro-electronics and its application to new processes and products, there has been rapid growth in the scope for national and global networking in the financial services industry in general. In some cases the emergent networks may involve only a pair of financial institutions, as in traditional banking correspondent relationships, while in other cases complex webs of banks and other financial or nonfinancial firms have been formed in a single network, as in credit card systems.

Delivery Systems

Penetration of a bank into retail banking abroad tends to fit into one of four categories:

- Banks that have followed the flag, and have remained in a developing country after the departure of the colonial powers
- A small group of banks that had foreign offices in various countries before any protective barriers favoring indigenous banks were laid down and were grandfathered in
- Banks that have bought foreign banks
- Banks that have adopted a niche strategy in foreign markets

Table 4-2 lists a number of issues that are critical to the ability to deliver retail financial services, which are by nature highly local, on an international or even global scale. First is the problem of market segmentation. Mass-market products and those targeted at specific market segments (e.g., Finns living in Sweden, the New York Puerto Rican community, those working in certain professions) are by definition highly local. For foreign-based institutions to compete they must offer better service (using almost entirely local resources), product differentiation, or lower price. Being "international" counts for nothing. Nevertheless, product differentiation can be accomplished, as NatWest USA has shown in catering to upper-income customers in the New York metropolitan area, Citibank dealing with consumer finance in Germany, and Hong Kong banks targeting Chinese communities in London, New York, and elsewhere. But it is not easy, and the burden of proof rests invariably with the foreign institution. Local consumer banking abroad is, by its very nature, a very localized uphill battle.

Product differentiation can also be achieved through distribution channels, and here a critical marketing question is whether financial services are "bought" or "sold." Payments services are typically "bought" in

Table 4-2 Delivering Retail Financial Services Internationally

Client segmentation	Market penetration vehicles
Mass market	On-the-ground greenfield
High net worth	Acquisitions
High net income (affluent)	Intercountry penetration (e.g., via mail
Profession-based market segments	or personal computer)
Other segmentation criteria	Joint ventures and strategic alliances
Points of sale	Sources of competitive advantage
Over the counter	Physical capital (e.g., installed distribu-
Specialized	tion outlets)
Joint (cross-selling)	Financial capital
Door-to-door	Human resources
Mail	Product technology
Personal computer and interactive video	Risk management technology
Economies-of-scale characteristics	Process technology
	Marketing/management knowhow
Economies-of-scope characteristics	Franchise
Cross-selling potential	

that the client actively seeks out a bank to provide them for a very clear need. Life insurance, on the other hand, is typically "sold" (like encyclopedias) in that the product can be complex and there may be no immediate perceived need. This means that selling over the counter, as in a bank, may be appropriate for some products and direct-mail selling, door-to-door selling by salespeople on commission, or selling by interactive video or home-shopping approaches for others.

Consumer marketing know-how is critical in retail financial services. What works in one country may, with modification, also work in another, and marketing technologies are relatively easy to transfer internationally. Institutions such as Citibank in the United States, Allied Dunbar in Britain, Compagnie Bancaire in France all have particular marketing approaches for various products that in many cases are not easy to emulate and that lend themselves to international transfer.

We have also noted that retail financial services are highly cost sensitive, and that means high levels of information and processing technology. The secret tends to be in the software, which differentiates cost structures among institutions using basically the same hardware and permits them to offer the same product at lower cost or lower losses.

Besides selecting promising products, client segments, and delivery systems, distribution economics in retail financial services are also highly sensitive to economies of scale and economies of scope. There is evidence that scale economies are more important in retail transactions than in other financial services because of the large transactions volumes involved. The existence of scope economies are clear when multiple products are pushed through the same relatively fixed-cost delivery systems, but less clear in terms of cross-selling potential and the "financial supermarket." Whether customers are willing to pay a higher "all-in" (i.e., "package") price for buying banking services, insurance, and mutual funds from the same institution instead of separately from a bank, an insurance company, and a stockbroker in many markets remains an open question. So is the incremental cost of cross-marketing—can the same individual effectively sell an array of (often complex) financial services as effectively as product specialists?

Table 4-2 also indicates some of the sources of competitive advantage in retail financial services, as well as alternatives for penetrating international markets. Clearly, physical capital in the form of point-of-sale outlets is critical in many cases, although independent agents selling on commission and direct-mail sales can reduce this requirement. The need for financial resources is obvious, both for credit extension and investment purposes. Capital is far more important, since finance for relending can usually be bought on the market at considerably lower interest rates than are earned on retail financial transactions. Financial capital is also critical for building up the ability to securitize, distribute and differentiate products and manage the attendant risks. Assuming management is willing to invest heavily and has the staying power to ride out the initial lean years in retail banking in a given market, the capital required to be a serious player in retail financial services may well provide protection from competitor incursions.

Entry into national markets and international distribution of retail financial services are closely related problems. The options are to proceed de novo, to buy a local bank or other financial services firm, to sell into another country from home (e.g., by mail or traveling salespeople), and to create joint ventures and strategic alliances. The first two are expensive. "Greenfield"—that is, de novo—projects may require creation of branch networks, and sellers of local financial institutions are not unaware of their value to foreign-based players and will charge accordingly. In cross-country selling it is not easy to overcome consumer risk aversion, and memories of horror stories like IOS and BCCI are ever present. Cross-country selling may also be impractical, although in Europe it is greatly facilitated by the financial liberalizations within the European Union and in North America under the North American Free Trade Agreement (NAFTA).

Joint ventures and strategic alliances may be more viable in the retail sector than in some other parts of the financial services industry. Banks in two or more countries can agree to honor each others' customers checks and credit cards, for example, to provide banking services to traveling tourists and business people. Initiatives along these lines include a 1989 arrangement between the Royal Bank of Scotland and Banco Santander of Spain. Another example involves a relationship developed in late 1986 between Citicorp and Dai-Ichi Kangyo Ltd. (DKB) of Japan. Each bank's customers are able to use the automated teller machines in the other's home country in their own language, and the two banks act as each other's agents in consumer loans and home mortgages (allowing customers of each to borrow quickly and easily from the other), with Dai-Ichi "support-ing" (distributing and processing charges for) Citicorp's MasterCard in Ja-pan. Each bank can tap into the information base and expertise of the other. The arrangement helps to establish a full-service presence in the oth-er's country. As noted, strategic alliances are most prevalent in truly inter-national retail businesses like bank cards, which require networks in order to operate effectively and organizations to run them.

Global Retail Banking?

The foregoing discussion raises the question whether most retail banking services really lend themselves to globalization, as do many wholesale banking and securities services discussed in other chapters of this book. We have pointed out that most retail services are really local and even regional in nature, and it is unclear what foreign-based institutions bring to the table. Whatever it is, it must be sufficiently superior in quality or lower in cost to convince mass-market customers to defect from their local institutions. Given the absence of patents, copyrights, and other statutory entry barriers in the financial services industry, sustaining such a basis for competitive advantage—assuming it can be achieved in the first place—is not easy in local markets around the world. Foreign-based institutions, in short, must win a local franchise against entrenched local competition, which may be quick to react to encroachments on what it regards as its turf. Either that, or foreign banks may simply buy good local franchises and run them essentially as portfolio investments. Failures in international retail banking are perhaps more common than successes.

Summary

The high-net-worth private banking client is likely to remain an important factor in international banking for the foreseeable future, although the pattern of wealth ownership will probably shift steadily from inherited wealth to that created by the current generation. The passing of property rights from one generation to another is constantly subject to fiscal and political challenge. At the same time, newly created wealth appears ever more acceptable alongside market-oriented economic policies. Economic structures are becoming increasingly competitive, which simultaneously di-minishes the chances of successive generations successfully retaining the wealth earned by their forebears and increases the chances that the newly wealthy will be sharper thinking and more international in outlook. Pri-vate banking players will have to adapt to these changes, remembering that their fate ultimately will be sealed by the quality of the human re-sources they are able to attract to what essentially remains a "people busi-ness."

Retail banking is one part of the financial services industry that does not lend itself particularly well to globalization. Some retail activities such as travelers checks and "plastic" are important exceptions. Others are highly idiosyncratic and local—Herr Mueller behaves differently from Monsieur Meunier, who behaves differently from Mr. Miller in terms of what he expects his bank to do for him—and this requires a great deal of adaptation of competitive advantages in products and processes. Indeed, the key success factors in retail banking may in the end be more related to a keen awareness of the market than to technology and systems.

Nonetheless, it is clear that international and even global niches exist in specific retail financial services, ranging from mortgage and consumer lending, stockbrokerage and mutual funds, to family financial planning. The jury remains out on whether there is a role for truly global retail financial services players in the future. And it is clear that "global branding," such as Coca-Cola or McDonalds, is possible in the financial services sector as well. So far, only American Express and perhaps Citicorp have succeeded in developing a global consumer franchise.

5

Assessment and Management of Cross-Border Risks

Various types of risk are faced by commercial and investment banks in their global operations. A few examples are credit risks in lending or investing in foreign entities, risks associated with project financing, risks in dealing foreign exchange, and funding risks related to balance-sheet management and off-balance-sheet exposures. By definition, international banking activities cross the political frontiers of sovereign national states and give rise to yet another source of risk in international banking—country risk.

The Nature of Country Risk

Suppose a New York bank makes a dollar loan to a Venezuelan company with satisfactory credit standing. When the time comes to repay the loan, however, the company finds it is unable to convert bolivares into dollars because its government has imposed exchange controls as part of a general declaration of economic emergency. In this case, the borrower is willing and able to meet its contractual obligations but country conditions effectively prevent it from doing so. In retrospect, *credit risk* was not a problem, but *transfer risk* (a form of country risk) was.

Or suppose a Japanese bank participates in a large syndicated Eurodollar credit to the government of Vietnam for infrastructure financing purposes. The bank has no credit risk, since it is lending against the full faith and credit of the government of Vietnam. But it does carry *sovereign risk*, since future circumstances may be such that the government may be unable or unwilling to provide debt service. This is another form of country risk.

All cross-border lending or investment activities by international commercial or investment banks and their clients thus involve *country risk*—the possibility that the future flow of returns from these activities may be impaired by economic or political events.

Credit risks associated with each borrower represent *unsystematic risk*. A bank or investor can reduce the overall level of risk to which it is exposed in that country by carefully building a diversified portfolio of exposures and ultimately drive the level of unsystematic risk close to zero. But because all exposures in a single country are linked by economic and political events, the lender or investor is stuck with a form of *systematic risk* that also falls into the category of country risk. Government may pursue fiscal, monetary, foreign exchange, or other policies that impair debt service on the part of multiple borrowers by affecting their profitability. The government may undertake nationalization or expropriation, impede access to foreign exchange, or carry out a host of other adverse policy measures. Systematic (country) risk thus limits the ability of a bank or investor to diversify away from unsystematic risk in the management of its portfolio in a particular country.

We have used two examples of country risk in the preceding hypothetical cases:

> *Transfer risk:* the possibility that the borrower may not be able to convert domestic currency into foreign currency
>
> *Sovereign risk:* loans or securities of governments, their agencies, or nongovernmental entities under government guarantee that eliminates credit risk, yet the government being unable or unwilling to service its foreign obligations

Foreign exchange risk does not confront the lender or investor directly if the obligation is denominated in nonlocal currency, yet exchange-rate movements can influence credit-worthiness of borrowers and issuers, and factors affecting exchange rates are often closely allied to those affecting country conditions in general.

Besides cross-border loans and securities holdings, a bank or investor may also have certain *direct* investments in a particular country. These may take the form of equity holdings in local companies, bank branches, joint ventures, or other types of ownership interests, all of which are subject to *foreign direct investment (FDI), risk* which can be quite different from the other country risk categories. Clearly, a country may be economically and politically sound, yet the government may decide to nationalize all foreign ownership interests in a certain sector as a matter of national policy. Country risk may be low, yet risk associated with FDI may be high under such circumstances. In cases where government places a very high priority on the direct foreign participation in a given sector—such as development of a nation's financial system—the reverse may be true.

Finally, a bank or investor that has a well-diversified portfolio of assets in a particular nation and yet remains troubled by its exposure to (systematic) country risk always has the option to diversify still further and distribute its holdings across a variety of different countries. This way, country risk becomes unsystematic as far as its overall portfolio is concerned, and this allows cross-country diversification strategies to reduce overall exposure to risk still further. Under *international portfolio diversification* (IPD), it simply puts its eggs in different country baskets, in the hope that one basket getting dropped will have little to do with what happens to others.

But are country futures indeed independent? Unfortunately, changes in oil prices, conditions on international financial markets, business cycles, protectionism, global or regional political events turn out to affect many countries at the same time, often in the same direction. Brazil's economic future may be quite independent of South Korea's, but both may simultaneously be affected by a major change in global interest rates. The risk associated with changes that transcend national political frontiers can be called *ambient risk*. This rule is systematic and inherent in the global environment. For practical purposes, ambient risk sets a limit on the extent to which IPD can succeed in reducing overall exposure to risk. The only way to reduce risk still further is to move into nonfinancial assets that have traditionally served as hedges in periods of global unease, such as gold or real estate, or to buy risk insurance. Unfortunately, neither is entirely free of ambient risk, and both tend to be rather costly alternatives.

We have defined six types of risk in three broad categories, all of which have to be considered in international portfolio management:

- *Credit risk* and *foreign direct investment risk* at the narrowest, unsystematic level, both relatively easily subject to diversification
- *Country risk*, of which *transfer risk, sovereign risk,* and *exchange risk* are components; systematic as far as individual cross-border loans and investments are concerned but can be made unsystematic through international portfolio diversification
- *Ambient risk*, which is generally systematic, transcends national frontiers, and thus effectively limits risk reduction via IPD

Problems associated with country exposures have proven to be hardy perennials.[1] As Table 5-1 shows, during the nineteenth century most international borrowing was associated with issuance of sovereign bonds. A good part of the proceeds from these was used for military purposes, with the losers of wars often ending up in default during the first great episode of cross-border credit difficulties in the 1820s. During the 1870s another period of sovereign bond defaults occurred from this reason combined with the unwise use of proceeds and political pressure by home governments on investors as part of foreign policies being pursued at the time. Bond defaults in the 1930s were mostly associated with the Great Depression, as country after country was unable to meet its commitments and

Table 5-1 Comparison of the Four Major International Debt Crises

	1820s	1870s	1930s	1980s
Countries of major private creditors	Britain	Britain, France, Germany	USA, Britain, Netherlands, Switzerland	USA, European countries, Japan, Canada
Major defaulters	Latin America, Greece	Egypt, Turkey, Spain, Latin America	Germany, Eastern Europe, Latin America	Latin America, Eastern Europe, Africa
Systemic factors	Lending to belligerents Lack of lending experience and information	Lending to belligerent or profligate rulers Strong political influence	Worldwide depression Trade wars	Oil and interest-rate shocks Worldwide recession Poor economic management
Main instrument	Bonds	Bonds	Bonds	Bank loans
Settlement process	Private negotiations	Private bondholders' councils	Private bondholders' councils	IMF, Paris Club, bank committees

Source: Salomon Brothers, Inc., *The Risks of Foreign Lending: Lessons from History.* New York: Salomon Brothers, Inc., 1993.

private borrowers cascaded into bankruptcy. As indicated in Figure 5-1, the postwar period was mainly closed to bond issuers outside the OECD countries, and bond investors were replaced by syndicated bank lending to countries that eventually ended up in major difficulties during the debt crisis of the 1980s.

Table 5-2 shows the cumulative periods of difficulty for countries that either were held in default or underwent major debt rescheduling, resulting in losses to lenders during the period 1800–1992. The bottom line is that country problems are not at all unusual, nor are they unconnected from each other. This suggests that both careful country assessment and the adoption of a careful portfolio approach to cross-border exposures is in order. In the 1990s, as emerging market debt and equity issues once again become significant and cross-border bank loans reappear, the lessons of the past should not be forgotten.

Country Exposure: Definition and Measurement

A basic prerequisite for effective global asset management is *exposure tracking*. Banks and institutional investors need to know their global exposure to risk along a variety of dimensions. It is important, for example, that a bank know its claims on all of its clients in a particular industry

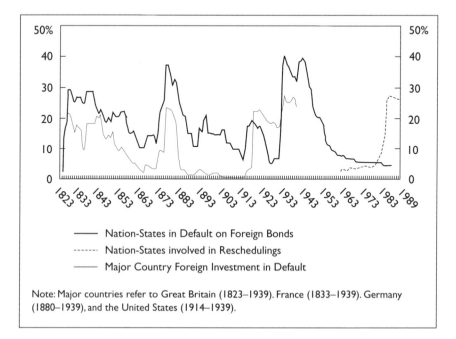

Figure 5-1. Sovereign default and rescheduling, 1823–1989. Source: Salomon Brothers, Inc.

Table 5-2 Cumulative Years and Periods of Default and Rescheduling, 1800–1992

Country	Periods	Years	Country	Periods	Years
Ecuador [a]	4	112	Egypt [a]	2	12
Honduras [a]	3	102	Jamaica	1	12
Greece	3	87	Netherlands	1	12
Mexico	5	78	Senegal [a]	1	11
Colombia	4	72	Spain	5	11
Nicaragua [a]	5	70	Uganda [a]	1	11
Peru [a]	5	70	Guyana [a]	1	10
Costa Rica	5	69	Japan	1	10
Bulgaria [a]	3	67	Madagascar [a]	1	9
Guatemala	4	66	Philippines [a]	1	9
Germany	2	64	Zambia [a]	1	9
Venezuela	5	57	Ivory Coast	1	8
Liberia [a]	4	49	Ghana	1	8
Dominican Republic [a]	3	48	Morocco	2	8
Chile	6	47	Mozambique [a]	1	8
El Salvador	3	47	Niger	1	8
Brazil [a]	6	44	Nigeria	1	8
Bolivia [a]	3	42	Tanzania [a]	1	8
Austria	4	37	Gabon [a]	2	7
Yugoslavia [a]	3	37	Guinea [a]	1	7
Paraguay [a]	5	36	South Africa [a]	1	7
Hungary	1	35	Viet Nam [a]	1	7
Turkey	6	31	Congo [a]	1	6
Romania	2	30	Italy	1	6
China	1	28	Malawi	1	5
Poland [a]	2	27	Angola [a]	1	4
Panama [a]	2	23	Russia [a]	4	4
Argentina [a]	3	22	Cameroon [a]	1	3
Portugal	3	22	Jordan [a]	1	3
Uruguay	5	22	Tunisia	1	3
Zaire [a]	2	17	Albania [a]	1	2
Czechoslovakia	2	15	The Gambia	1	2
Sierra Leone [a]	1	15	Iraq [a]	1	2
Zimbabwe	1	15	Iran [a]	1	1
Cuba [a]	3	14	Trinidad and Tobago	1	1
Sudan [a]	1	13			
Togo [a]	1	13			
Total				166	1,885
Total countries					72

Source: Salomon Brothers, Inc., *The Risks of Foreign Lending: Lessons from History.* New York: Salomon Brothers, Inc., 1993.
[a] Continuing in 1992.

such as petroleum, copper, or air transportation since worldwide, regional, or national developments at the industry level may affect multiple clients simultaneously. Groups of borrowers sensitive to certain economic or political conditions, such as energy-intensive companies, also require exposure measurement at the national, regional, or global level.

The difference between measurement of a bank's exposure to risk associated with particular firms or industries and its exposure to country risk is that the latter deals with cross-border financial flows, while the former is concerned with total claims and other exposures whether cross-border or not. For instance, a loan by a bank's branch in Buenos Aires to a local company, funded by Argentine peso deposits, incurs firm and industry risk but not country risk (although the bank's local branch does involve FDI exposure) yet the same loan originated by the bank's Paris office involves all three types of risk.

Figure 5-2 indicates, as a three-dimensional display, the kind of infor-

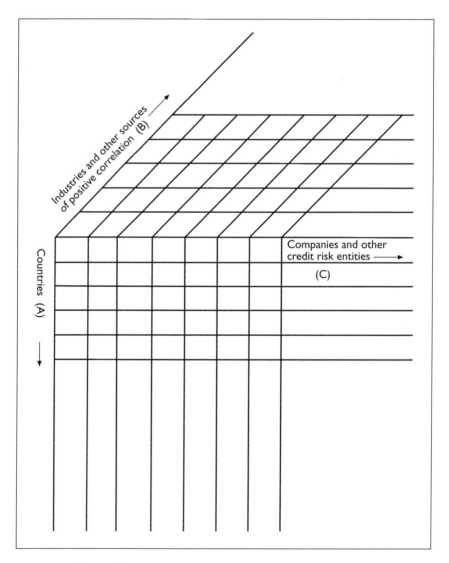

Figure 5-2. Three dimensions of global exposure tracking.

mation that is useful in keeping track of a bank's global exposure. With respect to exposure to country risk, the first category is lending exposure. Every cross-border loan, whether originated by the bank's head office or by offices anywhere else in the world, must be promptly reported and captured in the system. To double-check, it is useful to have each cross-border loan reported both by the originating office and by the office directly responsible for the country concerned. Exposures by country should then be broken down into appropriate maturity categories, loan commitments, and drawdowns or disbursements. It is also useful to know the extent to which the country has claims on the bank. These should not be netted against lending exposure, but it is important to be aware of them—in extreme cases, such claims may be used under the *right of set-off*.

Keeping track of lending activity by country is not only an important function of exposure-tracking systems, but it serves portfolio purposes as well. Figure 5-2 may also indicate subtotals by regions, wherein specific country groups may be captured as needed, for example, Central America, Southeast Asia, or sub-Saharan Africa. At the same time, such a system can track (in its B-dimension) lending by borrower type—banks, industries, public sector, private sector, energy-intensive companies, or other classifications of special interest. It may also include (in its C-dimension) exposure to corporate "families," for example, General Motors worldwide, as well. While only cross-border exposure is of interest with respect to country risk, total exposure is relevant for portfolio purposes and management of noncountry risk exposures.

The A-dimension of Figure 5-2 focuses on direct cross-border exposure. But suppose a bank loan to the Thai subsidiary of an American company is guaranteed by its parent. In that case the "country of lending" and the "country of risk" are different—one is the United States and the other is Thailand. Guarantees serve to transfer country exposure. "Comfort letters" or "keepwells," provided for example by corporate parents, do not transfer country exposure. Such exposure transfers are reflected in the A-dimension of Figure 5-2. Quite often, as in shipping loans, considerable judgment is required to determine the appropriate allocation of country exposure.

In making judgments about a country and its lending or investment opportunities, a bank or institutional investor will want to set limits on country exposure that should not be exceeded, usually in the form of overall *country limits* and *sublimits* for different maturities. Limits applied to individual borrowers, industries, or regions can also be incorporated here.

Nonlending exposure, either in the form of off-balance-sheet transactions, foreign exchange and derivatives exposures, equity interests in foreign firms, bank affiliates, branches, consortium arrangements, and portfolio investments, may also be recorded in an exposure information system generally under the A-dimension in Figure 5-2, although risk transfer may also be possible under home-country guarantees of parent companies, government agencies, or international organizations. Periodic exposure reports must be made available in regular intervals to bank officers, either in printed form or in on-line displays.

Valuation of Country Exposure

A bank or investor in debt instruments is naturally interested in the economic value of its exposure in a particular country. It is also interested in maximizing the economic value of its global asset portfolio, spread among a variety of different countries. Both decisions involve expected returns and possible future variance of those returns, as reflected in the degree of risk associated with them.

We can express this in the form of a conventional present-value equation, such as the following:

$$\text{NPV}_j \sum_{t=0}^{n} \frac{E(F_t) - E(C_t)}{(1 + i_t + \alpha_t)^t}$$

where NPV_j is the net present value of the future stream of expected returns to the bank or investor related to exposure in a particular country j, $E(F_t)$ and $E(C_t)$ denote the expected value of the stream of future returns and the associated collection costs at time t, respectively; i_t is the risk-free discount factor representing the bank's cost of funds (or another risk-free rate), and α_t represents a country-risk premium, which depends on the variance in returns on the bank's exposure in country j, relative to the variance in returns on an overall asset portfolio and on management's attitude toward risk. Prospective future developments in countries involving cross-border exposures will be reflected in the *means* as well as the *variances* of the probability distributions associated with these returns, and hence will influence both $E(F_t) - E(C)_t$ and α_t.

It is important to develop an accurate picture of the net expected returns, namely, $E(F_t) - E(C_t)$. One important component of returns is, of course, the repayment of principal. A second component covers the stream of interest payments, which usually involves either a fixed rate or the spread over LIBOR, the U.S. prime rate, or a similar floating base rate of interest. A third component of returns in bank loans is a share of commitment, participation, and management fees agreed on with the borrower. As noted in chapter 2, these may be quite substantial, especially for those involved in organizing and managing syndicated loans. And banks often lend to a particular borrower on fine terms in order to develop or maintain a "relationship." This involves existing and past banking ties, and focuses on the expectation of future earnings from a variety of activities, foreign exchange transactions, deposit balances, advisory services, custody business, and the like.

There is ample evidence of the importance of the "relationship" factor in international lending behavior, with regular scrambles by banks to get "close to" the borrower, directly and within syndicates, and in the tendency for losers of syndication mandates to participate anyway in the loans in order to maintain a relationship with the borrower. Similarly, borrowers can sometimes "encourage" banks to participate in loans that would not otherwise be attractive by suggesting that failure to do so may lead to loss of collateral business or pressure on their operations in host countries—thereby requiring the addition to apparent returns, in effect, of an insurance premium against possible future earnings losses elsewhere in the relationship. Particularly where a relationship with a particular government has been highly profitable in the past, and promises to be so in the future, such anticipated "indirect" or "soft" returns can be an important part of country lending programs.

A bank's lending to a particular borrower may also generate future returns with third parties which would otherwise be lost. For example, a particular loan to a company or government abroad may create opportunities for future trade financing or L/C business with home or third-country suppliers. A well-structured loan could strengthen a relationship with a particular domestic or foreign client in a way that promises additional future earnings.

Finally, there are collection costs. Loans that are delinquent or "nonperforming" because of conditions in countries where the exposure is lodged often involve sizable travel, legal, and other expenses. Particularly for bankers who take relatively small participations in major loans, collection costs can loom large in relation to expected returns in the event of problems. For fixed-income investors, defaulted bonds may pay off only a small fraction of the face amount.

It is clear, therefore, that expected returns of principal interest, fees, and the remaining less tangible earnings components, generated by country exposure, as well as expected collection costs form a multisided, probabilistic picture. Each element has its own time profile and expected value, so that $E(F_t) - E(C_t)$ in our formula is itself a highly complex composite. In addition to that, each element has its own measure of variability, so that the associated risk premium α_t is similarly complex. There are often trade-offs, as when the terms of loan agreements are relaxed at the borrower's insistence in exchange for higher expected returns in some other earnings components. Partly for such reasons, profit attribution in international banking tends to be extraordinarily difficult, and the returns facing individual banks that participate in syndicated transactions may well differ substantially from one to the other.

In measuring interest-rate risk, banks differentiate between floating-rate and fixed-rate loans. In floating-rate (e.g., LIBOR-based) loans or floating-rate bonds, a change in interest rates would show up both as a change in i_t and a change in $E(R_t)$, and therefore it would have a minimal effect on interest rate risk. In fixed-rate loans or bonds, $E(R_t)$ remains constant while i_t changes, causing a corresponding change in NPV. But even with floating-rate instruments, since spreads are fixed either for the life of the contract or for specific periods, there exists some residual interest-rate risk.

Apart from changes in interest rates, there exist a number of other contingencies.

1. The borrowing country may be unwilling or unable to fully pay back its debt. Nonperformance results in realized accounting losses of principal and/or accrued interest that must be booked against earnings, capital, and reserves after recovering what can be recovered. The consequences of nonperformance for the borrower's access to international capital markets and normal channels of credit are such that this event today tends to be triggered under relatively rare circumstances, as in bond or loan defaults.

2. The borrowing country may be unable to meet its external debt obligations and be forced to renegotiate the loan. By definition, the necessary refinancing or rescheduling under such circumstances cannot be accomplished *at market terms*. Since it occurs under duress, the original lenders are forced to extend further credit with the hope of avoiding accounting losses in the end. This may involve an extension of maturities, a new grace period, negotiation of new facilities, an adjustment in interest spreads, or other modifications. Even if this ultimately results in increased accounting returns, nonetheless the lender incurs an economic loss, since otherwise it would have used its assets—which are now tied up in the present portfolio—to construct the optimal portfolio.

3. The borrowing country may be willing and able to service external debt and avoid default and problems leading to reschedulings or forced refinancings, but something may happen that raises the perceived risk associated with the exposed assets from the lender's perspective. For example, an assassination of the head of state may have an unpredictable effect on debt service. Even though neither of the first two types of losses has been incurred by the lender, it has suffered a decline in the value of assets, since it cannot immediately reallocate them according to new perceptions of relative risks and returns. Such reallocation may be possible at the margin by running down exposures beginning with very short maturities; however, it is usually far from this type of instantaneous adjustment that is needed to avoid long-run downward adjustment in the value of the portfolio.

A number of country-related events may thus reduce NPV. Prospective defaults can be viewed as a reduction in $E(F_t)$ and an increase in $E(C_t)$. Anticipated rescheduling or refinancing losses are analogous to the forced introduction of higher valued t's that are less than compensated for by negotiated increases in $E(F_t)$, net of $E(C_t)$. Finally, losses from risk-class shifts reflect an increase in α_t if, as a result, the country is viewed by the market as being more risky.

Examples related to the difference between the book value of bank-country exposures and its respective economic value emerged in the latter phases of the LDC debt crisis of the 1980s. This can best be illustrated by figures and tables. Figure 5-3 indicates the size of the external debt of various developing and formerly centrally planned economies at the end

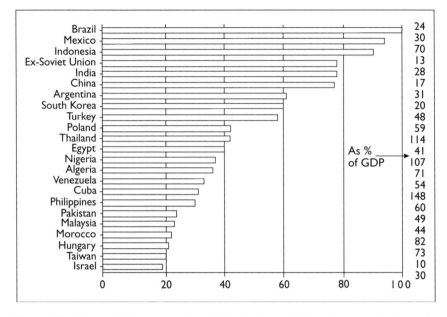

Figure 5-3. External debt outstanding of developing and formerly centrally planned economies, in billions of dollars, year-end 1992. Sources: Organization for Economic Cooperation and Development, World Bank, EIU.

of 1992, 10 years after the onset of the global debt crisis, with Brazil and Mexico in the lead in terms of total debt outstanding. Table 5-3 shows debt restructurings undertaken after 1990, involving exchanges of old bank debt for new "Brady" bonds that obliged the banks either to take a significant discount against the book values of their eligible debt exposure (floating-rate discount bonds) or exchange old debt for new bonds at face value (fixed-rate par bonds), or to lend additional amounts to the countries concerned. The bonds were supported by U.S. zero-coupon bonds, held in escrow and guaranteeing the bonds' principal, as well as a rolling guarantee with respect to interest coverage. In return, the banks had to take a hit either on principal or the rate of interest, while debtor countries had to undertake severe economic adjustments both in demand management and in adopting market-oriented growth policies.

The Brady restructurings accomplished a number of things. They increased the liquidity of external debt, as shown in trading volumes depicted in Figure 5-4 even as total debt outstanding was reduced via the discount bond conversion process. As Figure 5-5 shows, the negotiations had a uniformly positive effect on secondary-market debt prices as net expected returns increased and variance decreased, as perceived by investors and lenders—to the point where a year later, at the end of 1993, these prices had recovered significantly (Figure 5-6).

An additional factor was the development of an active secondary mar-

Table 5-3 Brady Plans Completed or in Final Stages, 1995 (U.S. dollars in billions)

Country	Bank Debt Covered Under Brady-Type Options	Debt Buyback Portion	Debt Converted to Bonds
Argentina	$26.4	$0	$16.6
Brazil	42.1	0	35
Mexico	47.9	0	35.8[a]
Nigeria	5.8	3.4	2.02
The Philippines (1990)	2.1	1.3	0.715
The Philippines (1992)	4.5	1.25	3.26
Venezuela	19.3	1.4	17.2

Data: Institute of International Finance and Salomon Brothers Inc. estimates.

[a]U.S.$20.3 billion was committed to the debt-reduction option, resulting in the issue of U.S.$13.2 billion in floating-rate discount bonds and a U.S.$7.1-billion decline in the face value of outstanding debt.

ket for bank loans in connection with debt-for-equity swaps and other debt-conversion transactions. The secondary debt market prices continued to be indicative of the economic value of bank exposures, so that it became possible to ascertain what exposures were actually worth. The purpose of country risk assessment is, of course, to obtain an estimate of $E(F_t)$, $E(C_t)$ and α_t. The more certain the bank is about the first two elements, the lesser the "true risk" that remains and the smaller is α_t.

Factors Affecting Country Risk

The country-risk problem that international banks or investors face is one of forecasting the future prospects of countries in which they have assets. It represents a strikingly complex task, requiring the construction of a social, political, psychological, historical, and economic composite assessment that may arise out of structural (supply-side) economic elements, demand-side macroeconomic and monetary elements, external economic and political developments, as well as the quality of the national economic management team and the domestic political constraints facing decision-makers.

A simple view of the problem could begin with an equation such as the following:

$$Y + M = A + X$$

representing real flows of goods and services in an economy, where Y is output, M is imports, A is domestic absorption (consumption, investment, and public-sector spending), and X is exports, all in real terms. Clearly, supply-side changes in Y will, with unchanged demand, require shifts in imports or exports. Reduced production capabilities at the national level, for example, may mean increased imports or a more limited capacity to export. In a similar way, demand-side shifts such as increased government spending will, for example, have to be met by expanded imports or diversion of export production to meet domestic needs. Monetary variables can affect the picture as well: growth in the domestic money supply will, unless offset by changes in exchange rates, tend to raise A relative to Y and therefore increase M, decrease X, or both.

To bring the money side into the picture more explicitly, we can develop an equally simple equation describing international financial flows:

$$VX - VM - DS + FDI + U - K = DR - NBR$$

Here, VX and VM represent the money value of imports and exports, respectively, DS represents debt-service payments to foreigners (usually part of VM in conventional balance-of-payments accounting), FDI is net flows of private and public-sector grants such as foreign aid, U is gifts and grants received from abroad, K is net capital flows undertaken by residents, DR is the change in owned international reserves of the country in question, and NBR is its net borrowing requirement. An overall negative balance on the left side of the equation clearly means that the country will

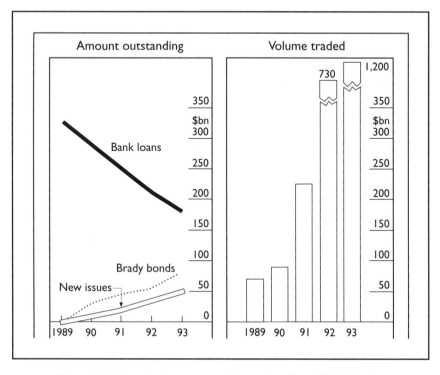

Figure 5-4. Developing country debt market. Data: World Bank.

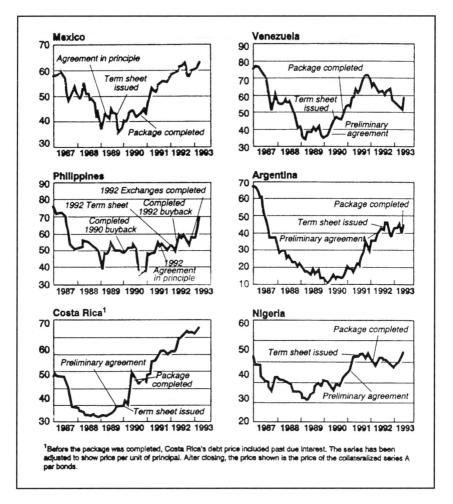

Figure 5-5. Secondary market prices for bank claims during negotiations of restructuring packages (%) of face value). Sources: Salomon Brothers and ANZ Bank Secondary Market Price Report; International Monetary Fund staff estimates.

have to increase its foreign borrowing or use up some of its international reserves. Increases in foreign borrowing brings about an increase in *DS* in future time periods.

Tying the two equations together are typical "country scenarios." Consider a government that comes under political pressure to increase spending for domestic social purposes. It does so by running a fiscal deficit, which it finances by issuing government bonds. Most of these bonds end up in the asset portfolio of the central bank, which in turn pays for them by increasing the money supply (central bank liabilities), representing monetization of debt. This puts upward pressure on the general price level of the economy and downward pressure on expected real interest rates, a result the government is reluctant to see reflected as a depreciation of its currency. The currency becomes "overvalued," made possible by the imposition of exchange controls and/or central bank intervention in foreign exchange markets. The whole process is likely to show up as an increase in A offset by an increase in M and/or a decrease in X in our first equation. The financial flows appearing in the second equation as a net reduction in the trade balance $(VX - VM)$ are financed by a reduction in reserve holdings DR (the central bank's external liabilities).

Many such scenarios could be sketched out, focusing on a wide variety of internal and external shocks that eventually lead to increased foreign borrowing, which, if sufficiently large and sustained, can in turn lead to debt-serving difficulties and economic losses for banks or investors. The problem is to evaluate the effect of these scenarios on the different variables as they evolve over time, and in particular, DS and NBR. This, together with the underlying political scenarios, is the essence of getting an estimate of the expected value and variance of exposure to a particular country.

Given the complexity of the problem, "well-rounded individuals," whose knowledge spans a variety of different fields such as economics, political science, sociology, and psychology, are very valuable to effectively assessing country risk. Low-quality estimates of $E(F_t) - E(C_t)$ and α_t yield

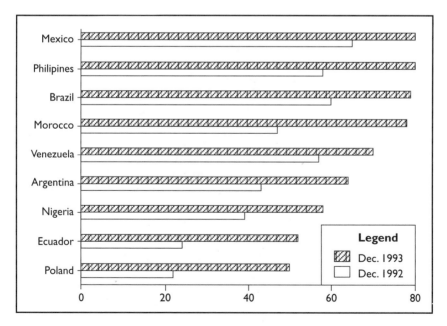

Figure 5-6. Secondary-market debt prices, par bonds (% of face value). Source: Salomon Brothers.

low-quality portfolio decisions and, ultimately, second-rate performance of a bank in the competitive marketplace.

National Economic Management

How do developments in the internal workings of a national economy, both on the supply and demand side, threaten a country's ability to service its external debt obligations? Of interest are the linkages between the supply side's ability to produce export, import-competing, and nontraded goods and the quantitative and qualitative dimensions of the labor force, the capital stock, the natural-resource base, the technology, and entrepreneurship, which are combined to determine this ability. Also of interest are the contributions of real capital inflows to these supply capabilities made possible by foreign borrowings, foreign direct investment, and other types of financial transfers.

Historical measures of *supply-side* economic performance are labor force growth and participation rates, unemployment rates, migration and labor force distributional trends, savings and investment trends, productivity trends, natural resource availability, and the like. The quality, timeliness, and comparability of the relevant data vary widely, but the real problem obviously lies in evaluating how good a predictor the past is for the future. Here, a great deal of judgment is required to identify and project various types of quantitative or qualitative labor-supply ceilings, possible market disruptions, social and economic infrastructure bottlenecks, capital availability problems, and natural resource constraints.

Of prime importance is the evaluation of government policies that will influence domestic savings and investment, capital flight and foreign direct investment, risk-taking in entrepreneurial activity, supply conditions in labor markets, adequacy of economic and social infrastructure, exploitation and value-added processing of natural resources, and the entire underlying complex structure of incentives and disincentives that is built into the nation's fiscal and regulatory system.

In many cases, such policies are anchored in government planning documents, so that evaluation of the degree of realism embodied in these plans is quite important. Government attempts to force the supply side of the economy into a mold that does not fit, but to which a political commitment has been made, can lead to severe domestic and international distortions in the real sector and skyrocket external borrowing, ultimately leading to debt servicing problems.

On the *demand side* of the national economy, country analysts are interested in factors affecting taxes, government expenditures, transfer payments, and the overall fiscal soundness of the public sector, as well as in prospective demand patterns for goods and services from the private and export sectors. Once again, historical data series covering consumption, government taxation and expenditures, gross national product or gross domestic product, and other conventional economic indicators are usually available on a reasonably timely basis to permit an evaluation of the demand picture over a number of years past. However, forecasts largely depend on the ability to predict government demand management and income distribution policies, as well as demand-side shocks that may be stemming from the foreign sector.

In attempting to develop a prognosis of the structural aspects of country futures, the analyst should start by acquiring the most accurate information possible on the historical and the current record of the domestic economy and then try to project both demand and supply-side dimensions. This may not be a particularly difficult problem in the short term, where the policy elements are relatively fixed. However, error sources multiply as the forecasting period is extended, and very few or none of the important determinants of economic performance can then be considered as constants. What will happen to taxes, fiscal transfers, government regulations, the use of subsidies and other market distortions, consumption and savings patterns, investment incentives, treatment of foreign-owned firms, and similar factors after 5 or 10 years? Everything is up for grabs, and forecasting has to rely largely on the basic competence of the nation's policymakers, their receptiveness to formal or informal outside advice, and the pattern of social and political constraints under which they operate. Assuming that the cast in a country's economic management team remains the same, past experience in domestic policymaking and reactions to outside shocks may not be a bad guide for the future—an assumption that nevertheless is often open to question.

A part of the task of projecting future economic management scenarios—maybe the most important one—lies in the *monetary sector*. Whereas most good country analyses contain extensive descriptions of the national financial system, the critical factors obviously relate to domestic prices and exchange rates. Useful indicators are the domestic monetary base, the money supply, net domestic credit, and available price indices, together with net foreign official assets and net foreign debt. Monetary disturbances may originate domestically or internationally. Apart from their inflationary and exchange-rate aspects, such disturbances may also have real-sector influences on consumption and savings, capital formation, income distribution, and expectations about the future.

Once again, whereas the mechanisms relating monetary developments to external debt service and transfer problems are well understood, and the requisite data usually are readily available, short-term assessments are much easier to make than a full-fledged, long-range outlook. It is, after all, possible to evaluate the relationship of the existing exchange rate to some hypothetical market-determined rate based on a calculated purchasing power parity index, and to project any deviation based on relative inflation trends. For example, in general the larger the degree of projected currency overvaluation, the greater the need for external borrowing, as well as the likelihood of reserve losses and/or the prospects for a tightening of controls on international trade and payments.

Much more difficult is the task of forecasting government responses to problem situations in the monetary sphere—devaluation, liberalization of exchange controls, and domestic monetary stringency—particularly the timing of such measures. In the long term, the problem once again comes down to the competence of the monetary policymakers and the political pressures that they clearly face.

The domestic economic management issues involved in country analysis by international banks are summarized in Figure 5-7. Complex as it is, this is still only part of the picture.

External Economic Aspects

Because of the importance of foreign exchange availability in projecting a country's debt service capabilities, country analysts must also pay attention to outside factors affecting its balance of payments and external finance. On the export side, this requires evaluation of both long-term trends and short-term instabilities. Increasing product and market diversification might be a sign of either greater export stability and reduced vulnerability to shifting economic and political conditions, or protectionist trends in the country's major markets. Shifts in the ratio of exports to gross national product may signal changing future debt service capabilities, and an analysis of demand and supply elasticities for major export products may indicate possible sources of future instability in export receipts. Domestic export-supply constraints and export-competing demand elements link back into the analysis of the previously outlined structural problems. Export policies pursued by export-competing national governments along with exchange-rate policies may also be very important. In general, we are interested in (1) alignment of a country's exports with its international competitive advantage, (2) diversification of export risk, and (3) home and third-country policies that might pose a threat to future export earnings.

On the import side as well, focus should be placed on both long-term trends and short-term instabilities. For example, the ratio of imports to gross national product per se indicates very little. However, abrupt and significant shifts in this ratio may be important. The ability of the government to compress imports in times of balance-of-payments trouble may be indicated by measures such as the ratio of food and fuel imports to total imports. Import price volatility, supplier concentration among trading partners, and trends in import-replacement production are among the other measures that can help identify possible problems originating in the import side. Here, as in the case of exports, the analyst should also be interested in the policy context—the structure of effective tariff and non-tariff protection and the impact of domestic resource allocation and efficiency on production.

The importance of foreign direct investment for the supply side of a national economy has already been noted, in terms of its contribution to aggregate and sectoral capital formation, technology transfer, development

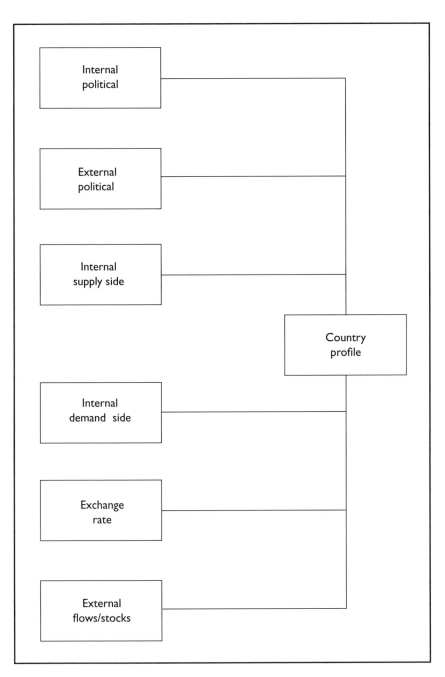

Figure 5-7. Summary of domestic economic management issues involved in country evaluations.

of human resources, management and entrepreneurial activity, access to markets, and access to supplies—the traditional multinational corporate "bundle" of services. Besides the balance-of-payments gains associated with FDI, induced exports and import-replacement production, outflows may occur via induced imports of goods and services and profit remittances. Each foreign investment project evidences a more or less unique balance-of-payments—in magnitude as well as in timing—profile. Policies affecting foreign direct investment (e.g., taxation, restrictions on earnings remittances, privatization, nationalization and expropriation) may alter this profile and thereby influence a country's prospects as perceived by international lenders and bondholders as well. Multinational companies are often extraordinarily sensitive to changes in national policies. Since such changes can trigger changes in the overall creditworthiness of countries as a whole, shifts in FDI patterns deserve careful attention. Moreover, capital outflows on the part of residents, which are frequently highly sensitive to the domestic outlook and to autonomous private lending by foreigners to domestic residents, can also have a substantial impact on a country's overall creditworthiness.

Finally, it may be important to analyze the magnitude and types of grants and concessionary (foreign aid) loans that a country receives from abroad, and the prospective future development of these flows. Certainly, in this case domestic conditions in the donor countries, donor-recipient relationships, and the economic and political attractiveness of the recipient countries is very important. And countries that are of strategic or economic importance are obviously prime candidates for future intergovernmental "rescues," which may to some extent backstop private investment or bank lending exposure in severe problem situations and increase the interest of major financial powers in successfully concluding "workout" situations. Figure 5-8 summarizes financial flows and their relationships to the domestic economic picture.

Liquidity and Debt Aspects

The aforementioned issues usually involve medium- and long-range forecasts of such measures as the balance of trade, the current account, and various other measures of "flow." These aggregates will naturally be reflected in a country's international reserve position and in its access to international financial markets for financing needs. Near-term "liquidity" assessments generally focus on such measures as changes in a country's owned reserves and IMF position and on ratios, such as reserves to monthly imports, intended to indicate in some sense the degree of "cushioning" provided by reserve holdings. The ability to borrow additional sums abroad, or to refinance existing debt, depends on the projected state of financial markets and assessment of country creditworthiness by international banks and official institutions at the time of need.

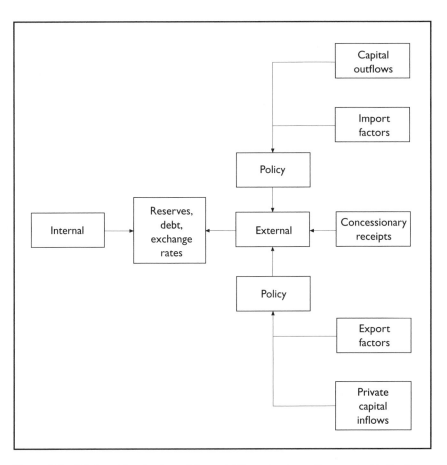

Figure 5-8. Relationship of external financial flows to domestic economic situation.

Analysis of the size and structure of country indebtedness and debt service payments is equally important in this regard. Ratios such as (1) total debt to exports or to gross national product and (2) long-term public debt to exports or to gross national product, are used in virtually all country analyses, as are the amount and trends in overall external indebtedness and current versus term debt.

The *debt service ratio*—debt service payments to exports or "normal" exports—is perhaps the most commonly used ratio. However, by using only exports in the denominator, the debt service ratio ignores the potentially equivalent contributions of import savings to a country's debt service capabilities. Consequently, for different countries a particular debt service ratio (say 0.3) may mean entirely different things about creditworthiness.

Another commonly used indicator is the so-called *cash flow index* (CFI), calculated as follows:

$$\text{CFI} = \frac{R + A + LC + T}{DS}$$

where R represents gross foreign exchange reserves held by the country's central bank; A denotes net foreign assets held by the commercial banks, LC represents undrawn loan facilities committed to the country, including interbank lines; T is the expected current-account balance; and DS represents debt service obligations for the year ahead. A CFI value of less than one indicates that additional borrowing will be required during the year to meet debt service obligations. Also commonly used ratios are:

- Foreign capital inflows to debt service payments
- Exports plus capital inflows and aid receipts to current debt
- Vital imports plus debt service payments to exports plus capital inflows and aid receipts ("compressibility ratio")
- The reciprocal of the average maturity of external debt ("rollover ratio")

All such ratios must be interpreted with caution. Ratios have different meanings for different countries and for the same country at different times and stages of development. There are absolutely no valid rules of thumb. Wise usage of ratios lies in their interpretation, in their changes over time, and in their specific context in a particular country situation. However, even if a good analyst recognizes the limitations of some of the listed indicators, she or he may nevertheless make use of them to understand and forecast how *other* banks or investors perceive the situation when a country comes into the market.

Figure 5-9 depicts the linkage between external "stock" factors and the policies that affect them. Domestic real or monetary changes may trigger trade or payments shifts, or vice versa, and both may affect external borrowing and reserves. Once a country borrows, the creditor takes a natural interest in the goings-on within the country; as the external debt builds up, there is widening monitoring and advice on behalf of the lenders, both in the public as well as in the private sector.

Political Aspects

Besides domestic structural and monetary variables and external stock and flow factors, country analysis related to term exposure always requires astute political forecasting. Most closely related to the economic variables just discussed is the "competence" or "wisdom" of national economic managers. Small casting changes can cause enormous changes in the quality of the play. There is also the question whether the technocrats have a full political mandate to "do what's necessary" from a debt service point of view, and ultimately, whether the government itself is firm and has the political will to carry out the necessary, often unpopular, programs. Evaluating and forecasting the political "overlay" of national economic poli-

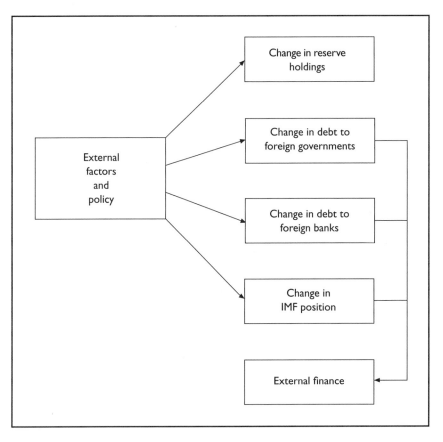

Figure 5-9. Internal-external linkages. IMF = International Monetary Fund.

cymaking (i.e., the degree of resolve, the power base, and the tools available for implementing sound policy decisions) cannot be overemphasized. Banks that are leaders in country analysis generally place a great deal of stress on this particular dimension, which requires an entirely different sort of forecasting and information base than some of the more mechanical aspects of the issue.

Of particular importance is the extent to which policymakers are receptive to outside advice. Politicians often find "business as usual" the best way to go, even when it is becoming clear that serious debt service problems are in the air. They certainly know that whatever needs to be done is probably going to have a substantial political cost (i.e., tax increases, monetary restraint, exchange-rate changes) and hope fervently that "something will turn up." However, rarely does anything ever turn up, at least in the short run, and foreign lenders are increasingly requested to offer advice as the country's debt grows. Very often, when the advice is well received the country makes its way out of the impending problematic situation, well before it becomes critical, despite the political costs involved. Sometimes the country engages outside advisors to help formulate sound economic plans and policies, improve its image in international financial markets, and perhaps take some of the domestic political heat. In severe cases, however, outside advice is often ignored, until any additional borrowing becomes considerably more expensive or not available at all, and a crisis looms.

At some point in this scenario—for domestic politicians later rather than sooner—the country will have to negotiate borrowing facilities with the International Monetary Fund. IMF involvement gives a certain degree of comfort to private banks and investors, and often their own extension of further credit is conditioned on the IMF stamp of approval on a country's plans. At the same time, the IMF may provide domestic policymakers with the necessary backbone to undertake unpopular yet necessary economic measures. Problems arise when even this external pressure fails to rectify the problem. In some cases the IMF can play a pivotal role in gradually rescuing countries from financial distress, but perhaps not in a timely fashion so as to save lenders or investors from economic losses.

In addition there are some rather fundamental political developments that need to be sorted out, monitored, and forecast as well.

Internal political change in a country may range from gradual to abrupt, systemic to nonsystemic, and cataclysmic to trivial, in terms of its importance to international lenders. For example, political drift to the right or to the left may be very important in terms of the internal and external operationality/soundness of the national economy and the quality of economic management. The symptoms can be clearly observed in domestic fiscal and monetary policies, in relations with foreign countries, in imposition of exchange controls, and the like. This may result in soaring levels of imports, reduced capacity to export, drying up of FDI, capital flight, aid cutoffs, and increasing problems of access to international capital markets. It is therefore necessary to look into the direction, magnitude, and timing of any political drift before one considers various future macroeconomic scenarios.

A more dramatic version relates to violent internal political conflict, which is destined to have serious direct economic consequences. Strikes, terrorism, sabotage, and popular insurrection seriously disrupt the operationality of the national economy, with potentially dramatic consequences for a country's balance of payments. Export industries (i.e., tourism) are particularly sensitive to those problems. The direct and indirect import requirements of government anti-insurgency efforts can be significant as well. It is clearly important to assess the strength of both the insurgency movement and the government in order to forecast the duration and outcome of such conflict. If the conflict results in systemic change, external debt may be repudiated.

External political conflict can likewise take a variety of forms, ranging from invasion and foreign-inspired or supported insurgency to border tension and perceived external threats. Threats from abroad often require far-reaching domestic resource reallocation in the form of an inflated defense establishment, which may cause adverse trade shifts and involve large direct foreign exchange costs. Military hardware, human resources, and infrastructure in an economic sense generally have low or negative productivity in terms of the domestic economy or the balance of payments and therefore contribute nothing to the basis of effective future debt service. Such distortions alone may have a serious bearing on the risk profile of a country as perceived by foreign banks.

These problems reside in both *potential* and *actual* external conflict. The latter simply magnifies the various distortions to which the supply-side possibilities of physical and human-resource destruction and dislocation, obsolescence, and reconstruction costs (unless partly offset by reparations or aid receipts) must be added. Even when external political conflict is over, there may be derivative internal political upheavals and possibly sizable costs of occupation or continued internal resistance and reparations obligations. All such assessments have to be undertaken in probabilistic terms, since they are of special interest in cross-border lending.

Shifting political alliances, regional political developments, and bilateral relations over such issues as human rights and nuclear proliferation can provide additional sources of political conflict. They are heavily influenced by global, regional, and national political events.

Political forecasting is an art which, despite its central role in plotting the future creditworthiness of countries, remains in its infancy. Indices of political stability developed by political scientists say little that is very reliable about the future or about the ultimate implications for debt service. The more sophisticated projections of possible sources of internal and external political conflict, while useful and necessary, usually leave the critical judgments largely up to the user of the information. And there are problems related to the completeness and timeliness of political information. Figure 5-10 shows the political factors considered in one major bank risk assessment of the People's Republic of China in 1994.

To summarize, country analysis is a process that requires careful assessment and weighing of internal economic and financial elements, external trade and monetary flows, and the impact of each on foreign debt and reserves—all in a political context that is itself often highly complex and difficult to gauge. As Figure 5-11 shows, each element in the analysis is linked to all of the others, and the task is to forecast the national politico-economic future with specific reference to the government's *ability* and *willingness* to service external debt.

Banks and other foreign debt holders, therefore, are principally concerned with *base-level* country scenarios, which permit evaluation of the net present value of country lending exposure. The problem becomes significantly more complex, if the task is to evaluate *project-specific* country scenarios related to equity investments, including the bank's own operations in the country in reference.

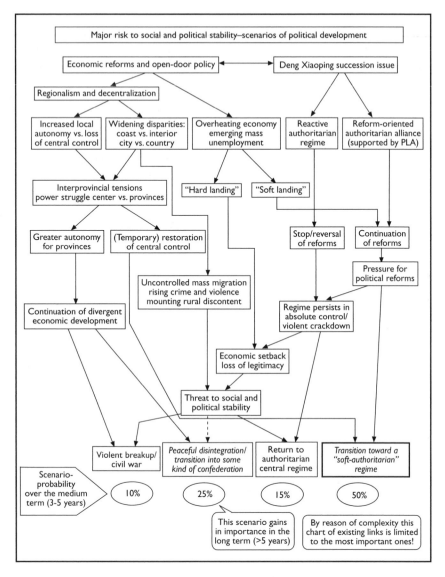

Figure 5-10. Example of political risk assessment of the People's Republic of China in 1994. Source: Swiss Bank Corporation.

Approaches to Country-Risk Assessment

Given the complexity of the factors affecting the creditworthiness of countries, how should international banks or institutional investors organize and evaluate the necessary flow of information within their own organizations' structures—and its assembly in a form that is useful from a decision-making point of view?

A truly definitive portrayal of a country's economic and political future, and its implications for creditworthiness, may require writing a book, maybe several books, about each nation. Such a review should be updated every six months or so, or whenever there is a significant change in lender/ investor interest or country circumstances. Encyclopedic analyses of this sort tend to be useless from a decision-making point of view, even though they would probably give the only correct and comprehensive overview of all of the critical variables, each highly country specific, and the various interrelationships among them—in other words, the ifs, ands, and buts that constitute an inevitable part of any exercise in politico-economic forecasting. However, banks and investors operate under pressure of time as well as fiscal and human-resource constraints. Given these realities, the following approaches to country analysis attempt to achieve a balance between completeness and accuracy, usability and feasibility.

Qualitative Assessments.   Closest to the custom-tailored, in-depth country analyses are purely "descriptive" country studies, which try to cover all of the political and economic underpinnings. They tend to be largely retrospective and subjective, and use no standardized format to avoid straitjacketing the discussion. This approach is particularly conducive to political risk evaluation, which tends inevitably to be "soft." Cross-country comparability suffers, however, if the focus on specific country attributes and prospects is maintained. Updating problems can be relatively

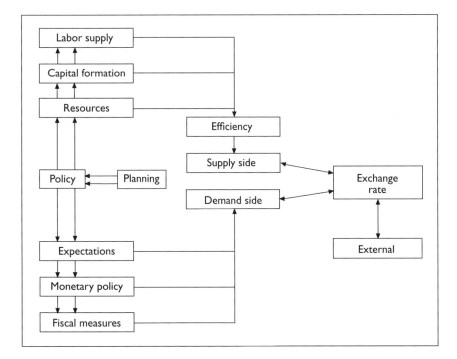

Figure 5-11. Domestic economic management issues involved in country analysis.

difficult because of the nature of the analysis and the level of detail, since there are great difficulties in distilling the essence of unstructured descriptive studies for use in exposure-setting decisions.

Structured Country Reviews.   Using a standard, relatively short format for all countries under consideration, this approach severely cuts back on the narrative and expands on the use of data analysis, standard ratios, and formalistic trend assessments. Qualitative elements are retained to an "optimal" extent and in an abbreviated format. An effort is made to retain country-specific elements in the analysis and to enhance usability by means of carefully formatted and tightly worded summaries. Besides conventional sources of country data, periodic country visits and information from representatives in the field are supposed to be used to update country files and improve the quality of the analysis. The standard format used in this approach is intended to facilitate cross-country comparisons without loss of significant qualitative country-specific information. Nevertheless, there is sometimes a tendency to deemphasize political risk and to adopt heavily retrospective focus.

Country Ratings.   So-called checklist country rating systems employ the same information base just discussed, often backed up by a formal narrative country study, in an attempt to assign "grades" both to quantitative and qualitative variables. Each grade is then assigned a weight, and one or several weighted summary scores are computed. These weighted summaries are supposed to capture not only the historical evidence, but also the future outlook as reflected in the score assignment and weighting process. This approach is basically an effort to facilitate country monitoring, cross-country comparisons, and performance auditing of the country assessment system. Besides weighted country scores, some approaches try to generate composite measures of debt service capacity, political stability and adaptability to external shocks, and the like, with weighted input measures used to generate "composite" indicators, which are then displayed in grid or matrix format.

Despite their advantages in country comparisons and usability in lending decisions, all such rating systems encompass a variety of disadvantages. Selection of indicators tends to be subjective and is often not based on coherent underlying models of politics or economics. Grading of indicators, likewise, tends to be subjective, as is the assignment of weights. Usually the same indicators and weights are used for all countries examined, which makes little sense. Nonquantifiable information is often ignored, which may throw out some country-specific elements that can have a strong bearing on risk. Political-risk grading systems, as developed in financial institutions and as they are available from advisory services, are even more tenuous in terms of validity. Perhaps the greatest potential problem lies in overreliance upon, and therefore, abuse of, such systems in exposure decisions. In an area where the use of forecasting in decision-making (especially in the long term), is akin to grasping at straws, this technique in the wrong hands may be particularly dangerous.

Country Evaluation Filters. This involves the use of "multiple discriminate analysis" to differentiate between countries that have encountered external debt problems in the past and those that have not. The objective is to avoid type 1 errors (predicting that a country will get into trouble when in fact it does not) and type 2 errors (predicting that a country will stay clear of problems when in fact it ends up in trouble). In the first case, a bank or investor may stay away when in fact it should have become involved, while in the second case it will go ahead when in fact it should have passed it up. If selected indicators, like the debt service ratio or the liquidity ratio, have been found to discriminate successfully between "trouble" and "no-trouble" countries in the past, then they may be used for this purpose in a forecasting context.

Despite their methodological sophistication, neatness, and usability of "yes/no" results, such filters have a number of limitations. They provide only partial coverage of the dependent variable of concern, namely, the possibility of a decline in the real economic value of exposure in a particular country. Empirically, they focus almost exclusively on past debt defaults or reschedulings. The wide economic differences among the countries in which banks have exposed assets, together with often rapid shifts in these countries over time, raise doubts about excessive reliance on such filters—or any limited set of indicators—even if statistical performance is reasonably good in evaluating historical experience of sample countries. Filters may, however, be useful for culling countries for close examination by one of the more in-depth techniques.

Outside Views. Aside from internal country evaluations, a bank or institutional investor may avail itself of outside services that monitor country conditions around the world. A number of political risk services and global country reviews are marketed by a broad array of firms, all of which claim special methodological expertise, information sources, or analytical competence. Individual consultants, particularly ex-public officials, offer similar services. Few, however, fully understand the international banking or investment business or have intimate knowledge of individual institutions, so that some of their advice is of limited value. On the other hand, outside consultants can provide useful "second opinions" and serve as a sounding board for internal views. From time to time, surveys of bank country ratings are combined into overall rankings of "what financial institutions think" of individual countries. Table 5-4 gives one example.

To summarize, Figure 5-12 depicts the kinds of country evaluation systems that are available to international banks and investors in terms of (1) their ability to capture country-specific details that may ultimately lead to losses in the value of bank exposures and (2) the usability of their respective informational outputs in decision-making. There is a clear trade-off: The more comprehensive the analysis, the less usable it is in an

Table 5-4 Institutional Investor's Country Credit Ratings: Example for 1994

Rank Sept. 1993	Rank March 1994	Country	Institutional Investor Credit Rating	Six-Month Change	One-Year Change	Rank Sept. 1993	Rank March 1994	Country	Institutional Investor Credit Rating	Six-Month Change	One-Year Change
1	1	Switzerland	92.2	0.2	0.2	34	34	Chile	53.6	2.1	4.7
2	2	Japan	91.0	-0.7	0.0	36	35	Oman	52.5	1.8	1.7
4	3	United States	89.7	0.5	1.1	33	36	Bahrain	52.0	0.4	1.0
3	4	Germany	89.4	-0.4	-0.9	35	37	Indonesia	51.7	0.2	0.6
5	5	Netherlands	88.4	-0.4	-0.8	37	38	Kuwait	51.5	2.3	2.6
6	6	France	88.2	0.0	0.6	38	39	Cyprus	51.1	2.3	2.3
7	7	United Kingdom	86.0	0.6	1.4	40	40	Czech Republic	49.7	3.1	5.1
8	8	Austria	85.6	0.3	0.3	39	41	Greece	49.1	0.5	1.2
9	9	Luxembourg	84.6	0.0	0.1	41	42	Mexico	46.9	1.3	1.7
10	10	Canada	81.9	-0.1	-0.1	43	43	Hungary	46.1	1.3	1.8
11	11	Singapore	81.4	0.5	1.2	44	44	Botswana	45.7	1.0	4.6
12*	12	Taiwan	79.0	0.9	0.5	42	45	Turkey	45.6	0.5	0.3
13*	13*	Belgium	78.8	-1.0	-1.5	46	46	Israel	43.4	2.9	3.8
14*	14*	Norway	78.8	0.7	1.7	45	47	Mauritius	43.3	2.3	4.9
15	15	Denmark	77.8	1.1	2.5	48	48	Tunisia	42.9	2.6	4.1
16	16	Spain	74.7	-0.5	-1.1	47	49	Colombia	42.4	2.0	3.6
17	17	Sweden	74.5	0.1	-0.7	49	50	India	40.0	1.6	1.4
18	18	Italy	72.6	-0.9	-2.5	50	51	South Africa	38.9	0.7	-0.9
19	19	Ireland	70.7	0.7	1.3	51	52	Venezuela	37.6	0.0	-1.0
20	20	Finland	69.9	0.5	0.3	52	53	Barbados	37.3	2.1	1.5
21	21	South Korea	69.5	0.6	0.9	53	54	Uruguay	36.0	1.8	2.3
22	22	Australia	68.9	0.8	1.0	54	55	Morocco	35.8	2.4	3.6
23	23	Portugal	67.3	0.6	1.2	55	56	Argentina	35.6	3.0	5.1
25	24	Malaysia	66.6	1.8	2.7	61	57	Slovenia	33.4	4.8	10.8
26	25	New Zealand	66.1	1.4	2.3	56	58	Papua New Guinea	32.8	0.4	0.4
24	26	Hongkong	66.0	-0.1	0.4	57	59	Slovakia	31.6	1.0	0.6
27	27	Thailand	61.1	0.3	1.1	58	60	Trinidad & Tobago	30.8	1.4	1.2
28	28	United Arab Emirates	59.9	1.6	2.0	64	61*	Philippines	30.5	2.5	3.4
—	29	Malta	58.7	—	—	62	62*	Poland	30.5	1.9	3.6
29	30	Saudi Arabia	58.6	0.7	0.6	67	63	Egypt	29.8	2.3	2.7
30	31	China	58.0	0.7	1.7	60	64	Libya	29.4	0.6	0.8
31	32	Iceland	55.8	0.9	0.7	68	65*	Paraguay	28.8	1.6	1.0
32	33	Qatar	54.7	1.8	2.5	66	66*	Pakistan	28.8	1.1	-0.1

65	67	Brazil	28.8	1.0	1.1
70	68	Zimbabwe	27.9	1.0	0.2
59	69	Iran	27.8	-1.6	-4.3
73	70	Sri Lanka	27.7	2.2	2.2
71	71	Costa Rica	27.6	0.8	2.8
63	72	Gabon	27.4	-0.8	-0.6
72	73	Ghana	27.1	1.1	2.9
74	74*	Swaziland	26.3	1.8	4.1
69	75	Algeria	26.3	-0.8	-1.9
75*	76	Romania	25.4	1.0	1.2
80	77	Seychelles	23.7	2.3	3.0
79	78	Jamaica	23.6	1.7	1.7
78	79	Nepal	23.2	1.1	1.5
77	80	Syria	23.1	0.4	0.7
76	81	Kenya	22.8	-0.2	-1.9
81	82	Ecuador	22.5	1.2	1.7
85	83*	Panama	22.1	1.2	1.7
83	84*	Jordan	22.1	1.0	1.1
88	85	Vietnam	21.9	2.4	4.4
90	86	Dominican Republic	21.0	1.8	2.5
86	87	Senegal	20.9	0.8	0.9
84	88	Estonia	20.7	-0.2	-0.7
97	89	Guatemala	20.1	2.0	1.3
95	90	Bangladesh	20.0	1.3	0.7
89	91*	Bulgaria	19.8	0.3	0.9
102	92*	Lebanon	19.8	2.7	5.7
81	93	Cameroon	19.7	-1.6	-2.1
87	94	Latvia	19.6	-0.4	0.1
94	95	Bolivia	19.5	0.8	1.4
91	96	Nigeria	18.6	-0.5	-1.7
93	97	Lithuania	18.4	-0.6	-0.5
92	98	Russia	18.1	-0.9	-2.1
98	99	Kazakhstan	17.7	0.1	1.9
109	100	Peru	17.5	2.5	3.6
101	101*	Malawi	17.4	0.1	1.2
107	102	El Salvador	17.3	2.0	2.1
99	103	Burkina Faso	17.2	-0.3	—

103	104	Benin	16.8	-0.1	—
107	105	Mali	16.7	1.4	—
104	106	Côte d'Ivoire	16.4	0.2	-0.3
106	107	Honduras	16.2	0.6	0.5
105	108*	Congo	15.5	-0.3	0.3
100	109*	Belarus	15.5	-2.0	-1.9
—	110	Togo	15.4	—	—
96	111	Ukraine	15.1	-3.1	-3.1
110	112	Uzbekistan	14.3	-0.1	-0.2
111	113	Tanzania	13.9	-0.1	1.0
114	114	Myanmar	13.3	0.3	0.9
116	115*	Zambia	13.1	0.7	1.4
111	116*	Guinea	13.1	-0.9	—
113	117	Croatia	12.8	-0.8	-1.4
115	118	Angola	10.7	-1.9	-3.0
120	119	Ethiopia	10.6	0.8	2.1
118	120**	Albania	10.3	-0.2	-0.8
121		Mozambique	10.3	0.6	1.9
123	122	Uganda	10.1	1.7	2.8
119	123	Afghanistan	9.9	-0.4	—
122	124	Nicaragua	9.1	0.4	0.8
117	125	Georgia	8.9	-2.8	
128	126	Grenada	8.5	1.0	1.2
127	127	Cuba	7.9	0.2	-0.3
125	128	Haiti	7.5	-0.5	0.2
130	129*	Sierra Leone	7.2	0.6	0.5
129	130*	Iraq	7.2	0.0	-0.2
126	131	Zaire	6.9	-0.8	-1.9
124	132	Yugoslavia	6.6	-1.7	-3.4
131	133	North Korea	6.5	0.2	-0.8
133	134	Sudan	6.1	0.4	-0.9
132	135	Liberia	6.0	0.0	0.0
		Global average rating	36.7	0.6	-0.1

* Order determined by actual results before rounding.
** Actual tie.

143

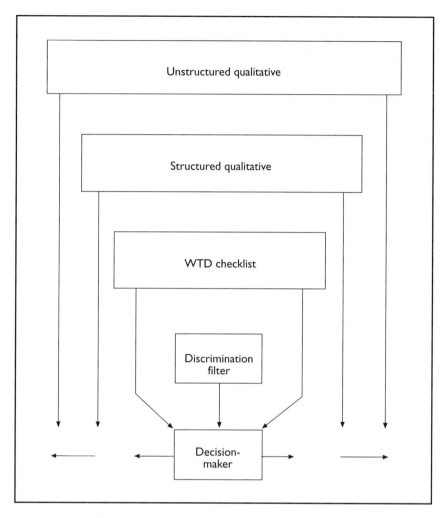

Figure 5-12. Breadth versus usability in country evaluation systems.

exposure-setting context. The more mechanical and formal the system, the less country-specific information it tends to capture, which may ultimately be the source of grief for the bank. Reconciling the two requisites for sound country evaluation systems—usability and completeness—is largely a matter of organizational design. Table 5-5 gives one example as applied to the People's Republic of China in 1994.

Institutional Design and Country Exposure Decisions

Figure 5-13 represents a simplified schematic of a decision system, one that will vary to some extent among international banks and investment

Table 5-5 Country Assessment Profile: People's Republic of China, 1994

Indicators		1990	1991	1992	Estimate 1993	Estimate 1994	Outlook 1995
Domestic Economy							
1. Real GDP growth	%	5.6	7.5	12.8	13.4	10.5	8.0
2. Investment/GDP	International average = 25%	38.2	37.8	40.5	41.7	42.0	41.0
3. Investment efficiency (1:2)	critical level ≤ 0.2	0.18*	0.20*	0.22	0.28	0.29	0.25
4. Inflation (retail prices, average)	%	2.2	2.8	5.3	13.0	20.0	14.0
5. Money supply growth M2	%	28.9***	26.7*	30.8*	23.6*	25.0*	down*
6. Real domestic credit creation	%	21.4***	22.2*	25.4*	11.0	10.0	down
7. Fiscal balance/GDP[1]	%	-2.1	-2.4	-2.6	-2.2	-1.7	up
External Economy							
8. Competitiveness (real exchange rate)	Index 1990=100	100.0	86.0	74.7	67.8	64.0	70.0
9. Trade balance (goods)	USD bn	11.4	11.3	8.38	-7.0**	-6.5	-4.0
10. Exports (goods + services)	USD bn	71.2	82.9	100.2	107.3	124.0	↗
11. Imports (goods + services)	USD bn	58.9	69.2	92.4*	116.9**	133.0	up
12. Current account balance	USD bn	12.6	14.6	8.95**	-8.2***	-7.5	-5.0
13. Exports/GDP	%	19.2	22.3	23.1	20.0	26.0	→
14. Export concentration (high=critical) to HK	%	42.1	44.6	43.5	24.0[2]	25.0	up
to USA		8.2	8.6	10.1	18.5[2]	20.0	down
15. Imports from Switzerland	CHF m	415	471	620	943+	950	→
Debt							
16. Total external debt (public + private)	USD bn	58.2	67.3	76.1	86.5	95.0	103.0
17. International reserves (excl. gold)	USD bn	29.6	43.7	20.6[3]	22.0	30.0	35.0
18. External debt service	USD bn	7.02	8.57	8.84	10.2	10.5	11.5
19. External debt/exports	critical level ≥ 150%	81.7	81.2	76.0	74.0	71.5	↗
20. External debt service/exports	critical level ≥ 25%	9.9	10.3	8.8	9.5	8.5	↗
21. Interest-adjusted current account/interest payments	%	484	484	342	-122*	-88*	↗*
22. International reserves/imports	critical level ≤ 3 mths	6.0	7.6	2.7*[3]	2.3*	2.7*	↗*
23. Political risk	points (1→10)	7*	6	6	7***	7*	↗*
24. Exchange rate (end-period)	CNY/USD	5.22	5.43	5.75	5.80+	8.70	9.00
25. Deposit rate (nominal; avg 1 yr)	%	9.9	8.6	7.9	9.4+	12.0	10.0

(continued)

Table 5-5 Country Assessment Profile: People's Republic of China, 1994 (continued)

* = Figure beyond critical level.
** = Figure in critical change vs. previous year.
*** = Figure in critical change and beyond critical level.
+ = Actual figure.
– = Due to the unreliability and deficiencies of Chinese statistics, most of the figures shown above are to be taken with caution!

[1] General government borrowing; including the refinancing of existing debt and financing of capital projects, the deficit would amount to CNY 129bn or 4.2% of GDP in 1994.
[2] The sharp fall in the share of China's exports to HK in 1993 is due to a change in the attribution of origin and destination to merchandise passing through HK between China and the USA and Japan, whereas the latter two's quota has been increased.
[3] Beginning July 1992, foreign exchange holdings of the Bank of China are excluded.

This Country Risk Monitor (CRM) provides economic and political indicators for short- and long-term transfer risk. The indicators have been chosen by empirical analysis. Occasionally, some of the indicators used in the CRM may vary from the standard set described below depending on availability and/ or usefulness.

We use three symbols as aids to monitoring risks:

* = Ratio has gone beyond an empirically determined critical level (applies to indicators 3, 19, 20 and 22); ** = Ratio both exceeds critical level and has undergone critical change within a 12-month period; *** = Value or ratio has deteriorated very sharply within a 12-month period (critical change). ➚ = improving ➘ = deteriorating

Outlook: → = unchanged ➚ = improving ➘ = deteriorating
* = Estimate NA = Not available

Note: The suggested critical values apply to developing countries only and do not necessarily reflect similar risks in the case of industrialized countries.

1. Real GDP growth: Change in Gross Domestic Product over a 12-month period in %, adjusted for inflation (i.e. in volume terms); growth measure.
2. Investment ratio: Gross fixed capital formation (fixed investment) as % of GDP or GNP. The higher the ratio, the higher the potential economic growth. International average: 25%.
3. Investment efficiency: 3-year moving average of real GDP growth (no. 1) divided by the average investment ratio (no. 2) for same period. The higher the value, the more efficient the economy; critical level ≤0.2 on average. (Note: values will tend to be lower for more developed countries.)
4. Inflation: Change in consumer prices as an annual average in %. One measure of quality of economic policy.
5. Money supply (M1 or other monetary control variable): Annual % change in money supply. Measure of monetary policy and early indicator for future inflation.
6. Real domestic credit: Annual % change of the domestic component of money supply (=M2 minus Net Foreign Assets), deflated by consumer price inflation. Measure of domestic monetary disequilibrium (in comparison to real GDP growth) and early indicator for balance-of-payments developments and exchange-rate changes.
7. Fiscal balance as % of GDP: General or (if unavailable) central government surplus or deficit as % of GDP. Fiscal policy measure. Since structural (permanent) deficits are more important than cyclical peaks and cross-country comparability is lacking, critical values are not determined.

146

8. International competitiveness index (Index of real effective exchange rate): Compares domestic with foreign inflation, adjusted for exchange-rate changes. Domestic inflation: GDP deflator. Foreign inflation: Trade-weighted changes of GDP deflators of major trading partners, adjusted for exchange-rate changes. A decline in the index (= a real devaluation) indicates an increase in competitiveness.

9. Trade balance: Exports minus imports of goods, in bn US$. Goods are valued at their prices as they leave the exporting country, i.e. f.o.b, without costs of insurance and freight. Chief determinant of the current-account balance (see no. 12).

10./11. Exports and imports: Exports and imports of both goods and services (e.g. tourism, transportation, interest), in bn US$.

12. Current account balance: Trade balance + balance of services + balance of unrequited transfers, in bn US$; a deficit shows the extent of a country's dependence on foreign resources to satisfy domestic demand, to be financed (a) by drawing down international reserves (see no. 17) and/or (b) by additional borrowing abroad (no. 16).

13. Share of exports in GDP: Exports of goods and services (see no. 10) as % of GDP. Index of the openness of the economy, indicating (a) the allocation of domestic resources to the tradable sector and the country's ability to service its external debt and (b) the country's vulnerability to foreign demand shocks.

14. Export concentration
Either: Share of main commodity exports in total exports. Main commodity exports (food and other agricultural products, raw materials and metals) as % of total exports. High value indicates high vulnerability to fluctuations in international commodity market conditions.
Or: Merchandise exports to main customers (countries) as % of total merchandise exports. High value indicates dependency on a few major customer markets.

15. Imports from Switzerland: Goods imports from Switzerland in m Sfr.

16. External debt: Total external debt (gross) of the reporting country in bn US$ at end of year. Includes short- and long-term debt, IMF lending and interest arrears.

17. International reserves: Total official international reserves at end of year, excluding gold. Foreign exchange, Special Drawing Rights, IMF reserves, Liquidity measure.

18. External debt service: Interest payments due on total debt + amortization payments due on medium- and long-term debt.

19. External debt/Exports: Total external debt as % of export receipts (goods & services). An important debt capacity indicator, since external debt ultimately has to be repaid out of export revenues. Critical level: ≥150; critical change: approx. 25% increase within a year.

20. Debt-service ratio: Annual interest and amortization payments on total external debt as % of export receipts (goods & services). Short-term liquidity measure. Critical level: ≥ 25%; critical change: approx. 50% increase within a year.

21. Interest coverage: Current account balance net of interest payments to foreign creditors, as % of interest payments. Indicator of debt-servicing capacity. 100% or more indicates net current account revenues technically sufficient to cover all interest obligations. 0 or less indicates net current account revenues technically too small to pay any interest.

22. Import cover: Official reserves at year-end (no. 17) divided by average monthly imports (see no. 11). Measure of how long imports could be financed from international reserves. Critical level: ≤ 3 months; critical change: approx. 50% decrease within a year.

23. Political risk: Social and political situation rated on a scale of 1–10 with regard to creditworthiness. Scores 1 to 3: no foreseeable/low risks; 4 to 6: acceptable/moderate risks; 7 to 9: high/higher risks; 10: unacceptable/extremely high risks.

24./25. Optional indicators: Any readily available risk-related indicator or any country-specific indicator.

Source: Swiss Bank Corporation

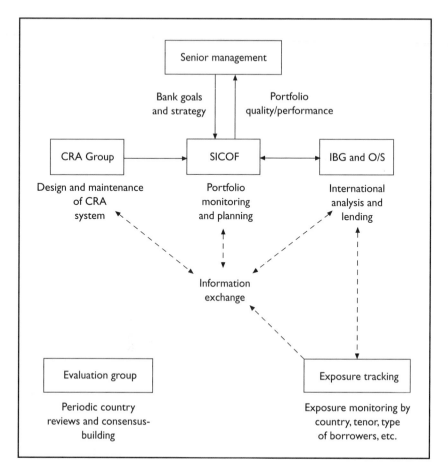

Figure 5-13. Schematic of a country decision. Solid lines represent reporting rela-
tionships; dashed lines represent information flows. CRA = country risk assessment;
SICOF = senior international credit offices; IBG = international banking group;
O/S = overseas offices.

firms. Information on cross-border exposure is maintained by a monitoring system at the head office, which receives and consolidates information
on the size and tenor of facilities granted, drawdowns, redeposits, and
other pertinent elements. As noted earlier, care must be taken so that exposure is correctly measured, frequently updated, and allocated in the light
of third-country guarantees, as well as certain other factors that might
shift the locus of risk.

The degree of decentralization of decision-making differs substantially
among institutions but the need to secure competitive advantages through
close client contact, quick response times, and adequate lending or investing authority can also lead to decentralization. This places a premium
on the existence of some type of centralized country assessment system,

which ensures that the global asset portfolio as a whole is in line with the institution's risk preferences and earnings targets, and at the same time does not inherently restrict activities in a highly competitive marketplace.

There will normally be a substantial two-way exchange of information between those responsible for the system and line bankers, insofar as they are not one and the same. In the event that a major change in exposure is contemplated, a shift in exposure limits seems justifiable by profitability, or an alteration in the perceived risk in existing exposure develops, an ad hoc country review group may be formed, consisting of responsible line officers, senior officials with regional responsibility, country economists and other specialists, and possibly other interested individuals under the chairmanship of a senior international credit adviser. Given the overall strategic goals of the bank or investment firm and its positioning in the target market as set by top management, such a review group may make a recommendation of appropriate action in the case involved. The purpose is to bring together as many different, often conflicting, viewpoints as possible, as, for example, between the country economist emphasizing the risks and the line officers emphasizing business opportunities, competition, and the associated returns. Ultimately, responsibility in such a system lies with the senior international adviser, who reports directly to top management and is charged with monitoring and planning the international portfolio within broad policy guidelines.

It is in the *use* of country evaluation that it becomes clear that whatever approach is adopted represents the beginning, not the end, of the task. Approaches that are too general may fail to concentrate on the true sources of risk in country exposure and on the specific concerns facing a particular institution's exposure. Risk on medium- and long-term exposure requires a far more complex analysis than exposure to short-term risk, or special purpose lending, which in turn is much more complicated than risk to any FDI exposure that a firm may have in a particular country.

The twin temptations of "quick and dirty" and "overloaded" country assessments seem to constantly confront international financial institutions. The first approach promises mechanical shortcuts and the use of low-priced talent to grind out country ratings at low cost. However, it often appears to succeed only in producing nonsense—there really is no substitute for high-quality analysis, flexibility, judgment, and familiarity. The second approach may rely on well-qualified internal personnel at high cost, yet encounter a dangerous narrowing of country expertise, possibly cause dissension in the ranks, and create bottlenecks in the decision-making process.

The conflicting demands of country assessment in international exposure management, ranging from high levels of usability, auditability, and comparability over the need to capture exceedingly complex and country-specific qualitative judgments over extended periods of time to the need to avoid abuse of the results in decision-making, probably means there is no such thing as an "ideal" country evaluation system. "Appropriate" systems will certainly differ for different institutions.

The key may reside as much on the training side as on the systems design. Training line bankers and portfolio managers to use sensible country assessments properly and to be sensitive to changing country-risk profiles as they go about their business may in the end contribute more to sound exposure decisions than comparable resources devoted to the design and implementation of more elegant systems.

Portfolio Aspects

We have focused in this chapter on the problems of exposure to country risk, what such exposure means from the standpoint of the real value of a bank's assets in a particular country, and the assessment of the risk. The discussion has concentrated mainly on country-by-country analysis—putting countries individually under the microscope to see what makes them tick and how this is likely to evolve in the future with regard to debt service.

However, international banks and investors are really in the business of managing a global portfolio of country exposures in the same way as they are managing a portfolio of the debt of companies, individuals, and other entities. This means maximizing returns on the entire portfolio subject to a given risk constraint set by management, or minimizing the level of risk to which the firm is exposed with a given target rate of return—the standard portfolio management problem. One difficulty in managing global portfolios of country exposures is that a country exposure, unlike stocks or bonds, often cannot easily be sold in broad and deep markets when risk or return perceptions change. It may be possible only to "run down" exposures over time as loans come due, for example, or in some cases are transferred through loan sales programs in the secondary loan market.

Yet the basic principles of portfolio approaches remain valid, since the institution is trying to maximize returns subject to risk in the *entire* portfolio, not on a country-by-country basis. It may very well be the case, for example, that increasing exposure in country X under relatively unfavorable risk-return conditions may still make a lot of sense if, by taking on that exposure, the *overall* level of risk on the portfolio decreases through the additional diversification. In particular, if the country has little in common with others in the portfolio (low covariances in expected returns), such an outcome may be very possible. It is the risks and returns associated with *global* portfolios that define the value of that portfolio to shareholders, although shareholders themselves may hold internationally diversified portfolios as well.

Country assessment and exposure setting should be a coherent managerial process that unambiguously focuses an institution's network of information and actively involves individuals with different functions and perspectives. The exercise itself will thus have tangible portfolio benefits of its own, quite apart from its more visible output in the form of defensible country-by-country evaluations. Mechanization and decentralization of the country review process will tend to cut down and perhaps eliminate this benefit, and may thereby help to stifle an environment conducive to sound global portfolio decisions.

Each institution's information-flow and decision-making setup is different, depending on such factors as the organization's size and structure. Some incorporate country assessments into portfolio decisions quite flexibly and informally, while others seem to rely on rigid and formalized review procedures. In some cases the review process is also closely tied to the annual budget cycle and the allocation of exposure authority to countries and regions. These again may be quite rigid in some institutions, while in others they are relatively easily altered as perceived market and risk conditions change.

While few international banks and investment firms fail to maintain adequate cross-border exposure measurement and monitoring, there seems to be far greater variability in the state of the country assessment systems themselves. Some are carefully thought through, while others remain largely cosmetic. Some are well integrated into the life of the organization, while others seem separate and even isolated. Whatever the approach, rational portfolio decisions with respect to country exposure management demand that forecasts of country futures be maintained on a comparable basis—and modified in the light of covariances arising out of common export markets or sources of supply, conditions in and access to international financial markets, and regional as well as global political developments.

Summary

Whereas country evaluation is itself an exceedingly difficult task, building country assessments into the design of international exposure portfolios that are in some sense "efficient" is even more complicated. Neither the risks nor the returns are clearly definable, and even exposure measurement is a difficult task. Portfolio ideas can contribute importantly in clarifying the risks. It also helps to identify dangers inherent in externally imposed evaluations for rational portfolio decisions, particularly when they stem from the regulatory system. At the same time, the development of informational and assessment capabilities as part of the country evaluation process can itself lead to improved international exposure decisions that implicitly embody portfolio concepts. Application of these also help pin down the link between risks and pricing of international loans and bonds. Portfolio theory says that the riskiness of any single cross-border exposure is not what is important, but rather the effect of that exposure on the risk of the overall portfolio.

Notes

1. For an excellent historical perspective on country problems, see Salomon Brothers, *The Risks of Sovereign Lending: Lessons from History.* New York: Salomon Brothers Inc, 1993.

6

Regulatory Issues

Banking is, and always will be, a regulated business. The reasons can be traced to its important fiduciary element—the use of other people's money—and the central role banking plays in the modern national and global economic and financial system. Banks cannot be allowed to impose politically unacceptable costs on society, either by failing those people deemed worthy of protection in financial matters or, through failure, contaminating other financial institutions and ultimately the economic system as a whole. Consequently, every country imposes regulations intended to ensure that banks are safe and sound, that they contribute to the efficient allocation of resources and economic growth, and that they deal with the public in a fair and honest way.

This requires striking a balance across the objectives depicted in Figure 6-1, and making often difficult choices between financial efficiency and creativity, institutional and systemic safety and stability, and the ability to ensure compliance and sound business conduct. And because the services provided by banks affect nearly everything in the economy, bank regulation is taken very seriously and regulatory failures become traumatic events for all concerned. The three objectives depicted in Figure 6-1 can be summarized as follows:

Financial-system performance may be explained in terms of static and dynamic efficiency of the financial system. Static efficiency, in turn, can be defined in terms of the all-in difference between what the ultimate saver in a financial system receives (net returns), and what the ultimate borrower has to pay (all-in cost of funds). The difference, termed the *all-in gross spread* (Figure 6-2), can be defined as the cost of financial intermediation and comprises costs associated with the intermediation process itself (labor, capital, etc.), the profits of the financial intermediaries, and losses that are not borne by the financial intermediaries' shareholders but rather are passed backward to the ultimate savers or forward to the ultimate users

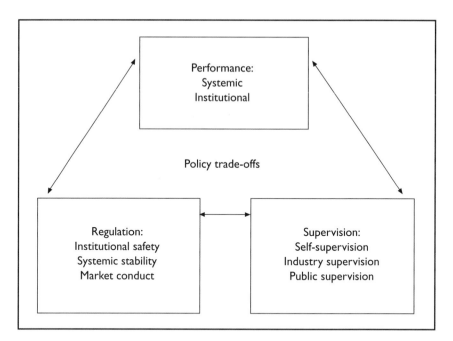

Figure 6-1. Trade-offs to be made between bank performance, regulation, and supervision.

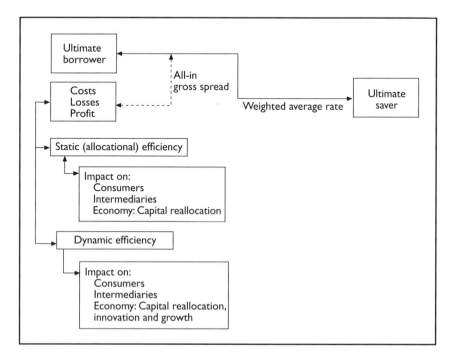

Figure 6-2. Efficiency in financial intermediation.

of funds. Some (arguable) indicators of efficiency in financial intermediation in various European countries are presented in Table 6-1, and a number of characteristics of financial system performance are listed in Table
6-2.

Regulation in Figure 6-1 has as its objective the maintenance of a safe
and sound banking system—one that is resistant to collapse and contami-
nation of the payments system and the credit allocation system—yet without precluding the failure of institutions that are not competitively viable
or are poorly managed. Additional objectives are safeguarding the assets
of uninformed retail customers who have deposited their savings in good
faith under the presumption of absolute safety backed by the institutions
themselves and by the state, and the assurance of fair dealing in financial
transactions—but without at the same time losing the value of caveat emp-
tor with respect to informed clients.

Difficult as these objectives are to achieve in a national banking environment, bank regulation in the international environment involves still
more complex issues, since the regulatory function is a matter of national
sovereignty, yet banks can and do operate across national jurisdictions, as
well as in offshore markets that can help avoid significant parts of the
regulatory net altogether. Regulatory burdens deemed excessive in one
country can prompt banks and/or their clients to move to another jurisdiction where the burdens are lighter—a form of "regulatory arbitrage" that
can both erode the gains associated with financial intermediation and
cause regulators to soften their approach, possibly excessively so. In this
chapter we explore the problems associated with bank regulation, specifically from the perspective of its impact on competitive performance of
financial institutions, both among themselves and against nonbank financial intermediaries.

Supervision in Figure 6-1 involves compliance with regulations and
the assurance that such compliance is achieved in the most effective and
efficient manner possible. Supervision can rely on managerial control by

Table 6-1 Banks'[a] Cost/Efficiency Measures, 1991

Country	Costs as Percentage of GDP	Costs per Head ($)	Real Increase in Costs, 1981–91 (%)	Cost/Income Ratio	Branches per Million Population
Germany	2.90	7.28	170	65.2	612
Norway	2.91	7.90	180	88.0	391
Denmark	3.02	8.26	160	62.6	516
Britain	3.46	6.44	130+	61.8	338
Holland	3.70	7.57	170	68.0	366
Sweden	4.88	1,448	320	117.5	356
Finland	5.61	1,374	300	125.6	534

Data: Organization for Economic Cooperation and Development (OECD), and Bank
for International Settlements (BIS).
[a] Including savings banks 1984–91.

Table 6-2 Some Characteristics of
"High-Performance" Financial Systems

Competitive markets and static efficiency
Low-cost structures
Effective risk management
Low excess returns
Exploited economies of scale and superscale
Exploited economies of scope
Market-driven dynamic efficiency
Product innovation
Process innovation
Optimum macroeconomic resource configuration
Minimum capital cost and sector allocation (static)
Preemptive and reactive structural adjustment (dynamic)
Global competitive performance
Financial sector
Real sector

the financial institutions themselves, in the knowledge that lapses can seriously erode the franchise value of the enterprise and damage its shareholders. Or supervision can be achieved by self-regulatory organizations (SROs) set up and operated by the financial services industry or by private-sector functions such as research analysts, auditing firms, rating agencies. Or supervision may be carried by the public sector through bank examinations carried out by the central bank or a bank supervisory agency and/or securities-related regulatory agencies.

The trade-offs depicted in Figure 6-1 should be apparent. Regulation such as capital adequacy rules, liquidity ratios, and exposure limits tend to reduce the efficiency of financial systems, as discussed in the following. There are no "free lunches" in this respect. Greater safety and stability almost always entail less static and/or dynamic efficiency in terms of criteria such as those listed in Figure 6-2. At the same time, some of the most easy-to-supervise regulations such as capital adequacy rules may cause significant efficiency losses, while difficult-to-supervise rules like "fitness and properness" criteria—that is, who is fit and proper to run a bank or to work in a bank—may be able to create safety and soundness with minimal efficiency losses. And finally, more intensive supervision almost always entails higher compliance costs and an erosion of efficiency.

It is not difficult to see why optimizing across the trade-offs depicted in Figure 6-1 is so difficult, especially when gains or losses in static and dynamic efficiency are often exceedingly difficult to measure, and when the costs of underregulation or undersupervision do not become apparent until it is too late. Nor is it difficult to see why, under such conditions, there is a persistent tendency for overregulation in the financial services sector.

In our discussion of regulatory issues, it is also useful to bear in mind the distinction between the regulatory environments of onshore and off-shore banking. *Onshore,* or *domestic, markets* for financial services are fully subject to national supervisory, regulatory, and monetary-policy controls. Whether and how foreign-based financial institutions may compete in these markets is strictly a matter for national political decisions. When domestic institutions are systematically protected from outside competition, they are frequently highly profitable. But they can also use that "artificial" profitability to cross-subsidize the penetration of other markets for financial services. These may also be relatively uncompetitive and inefficient by international standards.

Offshore markets for financial services are substantially beyond the reach of national authorities. They include Eurocurrency and Eurobond markets, and they are largely untaxed, unregulated, and highly efficient activities in which any number can play. While it seems fair to say that such characteristics have exposed the international economic and financial system to certain risks from time to time (some of them serious), offshore markets nevertheless set standards of performance in financial efficiency against which all other financial markets must be measured. It is important to recall, for example, that the Eurobond market and more recently the Euroequity market (see chapters 9 and 11) are the outcomes of confused and often muddled behavior on the part of national regulators since the 1960s. Authorities in European Union member nations were unable to agree, for example, on the establishment of an integrated European capital market in fulfillment of their obligations under the Treaty of Rome (until this was finally accomplished in the early 1990s). Individual national authorities permitted greater freedom of cross-border capital movement, yet excluded foreign borrowers and issuers from their national capital markets and drove them offshore.

All of these characteristics have combined to make financial services at the national level a "sensitive" industry, both as a central vehicle for the implementation of economic policy and as an industry subject to collective crises and failures by individual firms. The history of the United States, for example, records well over 15,000 bank failures—5,000 during the Great Depression of the 1930s alone and an average of well over 100 during the 1980s, not including massive failures of thrift institutions and a $150-billion taxpayer bailout in the late 1980s. Mismanagement or outright fraud have left prominent names like Banco Ambrosiano, BCCI, Bank Bumiputra, Crédit Lyonnais, Franklin National, Herstatt, Schroder Münchmeyer Hengst, Seafirst, and Continental Illinois among the failed or seriously damaged in recent years. Others, such as BankAmerica, and Crédit Suisse, have seen their competitive standing impaired, at least for a while. Governments are well aware of the inherent risks and potential conflicts involved in national and international banking; securities underwriting; and trading and dealing in financial instruments, foreign exchange, derivatives, and the like. Most notably in banking, these risks focus on the solvency of borrowers and the liquidity of institutions that are highly geared. Banking crises always carry with them negative externalities—damage imposed on individuals and institutions outside the firms directly involved and, in some cases, outside the industry itself. It is conventional wisdom that major banking crises can lead to severe damage to employment, income, economic growth, and related goals of society.

To protect themselves against such adverse consequences, countries have built elaborate "safety net" systems that are designed to provide liquidity to institutions in trouble, insure depositors, and sometimes bail out borrowers to help the bank maintain solvency. The operation of domestic financial safety nets invariably creates problems of efficiency and fairness; for example, how to distinguish between institutions that are TBTF (too big to fail) and those that are TSTS (too small to save), and how to neutralize competitive distortions that may result from people's expectations about the operation of the safety net. Even more important, the existence of a safety net creates potential "moral hazard" problems where management of financial institutions, knowing that they are likely to be bailed out, will behave in a less risk-averse manner and thus impose substantial contingent liabilities on those who hold up the safety net—the taxpayers and the general public.

To cope with this problem, and to ensure the safety and stability of national financial systems, governments apply various techniques of financial surveillance and control, ranging from careful bank-examination procedures, reserve requirements, mandatory asset ratios, and maximum lending limits to risk-related deposit insurance premiums, disclosure provision, securities laws, and moral suasion. Countries deal with this problem in different ways. Some simply nationalize all or major parts of the domestic financial services industry. As noted, regulation and control usually damage the efficiency of the domestic financial system, but this loss in efficiency can be considered as something of an "insurance premium" and is usually considered to be more than offset by the resulting gain in the safety and stability of the system.

Figure 6-3 summarizes the financial safety net that, in one form or another, typically provides stability to national financial systems. Problems arise when national financial institutions take some of their activities offshore into the Euromarkets or foreign markets. While home countries are supposed to regulate offshore branches, and host countries are supposed to regulate subsidiaries and other affiliates, the effectiveness of government regulation and control with regard to these activities remains the subject of intense debate.

Bank Capital Adequacy Controls

As global banking activities expanded, new financial products proliferated, with many of these being tradeable in the market. And as competition between banks from different countries grew, the difficulties in main-

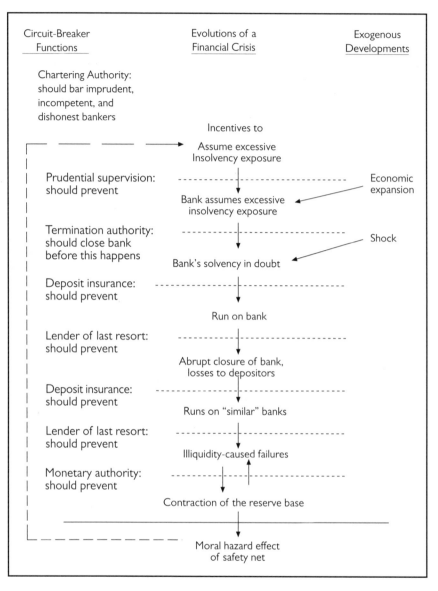

Figure 6-3. The safety net as a crisis prevention system. Source: Courtesy of Richard Herring, The Wharton School.

taining uniform standards for bank safety as well as "level" competitive conditions between banks from different countries became a serious problem. Regulatory differences, particularly those pertaining to capital adequacy, encouraged banks subject to less restrictive conditions to compete aggressively against other banks, which in turn pushed the more thoroughly regulated institutions to increase other forms of activities as a way of keeping up.

Achieving a "Level Playing Field"

Implementation of a truly level playing field in the financial services sector depends both on there being similar sets of restraints on the various types of lending that banks perform and on common definitions as to what is and is not bank "capital." The task is complicated by the structure of regulatory and prudential constraints already in place, and accepted, in each of the countries involved. These differ with respect to both lending practices and capitalization. There is a wide array of rules, for example, as to bank reserves—some countries permit "hidden" reserves against loan losses (in the form of deliberately undervalued assets)—and as to the regulation of domestic deposit rates, deposit insurance, domestic competition policies, and many other issues that can affect an institution's competitive positioning internationally. While these differences are comparable in nature to the competitive effects of subsidies and governmental participation in other industries, the differences are perhaps more serious in the banking sector. Moreover, in no other industry have uniform global standards been attempted.

Bank regulators have discussed the issue of standardization for years, confronting time and again the fact of national sovereignty in banking supervision and monetary control, and the entrenched interests of banks themselves. At a meeting in Amsterdam in October 1986, however, banking supervisors resolved to work toward the same minimum capital standards for all banks that do business across national borders, as a matter both of competitive fairness and of prudential soundness. Such a minimum would most probably also represent the maximum capital standards that countries will impose if their banks are not to suffer in international competition. Supervisors also agreed to work toward a uniform definition of capital, which in many cases included not only equity but also various forms of long-term debt, as well as greater commonality in loan-loss provisioning. Although the new standards, discussed below, have accomplished these tasks, it is nonetheless clear that the job is not finished. Regulatory coordination is likely to proceed in an attempt to reach an agreement on sanctions (including exclusion from specific businesses and markets) for institutions that violate or circumvent banking rules, questions of prudential requirements governing market risk, and the problem of one set of standards being applied to the banking sector and another, looser set of rules for the nonbanking financial services sector.

The BIS Capital Adequacy Rules

In January 1987, following three months of discussion, the Bank of England and the U.S. federal banking regulatory authorities (the Federal Reserve, the Federal Deposit Insurance Corporation, and the Comptroller of the Currency) announced that they had reached agreement on proposals for a common measure of capital adequacy for banks. The proposals were for a risk-related approach similar in many respects to that already in use in the United Kingdom and that proposed in papers released by the U.S. regulatory authorities in January 1986. The proposals also drew on work of the Banking Regulations and Supervisory Practices committee of the Bank for International Settlements (BIS) in Basel.

The Basel Committee's approach was to seek a convergence of the various regulatory methods to form a package that could be used by banking regulators from all of the Group of Ten (industrialized) countries plus Switzerland and Luxembourg. The issues involved were controversial, and the goal of the Committee was ambitious. The 1987 U.S.–U.K. proposals were circulated for comment, then adopted by the Basel Committee as a whole in July 1988 and subsequently ratified by each country. The Federal Reserve announced its final version of the guidelines in January 1989. In its announcement of the new guidelines, the Fed noted that they had been designed to achieve certain important goals:

• Establishment of a uniform capital framework, applicable to all federally supervised banking organizations
• Encouragement of international banking organizations to strengthen their capital positions
• Reduction of a source of competitive inequality arising from differences in supervisory requirements among nations

The guidelines were intended to establish a systematic analytical framework that makes regulatory capital requirements more sensitive to differences in risk profiles among banking organizations, takes "off-balance-sheet" exposures into explicit account in assessing capital adequacy, and minimizes disincentives to holding liquid, low-risk assets.

Off-balance-sheet items represent contingent assets (or liabilities) that the accounting profession does not require to be entered on the face of a bank's financial statements because of the uncertain nature of the contingencies that determine whether these items become due and payable (i.e., move onto the balance sheet). Most accountants do require that, as contingent items, they be disclosed in footnotes to the financial statements, but they escape being included in regulatory ratios. Off-balance-sheet transactions are listed in Table 6-3.

Since many financial products, such as note issuance facilities, swaps, and financial futures transactions involve contingent obligations, they are not included on balance sheets. The rapid growth in off-balance-sheet items, however, has been a cause of concern to regulators, which has led to an effort to "capitalize" off-balance-sheet items so as to include them in the overall grasp of bank supervisory regulations.

In principle the BIS approach is a simple one, although the actual structure is fairly complex. The basic idea is to assign each asset owned by a bank (or accounted for on an off-balance-sheet basis) to one of four "risk categories." Each risk category is assigned a "risk weight," which is

Table 6-3 Summary of Off-Balance-Sheet Activities

Contingent Claims	Financial Services
Loan commitments	Loan-related services
Overdraft facilities	Loan origination
Credit lines	Loan servicing
Backup lines for commercial paper	Loan pass-throughs
Standby lines of credit	Asset sales without recourse
Revolving lines of credit	Sales of loan participants
Reciprocal deposit agreements	Agent for syndicated loan
Repurchase agreements	Trust and advisory services
Note issuance facilities	Portfolio management
Guarantees	Investment advisory services
Acceptances	Arranging mergers and acquisitions
Asset sales with recourse	Tax and financial planning
Standby letters of credit	Trust and financial managements
Documentary or commercial letters of	Management of pension plans
credit	Trusteeships for unit trust, pension
Warranties and indemnities	plans, and debentures
Endorsements	Safekeeping of securities
Financial support to affiliates or subsidi-	Offshore financial services
aries	Brokerage/agency services
Swap and hedging transactions	Share and bond brokerage
Forward foreign exchange contracts	Mutual fund (unit trust) brokerage
Currency swaps	General insurance brokering
Current futures	Life insurance brokering
Currency options	Real estate agency
Cross-currency swaps	Travel agency
Interest-rate swaps	Payments services
Cross-currency interest-rate swaps	Data processing
Interest-rate options	Network arrangements
Interest-rate caps, floors, and collars	Clearing house services
Investments banking activities	Credit/debit cards
Securities underwriting	Point-of-sale systems
Securities dealership/distribution	Home banking
Gold and commodities trading	Cash management systems
Market-making in securities	Export/import services
	Correspondent banking services
	Trade advice
	Export insurance services
	Countertrade exchanges

used to multiply the amounts in each risk category to determine the amount of "capital" required by the bank. Table 6-4 shows risk categories and risk weightings and examples of the types of assets in each category.

Capital is divided into tier 1 or "core" capital (consisting of retained earnings, common stock, and qualifying perpetual preferred stock and minority interests in equity accounts of consolidated subsidiaries, minus

Table 6-4 Summary of Risk Weights and Risk Categories for State Member Banks

Category 1: Zero percent
1. Cash (domestic and foreign) held in the bank or in transit
2. Balances due from Federal Reserve Banks (including Federal Reserve Bank stock) and central banks in other Organization for Economic Cooperation and Development (OECD) countries
3. Direct claims on, and the portions of claims that are unconditionally guaranteed by, the U.S. Treasury and U.S. government agencies[a] and the central governments of other OECD countries, and local currency claims on, and the portions of local currency claims that are unconditionally guaranteed by, the central governments of non-OECD countries (including the central banks of non-OECD countries), to the extent that the bank has liabilities booked in that currency
4. Gold bullion held in the bank's vaults or in another's vaults on an allocated basis, to the extent offset by gold bullion liabilities

Category 2: 20 percent
1. Cash items in the process of collection
2. All claims (long- or short-term) on, and the portions of claims (long- or short-term) that are guaranteed by, U.S. depository institutions and OECD banks
3. Short-term claims (remaining maturity of one year or less) on, and the portions of short-term claims that are guaranteed by, non-OECD banks
4. The portions of claims that are conditionally guaranteed by the central government of OECD countries and U.S. government agencies, and the portions of local currency claims that are conditionally guaranteed by the central governments of non-OECD countries, to the extent that the bank has liabilities booked in that currency
5. Claims on, and the portions of claims that are guaranteed by, U.S. government-sponsored agencies[b]
6. General obligation claims on, and the portions of claims that are guaranteed by the full faith and credit of, local governments and political subdivisions of the U.S. and other OECD local governments
7. Claims on, and the portions of claims that are guaranteed by, official multilateral lending institutions or regional development banks
8. The portions of claims that are collateralized[c] by securities issued or guaranteed by the U.S. Treasury, the central governments of other OECD countries, U.S. government agencies, U.S. government-sponsored agencies, or by cash on deposit in the bank
9. The portions of claims that are collateralized by securities issued by official multilateral lending institutions or regional development banks
10. Certain privately issued securities representing indirect ownership of mortgage-backed U.S. government agency or U.S. government-sponsored agency securities
11. Investments in shares of a fund whose portfolio is permitted to hold only securities that would qualify for the zero or 20-percent risk categories

Category 3: 50 percent
1. Loans fully secured by first liens on 1–4 family residential properties that have been made in accordance with prudent underwriting standards, are performing in accordance with their original terms, and are not past due or in nonaccrual status, and certain privately issued mortgage-backed securities representing indirect ownership of such loans (loans made for speculative purposes are excluded)
2. Revenue bonds or similar claims that are obligations of U.S. state or local governments, or other OECD local governments, but for which the government entity is committed to repay the debt only out of revenues from the facilities financed
3. Credit equivalent amounts of interest-rate and foreign-exchange-rate related contracts, except for those assigned to a lower risk category

(continued)

Table 6-4 (continued)

Category 4: 100 Percent

1. All other claims on private obligors
2. Claims on, or guaranteed by, non-OECD foreign banks with a remaining maturity exceeding one year
3. Claims on, or guaranteed by, non-OECD central governments that are not included in item 3 of Category 1 or item 4 of Category 2; all claims on non-OECD state or local governments
4. Obligations issued by U.S. state or local governments, or by other OECD local governments (including industrial development authorities and similar entities), repayable solely by a private party or enterprise
5. Premises, plant, and equipment; other fixed assets; and other real estate owned
6. Investments in any unconsolidated subsidiaries, joint ventures, or associated companies—if not deducted from capital
7. Instruments issued by other banking organizations that qualify as capital—if not deducted from capital
8. Claims on commercial firms owned by a government
9. All other assets, including any intangible asets that are not deducted from capital

---

Source: Federal Reserve Board.

[a] For the purpose of calculating the risk-based capital ratio, a U.S. government agency is defined as an instrumentality of the U.S. government whose obligations are fully and explicitly guaranteed as to the timely payment of principal and interest by the full faith and credit of the U.S. government.

[b] For the purpose of calculating the risk-based capital ratio, a U.S. government-sponsored agency is defined as an agency originally established or chartered to serve public purposes specified by the U.S. Congress but whose obligations are not explicitly guaranteed by the full faith and credit of the U.S. government.

[c] The extent of collateralization is determined by current market value.

"goodwill") and tier 2 capital (various forms of "supplementary" capital). Table 6-5 presents a summary of definitions of qualifying capital for Federal Reserve-supervised banks.

Before these proposals were adopted, the principal means of assessing capital adequacy for U.S. banks had been to divide "total capital" (which included retained earnings, common and preferred stock, and certain forms of subordinated debt) by "total assets." The Federal Reserve and other banking supervisory bodies set different ratio requirements for different types of banks. At the beginning of 1989, when the final guidelines were announced, U.S. money-center banks were required to maintain a 6-percent capital/total assets ratio, although many banks were not in compliance at the time. By the early 1990s virtually all U.S. banks had been brought into compliance.

The face amount of an *off-balance-sheet* item (such as a letter of credit, a swap, or a foreign exchange obligation) is taken into the risk-based capital ratio by multiplying it by a "credit conversion factor." The resultant "credit equivalent amount" is assigned to the appropriate risk category (according to the identity of the obligor or guarantor). Among those items converting to credit risks at 100 percent of face value are all direct credit substitutes, risk participations in bankers acceptances or di-

Table 6-5 Summary Definition of Qualifying Capital for State Member Banks Using the Year-end 1992 Standards

Components	Minimum Requirements After Transition Period
Core capital (tier 1)	Must equal or exceed 4% of weighted risk assets
Common stockholders' equity	No limit
Qualifying noncumulative perpetual preferred stock	No limit; banks should avoid undue reliance on preferred stock in tier 1
Minority interest in equity accounts of consolidated subsidiaries	Banks should avoid using minority interests to introduce elements not otherwise qualifying for tier 1 capital
Less: Goodwill[a]	
Supplementary capital (tier 2)	Total of tier 2 is limited to 100% of tier 1[b]
Allowance for loan and lease losses	Limited to 1.25% of weighted risk assets[b]
Perpetual preferred stock	
Hybrid capital instruments and equity contract notes	No limit with tier 2
	No limit with tier 2
Subordinated debt and intermediate-term preferred stock (original weighted average maturity of 5 years or more)	Subordinated debt and intermediate-term preferred stocks are limited to 50% of Tier 1,[a,b] amortized for capital purposes as they approach maturity
Revaluation reserves (equity and building)	Not included; banks encouraged to disclose; may be evaluated on a case-by-case basis for international comparisons; taken into account in making an overall assessment of capital
Deductions (from sum of tier 1 and tier 2)	
Investments in unconsolidated subsidiaries	
Reciprocal holdings of banking organizations capital securities	
Other deductions (such as other subsidiaries or joint ventures) as determined by supervisory authority	On a case-by-case basis or as a matter of policy after formal rule-making
Total Capital (tier 1 + tier 2 deductions)	Must equal or exceed 8% of weighted risk assets

Source: Federal Reserve Board.

[a] All goodwill, except previously grandfathered goodwill approved in supervisory mergers, is deducted immediately.

[b] Amounts in excess of limitations are permitted but do not qualify as capital.

rect credits substitutes (such as letters of credit), sale and repurchase agreements, and certain forward agreements.

Those items entitled to 50-percent conversion factors include transaction-related contingencies, revolving credit agreements, and note issuance facilities and similar arrangements. Items converted at 20 percent include short-term self-liquidating trade-related contingencies. Items converted at zero percent include unused portions of commitments with an original maturity of one year or less, or which are unconditionally cancelable at any time.

Table 6-6 shows credit conversion factors for various types of off-balance-sheet items. The guidelines include among off-balance-sheet items all interest-rate and foreign exchange contracts, for which credit equivalent amounts are calculated in the case of each individual contract.

The BIS rules included a schedule for implementing the new system, with a ratio of 8 percent (of which at least 4 percent must be in the form of tier 1 capital) in effect beginning on January 1, 1993. They now provide a common standard for safe and prudent banking capitalization, Once countries have agreed on the same minimum base, there is no advantage in being undercapitalized or for countries to unduly subsidize banking institutions, for example, by setting interest-rate controls to allow banks to accumulate excess profits as a cushion against future losses, at the expense of economic growth and efficiency. Riskier instruments have become more costly to hold, lessening the chances of excessive exposure and the prospect that regulators will have to step in to provide support in a crisis. There is less incentive to underprice off-balance-sheet commitments. Given

Table 6-6 Credit Conversion Factors of Off-Balance-Sheet Items for State Member Banks

100-Percent Conversion Factor
1. Direct credit substitutes (include general guarantees of indebtedness and all guarantee-type instruments, including standby letters of credit backing financing obligations of other parties)
2. Risk participations in bankers acceptances and direct credit substitutes, such as standby letters of credit
3. Sale and repurchase agreements and assets sold with recourse that are not included on balance sheet
4. Forward agreements to purchase assets, including financing facilities, on which drawdown is *certain*
5. Securities lent for which bank is at risk

50-Percent Conversion Factor
1. Transaction-related contingencies (include bid bonds, performance bonds, warranties, and standby letters of credit backing nonfinancial performance of other parties)
2. Unused portions of commitments with original maturity[a]
3. Revolving underwriting facilities (RUFs), note issuance facilities (NIFs), and similar arrangements

20-Percent Conversion Factor
1. Short-term, self-liquidating trade-related contingencies, including commercial letters of credit

Zero-Percent Conversion Factor
1. Unused portions of commitments with original maturity[a] of one year or less, or which are unconditionally cancelable at any time, provided a separate credit decision is made before each drawing

Source: Federal Reserve Board.
[a] Remaining maturity may be used until year-end 1992.

the rate of financial innovation and the deluge of new instruments, it was necessary that the guidelines provide regulators with a coherent framework into which to slot new types of exposures as they evolve, instead of always lagging events by as much as several years. Each new type of instrument is assigned to the highest risk category until such time as the regulators rule otherwise.

The BIS risk-based capital approach increased pressure on banks to charge higher spreads or fees for financial transactions in which they participate, in order to recover the incremental cost of the additional capital needed to support specific loans and advances, or simply to recover the higher overall cost of capital. This condition was seen by many banks to place them at a substantial disadvantage relative to securities firms, with which they are increasingly in direct competition. Securities firms, not being regulated by banking authorities who must look after the deposits they are guaranteeing, are not subject to the new rules or to any similar constraints. Coordination with authorities regulating the securities industry is essential if competitive rules under which firms in the two sectors (banking and securities) of the industry operate are not to serve as further distortions to competitive conditions in the case of financial services that are performed by both banks and nonbanks.

Nor are the provisions of the BIS accord uniform between banks of different countries. For example, wide international differences exist in the availability of information on bank performance, which may influence their relative competitive positioning and certainly affects the ability to determine whether the international competitive playing field is in fact relatively level. Transparency in U.S. accounting for banks is assured by the regulatory structure, and any disclosure problems are relatively quickly remedied—including cross-border exposures and off-balance-sheet exposures in such transactions as swaps. In other countries disclosure is far less extensive, and in some cases relatively meaningless. Disclosure of off-balance-sheet exposures in many cases is absent altogether, and many home countries of multinational banks fail to disclose their worldwide operations on a consolidated basis. Another issue is whether banks may emerge among the nonparticipating countries that would challenge banks from the participating countries for business and possess a competitive edge over the participating banks through less rigorous regulatory standards. Conceivably, banks could migrate to unregulated areas for the purpose of competing with the banks from the major countries. However, since only a small percentage of the world's international banking assets are booked outside the participating BIS countries, the impact of such a migration would not appear to be large.

Finally, it has been argued that coordinated risk-based capital requirements can actually be counterproductive, since assets categorized in the same risk class may have vastly different risk profiles. Moreover, since different assets and off-balance-sheet exposures require different levels of capital, the result may well be distortions in banking decisions—for example, loading up on highly interest-rate-sensitive U.S. government securities that require less capital backing than perhaps less volatile asset deployments—decisions that ultimately may lead to increased, rather than decreased, vulnerability of individual institutions. It could also reduce financial innovation and, as noted, place banks at a competitive disadvantage against nonfinancial institutions operating in the securities markets that are not subject to similar requirements.

In general, by the mid-1990s banks in most of the advanced countries had attained the BIS guidelines with greater or lesser difficulty. Banks in each country faced more or less unique difficulties associated with, for example, loan losses related to real estate and country lending in the United States and various European countries, stock-market collapse and the end of the "bubble" economy in Japan, the simultaneous creation of a single market in financial services under universal banking conditions in the European Union. Table 6-7 indicates the degree of compliance of major banks in various countries with the BIS capital adequacy standards in mid-1994.

The Problem of Derivatives Exposure and Position Risk

The rapid growth in bank holdings of interest-sensitive instruments such as government bonds at a time of declining rates—in part encouraged by zero weighting of government securities under the BIS rules—in addition

Table 6-7 Capital Adequacy of Top Banks in Selected Countries, 1994

Bank	Total Assets (billion)	Total Equity (billion)	Total Equity/ Assets	Risk-Weighted Capital Ratios (1993 Basis)	
				Tier 1	Total
Argentina (APs)					
Banco de Galicia y Buenos Aires	5412.5	463.0	3.6%	NA	NA
Banco Frances y Rio de la Plata	2516.4	426.2	16.9	NA	NA
Australia (A$)					
ANZ Banking Group	100.0	5.1	5.1%	5.9%	10.8%
Commonwealth Bank	87.4	5.5	6.3	6.3	9.9
National Australia	117.3	8.5	7.8	7.7	11.4
Westpac Banking	104.7	7.1	6.8	7.4	12.3
Britain (£)					
Abbey National	79.9	3.4	4.2%	9.4%	10.5%
Barclays Bank	163.1	6.0	3.7	6.0	9.8
Lloyds Bank	71.6	3.6	5.0	6.6	10.6
National Westminster	152.3	5.9	3.9	5.7	10.8
HSBC Holdings	206.0	9.3	4.5	7.9	13.2
Canada (C$)					
Bank of Montreal	116.9	5.7	4.7%	7.4%	10.3%
Canadian Imperial	141.3	7.9	5.6	6.9	9.7

(continued)

Table 6-7 (continued)

Bank	Total Assets (billion)	Total Equity (billion)	Total Equity/ Assets	Risk-Weighted Capital Ratios (1993 Basis) Tier 1	Total
National Bank	42.7	2.0	4.8	6.2	9.0
Royal Bank	164.9	7.9	4.8	5.9	9.3
Scotiabank	107.6	5.9	5.5	6.5	10.4
Toronto Dominion	85.0	5.0	5.9	7.0	10.2
Chile (ChPs)					
Banco O'Higgins	1,032	87.5	8.5%	NA	NA
France (Ffr)					
BNP	1,486.1	62.9	3.3%	5.6%	9.6%
Paribas	1,356.0	59.5	2.8	7.6	9.0
Crédit Lyonnais	1,993.0	40.5	3.0	5.0	8.2
Société Generale	1,534.0	47.8	3.1	5.0	9.1
Germany (DM)					
Commerzbank	285.0	11.2	3.9%	5.1%	8.9%
Deutsche Bank	556.6	22.9	4.1	5.7	11.3
Dresden Bank	380.3	13.3	3.5	5.6	9.1
Japan (¥)					
Dai-Ichi Kangyo Bank	59,368	2,054	3.5%	4.9%	9.4%
Bank of Tokyo	29,108	1,027	3.5	5.0	9.8
Sakura Bank	59,990	1,784	3.0	4.4	8.9
Mitsubishi Bank	53,316	1,755	3.3	4.6	9.1
Fuji Bank	55,805	1,950	3.5	4.9	9.3
Sumitomo Bank	56,889	2,285	4.0	6.3	9.4
Sanwa Bank	54,839	1,922	3.5	4.9	9.4
Mexico (PS)					
Banacci	133.6	9.4	7.8%	7.5%	11.6%
Grupo Financiero Bancomer	114.5	3.0	6.9	5.3	9.5
Panama (US$)					
Bladex	3.07	0.2	7.8%	29.3%	32.6%
Spain (Pts)					
Argentaria	10860	512	4.7%	11.7%	12.9%
Banco Bilboa Vizcaya	11635	608	5.2	11.9	12.5
Banco Popular	2806	242	8.6	14.0	14.0
Banco Santander	10442	353	3.4	9.5	12.5
Banco Central Hisp.	10386	590	5.7	7.4	9.0
Switzerland (Sfr)					
CS Holding	346.5	15.8	5.6%	7.1%	10.3%
Swiss Bank Corp.	207.0	13.1	6.2	8.7	11.2
UBS	311.3	20.9	6.7	8.3	10.2
Safra Republic (US$)	11.3	1.3	11.3	NA	NA
U.S.A. (US$)					
Bankers Trust NY Corp.	92.1	4.5	4.9%	8.3%	14.1%
Citicorp	216.6	13.9	6.4	6.5	11.2
J.P. Morgan & Co.	133.9	9.9	7.4	8.3	13.0

Source: Salomon Brothers, August 24, 1994.

to the enormous growth in over-the-counter and exchange-traded derivative instruments such as swaps, futures, options, and various types of structured financial instruments, raised the issue of *position risk*. This is the risk that financial instruments of contingent obligations held by banks on or off the balance sheet could change dramatically in value as a result of changes in interest rates, for example, raising the danger of substantial losses once the positions are unwound or replaced. Historical values may not be a good guide to actual values, especially in times of volatile interest rates and exchange rates. This is an effect that the BIS capital adequacy rules do not capture, since they deal only with the problem of credit or counterparty risk.

This problem was addressed by the Basel Committee on Banking Supervision in a report issued in mid-1994, specifically addressed to market risk associated with derivatives exposures. The report noted that BIS capital adequacy rules were addressed to traditional credit exposures on and off the balance sheet, but ran the risk of requiring too little capital for new types of derivatives, especially equity and commodity derivatives. The proposals suggested that significant additional capital should be maintained against such derivatives, as well as longer-term derivative positions that can cause major losses under volatile market conditions.

The proposals would take effect in mid-1995, and would be partially offset by modifications in the 1988 BIS capital adequacy standards by permitting "netting" of off-balance-sheet transactions with a given derivatives counterparty. Netting would allow banks to base their risk-adjusted capital requirements with that counterparty on the difference between the value of buy and sell contracts, that is, the "net" exposure. This would reduce the capital requirements associated with a "typical" portfolio of interest-rate and currency swaps by 25 to 40 percent, but only in the case of banks based in countries whose bankruptcy laws recognize netting.

Additionally, it was proposed in 1994 by the Institute of International Finance—a grouping of banks that account for the bulk of over-the-counter derivatives activity—that new standards of disclosure be applied to derivatives, including (1) the total replacement value of contracts, segregated by counterparties with different credit ratings; (2) the value of contracts in each category of derivatives, such as currency swaps and interest-rate options, as well as a breakdown of maturity profiles; and (3) an analysis of each institution's method of accounting, risk management, netting of contracts, and methods of trading, as well as management controls.

As Table 6-8 suggests, capital adequacy rules represent but one of the techniques used by regulators in an attempt to ensure safety and soundness. Other regulatory options include fitness and properness standards applied to the ownership and management of banks, involving who may own a bank and who may work in banking. This issue became particularly important with the unfolding BCCI scandal in the early 1990s and involved fitness and properness criteria for establishment within national jurisdictions, continuation of permission to operate, forced closure and with-

Table 6-8 Regulation Options

Risk-based capital standards
Fitness and properness standards
Criteria
Certification, continuation, closure
Jurisdiction: home vs. host
Credit-related regulation
Position risk regulation
Liquidity risk regulation
Market-to-market accounting
Line-of-business regulation
Banking vs. securities
Banking vs. insurance
Banking vs. industry

drawal of a banking license, and the question of jurisdiction: BCCI was chartered in Luxembourg, a jurisdiction with lax fitness and properness criteria and limited ability or willingness to supervise the bank's activities outside the country, where virtually all of the damage occurred. Subsequent to the BCCI case a number of jurisdictions, including the United States at the federal and state levels, made efforts to tighten the oversight of foreign-based financial institutions.

In terms of Table 6-8 there are also standard credit-related regulations involving lending limits, for example regulation of position risks such as asset-liability mismatches, regulation of liquidity such as reserve requirements, and finally, mark-to-market accounting under which certain assets would be carried on the books at their replacement values as opposed to their historical cost. The latter option remains highly controversial in banking, although, as noted, it has found its way into a number of the BIS initiatives.

In addition to the basic regulatory framework of banking, there is also line-of-business regulation, which deals with what types of businesses banks may engage in, and how they may engage in them. Table 6-9 lists the basic issues. Should banks be allowed to underwrite and distribute securities? If so, should this be done in the bank itself or though a separately capitalized subsidiary? Should banks be allowed to underwrite life insurance or property and casualty insurance, either directly or through insurance subsidiaries? Should banks be allowed to own industrial companies, and vice versa? If so, how? Each of these questions requires answers that are complex and often themselves give rise to new questions. There is, for example, the problem of regulatory conflict between banking and insurance regulators and between banking and securities regulators, which may require the use of separate subsidiaries and regulation by function. Clearly, different countries have approached these problems in very different ways, ranging for example from relatively strict separation of functions in the United States to universal banking in most of Western Europe.[1] We

Table 6-9 Line-of-Business Regulation

Banking vs. securities
Banking vs. insurance
Banking vs. industry
    Should banks control industrial firms?
        Asymmetric information
        Monitoring function
        Chinese walls and firewalls
        Concentration of power
    Should industrial firms control banks?
        A socialized safety net for industry?
        Alternative structural forms
            Integrated structures
            Holding company structures
    The role of firewalls
Geographic constraints
Product and client-based constraints

shall return to these issues in chapter 14. In addition, many countries impose geographic restrictions on where banks may operate, client-based restrictions on whom they may deal with, and product-based restrictions on the kinds of financial services they may provide. These are often protectionist in nature, and frequently impact disproportionately foreign-based financial institutions.

Regulatory Determinants of Financial Structures

Global financial flows are affected dramatically by regulatory factors such as those discussed here. We have noted that financial services comprise an industry that has usually been, and will inevitably continue to be, subject to significant public-authority regulation due to its fiduciary nature and the possibility of social costs associated with institutional failure. Indeed, small changes in financial regulation can bring about truly massive changes in financial activity.

When analyzing the effects of regulation on the level of activity in a given country's financial system, it is useful to think of regulation as imposing a set of "taxes" and "subsidies" on the operations of financial firms. On the one hand, the imposition of reserve requirements, capital adequacy rules, and certain forms of financial disclosure requirements, for example, can be viewed as imposing additional implicit "taxes" on a financial firm's activities in the sense that these regulations increase the bank's costs of financial intermediation. On the other hand, regulator-supplied deposit insurance and lender-of-last-resort facilities serve to stabilize financial markets and reduce the risk of systemic failure, thereby lowering the costs of financial intermediation. They can therefore be viewed as implicit "subsidies."

The difference between these "tax" and "subsidy" elements of regulation can be viewed as the *net regulatory burden* (NRB) faced by a bank or other financial firm in any given regulatory jurisdiction. Private, profit-maximizing financial firms tend to migrate toward those jurisdictions where the NRB is lowest, assuming all other economic factors are the same. Thus at any point in time, NRB differences will induce firms to relocate as long as NRB savings exceed the transaction, communication, information, and other economic costs of relocating. Since one can argue that, in today's global financial marketplace, transaction and other economic costs of relocating are likely to be small, one can expect financial market participants to be extremely sensitive to changes in current and perceived NRBs among competing regulatory domains. To some extent, the regulators responsible for particular jurisdictions (nations, states, cities) appear to recognize this sensitivity and in their competition for employment, creation of value-added taxes, and other revenues, have engaged in a form of competition over their levels of NRB.

In an individual, closed economy with a single regulatory body, competition will spark a dynamic interplay between demanders and suppliers of financial services, much as in any market situation. Users of financial services will vote with their feet, seeking similar or superior services if justified by cost and risk considerations. Private firms will seek to reduce their NRB and increase their profitability. If they can do so at low cost, financial firms will actively seek product innovations and new venues that (legally) avoid cumbersome regulations. However, the familiar story of competitive equilibrium must be extended in two directions: to the case of multiple and sometimes overlapping domestic regulatory bodies, and to the case of many countries, with many suppliers of financial services and many regulatory bodies.

A single economy may have multiple regulatory bodies, complemented by a host of other regulatory groups at the state and local levels in countries organized politically along federal lines. In the case of the United States, at the federal level financial activities could fall under the domain of the Federal Reserve Board, the Comptroller of the Currency, the Securities and Exchange Commission, and the Commodity Futures Trading Commission, to name only the major regulatory agencies. Each of the 50 states has its own regulatory bodies to deal with banking and insurance. Every city and municipality has an agency responsible for local income taxes, real estate taxes, transfer taxes, stamp duties, and so on, all of which affect the NRB falling on financial institutions. In practice, the situation is complicated still further by ambiguity regarding the definition of a "bank," a "security," an "exchange," and so forth—which may blur the categorization of a financial service, as well as raise questions about which regulatory agency holds jurisdiction.

It has been argued that regulation itself may be thought of in a market context. Via a political process, regulatory bodies may be established along geographic, product, or functional lines.[2] These regulators then compete with one another to extend the reach of their regulatory domains. Domestic financial firms understand this competition, which widens their scope for reducing the NRB and for enhancing their market share or profitability. In this setting, domestic regulators are likely to respond to private initiatives with reregulation in an effort to recover part of their lost regulatory domain.

In an open, international economy with many governments and many regulatory authorities, we find a still more fertile ground for firms to reduce their NRB. National regulatory authorities may compete among themselves on the basis of NRB to preserve or reclaim their regulatory domain. Again, private firms benefit from such international competition, especially if financial innovation and technological change allows them to operate successfully at a distance from their home bases. Users of financial services also benefit to the extent that competition forces financial firms to pass through to them the lower NRB. An important question (discussed later in this chapter) is whether society as a whole gains or loses as a result of the lower NRB brought about by regulatory competition.

Competition among Regulators and Contestable Markets

Compliance with regulations in onshore financial markets creates opportunities to develop a parallel, offshore market for the delivery of similar services. Barriers must exist to keep a large proportion of financial activity from migrating offshore. In this case, political risk and minimum transaction size temper the flow of deposits and investments offshore, while size and credit quality perform a similar role for borrowers. In addition to the narrow provision of bank deposits and loans, offshore markets can be used to replicate a variety of nonbank and financial instruments, many of which may also be regulated by onshore financial authorities. Consequently, offshore markets raise a general competitive threat to onshore financial services activities.

The rise of offshore markets underscores the fact that market participants face a range of alternatives for executing transactions in any of several financial centers. Consequently, if domestic regulators desire to have the transactions conducted within their respective financial centers—driven by their regulators' desire to maintain an adequate level of prudential regulation, to sustain their revenues from the taxation of financial services, to support employment and output in the financial services industry and linked economic sectors, or simply to maximize their regulatory domain—the regulatory requirements cannot be set arbitrarily.

Indeed, it can be argued that domestic financial regulations are determined competitively after taking account of regulations (both present and prospective) in other financial centers. Thus, the movement to liberalize regulations affecting financial institutions is not the result of a sudden out-pouring of laissez-faire behavior but rather of an endogenous process as national regulators vye for market share. The market for financial regula-tion is contestable in the sense that other national regulatory bodies offer (or threaten to offer) rules that may be more favorable than those of the domestic regulator. This actual or threatened competition may serve to constrain the actions of financial regulators and tax authorities.

This view results in what has been referred to as a "regulatory dialec-tic"—a dynamic interaction between the regulator and the regulated, where there is continuous action and reaction by all parties. The players in this setting may behave aggressively or defensively. To the extent that they behave adaptively, even if underlying factors (such as communications technology and the level of financial transactions, for example) remain constant, considerable time is likely to be required for an equilibrium regu-latory structure to emerge.

In a changing environment, players will adapt with varying speed and degrees of freedom:

- Less regulated players move faster and more freely than more tightly regulated ones.
- Private players move faster and more freely than governmental ones.
- Regulated players move faster and more freely than regulators.
- International regulatory bodies move more slowly and less freely than all other players.

Given this ordering of adaptive efficiencies, we expect that the lag between a regulation and its avoidance is on average shorter than the lag between the avoidance and reregulation. The lag in reregulation may be shorter for industry-based, self-regulatory groups than for governments. It may be longest when international regulatory efforts are involved.

Net Regulatory Burden and Structural Arbitrage

Financial firms thus constantly monitor their NRB, and may transfer activ-ities into another regulatory regime when NRB can be reduced. In a per-fect international capital market with no entry or exit costs, no transaction costs, no barriers between countries, and no sovereign risk, we would pre-dict that all banking and securities activities will migrate to the country with the lowest NRB, inclusive of taxes. In the real world, a variety of imperfections exist that permit some dispersion of NRB across countries. For example, when transactions costs and information costs are positive, firms will need to be located in those countries where they intend to sell financial services. Nevertheless, this dispersion among NRBs cannot be too great, otherwise private firms will have an incentive to relocate their activi-ties. Entry and exit costs, currency conversion costs, and distance-related delivery costs, plus uncertainties surrounding these costs and other control measures, act as effective barriers to complete NRB equalization across countries. Technological change that has markedly lowered communications and information-processing costs, combined with the rapid growth of international financial transactions, has cut the gap in NRB needed to induce regulatory arbitrage.

In a similar fashion, regulators have also become more willing to compete on the basis of NRB. The regulator must ensure that its regulatory revenues (when combined with supplementary budgetary support that comes willingly from informed taxpayers) are sufficient to produce a given set of regulatory services. If this condition is not met, the regulatory burden is not sustainable and reregulation will force it back into line. However, if the regulator is generating more than enough revenues to cover costs, it needs to be concerned that private firms will migrate to lower NRB regions unless the associated transactions costs and information costs exceed the tax savings and/or regulatory savings. In this case, the regulator could either lower the NRB or impose taxes and controls to stop the migration of financial activity. Since taxes and controls are easily avoided, the policymaker is likely to alter the NRB. The question is therefore: What is the long-run, equilibrium, sustainable value of the net regulatory burden?

A somewhat separate but related question involves social welfare and whether a reduction in the NRB that shifts the fiscal burden from financial market participants to other segments of society serves general welfare goals. As any factor of production or economic activity gains mobility, it becomes increasingly difficult to subject it to tax. Of necessity, the fiscal burdens will be redistributed onto less mobile factors or activities. Regulations impose costs that, in part, will be transferred to clients. Costly regulations create incentives for financial firms to innovate in order to reduce their costs and capture a larger market share. Money-market mutual funds and off-balance-sheet financing techniques are two well-known domestic examples that exist in a number of countries, as discussed in chapter 7. The greater the regulatory costs, the greater is the incentive to innovate or to avoid the domestic financial system. In the United States, for example, the 1,200-mile shift of Citibank's credit card operations from New York to South Dakota (in part, to escape New York's usury ceilings) illustrates this kind of mobility among federal states.

In the international setting, the scope for governments to collect excessive regulatory taxes is reduced because there is greater competition among national regulatory environments. Each domestic financial center faces competition from foreign and offshore financial centers. As transactions costs and information costs decline, the cost of using an offshore financial center declines as well. The development of offshore currency and bond markets in the 1960s represents a case in which borrowers and lenders found that they could carry out the requisite market transactions more efficiently and with sufficient safety by operating offshore—in a parallel market.

In the past, policymakers have often set financial regulations as if no international feedback effects would occur. The obvious point is that in today's world, communication costs are low and capital mobility is high, so that it has become less feasible for a state or a nation to impose an NRB that stands too far apart from world norms. In the 1970s and 1980s, U.S. and European financial institutions have moved a large part of their operations offshore, suggesting that they judged the cost of domestic financial regulations to be excessive. If we assume that transactions costs, information costs, and communication costs continue to decline, it follows that the NRB tolerated by financial institutions must approach zero, that is, that a financial institution will migrate rather than pay any positive regulatory tax.

However, it is likely that a long-run equilibrium can be maintained with a *positive* NRB. Financial transactions involve uncertainty—about the monetary unit of account, about the creditworthiness of the financial institutions and other counterparties, and about the political stability of the financial center. Financial institutions ought to value their access to lender-of-last-resort facilities, deposit/liability insurance, the opportunity to be headquartered in a stable political climate, and the like. Indeed, we observe that those markets that are almost fully unregulated, with a NRB approaching zero, have not in fact completely dominated financial transactions subject to location shifting, such as the Eurocurrency markets. If financial institutions find it in their interest to pay some level of regulatory tax, the economic question then concerns the sustainable magnitude of this tax.

NRB and the Specialness of Financial Institutions

It has been argued extensively that financial services firms are "special," either in view of their fiduciary responsibilities to clients or in terms of the macroeconomic role performed by banks at the core of the national and international payments and credit system. As noted earlier, firm or systemwide failure can impose costs on those insufficiently informed to make rational financial choices or on society at large as the credit and monetary base contracts. Alternatively (or in addition) the degree of control that financial firms exercise over other parts of the economy may be deemed excessive in a political context.

"Specialness" can be considered in both a narrow and a broad sense. In the former, specialness is considered to encompass only the deposit/credit and monetary policy dimensions, and therefore applies only to "commercial banks" under the U.S. or Japanese institutional definition, but not to other types of financial services firms. However, to the extent that either of these dimensions bear on other types of financial services firms as well, or on sectors such as housing that are viewed as being socially desirable, other financial services firms such as savings institutions can also be considered special. Moreover, all financial services firms vulnerable to crises of confidence or failure-related negative externalities could be considered special and therefore subject to certain assistance and regulatory treatment on the part of government that need not apply to other types of firms such as industrial companies.

We have seen that a variety of constraints ranging from capital adequacy standards to liquidity requirements and periodic compliance reviews are usually set in place to mitigate concerns related to specialness. Each may involve economic costs, and may therefore erode the static or dynamic efficiency properties of all or parts of the financial services industry. Whether the social gains in terms of improved firm and industry stability and fiduciary performance exceed these costs is a complex and difficult matter for debate.

Moreover, since such improvements can only be measured in terms of events that *did not occur* and costs that were successfully *avoided,* the argumentation is invariably based on "what if" hypotheticals. There are no definitive answers with respect to optimum regulatory structures. There are only "better" and "worse" solutions as perceived by the electorate and their representatives. Consequently, collective risk aversion and political reaction to past regulatory failures in the financial services sector can easily produce overregulation. This is also reflected in the reward system of bureaucrats charged with operating the regulatory structure, which causes them to be excessively risk averse and prone to overregulation.

Financial Deregulation: Benefits and Costs

On the basis of efficiency gains and NRB-linked functional and geographic competition, deregulation in financial services has become a fact of life in the United States and in various other countries such as Japan and the EU under the 1992 single-market initiatives. Information and transactions costs have declined. New competitors have entered the financial services field, while others sought exit or combined with viable players as elegantly as possible. New financial products have come on-stream almost daily, their number and variety limited only by the human imagination. Artificial barriers to competition, some of which have been in place for decades, have been subject to steady erosion. Competitors have bid actively for human as well as financial resources, even as product, process, applications, management, and marketing technologies have evolved faster. In short, the environment is one of vigorous competition, based at its core on concepts like institutional competitive advantage, specialization, economies of scale, and economies of scope. If the process is permitted to work itself out, a far stronger and more efficient financial system eventually evolves, where excess profits ultimately disappear, transactions costs are driven to a bare minimum, information becomes much more readily available, the basis for rational decision-making improves, and only the fittest competitors are able to prosper for very long. The process of financial allocation in the national economy will improve materially, and the gap between what the ultimate saver receives and what the ultimate investor has to pay for funds will be narrowed to the finest possible margin. Perhaps even more important, deregulated financial systems will improve availability of resources to new and emerging industries, strip away resources from declining and uncompetitive sectors and firms sooner, quite possibly enhance the underlying incentives to save and to invest, accelerate technological change, bolster the ability to lay off risk and perhaps swallow economic and financial shocks with less social damage, and generally support the process of sustainable economic growth.

If deregulation is to be justified in economic terms, that justification must come in large part through substantive change in competitive performance in the provision of corporate financial services. The Glass–Steagall provisions of the Banking Act of 1933 in the United States (or Article 65 in Japan) notwithstanding, for example, the 1980s saw substantial competition between securities firms and commercial banks for a wide variety of financial services, especially in the international capital market. In areas without artificial barriers to competition, the degree of efficiency and innovativeness that characterizes the various competing financial services firms has been very high indeed, with commensurate benefits accruing directly to the users of the services and more broadly to the economic and financial system as a whole.

Economists generally work under the assumption that any limitation of competitive opportunity favors those who benefit from protection, as well as reduces the efficiency with which financial and human resources are allocated—the so-called *static* "deadweight losses" associated with protected markets. There are also adverse *dynamic* consequences (such as reduced financial innovation) that make themselves felt over time and ultimately are likely to be substantially more important. Evidence on the size and stability of underwriting fees, artificially wide banking spreads, the quality of services provided to small issuers, and the underpricing of new issues in protected markets usually follows the pattern one would expect to see in such situations. The conclusion that more competition is better than less comes as no great surprise either from the standpoint of efficiency or fairness, and seems well justified in terms of the inferential evidence presented on concentration and competitive structure. The evidence does suggest that statutory competition barriers generate costs, and that deregulation generates material benefits to the users of financial services and to the economy at large.

If there are potential benefits associated with the deregulation of financial services, there are also potential costs with respect to both economic efficiency and equity dimensions. Potential costs include lessened stability of the financial system and the exploitation of conflicts of interest on the part of financial institutions engaged in both commercial and investment banking activities, for example. The magnitude of the first of these potential costs depends, in part, on the riskiness of various ventures that might be undertaken by financial institutions. That many financial activities involve risks is clear. If there were no risks, they would produce few gains, both to the direct participants and to society at large. However, risk can be managed through astute evaluation, diversification, and exposure limits, as well as a growing array of hedging vehicles. In the securities business, for example, the major risks involved concern the potential losses associated with securities underwriting and dealing, their bearing on the safety and soundness of individual financial institutions and the system as a whole, and the nature of the risk/return trade-offs in the market for corporate securities. However, with the addition of a new range of financial services activities whose returns are not perfectly correlated with those of traditional banking activities, the ability of commercial banks to engage in corporate securities business may well enhance the earnings stability of the institutions as a whole. This suggests that safety and stability of financial environment depends fundamentally on careful balance and breadth of scope of activities, rather than on traditional notions of narrowly defined activity limitations and controls.

In addition to questions relating to the potential impact of interpenetration between financial institutions on financial stability, there is also the nagging issue of potential conflicts of interest when various types of activity are housed in the same institution—for example, investment banking, commercial banking, and trust banking. Various institutional and legal safeguards exist to limit conflict exploitation, and these safeguards can be made adequate to cope with significant deregulation of activity limits.

A careful examination of the structure of incentives and disincentives that underlies the exploitation of conflicts of interest usually shows that such exploitation is fundamentally inimical to the economic interest of the firm and its shareholders—the value of the enterprise as a going concern. Insulation of commercial banking units from securities affiliates of universal banks, for example, as well as the competitive nature of the markets for financial services and the ready availability of performance information, provide sanctions against deviations from this standard that are both timely and painful. Moreover, institutional factors that influence the behavior of managers, such as the structure of bonus schemes, the use of profit centers, and the market for corporate control, tend to ensure that behavior at variance with basic corporate and client interests is not tolerated for long.

If the evidence on the characteristics of a particular type of financial service shows that the risks are both limited and manageable, if activity diversification enhances the earnings stability of financial institutions, and if economic incentives and legal constraints provide effective insulation and safeguards against conflicts of interest, then the case for permitting financial institutions to engage in a broad range of activities in order to maximize economies of scale and scope would appear to be very strong indeed.

Evidence suggests that efforts to foster financial safety and soundness through activity separation, as Glass–Steagall in the United States and Article 65 in Japan have attempted to do, sacrifice the diversification (and hence stability) gains from interpenetration of commercial and investment banking activities. Any stability benefits attributable to activity separation are thus partially or wholly offset by stability losses due to reduced diversification of earnings streams. The evidence also suggests that financial regulation generates efficiency losses. At the level of the firm, regulation prevents management from optimally deploying the institution's capital and human resources, designing optimal financial and organizational structures, and developing optimal business strategies. At the level of society, regulation fosters misallocation of resources, stifles innovation and international competitiveness, and constrains the contribution of the financial system to economic growth. The objective is to capture for society the efficiency gains from greater competition and market interpenetration between commercial and investment banking *without* at the same time compromising the safety and stability of the nation's financial system.

Financial Supervision

We noted in Figure 6-1 at the beginning of this chapter that three issues need to be addressed in assessing the regulatory framework of financial services, whether in a domestic or international context. We have so far discussed two of these in some detail, performance, that is, financial efficiency, and regulation. The third element is supervision and oversight of financial institutions and markets.

Table 6-10 identifies the various options that are available with respect

Table 6-10 Oversight Options

Self-control
Franchise value of the firm
    Reputation effects
    Importance of market for corporate control
Ethical standards
Compliance function
Conflict management

Industry oversight
    Self-regulation: value and credibility
    Role of external auditors and law firms

Public oversight
    Role of bank supervisors
    Role of securities watchdogs
    Civil penalties
    Criminal prosecution
    Supervisor qualification and compensation

Cross-regulation and turf battles

Political immunization

Public credibility vs. practical expertise

to oversight of institutions engaged in the provision of financial services. *Self-control* refers to resistance to financial failure, abuse of fiduciary responsibilities, and other lapses in management. Good management is embedded in the franchise value of the firm, notably its market value in relation to its book value. Managerial problems should be reflected in the reputation of the firm, which in turn will be reflected in its value. Thus, an important responsibility of management is to maximize its franchise value, and to put in place the necessary safeguards against its erosion. If the institution is subject to a high level of transparency via disclosure rules, equity research analysis, rating by agencies, investigative financial reporting, and so on, as well as the threat of a hostile takeover in a contestable market for corporate control, the pressure on management to enforce safe and sound practices and high standards of conduct may obviate to a significant degree external supervision that could entail greater regulatory burdens. This would include inculcating high ethical standards on the part of employees, the maintenance of a strong internal compliance function, and careful attention to avoidance of conflicts of interest. *Industry oversight* refers to supervision by industry associations and self-regulatory organizations (SROs) to encourage and enforce high standards of conduct among members. Depending on their ability to enforce standards on their members and to discipline them for noncompliance, it may be that SROs—together with external audits by public accounting firms and the threat of lawsuits by disgruntled private parties—can alleviate shortcomings in self-regulation without incurring some of the regulatory costs associated with external supervision. *Public oversight* refers to supervision by agencies set up for that purpose whose mandates are anchored in regulatory statutes. This requires an infrastructure of qualified, motivated banking and financial examiners and securities regulators who have at their disposal both civil and, where necessary, criminal penalties. Most financial systems have found that a structure of external supervision is necessary, no matter how effective self-supervision and SRO supervision turn out to be, since there are always gaps that could lead to instability and breaches of appropriate conduct in financial markets.

As Table 6-10 suggests, problems in supervision of financial institutions and markets will arise no matter which system is adopted. There will be regulatory conflict in the case of multiple or overlapping regulators, each of which is highly protective of its "turf" and anxious not to be blamed for problems that may slip through the supervisory net. There is also the problem of politics, and the possibility that elected representatives will "lean" on banking and financial examiners and supervisors to "go easy" on particular institutions that are politically well connected. And finally, whatever supervisory approach is adopted, it must be credible to the general public. External public supervision is arguably the most credible, yet least likely to be able to keep up with the latest financial products and practices in a rapidly evolving market, as against the firms themselves and industry watchdogs.

Summary

Banking and finance comprise a highly sensitive sector of the economy. There is an inherent element of price and liquidity risk in maturity-mismatching in asset and liability management, trading, and merchant banking activities. Despite careful diversification in asset deployment, exposures incurred in lending activities always involve solvency risk. The very role of financial intermediation entails the assumption of risks. Moreover, fraud, misrepresentation, financial collapse, predatory behavior, self-dealing, bubbles, busts, and shocks have afflicted financial systems over the centuries, in the United States, Europe, and elsewhere in the world. Problems that afflict an individual institution may spill over to damage the entire fabric of the national financial and economic system. To cope with this problem, countries have tried to establish safeguards that are robust enough to contain external damage triggered by crises in the financial sector, yet that do not materially impair financial efficiency or the creative forces of private enterprise. Deposit insurance limits erosion of confidence by banking customers. The central bank as official lender of last resort exists to inject liquidity into individual institutions in trouble (e.g., via its discount facilities) and into the financial system as a whole (via open market operations and changes in reserve requirements).

Along with institutional safeguards comes regulation to further support the safety and soundness of the financial system. The apparatus is familiar—reserve requirements, bank examination and supervision, maximum lending limits, securities regulation, activity limitations on commercial and investment banks, mutual savings banks and savings and loan institutions, and interest-rate ceilings, among the traditional techniques. Countries use different kinds of safeguard structures, but the need for them is universally recognized. Indeed, some use bank nationalization to "socialize" both the risks and the returns, and not coincidentally to achieve a direct government role in credit allocation.

The problem with financial regulation and control is that it invariably erodes the *efficiency* of the system. All regulatory and supervisory measures have the potential of displacing financial resource allocation from that which is most efficiently driven by the free interplay of market force. This is as true of reserve requirements as it is of interest-rate ceilings on deposits. Further costs are associated with eroded innovativeness and competitive vitality of the industry. So the combination of financial safeguards and regulation results in a lessening of financial efficiency and dynamism. Greater security is never free—there is always a price to be paid. Here we are buying increased safety with respect to the national financial system and paying for it in the form of reduced financial market efficiency. This is a logical trade-off. Yet there is always the question whether we are paying too high a price for the increased financial stability we are purchasing through regulation and control. Many countries would surely regard bank nationalization as an extortionate price to pay for any prospective increase in financial safety that would create.

These issues become especially difficult in the international environment, although much progress has been made to create a more coherent regulatory apparatus and at the same time a more level playing field. This has focused on more careful assignment of regulatory responsibility to branches and affiliates, coordination of national prudential policies, and perhaps most important, alignment of capital adequacy standards.

Notes

1. For a detailed discussion of these issues, see Anthony Saunders and Ingo Walter, *Universal Banking in the United States*. New York: Oxford University Press, 1994.

2. Edward Kane, "Competitive Financial Reregulation: An International Perspective," in R. Portes and A. Swoboda (eds.), *Threats to International Financial Stability*. London: Cambridge University Press, 1987.

7

Structural Change in Global Financial Flows

The previous chapters have focused in some detail on the structure of *intermediated* global financial flows, that is, flows that run through the balance sheets of financial intermediaries such as commercial banks. The cost of financial intermediation, including the regulatory costs, was identified in chapter 6 as the all-in differential between the returns obtained by ultimate savers and the cost of funds to ultimate borrowers. This differential comprises the operating costs, losses, and profits incurred in the intermediation process. The lower this differential, the more efficient is the intermediation process. Banks (and banking systems) compete with each other to a significant degree on the basis of intermediation efficiency, which in turn is driven by their respective comparative advantages and regulatory burdens. They also compete with alternative forms of financial intermediation, notably securities transactions, both within national financial systems and globally. In this chapter we shall outline the dynamics of alternative financial intermediation flows, their dramatically shifting patterns in recent decades, and their prospective future development. These dynamics, in turn, have a pivotal effect on the strategic positioning and performance of banks and other financial firms, their wholesale and retail clients, and the competitiveness of entire financial systems, as discussed in chapters 14 and 15.

Stylized Process of Financial Intermediation

The central component of any model of a modern financial system is the nature of the conduits through which the financial assets of the ultimate savers flow through to the liabilities of the ultimate users of finance, both within and between national economies. This involves alternative and competing modes of financial intermediation, or "contracting," between counterparties in financial transactions. Here we shall discuss the intermediation framework in terms of a model that can be useful in explaining and forecasting structural shifts in national and global banking and financial markets through time as well as the strategies of individual financial services firms.

Figure 7-1 is a guide to thinking about financial contracting and the role of financial institutions and markets. It depicts the financial process (flow of funds) among the different sectors of the economy in terms of underlying environmental and regulatory determinants or drivers as well as the generic advantages needed to profit from three primary linkages:

1. Savings/commercial banking and other traditional forms of intermediated finance
2. Investment banking and securitized intermediation
3. Various financial direct-connect mechanisms between borrowers and lenders

Ultimate *sources* of surplus funds arise in the household sector (deferred consumption or savings), the corporate sector (retained earnings or business savings), and the government sector (budgetary surpluses).

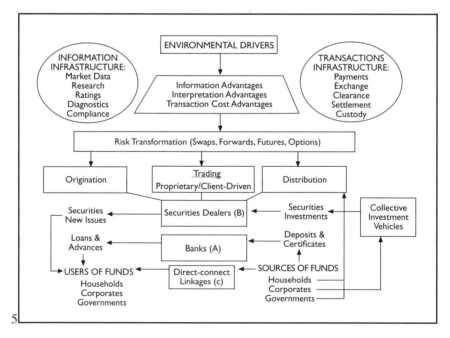

Figure 7-1. Financial intermediation dynamics.

- Under the first or "classic" model of financial intermediation, savings (or funds sources) are held in the form of deposits or alternative types of claims issued by commercial banks, savings organizations, insurance companies, or other forms of financial institutions entitled to finance themselves by placing their liabilities directly with the general public. Financial institutions then use these funds flows (liabilities) to purchase domestic and international assets issued by nonfinancial institution agents such as firms and governments.
- Under the second model of funds flows, savings may be allocated directly to the purchase of securities publicly issued and sold by various governmental and private sector organizations in the domestic and international financial markets.
- Under the third alternative, savings surpluses may be allocated directly to borrowers through various forms of private placement and other direct-sale mechanisms.

Ultimate *users* of funds comprise the same three segments of the economy—the household or consumer sector, the business sector, and the government sector.

- Consumers may finance purchases by means of personal loans from banks or by loans secured by purchased assets (hire-purchase or installment loans). These may appear on the asset side of the balance sheets of credit institutions on a revolving basis, for the duration of the respective loan contracts, or they may be sold off into the financial market in the form of securities backed by consumer credit receivables.
- Corporations may borrow from banks in the form of unsecured or asset-backed straight or revolving-credit facilities and/or may sell debt obligations (e.g., commercial paper, receivables financing, fixed-income securities of various types), or equities directly into the financial market.
- Governments may likewise borrow from credit institutions (sovereign borrowing) or may issue securities directly.

With the exception of consumers, other borrowers such as corporations and governments also have the possibility of privately issuing and placing their obligations with institutional investors, thereby circumventing both credit institutions and the public debt and equity markets. But even consumer debt can be repackaged as asset-backed securities and sold to private investors, as discussed later in this chapter.

Alternative Modes of Financial Contracting

In the first mode of financial contracting (mode A in Figure 7-1), depositors buy the "secondary" financial claims or liabilities issued by credit institutions, and benefit from liquidity, convenience, and safety through the ability of financial institutions to diversify risk and improve credit quality through professional asset management and monitoring of their holdings of primary financial claims (debt and equity). Savers can choose among a set of standardized contracts and receive payments services and interest that may or may nor be subject to varying degrees of government regulation.

In the second mode (mode B), investors may select their own portfolios of financial assets directly from among the publicly issued debt and equity instruments on offer. This may provide a broader range of options than standardized bank contracts and permits larger investors to tailor portfolios more closely to their objectives while still achieving acceptable liquidity through rapid execution of trades—aided by linkages with banks and other financial institutions that are part of the domestic payments mechanism. Small investors may choose to have their portfolios professionally managed, for a fee, through various types of mutual funds, designated as collective investment vehicles in Figure 7-1.

In the third mode (mode C), investors buy large blocks of privately issued securities. In doing so they often face a liquidity penalty, due to the absence or limited availability of a liquid secondary market, for which they are rewarded by a higher yield. On the other hand, directly placed securities can be specifically "tailored" to more closely match issuer and investor requirements than can publicly issued securities. Moreover, recent institutional and regulatory developments have added to the liquidity of some direct-placement markets.

Value to ultimate savers and investors, inherent in the financial processes described previously, accrues in the form of a combination of yield, safety, and liquidity. Value to ultimate users of funds accrues in the form of a combination of financing cost, transactions cost, flexibility, and liquidity. This value can be enhanced through credit backstops, guarantees, and derivative instruments such as forward-rate agreements, caps, collars, futures, and options. Furthermore, markets can be linked functionally and geographically, both domestically and internationally.

- *Functional* linkages permit bank receivables, for example, to be repackaged and sold to nonbank securities investors. Privately placed securities, once they have been seasoned, may be sellable in public markets.
- *Geographic* linkages make it possible for savers and issuers to gain incremental benefits in foreign and offshore markets, thereby enhancing liquidity and yield or reducing transactions costs.

If permitted by financial regulation, various kinds of financial firms emerge to perform one or more of the roles identified in Figure 7-1— commercial banks, savings banks, postal savings institutions, savings cooperatives, credit unions, securities firms (full-service firms and various kinds of specialists), mutual funds, insurance companies, finance companies, finance subsidiaries of industrial companies, and various others. Members of each *strategic group* compete with each other, as well as with members of other strategic groups. Assuming it is allowed to do so, each organization elects to operate in one or more of the three financial-process modes identified in Figure 7-1, according to its own competitive advantages, that is, its comparative efficiency in the relevant financial production mode compared with that of other firms.

Static and Dynamic Efficiency Aspects

Issues relating to the static and dynamic efficiency of the three alternative financial processes are summarized in Figures 6-2 and 6-3 of the previous chapter.

Static efficiency is modeled as the all-in, weighted average spread (differential) between rates of return provided to ultimate *savers* and the cost of funds to *users*. This gap, or *spread,* depicts the overall cost of using a particular mode or type of financial process and is reflected in the monetary value of resources consumed in the course of financial intermediation. In particular it reflects the direct costs of production (operating and administrative costs, cost of capital, etc.). It also reflects losses incurred in the financial process, as well as any monopoly profits earned and liquidity premia. Financial processes that are considered "statically inefficient" are usually characterized by high spreads due to high overhead costs, high losses, barriers to entry, and the like.

Dynamic efficiency is characterized by high rates of financial product and process innovation through time.

Product innovations usually involve creation of new financial instruments (e.g., caps, futures, options, swaps) along with the ability to replicate certain instruments by bundling existing ones (synthetic securities) or to highlight a new financial attribute by rebundling existing instruments. There are also new approaches to contract pricing, passive or index-based portfolio investment techniques, that also fall under this rubric.

Process innovations include contract design (e.g., cash-settlement futures contracts); methods of clearance, settlement, and trading; and techniques for efficient margin calculation.

However, costs may be associated with financial innovation as well. Examples include financial instruments that take substantial resources to develop but ultimately fail to meet a need in the marketplace. Research during the 1980s shows a wide variety of derivative securities failures, such as a futures contract based on the retail price index.

Successful product and process innovation broadens the menu of financial services available to ultimate issuers, ultimate savers, or other agents along the various financial channels described in Figure 7-1. Probably the most powerful catalyst affecting the competitive dynamics of the financial services industry has been technological change.

It is against a background of continuous innovation and pressure for dynamic efficiency that financial markets and institutions have evolved and converged. Global financial markets for foreign exchange, debt instruments, and to a lesser extent equity have developed various degrees of "seamlessness," as depicted in Figure 7-2. Indeed, it is arguable that the most advanced of the world's financial markets are approaching a theoretical, "complete" optimum where there are sufficient financial instruments and markets, and combinations thereof, to span the whole state-space of risk and return outcomes. Financial systems that are deemed *inefficient* or *incomplete* are characterized by a limited range of financial services and obsolescent financial processes.

Both static and dynamic efficiency are obviously important from the standpoint of national and global resource allocation, not only within the financial services industry itself but also as it affects *users* of financial services. That is, since financial services can be viewed as "inputs" to the

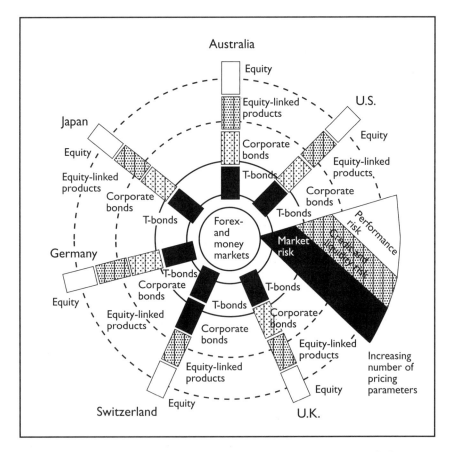

Figure 7-2. Seamlessness of financial markets. Source: McKinsey & Co.

overall real production process (along with labor and capital), the level of national output and income—as well as its rate of economic growth—are directly or indirectly affected by the static and dynamic efficiency attributes of the financial system. A "retarded" financial services sector can represent a major impediment to a nation's overall real economic performance.

Such retardation represents a burden on the final consumers of financial services and potentially reduces the level of private and social welfare. It also represents a burden on producers, by raising their cost structures and eroding their competitive performance in domestic and global markets. These inefficiencies distort the patterns of allocation of labor as well as capital. One major reason for progressive deregulation in many countries during the 1980s was an attempt to capture, for the countries involved, static and dynamic efficiency gains—and at the same time to maximize the real value-added generated in the financial services industry itself.

Globalizing the Model

The stylized model of financial intermediation presented in Figure 7-1 is cast implicitly in the context of domestic financial systems. The discussion can, however, easily be globalized:

- Sources of funds in national economies can be accessed by users of funds resident abroad. Examples include purchases of foreign securities by institutional investors and by domestic households, either as individual securities or through collective investment vehicles such as mutual funds. International access to national savings pools is of particular importance in view of the wide differences that exist in savings rates among countries.
- Users of funds ranging from international organizations and government entities to corporations and even households (through asset-backed securities collateralized by consumer credit, mortgages, etc.) can access foreign sources of financing by borrowing or issuing securities outside the home country, either in foreign markets or in the offshore markets. International financings are particularly important in the light of large differences that exist in national levels of consumer, corporate, and governmental borrowing requirements.
- Financial intermediaries connecting sources and users of funds operate internationally as well as domestically. Cross-border lending and foreign currency funding are forms of international banking via the classic financial intermediation mode. New issues of securities undertaken abroad or offshore, or domestic issues incorporating international tranches, link issuers and investors across financial markets.

The role of derivatives and other hedging instruments—and portfolio diversification for investors—is substantially more important as well when the model is internationalized rather than remaining purely domestic, due to the existence of different national currencies, macroeconomic environments, and financial market conditions. This is discussed in greater detail in this chapter and in chapter 10.

Structural Shifts in the Intermediation Process

As noted earlier, unless prevented from doing so by regulation, the three alternative channels of financial funds flows identified in Figure 7-1 compete vigorously with each other for transactions volume in the financial intermediation process. The winners and losers among institutions competing in this process tend to be relatively consistent across national and international financial markets.

Taking the United States as an example of a large, integrated financial market (notwithstanding any geographic barriers or line-of-business constraints imposed on financial intermediaries by the regulatory authorities), the shifts that have taken place over almost half a century are presented in Table 7-1. It is evident that fully intermediated financial flows (mode A in Figure 7-1) have dramatically given way to partially disintermediated flows via the securities markets (more closely fitting mode B). Note the decline in the shares of traditional financial institutions such as commercial banks, thrifts, and insurance companies from 1946 to 1990, and the

Table 7-1 Financial Assets of Selected Financial Institutions (percent of total)

Institutions	1946	1950	1960	1970	1980	1990
Commercial banks	57.3	51.2	38.3	38.6	36.7	31.2
S&L associations	4.4	5.8	11.9	12.9	15.4	10.2
Mutual savings banks	8.0	7.6	6.9	5.9	4.2	2.5
Credit unions	0.2	0.3	1.0	1.3	1.7	2.0
Life insurance companies	20.3	21.3	19.3	15.0	11.5	13.1
Private pension funds	1.5	2.4	6.4	8.3	11.6	10.9
State and local pension funds	1.2	1.7	3.3	4.5	4.9	7.4
Other insurance companies	3.0	4.0	4.4	3.7	4.3	5.0
Finance companies	2.1	3.2	4.6	4.8	5.0	5.3
Real estate investment trusts	0.0	0.0	0.0	0.3	0.1	0.1
Mutual funds	0.6	1.1	2.8	3.5	1.5	5.7
Money-market mutual funds	0.0	0.0	0.0	0.0	1.9	4.6
Securities brokers and dealers	1.5	1.4	1.1	1.2	1.1	2.0
Total[a]	100.0	100.0	100.0	100.0	100.0	100.0
Total ($billions)	234	294	600	1,342	4,040	10,751

Source: Board of Governors of the Federal Reserve System, *Flow of Funds Accounts*, various editions.

[a] Columns may not add to exactly 100 percent because of rounding.

dramatic rise in shares of finance companies, pension funds, and mutual funds that allow issuers and investors more direct access to primary securities markets—presented graphically in Figure 7-3 for 1973 and 1993.

Regarding the left-hand (borrower) structure of Figure 7-1, it is evident from Figure 7-4 that there has been very rapid growth in U.S. commercial paper (USCP) outstanding (discussed in chapter 2) as the closest substitute to bank credit lines. Comparable growth can be found in the share of domestic bond issues, most notably corporate obligations issued under medium-term-note (MTN) programs, discussed in chapter 9. Regarding the right-hand (investor) side of Figure 7-1, it is clear from Figure 7-5 that there has been correspondingly rapid growth in money-market mutual funds, the closest substitute to interest-bearing bank and savings institution deposits.

The reason for this migration of financial flows from one intermediation process to another arguably has much to do with changes in the relative static and dynamic efficiency characteristics and costs (or spreads) of intermediation via traditional financial institutions, as against more direct securities market processes. As we have noted, these processes compete with each other on static and dynamic efficiency criteria, resulting in the significant long-term shifts in market shares evident in Table 7-1.

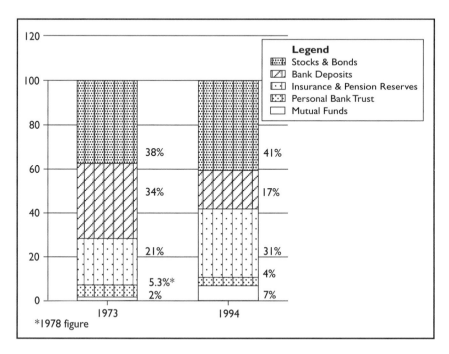

Figure 7-3. Change in investments of household financial assets from 1973 to 1994. Source: Federal Reserve Board, Flow of Funds, 3rd quarter, 1994.

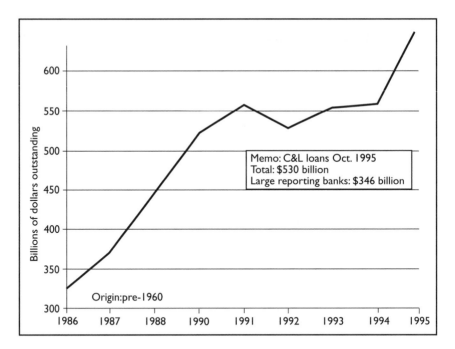

Figure 7-4. U.S. commercial paper market. Data: Federal Reserve Board.

The other development promoting the shift from intermediated to disintermediated finance in the United States has been securitization—the issuance of traded financial instruments against anticipated cash flows of interest and principal from various kinds of receivables.

Securitization is a term frequently used to describe a major change that has taken place in the international banking and capital markets. Strictly speaking, the term refers to the process of packaging illiquid financial assets held on the books of banks, savings associations, mortgage lenders, insurance companies, and other financial institutions in such a way as to be able to sell participations in the package to capital market investors. A number of residential mortgages, for example, can be sold to a single-purpose trust, and the trust pays for these mortgages out of the proceeds from the sale of trust certificates representing proportionate ownership of the trust assets. In a broader context, securitization has come to represent a general trend of moving nonmarketable assets off the balance sheets of financial institutions into the vast pool of liquid assets in the securities market.

Securitization occurs when an asset holder finds it desirable to liquidate or restructure its investment portfolio—for reasons of profitability, because of mismatches between assets and the availability of funding for them, or because of the need to adjust the overall size and capacity of its balance sheet. Securitization also occurs when the traditional customers of financial institutions discover alternate ways to finance at lower costs from other sources. When this occurs, the inflow of business to the traditional institutions is reduced. The process of securitization of loans has been greatly accelerated by the considerable structural changes that have occurred in the international capital markets over the past two decades.

An early example of securitization was the growth in commercial paper outstandings in the United States in the late 1960s. During this period, regulations limited the interest rates banks could pay on deposits. The effect was to drive large corporate depositors to the commercial paper market where "market" rates could be obtained. These regulations and other monetary policies at the time reduced the growth rate of bank loans, driving those companies needing working capital financing into the commercial paper market. Short-term loans, then, were flowing from the banks into the market where they were financed by nonbank sources, namely other financial institutions and corporations. Consequently, the decline in the share of new credit financing bypassing banks particularly in the United States has been particularly dramatic. The reasons are numerous:

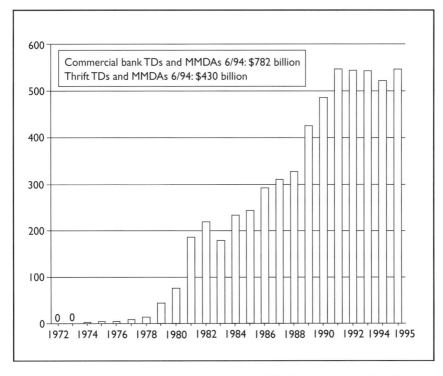

Commercial bank TDs and MMDAs 6/94: $782 billion
Thrift TDs and MMDAs 6/94: $430 billion

Figure 7-5. Assets of money-market mutual funds, 1972–95. Source: MMDA, Federal Reserve Bulletin, various issues.

- A general decline in long-term interest rates after 1981 from the high rates that had been pervasive in the late 1970s, and a restoration of a positively sloped yield curve, which increased the attractiveness of fixed-rate financial instruments.
- The poor quality of U.S. bank balance sheets after they had overextended themselves on developing country loans and numerous other problem sectors. This eroded the credit standing of bank certificates of deposit and raised their funding costs as investors began looking for alternatives—in short, it meant that many high-grade companies could sell their own securities at rates lower than the rates at which banks could raise funds, thus making bank financing a high-cost source of funds.
- The growing LDC debt burden forced many banks to restrict growth in assets in order to protect their deteriorating capital ratios, and to take more seriously the issue of liquidity—on the asset side by selling off loans already on their books, on the liability side by funding themselves in nontraditional ways with term debt. Thus, banks themselves became important borrowers in international capital markets, motivated by a need to issue new capital to strengthen their capital bases and to achieve better matches between asset and liability maturities, as well as to take advantage of capital market conditions to lower their overall cost of funds.
- Constraints on the banks led to a very large increase in off-balance-sheet activities, or contingent liabilities to offer financing in the future under specified circumstances, which for regulatory and accounting purposes were not recorded on the face of bank balance sheets. They included guarantees, letters of credit, activities as lessors, and participations in interest-rate and currency swap transactions and various forms of standby and back-up note issuance facilities. These activities permitted the banks to recapture some of the business lost to securitization, to increase their returns on assets, and to improve capital ratios. At the same time, off-balance-sheet activity and securitization increases the difficulty of determining a banker's aggregate risk exposure, a matter that has led to new rules for preserving bank capital adequacy.
- The growth in the volume, depth, and turnover of capital markets caused by the increased globalization, deregulation, and institutionalization created a large pool of financial assets seeking investment opportunities. These were found in Eurocommercial paper, mortgage-backed securities, junk bonds, and more recently in bonds backed by a wide variety of different types of assets. Capital market activity, because of the appeal of lower rates, more suitable maturity structures, and other special features drew even more business away from traditional lenders in a classic example of disintermediation.

The earliest form of securitization activity began in the mortgage market. Its success prompted many firms to apply the same procedure to other types of loans and receivables—in essence, a form of trust financing that turns illiquid mortgage assets or secured loans into tradable financial instruments backed by the security that supported the original loans. Thus far, residential and commercial mortgage loans, automobile loans, credit card receivables, loans to finance recreational vehicles and boats, and computer and manufacturing leases as well as financial receivables have all served as collateral to back new securities issues, as noted in Table 7-2. There are three basic types of loan-backed securities, all of which developed from the secondary mortgage market—pass-throughs, mortgage-backed bonds, and pay-throughs.

In a *pass-through*, a portfolio of mortgages that have similar maturity, interest rate, and credit quality is placed in trust and investors purchase certificates of ownership in the trust. The mortgages associated with the portfolio are assigned by the loan originator to the trust, and the trust collects interest and principal and passes it on to investors. For these services the originator extracts a servicing fee or passes this function on to another servicing institution. Pass-throughs are owned by the final investor; since they are not debt obligations of the originator, they do not appear on the originating bank's balance sheet. The best-known pass-throughs are backed by the Government National Mortgage Association (GNMA), or "Ginnie Mae," and are collateralized by mortgages guaranteed by the Federal Housing Administration (FHA) or the Veterans Administration (VA). GNMA guarantees the payment of both interest and principal. Since Ginnie Maes are backed by government guaranteed mortgages

Table 7-2 Securitized Asset Classes

1970	Mortgages
1985	Autos Boats Equipment leases
1986	Recreational vehicles Light trucks
1987	Credit card receivables Consumer loans Trucks Trade receivables
1988	Affiliate notes Insurance policy loans Hospital receivables
1989	Home equity loans Time shares Junk bonds
1990+	Middle market commercial and industrial loans LDC debt

and also have the counterguarantee of a federal agency, there is little or no default risk associated with them. For this reason there is an active and well-developed domestic and international secondary market that assures liquidity.

Mortgage-backed bonds (MBBs) are securities collateralized by a portfolio of mortgages that is a debt obligation of the issuer. MBBs therefore are reported as liabilities on the issuer's balance sheet, while the mortgages themselves act as collateralization and represent the issuer's assets. MBBs generally have a maturity of 5 to 12 years, with interest paid semiannually. Unlike pass-throughs, the cash flows associated with the mortgage do not go directly to the investors, and the credit risk of the mortgages remains with the financial institution concerned. Mortgage-backed bonds are typically overcollateralized; if the collateral cover falls below a certain level stated in the bond indentures, the collateral must be topped-up by the issuer. Overcollateralization allows the investor additional protection against default on individual mortgages in the portfolio. Overcollateralization also provides protection to bondholders from a fall in the market value of the collateral between valuation dates (usually every quarter). While bondholders could alternatively be covered for the risk of collateral erosion and default risk by extra yield, issuers tend to prefer overcollateralization, since they regularly receive principal and interest flows that can then be reinvested. MBBs are common in both the private and the government-backed sector in the United States. They are issued by savings and loan institutions as well as by mutual savings banks. They are less attractive than pass-throughs due to the fact that they remain on a financial institutions' books and thus do not avoid all of the intermediation costs, including capital requirements, reserve requirements, and insurance charges.

The *pay-through mortgage-backed security* can be viewed as a hybrid of the pass-through and the MBB. The securities are collateralized by mortgage loans and remain on the originators balance sheet as debt. The principal and interest payments from the mortgages are in turn dedicated to the servicing of the bonds. The most common pay-through is the collateralized mortgage obligation (CMO). The first CMO was issued by the Federal Home Loan Mortgage Corporation ("Freddie Mac") in 1983, and there have been a large number of variations. In the initial Freddie Mac CMO there were three maturity classes. Class 1 bondholders received the first installment of principal payments and any prepayments until Class 1 bonds were paid off, and so on with Class 2 and Class 3. Class 1 bonds were repaid within 5 years, Class 2 within 12 years, and Class 3 within 20 years. This particular structure essentially gives bondholders protection against the bonds being called by the issuer. Because of this cover as well as the range of maturities available, pay-throughs have attracted a segment of the investor base that was otherwise uninterested in mortgage-backed securities.

Since use of the first pass-through bonds involving government agencies as quasi-guarantors to securitize U.S.fixed-rate mortgage loans in the early 1970s, the securitization technique has been successfully extended to a variety of other markets as well. As the transactions costs of using securitization technology have declined and the advantages to financial institutions have become more apparent (e.g., increased asset liquidity and a superior ability to manage interest-rate risk exposures), potentially all bank loans have become securitizable either through pass-throughs, collateralized mortgage obligations, asset-backed securities, or loan sales.

There are three generic benefits for corporations that engage in asset securitization. The first is liquidity, an important characteristic of marketable financial assets particularly in times of uncertainty. Financial assets that are illiquid have limited attractiveness and have to be compensated for with a commensurately increased yield. Securitization allows investors to turn future uncertain payment streams into cash. In general, the higher the degree of interest-rate volatility of these assets, the more attractive they are for securitization.

Second, securitization allows corporations and other issuers to access various new segments of the securities markets that can be more efficient in terms of transactions costs. Securities markets tend to be cheaper for issuers than direct loans, particularly when there is a wide spread between the credit ratings of a company and that of its clients. Issuers have been able to reduce their cost of financing substantially.

Third, securitization of a company's receivables allows it to diversify its investor base and allow them to exploit new sources of capital, while leaving older sources unimpaired. Securitization is also attractive due to its arm's-length nature as far as a bank and a customer are concerned. The servicing of the obligation can continue without the client ever knowing that his or her debt has been sold. Securitization shrinks balance sheets and allows better use of capital.

The securitization process has significant effects on corporations. High-technology and smaller companies can use their relationships with customers to raise capital at competitive rates. A firm's ability to sell receivables will have implications for how the company sells to clients, and in the overall terms of credit it is able to extend to customers. The corporation can lengthen the terms for the clients, safe in the knowledge that it will be able to sell the receivables off at a later stage and remove them from its balance sheet at short notice. This may give such firms advantages against their competitors. It has allowed small, independent companies with creditworthy customers the opportunity to access customer financing independent of its own balance sheet by securitization of its receivables.

Securitization is most attractive for corporations with sizable differentials between their own credit standing and that of their clients. The larger the differentials, the larger the scope for a reduction in the cost of financing. In the case of automobile companies, their balance sheets are reduced, and with servicing fees still coming in they can achieve a substantial increase in return on assets.

In addition to the advantages available to nonfinancial firms, securitization is attractive to financial institutions actively involved in their origination due to the possibility of reducing net regulatory burden, as discussed in chapter 6. If a financial institution can sell a mortgage pass-through, it eliminates the underlying mortgage from its balance sheet and will no longer have to hold capital against that asset, thus freeing the capital for other uses. Similarly, as the proceeds from the sale are not deposits, the issuer will not have to hold reserves or pay for deposit insurance against the proceeds.

Risk and Return Considerations

The return on an asset-backed security obviously depends on its price and its coupon, both of which are related to the risk of the underlying assets. In situations where a security's yield is greater than that of the underlying loan, securitization offers no benefits. Several options are available to change risk/return relationship associated with securitized assets. In the case of loan-backed bonds, for example, overcollateralization will reduce risk as well as return. There is also the possibility of insuring the securities themselves, in which case it is the insurer who bears the default risk: the insurer will have to evaluate the portfolio, and will charge a premium commensurate with that evaluation.

This indicates the importance of the ability to evaluate the pool of loans that underlies asset-backed securities. The securitization process is clearly dependent on rating agencies' and investors' abilities to understand the loans. Highly complex loan portfolios or loans that have complex credit characteristics are unlikely to be well suited to securitization. The success of securitization will also depend on the payment patterns and maturities. Loans with poorly defined payment patterns and with maturities of less than two years are less attractive candidates for securitization, because the costs of securitization are more difficult to recoup over a short period and investors are not as attracted by short maturities, although credit card-backed securities are a notable exception.

The costs of securitization consist of administrative costs—primarily investment banking fees—and the costs associated with providing information to investors and rating agencies. The benefits from securitization include protection from interest-rate risk, increased liquidity for original lenders and for investors, a more efficient transfer of resources from surplus to deficit financial sectors, and new and less expensive sources of capital for the original lenders. Securitization also serves to liquify a bank's balance sheet and to provide additional funding sources. Securitization is particularly common in the case of smaller loans, which would be difficult to sell individually. Investors can achieve higher levels of diversification because, with the same nominal exposure, a bank in fact takes the credit risk of a large number of different borrowers, thus achieving greater diversification. As the players have become more experienced in the securitization process, the costs of securitizing have tended to fall significantly.

Finally, one of the driving forces behind the growth in securitization has been the rating agencies, which have developed the capability to assess the risk inherent in these structures. Their analysis is conducted on two fronts, legal and credit. On the legal front, it is critical that the issuer of the securities, which is generally a shell company, be independent of the owners of the original securities. On the credit front, the major concern is the quality of the assets pledged, rather than the creditworthiness of the original owners.

As Figure 7-6 shows, there remain wide differences in securitization across financial markets.

That the shift away from the traditional intermediation mode has not been confined to the United States is shown in Figure 7-7. This figure

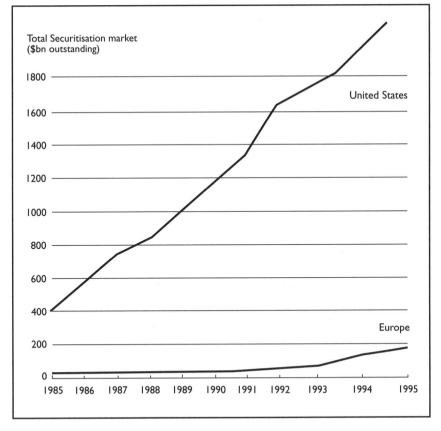

Figure 7-6. Total securitization market in Europe ($ billion outstanding). Source: Citibank.

indicates the relative rise in household financial assets maintained in securitized form in a number of countries—gains that have come at the expense of banks and other intermediaries.

The trend toward securitization internationally is likely to grow as well, as governments in various countries change bank and securities regulations to allow securitization to proceed, and as pressure mounts from financial services firms as well as nonfinancial firms for access to this technology. Thus a major integrating factor in the international securities markets is likely to come from the direct recycling of bank loans through one of the many available securitization vehicles.

The next set of developments in some of the most innovative financial markets is likely to involve replacement of traditional banking and securities forms of financial intermediation by the pure direct-connect mechanisms identified by mode C in Figure 7-1, including direct intercompany payments and electronic funds (see Figure 7-8), increased private placements of securities, and the like—that is, direct financial links between sources and users of funds that have the potential of further cutting out

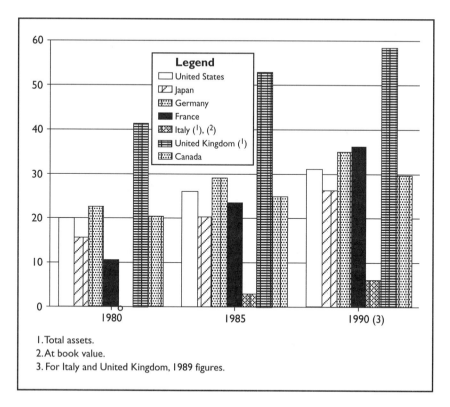

Figure 7-7. Change in total institutional assets (as a percentage of household financial assets in seven countries. Source: Bank for International Settlements Annual Report, 1992.

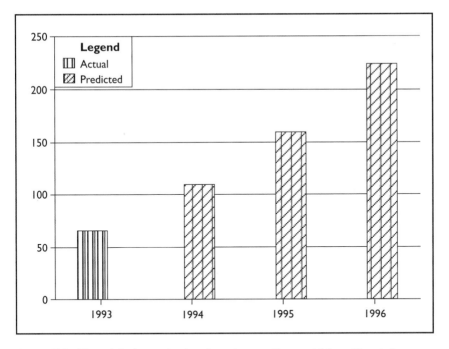

Figure 7-8. Financial electronic data interchange (fees paid in millions). Sources: EDI Group Ltd., The Resource Alliance.

traditional financial intermediaries. Figure 7-9 shows the development of the U.S. private placement market, including placement under Securities and Exchange Commission (SEC) Rule 144A (see chapter 9).

The three intermediation modes in Figure 7-1 thus compete with one another in a modern financial system on the basis of static and dynamic efficiency, although they are often closely interrelated. For example, the provision of liquidity via mode B is an important aspect of the viability of privately placed securities via mode C. Similarly, credit backstops and guarantees by banks via mode A represent an important aspect of various kinds of securities transactions conducted via mode B.

Financial Derivatives, Swaps, and Synthetics

The volume of financial derivatives has grown rapidly in recent years in response to prevailing patterns of interest-rate and exchange-rate volatility, equity market developments, and the gains inherent in arbitraging investment and financing opportunities across currencies and fixed/floating debt pricing. Derivatives and the kinds of synthetic securities they make possible are at once linked to trading in the underlying cash securities and to a

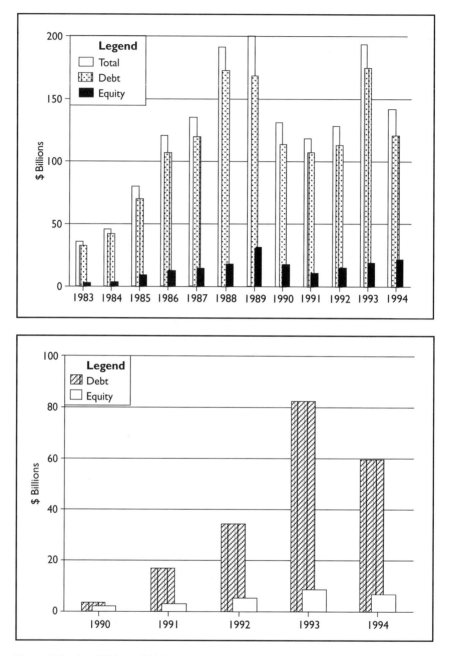

Figure 7-9. (top) Value of U.S. private placements, 1983–94. (bottom) Rule 144A U.S. private placements, 1990–94. Source: Securities Data Co.

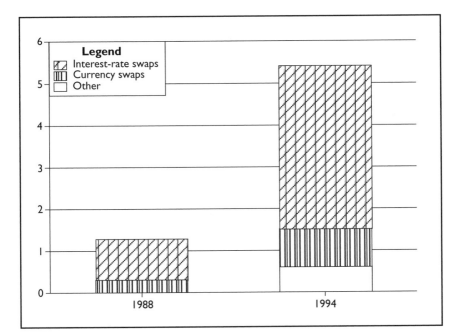

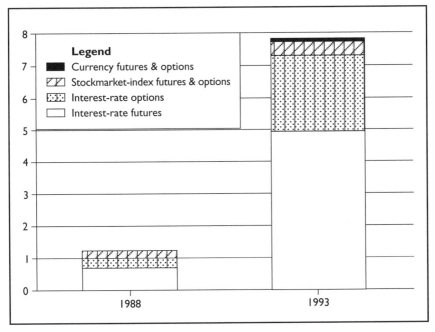

Figure 7-10. Notional principal amount of (top) over the counter derivations ($ trillions) and (bottom) exchange-traded derivatives (amount outstanding, $ trillions). Source: Bank for International Settlements, annual reports.

degree substitute for them as investment vehicles. Figure 7-10 indicates the notional principal amount of over-the-counter (OTC) and exchange-traded derivatives outstanding at the end of 1988 and 1992, respectively. Suffice it here to point out the volumes involved—almost $4 trillion in swaps and swap-related structures securities and almost $7 trillion in futures and options contracts. These instruments provide the core of global risk management and positioning vehicles and clearly affect each of the functions specified in Figure 7-1—even at the retail level as, for example, mortgage borrowers seek protection from rising interest rates.

A variety of derivatives contracts provide good substitutes for the underlying securities, involving lower transactions costs, and may affect the demand for underlying securities. They are regarded as a major area for growth on the part of institutional investor activity. This applies to exchange-traded futures for asset-allocation shifts between countries, to foreign exchange forwards (used as "overlays" to the underlying investment portfolios), as well as to some OTC options.

Financial Market Infrastructure

Finally, in the context of Figure 7-1 the efficiency characteristics of the financial intermediation process discussed here is significantly affected by the "value-chain" of securities market services related especially to mode B in Figure 7-1. These include (1) information gathering and dissemination, (2) provision of analytics and research, (3) establishment and maintenance of efficient physical or electronic trading systems, (4) transactions clearance and settlement, and (5) posttrade custody and safekeeping, including credit-related aspects of the process.

The top left part of Figure 7-1 lists the principal components of the information infrastructure. This includes provision of market information—economic and political facts and interpretation, market prices and volumes, and related data of importance to financial market participants. The vendors, including Reuters, Telerate, and Bloomberg, compete aggressively in ferreting out information and making it available on-line in proprietary systems that sometimes permit users to run their own software on real-time market data. Competition among information vendors has meant that information advantages—asymmetric information—arguably plays less of a role today than it once did in separating winners from losers in the global financial services environment.

Also included in the information infrastructure is research, critical in interpretation of what is going on in the national and international economy, in national and global industries, in corporations, and so on. Research makes it possible to improve the valuation of assets, build efficient portfolios, and optimize financial strategies and a range of other financial operations—even as it makes financial markets more transparent and fair. Researchers in high-performance financial systems compete vigorously with each other in terms of the accuracy of their interpretation and forecasts, and their skills tend to be quite portable. In this sense, top-flight researchers can be considered "free agents" whose views are less likely, for example, to be suborned by pressure for research reports that support their employers' interests rather than those of investors and others who rely on the researcher's objectivity.

The same is true with regard to the rating agencies—Standard & Poor, Moody's Investor Service, Fitch's, IBCA, and other generalist and specialist agencies. Most are paid by the issuer, yet work for the investor, a conflict of interest that most be resolved in favor of the investor if the rating agency is not to destroy its franchise. Again, vigorous competition among rating agencies reduces information and interpretation problems in financial markets, and enhances their transparency and fairness.

Two other services complete the information infrastructure of financial markets. One is portfolio diagnostics, which measure portfolio performance against benchmarks and alternative portfolios. A number of firms and publications periodically report on the risk and return performance of mutual funds, for example, leaving fund managers with no place to hide and providing a much more competitive playing field for even the retail investor. Finally, there is the compliance infrastructure, which ensures that financial transactions are in alignment both with external regulation and internal policies, violation of either of which could create severe damage.

The top right of Figure 7-1 lists transaction infrastructure services. These include the payments system, which is relied on both domestically (e.g., Fedwire and CHIPS in the United States) and internationally (e.g., SWIFT) to channel payments for both real and financial transactions at low cost, low rates of error, and high levels of security and confidentiality. These organizations are usually run by public agencies such as central banks or user cooperatives, with the purpose of providing optimum service at minimum cost. They are also central to the operation of free markets, with failures having potentially disastrous consequences for the financial system and the economy as a whole, and therefore are properly regarded as utilities.

No less important are efficient exchange systems, spanning a range of options from open-outcry pit-based trading and the use of specialist market-makers to electronic screen-based and over-the-counter trading. Vigorous debates rage about the strengths and weaknesses of different trading systems in terms of price discovery, transparency, resistance to manipulation, transaction efficiency and immediacy, and other characteristics of high-performance, fair, and stable markets. Different trading systems—private, public, cooperative, or informal—compete with each other on the basis of these criteria, and those with superior performance tend to draw transactions from less capable rivals.

The clearance, settlement, and custody infrastructure performs an equally crucial function in the financial system and helps increase the availability and lowers the cost of risk capital. This is accomplished by allowing investors a high degree of portfolio diversification and asset-reallocation opportunities as well as significant liquidity, which means that investors will be much more willing to invest in assets that, on their own, would seem risky and illiquid. An efficient securities clearance and settlement system does so promptly at low cost, with a minimum of errors and a maximum degree of certainty that the transaction will be concluded on the precise terms agreed to in the trade. Because friction-free securities transactions can remove major barriers to trading, the clearing and settlement infrastructure can play a key role in the evolution of both domestic and international financial markets. Similarly, efficient and secure custody services reduce costs and risks in domestic and international securities transactions, and handle problems like withholding tax issues and corporate events.

Many of the benefits associated with efficient financial markets may be reaped by removing barriers to capital flows and financial services, allowing international capital markets for fixed income securities and equities to allocate capital more efficiently among issuers. Recognizing this, many countries are seeking to improve their financial market infrastructure services by aligning them progressively with international standards. This suggests that financial markets compete with each other globally in terms of the quality of their infrastructures as well as the quality of financial products and services themselves.

Borrower and Investor Alternatives

In the modern financial environment of today, borrowers face a range of alternatives for obtaining financing, depicted in Figure 7-11. Obviously, not all borrowers have access to all of these (Figure 7-12). But we have already noted that even retail borrowers and small or medium-size companies that are basically limited to bank borrowing can subsequently have their loans securitized and benefit from both access to a much broader pool of funding sources and conversion of illiquid bank loans into liquid securities forms. The gains from both activities will tend to be partially passed backward to the borrower.

Similarly, today's modern financial system provides a wide range of opportunities and services to investors (see Figure 7-13), which allow them to optimize their asset portfolios by taking advantage of the domestic and international portfolio diversification inherent across the range of financial instruments being offered, as well as improvements in the securities market infrastructure services discussed in this chapter. Again, even the retail investor can access these investment alternatives and process-technology improvements by taking advantage of the broad array of mutual funds, unit trusts, and other collective investment vehicles being aggressively marketed to households—in many cases by means of imaginative, high-technology, nonstationary distribution techniques.

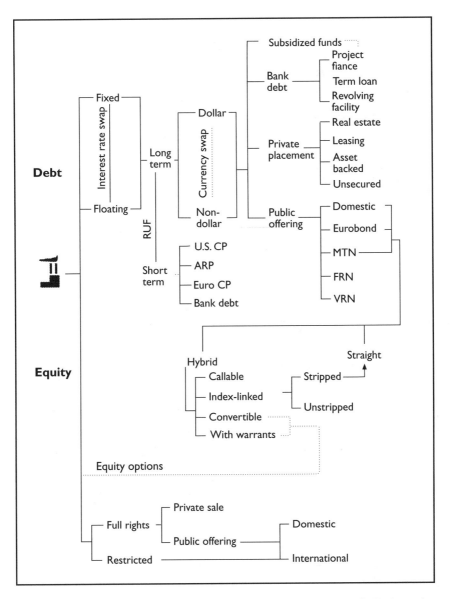

Figure 7-11. Financing alternatives available to major corporations. RUF = revolving underwriting facility; MTN = medium-term notes; FRN = floating-rate note; VRN = variable-rate note.

Summary

In this chapter we have outlined the "roots and branches" of financial intermediation, whether domestic or global, using the flow-of-funds diagram in Figure 7-1 as a basic framework. We have sketched out the causes, course, and consequences of disintermediation and securitization in terms

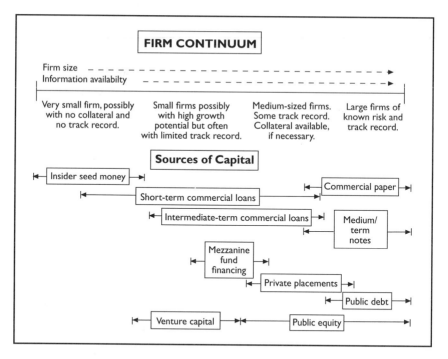

Figure 7-12. Continuum of financing alternatives depending on company size and prospects. Source: Gregory F. Udell.

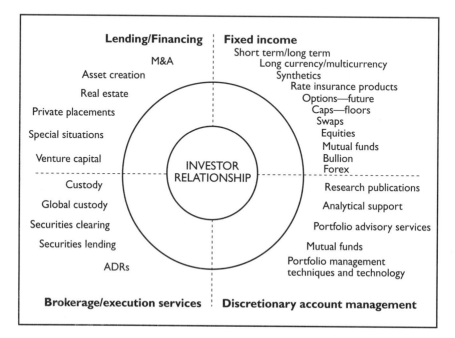

Figure 7-13. Services provided to investors in the modern financial system. M & A = mergers and acquisitions; ADR = American depository receipts.

of the comparative efficiencies of competing intermediation channels. A more efficient intermediation conduit will gain financial flows at the expense of a less efficient one—efficiency being defined both in the cost of intermediation and in the quality of the services provided. Similarly, national financial systems that are less efficient will lose financial flows to more efficient ones, as borrowers/issuers and savers/investors seek other venues where their costs are lower or their risk-adjusted returns are higher. And they are under constant pressure to do so, either to reduce the cost of capital or to better serve their fiduciary obligations to the ultimate asset holders.

Global finance thus involves two battles that go on simultaneously. The first is the battle between alternative intermediation channels. The second is the battle between national financial systems and between these systems and offshore financial intermediation. And, while retail transactions differ in many ways from wholesale transactions, securitization brings them ever closer together—there is no reason why a consumer purchase in the United States, resulting in a credit card charge, cannot be partially financed by a household in Japan that invests in a mutual fund that holds U.S. asset-backed securities swapped into yen.

Banks, securities firms, investment managers, infrastructure services vendors, and other participants in national and global financial markets must "go with the flow" by trying to determine future patterns of financial intermediation and position themselves optimally to take advantage of them.

II

INTERNATIONAL CAPITAL MARKET SERVICES

8

International Money and Foreign Exchange Markets

As long ago as the fifteenth century, organized international money and foreign exchange markets existed. Merchants in Italy, for example, wanting to import tapestries made in Belgium from wool gathered in England, had to find ways to finance these transactions that occurred outside their own country. Italian banks, such as the Medici, set up foreign branches to effect payments and arrange for the delivery of the goods on behalf of their clients. The banks had to deal in currency exchange and in deposit collecting and loan-making in countries outside of Italy. These activities have continued throughout the nearly 500 years of modern banking history, though during the past 20 years or so they have been especially subject to new developments, growth, and change.

Just as international banking refers to activities of banks outside their domestic national markets, international money-market and foreign exchange transactions deal with the issuance and trading of money-market instruments in various currencies in markets other than their domestic national markets. In the domestic U.S. market, money-market instruments include U.S. government and government agency paper of approximately one year or less maturity, as well as commercial paper, bankers' acceptances, and bank certificates of deposit. These instruments conform precisely to U.S. regulatory requirements and market practices; if foreigners wish to buy them, they must take them as they are—in registered form, in which the identity of the purchaser is disclosed, and subject to withholding taxes on interest and bank reserve requirements. If these conditions are not satisfactory, alternative instruments will be sought; if these don't exist, they will be invented through the creative processes inherent in a free-market system that allows capital to cross borders without impediment.

Origins of Eurocurrencies

The history of the international money market, since its modern (postwar) rebirth in the 1960s, is a confluence of three parallel and mutually influential events: major changes in the international monetary system, the evolution of an international investor base, and continuing deregulation of domestic capital markets in major countries to conform to overpowering international alternatives.

In 1944, at Bretton Woods, New Hampshire, the Allied Powers agreed to a postwar international monetary system in which the dollar would be the principal reserve currency (i.e., used as reserves by other countries). The dollar was to be pegged to gold, at the rate of $35 per ounce, and all other currencies were to be fixed to the dollar. When balance-of-payments difficulties arose, it was understood to be the obligation of both the deficit and the surplus countries to modify their domestic fiscal and monetary policies so as to reduce the problem. Governments periodically intervened in foreign exchange markets to help the process along, but usually they relied on broad economic policy changes to effect adjustment. If the imbalance could not be redressed after suitable effort, then the currency could be refixed to the dollar, after which it would have to be defended at the new rate. For the system to work, the world's principal economies would have to grow at about the same rate and the world's military and other burdens would have to be shouldered equally, which was not the case. Further, at the national level, strict economic discipline and controls would be needed, and voting publics would refrain from blaming others for problems and would understand that it was necessary from time to time to take bitter medicine in the interest of their country's long-run well-being. These conditions were not commonly found in the 1950s and 1960s any more than they are now.

In 1971, after several years of large U.S. balance-of-payments deficits, the Bretton Woods system collapsed. It was replaced by a floating-rate mechanism, in which all currencies were to be priced continually by the market and economic imbalances would generate corrective pressures on the foreign exchange rate. The mechanism obviated the need for capital market controls that restricted cross-border transfers, as harsh policies were no longer necessary—the market would administer the medicine that countries were unable to administer to themselves. In time, all the major industrial nations removed their controls on international capital movements. This meant that users and providers of capital could look overseas for capital market opportunities that were superior to what was available at home. It also meant, however, that interest-rate and foreign exchange market volatility would be much greater in the new floating exchange rate environment than in the old fixed-rate regime. Increased volatility led to a great expansion of trading activities and hedging strategies, by banks and other market-makers.

The postwar investor population was affected by these events and by the rapid institutionalization of markets in the United States, the United

Kingdom, and some other European countries. There was also a large increase in the population of otherwise law-abiding Europeans who wanted to transfer funds into foreign bank accounts that were beyond the scrutiny of tax authorities in their countries, as well as an increase in irregular or illegal accumulation of funds in tax-haven countries by corrupt government officials, flight capitalists, and criminals. These individuals, mostly investing through banks in Switzerland, Luxembourg, and other European centers, were highly focused on preserving their anonymity. The institutions, though not subject to tax concerns, were sophisticated investors looking for underpriced investments. Together, these investors were looking for opportunities that were not available in the United States.

Such opportunities were soon discovered in the Eurocurrency markets—an informal, unregulated, over-the-counter market made up of banks and other professional dealers from around the world transacting in instruments that were not available in national markets. Occasionally the Eurocurrency market would devise a financial instrument that was not available in the home market, and it would attract a large volume of activity on the part of home market nationals. Soon the pressure to deregulate the domestic market to make the same type of financing available became too great to contain. Often involuntarily, most countries have had to give in to the process of imported innovation. The result has been a large increase in the number and type of financial instruments available in international and foreign markets.

Eurodollars

Though there was some activity in Eurodollars before World War II, it did not become significant until the early 1960s. At this time, dollars were accumulating in Europe as a result of increased economic growth and investment, the U.S. balance of payments deficits, and investor preference to hold dollars but not in the United States. A dollar-denominated bank deposit outside the United States, for example, in London (or Frankfurt or Zurich), was called a Eurodollar. If you wanted a Eurodollar investment, you had to have it in the form of a bank deposit—in the beginning that was all there was. Eurodollars (and all Eurocurrencies) are priced in terms of the London Interbank Offered Rate (LIBOR), which is the rough equivalent of the Federal Funds rate in the Euromarket: the rate a bank will offer for a loan to another major bank for a specified maturity, such as 30 or 60 days. Major banks post their own rates daily. The rate to be paid on a deposit from another bank is expressed in terms of the London Interbank Bid rate (LIBID). A nonbank borrower can expect to pay a premium over LIBOR (e.g., LIBOR + ¼ percent), and a nonbank depositor would receive a rate reflecting a discount (LIBID − ¼ percent). The spread between LIBOR and LIBID has generally been about ¼ percent, much less than the difference between U.S. prime rate and bank deposit rates.

Other Eurocurrencies

Banks also quote rates for loans and deposits in other currencies, which in a way they manufacture synthetically. They do this by adding the cost or benefit of a forward foreign exchange contract for the prescribed maturity in the desired currency to the U.S. dollar LIBOR rate. If a customer wants a loan based on 60-day sterling LIBOR, the bank first acquires the required amount of sterling in the spot market, then sells sterling forward against dollars in 60 days, and the cost or benefit of this transaction (in percentage) is added to the dollar LIBOR cost.

Euro Certificates of Deposit

Banks, especially U.S. banks, were eager to build up their Eurodollar deposits as a source of funding for their growing international activities. The deposits could be used to fund Eurodollar bank loans or loan syndicate participations. They could be loaned to branches in the United States to support lending activity there, if and when the rates were right. And they could serve as a means of diversifying the banks' wholesale source of funding for their overall deposit base. Investors were other banks (there were more than 400 foreign bank branches in London in 1980, all looking to "buy" assets in the interbank market), multinational institutions, and corporations with temporary funds to invest.

In 1961 Citibank devised the first transferable Euro certificate of deposit (ECD). This was a major innovation that soon led to secondary market trading in dollar instruments and to the creation of the Eurosecurities market. The first Eurobond was offered in 1963, and was sold to investors willing to extend their investment for 15 years, at somewhat higher rates. Both ECDs and Eurobonds were in bearer form (identity of purchaser not disclosed) and were free of withholding taxes on interest.

During the next 30 years the Euromarket was a constant source of innovation, with new instruments being introduced as soon as changing regulatory or investor preferences dictated. Inevitably, ECDs and Eurobonds were introduced in currencies besides the dollar. The Eurobond market soon took off on a continuous expansion that has made it into one of the world's principal sources of finance (see chapter 9).

A Euro Money Market

The money market, however, developed much more slowly than the Eurobond market. In part this was because in the Euromarket well-known international banks had a lock on the market for short-term investments. The banks were also prepared to offer ECDs of whatever maturity an investor might wish. Mostly there was little demand for trading the instruments; the investors were happy to hold them until maturity unless a special requirement to sell them arose.

Investors were extremely quality conscious at a time when limited international investment-grade rating information was available. Unlike domestic markets, the U.S. and European governments did not offer short-term securities internationally, so investors had to make do with banks and other corporate issuers.

If they were prepared to go out a bit in maturity, investors could buy outstanding or newly issued Eurobonds of high-grade, well-known issuers, including some major European governments. The issuers began to shorten the maturities of their bonds (e.g., to two or three years in some cases) to attract these investors as well as to avoid the extremely high interest rates of the late 1970s. As trading volume increased in the secondary markets, investors began to accept that they could rely on the liquidity in the market to facilitate a sale of Eurobonds before maturity.

Eurobonds, however, had certain characteristics that limited the flexibility that many issuers wanted. The bonds were of a fixed amount, underwritten, and sold all at once, and they involved considerable expense. Some issuers instead preferred continuous offerings of their paper to the market on a nonunderwritten basis. They wanted to simply post rates for a range of different maturities, based on advice from one or more dealers, and then see how many notes the dealers could sell. They could raise or lower the rates based on demand. This is the mechanism used in the U.S. commercial paper market, and in the early 1980s it was applied to the Euromarket as Euro commercial paper (ECP).

At first it was slow going. The best known borrowers could often issue commercial paper in the much more liquid market in the United States at lower rates; those who couldn't were not so attractive to the name-conscious market. Some commercial paper was offered with bank guarantees or letters of credit, but still it took time for the market to build up significant volume. The effort was encouraged by the intervention of banks into the market with various forms of note issuance facilities (NIFs), under which a bank loan could be replaced by marketable notes that would be sold through a syndicate of banks.

Next came the introduction in the mid-1980s of the Euro medium-term notes (EMTNs), which were similar to the medium-term note programs then increasing in popularity in the United States. EMTNs cover maturities from less than 1 year to about 10 years. They were issued, like Eurobonds, by large corporations and by governments and their agencies from all around the world. Though EMTNs had longer maturities, they retained some of the characteristics of commercial paper.

These various instruments, now available (directly or through simultaneous swaps) in most major currencies, constitute a family of Eurosecurities that makes up a broad and diverse money market. The volume of outstanding paper in these instruments, as well as the secondary market trading in them, has increased steadily, as shown in Table 8-1. At the end of 1993, $256.9 billion of such securities (exclusive of bank ECDs) were outstanding.

Money-Market Instruments

The following is a description of the different international money-market instruments traded in the Euro securities market.

Euro Certificates of Deposit

ECDs are issued by banks directly or through dealers or brokers. Banks prefer to sell their own ECDs to their clients and correspondent relationships, but often, to extend the market and increase the volume of ECDs outstanding, they resort to dealers to sell the paper for them, for a modest commission. The banks post their own rates for a spectrum of maturities. These rates are closely tied to LIBOR, which is quoted in most major currencies. Newspapers such as the *Financial Times* of London publish averages of these posted rates daily (see Table 8-2).

Banks will often negotiate with large customers for special rates for ECDs with custom-made maturities or other terms. The bank's posted rates may be slightly higher or lower than rates posted by similar banks, reflecting the bank's greater or lesser desire to take in funds at particular maturities. Such decisions are made by the bank's treasury department, which has to balance the entire bank's requirement for funds and currencies at particular maturities. For most banks, the treasury function in the London branch will conduct most of these Euro funding operations, generally in close contact with the central office.

The secondary market in ECDs is very active. Banks maintain markets in their own ECDs, and encourage their customers to trade with them. As rates change, banks will either increase their issuance of ECDs or attempt to buy in outstanding paper. Brokers may work with the banks as agents, on a nonexclusive basis, to place or buy in ECDs for a commission of a few basis points. Such brokers do not take positions in the bank's ECDs for their own account. Often the brokers represent individual investors seeking the best rates for deposits. Dealers, on the other hand, purchase and sell bank ECDs for their own account. They hope to create opportunities for capital gains from trading in the ECDs, as they would in all money-market instruments. Dealers will call the bank in the morning and offer to buy or sell ECDs at particular rates. Then they lay off their positions to customers, or hold them for a few days to wait for an expected market change to occur. Large dealers offer ECDs along with a complete menu of other Euro money-market instruments to customers on a continuous basis.

As an example, a dealer such as Salomon Brothers might be aware that Mitsui Life Insurance Company is seeking to place $100 million in high-grade short-term investments tomorrow morning, Tokyo time. Mitsui actually wants the investments to have a maturity of 75 days. The posted

Table 8-1 Volume of Euro Money Market Instruments Outstanding (amounts outstanding at year-end, $ billions)

	Market Opening	1986	1987	1988	1989	1990	1991	1992	1993	1994	Compounded Growth Rate
Euro commercial paper and other short-term notes (NIFs and RUFs)	Early 1980s	29	50.2	66.7	69.6	89.4	106.4	115.7	110.3	114.1	18.7%
Euro-medium-term notes	Mid-1980s	0.4	2.6	5.6	9.6	21.9	38.5	61.1	146.6	292.0	128.0%
Total		29.4	52.8	72.3	79.2	111.3	144.9	176.8	256.9	406.1	38.8%

Source: Bank for International Settlements.

Table 8-2 Euro Currency Interest Rates

Apr. 13	Short Term	7 Days Notice	One Month	Three Months	Six Months	One Year
Belgian Franc	$5^{1}/_{16}$–5	$6^{1}/_{2}$–$6^{3}/_{8}$	5–$4^{7}/_{8}$	$5^{1}/_{4}$–$5^{1}/_{8}$	$5^{1}/_{2}$–$5^{3}/_{8}$	$5^{7}/_{8}$–$5^{3}/_{4}$
Danish Krone	7–$6^{3}/_{4}$	7–$6^{3}/_{4}$	7–$6^{3}/_{4}$	7–$6^{3}/_{4}$	$7^{1}/_{8}$–$6^{7}/_{8}$	$7^{1}/_{4}$–7
D-Mark	$4^{5}/_{8}$–$4^{1}/_{2}$	$4^{9}/_{16}$–$4^{7}/_{16}$	$4^{9}/_{16}$–$4^{7}/_{16}$	$4^{11}/_{16}$–$4^{9}/_{16}$	$4^{3}/_{4}$–$4^{5}/_{8}$	$5^{1}/_{16}$–$4^{15}/_{16}$
Dutch Guilder	$4^{7}/_{16}$–$4^{5}/_{16}$	$4^{5}/_{8}$–$4^{3}/_{8}$	$4^{5}/_{8}$–$4^{1}/_{2}$	$4^{3}/_{4}$–$4^{5}/_{8}$	$4^{7}/_{8}$–$4^{3}/_{4}$	$5^{1}/_{8}$–5
French Franc	$7^{3}/_{4}$–$7^{1}/_{2}$	$7^{13}/_{16}$–$7^{9}/_{16}$	$7^{3}/_{4}$–$7^{1}/_{2}$	$7^{5}/_{8}$–$7^{3}/_{8}$	$7^{1}/_{8}$–$6^{7}/_{8}$	$7^{1}/_{16}$–$6^{13}/_{16}$
Portuguese Esc.	$9^{3}/_{8}$–$8^{7}/_{8}$	$9^{5}/_{8}$–$9^{1}/_{4}$	$10^{11}/_{32}$–$10^{5}/_{32}$	$10^{13}/_{16}$–$10^{1}/_{8}$	$11^{1}/_{4}$–$10^{1}/_{2}$	$11^{5}/_{8}$–$11^{1}/_{4}$
Spanish Peseta	$8^{23}/_{32}$–$8^{19}/_{32}$	$8^{3}/_{4}$–$8^{5}/_{8}$	9–$8^{7}/_{8}$	$9^{15}/_{32}$–$9^{11}/_{32}$	$9^{3}/_{4}$–$9^{5}/_{8}$	$10^{13}/_{32}$–$10^{9}/_{32}$
Sterling	$6^{3}/_{4}$–$6^{1}/_{4}$	$6^{3}/_{16}$–$6^{1}/_{16}$	$6^{1}/_{4}$–$6^{3}/_{16}$	$6^{11}/_{16}$–$6^{9}/_{16}$	7–$6^{15}/_{16}$	$7^{9}/_{16}$–$7^{7}/_{16}$
Swiss Franc	$3^{1}/_{2}$–$3^{3}/_{8}$	$3^{1}/_{2}$–$3^{3}/_{8}$	$3^{1}/_{2}$–$3^{3}/_{8}$	$3^{1}/_{2}$–$3^{3}/_{8}$	$3^{5}/_{8}$–$3^{1}/_{2}$	$3^{11}/_{16}$–$3^{9}/_{16}$
Can. Dollar	$8^{1}/_{16}$–$7^{7}/_{8}$	8–$7^{13}/_{16}$	8–$7^{7}/_{8}$	8–$7^{7}/_{8}$	$7^{15}/_{16}$–$7^{13}/_{16}$	$7^{15}/_{16}$–$7^{13}/_{16}$
U.S. Dollar	6–$5^{7}/_{8}$	$6^{1}/_{16}$–$5^{15}/_{16}$	$6^{1}/_{8}$–6	$6^{1}/_{4}$–$6^{1}/_{8}$	$6^{7}/_{16}$–$6^{5}/_{16}$	$6^{11}/_{16}$–$6^{9}/_{16}$
Italian Lira	$10^{1}/_{4}$–$9^{3}/_{4}$	$10^{5}/_{16}$–$10^{3}/_{16}$	$10^{3}/_{8}$–$10^{1}/_{4}$	$10^{5}/_{8}$–$10^{1}/_{5}$	11–$10^{7}/_{8}$	$11^{7}/_{16}$–$11^{15}/_{16}$
Yen	$1^{7}/_{8}$–$1^{3}/_{4}$	$1^{13}/_{16}$–$1^{3}/_{4}$	$1^{3}/_{4}$–$1^{11}/_{16}$	$1^{11}/_{16}$–$1^{5}/_{8}$	$1^{5}/_{8}$–$1^{9}/_{16}$	$1^{5}/_{8}$–$1^{9}/_{16}$
Asian $Sing	$3^{7}/_{8}$–$3^{3}/_{4}$	$3^{1}/_{4}$–$3^{1}/_{8}$	$2^{13}/_{16}$–$2^{11}/_{16}$	$2^{15}/_{16}$–$2^{13}/_{16}$	3–$2^{7}/_{8}$	$3^{3}/_{8}$–$3^{1}/_{4}$

Source: Financial Times, April 18, 1995.
Short term rates are call for the US Dollar and Yen, others: two days' notice.

rate for 60-day ECDs might be 4 percent, and for 90 days 4.3 percent. Salomon will call a dozen or more high-grade banks the evening before the opening in Tokyo to offer to buy 75-day ECDs at a rate of 4.25 percent, in order to offer them at, say, 4.20 percent, to Mitsui Life. Many banks will turn Salomon down, but one or two may have a need of their own for a large placement of 75-day ECDS and be willing to pay the somewhat higher rate. Such intense market coverage together with the willingness of dealers to position paper of all types has greatly improved the efficiency of the Euro money market in recent years. The improving efficiency of the market largely explains its rapid growth since the early 1980s.

Floating-Rate Notes

In the early 1980s, many banks began to offer floating-rate notes (FRNs) as a supplement to their funding activities. These notes were not deposits, and therefore were subordinate to them. The FRNs might have a maturity of 10 years, but interest would be reset every 90 days at three-month LIBOR (say, 4.5 percent) plus a small spread (say, $\frac{1}{8}$ percent). Because of the continuous resetting, the price of the notes was expected to return to par (100 percent) every 90 days, assuming that the reissue rate continued to be LIBOR + $\frac{1}{8}$ percent. An investor was now given a choice between 90-day ECDs (say, at 4.3 percent) and purchasing and reselling 90 days later a FRN at a rate of 4.625 percent, a difference of 32.5 basis points. The investor would have to realize that there was a risk that the FRNs could not be sold at 100 percent 90 days later, so part of the 32.5 basis points was a reserve to protect against selling it at a price below par, plus commissions. The investor might ask a dealer to quote a repurchase rate at which the firm would agree to buy the FRNs back 90 days hence, and if a positive spread still existed (and the investor was willing to take the credit risk of the dealer meeting this obligation 90 days later) the investor might prefer the FRN trade to the ECD. On the other hand, the investor may prefer to remain a depositor in the bank, rather than a general creditor, and therefore accept a lower rate for the increased security.

To some extent, therefore, the FRN market competed with the ECD market. However, as fear about the credit quality of banks emerged in the early 1980s, there was less assurance about the ability of bank's to roll over funding at the same spread over LIBOR, and the FRN market weakened considerably. So too did the market in ECDs, relative to other instruments.

Euro Commercial Paper

Commercial paper, which has been issued actively in the United States since the 1860s, first appeared in Europe in the early 1970s. It was aimed initially at U.S. corporations, which were required then by government regulations to finance all overseas investments with foreign borrowings, to provide a money-market alternative to bank borrowing. The effort was not successful. After commissions and set-up expenses, the cost of funds to the issuer was about the same as the cost of a comparable LIBOR-based bank loan. Euro investors were cautious; they were hesitant to buy the paper of companies that were not already well known and were unimpressed by the limited liquidity in the market. In 1974, the regulations requiring U.S. companies to finance overseas were repealed, and the market died away. The economics were simply not there—there was very little benefit to using the market at the time.

In the early 1980s, a new attempt was made to develop the ECP market. This time the initiative was aimed at banks that needed higher and safer returns on their money-market investments, and at corporate and institutional investors, which were increasingly concerned by the deterioration in bank credit ratings in the United States and wanted to diversify their cash management programs into nonbank investments. Dealers, aware of these concerns, began to approach European money managers with proposals that they switch from ECDs or FRNs to ECP of top-name companies like AT&T and Exxon. They were earning only LIBID less $\frac{1}{4}$ percent from their bank deposits, but now they could diversify into higher grade paper, such as that issued by companies with AAA bond ratings, at a better rate, say, LIBID less 10 basis points. Or, if they were prepared to take corporate bond ratings of AA or A (with top grade U.S. commercial paper ratings of A1 and P1) they could look for an even higher rate, say, the mean between LIBID and LIBOR.

In 1985, as bank credit worries increased and a greater supply of nonbank paper was offered, the market began to develop in earnest. As it did, the recognized rating agencies, Moody's and Standard & Poor's, increased their involvement in ECP ratings and investors became more aware of them. To be rated, issuers had to be able to demonstrate that they had unused bank lines of credit available to provide liquidity to an issuer should a major market interruption occur in which it would not be possible to roll maturing ECP over. Committed credit facilities in same-day funds, called "swinglines," must be in place to cover a few days of maturities, with "back-up" lines, often uncommitted, available for the rest of the maturities.

Unrated paper soon required up to 10 basis points higher interest rates than lower rated (A2, P2) ECP, which itself required 5 to 10 basis points more interest than A1- to P1-rated paper. Ratings became increasingly important after several major defaults in 1989–1990. By 1990 the ECP market had increased to about $70 billion of outstandings. Citibank, a major ECP dealer, estimated at the time that banks comprised about 44.7 percent of the investor market, corporations 27.8 percent, and money managers and financial institutions 27.5 percent. Among the banks were those that managed substantial investment funds for their clients.

From the issuer's point of view, ECP provided cheaper funds, because the market was pricing it and the issuer did not have to pay significant commitment fees to banks. Accessing the ECP market permitted an issuer to tap in to the principal investor base in the Euromarket and represented a diversification of the issuer's sources of funding.

Dealers initially were enthusiastic about the rapidly expanding ECP market. They wanted to assist existing and new clients for Euromarket services; to appear well placed in the competitive rankings, or "league tables"; and to profit from the growth in the new market. Intense competition forced spreads down, squeezed commissions, and spread too many programs among several dealers. Profits were hard to come by. Of the top 10 dealers at the end of 1987, four (Merrill Lynch, CS First Boston, S.G. Warburg, and Salomon Brothers) had withdrawn from the market by the end of 1990. Subsequently, competitive conditions settled down into a rated-only market with fixed commissions of 3 to 5 basis points paid by issuers to dealers.

ECP market developments also affected domestic markets. By the mid-1980s it was possible for issuers to swap dollar-denominated commercial paper into paper denominated in any other major currency. Thus a market grew in "synthetic" Euro-DM, Euro-Sterling, and other Eurocurrency commercial paper including ECUs. Such paper began to appeal to issuers from various European and other countries, and this in turn put pressure on local regulators to permit the development of domestic CP markets in several countries, such as Japan, Germany, Britain, and France, that had never had commercial paper markets before. Table 8-3 shows the growth in domestic CP outstandings since 1986. The table indicates that domestic CP volume outstanding in 1993 in countries that did not have CP markets before 1980 (Japan, Germany, Britain, France, Spain, and others) totaled more than $140 billion, compared with $110 billion of ECP and Euronotes combined. In a Europe of no capital controls, the distinction between domestic commercial paper and ECP may become moot. It is not moot, however, when substantial noninterest factors apply to one but not to the other. USCP, for example, is limited by law to borrowings for working capital purposes only for maturities up to 270 days. USCP is subject to income tax withholding on interest and is issued in book-entry form. ECP is exempt from maturity and use-of-proceeds restrictions, is not subject to withholding taxes, and is offered in bearer form. Thus a substantial difference exists between domestic CP and ECP denominated in dollars. Often the difference results in an interest rate differential.

The development of the ECP market has been one of the more significant innovations in international finance during the past decade. The market developed to fill a need by international investors for a spectrum of bearer money-market paper that was free of withholding and other taxes. Gradually the spectrum widened to include lesser quality names, including some speculative Latin American issuers, that were appropriately priced by the market. The new market was successful enough to generate further

Table 8-3 Domestic and International Markets for Commercial Paper and Medium-Term Notes (amounts outstanding at year-end, $ billions[a])

Items	Market Opening	1986	1987	1988	1989	1990	1991	1992	1993
Commercial-paper markets									
United States	Pre-1960	326.1	373.6	451.8	521.9	557.8	528.1	545.1	553.7
Japan	End-1987		13.8	73.8	91.1	111.2	84.3	82.7	72.4
France	End-1985	3.7	7.6	10.4	22.3	34.3	39.6	36.1	28.5
Spain[b]	1982	6.3	4.3	6.3	8.3	25.0	27.2	32.6	27.9
Canada	Pre-1960	11.9	14.9	21.0	25.0	24.8	24.8	22.4	23.6
Germany	Early 1991						5.4	10.5	7.8
United Kingdom	1986	0.8	3.8	5.7	5.7	6.3	6.1	6.3	8.6
Other		9.3	21.8	26.0	37.4	48.5	49.2	47.8	49.5
Total Domestic		358.1	439.8	595.0	711.7	807.9	764.7	783.5	772.0
Eurocommercial paper and other short-term Euronotes (NIFs and RUFs)	Early 1980s	29.0	50.2	66.7	69.6	89.4	106.4	115.7	110.3
Total		387.1	490.0	661.7	781.3	897.3	871.1	899.2	882.3
Medium-term note markets									
United States	Early 1970s	35.0[c]	50.0[c]	65.0[c]	76.0	100.0	142.3	175.7	210.3
United Kingdom	Mid-1990					0.7	1.9	4.9	11.9
Euro medium-term notes	Mid-1980	0.4	2.6	5.6	9.6	21.9	38.5	61.1	146.6

Data: Bank for International Settlements.
[a] Converted at current exchange rates.
[b] Up to 1991, nonfinancial institutions only.
[c] Estimate.

innovation, standardized documentation, and (in time) mature pricing and distribution methods. Its reach extended into note issuance facilities and medium-term notes (see below) and stimulated the development of domestic CP markets almost immediately all over the world. These impressive achievements are examples of the fungibility of money in a marketplace in which capital movements are not restricted and transactions flow to where they may be most efficiently effected.

NIFs and RUFs

Meanwhile, some of the large wholesale banks began to see ECP as a threat to their basic business of providing short-term credit to major industrial and government borrowers. As clients moved into ECP, they left their bank loans behind. The banks did furnish the backup credit lines and swinglines needed to access the ECP market, but the profitability of these facilities was small in relation to customary bank loans. Banks began to fear a repeat of their experience in the United States, in which the commercial paper market grew rapidly at the expense of the banks.

So, to remain competitive in offering short-term credit to their customers, the banks introduced a family of revolving-credit facilities, called note issuance facilities (NIFs), in which the customer had the choice of drawing down a loan at an agreed spread over LIBOR or selling notes (ECP) through the banks at a lower rate. The NIFs were seen by customers as a souped-up version of an ordinary ECP program, in which all of the benefits of ECP were retained while the benefits of a committed bank facility were secured. Competition among banks for NIFs resulted in a tightening of the market: Fees (a one-time fee for arrangement, and annual fees for participation and commitment) were squeezed, as were the lending spreads over LIBOR on loans drawn down under the facility.

A NIF works as follows: An issuer enters into an agreement with a bank for a $200-million revolving-credit facility for, say, seven years. The lead bank syndicates the facility with other banks, according to the normal syndication process. Funds drawn down under the facility can be repaid at will, without penalty. The issuer agrees to obtain commercial paper ratings, which in this case we can assume are A1 and P1. If the issuer decides to draw down $100 million for six-months, probably to roll it over continually, it notifies the bank that it wishes, as of a prescribed date, to either take down a six-month loan at the rate provided in the loan agreement, say LIBOR + ¼ percent, or to issue promissory notes in ECP form to a predetermined group of banks and dealers (usually led by the NIF's arranging bank) at whatever rate the dealer group may offer for distribution to investors. If an ECP alternative superior to the bank loan does not result, the banks are obligated to make the loan. Thus, for a modest set of fees, the issuer can have his cake and eat it too. That is, he can have the lower rates of the ECP market and the guaranteed assurance that funds will be forthcoming, regardless of market conditions.

NIFs come in various forms and with different features. The principal difference in form is in the method by which the ECP market is accessed. Most NIFs have "tender panels," a group of banks and dealers selected by the lead bank (and the issuer) who are obligated to bid for the ECP notes at an auction to be held when the notes are issued or to be renewed. Another approach is through a revolving underwriting facility (RUF), which differs from a NIF mainly in using a designated placement agent(s) to distribute the notes at market rates. Members of the tender panel and the placement agents can bid whatever rates they want, so their role is largely best efforts, but they can be replaced by the issuer if they fail to perform satisfactorily. The idea, however, is to get enough competent dealers to participate so that the auction process will result in bids that will provide money-market rates to the issuer. As discussed previously, money-market rates for ECP may be substantially less than the lending rates offered by banks. In an aggressive market environment, the issuer just described may be able to receive bids of $100 million of ECP at a rate of London Interbank mean (LIMEAN) (between LIBOR and LIBID) or less, thus saving $3/8$ to $1/2$ percent on the alternative bank loan. If the annualized fees are no more than the normal 10 basis points or so, the issuer is still well ahead of the game. Figure 8-1 illustrates the Euronote issuance process.

Large well-known, highly rated issuers may decide to forego the underwriting feature offered by NIFs and rely on their ability to continually resell maturing ECP. Such issuers save the arrangement and participation fees charged by the banks, but they must still pay something for backup and swinglines. Over the years, the market has developed efficient pricing for the underwriting function.

A variety of additional NIF features have been introduced by innovative banks since the mid 1980s. Among these are the ability to utilize NIFs more comprehensively, that is, for notes issued either in the U.S. commercial paper or the ECP market, for nondollar denominations of drawdown or rollovers, and for bank letters of credit to be used to provide credit backing for issuers unable to obtain satisfactory ratings. "Tap" issuing features have also been provided to allow notes to be issued frequently in small amounts to satisfy dealer demand. Such issues can involve "continuous tender panels" in which the placement agent announces daily a rate level at which all bids will be accepted. Aggressive dealers will bid below that rate to be sure to obtain the paper being auctioned.

Large U.S. commercial paper issuers, especially those issuing directly (without dealers) often utilize the tap issue method to obtain the best rates and to spread maturities widely. Direct issuers in the United States account for more than half of all U.S. commercial paper outstandings. Direct issuance is much less common in the ECP market, but increasingly large issuers are resorting to self-underwritten tap issues to effect the most efficient use of the market.

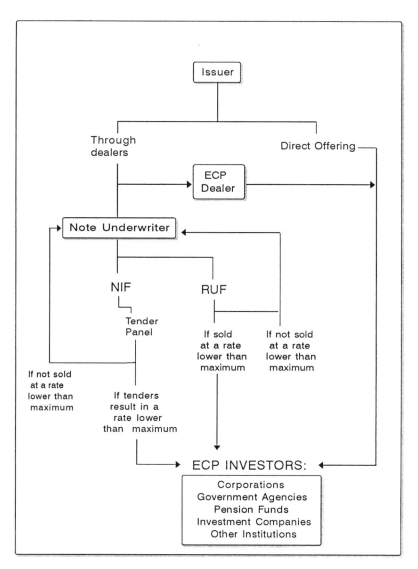

Figure 8-1. Euronote issuance process. ECP = eurocommerical paper; NIF = note issuance facility; RUF = revolving underwriting facility.

Euro Medium-Term Notes

Next in the continuous evolution of new money-market products was the Euro-medium-term note (EMTN), which followed in the wake of an expanding ECP market and the development of enhanced market activity for medium-term notes in the United States. EMTNs offer an extension of ECP market practices over greater maturities. EMTNs have had the effect of erasing the traditional boundaries between the short-term money market and bond markets.

Medium-term notes have been available in the United States since the early 1970s, but initially they were limited in use because of registration requirements and lack of a well-developed investor base for one- to five-year maturities. The introduction in 1984 of Rule 415, providing for "shelf registration" in the U.S. market, made it possible to offer MTNs continuously in the public bond market. Distribution was through dealers or directly by large issuers such as General Motors Acceptance Corporation. Rising interest rates of the 1970s, increased volatility in the fixed-income securities market, the sharp yield curves prevalent in the 1980s, and increasing sophistication of fixed-income traders attracted many investors to MTNs in the mid-1980s. Further innovations in product design by dealers and issuers, such as offering floating-rate as well as fixed-rate returns, deep-discount zero coupons, and multicurrency options, made the MTN into a highly flexible and desirable investment vehicle. The domestic U.S. MTN market matured during the period 1988–1994, during which new issue volume nearly quadrupled to $280 billion.

Similarly, the EMTN market snapped to life during the 1990–1994 period, during which sales increased tenfold to $260 billion. Globally, MTN programs exceeded $540 billion at the end of 1994. In 1990, the global total of MTN programs was only $110 billion. This growth was largely because of the flexibility that MTN programs offer large, frequent borrowers, which in the Euromarket tend to be sovereign governments and multinational institutions such as the International Finance Corporation (an affiliate of the World Bank) or the European Bank for Reconstruction and Development. Such borrowers have continuous financing requirements and use the full spectrum of the yield curve to obtain it. Changes are frequently made in their borrowing "strategies," which result in changing the maturities of outstanding liabilities to pursue opportunities for lower funding costs or to hedge against expected interest rate or foreign exchange movements.

In considering how to obtain the lowest overall cost of borrowing, such issuers also must consider the cost of issuance. EMTNs involve very low documentation costs and may be issued on a continuous, nonunderwritten basis, in which the issuer pays only a commission of a few basis points or distributes the notes itself.

In a normal Eurobond offering, an issuer must pick a time, an amount, and a currency and then auction the bonds off to the highest bidder, that is, at the lowest interest rate. The issue will be large enough (typically $150 million to $300 million) to satisfy financing requirements for at least several months, and will involve payment of underwriting and placement commissions to an underwriting group. In an EMTN program, the issuer announces to the market a program for the issuance of debt securities (PIDS) through continuous offerings over an extended period during which it hopes to raise up to a maximum amount of funds, often as much as several billion dollars. A document, similar to a U.S. Rule 415 shelf registration, is issued providing details of the program, and a one-page supplement is issued when securities are issued under it. The program is rated by the agencies, and sometimes some sort of road show is put together to inform potential investors about the issuer. When the program is ready to go, the issuer can bring out large "tranches" (say $200 million to $300 million each) under normal Euromarket underwriting methods, or resort to tap issues, or both. During 1992 only about 20 percent of all EMTN issues were done through Eurobond underwritings. The issuer can post rates, or have dealers post them, at which it is willing to take all offers. Or it can auction them off a day at a time, in any Eurocurrency it likes. If the market fails to take the paper at a maximum rate, the issuer can require its syndicate of banks to take it, if it has provided for a NIF. If the U.S. market is cheaper, the issuer might go there if a shelf registration is in effect. There are a great many options.

Treasury Securities

International money markets also include domestic short-term securities purchased by international investors. Mainly such investors are interested in government (Treasury) bills and notes because of their liquidity and high quality. These securities are available in all industrialized countries and in many less developed countries. Except during brief periods when foreign exchange markets are in turmoil pending a realignment, foreign investors rarely comprise more than a nominal percentage of the investment demand for domestic government securities. Even in the United States during the period 1984–1987, when Japanese and other foreign investors (both central banks and private sector investors) were at their most active, all foreign holdings of U.S. Treasury securities never exceeded 7 percent of the outstanding supply, of which perhaps half were official holdings of dollar reserves by foreign central banks. It is true, however, that foreign buying can be concentrated for a time on single auctions of newly issued paper, at which time the foreign demand can have a significant effect on the price of the paper being sold. Nonetheless, such concentrations of buying (or selling) power rarely last for long.

Investors acquire foreign Treasury securities for essentially two reasons. One is to take a position in a liquid instrument that is subject to an expected price change because of changing interest or foreign exchange rates. Such investments are "uncovered," or unhedged positions. The investor *wants* the risk that the deutsche mark will increase in value relative to the dollar, and that foreign "speculators" will bid up the price of German Treasury securities. The other reason is to take a "covered" position, through which the investor might pick up several basis points of yield. If the investor can buy a six-month German Treasury bill, which, when swapped into dollars, yields more than six-month U.S. Treasury bills, he may be better off. A well-informed investor will scan the world's Treasury and swap markets frequently looking for such opportunities. For a start, the investor can consult the daily posting in the *Financial Times* of world money rates, which are mainly reflections of secondary market prices for Treasury bills in the various cities (i.e., countries) indicated (Figure 8-2).

Wholesale banks in most countries are very actively involved in domestic, and frequently international, Treasury securities. A substantial portion of the large volume of trading profits reported by large U.S. banks comes from trading in U.S. government securities. Originally these banks entered into the business to provide services to customers and to effect their own transactions in the government securities market. In recent years, however, trading for the banks' own accounts has become a major business. The large market liquidity and the wide range of securities available make these securities ideal for trading. Large universal banks in most European countries and large investment banks also trade extensively in the government securities markets of several countries, often serving as a registered market-maker. Several foreign banks are registered primary market dealers in U.S. government securities.

Foreign Exchange Markets

Dealing in foreign exchange has become an increasing important activity for all international bankers and money-market investors. This is due to the continuous increase in world trade and cross-border financial flows in support of the real economy in a time of high volatility in foreign exchange markets. Customers of banks need assistance in managing and hedging their international cash flow, and banks have long been in the business of assisting them. In addition, funds flows in support of cross-border financial investments have increased substantially as a result of greater appreciation of international investment opportunities and easier mechanics through which to make them. The sums involved have been growing rapidly during the last several years and continue to do so. Investors need to fund these investments and to hedge them from time to time. Market-making by banks in foreign exchange has been an essential and profitable service to customers in both the manufacturing and financial sectors. Finally, banks and investment banks, and some investment funds, have found dealing for their own accounts to be an attractive source of potential profits. As in most trading markets, high volume and volatility make for an ideal environment for skillful participants.

Some years ago government officials, in discussing the foreign exchange markets, would refer to participants as "legitimate" commercial users, or as "speculators," presumably meaning that the latter group was something other than legitimate. This distinction, probably never very useful, is no longer used as market practices have become better understood.

■ THREE MONTH EURODOLLAR (IMM) $1m points of 100%

	Open	Sett price	Change	High	Low	Est. vol	Open int.
Jun	94.74	93.65	+0.01	93.76	93.65	113,687	515,548
Sep	93.61	93.58	+0.02	93.64	93.58	138,694	354,331
Dec	93.40	93.39	+0.04	93.48	93.39	123,591	267,386

■ US TREASURY BILL FUTURES (IMM) $1m per 100%

Jun	94.33	94.29	+0.07	94.33	94.29	1,566	14,476
Sep	94.16	94.12	+0.13	94.18	94.12	248	10,986
Dec	94.03	93.97	+0.02	94.04	93.97	56	9,958

All Open Interest figs. are for previous day

US INTEREST RATES

4pm

		Treasury Bills and Bond Yields			
		One month	5.62	Two year	6.48
Prime rate	9	Two month	5.70	Three year	6.59
Broker loan rate	6 1/2	Three month	5.79	Five year	6.80
Fed.funds	6 1/8	Six month	5.99	10-year	7.03
Fed.funds at intervention	6 1/8	One year	6.19	30-year	7.39

WORLD INTEREST RATES

MONEY RATES

April 13	Over night	One month	Three mths	Six mths	One year	Lomb. inter.	Dis. rate	Repo rate
Belgium	4 7/8	4 15/16	5 1/4	5 7/16	5 13/16	7.40	4.00	–
week ago	5 1/16	4 15/16	5 3/16	5 11/16	5 15/16	7.40	4.00	–
France	7 11/16	7 5/8	7 3/8	7	6 7/8	5.00	–	8.00
week ago	7 11/16	7 5/8	7 1/2	7 3/16	7 3/16	5.00	–	8.00
Germany	4 17/32	4 15/32	4 19/32	4 3/4	4 7/8	6.00	4.00	4.50
week ago	4.53	4 15/32	4.68	4.70	4.95	6.00	4.00	4.85
Ireland	5 15/16	6 7/16	6 5/8	6 13/16	7 5/16	–	–	6.25
week ago	5 1/8	6 7/16	7	7 1/16	7 9/16	–	–	6.25
Italy	10 1/4	10 7/16	10 9/16	10 29/32	11 1/4	–	7.50	10.46
week ago	10	10 7/16	11	11 3/8	11 3/4	–	7.50	10.44
Netherlands	4.48	4.50	4.68	4.80	5.04	–	5.25	–
week ago	4.56	4.50	4.71	4.83	5.06	–	5.25	–
Switzerland	3 1/4	3 3/8	3 3/8	3 1/2	3 5/8	6.625	3.00	–
week ago	3 1/4	3 3/8	3 3/8	3 7/16	3 9/16	6.625	3.00	–
US	5 15/16	6 1/16	6 3/16	6 3/8	6 5/8	–	5.25	–
week ago	6	6 1/16	6 3/16	6 3/8	6 11/16	–	5.25	–
Japan	2 1/16	1 21/32	1 17/32	1 1/2	1 1/2	–	1.75	–
week ago	2 1/16	1 21/32	1 9/16	1 9/16	1 9/16	–	1.75	–
■ $ LIBOR FT London								
Interbank Fixing	–	6 1/8	6 1/4	6 7/16	6 11/16	–	–	–
week ago	–	6 1/8	6 1/4	6 7/16	6 3/4	–	–	–
US Dollar CDs	–	5.88	6.02	6.21	6.51	–	–	–
week ago	–	5.88	6.06	6.26	6.59	–	–	–
SDR Linked Ds	–	4 15/16	5	5 1/16	5 1/16	–	–	–
week ago	–	4 15/16	5	5 1/16	5 1/16	–	–	–

ECU Linked Ds mid rates: 1 mth: 6 1/8; 3 mths: 6 3/16; 6 mths: 6 5/16; 1 year: 6 9/16. $ LIBOR Interbank fixing rates are offered rates for $10m quoted to the market by four reference banks at 11am each working day. The banks are: Bankers Trust, Bank of Tokyo, Barclays and National Westminster.
Mid rates are shown for the domestic Money Rates, US $ CDs and SDR Linked Deposits (Ds).

Figure 8-2. Example of money rates table. Source: *Financial Times,* April 18, 1995.

All players are simply investors; some have mundane reasons for playing, perhaps, and others have more sophisticated ones, but they cannot be distinguished in the market, which attracts transactions only because of changing investment conditions.

Increasing Turnover

The large and active foreign exchange market is like any other "free" marketplace, except for an important difference. Governments, through their central banks, intervene to regulate foreign exchange rates. Their purchases and sales, especially when there is international coordination, can make a significant difference in rates and (more important sometimes) in the expectation for future rates. Most nongovernment players see the government role as placing an artificial limit on price movements in one direction or another, and thus attempt to position themselves to benefit from it. Playing against the governments, in other words, can be extremely profitable for dealers and investors, and this (during a time of significant amounts of government intervention) has helped to increase the volume of turnover in the world foreign exchange markets considerably. As of the end of 1992, after a major foreign currency crisis involving the ERM, average *daily* foreign exchange turnover exceeded *$1 trillion*. It has increased significantly since then. Thus, the foreign exchange market is by far the world's largest financial market (Table 8-4).

Market Organization

The foreign exchange market is an informal, over-the-counter market organized into trading centers around the world. The market has no central clearinghouse or exchange, and operates only through dealers. Interdealer transactions constitute approximately 75 percent of all trading in the major centers. The dealer market is highly concentrated, with the 10 leading dealers in each major center accounting for roughly 40 percent of the market. Dealers sometimes specialize in only a few currencies, although some are more broadly active. Dealers make markets in a variety of foreign exchange products, including spot and forward rates, swaps, and other derivatives.

Table 8-4 Net Foreign Exchange Market Turnover
($ billion per day)

Country	March 1986	April 1989	April 1992	April 1995
United Kingdom	90	187	300	460
United States	59	129	192	240
Japan	48	115	128	160
Singapore	—	55	74	102
Hong Kong	—	49	61	100
Switzerland	—	57	68	98
Germany	—	—	57	96
France	—	26	35	85
Australia	—	30	30	35
Canada	9	15	22	28

Source: International Monetary Fund, April 1995.

Though the foreign exchange market is unregulated, central banks are active participants and are able to keep an eye on the behavior of banks to which regulatory controls apply, and other players from their countries. The leading center for foreign exchange trading is London, mainly because London is the center of the Eurocurrency market and overlaps both the New York and Tokyo time zones. In 1992 London accounted for about 30 percent of global forex turnover. The United States accounted for about 19 percent, Japan 13 percent, and Switzerland and Singapore 7 percent each of 1992 global forex turnover.

Market Functions

Transactions in the "spot" market reflect simple buying and selling of currencies for immediate delivery. The spot rates reflect the daily foreign exchange rates between currencies. Spot rates between various currencies comprise "exchange cross rates," a table of which is published in financial newspapers daily, and which are available on screens to market-markers in real time. "Forward" rates are spot rates plus (or minus) a "premium" that reflects the discount differential in interest rates between the currencies for the period involved. Market-makers will buy and sell forward contracts if they get out of line with their covered interest parity through arbitrage transactions.

Table 8-5 shows dollar spot and forward rates and exchange cross rates for April 17, 1995. Dealers also make markets in indexed currency "units," such as the European currency unit (ECU), the official monetary denomination of the EU, and the special drawing right (SDR) used by the IMF.

In addition to spot and forward rates, dealers also trade in currency swaps and currency options, futures, and customized currency derivative securities.

Beating the System

Dealers, on their own behalf and for the benefit of customers, often propose forex trading strategies that are intended to take advantage of the market intervention activities of central banks. Such intervention, which can be in market purchases of spot and forward contracts or in futures or options markets, can also involve resetting domestic interest rates to affect forex rates. Intervention can occur whenever economic officials of one or more countries are unhappy with the exchange rates between their currencies, and seek to adjust them. Mostly intervention takes place in the European monetary system when one or more currencies move outside the prescribed bands within which they are supposed to trade. The central banks of the EU countries are required by agreement (the exchange rate mechanism, or ERM) to support their own or other currencies when these bands are approached. As there are numerous EU countries and the movement

Table 8-5 Dollar Spot, Forward, and Cross Rates

Dollar Spot Forward Against The Dollar

Apr. 17		Closing Mid-point	Change on Day	Bid/Offer Spread	Day's Mid High	Day's Mid Low	One Month Rate	One Month %PA	Three Months Rate	Three Months %PA	One Year Rate	One Year %PA	J.P. Morgan Index
Europe													
Austria	(Sch)	9.6506	−0.1301	464–548	9.6548	9.6464	9.6391	1.4	9.6191	1.3	9.5256	1.3	107.6
Belgium	(BFr)	28.4130	−0.162	960–300	28.5700	28.3960	28.3875	1.1	28.341	1.0	28.193	0.8	109.9
Denmark	(DKr)	5.4014	−0.0601	004–024	5.4565	5.3995	5.4054	−0.9	5.4129	−0.9	5.4379	−0.7	109.2
Finland	(FM)	4.2198	−0.0597	173–223	4.2764	4.2173	4.2218	−0.6	4.2231	−0.3	4.2273	−0.2	86.3
France	(FFr)	4.7980	−0.055	960–000	4.8430	4.7960	4.8035	−1.4	4.811	−1.1	4.804	−0.1	109.9
Germany	(DM)	1.3715	−0.0185	710–720	1.3885	1.3700	1.3698	1.5	1.3661	1.6	1.3493	1.6	112.3
Greece	(Dr)	222.960	−2.78	910–010	225.490	222.640	225.26	−12.4	229.21	−11.2	246.46	−10.5	68.1
Ireland	(I£)	1.6440	+0.0105	435–445	1.6465	1.6335	1.6445	−0.4	1.6461	−0.5	1.6547	−0.7	—
Italy	(L)	1691.12	−13.88	023–200	1700.50	1690.28	1697.37	−4.4	1710.62	−4.6	1770.12	−4.7	63.8
Luxembourg	(LFr)	28.4130	−0.162	960–300	28.5700	28.3960	28.3875	1.1	28.341	1.0	28.193	0.8	109.9
Netherlands	(Fl)	1.5375	−0.0187	370–380	1.5520	1.5321	1.5357	1.4	1.5319	1.5	1.5138	1.5	109.5
Norway	(NKr)	6.1447	−0.0728	437–457	6.2307	6.1425	6.1382	1.3	6.1284	1.1	6.1022	0.7	98.2
Portugal	(Es)	144.475	−2.475	380–570	146.450	144.340	145.075	−5.0	146.225	−4.8	151.525	−4.9	96.7
Spain	(Pta)	122.150	−1.325	950–350	123.100	121.950	122.44	−2.8	123.1	−3.1	126.375	−3.5	79.5
Sweden	(SKr)	7.2043	−0.0898	993–093	7.3094	7.1988	7.2184	−2.4	7.2498	−2.5	7.4128	−2.9	76.3
Switzerland	(SFr)	1.1295	−0.0205	290–300	1.1505	1.1285	1.1268	2.8	1.1213	2.9	1.095	3.1	113.4
UK	(£)	1.6155	+0.0125	150–160	1.6175	1.6055	1.6153	0.1	1.6142	0.3	1.6038	0.7	84.1
Ecu		1.3395	+0.0118	380–410	1.3410	1.3253	1.3396	0.0	1.3397	−0.1	1.3387	0.1	—
SDR†		0.63680	—	—	—	—	—						
Americas													
Argentina	(Peso)	1.0008	−0.0002	007–008	1.0008	1.0007	—						—
Brazil	(R$)	0.9055	−0.002	050–060	0.9060	0.9050	—						—
Canada	(C$)	1.3644	−0.0041	641–646	1.3703	1.3641	1.3667	−2.0	1.3711	−1.9	1.3834	−1.4	80.8
Mexico	(New Peso)	6.2650	−0.03	500–800	6.2800	6.2500	6.2672	−0.4	6.2704	−0.3	6.2753	−0.2	—
USA	($)	—											89.3
Pacific/Middle East/Africa													
Australia	(A$)	1.3499	−0.0002	495–504	1.3575	1.3492	1.3515	−1.4	1.3554	−1.6	1.3766	−2.0	80.7
Hong Kong	(HK$)	7.7326	−0.0009	321–331	7.7331	7.7321	7.7314	0.2	7.7356	−0.2	7.7711	−0.5	—
India	(Rs)	31.4050	+0.05	000–100	31.4120	31.3700	31.485	−3.1	31.73	−4.1	—		—
Israel	(Shk)	2.9461	−0.0125	436–486	2.9709	2.9436	—						—
Japan	(¥)	82.0750	−1.245	500–000	82.8500	81.6000	81.775	4.4	81.115	4.7	78.02	4.9	172.4

236

		Closing mid-point		Change on day	Bid/offer spread					
Malaysia	(M$)	2.4635	1.0	-0.0015	625-645			2.4535	0.4	—
New Zealand	(NZ$)	1.4817	-2.8	-0.0064	810-826			1.5111	-2.0	—
Philippines	(Peso)	26.0500	—	-0.05	500-500	25.9500			—	—
Saudi Arabia	(SR)	3.7500	-0.3	-0.0005	499-501	3.7503	3.753	3.765	-0.4	—
Singapore	(S$)	1.3947	4.5	-0.0006	942-952	1.3970	1.3812	1.3547	2.9	—
South Africa	(R)	3.6065	-6.0	+0.0027	040-090	3.6090	3.6618	3.8558	-6.9	—
South Korea	(Won)	768.700	-4.7	-0.75	600-800	768.500	775.2	793.7	-3.3	—
Taiwan	(T$)	25.3378	-0.9	-0.014	255-500	25.2570	25.3978		-3.4	—
Thailand	(Bt)	24.5250	-1.0	-0.03	000-500	24.5000	24.5725	24.66	-0.6	—

†SDR rate per $ for Apr. 13. Bid/offer spreads in the Dollar Spot table show only the last three decimal places. Forward rates are not directly quoted to the market but are implied by current interest rates. UK, Ireland & ECU are quoted in US currency. J.P. Morgan nominal indices Apr. 13. Base average 1990=100.

Cross Rates and Derivatives

Exchange Cross Rates

Apr. 17	BFr	DKr	FFr	DM	I£	L	Fl	NKr	Es	Pta	SKr	SFr	£	C$	$	¥	Ecu
Belgium (BFr)	100	19.01	16.89	4.828	2.142	5952	5.412	21.63	508.5	429.8	25.36	3.976	2.179	4.802	3.519	288.9	2.627
Denmark (DKr)	52.60	10	8.883	2.540	1.127	3131	2.847	11.38	267.5	226.1	13.34	2.091	1.146	2.526	1.851	152.0	1.382
France (FFr)	59.22	11.26	10	2.859	1.268	3525	3.205	12.81	301.1	254.5	15.02	2.355	1.290	2.844	2.084	171.1	1.556
Germany (DM)	20.71	3.938	3.498	1	0.444	1233	1.121	4.480	105.3	89.03	5.253	0.824	0.451	0.995	0.729	59.84	0.544
Ireland (I£)	46.69	8.877	7.885	2.254	1	2779	2.527	10.10	237.4	200.7	11.84	1.857	1.017	2.242	1.643	134.9	1.227
Italy (L)	1.680	0.319	0.284	0.081	0.036	100.	0.091	0.363	8.543	7.222	0.426	0.067	0.037	0.081	0.059	4.854	0.044
Netherlands (Fl)	18.48	3.513	3.120	0.892	0.396	1100	1	3.996	93.96	79.43	4.686	0.735	0.403	0.887	0.650	53.38	0.486
Norway (NKr)	46.24	8.790	7.808	2.232	0.990	2752	2.502	10	235.1	198.8	11.73	1.838	1.007	2.220	1.627	133.6	1.215
Portugal (Es)	19.67	3.739	3.321	0.949	0.421	1171	1.064	4.253	100.	84.53	4.987	0.782	0.428	0.944	0.692	56.81	0.517
Spain (Pta)	23.26	4.423	3.929	1.123	0.498	1385	1.259	5.031	118.3	100.	5.900	0.925	0.507	1.117	0.819	67.21	0.611
Sweden (SKr)	39.43	7.497	6.659	1.904	0.845	2347	2.134	8.528	200.5	169.5	10	1.568	0.859	1.893	1.387	113.9	1.036
Switzerland (SFr)	25.15	4.781	4.247	1.214	0.539	1497	1.361	5.439	127.9	108.1	6.378	1	0.548	1.208	0.885	72.66	0.661
UK (£)	45.90	8.726	7.751	2.216	0.983	2732	2.484	9.927	233.4	197.3	11.64	1.825	1	2.204	1.615	132.6	1.206
Canada (C$)	20.83	3.959	3.517	1.005	0.446	1240	1.127	4.504	105.9	89.52	5.281	0.828	0.454	1	0.733	60.16	0.547
US ($)	28.42	5.403	4.799	1.372	0.609	1692	1.538	6.147	144.5	122.2	7.207	1.130	0.619	1.365	1	82.11	0.747
Japan (¥)	34.62	6.581	5.845	1.671	0.741	2060	1.873	7.486	176.0	148.8	8.778	1.376	0.754	1.662	1.218	100.	0.910
Ecu	38.06	7.235	6.427	1.837	0.815	2265	2.060	8.231	193.5	163.6	9.652	1.513	0.829	1.828	1.339	110.0	1

Source: Financial Times, April 18, 1995.

Danish Kroner, French Franc, Norwegian Kroner, and Swedish Kronor per 10; Belgian Franc, Yen, Escudo, Lira and Peseta per 100.

of currencies within the ERM can at times be considerable, there is ample room for intervention by EU central banks. Intervention can also occur in the U.S. dollar market relative to major currencies, such as the yen or the deutsche mark, when such currencies move toward extreme values relative to the dollar. In recent years the U.S. government has resisted intervention in order to let market forces work to effect stabilizing changes in trade flows, even at the "cost" of a weaker dollar.

Most of the action in recent years has been with the ERM currencies. In September 1992 and again in June 1993, major currency realignments forced the withdrawal of the pound from the ERM (along with a substantial devaluation of it by the market), the refixing of several currencies' support levels, and ultimately (after a fierce attack on the French franc) a major widening of the support bands from 2.5 percent to 15 percent, which had the effect of suspending the ERM entirely. These events are discussed in greater detail in chapter 6.

During this period of currency intervention, great sums were invested by central banks in support mechanisms (approximately £50 billion was expended unsuccessfully in support of sterling by the central banks of Britain and Germany), and great fortunes were made by bold investors who invested heavily against them. A prominent American investor (a hedge fund manager) is thought to have made profits of $1 billion from the sterling crisis. Many banks and dealers made large profits as well.

There are principally two trading strategies used by private investors during such crises. One is to sell the vulnerable currency forward for one or two months, often against the stronger currency. Large positions must be taken to make meaningful profits, because even if the weaker currency is devalued, it may not be by more than a few percent. These positions are taken with borrowed funds requiring credit agreements, since forward contracts do not require cash outlays. A large gain could occur if, say, sterling were devalued relative to the deutsche mark by 10 percent over a three-week period. The costs of the position are principally the costs of borrowing sterling at a high interest rate (the burden of the weaker currency) less interest income from German Treasury bills, which usually carry relatively low interest rates during currency crises, plus transaction and margin costs. If the investor bets right, there is an ample margin to fund the interest differential and transaction costs, but if sterling manages to resist devaluation and survive the crisis, the investor's loss will be limited to the interest differential. Once the crisis is past, however, sterling might rally relative to the DM, so it is important to be flexible enough to get out of the position on a timely basis.

Another strategy is to establish interest-rate positions in the weak currency (e.g., through purchases of bonds or through forwards or futures contracts) once the crisis has begun, on the expectation that after the crisis interest rates in the devalued currency, pushed up during the effort to prevent devaluation, would drop sharply causing a corresponding increase in bond values.

The two strategies are different, and involve different risks. To make money, however, both depend on the weaker currency being devalued. Other strategies that bet on the weaker currency surviving the crisis unchanged are also possible. Such a strategy, for example, could involve borrowing deutsche marks (at relatively low rates) to buy U.K. Treasury bills at relatively high rates.

Competing in Money-Market and Foreign Exchange Trading

There are a great many competitors in the international money and foreign exchange markets. Some firms specialize in these activities, but most conduct them as a part of a broader commitment to financial market-making. Commissions are very thin in these high-volume markets, and most firms make their money from trading.

In money markets in particular, trading success depends on an effective distribution system through which positions can be bought and sold at reasonable prices. This usually means being closely in touch with investors, corporations, and end-users in general. (Nobody gets rich trading only with market-makers like Salomon Brothers). It also depends on having good information, through salesperson feedback and from contact with other dealers and issuers. Telecommunications systems have to be as modern as possible to stay in contact with market players all around the world. Indeed these are so important that many firms regard their own as "competitive weapons."

Foreign exchange trading inevitably means substantial position-taking, if a dealer expects to make much money. This is a risky and volatile business for most dealers, and all ways possible to minimize risk by hedging and by using derivatives and technical trading strategies are utilized. Most of the larger players are commercial banks, which have a natural competitive advantage in comparison with nonbank dealers in the daily foreign exchange order flow from their customers. Being able to trade with customers in large volumes helps to protect the bank's overall dealer spread (between the buy and sell rates quoted), and serves to ensure at least a minimal level of profitability. Adding more aggressive trading for the bank's own account, in which large speculative positions are taken, can boost trading revenues considerably. Table 8-6 shows the foreign exchange trading income of several major U.S. banks from 1984 through 1993.

The table illustrates several interesting aspects of the foreign exchange activities of these banks. First it shows that the business, however risky, has been profitable for all ten banks in every year since 1984. All but two of the banks earned more than $100 million from foreign exchange trading in 1992. Citibank earned over $1 billion in foreign exchange in 1992; but in 1989 its $471 million of income was 25 percent less than the year before. Bankers Trust has shown substantial volatility in its foreign exchange trading income all through the period. All of the banks except

Table 8-6 Foreign Exchange Trading Income of Major U.S. Banks[a]

Bank	1990	1991	1992	1993	1994
Bank of America[a]	207.0	246.0	300.0	325.0	237.0
Bankers Trust	425.0	272.0	331.0	191.0	(54.0)
Chase Manhattan Bank	217.2	215.0	327.0	356.0	280.0
Chemical Bank	207.2	289.0	363.0	302.0	152.9
Citibank[b]	657.0	709.0	1005.0	995.0	573.0
First Chicago	102.8	95.1	109.5	104.9	42.0
Bank of New York	47.6	47.0	66.0	54.0	27.0
Marine Midland	3.4	3.1	3.2	7.3	3.6
J. P. Morgan & Co.	309.0	218.3	359.6	304.4	131.0
Republic New York Corp.	77.3	81.4	102.6	111.6	91.0
Total	2,253.5	2,175.9	2,966.9	2,751.2	1,483.5

Data: Annual Reports/10Ks/Call Report Data.
[a] Millions of dollars exclusive of translation income.
[b] Includes translation gains and losses.

Marine Midland, a subsidiary of Hongkong Shanghai Bank, have clearly placed heavy emphasis on foreign exchange trading as an important source of noninterest income. The group as a whole increased foreign exchange trading income fourfold during the period, from $743 million in 1984 to over $2.7 billion in 1993.

Consultants and other experts who offer services predicting market behavior, or access to "inside thinking" on the part of government officials, make a good living, but there is little evidence that they know any more than the market reveals in the price of the instruments and contracts. Technical trading strategies can be successful, but like all trading, success seems mainly to depend on discipline, courage, capital, technical skills, and experience. Most market-makers would also add that good luck plays a major role in successful trading. Most of their supervisors would add that effective internal control procedures are also essential.

Summary

International money and foreign exchange markets have developed enormously over the past several years. This is largely the result of increasing trade and international investment, but it also reflects improvements in technology and know-how on the part of the major banks and their clients. The once modest Eurocurrency money market has now emulated its U.S. counterpart in variety of instruments available for trading, in types of investors served, and even in volume of trading. Global investors and issuers of securities now have a very large choice of instruments and rates, and they may move from one market to the next in search of a better deal. Such choices serve to bring rates together and thereby integrate the money markets in the United States with those outside it. As the Eurocurrency market has developed in size and complexity, money has been drawn away, or disintermediated, from commercial banks. To address this competitive threat, many major international banks have adapted their products to the markets and have become active suppliers of ECP and EMTNs to their customers.

Foreign exchange trading has also grown substantially during the past several years with increasing volatility and cross-border investment activity. Banks have benefited from the many market-making opportunities that these developments have presented. Some nonbank financial service firms have also been attracted to the foreign exchange markets for the first time and have prospered in it. In both foreign exchange and money markets, trading skills are increasingly useful, and the most successful banks have made their trading activities into one of their most important noninterest activities.

9

Eurobonds and Other International Debt Issues

Before 1963, the method used to raise long-term capital from international sources was to float a bond issue in some other country, denominated in the currency of that country and issued in accordance with the standard procedures of the bond market there, usually at a premium interest rate reflecting the exotic nature of the borrower and/or the possibility of difficulties in collecting payments due. Such issues are and have long been called "foreign bonds."

In the Beginning, Foreign Bonds

Today when foreigners issue dollar-denominated bonds registered with the U.S. Securities and Exchange Commission the bonds are called "Yankee bonds"; those registered with the Japanese Ministry of Finance and denominated in yen are "Samurai bonds"; those involving sterling in the United Kingdom are "Bulldog bonds"; and so on. They are all, however, foreign bonds. Each must comply exactly with the capital market registration and distribution requirements of the country concerned. This usually means publication of a prospectus in the language of the country, adherence to disclosure and accounting requirements, and adoption of local underwriting and securities distribution methods.

The total annual volume of foreign bonds averaged only $2.6 billion during the period 1964–1974. Then, after the removal of certain U.S. capital market controls in 1974, volume jumped sharply and averaged about $16 billion annually for the rest of the 1970s. By the end of the 1980s, foreign bonds, stimulated by the appearance of the Samurai market and much greater usage of the Swiss market (the Swiss do not allow Swiss franc-denominated bonds to be issued outside Switzerland), accounted for about $30 billion to $40 billion of new issues each year, and about twice that amount just a few years later. Though current volumes are large by foreign bond standards, they still represent a relatively small part of the total international bond market.

The growth of foreign bonds was hampered by a number of disadvantages to issuers and investors alike. International issuers had to meet local registration disclosure requirements at considerable expense; delays were usually involved while issuers prepared the necessary documents and translations or waited for permission to proceed. Underwriting fees and other expenses of issuance were often high. The effect of these requirements and practices led issuers to look for other ways to raise funds abroad.

Pioneering Days

By the early 1960s, an alternative form of bond issue had developed, the Eurobond, which minimized these disadvantages while offering international investors a better selection of currencies, maturities, and familiar names. The Eurobond market became the preferred international market for most issuers after 1980. Today this market is far larger than the foreign bond market (together these two types of bonds—foreign and Euro—are referred to as "international bonds") and is comparable in size to the U.S. investment-grade corporate bond market (see Figure 9-1, Table 9-1). The

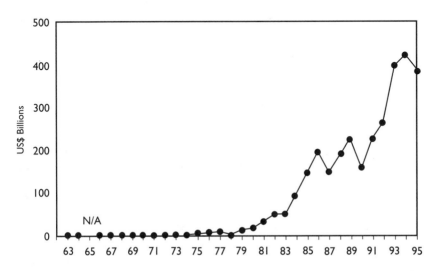

Figure 9-1. Increase in new issues of Eurobonds, 1963–95. Source: IFR securities data as reported by *Institutional Investor.*

Table 9-1　The Maturing Eurobond Market, Volume of New Issues ($ billions)

	1990	1991	1992	1993	1994	1995
U.S. bonds, total	418.71	670.04	976.10	1225.40	792.7	756.5
Corporate (Baa and above)	106.72	193.74	271.20	389.20	342.5	417.3
International bonds	224.86	267.40	342.13	482.70	485.2	385.1
Eurobonds	159.19	228.02	265.79	388.00	425.9	322.4
Foreign bonds	65.65	39.38	76.34	94.70	59.3	62.7

Data: Securities Data Corp. and IFR.

combined U.S. bond market includes U.S. Treasuries, corporate bonds of varying quality, various forms of collateralized securities, and tax-free municipal securities.

Eurobonds originally were fixed-rate, unsecured promissory notes denominated in United States dollars that were issued by a corporation or government entity. They were issued outside the United States and therefore were not required to be registered with the SEC or any other national securities authority. Not being registered with the SEC, however, these bonds could not be sold in the United States or to U.S. citizens. Instead, they were sold to non-U.S. residents, principally wealthy individuals and international institutions, who wished to invest in high-grade U.S. dollar-denominated securities. Investors paid for the bonds by charging a Eurodollar deposit account in a European bank, or in a European branch of a U.S. bank. The dollar deposits in banks had accumulated outside the United States (because of the growing U.S. balance of payments deficit and regulatory factors) and as most of these were in Europe, they became known as Eurodollar deposit accounts, or Eurodollars. Once Eurodollars came into existence, they had to be invested in loans or other instruments. Banks sought out Eurodollar borrowers, and soon the Eurodollar certificate of deposit appeared. It was only a matter of time before a fixed-rate, medium-term, high-grade instrument denominated in Eurodollars would appear.[1]

Inspired by U.S. Capital Controls

These were the days of the Bretton Woods fixed-exchange-rate system in which the noncommunist world's currencies were linked to the U.S. dollar and the dollar was pegged to gold. Countries often defended their exchange rates by the imposition of foreign exchange and/or capital controls. In 1963, in an attempt to stem the outflow of dollars, the United States imposed an interest equalization tax, intended to deter foreign governments and corporations from borrowing in the United States foreign bond markets. Later, controls imposed by the Commerce Department's Office of Foreign Direct Investment required U.S. companies investing abroad to raise the money outside of the United States. So a supply of borrowers— Europeans who could no longer borrow in the United States and U.S. companies that now had to borrow outside the United States—met with a growing supply of funds in the form of Eurodollars.

The First Eurobond

The first Eurobond was a $15 million issue for Autostrade, an Italian toll road authority guaranteed by an Italian government agency. The issue was managed in June 1963 by the London firm of S.G. Warburg and co-managed by banks in Belgium, Germany, the Netherlands, and Luxembourg. It was underwritten according to the U.S. underwriting system, in which the issue is announced, syndicated, and marketed for about two weeks before it is priced (as opposed to the British system in which the issue is priced, syndicated, and then offered to subscribers, with the underwriters liable for the unsubscribed portion of the issue). The banks could not offer the bonds to the general public (they were not registered in any of the European countries) but did make them available "privately" to their investment clients, many of whom had granted discretion over their investments to the banks involved. The bonds were listed on the Luxembourg Stock Exchange where the banks and their investors could check secondary market prices from time to time.[2]

The Autostrade issue became the prototype for many other issues by various European entities, almost entirely government-related credits. U.S. investment banks with sales offices throughout Europe became active participants in the market, having sharpened their selling skills by distributing foreign bonds issued in the United States by European government and agencies to investors elsewhere in Europe.[2]

Investor Anonymity

U.S. corporates were held in high esteem by investors, and when they and their bankers volunteered responsible standards of disclosure and investor protection these were accepted without question. However, most of the early investors were wealthy families or privately owned businesses, whose financial affairs were managed by banks in Switzerland, Luxembourg, Belgium, France, and to some extent the United Kingdom. Many such investors were unwilling to purchase U.S. corporate securities, despite their high regard for the corporation issuing the paper. Their reluctance came partly from the fact that in the United States issuers were required to withhold part of the required interest payment due to foreigner investors (to ensure that any U.S. taxes due would be paid). The amount withheld could often be reclaimed by filing a tax return in the United States, but few European investors were willing to do that. They were also reluctant to purchase registered bonds, which required them to disclose their name and address to the issuing company. They preferred bonds that were payable to the bearer, which did not require any such disclosure of the identity of the investor. In the United States only registered bonds were available. Eurobond buyers, however, were concerned that the Internal Revenue Service, the corporation, or some other entity might someday pass information on file about them to the tax officials of their country and reveal wealth or other transactions that the investor was trying to conceal. To attract these investors, there could be no withholding tax and no registered bonds, which meant that American companies would have to issue their bonds in bearer form through subsidiaries in various tax-haven jurisdictions, usually the Netherlands Antilles, guaranteed by the parent companies. The United States repealed the withholding tax on interest paid to foreigners in 1984, thus ending the requirement for issuing Eurobonds through tax haven subsidiaries.

Eurobonds after the Collapse of Bretton Woods

Thus the Eurobond market had an early assist from regulations imposed by the U.S. government. Exchange controls erected to assist in managing the balance of payments forced both U.S. and non-U.S. issuers to use the Eurobond market, despite the fact that interest rates were higher there than in the United States. The incorporation of issuing subsidiaries outside the United States enabled corporations to avoid the withholding tax and as a result substantially increased investment demand for the securities, even though the rates the investors would receive might be below comparable rates available in the home market.

By 1971 the world financial system installed at the 1944 Bretton Woods conference was no longer able to cope with the pressure brought on the dollar by the U.S. balance-of-payments deficits and the fixed-exchange-rate system broke down. The United States closed the "gold window" by refusing to exchange gold for dollars with foreigners, and as a result the dollar was "floated." This instituted the floating-exchange-rate system, in which the foreign exchange market would set the exchange rates for different currencies on the basis of balance of payments and other funds flows. It was thought that the changing price of foreign exchange would, over time, adjust balance-of-payments disequilibria. Accordingly, there was no further need for such capital controls as the interest equalization tax and foreign direct investment regulations, both of which were abolished in 1974.

But the pool of Eurodollars did not dissipate. Owners of dollars were permitted to sell them in the market, transfer them to accounts in New York, or purchase other assets with them. Many holders of dollars, particularly individuals, retained them in Eurodollar investments for the tax and secrecy advantages. In the aftermath of the first oil shock of October 1973, the trade surpluses of the London-oriented Organization of Petroleum Exporting Countries (OPEC) became a primary source of Eurodollar balances. The Eurobond market then began in earnest, as liquidity built up and trading in Eurodollars and other instruments increased. These conditions, in turn, began to attract European and multinational *institutional* (as opposed to *individual*) investors to the market in a significant way.

The Eurobond Boom, 1981–1985

By 1980 institutional participation in the market was at such a high level that an infrastructure began to develop to support it. Purveyors of such services as bond brokerage (arranging for the sale and purchase of bonds between dealers), "when issued" trading (or "gray-market trading"—i.e., buying and selling of primary securities before the actual offer date), and bond market research began to arrive in London like waves of an assault force. More capital was committed and more traders and sales personnel were hired. It became important to many banks to be "seen" in the right issues. Some of this was nonsense, but it expanded the market nevertheless, and as the dollar turned, after tighter monetary policies were introduced in 1979 and Ronald Reagan was elected president in 1980, from a scorned and underappreciated currency to a much admired and overvalued one, the Eurobond market soared. The dollar became one of the world's strongest currencies, and unlike strong currencies in the past, yielded very high rates of interest, so the demand for Eurobonds rose to a point where European investors would pay more for a U.S. corporate obligation than American investors would.

Lower Rates Offered to Issuers

This enthusiasm for Eurobonds was spurred by competition and by the expectation that total investment profits would include attractive foreign exchange gains. It was also greatly influenced by the fact that investors could buy Eurobonds of top-grade U.S. companies free of withholding taxes on interest whereas they couldn't buy U.S. Treasury securities on the same basis. So high-grade corporates became the substitutes for U.S. government securities in the eyes of Euro investors. In the end, a kind of competitive bidding to get the top names developed among investors and the retail investors, as might be expected, won out—that is, they bid the highest prices, or the lowest interest yields for the bonds. Thus, during the 1981–1985 period it was quite common for U.S. companies rated AA and better to borrow 5- to 10-year money in Europe more cheaply than they could in the United States, and in some cases, more cheaply than the U.S. Treasury could borrow. This condition resulted in a surge of Euro issues. In 1982, for example, several U.S. investment banks found that they had sold more corporate bonds at new issue in London than they had in New York—a fact many firms found hard to believe, and that few would duplicate in the years after 1983.

Participation by Institutions

This feeding frenzy, however, occurred at a time when U.S. nominal interest rates were declining and the dollar was rising. Treasury securities were readily available as the growing fiscal deficit brought the government to market more and more often. (If this did not crowd U.S. companies out then perhaps it nudged them toward Europe.) It was not important whether an issuer was known as a multinational corporation—many companies that were entirely domestic, including some U.S. public utilities and even savings and loan associations, came in. And the investors began to include insurance companies from Birmingham, bond funds from Lyons, pension fund managers in Melbourne, and agricultural cooperatives in Osaka. Some of these investors had only recently been allowed to invest overseas by their home governments, which were following patterns occurring elsewhere and dismantling overseas investment restrictions. These institutions were increasingly interested in secondary market liquidity and sophisticated trading ideas, neither of which had been especially important to the retail customer base. Retail investors wanted simple issues of well-known companies that they could hold until maturity.

During the 1980s, the effort to involve the institutions resulted in much emphasis on new investment ideas and market-making. Bonds with warrants to purchase additional bonds, zero-coupon bonds, and floating-rate notes appeared at this time. New issue volume increased, and so did the size of individual issues, from an average below $100 million in 1983 to over $200 million by the end of 1992. Market-making, however, was difficult, in part because of the high volume of aggressively priced new issues that often were out of line with secondary market price levels, and because the float in Eurobonds was thin. Though no precise data exist as to the extent of this participation, certain Swiss banks have estimated that during the 1980s some 40 to 60 percent of all Eurobonds ultimately found their way into Swiss-managed accounts of individuals, where for the most part they were held until maturity. By contrast, less than 5 percent of U.S. corporate bonds are ever bought by individuals. During this period, opportunities for hedging and borrowing bonds for short-selling by market-makers were limited.

The World's Only Unregulated Capital Market

The Eurobond market is virtually unregulated. It is, however, subject to self-imposed standards of practice. Eurobonds are typically listed on the London or Luxembourg stock exchange in order to attract investors, and each stock exchange has its own specific disclosure requirements. The issues themselves are typically made subject to U.K. law. And the Association of International Bond Dealers (AIBD), a nongovernmental industry association, sets minimum trading standards.

These standards differ from legal requirements. Whereas individual firms may be regulated by their national authorities, there are no legal requirements on the part of the issuer or bankers to provide for investor protection, orderly markets, or courts of law in which to deal with disputes or abuses. Until 1987 there were no financial regulations that applied to the market, such as queuing, capital requirements for underwriters, or margin rules. However, the Financial Services Act, passed by the British Parliament in 1987, provides for certain capital and other requirements for all Eurobond market participants using London as a base. There is also a draft EC directive proposing minimum capital requirements for securities dealers that would parallel the capital adequacy standards adopted for banks, especially in the area of swaps and other derivative securities (see chapter 10).

Market conduct has been self-regulated and as such has performed remarkably well. As distinct from normal domestic securities markets, however, the Euromarket is substantially a wholesale market in which sophisticated issuers and investors participate, and offenders can only be punished by rejection. The market is easy to enter as a competitor, and competition between dealers has always been sharp. Risk-taking and new product innovation, and quick copying, have been as well developed in the Euromarket as anywhere in the world. It has never been an easy market to make money in and requires a substantial commitment of talent and capital. Thus it has tended to be dominated by 25 or so primary players who have set the rules and procedures that the market must follow. The market as a whole has a practical stance; emphasis has always been on doing what works in a manner so as to permit doing it again. Recently, large U.S. institutional investors have found the Eurobond market attractive as a source of nondollar investments and arbitrage opportunities.

The absence of regulation, the lack of barriers to competition, and the variety of players have made the Eurobond market a hothouse for innovation. Many of the best ideas to influence the U.S. bond markets had their origin in the Eurobond market: the "bought deal" (see "New Issue Procedures" later in this chapter), the zero-coupon bond, the floating-rate note, currency option bonds, bonds with swaps, and convertible put bonds are just some of the successful innovations in Europe that have been copied in New York. The Section 415 underwriting rules introduced by the SEC in 1984, which provide virtually immediate access by companies to the U.S. bond market (which permitted the bought deal to be imported to the United States) are also a result of imported innovation that led to significant deregulation. Similar rule revisions have occurred in other countries, especially Japan, which has imported almost all of its new capital market products during the past 15 years or so.

The Market Matures

These new investors included European pension and insurance funds of U.S. and other companies, bank trust departments, investment companies, supranational financial institutions such as the World Bank and central banks of various countries, and increasingly, after 1973, Middle East funds managed by Western financial institutions. After the election of Margaret Thatcher in 1979 and the removal of British foreign exchange controls soon thereafter, U.K. institutional investors also began to enter the market, although modestly at first.

Although Eurodollar bond issues have been floated throughout the past 30 years during times of both a strong and a weak dollar, the bulk of market activity has remained in dollars even during times when the currency has been weak. The foreign exchange situation has always had a significant effect on the Eurobond market, which of course is not the case in the U.S. domestic bond market. Figure 9-2 shows how the market for nondollar issues increases during periods of a weak dollar—as best demonstrated in 1991, when less than 40 percent of all new Eurobond issues were dollar denominated.

The Eurobond market began to broaden during the late 1980s as globally oriented institutions began to participate more actively, especially in the nondollar sector. These institutions were capable of bond arbitrage, using options and futures to hedge positions and managing portfolios according to the latest techniques. In addition, they were offered an increasing supply of interesting and relatively liquid investment opportunities in deutsche marks, yen, ECUs, and other nondollar instruments. The Euro-

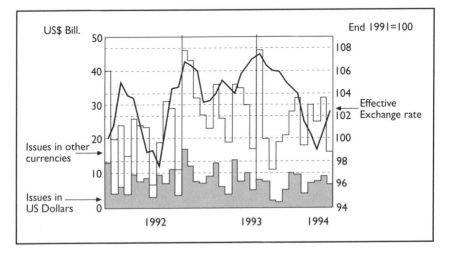

Figure 9-2. Issuing activity in the bond market (straight fixed-rate issues, on an announced basis) and the U.S. dollar effective exchange rate. Source: Bank of England and the Bank for International Settlements.

bond market, noted the *Institutional Investor* in an article commemorating its thirtieth year, is

> maturing into a more efficient, forthright citizen of the globe. What the first dealers knew as an offshore dollar market with a retail investor base of tax-dodging Continental coupon clippers is now something else altogether. [Dealers] . . . think in terms of world-wide capital flows, powerful institutional investors and a broader mix of borrowers than exists in any domestic market.

Eurobond Issuers

Eurobond issuers represent a vast variety of governmental and corporate organizations from all over the world, which find capital-raising opportunities in this market to be superior, or supplementary, to markets at home. Supranational institutions (such as the World Bank and the European Union) are frequent borrowers, as are agencies of European, Asian, Australasian, Latin American, and other governments. Large banks have used the floating rate note (FRN) market, which accounts for about 40 percent of all new issues, to fund their own lending books or for swaps. FRNs pay a rate tied to the London Interbank Offered Rate, or LIBOR, and are repriced every three months or so, so as to allow the notes to trade at par. Industrial corporations and their captive finance subsidiaries are also active borrowers.

Bonds are issued in fixed- and floating-rate form, in a variety of currencies, often accompanied by interest-rate or currency swaps. Maturities tend to be less than 10 years, averaging around 5 to 6 years. Most bonds are offered in *plain vanilla* form, that is, with no early call provisions or no sinking funds. Bonds with special features, called *bells and whistles,* are less frequent but do appear in force when market conditions are ripe. Most bonds are rated by Moody's and Standard & Poor's, even those issued by non-U.S. companies and governments. Clearance and settlement of Eurobond trades is generally done on a book-entry basis by one of two efficient private companies, Euroclear and Cedel.

Tables 9-2 and 9-3 show the volume of Eurobonds in 1994 broken down by types of securities and country of issuance, and by currency of issuance.

The Financial Times of London on June 1, 1993, listed more than 50 bonds in its daily "New International Bond Issues" table, including issues in 13 different currencies (or currency units like the ECU) (see Table 9-4). The figure includes nine issues by Japanese companies. During the latter part of the 1980s and the early 1990s, Japanese companies were the most frequent of all issuers.

Japanese companies face a highly regulated and expensive corporate bond market in Tokyo and as a result have made heavy use of the Euromarket compared with their domestic alternative. During the period 1984–

Table 9-2 Country Versus Type of Security, Eurobond New Issues, 1994

| | All Issues | | Straight Bonds | | Floating Rate Notes | | Equity Related | | | |
| | | | | | | | Convertibles | | Equity Warrants | |
	Amount[a]	No. of Issues	Amount[a]	No. of Issues	Amount[a]	No. of Issues	Amount[a]	No. of Issues	Amount[a]	No. of Issues
Japan	40.8	630	19.8	322	7.4	143	4.8	72	8.5	93
Supra/Multinat'l	32.9	146	30.2	127	2.6	19	—	—	—	—
France	30.1	234	24.6	195	3.8	29	1.5	8	0.2	2
United Kingdom	27.9	142	17.1	81	9.9	56	8.4	5	—	—
United States	59.7	296	33.3	195	24.0	93	2.3	8	—	—
Germany	47.3	355	43.2	321	3.6	28	0.1	1	0.3	5
Canada	19.3	63	13.0	53	6.2	9	0.2	1	—	—
Finland	9.1	37	5.5	20	3.2	13	0.3	4	—	—
Sweden	21.2	105	13.0	81	8.1	23	0.1	1	—	—
Austria	8.7	56	7.6	44	0.8	10	—	—	0.2	2
Italy	17.1	63	9.6	35	7.0	25	0.5	3	—	—
Netherlands	18.7	162	16.6	140	0.8	11	1.1	8	0.2	3
Norway	0.8	6	0.7	5	0.1	1	—	—	—	—
Spain	7.4	19	6.4	13	1.0	6	—	—	—	—
Mexico	6.2	33	3.2	18	2.0	11	1.0	4	—	—
Australia	11.8	108	7.8	87	3.9	20	0.1	1	—	—
Brazil	3.4	47	2.7	39	0.5	6	—	—	0.2	2
Denmark	2.1	29	1.7	25	0.2	3	0.2	1	—	—
Switzerland	6.5	42	3.9	27	0.9	8	0.1	2	1.7	5
Belgium	8.4	139	8.2	136	0.2	3	—	—	—	—
Argentina	4.3	39	3.0	29	0.8	7	0.2	2	0.2	1
Others	42.5	354	13.0	107	20.3	141	1.7	103	0.3	3
Total	425.9	3105	284.1	2100	107.4	665	22.5	224	11.8	116

Data: IFR 1063, January 7, 1995.
[a]U.S. dollars in billions.

Table 9-3 Currency versus Type of Security, Eurobonds/International Issues through December 31, 1994

| | All Issues | | Straight Bonds | | Floating Rate Notes | | Equity Related | | | |
| | | | | | | | Convertibles | | Equity Warrants | |
	Amount[a]	No. of Issues	Amount[a]	No. of Issues	Amount[a]	No. of Issues	Amount[a]	No. of Issues	Amount[a]	No. of Issues
US $[b]	163.3	841	76.1	356	70.7	370	11.1	82	5.1	30
Japanese yen[c]	70.3	675	57.9	557	9.2	103	2.2	14	1.0	1
Deutsche mark	33.0	133	24.6	80	7.7	44	0.03	1	0.6	8
Pound sterling[d]	30.5	150	17.7	80	12.0	64	0.9	6	0.0	0
French franc	25.3	91	22.0	73	1.4	8	1.5	8	0.4	2
ECU	7.3	33	7.3	33	0.0	0	0.0	0	0.0	0
Swiss franc	21.6	313	12.2	123	1.3	25	3.5	91	4.6	74
Canadian $	14.0	123	12.7	115	1.4	8	0.0	0	0.0	0
Italian lira	19.9	150	17.9	134	1.5	13	0.5	3	0.0	0
Dutch guilder	12.5	77	11.8	68	0.2	2	0.5	7	0.0	0
Luxembourgian franc	11.9	317	11.7	311	0.1	3	0.02	2	0.1	1
Australian $	7.6	109	7.2	104	0.4	5	0.0	0	0.0	0
Spanish peseta[e]	1.6	14	1.4	11	0.2	3	0.0	0	0.0	0
Austrian schilling	1.4	9	1.0	7	0.4	2	0.0	0	0.0	0
Swedish krona	2.1	19	2.1	19	0.0	0	0.0	0	0.0	0
Danish krone	0.8	14	0.6	13	0.0	0	0.2	1	0.0	0
Portugese escudo[f]	0.4	7	0.1	2	0.3	5	0.0	0	0.0	0
New Zealand $	0.1	2	0.1	2	0.0	0	0.0	0	0.0	0
Hong Kong $	2.5	35	0.7	15	1.8	20	0.0	0	0.0	0
Irish punt	0.1	3	0.1	3	0.0	0	0.0	0	0.0	0
Finnish markka	0.7	5	0.3	1	0.0	0	0.3	4	0.0	0
Total	427.0	3120	285.6	2107	108.4	675	20.8	219	11.8	116

Data: IFR 1063, January 7, 1995.
[a] U.S. dollars in billions.
[b] Including Yankee issues.
[c] Including Samurai and Shibosai issues.
[d] Including bulldogs.
[e] Including matadors.
[f] Including navigator.

Table 9-4. New International Bond Issues

Borrower	Amount m.	Maturity	Coupon %	Price	Yield %	Launch Spread bp	Book Runner
U.S. Dollars							
Chugal Pharmaceutical Co.(a)Φ	220	Jun. 1997	1.125	100	—	—	Nomura International
C. Italiano, Hong Kong(c)‡	50	Jun. 2003	(c)	99.75R	—	—	Credito Italiano, Milan
Asian Development Bank	500	Jun. 2003	6.375	99.28R	6.475	+23 (6¼%–03)	Lehman/JP Morgan
Nissan Intl. Finance (Neths.)‡	125	Jun. 2006	(f)	100R	—	—	IBJ International
Gatic(g)	35	Jun. 1995	11	99.4R	11.500	+735 (37/8%–95)	Paribas Capital Markets
JDC Corp.(j)Φ	140	Jun. 1997	1.125	.100	—	—	Nikko Europe
American Express TRS Co.(k)‡	125	Jun. 1998	(k)	99.9R	—	—	Lehman Brothers Intl.
Amer Group(l)§	75	Jun. 2003	6.25	100R	—	—	NatWest Securities
Cemex	1bn	Jun. 1998	8.875#	99.53R	8.994	+370 (53/8%–98)	JP Morgan Securities
Republic of Italy(q)	300	Jun. 2003	6.625	97.915R	6.921	+75 (6¼%–03)	Morgan Stanley Intl.
Banespa	130	Jun. 1996	11#	100R	11.000	+650 (4¼%–96)	CSFB
Banco Safra(r)	55	Jun. 1998	8.625#	99.615R	8.800	+450 (r)	Bear Stearns Intl.
Bitumenes Orinoco(u)*‡	50	Nov. 1996	(u)	100	—	—	JP Morgan Securities
Vattenfall Treasury	500	Jun. 1998	6	99.838R	6.038	+62.5 (53/8%–98)	CSFB
Kotobuklya Co.†	30	Jun. 1998	(v)	100	—	—	LTCB International
Yen							
Mitsubishi Corp. Finance	10bn	Sep. 1996	4.35	100.1R	4.32	—	Sanwa International
Nissho Iwai Europe(w)	3bn	Sep. 1994	3.55	100R	3.550	—	IBJ International
Nissho Iwai Europe‡	3bn	Sep. 1994	(x)	100R	—	—	IBJ International
D-Marks							
Conti-Gummi Finance(h)Φ	250	Jul. 2000	7.5	120.25	—	—	Deutsche Bank
Deutsche Finance Netherlands	500	Jun. 1998	6.5	101.85	6.060	—	Deutsche Bank
French Francs							
Inter-American Dev. Bank	1.2bn	Sep. 2000	7	99.3R	7.135	+22.5 (8½%–00)	BNP Capital Markets
Société Générale(l)§	1.5bn	Jan. 2000	3.5	(i)	—	—	Société Générale

	Amount	Maturity	Coupon	Price	Yield	Spread	Bookrunner
Sterling							
Abbey Nat. Treasury Services	500	Jun. 1998	7.75	99.66R	7.835	+60 (7¼%–98)	UBS/SG Warburg Secs.
Bristol and West BS	75	Jun. 2018	10.75	99.601R	10.797	+190 (8¾%–17)	Baring/Hoare Govett
Barclays Bank(m)	100	(m)	9.875	98.951R	10.007	+135 (9%–08)	Barclays de Zoete Wedd
Britannia Building Society(n)‡	100	Jun. 1997	(n)	99.43R	—	—	Samuel Montagu & Co.
Sedgwick Group(s)§	41.5	May 2008	7.25#	100R	—	—	NM Rothschild/Warburg
Canadian Dollars							
Banque Nationale de Paris	125	Jul. 1999	7.5	99.266R	7.657	+50 (6½%–98)	ScotiaMcLeod
De Nationale Investeringsbank	100	Jul. 1998	7.5	99.68R	7.579	+45 (6½%–98)	RBC Dominion Securities
Italian Lira							
Bank for Dutch Municipalities	150bn	Jun. 2003	10.5	101.1	10.319	—	Deutsche Bank London
LKB Baden-Württemberg Fin.	150bn	Jun. 2000	10.375	101.5	10.066	—	Bca. Nazionale del Lavoro
Daimler-Benz Intl. Finance	125bn	Jun. 2000	10.5	101.275	10.236	—	Deutsche Bank London
Ecus							
Compagnie Bancaire(o)	100	Jun. 1998	7.25	99.8R	7.299	+40 (7¼%–98)	Paribas Capital Markets
Guilders							
Bayerische Vereinsbank	200	Jun. 2003	7	100.25R	6.964	+30 (6½%–03)	Rabobank Nederland
Spanish Pesetas							
De Nationale Investeringsbank(e)	10bn	Jun. 1999	11.5	101.1	11.238	—	Bco. Negoclos Argentaria
Bancomext(e)	10bn	Jun. 1998	12.65	100.625	12.475	—	Bco. Santander Negoclos
Swedish Krona							
Nordic Investment Bank	500	Jun. 2000	8.5	99.75R	8.549	—	Morgan Stanley Intl.
Swedish Export Credit(y)	200	Jun. 1994	9.5	100	9.5	—	Morgan Stanley Intl.
Swiss Francs							
Sagami Chain Co.(b)*Φ	40	Jun. 1997	1	100	—	—	Nomura Bank (Switz.)
Eurofima(d)	400	Jun. 2003	5	102	4.744	—	Swiss Bank Corp.
Aegon	100	Jul. 1998	4.75	102.125	4.269	—	Swiss Bank Corp.
GECC*	100	Jul. 1998	4.75	101.875	4.325	—	Banque Paribas (Suisse)
West Japan Railway Co.	200	Jun. 2000	4.75	100.75	4.622	—	UBS
Taisei Oncho Co.(p)*§	70	Sep. 1997	1.875#	100	—	—	Nomura Bank (Switz.)

(continued)

Table 9-4. New International Bond Issues (continued)

Borrower	Amount m.	Maturity	Coupon %	Price	Yield %	Launch Spread bp	Book Runner
Aoki International Co.(t)*Φ	300	Jun. 1997	1.25	100	—	—	Nomura Bank (Switz.)
Daimler-Benz Nth.America *	150	Jul. 1999	4.75	101.75	4.412	—	Credit Suisse
Council of Europe ‡	100	Jul. 1994	(z)	100.5	—	—	UBS
Luxembourg Francs							
SNCI, Luxembourg	1.5bn	Jul. 2001	7.125	101.95	6.801	—	BIL
CSFB Finance	2bn	Jul. 2003	7.75	102.05	7.452	—	Kredietbank Luxembourg
Tractebel Invest Intl.	1bn	Jul. 2001	7.25	101.5	6.999	—	Cregem Intl. Bank
Arbed	1.5bn	Jul. 2000	7.75	100.9	7.580	—	BGL

Source: Financial Times, June 1, 1993.

Final terms and non-callable unless stated. The yield spread (over relevant government bond) at launch is supplied by the lead manager. * Private placement. § Convertible. Φ With equity warrants. ‡ Floating rate note. # Semi-annual coupon. R: fixed re-offer price. a) Denom.: $10,000 + 2 warrants. Exercise price: ¥1579. FX: 111.5¥/$. b) Denom.: SFr50,000 + 50 warrants. Exercise price: ¥2348. FX: 76.09¥/Sfr. Callable on 3/6/95 at 102% declining by ½% semi-annually. c) Issue launched on 18/5/93 was increased to $150m. Coupon pays 6-month L/bor − 0.125%; minimum 6%, maximum 10%. d) Callable on 30/6/01 and on 30/6/02. e) Matador bond. f) Coupon pays 6-month L/bor + 0.375%. g) Quarterly coupon. Puttable in 9 months at 99⅜% increasing by ⅛% quarterly. h) Denom.: DM5000 + 24 warrants. Each warrant is exercisable into 1 Continental share at DM199. i) International tranche of FFr3.bn domestic deal. Shareholders have priority subscription rights on FFr1.5bn of bonds on the basis of 1:25 of their shareholdings. Bond price: FFr660. Redemption price: FFr800. Conversion ratio 1:1. Callable from 1/1/97 at a yield of 6.22% subject to share price condition. j) Final terms fixed on 2/6/93. k) Coupon pays 3-month L/bor + 0.375%. Callable at par on interest payment dates from June 1996. l) Conversion price: Markka 144. Exchange rate: 5.5243 Markka/$. Callable at par from 6/7/98. m) Fungible with the outstanding £200m launched on 7/4/93. Undated subordinated issue. Plus 43 days accrued interest. Callable at par in 15 years, then every 5 years. If not called, coupon will be reset. Yield and spread calculated to first call. n) Coupon pays 3-month L/bor + 0.15%. Deal was launched with additional detachable interest rights (ADIRs) which were privately placed. The ADIRs entitle holders to receive 5%–3-month L/bor. o) Spread was over BTANs. p) Final terms fixed on 1/6/93. Callable on 30/6/95 at 102% declining by ½% semi-annually. Acceleration clause. Conversion price revision clause. q) Fungible with new 10-year bonds created in the current exchange offer. r) Callable and puttable on 3/12/95 at par. t) Final terms fixed on 3/6/93. Callable on 16/6/95 at 102% declining by ½% semi-annually. u) Average life years: 2.6 years. Coupon pays 6-month L/bor + 3%. Callable. v) Coupon pays 6-month L/bor + 0.375%. w) Quarterly coupon. x) Coupon pays 3-month L/bor + 0.125% from 3/6/93–7/9/93, 6.75%–3-month L/bor to 7/3/94 and 3-month L/bor thereafter. y) Redemption proceeds are determined by formula: 100% + 15% × (7.85%–3-year swap offer yield). z) Coupon pays 3-month L/bor − 0.15%. Note: Yields are calculated on ISMA basis.

256

1990, Japanese corporations floated issues of straight and convertible bonds, and bonds with equity purchase warrants, in the Eurobond market totaling ¥62.6 trillion (approximately $500 billion), compared with issues totaling ¥54 trillion in the Tokyo market. Japanese companies are attracted by convertible debentures and issues of debt with stock purchase warrants, which enable them to "repay" the debt in the future when the investors convert the debentures or exercise their options to acquire more shares by turning in their bonds. While Japanese stock prices were high and rising this method of financing was thought to be too good to resist; however, after the fall of the Japanese equity market beginning in December 1989, repayments had to be made in cash because the share prices were too low for the bonds to be converted. Nevertheless, some companies still found this method of financing attractive as late as mid-1993.

Japanese corporations are able to avoid restrictions in the Tokyo market by issuing securities abroad—often at lower cost than in Tokyo—through Japanese securities firms in London. These firms, in turn, often sell all or most of the securities to Japanese investors in Tokyo. Because of this recycling capacity, many Japanese companies have avoided using the Japanese capital market altogether. This has brought considerable pressure on Japanese government officials to further deregulate new issues procedures to reattract Japanese issuers. Little by little, this is occurring.

Eurobond Investors

The Eurobond market today is broad and complex, with various different and changing components that tend to be defined by investor types or their location.

Retail Investors

The term *retail investor* means a private individual who usually entrusts his or her money to a bank that invests it, according to some general instructions. The typical retail investor in Europe used to be described by the market as a "Belgian dentist," that is, a middle-class European professional who had been able to move some money for investment outside of his home country. He would invest in round lots of 100 bonds through a bank in Switzerland or Luxembourg in which he maintained a private account. Such accounts often can be maintained with very high degrees of secrecy, and therefore are attractive to various types of individuals and corporations seeking to hide funds from the eyes of others. Retail investors have now grown to include wealthy individuals from all over the world whose money is invested for them anonymously by European banks. Some of these clients have included well-known, if notorious figures, such as the former shah of Iran, former Philippine president Ferdinand Marcos, and

Panamanian general Manuel Noriega. Swiss banks are the best known and largest institutions managing retail investment accounts, although they have their equivalents in all the other European countries. They charge relatively high fees for their services and do not have an outstanding reputation for investment performance, since their true function is to preserve capital and confidentiality. The three or four largest Swiss banks alone are reported to have over $750 billion dollars of customer funds in their custody. A very high percentage of these funds is invested outside Switzerland.

Retail portfolio managers have a strong preference for "household" issuer names because their cautious and risk-averse customers insist on dealing only with well-known companies or governments. The portfolio managers do, however, have more than a little discretion in handling their customers' accounts, and accordingly they also participate in the occasional special or less well-known situation, especially if the issue is being managed by the bank.

In recent years wealthy Japanese individuals have likewise become bond market participants, particularly in zero-coupon issues where—under the Japanese tax code—they do not have to pay taxes on the imputed interest. Japanese demand for zero-coupon Eurobonds became so strong that the Japanese Ministry of Finance imposed a regulation restricting the percentage of any issue that could be sold into Japan. Individuals invest in Eurobonds mainly through Japanese securities firms, whose role in the Euromarket has expanded, reflecting the strong demand for Eurobonds of all types in Japan during the 1980s.

Institutional Investors

The institutional sector of the Eurobond market is not too different from its counterpart in the United States. London has long been a center for professional money managers who, for example, manage corporate and other pension funds, mutual funds, and private wealth. Other European financial institutions, such as the European Investment Bank and other EU entities, central banks, insurance companies, banks (especially foreign banks without an active customer base in Europe that need to acquire lending opportunities in the market), a growing array of European and American mutual funds, and corporations with excess cash have a trading and performance orientation that is similar (though not quite so intensive) to that of the U.S. market. In the late 1980s, large Japanese insurance companies, trust banks, and other institutions began to participate in the market for the first time. Because of the large amount of funds available for investment and the Japanese practice of acting more or less in the same way at the same time, Japanese institutions had a very large impact on the market over the past 10 years.

Investor Bias

On the whole, both institutional and individual investors have a heavy bias in favor of the better quality names and shorter maturities. They fear defaults because they do not wish to expose themselves to uncertainties, delays, and disclosures by seeking recovery in bankruptcy proceedings. There have been times when a Baa-rated Eurobond issue has done well, but this is a much less frequent occurrence than with Baa-rated U.S. bonds. Still, there are some who predict that with the right sales effort, a Euro-junk-bond market might emerge. So far it has not done so. Those relatively few Europeans who wish to buy junk bonds can purchase them in New York.

As the dollar weakened relative to the traditional hard currencies after 1985, the volume of new Eurobond issues in other currencies and the ECU increased proportionately. ECU-denominated issues were principally aimed at the institutional sector of the market. Since the ECU is a currency accounting unit that contains, on a weighted basis, only the currencies of the EU member countries, it is free of the effect of the U.S. dollar. Accordingly it is the only currency unit that was all-European at a time when serious efforts were under way to secure a form of monetary union. The ECU, in particular, gained importance to both issuers and investors as more European governments, corporations, and institutions endeavored to eliminate dollar risk as much as possible form their financial assets and liabilities. Banks now make loans in ECUs, to the extent of $35 billion in 1991; governments and corporations issue both international ($33 billion in 1991) and domestic ($10 billion) bonds in ECUs; and markets in ECU Euronote facilities and Treasury bills and notes are developing rapidly. Secondary market trading in ECU instruments grew by 80 percent in 1991, and ECUs were increasingly used in currency swaps and futures and options contracts (Table 9-5).

Table 9-5 The Private ECU Market (U.S.$ billions)

	1989	1990	1991	1992	1993	January–September 1994	Stock at end September 1994
Total bank lending[a]	24.6	24.9	35.2	8.9	0.4	(18.6)	219.0
International bond issues	12.0	17.6	32.6	22.0	8.2	5.5	
Net Euronote placements		4.1	3.6	(2.4)	(0.9)	(0.4)	8.0
Domestic bond issues	10.3	15.0	9.9	11.8	15.0	14.8	
Short-term domestic treasury bills and notes	19.5	20.2	18.7	19.1	18.0	10.8	

Data: Bank of England, ISMA, Euroclear, national authorities, and BIS.
[a] Changes at constant end-of-period exchange rate.

Eurobonds with Swaps

It is clear that the U.S. and international markets are already very closely linked, not just in terms of the relationship between domestic and Euro-dollar interest rates, but also through the newer forms of linkage that the interest-rate and currency-swap markets provide. During the 1980s a system for swapping interest rate and foreign currency obligations among debt obligors around the world developed (see chapter 10). It is now possible—indeed there is a large volume of this type of business—for a company that owes floating-rate debt to swap the interest portion of the debt with another company that has a fixed-rate obligation. Thus without actually doing a financing a company can switch its future interest-rate exposure from fixed to floating or vice versa. This is a very useful tool for managing financial liabilities. It is also a useful tool for managing assets—a pension fund investor can swap fixed-interest payments from a bond for a contract to receive a floating rate of interest. Some use swaps more aggressively than that—for example, an AA-rated Japanese bank may issue a Eurobond at a very low fixed-interest rate and swap it with a Baa-rated issuer like Boston Edison Power Company, a lesser quality credit but one that can still borrow from a bank at a small spread over LIBOR. The Japanese want to generate floating-rate funding at a rate *below* LIBOR, which they do by offering their attractively priced fixed-rate obligation to Boston Edison at a premium. Boston Edison can afford this because it cannot at the time borrow fixed rate in the United States or Europe on quite as fine terms as the Japanese bank can (see Figure 9-3). A sizable market for swaps of all kinds now exists, and arranging the transactions is not difficult. With such techniques, companies can alter the whole structure of their liabilities on very short notice, or they can use them to lower their costs of funds, as discussed in chapter 10. It is easy to see how an aggressive banker might line up Boston Ed to do the swap, then immediately offer the sub-LIBOR package to the Japanese bank, the execution of which would provide the banker with an attractive Eurobond issue to lead manage.

Swaps can also be used to exchange foreign currency obligations, sometimes in very unusual ways. In 1985, for example, Walt Disney Corporation issued a bond denominated in ECUs. This was immediately swapped with a French government agency for a yen obligation that it had obtained a year earlier through the issuance of a Samurai bond in Japan. Disney ended up with a low-cost yen obligation, which it repaid out of its yen royalty income from Tokyo Disney World, and the French switched out of a yen exposure into an obligation it preferred in managing its liabilities.

One can now create "synthetic" dollar assets or liabilities through nondollar bond issues combined with an appropriate currency swap, or synthetic fixed-rate securities by combining a floating-rate note with an interest-rate swap. The search for lower-cost liabilities and higher-yielding

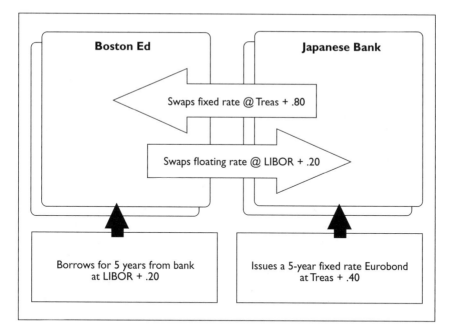

Figure 9-3. Fixed rate—floating rate swap transaction.

assets is extensive on the part of corporations and financial institutions, so that the spreads between true and synthetic paper are narrowing as arbitrage transactions take place in the markets involved for these varied and numerous transactions. It is generally recognized by investment bankers that approximately 60 percent to 70 percent of all Eurobond transactions since about 1986 have involved swaps of one sort or another.

New Issue Procedures

In the United States, securities issues must be filed with the SEC, which must declare issues "effective" before they can be sold to the public. To be declared effective, issues must meet disclosure and procedural requirements. In the past the SEC would routinely take a few weeks to review filings placed with it. Today, as a consequence of Rule 415, many companies can file shelf registration statements that, when effective, will provide an issuer with the means to come to market at any time on very short notice. Issuers must distribute securities through investment bankers acting as underwriters who usually (but not always) will syndicate issues with other bankers. The issue, when ready to be launched, will be priced and a "fixed" (i.e., nondiscountable by the other underwriters) underwriting discount will be established by negotiation between the issuer and the lead underwriter.

Thereafter the issue will be allocated among underwriters by the lead underwriter. The underwriters will then commence to sell the issue to investors, virtually all of whom are experienced institutional investors who know the secondary market trading levels. All sales to investors must, by terms of the agreements between underwriters, be at the fixed offering price until such time as the lead underwriter "releases" the issue for free trading at whatever price the market may then command.

Issues may be brought as "bought deals," in which one or a few underwriters purchase the entire issue (which may or may not subsequently be syndicated), or they may follow the more traditional practice in which the issue is purchased from the company by the entire syndicate following pricing negotiations. Bought deals may be awarded to the lowest bidder following a competitive process, or they may be awarded without competition if the issuer likes the proposal made to it and wants to avoid taking any risk that the market may move against it before the issue is priced.

In the Eurobond market, there are a number of different practices. There are no requirements for filing an issue with any regulatory bodies except for the listing requirements of the London or Luxembourg stock exchange. In earlier years most issues were "mandated" by a corporation to a particular lead manager who would form a syndicate, test the market for a week or two with "road show" visits to principal European cities with senior officers of the issuer, and then agree on price and gross spread with the issuer. Today, most issues are bought deals that are mandated to the underwriter offering the best net cost of funds in the currency that is ultimately desired by the issuer.

A Eurobond Pricing Example

For example, a company may inform those who ask that it is "thinking about" raising $100 million with a maturity of five to seven years. It may actually communicate this message to three or more underwriters to get their best ideas. Each underwriter will discuss the situation internally to come up with the most accurate assessment possible of the rate at which the issue could be completely sold within a day or two. For example, an issuance of ordinary five-year notes, noncallable with interest payments only until maturity (these terms are variables as far as the underwriter is concerned, to be adjusted as necessary to determine the optimal combination of attractiveness to the issuer and to investors), is estimated to sell in the market to knowledgeable investors at, say, an *annual* yield of 7.25 percent. The issuer would expect to incur a "cost-of-funds" of a bit more than that, say, 7.30 percent, which would include the underwriters' discount, or "gross spread." The annual coupon is a traditional practice in the Eurobond market, originally offered in place of the semiannual coupons that are common in the United States, as an accommodation to Swiss banks and their customers who don't like to be bothered with too frequent coupon clipping of bearer bonds.[3]

With an annual coupon of 7.00 percent, such an issue would provide a cost of funds to the company of 7.31 percent at an all-in (including underwriter's discount) price of 98.74 percent. If the underwriter can resell the bonds at a price of 98.98 percent, its customers will obtain a yield of 7.25 percent. The underwriter's profit is 0.24 percent (98.98 percent − 98.74 percent). This is the way bonds are priced in the United States, but there the underwriters agree (in writing) with each other that none will sell at a price other than 98.74 percent except to other dealers. Thus the price of 98.74 percent is "fixed" during the offering period, until the lead manager disbands the syndicate formed for the issue.

In the Euromarket, however, "traditional" (but now rapidly fading) practices require that a gross spread of 1⅞ percent would apply to a seven-year issue such as the example given here. However, this extremely high level of gross spread is largely fictional to all but the continental European bankers participating as underwriters in the deal. Only these banks can hope to retain the full spread, because they simply put the bonds into their clients' accounts at a price of 100 percent, with the 1⅞ percent difference between the price at which the banks were able to acquire the bonds, that is, 98.125 percent, and 100 percent being the bank's profit. But to maintain the spread of 1⅞ percent and still provide a competitive cost of funds to the issuer (7.31 percent), the bank must lower the coupon to 6.85 percent (which at 98.125 percent yields 7.31 percent over five years). Private clients or retail investors may be willing to accept a yield of 6.85 percent on the bonds, but institutions, focusing as they do on secondary market trading levels and required spreads over Treasury securities, would not. In traditionally priced Eurobonds, most non-Swiss underwriters are unable to sell bonds at 100 percent. Their clients will not pay more than 98.37 percent for the 6.85 percent coupon bond (which will yield 7.25 percent), so the bankers have to discount the bonds to them. This difference in pricing methods is called a two-tiered pricing structure (see Table 9-6), though since 1989, and with rising levels of secondary market trading (see Figure 9-4), most of the major Eurobond issues have been offered in the American fixed-price manner to effect better institutional distribution.

The fixed-price-offer method essentially takes the pricing structure for the sale of Eurobonds to institutional investors and locks it into an agreement among underwriters not to sell at any other price so as to preserve the spread. However, it also eliminates the 0.125 percent praecipium, or special portion of the management fee due the lead manager, and the practice of charging all the after-market stabilization expenses to the other underwriters, both traditional practices of the Eurobond market that came to be much disliked. The far more transparent fixed-price method is virtually identical to the method used to price issues in the U.S. market.

But to win the mandate, the lead underwriter probably has to come up with a rate to the issuer below the market rate of 7.30 percent. There are several ways this can be done.

Table 9-6 Different Eurobond Pricing Methods

	Traditional Pricing Method for Continental Banks	Fixed-Price Offering Method for Institutional Investors
Annual coupon	6.850%	7.250%
Gross spread	1.875%	0.250%
Cost of funds to issuer	7.310%	7.310%
Price bought by investor	100.000%	100.000%
Yield to retail investor	6.850%	—
Gross underwriter's discount	1.875%	0.250%
Rebate to institutional investors	(1.625%)	—
Yield to institutional investors	7.250%	7.250%
Net underwriter's profit	0.250%	0.250%

[a] Both methods produce the same cost of funds to the issuer (7.31 percent), and the same yield to the institutional investors (7.25 percent) at a net profit to the underwriter of 0.25 percent. The artificially large gross spread of 1.875 percent charged by the Continental Bank is applied to a lesser bond coupon (6.85 percent) to provide the required cost of funds. Thus, the retail investor pays a much higher price for the bonds, as compensation to the Continental Bank.

First, an investor somewhere around the world, in Japan or the Middle East for example, might be found that was prepared to purchase the bonds at a lower yield, thereby allowing the underwriter room to lower the cost of funds to the company. Sometimes, before bidding an underwriter will spend the preceding night scouring the investors in different time zones to see if demand can be found at the better price levels. Often it can.

Second, the underwriter may find a way to create a synthetic dollar bond using swaps that would cost the company less than 7.30 percent. Again, the underwriter must scan the world: Is there an opportunity to issue bonds in, say, Australian dollars and simultaneously enter into a U.S.$/Australian$ currency swap to obtain a lower cost of funds? There are many possibilities on any given day, and many must be checked out in detail. The underwriter could also decide to purchase the bond from the company at an aggressive rate, say at break-even, or 7.25 percent, because it is convinced that interest rates will decline and its profit will be "bailed out" by the rising market (an event that is not assured). Finally, the underwriter may decide to offer to purchase the bonds at an even lower rate, say below 7.25 percent, because of an opportunity to use it in connection with a favorably priced swap transaction, or simply as a means to buy market share.

Syndication and Underwriting Risk Management

Once an issuer selects one of the available offers it will usually confirm and accept the terms proposed on the telephone. If so, the transaction

$ trillions

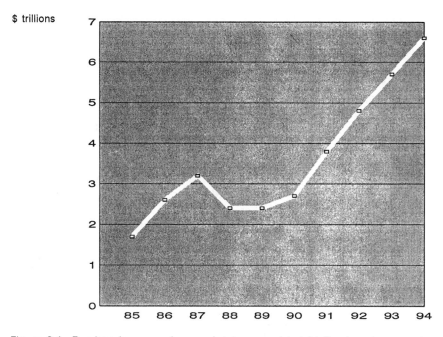

Figure 9-4. Eurobonds—secondary market turnover (straight Eurobonds, convertibles and floating-rate notes). Source: ISMA as reported by *Institutional Investor*.

becomes a "bought deal"—the underwriter has agreed to purchase the issue outright. There are no outs for syndication, investigation into the issuer's business, documentation, or market changes. The underwriter owns the entire issue itself. In other cases the issuer will only mandate an underwriter to proceed with the transaction, usually subject to a rather precise understanding as to when the issue will be priced and underwritten.

Either way, the underwriter's next step is to arrange for a syndicate of other underwriters to share the risk. It may be that the issuer has imposed on the transactions group co-lead managers of the issuer's own selection. Such co-lead managers are functionally the same as co-managers in U.S. transactions—they share in the management-fee portion of the gross spread and appear prominently at the top of the list of underwriters alongside the lead manager, or "book running manager" in U.S. terms. A lead manager will usually not propose or initiate the inclusions of co-lead managers for competitive reasons. It will, however, look for co-managers that are functionally about the same as U.S. "special bracket" underwriters, which rank just ahead of traditional "major bracket" underwriters. In Eurobond issues large numbers of co-managers have become common, with 8 to 12 not unusual. The lead manager will try to lay off as much as 90 percent of the underwriting risk of the issue, keeping about 10 percent for itself. Some issues are completely syndicated among the managers, but in most cases a general underwriting group, representing about 50 percent of the underwriting, is invited. If an issue is too overpriced (too little yield), the lead manager may not be able to syndicate the issue fully, and will have to increase its own underwriting by the amount of any shortfall.

Once syndication has begun and terms are known, the issue will appear in the gray market. This is an informal, unauthorized, electronic quotation service that is provided to the market by certain bond brokers over the Reuters, Bloomberg, and other information networks. On one or more Reuters' "pages" there will appear a list of all of the latest issues that have been announced, together with a brief summary of their terms and any recent news concerning syndication. Individual bond brokers will have their own pages on which they post prices. All market participants and most institutional investors stay tuned to the gray-market pages continuously to keep abreast of market developments. Before fixed-price issues became widely in use, the gray-market data would include the bond brokers' indicative bid-and-asked quotations, expressed in terms of a percentage discount from the offering price, or in terms of a percent of par value (100 percent). These quotations would often show substantial discounts from the offering price, sometimes greater than the gross underwriting spread.

Co-managers (and other underwriters) finding themselves being allocated bonds in poorly priced issues may decide that they do not wish to retain the market risk of holding the bonds in inventory, and therefore elect to sell the bonds in the market. The easiest market to access is the gray market. If the issue is tightly priced and the co-manager has no demand from its customers, it may call a bond broker to arrange a sale of the bonds on a confidential basis. This way the issuer and the lead manager will not know for sure that the co-manager was unable to sell the bonds allocated to it. The bond broker will immediately call the lead manager of the issue and ask it to buy the bonds back at the gray-market price quoted by the broker. If the lead manager wishes to stabilize the issue around the gray-market level, it will purchase the bonds. Depending on the lead manager's response, the bond broker may adjust his quotes. This process can often have the effect of repricing an issue and causing a substantial portion of the entire issue to be reacquired (frequently at a loss) by the lead manager.

Such lead manager's stabilization purchases, in effect, are for its own account, not for the account of the whole syndicate, because stabilization losses can only be charged to the syndicate up to the amount of the underwriting commission. This is because in a traditional variable-price underwriting, stabilization prices will vary resulting in profits or losses, which may be substantial. It becomes difficult for the lead manager to separate transactions made for its own account (i.e., regarding its own bonds) and those of the syndicate. Accordingly, if more than a minimal amount of stabilization is to occur it will be performed by the lead manager acting on its own and at its own risk.

It is often in the interest of the lead manager to stabilize issues—it prevents the gray market from collapsing to levels below the full amount of the gross spread, and it buys time for the marketwide sales effort to take effect. If the stabilization effort is persuasive the issue will respond; if not it may drop in price, which is most injurious to the manager holding the largest amount of bonds—usually the lead manager. If the issue is clearly mispriced, however, the lead manager may be better off to attempt to hedge the issue as early as possible, for example by selling Treasuries or by selling ("shorting") a similar Eurobond issued by another company, and then let the market manage on its own without accumulating additional bonds through stabilization. If the cost of financing the inventory of bonds is less than the income received on them, some participants are willing to carry the unsold bonds for as long as several months, until they can be sold off at higher prices when opportunities present themselves. Sometimes they can only liquidate such positions at a loss—often a large loss.

Clearly the risk exposure of a lead manager was considerable under the gray-market-dominated, variable pricing system. Lead managers accordingly experimented with several methods of imposing syndicate "discipline," usually without satisfactory results. However, syndicate practice permitted the lead manager to charge the expenses of the issue, including some stabilization charges, to underwriter accounts, that is, against the portion of the gross underwriting spread allocated to each syndicate member for agreeing to take on the underwriting risk. Before long the lead managers had depleted the entire underwriting fee by stabilization charges, much to the annoyance of the other underwriters. By the early 1990s, the fixed-price underwriting method was introduced and became widely accepted. It ended the wild activities of syndicate members and managers, though the gray market continues to exist and to act as a reality check for all participants.

Asset-Backed Securities

In the early 1980s, "mortgage-backed" securities were first introduced in the United States. These were originally called pass-through securities. They were paid by the monthly cash flows generated by a pool of residential mortgages. These payments, consisting of interest and principal, were subject to the considerable uncertainties of prepayment, which greatly altered the maturity of the security. Pass-throughs were followed in the market by collateralized mortgage obligations, or CMOs, in which the pool of mortgages was divided into tranches that were to be repaid sequentially to reduce the uncertainty associated with repayment of the bonds. CMOs became extremely popular and led to further innovation and an enormous expansion of the mortgage securities market in the United States. Soon the same principals were applied to other types of asset-backed securities, such as those based on pools of automobile and credit-card receivables, commercial bank loans, and many other types of financial assets.

All asset-backed securities share most of the following characteristics: they are off balance sheet for the asset provider, the assets physically are deposited into a trust supervised by an independent trustee, the pool of assets is somewhat greater than the face value of the security—a condition called "overcollateralization," and the value of the assets in the pool is marked to market periodically. If the value of the assets in the pool falls below a minimum, the provider must contribute additional assets to meet the required standard. Many asset-backed securities have "credit enhancement" features, such as a guarantee of a bank or an insurance policy with one of the mortgage insurance groups operating in the United States. As a result of all of these features, the security is usually able to receive AAA or AA bond ratings. The securities are sold in the market, however, at a premium over the corresponding rate for comparably rated finance company securities. The securities are relatively safe, but they are also complex and subject to thin secondary market trading. Accordingly they require a higher rate to be sold to institutional buyers. In 1993, $480 billion of asset-backed securities were issued in the U.S. market, compared with $389 billion of corporate bonds. In that year, they represented the largest segment after U.S. government securities of all capital market activity in the United States.

The international market has been much slower to adopt asset-backed securities, though considerable progress has been made since 1989. The securities are mainly bought by international institutional investors; they are too complex for Belgian dentists and other retail investors. During most of the 1980s, international institutional investors were able to acquire asset-backed securities in the U.S. market, and did so. By the end of the decade such investors accounted for an estimated 30 percent of the U.S. market for asset-backed paper. Thereafter, as these institutions increased their share of total international bond market activity, more asset-backed issues were pitched to Euromarket investors.

Euromarket asset-backed securities contain all of the structural features of similar securities issued in the United States. A number of U.S. issuers (such as Citicorp, American Express, and General Electric Capital Corp.), seeking to diversify their sources of funds, offer securities in both markets. Other European names find it easier to come to the Euromarket than to the U.S. market, because of name recognition, registration requirements, and other reasons. Many large U.K., Scandinavian, and other banks and leasing companies have issued asset-backed Eurobonds. Certain third-world borrowers (Mexico, Argentina, Turkey) have found assets-backed securities more acceptable to the market than their uncollateralized paper. Many different and unusual asset pools have been attempted, including Mexican telephone receivables, commercial real estate loans, and aircraft leases.

Increasingly the effect of this activity is loosening resistance to asset-backed securities in European and other countries. Various accounting practices (to permit off-balance-sheet treatment) and financial regulations (pertaining to minimum capital rules) have to be adjusted to permit asset-backed securities to be issued in local markets, but this is beginning to occur throughout Europe, especially in the United Kingdom where several sterling-denominated asset-backed securities have been issued. Issues have also occurred in France and Sweden.

Jumbos, Globals, and Private Placements

By the mid-1980s, issues exceeding $1 billion became common in the Eurobond market. These were usually floating-rate note issues by sovereign governments or large banks, which, because of their size, were called "jumbos." By the late 1980s, some fixed-rate jumbos had appeared, after which the World Bank issued the first "global" bond issue, in which several separate markets (the Eurobond, the U.S. public debt market, the Japanese public debt market, etc.) were approached simultaneously at the same terms and rate. The World Bank issue had a lead coordinator for the issue and several different book runners for the respective tranches. The issue was successful and followed by others like it. One of these was a $5.5 billion two-part offering of 10-year notes and 30-year bonds by the Republic of Italy in September 1993. The issues were part of a $10 billion shelf registration filed with the U.S. SEC in July 1993 to be marketed over the following 10 years. The issues were structured to be acceptable as global bonds, that is, they were to be tradable around the world, registered in such countries as required it, and part of a paperless book-entry system that required the bonds to be registered. The filing of the U.S. registration statement was followed by a "road show" of Italian government officials to various U.S. and foreign cities to meet investors. Italy had a long-term debt rating of A-1 from Moody's and AA from Standard & Poor's. As the road show progressed, market conditions improved and the underwriters saw considerable demand for the issues building up. The 10-year issue was priced to yield 0.62 percent over 10-year U.S. Treasuries, and the 30-year issue was priced at 0.80 percent over 30-year Treasuries. These rates were approximately comparable to those of a high-grade U.S. corporate bond. U.S. investors accounted for about 40 percent of the total demand for the bonds. The rest were sold to Euromarket and Asian investors. This was the largest global bond issue undertaken to date; its success invited additional issuers, particularly sovereigns, to try the market.

Various European and Latin American governments also sold global, jumbo bonds that were principally targeted at the Eurobond market but also offered in other markets. Often the Latin American bonds were rated below investment grade, but because of economic recovery in Mexico, Argentina, and elsewhere the bonds were well received. Frequently access to the U.S. market was provided through private placements (arranged by the lead manager of the Eurobonds) under Rule 144a, which permitted the sale and resale of unregistered securities in the United States to certain qualified institutional buyers.

Because the various bond markets around the world had been subject to extensive integration through arbitrage trading and institutional participation, the bonds could be sold at the same yield in all the markets, though demand would vary from place to place for a variety of reasons including currency, rating, and maturity preferences.

Competition in European Bond Markets

The many different participants bring many different strengths and other characteristics to the Euromarket. Thus many banks, investment banks, and brokers have had the chance to operate in the market with certain important competitive advantages. Swiss and certain other European banks have the advantage of considerable in-house placing power. They are able to "encourage" their retail customers to purchase Eurobonds that they bring to the market, and for which they can charge full fees. This placing power naturally draws prospective issuers to them. U.S., Japanese, and British investment and merchant banks have the advantage of influential relations with their home-country issuers and with institutional investors. Other specialized participants appear from time to time—U.S. commercial banks, for example, have been key participants in floating-rate markets and in swaps, where they have been able to use their large funding base and trading books to considerable advantage. Japanese banks and securities firms have benefited not only by a steady flow of Japanese issuers in the market (many of which are guaranteed by a Japanese bank) but also by the large appetite for Eurobonds that occurs from time to time on the part of financial institutions in Japan. Table 9-7 lists top U.S. underwriters and Eurobond lead managers in 1993 and 1994.

In the United States, the 10 leading underwriters of corporate bonds & equity together managed approximately 83 percent of the total market in 1994, a figure that has not changed much during the past 10 years. In the Eurobond market, on the other hand, the top 10 firms accounted for only 44.5 percent of the market in 1994, and the firms comprising the top 10 varied considerably from the rankings of 1993. By almost any method of comparison, the levels of competition in the Eurobond market are far greater—perhaps twice as great—as in the U.S. bond market.

As markets change to reflect investor preferences—for dollars over other currencies, for fixed over floating rate, for straight debt over equity-related securities—the competitive picture changes and different institutions emerge as having the greatest comparative advantage. Firms that have built strong distribution, trading, and investment banking capabilities in various different markets will probably do best over the long run. Cer-

Table 9-7 Top U.S. Underwriters and Eurobond Lead Managers, 1995 and 1994

Manager	January 1, 1995–December 31, 1995				January 1, 1994–December 31, 1994			
	Amount ($Millions)	Rank	%	Issues	Amount ($Millions)	Rank	%	Issues
All Domestic Capital-Raising Issues * *(Full Credit to Lead Manager)*								
Merrill Lynch	96,773.3	1	18.3	745	80,282.3	1	18.5	526
Morgan Stanley	61,213.5	2	11.6	478	48,400.7	4	11.1	374
Salomon Brothers	55,549.4	3	10.5	443	38,021.0	6	8.7	389
Goldman, Sachs	54,675.6	4	10.3	395	50,033.3	3	11.5	342
Lehman Brothers	49,767.7	5	9.4	433	51,373.7	2	11.8	435
CS First Boston	39,449.9	6	7.5	278	45,077.9	5	10.4	355
J.P. Morgan	30,015.5	7	5.7	255	18,442.7	7	4.2	142
Smith Barney	17,325.7	8	3.3	240	10,426.0	9	2.4	151
Bear, Stearns	13,837.2	9	2.6	196	10,931.9	8	2.5	139
First Tennessee Bank, N. A.	13,403.1	10	2.5	231	7,302.8	12	1.7	101
Donaldson, Lufkin & Jenrette	13,296.0	11	2.5	138	9,960.9	10	2.3	143
NationsBank	8,757.7	12	1.7	112	1,421.8	25	0.3	23
Chase Manhattan	6,238.2	13	1.2	115	1,677.2	23	0.4	15
PaineWebber	6,181.4	14	1.2	106	9,557.8	11	2.2	149
UBS	5,970.0	15	1.1	120	5,039.9	13	1.2	74
Industry Totals	528,994.8	—	100.0	5,930	434,874.8	—	100.0	4,935
Total Top 10	488,500		92.3					
Eurobonds								
SBC Warburg	17,966.1	1	6.4	97	19,406.0	1	6.0	119
Deutsche Morgan Grenfell	15,637.4	2	5.6	69	13,030.2	7	4.0	74
Merrill Lynch	14,820.3	3	5.3	88	16,612.4	4	5.2	103
ABN Amro Hoare Govett	14,054.3	4	5.0	87	9,274.6	12	2.9	66
J.P. Morgan	13,138.7	5	4.7	79	14,149.1	5	4.4	81
Morgan Stanley	12,059.9	6	4.3	78	13,668.5	6	4.2	87
CS First Boston/Credit Suisse	11,891.0	7	4.2	59	18,191.6	2	5.6	69
Lehman Brothers	11,383.3	8	4.1	65	8,495.6	14	2.6	44
Goldman, Sachs	11,151.4	9	4.0	47	17,657.1	3	5.5	77
Banque Paribas	10,235.1	10	3.7	57	9,385.5	11	2.9	52
Dresdner Bank AG	9,756.9	11	3.5	33	4,198.4	22	1.3	19
UBS	9,353.3	12	3.3	61	11,209.2	10	3.5	47
Commerzbank AG	8,747.5	13	3.1	31	3,500.1	26	1.1	17
BZW/Barclays PLC	8,264.6	14	2.9	57	6,961.7	16	2.2	52
Nomura Securitie	8,235.6	15	2.9	60	12,314.8	8	3.8	77
Industry Totals	280,399.3	—	100.0	1,840	322,417.4	—	100.0	2,028
Total Top 10	235,999.0		84.3					

* All issues excluding mortgage and asset backed securities. Also excludes closed-end fund offerings and secondary shareholder offerings.

tainly, however, the Eurobond market is not one that can be dominated by any single firm, or small group of firms, for any length of time. The vigorous competitive action of the unregulated, innovation-oriented market will keep it that way.

All banks and investment banks seeking to compete in the international market must come to terms with three basic factors: (1) the new issue business for investment grade bonds has become global; (2) globalization has made the business extremely competitive and realized underwriting profits have declined accordingly; and (3) firms must regard new issues, secondary market-making and trading, hedging, swaps, and arbitrage related to bonds all as one integrated business.

That the business has become global is no surprise today. Borrowers, when discussing possible financings with their bankers, want to know what is the cheapest way to raise funds from whatever source. A competitor, for example, who does not operate in the U.S. and/or the Eurodollar bond market, or the Swiss franc market, or in Japan will be at a significant disadvantage compared with a firm that is active in all of these markets. Becoming involved in these markets entails a substantial threshold of cost, personnel, and supervision without which a firm is, in effect, only an occasional participant in the global debt markets.

Will the Eurobond Market Die with Further Financial Deregulation?

During the past decade there has been substantial deregulation of most of the national capital markets in the OECD countries. This is partly the result of involuntary "imported deregulation," and partly because of a desire by financial authorities to upgrade the quality and efficiency of national capital markets. A question often asked is, will such deregulation, if continued, obviate the need for the Euromarket?

This subject has received much attention. Those who believe the Euromarket will wane with the rising importance of deregulated national markets consider that issuers prefer domestic markets when they are competitive, and that because of greater secondary market liquidity international investors prefer them as well. Those who are doubtful that the Euromarket is on its last legs believe, to the contrary, that there will always be enough regulation in most national markets to be able to reward those who attempt to escape them, and that in a world of very diverse internationally minded investors, bargains will be offered from time to time to attract business into the great unregulated and untaxed arena of international bond and capital markets.

There is developing evidence, moreover, that the best prices are obtained in markets with the greatest amount of secondary market liquidity. Different currencies will of course offer different rates, but through currency swaps these rates will be arbitraged into parity with the dollar, the

ECU, and other preferred currencies. Only the U.S. bond market can at present offer as much secondary market liquidity as the Eurobond market, and investors in the United States are increasingly accustomed to investing in Eurobonds as an adjunct market to (if not an integrated part of) the U.S. bond market. Thus it appears likely if current trends continue that rising liquidity in national bond markets will result in further integration with the Euromarket, in which case the borders between the markets may become very indistinct indeed.

Summary

The international bond market has experienced phenomenal growth for over a quarter of a century, primarily in the Eurobond sector. As an unregulated market bringing together from all parts of the world high-quality issuers with a widely diverse and changing body of investors, the market is historically unique. The Eurobond houses, based in London but coming from all corners of the world, compete to offer issuers rapid access to low-cost funds. Their success has furthered international financial integration and has contributed to the drive for deregulation. In the future, developments related to the creation of a common "internal" market by the EU countries should cause capital market activity in Europe to expand greatly. Such increased activity may further diminish the differences between on-shore and offshore debt financing as it increases the worldwide selection of debt instruments.

Notes

1. Another reason Eurodollars came to be was that certain holders of dollars did not wish to deposit them in the United States, or invest in U.S. securities, because they feared the funds might be blocked for political reasons. The Moscow Narodny Bank in London, for example, was an early investor in Eurodollar deposits and Eurobonds.

2. For a brief but interesting history of international bond markets see F.G. Fisher, *International Bonds*, Euromoney Publications, 1981, pp. 15–27.

One of the U.S. firms that was very active in selling U.S. securities through offices in Europe was White Weld & Co., Inc. Subsequently White Weld's European operations were separately incorporated as White Weld Ltd., which formed a joint venture with Crédit Suisse, a prominent Swiss bank. The joint venture, called Crédit Suisse White Weld, specialized in Eurobonds. It was recapitalized into a new company, Crédit Suisse First Boston, in 1978 when White Weld & Co. was sold to Merrill Lynch.

3. Yields and cost of funds for Eurobonds are often expressed in terms of semiannual coupon equivalents for the benefit of those issuers whose alternative financing sources are expressed in semiannual terms. An annual coupon yield of 9.25 percent would have a semi-annual equivalent of 9.05 percent.

10

Swaps and Related
Derivative Securities

Few events have stimulated international capital market activity as much as the development, beginning in the early 1980s, of "derivative" securities. *Derivatives,* which include futures, options, and swaps, are special contracts whose values reflect changes in the price of underlying assets (stocks, bonds, or commodities) traded on exchanges or in over-the-counter markets. Derivatives are used to manage the various risks associated with financial assets and liabilities, the market values of which can fluctuate widely. Globalization of financial markets has resulted in the spreading of derivatives to market centers all over the world, and in the extremely rapid growth in contracts outstanding, which were estimated by the Bank for International Settlements at the end of 1993 to exceed $16 *trillion* in notional value. *Notional value* means the principal amount that is hedged, not the actual value of the derivative instrument itself, which is far less than the notional amount.

Derivatives packaged together with cash market securities can create "synthetic" securities with characteristics that differ substantially from those of the original cash market instrument. Thus derivatives are used to alter the investment characteristics of a security without requiring the security to be sold and the proceeds reinvested. Derivatives traded on exchanges in the United States, Europe, and Asia are large-volume, commodity-like instruments that include interest-rate and currency *futures* contracts, and interest-rate and currency *options* (including options on futures contracts). Derivatives traded in over-the-counter markets include interest-rate swaps (over $6 trillion of notional value outstanding at the end of 1993), currency swaps ($900 billion notional value outstanding), other swap-related derivatives ($1.4 trillion outstanding), and a variety of small-volume, customized instruments used to hedge interest-rate, equity,

Table 10-1. Financial Derivative Instruments Outstanding

	Notional Principal Outstanding (in billions of US dollars)					
	1989	1990	1991	1992	1993	1994
Exchange-traded instruments	1,766.6	2,290.2	3,518.8	4,632.5	7,760.8	8,837.8
Interest rate futures	1,200.8	1,454.5	2,156.7	2,913.0	4,942.6	5,757.4
Interest rate options[1]	387.9	599.5	1,072.6	1,385.4	2,362.4	2,622.8
Currency futures	15.9	16.9	17.9	24.9	32.2	33.0
Currency options[1]	50.2	56.5	62.8	70.9	75.4	54.5
Stock market index futures	41.3	69.1	76.0	79.7	109.9	127.7
Stock market index options[1]	70.6	93.7	132.8	158.6	238.3	242.4
Over-the-counter instruments[2]	—	3,450.3	4,449.4	5,345.7	8,474.6	14,400
Interest rate swaps	1,502.6	2,311.5	3,065.1	3,850.8	6,177.3	10,800
Currency swaps[3]	449.1	577.5	807.2	860.4	899.6	2,100
Other swap-related derivative[4]	—	561.3	577.2	634.5	1,397.6	1,500

Sources: Futures Industry Association, various futures and options exchanges, ISDA and BIS calculations.

[1] Calls and puts.

[2] Data collected by the International Swaps and Derivatives Association (ISDA) only; the two sides of contracts between ISDA members are reported once only.

[3] Adjusted for reporting of both currencies; including cross-currency interest rate swaps.

[4] Caps, collars, floors and swaptions.

and foreign exchange risks (Table 10-1). As a proportion of the international assets of BIS reporting banks, the notional volume of derivative contracts on interest rates and currencies rose from around 25 percent in 1986 to nearly 75 percent in 1990. Perhaps even more significant, trading in derivatives has in many instances exceeded that of the underlying cash markets.

This chapter addresses swaps and related derivative instruments, which can be tailored to reflect almost any interest rate or currency outlook and create an appropriate risk exposure. Equity-related derivatives are discussed in chapter 11. Figure 10-1 provides definitions of the most common terms used in connection with derivative instruments.

Swaps

Swaps are over-the-counter instruments involving the exchange of one stream of payment liabilities for another. Before 1980 swaps scarcely existed. By 1985 they were seen to offer great advantage to issuers (and investors) of debt securities because, with them, a party could lower the cost of financing in bond markets, or raise the yield on bond investments, through arbitrage and by exploiting comparative advantages. Indeed, swaps had become so much a part of the international financial scene that Eurobond transactions involving swaps were responsible at times for more that half of all new issues. Also, since about 1987 banks and other finan-

Figure 10-1 Common Terms in the Derivatives Market

Derivative

A financial contract whose value is designed to track the return on bonds, stocks, currencies or some other benchmark. Generally, derivatives fall into two broad categories—forward-type contracts and option-type contracts—and may be listed on exchanges or traded privately.

Option

A contract for which the buyer pays a fee in exchange for the right to buy or sell a fixed amount of a given financial instrument at a set price within a specified time. Options are "price-insurance" contracts because they protect buyers from adverse swings in the price of the underlying asset. The buyer can never lose more than the price paid for the option, but the seller's losses are potentially unlimited.

Cap

An option that protects the buyer from a rise in a particular interest rate above a certain level.

Floor

An option that protects the buyer from a decline in a particular interest rate below a certain level.

Exotic options

A wide variety of options with unusual underlying assets or peculiar terms or conditions. For example, a lookback option confers the retroactive right to buy a given financial instrument at its minimum price, or sell at its maximum price, during a special "lookback period." A compound option is an option such as a put on a call, a call on a put, a put on a put, or a call on a call.

OTC derivatives

Derivative transactions take place "over-the-counter," or off organized exchanges, and usually by telephone.

Forward

An OTC contract obliging a buyer and a seller to trade at a set price on a future date a fixed amount of a particular commodity, currency or other financial instrument. Forwards are "price-fixing" contracts, because they saddle the buyer with the same returns as owning the underlying asset. Normally, no money changes hands until the delivery date; then, the contract is usually settled in cash rather than through exchange of the actual asset.

Swap

A forward-type contract in which two parties agree to exchange streams of payments over time according to a predetermined rule. In an interest rate swap, one party agrees to pay a fixed interest rate in return for receiving a floating interest rate from another party. An equity-index swap may involve swapping the returns on two different stock-market indexes, or swapping the return on a stock index for a floating interest rate.

Future

Basically, an exchange-traded forward contract. Futures contracts are highly standardized, and the exchange acts as a counterparty to both buyer and seller, guaranteeing payment in case one of them defaults. In return, buyer and seller are required to put up collateral, or margin, equal to a certain percentage of the underlying value of the contract which is marked to market daily.

Source: The Wall Street Journal, August 10, 1993.

cial intermediaries have found swaps extremely beneficial in managing the special risks of interest-rate and currency exposures from loan or investment portfolios. Swaps are enormously accommodating—they enable parties to change their financial assets and liabilities at will and at low cost, for example, to change a fixed-interest payment obligation into a variable one, or to change a dollar-payment obligation into a deutsche mark one.

Swaps constitute valid and binding agreements between participants to exchange one stream of future interest (and sometimes principal) payments for another. Swaps, however, represent contingent values and therefore do not appear on balance sheets, except in footnotes. Since 1985 they have been transacted according to standardized documentation, and almost always involve counterparties of high creditworthiness. The growth of interest-rate and currency swaps has been exceptional since their origin, as indicated in Figure 10-2.

The Origin of Swaps

As discussed in earlier chapters, in the early years of modern international capital markets, around the mid-1960s, foreign exchange controls that blocked or impeded the flow of funds across borders were abundant. In the days of fixed exchange rates, the conventional method of preventing funds from exiting or entering one's country was to surround the country with a ring of exchange controls. For example, if a British pension fund manager wanted to invest in the U.S. equity market, he or she would either have to sell an existing overseas asset to pay for the new investment or purchase international "investment currency" to do so. Investment currency was rigged to be

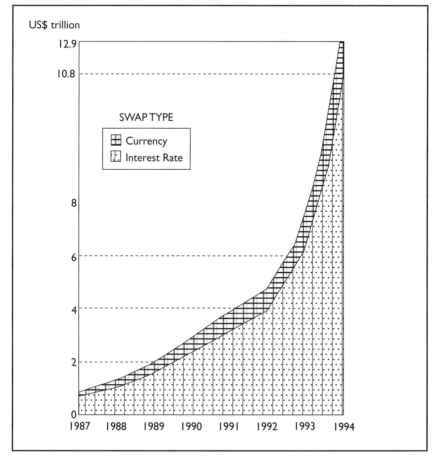

Figure 10-2. Swap market growth from 1987 to 1994, total notional U.S. dollar amount (in trillions) outstanding. Source: International Swap Dealers' Association.

more expensive than domestic currency, and buying it was in effect the same as buying dollars for the U.S. investment at a premium or paying a higher rate for the dollars than otherwise prevailed. Similarly, if a U.S. company wanted to make a capital investment in its manufacturing facility in Manchester, it was under considerable pressure from U.S. authorities (finally legalized by regulations issued by the Commerce Department's Office of Foreign Direct Investment, now extinct) to finance the investment with funds borrowed outside the United States, even if that should mean (as it did until the late 1970s) that the cost of financing would be greater than what was available to the company domestically.

To accommodate the requirements of both such parties, the "back to back" or "parallel" loan was devised. The U.S. firm would lend an agreed amount of dollars to a U.S. affiliate of the British pension fund, and in a separate but "parallel" transaction the U.K. pension fund would lend the same amount in sterling to a U.K. affiliate of the American company. Two loan agreements were required, both containing substantially the same terms and conditions, often including provisions for "topping up," or reducing the amount of one loan as an offset to the changed market value of the other. Such changes would occur because of changes in the dollar/ pound sterling rate. The loans did provide substantial value to each party, but the cost of arranging and executing them consumed a large portion of this value, especially when the principal amounts were small, which was often the case. Credit considerations were complex, even though the loans provided for a mutual offset in the case of default, and agreement on interest rates was often difficult to achieve when the maturities involved exceeded the one- to 2-year periods for which forward foreign exchange rates could reliably be obtained. Banks were often asked to stand in the middle, to ease questions of counterpart credit exposure, though such arrangements added further to the cost of the transactions. Accountants ruled that because of the offsetting provisions, the loans would not have to be included on the face of the companies' financial statements, which provided an advantage that direct borrowing from a foreign bank would not. After a time, much of the process was made easier by the familiarity of participants and the standardization of some of the procedures, but the overall volume of parallel loans was very modest by current standards.

After the collapse of the Bretton Woods fixed-exchange-rate system and the adoption of floating exchange rates, controls governing the international transfer of funds became obsolete and began to be removed. The U.S. regulations were rescinded in 1973, the British government abolished exchange controls in 1979, and other countries followed suit thereafter. Parallel loans were no longer necessary, and immediately disappeared. Some of the financial principles underlying the parallel loan market, however, were deemed to have wider application and served as the basis for the swap markets that succeeded them.

Currency Swaps.   A few years later, in August 1981, a significant transaction took place in which IBM and the World Bank agreed to exchange the future liabilities associated with borrowings in the Swiss franc and U.S. dollar bond markets, respectively. IBM was then perceived in Switzerland as one of the two or three best "names" from the United States and was therefore able to borrow Swiss francs in the Swiss market on extremely favorable terms compared with all other foreign borrowers—that is, at about the same rate as the Swiss government. The World Bank, having used the Swiss market several times in recent years and being involved with third-world loans, was not regarded quite so favorably by the Swiss and was therefore required to pay a higher rate than the best U.S. credits— about 20 basis points above the Swiss government rate. On the other hand, the World Bank, like IBM at the time, carried an AAA rating and was well respected as a credit in the U.S. dollar markets because of the backing of the U.S., German, Japanese, and other governments. The World Bank could borrow in the United States at rates only narrowly higher (e.g., 40 basis points) than those of U.S. Treasuries, but IBM would have had to pay a slightly higher rate than this.

Thus, if each borrowed in the market in which its comparative advantage was the greatest—that is, if IBM borrowed Swiss francs and the World Bank borrowed dollars—both borrowings would be at rates superior to the available alternatives. If they then swapped the liabilities each had incurred, the World Bank would create Swiss francs synthetically at a bargain rate, saving 10 basis points on the transaction, and IBM would save 15 basis points with its synthetic dollar financings. The parties had similar credit ratings so counterparty risk was offset.

The way it worked was this: The World Bank borrowed at 5 basis points more advantageously than IBM could have done in dollars, and IBM borrowed at 20 basis points better in Swiss francs than the best rate offered the World Bank. IBM relent its Swiss francs to the World Bank at 10 basis points more than it paid for them. The World Bank thus gained, net, a 10-basis-point advantage over its alternative Swiss franc borrowing cost, and IBM gained a net, a 15-basis-point advantage by combining the World Bank's 5-basis-point advantage in dollars with the 10 basis points that it kept for itself on the Swiss franc financing (see Figure 10-3). The value received by each party was the product of negotiation; since then, market-makers quote prices for swaps that reflect the net demand of thousands of different market users.

Each party swapped its fixed-rate funding obligation for a different fixed-rate obligation, which changed its liability into something quite different. (Today, currency swaps involving fixed rate to floating rate are also available.) The World Bank had created a synthetic Swiss franc security for itself that had all of the properties of the real thing, and IBM had done the same in dollars.

In the period preceding the IBM–World Bank currency swap, it was possible to arrange for foreign exchange purchases and sales in the forward markets, although as indicated, these markets did not always operate beyond one- to two-year maturities. Swaps are now the preferred instrument for hedging foreign exchange exposure beyond a year. The growth of this market segment has put pressure on governments with restrictions on foreign exchange transactions to drop such restrictions, which the swap market can easily frustrate. Accordingly considerable growth in nondollar currency swaps has occurred in recent years. Swaps in virtually all major currencies are now available, as shown in Table 10-2.

Interest-Rate Swaps. Having observed currency swaps develop, some bankers began to think of ways to apply the same idea to transactions involving short- and long-term dollar borrowings. They were encouraged by the existence of different credit risk premia in the fixed-rate and floating-rate term debt markets. For example, a weaker credit such as a BBB-rated industrial company would have to pay as much as 70 basis points more than an AAA-rated bank for a five-year bond issue, but it would have to pay only 30 basis points more for a five-year bank loan based on LIBOR. So the BBB company could maximize its comparative advantage by borrowing from its bank and swapping the floating-rate interest payment obligation with, say, a Japanese bank for a stream of fixed-rate interest payments that the Japanese bank had incurred through the

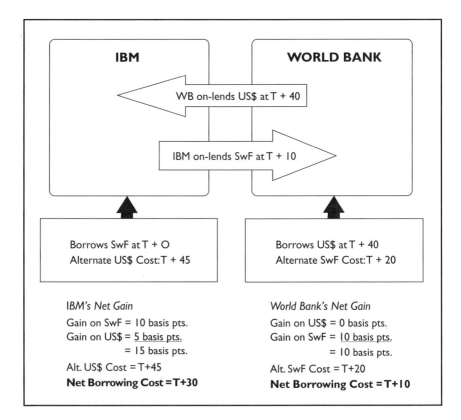

Figure 10-3. The first currency swap between IHBM and the World Bank, April 1981. T = Treasury; SwF = Swiss franc.

Table 10-2 Composition of Currency Swaps Outstanding as of 1993
(U.S. $ billions)

Currencies	Total Notional Amount[a,b]	Of Which Against		Of Which	
		USD[b]	Other Currencies	End-User	Fixed/Floating
Japanese yen	317.6	205.9	111.7	211.1	144.1
Swiss franc	146.5	72.5	74.0	115.5	57.0
Deutsche mark	139.3	65.7	73.6	113.7	61.4
ECU	73.5	38.9	34.6	59.2	42.9
Canadian dollar	70.7	57.9	12.8	58.3	43.8
Pound sterling	88.3	49.4	38.9	74.0	35.3
Italian lira	45.4	25.8	19.6	35.0	27.2
Subtotal	881.3	516.1	365.2	666.8	411.7
Other	277.4	124.0	30.7	219.9	109.7
Minus double-counting of nondollar swaps	−259.1		−259.1	−205.6	−73.2
Total	899.6	640.1	136.8	681.1	448.2

Source: International Swap Dealers' Association.

[a] Hypothetical underlying amount on which swap payments are based.

[b] Adjusted for double-counting of positions reported by International Swap Dealers' Association.

issuance of Eurobonds. The Japanese bank would pass on its fixed-rate obligation to the BBB company at, say, its cost of funds plus a premium of 50 basis points. The BBB company would then be able to create a synthetic five-year fixed-rate borrowing at 20 basis points less than its alternative cost of funds. The Japanese bank assumes the BBB company's floating-interest-rate obligation to pay LIBOR plus 30 basis points, but it reduces this by the 50-basis-point spread that it made in the fixed-rate bond swap, resulting in a net cost of funds of LIBOR minus 20 basis points (see Figure 10-4). In this way an interest-rate swap was created. Many more followed, with further modifications and improvements. A secondary market in swaps subsequently developed. New applications were introduced rapidly as volume built up and the number of participants and intermediaries increased sharply.

Two basic types of interest-rate swaps have become common since 1981, "coupon swaps" (of fixed-rate to floating-rate swaps such as the one just illustrated), and "basis swaps," in which floating-rate obligations indexed to different reference rates are exchanged. An example of the latter is a swap between a rate indexed to U.S. Treasuries and one indexed to LIBOR. Basis swaps also include exchange of rate obligations indexed to the same reference, but for different maturities (e.g., 30-day LIBOR vs. 90-day LIBOR).

Through the end of 1982, the interest-rate swap market had operated in mainly an international context. During 1983, however, a large volume of swaps developed between exclusively domestic U.S. counterparties. Top-

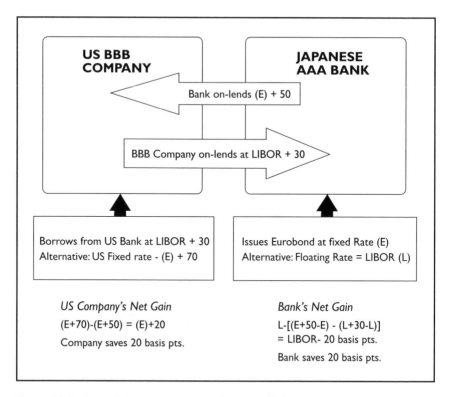

Figure 10-4. An early interest-rate swap between U.S. company with a BBB rating and a Japanese bank with an AAA rating. LIBOR = London Interbank Offered Rate.

quality borrowers, such as Student Loan Marketing Association, would issue fixed-rate securities to swap them into floating-rate obligations to fund their essentially floating-rate loan portfolio at a lower cost.

Then a major new use for interest-rate swaps was found in the distressed U.S. savings and loan industry. These organizations had fallen into great difficulty as a result of financing fixed-rate home mortgages from the proceeds of floating-rate deposits. When interest rates soared in the late 1970s, many savings and loan institutions suffered heavy losses. As rates began to decline again in the early 1980s, some S&Ls sold fixed-rate debt securities, collateralized by mortgages, to pay down variable-rate liabilities. Others simply swapped their existing floating-rate funding obligations into fixed-rate obligations, again offering existing mortgages as collateral.

Swaptions, Caps, and Floors

As the market for swap transactions grew, comparable developments were occurring in the field of financial futures and options. Financial futures became available in many different currencies and instruments and came to be traded on futures exchanges in London, Paris, Zurich, Frankfurt, Singapore, and Tokyo, in addition to the futures markets in the United States. Through sophisticated use of financial and foreign exchange futures contracts, new ways of hedging against interest-rate and foreign exchange exposures were developed. Ultimately, these resulted in the ability of dealers to sell options on hedged positions, which they carried on their own books.

Soon, markets were being made in option contracts in which purchasers could, in effect, acquire insurance against future risk exposures. The ability of the dealer to price options that it was selling to others became crucial to the dealer's operation. Whereas the dealer collects the premium at the outset, the actual result of the contract would not be known for some time, often for several months. If the dealer had misjudged the value of the options that were sold at the beginning of the year, it might not know it until nearly the end of the year—although after a time the development of an active secondary market in various types of options clearly revealed the value of the positions.

Gradually, the financial market environment became much more sensitive to and aware of sophisticated hedging devices and strategies. Many of these were based on the improving understanding in the market of the many uses and values of swaps, futures, and options transactions used in various combinations, called *swaptions*. The swaption market includes any option that gives the buyer the right, but not the obligation, to enter into a swap on a future date. It also includes any option that allows an existing swap to be terminated or extended by one of the counterparties. Some of the more recent swaptions have included forward swaps, caps and floors, collars, callable/putable swaptions, and contingent swaps.

Forward Swaps.   *Forward swaps* are swaps in which the payment accruals commence at some specified time in the future. They can be used to fix funding costs in the future, as for example after the construction phase of a real estate project has been completed. There are many other uses as well, as illustrated by Figure 10-5, which shows a forward swap used in conjunction with the issuance of a callable bond to provide the issuer with greater flexibility and a lower overall financing cost. In this case a French bank issued 7.5 percent yen bonds. The bonds, callable after five years, would mature in eight years. On issuance of the yen bonds, the French bank entered into a currency swap (swap A) in which it would receive yen and pay ECUs.

After three years the yen had strengthened substantially against the ECU and yen interest rates had declined. The value of the contract to pay ECUs and receive yen was worth more than when the contract was originally written. Because the yen/ECU swap had appreciated, the French bank wanted to realize this value in some way. It could do so by, in effect, repaying the first swap (that is, selling it in the market at a capital gain reflecting its increased value) and replacing it with another one at current, more favorable rates. Or it could gain more flexibility for itself by entering into a second swap (forward swap B), a forward ECU/yen swap that would come into effect in two years (at the call date) and then last for three years (until the bonds mature). The plan is to call the yen bonds in two years and replace them as a funding source for swap A with swap B, then coming into effect. Then the French bank locks in an income differential that is the equivalent of a three-year annuity instead of a capital gain. Alternatively, if rates had continued to improve the bank could decide not to call the yen bonds, and sell swap B at a profit instead.

Caps and Floors. *Caps* and *floors* involve the purchase of a series of options on short-term interest-rate indexes, which enables the purchaser to fix the upper or lower rate to which it would be exposed. In combination with other instruments, a cap or floor for almost any kind of asset or liability exposure to interest or exchange rates can be created.

Collars. A combination of a cap and a floor in a single transaction to limit both upside and downside risk is called a *collar.*

Callable/Putable Swaptions. Customized swaps can be created by the addition of call or put features. In a *callable swaption,* which is made up by combining a regular interest-rate swap and an option (at some additional cost for the option premium) on a reverse of such a swap, a hedge can be established at the outset of a swap transaction involving, for example, a callable Eurobond issue, where the call feature is deemed to have high value.

Contingent Swap. This is in essence an option on a swap with particular characteristics that could be exercised if, for example, bond purchase warrants attached to a Eurobond issue to lower its cost should be exercised.

In these and similar cases involving combinations of swaps with other instruments, the desired customized package can be purchased from swap dealers who create them by taking counterpart, or "mirrored," positions, on their own books.

Other Innovations

With increasing use, the swap market has attracted a considerable array of new products and innovative applications.

> *Amortizing Swaps.* A swap with a variable notional balance, for example, balances that match the expected cash flow of a financing

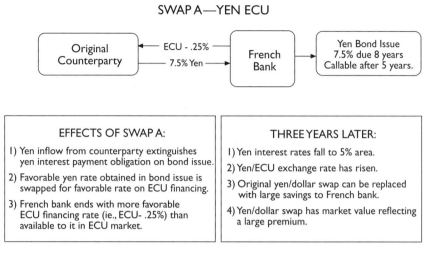

SWAP A—YEN ECU

| Original Counterparty | ← ECU - .25% ← / — 7.5% Yen → | French Bank | → | Yen Bond Issue 7.5% due 8 years Callable after 5 years. |

EFFECTS OF SWAP A:

1) Yen inflow from counterparty extinguishes yen interest payment obligation on bond issue.

2) Favorable yen rate obtained in bond issue is swapped for favorable rate on ECU financing.

3) French bank ends with more favorable ECU financing rate (ie., ECU- .25%) than available to it in ECU market.

THREE YEARS LATER:

1) Yen interest rates fall to 5% area.

2) Yen/ECU exchange rate has risen.

3) Original yen/dollar swap can be replaced with large savings to French bank.

4) Yen/dollar swap has market value reflecting a large premium.

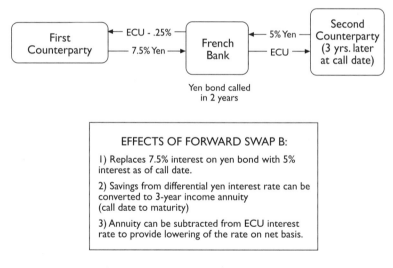

FORWARD SWAP B— LOCKING IN PREMIUM VALUE

| First Counterparty | ← ECU - .25% ← / — 7.5% Yen → | French Bank | ← 5% Yen ← / — ECU → | Second Counterparty (3 yrs. later at call date) |

Yen bond called in 2 years

EFFECTS OF FORWARD SWAP B:

1) Replaces 7.5% interest on yen bond with 5% interest as of call date.

2) Savings from differential yen interest rate can be converted to 3-year income annuity (call date to maturity)

3) Annuity can be subtracted from ECU interest rate to provide lowering of the rate on net basis.

Figure 10-5. Forward swap-callable bond transaction. ECU = European currency unit.

project or the prepayment schedule of a mortgage asset or liability.

Step-Up/Down Swaps. A swap in which the fixed payment level varies—increasing or decreasing—for some portion of the swap term. For example, the fixed-rate portion may be set below the market for the first two years, with an above-market rate for the remainder of the term.

Mortgage Swaps. A swap structured to replicate all or a portion of the yield or return characteristics of mortgage securities. In the most straightforward structure, a mortgage yield is exchanged for a floating-rate return, and the notional balance is amortized according to either a specific prepayment assumption or the actual prepayment experience of the underlying mortgage pool.

Commodity Swaps. A swap exchanging payments based on the value of a particular commodity (e.g. gold or oil). One party pays a fixed price for the commodity and receives the spot price of the commodity on the reset date.

Repackaged Securities

There have been recent occasions when a particular issue of floating-rate securities has gone awry in the secondary market, because of credit deterioration or regulatory concerns that have affected the market, and the issue has traded at unusually depressed prices. On such occasions dealers have stepped forward with the intention to tender for the floating-rate securities (which pay, say, LIBOR) at a discount, so the effective yield becomes, say, LIBOR plus .35 percent. The securities are then transferred to a newly formed trust in which the notes are held as collateral. The trust, which may be owned by the investment banker/dealer, would then enter into an interest-rate swap with a counterparty exchanging floating-rate payments for fixed-rate. The trust will fund the fixed-rate part of the swap by offering fixed-rate bonds in the market as an asset-backed security, at, say, a rate of U.S. Treasuries plus 80 basis points. The swap thus makes possible the removal of the securities from the distressed floating-rate note market into the more healthy fixed-rate bond market, and the banker organizing the transaction profits from the difference in values (Figure 10-6).

Risks of Swaps

Several types of risks are associated with swaps. With the explosively increasing volume of swaps, these risks have become of concern to bank regulators around the world and to investors in those financial intermediaries most involved with swaps and related products. Regulators, often slow to fully understand new technologies and market activities that develop quickly, fear that global exposures are so large that the entire financial system may be at risk to a sudden failure. The risks may have gotten out of hand, some regulators in the United States and Europe have said, and have to be reined in. Market practitioners, on the other hand, claim that far from increasing risk, derivatives improve market efficiency and provide essential tools for managing, and even reducing, total risk to the financial system. For brief definitions of the many types of risks related to derivatives, see Table 10-3.

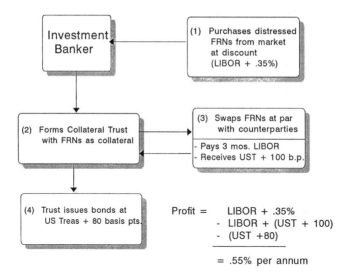

Figure 10-6. A repackaged securities transaction. FRN = fixed-rate notes; LIBOR = London Interbank Offered Rate; UST = U.S. Treasuries; b.p. = basis points.

Counterparty (Credit) Risk

Interest-rate swaps involve only a contractual exchange of interest payment obligations. No principal is exchanged. Currency swaps, however, do involve principal—they are mutual obligations to exchange all debt service payments (interest and principal) as each comes due. If one party defaults, the other can declare its swap payable and offset the defaulted obligation. Depending on interest and exchange-rate movements between the date of swapping and the default, which would affect both interest and principal payments due, one party or the other would be owed a balance (a premium over the notional amount) after offsetting. Because of the offsetting feature, the amount of exposure to default risk is usually equal to only a small percent (generally expected not to exceed 5 percent) of the notional values exchanged.

To preserve the hedge provided by the original swap, the nondefaulting party would most likely enter into a replacement swap with another counterparty, but in doing so would lose the premium due it. For example, if the BBB company (Figure 10-2) defaults on its obligation to exchange payments with the Japanese bank—which has funded its commitment with a fixed-rate Eurobond—the Japanese bank finds itself with a sudden reversal of its funding; from LIBOR minus 20 basis points to a fixed rate. If the Japanese bank has used the swap to fund a floating-rate loan to a Japanese client, it no longer has a locked-in spread on the loan over its cost of funding. Instead it has what might be a substantially differ-

Table 10-3 The Different Flavors of Derivative Risk

Counterparty risk
Also known as credit risk, the risk that one party in a derivatives contract will fail to perform, causing the counterparty to suffer a loss

Liquidity risk
The risk that a financial instrument, or a derivative based on that instrument, cannot be sold except at a sharp loss

Market risk
The risk of an abrupt change in the price of an asset underlying a derivatives contract

Operational risk
The risk of losses resulting from inadequate controls, human error, or management failure; includes the risk that the theoretical models used in pricing, tracking, hedging, and estimating the risk of derivatives will turn out to be flawed

Settlement risk
The risk that an expected settlement payment on a derivative contract won't be made on time because of a default or a technical foul-up; this exposes the counterparties to market, liquidity, and credit risk

Systemic risk
The risk that a disruption—at a firm, in a given financial market, or to a settlement system—will cause widespread difficulties at other firms in other markets or in the whole financial system

---

Source: The Wall Street Journal, August 10, 1993.

ent interest-rate differential on the loan, plus an unhedged exposure to the future movement of fixed-rates versus LIBOR.

The Japanese bank must call the Eurobond (if that is possible) and replace it with floating-rate funding at whatever rates the market then requires for the remaining period to maturity of the original Eurobond. Or it could replace the defaulted swap with another at whatever rates for swaps of the appropriate maturity then apply. Thus, the simplest measure of the risk to a party engaging in a currency or interest-rate swap is the cost of replacing the swap in the market. If there has been no change in interest or currency rates since the original transaction, then the replacement cost, or the value to be obtained in selling the swap to another party, would be nil. Swaps only have positive or negative value to the extent that interest rates have changed since the original swap was transacted. Therefore, the replacement cost will be either higher or lower than the original cost, resulting in either a potential gain or loss.[1] The risk exposure is limited to the cost of replacing a swap at a loss.

The replacement value establishes the market value of the swap at any given time. When marked to market, swaps are therefore either "in the money" or "out of the money" to the extent that they would gain or lose in the event of default and replacement. Net replacement value thus has become the market value of existing swaps, and reflects the value of the contingent asset or liability associated with the transaction.

The replacement cost of an interest-rate swap, however, can never come close to its notional value (or principal equivalent amount) even when interest-rate changes are considerable. The risk exposure of swaps, therefore, is small in relation to their notional values. According to a survey conducted by International Swap Dealers Association, the total defaults and losses on more than $3.1 trillion (notional) of swaps surveyed through the end of 1991 has so far been about $358 million (actual, not notional), or only 0.0115 percent. To minimize counterparty risk, market-makers in swaps generally require that principals be themselves high-quality credits or that well-known banks act on behalf of their clients of lesser quality.

The replacement cost of a currency swap, even if it does not approach its full notional value, may be different from that of an interest-rate swap, because the exchange of principal payments is also involved. Risk exposures of interest-rate swaps of longer than one year for which capital must be set aside have been set at 0.5 percent of notional amount by the BIS and the central banks of the OECD and some other countries; for currency swaps of more than one year the ratio is 5 percent of principal amounts. As a contingent asset or liability, the swap is not recorded on the balance sheets of the participants. As the volume in swaps has grown so considerably in recent years, so has the value of the contingencies associated with them. These contingencies now represent substantial amounts and therefore pose important control issues to bank regulators. These matters are discussed later in this chapter.

Liquidity Risk. Theoretical replacement values depend on liquid markets to be realized. If markets should dry up, especially the over-the-counter markets, because of some kind of direct or indirect shock to the system, then all valuations could fall into question.

Basis and Market Risks. In the examples provided (Figures 10-1 and 10-2) the parties involved were creating synthetic liabilities in fixed- or floating-rate dollars to fund asset purchases in identical instruments, that is, fixed- or floating-rate dollars. Once matched up, only counterparty risk remained. A swapper, however, can choose to select swaps that provide exposures to other risks.

Basis risk involves swapping so as to have exposures to differently determined market indices. An example would be the BBB-rated company not actually borrowing from the bank at LIBOR plus 30 basis points, which could be done, but instead arranging even cheaper funding for its side of the swap by using the U.S. commercial paper market. Though the company is still obligated to receive LIBOR plus 30 from the Japanese bank in exchange for paying 50 basis points over the Japanese bank's fixed-rate Eurobond cost, its own funding cost is now dependent on the U.S. commercial paper rates, not LIBOR. This difference may or may not be advantageous to the BBB company in the future; because the company believes that it will be, it proceeds knowing that if the relationship between LIBOR and commercial paper changes, the company could experience a further gain or loss on its position.

Similarly, when the difference is not between instruments, but between maturities, *market risk* develops. If the BBB company's own funding had been at 30-day LIBOR, instead of the more standard three-month LIBOR, rate differences could also arise that would provide additional potential gains or losses. Frequently these types of risk exposures are taken deliberately by principals to provide higher returns. In efficient markets there is usually not much benefit in a totally risk-free position, so to create some benefit for modest risks, some players frequently expose themselves to basis and market risks.

Operational Risk.   This is the risk of things going wrong in the rapidly moving, high-tech trading environment of derivatives due to staff error (e.g., in pricing or valuing swaps), or sloppy accounting or control procedures. These risks extend to understanding the contractual legality for swap transactions, especially when dealing with state-owned counterparties and when exposed to the bankruptcy laws of different countries, and to ensuring complete documentation.

Settlement Risk.   This is the risk that the required payments are not made on time, for whatever reason. Payments due across time zones can create settlement complications, as can technical or operational difficulties. Nonpayment can force a counterparty default, triggering a repricing possibly involving losses.

Systemic Risk.   Derivative transactions involve different markets and instruments, and can spread an individual bank's difficulties as well as general liquidity risks throughout the global financial system. Individual banks must, therefore, be able to monitor and regulate their aggregate exposures to other banks, markets, and instruments. This is an extremely complex task that not all banks are presently capable of managing.

Risk Management

Regulatory issues related to risk management of derivatives have continued to be both complex and controversial. Many such issues relate to equity and commodities derivatives, which are usually not connected directly to markets for interest-rate and currency products offered by banks. In 1992, senior bank regulators from several countries began to issue warnings to the banking systems under their control to beware of excessive growth in the derivatives field. Too many banks, they said, were not prepared to monitor and supervise their own positions, and could be subject to surprise discoveries or vulnerable to shocks generated elsewhere in the system of which they were a part. This expression of concern led to a special study by the Group of Thirty (a nonofficial think tank composed of former public and private sector senior banking officials), which published a report written for market practitioners. This report made several recommendations as to the management and control of derivative businesses, including suggesting that senior management assume responsibility for derivative positions, that dealers mark their positions to market daily, that stress simulations be run periodically to see how the portfolio would hold up, that credit functions be strengthened and made independent of dealing functions, and that netting provisions for credit and other exposure management practices be used. The report, in the view of many regulators and practitioners, seemed very much on target and possibly would be influential with bank examiners and supervisors, but it held no official standing.

Not fully satisfied by these recommendations, however, the BIS's Basel Committee on Banking Supervision proposed in April 1993 that banks apply capital charges to meet market risks on derivative (and other) positions and that a standardized framework applicable to all banks be devised. Two years later the committee, with the approval of the central bank governors of the Group of Ten countries, proposed changes to the original capital adequacy measures to accommodate market risk, the committee also proposed that banks be permitted to use their own in-house risk measurement models, if these met certain tests. Principally, such models must attempt to measure the amount of *value-at-risk* under conditions of substantial market change. Such models calculate the probability of losses as well as their correlation in the performance of different financial instruments.

The Users of Swaps

The widespread availability and simplicity of swaps have attracted a variety of users from around the world who enter into swap contracts for a wide range of reasons. The more active the market, the more innovative it has become. New applications involving swaps appear continuously. The result has been a substantial broadening of the range of opportunities available to both borrowers and investors.

The effect of such an enlarged financial menu has been to globalize the palate of virtually all capital market users. Each borrower preparing a financing must check several different markets before it can be sure that it has selected the optimal course for its requirements. Not only does the prospective borrower determine what the rates, terms, and conditions of a transaction in its own domestic market would be, it must also check the comparable opportunities in the Eurobond markets and all of the synthetic possibilities that can at the time offer competitive alternatives. Clearly the ability to monitor, understand, and execute such a wide variety of different financings requires a substantial upgrading in the financial skills of the borrower's treasury department personnel.

Corporate Issuers

As an example, consider a frequent financer, such as General Electric Capital Corporation, which in the course of a single year will routinely borrow several billions of dollars. The financial staff of G.E. Capital will daily receive calls and faxes from dozens of bankers suggesting different types of financings. All domestic markets will be covered, together with the Eurobond market, which will often contain a special "bargain" such as an offer to raise money in nondollar Eurobonds denominated in yen; Australian, Canadian, or New Zealand dollars; or Swiss francs, together with a swap back into U.S. dollars for the desired maturity at an especially attractive rate that would generate below-market financing opportunities. From this profusion of opportunities, G.E. Capital must select the choice that serves it best, knowing that during the course of the year it will be doing many additional financings and will want to balance its use of any single market appropriately. G.E. benefits by spreading its total financing needs across all of the world's capital markets, which ensures that it is achieving the lowest cost of financing possible.

Other companies with high debt ratings but a small requirement for new financing might decide to utilize their "excess" debt capacity to benefit from arbitrage profits. Such a company might issue a fixed-rate dollar Eurobond at an attractive rate relative to its alternative in the United States and swap the issue into a floating-rate obligation carrying a net interest rate of, say, LIBOR minus 25 basis points. The proceeds from the original financing might then be used to purchase a floating-rate obligation from, say, a high-grade Japanese bank at LIBOR plus 10 basis points, resulting in a spread of 35 basis points. Naturally, companies do not participate in interest-rate arbitrage to the point where it might interfere with their own borrowing requirements, but should an unexpected requirement arise, the swaps can always be reversed or the positions unwound.

Banks

Banks are very active users of swaps as a means to lower their cost of funds to improve lending profits and manage their funding gaps. They are also able to take advantage of natural swapping opportunities from their loan book, and the requirements of their clients. As a result, banks, especially U.S. banks, have become extremely large holders of swaps and related derivative products, with four such banks having "exposures," or positions, in notional terms in excess of $1 trillion each as of December 31, 1993. (Table 10-4). From the size of these exposures it is easy to understand the concerns of bank regulators.

Alternatively to trading on their own books, some banks and other dealers in swaps retain portfolios of "matched swaps" as an off-balance-sheet revenue-producing asset. Such banks usually will manage the portfolio actively, buying and selling extant swaps at prices they consider attractive while also adding to the portfolio new swaps they have created. Many banks like to create swaps for their transaction value more than they like to retain them as a portfolio investment. Thus, originating banks are able to sell swaps to nonoriginators much like they sell bank loans. Beginning in 1992, several large investment banks created special off-balance-sheet subsidiaries to remain competitive with the large commercial banks in the swaps area. These subsidiaries were capitalized in such a manner as to receive AAA ratings (thus being highly acceptable as a counterparty), and would house the firms' swap and other derivative positions.

Dealing in derivative instruments became an increasingly important source of revenues to banks and investment banks during the early 1990s. Merrill Lynch, for example, disclosed in its 1993 annual report that its revenues from trading swaps and other derivatives was $761 million, a 57 percent increase over the results for 1992. The derivatives revenue for Merrill Lynch was greater than its revenues from trading stocks and represented 26 percent of Merrill's $2.92 billion total revenues from principal trading in 1993. The notional value of Merrill's positions in swaps and derivatives in 1993 was $891 million, up 28 percent from the previous year.

Investment Managers

Finally, managers of large investment portfolios are swap users. A bond portfolio manager may find it is more advantageous to swap the future payments from a German government deutsche mark bond for the future payments from a U.S. Treasury bond than it is to buy the Treasury bond outright. Likewise, he may decide that he likes the liquidity of a portfolio of money-market securities but wants to fix rates before a market change and therefore enters into an interest rate swap to do so. Asset managers

Table 10-4 Derivatives Exposure Top US Commercial Banks, December 31, 1993 (U.S. $ billions)

Bank	Total Notional Value of Contracts Originated	Total Replacement Value of Contracts
Chemical Banking	$2,288	$24.2
Citicorp	1,835	22.2
Bankers Trust	1,526	21.5
J. P. Morgan	1,470	30.7
Chase Manhattan	887	13.7
Bank America	882	14.2
First Chicago	390	6.5
Nationsbank Corp.	154	1.0
Republic New York Corp.	145	1.5
Continental Banking	119	1.9

Data: Standard & Poor's.

are less advanced in their use of swaps than liability managers, but many believe they will catch up quickly once they become accustomed to handling the wide range of opportunities that swapping provides.

Many observers believe that substantial future growth will occur as more end-users from among both asset and liability managers discover the benefits of swaps for interest-rate and currency hedging, and new users from the real estate, mortgage finance, and international governmental, investment management, and corporate sectors become involved in the market.

Swap Pricing

Pricing of swaps during the early days of the market was based on sharing of the comparative rate advantages realized through the swap process. As the users of swaps have multiplied, however, so have the influences on pricing. Counterparties use swaps for vastly different applications, and they compete with each other on a price basis for the same basic product (e.g., a LIBOR vs. five-year Treasury swap). Also, the market now has a significant number of market-makers, or swap traders, who are continually positioning in anticipation of market changes. This professional market trading has established a commoditylike price level for basic swap products. For less liquid, noncommodity swaps, a premium can be expected to be paid.

The price of a swap is generally quoted as the all-in fixed rate for a particular maturity to be exchanged for, say, three-month LIBOR. This price will be affected by changes in the basic U.S. Treasury rate, by changes in the yield curve, and by hedging costs and the level of new issue spreads for domestic and Eurobond issues. Over-the-counter and custom-designed swaps can be more difficult to value because actively traded markets for them may not exist. In such cases models that calculate the present value of payments to be received net of those to be paid can be used to determine the replacement value. This process is more complex when swaps of various types are involved.

Accounting and Tax Issues

There are many types of swaps, and the accounting procedures used for these can differ. In general, however, the central accounting issue concerning swaps is that of their disclosure. Both interest-rate and currency swaps do not have to be disclosed in financial statements in the United States and other countries unless individually or together they are considered to be material to the financial position of the company as a whole, in which case they must be described in the footnotes to the financial statements. So for financial reporting purposes, swaps are considered off-balance-sheet items in most cases. For income statement purposes, swap payments typically are reported as adjustments to interest expense, with gains, losses, or lump-sum payments being amortized over the life of the original transaction. A swap ordinarily does not involve any exchange of principal, and consequently the cash flows on the swap are treated for tax purposes, in most countries, as ordinary income or expense, with gains, losses, or lump-sum payments being taken as adjustments to income in the period incurred.

Regulatory Issues Involving Swaps

As discussed more fully in chapter 20, the BIS proposals for improving bank capital adequacy that were adopted in 1988 by the 12 leading banking nations were aimed at "strengthening the stability of the international banking system and removing a source of competitive inequality for banks arising from differences in supervisory arrangements among countries." Among the elements of the Basel proposals were a weighting system for relating capital to banking risks, including off-balance-sheet exposures.

The latter included procedures for calculating the "credit equivalent amounts" of interest rate and currency swaps as well as of certain forward market transactions.

The credit equivalent amounts, as finally adopted by the Basel Committee and against which capital must be reserved, are to be calculated by adding together the "current exposure" of a contract and the "potential future exposure." The Basel proposals did not reflect a final consensus on valuing the current exposure of swaps. The Committee agreed that bank regulators could use discretion but should rely on either the marked-to-market or replacement-cost method in doing so. In calculating the marked-to-market exposure of a swap contract, only negative exposure counts. That is, if the swap is in the money, or has positive market value, it cannot be used to offset current negative exposures of out-of-the-money swaps. Potential future exposure is determined by multiplying the notional value of the contract by a risk factor as follows:

Remaining Maturity	Interest Rate Swap Contracts	Currency Swap Contracts
Less than 1 year	0	1.0%
1 year and over	0.5%	5.0%

The difference in the risk factors reflects both maturities and the structural differences between interest-rate and currency swaps, the latter involving principal payments and cross-currency foreign exchange exposure. In April 1995, the BIS also proposed additional capital requirements to reflect the market risk of banks' derivative and other holdings, as previously described.

In March 1988 the Federal Reserve Board adopted a joint interagency proposal for implementing the Basel proposals in the United States. The Federal Reserve's regulations apply only to U.S. banks and bank holding companies, though similar requirements have been imposed on banks from all of the principle industrialized nations. None of these, however, as yet applies to nonbank financial institutions such as investment banks, insurance companies, or financial or commercial corporations in the United States or in other countries. Current discussions among EC, BIS, and U.S. banking regulators indicate that nonbank institutions will also be subject to similar restrictions in the near future.

The net effect of the capital standards is to increase the amount of capital that banks must have to maintain their swap portfolios. Some observers note that the measures will not fall evenly on the banks—that German, French, and Japanese banks may have to reserve greater amounts of capital to maintain their portfolios than would others. Others, possibly including nonbanks, may be able to avoid capital restrictions to some degree.

Swaps as Bridges between Markets

Swaps are a means of integrating markets that would otherwise remain substantially independent of one another. In the early days of the Eurodollar bond market, substantial differentials existed between its rates and other terms of borrowings and those of the domestic dollar bond market. The European investor base was quite different and greatly influenced by such factors as exchange rates, tax factors, and the need for anonymity. In recent years the Eurodollar and U.S. dollar bond markets have become substantially integrated. The original distinguishing factors remain important, but investors have less leverage over borrowers now than they had previously because borrowers enjoy greater flexibility. Among these alternatives are interest-rate and currency swaps, which permit the creation of synthetic securities in which the interest rate is set in the most favorable market.

Interest-rate swaps link short-term and long-term rates, or capital market rates and bank lending rates. When the spreads between the rates available become great enough they attract enough business to reduce them. In any case, however, the market for plain vanilla interest-rate swaps is sufficiently liquid that dealers now quote very narrow (e.g., 5 to 6 basis points) bid/asked spreads. In the cap market, spreads range from about 6 basis points for 2 years to about 35 basis points for 10 years. Thus, large volumes of market activity can compress the rate differentials between fixed- and floating-rate dollar instruments.

In the same way, currency swaps link long- and short-term dollar and nondollar rates. More accurately, perhaps, it could be said that currency swaps link dollar bond market borrowing rates and conditions with those of various nondollar bond markets.

The swap market has become very efficient in scouring the world's capital markets on a 24-hour a day basis to locate swapping possibilities that provide valued-added to participants, and in quickly communicating these possibilities to clients. Once a transaction is completed, the market is aware of it immediately and any "new" aspects of the deal are quickly assimilated. A few more transactions of the same type occur bearing higher fees or other costs, reflective of the innovation. Then, usually after a relatively short period, the spreads close, the advantages disappear, and the market goes looking for the next opportunity. Such speed and efficiency is made possible by competitive forces, by excellent telecommunications facilities, and by a major increase in the market sensitivities and technical competence of both the bankers and their clients. The more rapidly and efficiently markets work, the more efficient the linkages.

Figure 10-7 diagrams the linkages swaps create in the international capital markets.

Competing in Swaps and Derivatives

There are many different competitors in the market for swaps and other derivative securities. These include banks, investment banks, finance companies, insurance companies, and dealers from the United States, the United Kingdom, continental Europe, Japan, Canada, and other parts of Asia. Their roles are essentially that of end-users and swap arrangers and providers. Many large banks and other financial houses act as both users and providers. Competition is driven by innovation in application of swap technology to new uses, improved terms and pricing, and the ability to cover market opportunities all over the world.

In the early days of the market, investment bankers tended to act as agents and commercial banks as principals. Competitive pressure, however, quickly drove a number of investment banks to position swaps that they were trying to arrange in order to complete a particular, fast-moving deal in which they were competing with other firms. Thus, if CS First Boston was trying to arrange for a seven-year interest rate swap for Alcoa, it might decide to wrap up the business by taking the Alcoa exposure on its own books with the intention of selling it or matching it with another swap later on. In time, CS First Boston might sell the package of Alcoa's obligation to it, and its obligation to Alcoa (together called a "matched swap") to another bank, or repackage the swap by selling one obligation with or without a match and keeping the other for its own portfolio to be matched with another swap priced more advantageously.

By skillful management of its matched book of swaps, CS First Boston could earn revenues, stay on top of the market in swaps so as to compete

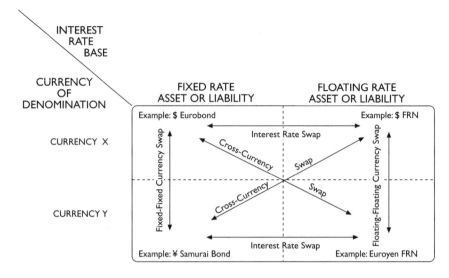

Figure 10-7. How swaps link the international capital markets. FRN = fixed-rate note.

more vigorously, and offer its clients swaps as principal so as to minimize the risk of the business being done with another party. Disadvantages include substantial administrative costs associated with keeping track of all the swaps passing through CS First Boston's hands, and risks associated with swap counterparty failure and the possibility of swaps requiring an allocation of regulatory capital in the future. Many of the major U.S. investment banks operate in the swaps business as principal, and of course virtually all of the international commercial banks do so as well.

Competitors recognize that to be successful, firms must enlarge on the linkages that exist between the swaps desk and other financing departments of the firm. Swaps have become commodities applicable to transactions involving corporate finance, mortgage and real estate finance, project finance, asset management, foreign exchange, and virtually all other areas of a firm's business that involve the putting together of sophisticated financial packages. The global capital markets department is in daily contact with a large number of potential bond issuers. The fixed-income department is in daily contact with a large number of asset managers. The type of transaction to be selected by such issuers or investors may involve one or more swaps. To quote a deal to the client requires hands-on attention of the swaps desk, and a very short response time.

Despite the extraordinary growth of the past few years, swap markets are still in an early stage of development. More end-users are attracted to the market every year. More intermediaries are learning how to use swaps to help them provide more efficient services to their clients. The market will continue to welcome new ideas and further applications for swaps. As in virtually all financial services today, competition is extensive and favors those who are able to create value for their clients, to manage their own exposures efficiently, and to keep abreast of—and contribute to—the fast moving technology of the market.

Summary

Unknown before 1980, swaps and their family of related transactions have become a large and important part of the global financial landscape today. They are useful to issuers of securities and to investors as a means to manage financial market risk exposures and to lower costs of funds, or increase return on investment, respectively. They enable participants to bridge (and thus aid in integrating) financial markets across maturities, currencies, and forms of payment. Swaps have a multitude of applications and therefore have proliferated widely since their introduction. Swaps are comparatively cheap, quick to arrange, involve standardized and simple documentation, and expose their participants to only modest risk levels in relation to the notional amounts involved, which nonetheless must now be accounted for by banks under the current capital adequacy rules.

Notes

1. As the value of the swap depends on the *change* in interest or exchange rates, it is a first derivative (in calculus terms) of the rates, hence it is a "derivative security."

11

International Equity Securities

International transactions in equity securities have expanded enormously since the mid-1980s, as reflected in the substantial increase in the volume of cross-exchange transactions in secondary markets, of cross-border mergers and acquisitions, and of new issues offered to investors under one of several different "globalized" distribution techniques. Total foreign share trading exceeded $3.0 *trillion* in 1993, up from less than $1 trillion in 1986—a growth rate of 17 percent. The United States has been prominently involved in these developments: total worldwide purchases by foreigners of U.S. shares also expanded at a compound growth rate of 17 percent for the 10-year period 1980–1990; however, U.S. purchases of foreign equity securities grew at a 30 percent compound rate.[1] Global equity market capitalization has also grown during the last several years, from $7.8 trillion in 1987 to more than $14 trillion in 1993 (Table 11-1).

Behind the Growth

This extraordinary growth in the appetite for investment in international stocks has been very widespread. Not only are investments in the United States, Japan, and the major European countries in demand, but also investments in shares from other European countries—West and East—and from a variety of new "emerging" markets, from Argentina to the People's Republic of China. These developments reflect the many factors that have led toward the integration of capital markets around the world—powerful forces such as the opening up of national markets through various deregulatory processes; substantial improvements in financial reporting, information gathering, and dissemination technology; and greatly improved trading environments. The growing involvement of major financial institutions, especially those from the United States and Japan, as investors and

Table 11-1 Global Equity Markets Capitalization

Market Value

	1987		1988		1989		1990		1991		1992		1993		1994	
	U.S. $ billions	%	U.S. $ billions	%	U.S. $ billions	%	U.S. $ billions	%	U.S. $ billions	%	U.S. $ billions	%	U.S. $ billions	%	U.S. $ billions	%
United States	2,589	33.1	2,794	28.7	3,506	29.9	3,090	32.8	4,099	36.3	4,498	41.2	5,224	37.0	5,082	33.5
Japan	2,803	35.8	3,937	40.5	4,393	37.5	2,918	31.0	3,131	27.7	2,399	22.0	3,000	21.3	3,720	24.5
United Kingdom	681	8.7	771	7.9	827	7.1	849	9.0	988	8.7	927	8.5	1,152	8.2	1,210	8.0
France	172	2.2	245	2.5	365	3.1	314	3.3	348	3.1	351	3.2	456	3.2	451	3.0
Germany	213	2.7	252	2.6	365	3.1	355	3.8	393	3.5	348	3.2	463	3.3	471	3.1
Canada	219	2.8	242	2.5	291	2.5	242	2.6	267	2.4	243	2.2	327	2.3	315	2.1
Switzerland	129	1.6	141	1.4	171	1.5	160	1.7	174	1.5	195	1.8	272	1.9	284	1.9
Hong Kong	54	0.7	74	0.8	77	0.7	83	0.9	122	1.1	172	1.6	385	2.7	270	1.8
Netherlands	86	1.1	114	1.2	158	1.3	120	1.3	136	1.2	135	1.2	182	1.3	283	1.9
Australia	106	1.4	138	1.4	141	1.2	108	1.1	145	1.3	135	1.2	204	1.4	219	1.4
Italy	120	1.5	135	1.4	169	1.4	149	1.6	159	1.4	129	1.2	136	1.0	180	1.2
Spain	71	0.9	91	0.9	123	1.1	111	1.2	148	1.3	99	0.9	119	0.8	—	—
Sweden	71	0.9	100	1.0	119	1.0	92	1.0	97	0.9	77	0.7	107	0.8	—	—
Other developed markets	199	2.5	212	2.2	271	2.3	220	2.3	239	2.1	255	2.3	438	3.1	744	4.9
All emerging markets	319	4.1	483	5.0	738	6.3	612	6.5	851	6	957	7.4	1,636	11.6	1,929	12.7
World	7,832		9,729		11,714		9,423		11,297		10,920		14,101		15,186	

Source: International Finance Corp.

as providers of services to the markets, reflects a substantial change in their behavior from the more conservative practices of the past (before about 1980) during which investment horizons were limited to domestic markets.

Market Liberalization and Deregulation

The much-resisted abolition of fixed commission rates by the New York Stock Exchange (NYSE) on May 1, 1975—an event then called "Mayday"—generated a number of fundamental changes in the way equity markets operate all over the world. The basic principle involved was that a stock exchange could not operate as a private club with rules that prevented market access by nonmembers and required fixed minimum, nonnegotiable per-share commission rates, irrespective of trading volume.

As institutional trading grew during the 1960s, many large investors began to complain about the high cost of commissions and their inability to recover these by becoming members of the exchange. The SEC and the Antitrust Division of the U.S. Justice Department took an interest in the issue, and ultimately forced the NYSE to rescind its minimum commission rules, to allow foreign brokerage firms to become members, and to include nonmembers on its board of directors. Immediately after these rule changes, institutional commission rates plummeted (they are now down to less than 5 percent of pre-Mayday levels on large institutional transactions) and many firms were required to reorganize and improve their competitive capabilities. In response to such pressures, the NYSE member firms introduced many innovations and provided much more extensive and more valuable services to customers, thereby improving the quality and efficiency of the markets considerably. In 1975, the daily trading volume on the NYSE, which accounted for 85 percent of all shares traded in the United States, was 18.6 million shares, annual market turnover was valued at $127 billion, and the market capitalization of listed companies was $134 billion. By 1994, daily NYSE trading volume averaged 291.4 million shares, annual market turnover was $2.5 trillion, and market capitalization was $5 trillion. However, by 1994, the development of electronic, screen-based markets like the National Association of Securities Dealers Automated Quotation Service (NASDAQ), increased regional exchange trading, and off-market trading arrangements had reduced the NYSE share of total U.S. equity trading to about 50 percent.[2]

The "Mayday effect" was not lost on other countries. In the late 1970s, the Labour government in Britain instituted a lawsuit against the London Stock Exchange (LSE) alleging that its clublike operations were in restraint of trade. The Conservative government of Margaret Thatcher inherited this lawsuit and settled it with the Exchange in 1983. Under the terms of the settlement, the LSE agreed by October 27, 1986 to abolish membership restrictions and the requirement that members act only in a "single capacity," that is, as either dealer or broker, but not both. This settlement changed the economics of the U.K. securities business fundamentally, and led to what the British press called the "Big Bang" in London, a total transformation of the securities markets in the United Kingdom. Under the system that replaced the old rules, any qualified firm (including commercial and merchant banks and foreign securities firms) could join the LSE, firms could act as both brokers and dealers (as in New York), and commission rates were fully negotiable.

The Bank of England, wishing to take advantage of the coming changes to improve the efficiency of capital markets in the United Kingdom (especially for government securities, and in anticipation of large privatization issues to come), and to firm up London's position as Europe's most active financial center, also contributed to the "reregulation" of London financial markets by revising the capital requirements for market-making in government and corporate debt securities, and in equities. And the British Parliament passed a landmark, omnibus securities regulation bill, the Financial Securities Act of 1986, to set up an institutional framework for securities market regulation.

In consequence, trading volume in the United Kingdom more than doubled; commissions were slashed; many of the British brokers and dealers merged into other, stronger groups; competition increased greatly; and large integrated securities firms, such as S. G. Warburg, Merrill Lynch, and Goldman Sachs, increased their market share. The benefits of the reforms, as in the early days after Mayday in New York, were seen to flow mainly to the users of securities market services at the expense of the providers of such services. The competitive difficulties caused by Big Bang were heightened after the worldwide stock market crash of October 17, 1987.

The rest of Europe was very mindful of the market changes in London. By this time, preparations were under way for the implementation by the EC of the Single Market Act by the end of 1992, and the Commission was in the process of promulgating directives for the future conduct of banking and other financial services. Liberalization to accommodate greater competition was the key to the EU reforms, and in all countries some form of financial market deregulation occurred. Extensive though far less comprehensive changes than those that occurred in Britain were made in France, Germany, Italy, and Switzerland. Similar changes were also adopted in Canada, Australia, and New Zealand, and ultimately in Japan, where regulatory changes were more difficult to make because of a competitive impasse between banks and securities firms that had been separated by Article 65 of the Securities and Exchange Law of 1947.

In general, a decade after the Big Bang settlement was reached, the principles of open access and negotiated commissions were adopted (at least in significant measure) by almost all countries that had important stock exchanges. In Japan, fixed commissions still existed, but a system of progressively increasing discounts for large trades in effect did away with minimum rates by 1992. This wide acceptance of competitive and regulatory practices reflects a degree of global convergence that had not occurred before, one that has become increasingly difficult for individual countries to oppose. This is because market forces can now create alternative trading venues to those blocked by local regulation. If Britain should impose a stamp tax on stock trading, henceforth much of the LSE trading business would be conducted elsewhere, for example, in New York where over-the-counter market-makers can quote tax-free prices to U.K. investors. Rather than lose its stock-market business to New York, the British would more likely drop the stamp tax. Also, countries now lobby other countries to offer reciprocal access to financial services markets or suffer denial of access to financial services by nationals of their country. Between market forces and political pressures, it has become extremely difficult for any country to drag its feet indefinitely in opposition to the emerging global standard of stock market reforms.

Improved Information Flows

Advances in information and communications technology have been essential to the growth in the international equities markets. Market information of all types is now available internationally, through newspapers, screens, and contact with brokers. Securities can also be traded internationally in most OECD countries with a high degree of reliance on trouble-free payment and delivery, which was rarely the case before 1980 when dealing outside the United States, the United Kingdom, and Canada. It is now possible to receive a reliable quote on virtually any stock whose home market is one of the major financial centers, from just about anywhere, on the telephone. Quotes are also available for securities from many other countries on very short notice.

The recent computerization of various national markets, such as in Britain, France, Switzerland, and Germany, has introduced a variety of new technological capabilities for screen trading, futures and options transactions, and paperless trading that did not exist before Big Bang. These developments has had the effect of linking international marketplaces, making possible a level of expansion that probably could not otherwise have occurred.

With these developments has come a large increase in the number of trained professionals who provide the many services needed to sustain a growing market: These services include such front office activities as providing investment research information (about an increasing number of different companies and securities from an increasing number of countries), block and program trading and portfolio insurance services offered to institutional clients, indexing and other services offered to investment companies and mutual funds, and an increasing use of derivative securities for customer risk management programs. Internal and back-office capabilities include various firmwide exposure risk management and hedging functions, optimal financing of trading positions, improved payment and settlement activities, and more efficient record keeping, management control, and information services.

Better Trading Markets

Trading markets in international equity securities have improved steadily since the early 1980s. Before that, secondary trading in international stocks was limited. The level of trading activity in the home markets, especially in continental Europe, was often low and liquidity limited. The American Depository Receipt (ADR) market was useful for some stocks, mainly British, Japanese, and Canadian, but prices were still set in the home market, and gradually U.S. investors shifted their business there. A few multinational companies were listed on the NYSE and the Tokyo Stock Exchange (TSE), more on the LSE, but trading volumes in the foreign markets was rarely significant compared with those in the home market. Frequently foreign companies chose not to list on the NYSE because of the expense and the awkward disclosure requirements associated with becoming an SEC "reporting company." Many companies instead passively allowed their shares to be traded in the NASDAQ system or in over-the-counter markets by firms specializing in international stocks.

For years, the principal international trading activity was foreign stock arbitrage, in which one would buy an (ADR)[3] of, say, a Dutch stock and simultaneously sell the number of underlying shares represented by the ADR in Amsterdam. To do this profitably one had to be a master of the details involved. The purchase in dollars after commissions had to cost less than the proceeds of the sale of the shares, after commissions and transfer expenses, and after the foreign exchange costs of converting back into dollars. Such arbitrage activities kept prices of international shares around the world in line with their home market values.

The next development was to provide improved market-making services to customers interested in buying foreign securities that were not available on exchanges. For example, a U.S. pension fund might want to buy shares in Fujitsu Ltd., which was not listed on any U.S. exchange or in NASDAQ but for which ADRs were available. The pension fund might call a Japanese broker based in New York who could say, "We will take your order and purchase Fujitsu shares in Japan overnight. We will confirm tomorrow and tell you at what dollar price the order was executed. We will then deposit the shares with the agent bank in Japan and have ADRs put into your account in New York." Alternatively the pension fund might call a U.S. market-maker in Fujitsu and be told, "We will sell you Fujitsu dollar ADRs right now for $x." The U.S. broker, if he or she does not have Fujitsu ADRs in inventory, will try to buy them in the New York market or trade with a Japanese broker overnight to get the shares to deliver to the pension fund. The market-maker's price will reflect the various uncertainties to contended with. Such international block trading services soon became popular with major U.S. and European institutional investors. Certain stocks became international favorites, and the U.S. and British firms quickly offered research coverage of them. Soon these services were offered to investors all over Europe and in Japan. Over time the trading volume in international equities built up considerably and pricing was tightened up accordingly.

Now, with foreign membership available on exchanges in Europe and the Far East as well as North America, it is possible for participating firms to be active market-makers in U.S., European, and Asian stocks around the clock. Such firms are able to balance orders from around the world, not just from their home market. They are also able to limit their market-making activities to stocks for which they see international demand, and not find themselves in the position of being a market-maker for all comers, as some national dealers feel they must do. The commitment to dealing in international equities by major firms is now very substantial and is reflected in the number of personnel that have been added in research, trading, sales coverage, systems, and back office and foreign exchange by major U.S., British, Japanese, and other firms. A very large increase in market infrastructure has occurred, which not only makes improved services possible but also provides competitive energy in the market as all of these new employees seek to advance their careers.

The result of these developments has been a substantial increase in the value of worldwide equity trading volume, which increased 26 percent from $5.8 trillion in 1987 to $7.3 trillion in 1993. This increase reflected a large increase in trading volume in Japan, which exceeded the total volume of U.S. equity trading in 1988 and 1989. After 1989, however, because of the precipitous drop in share prices, Japanese trading substantially dried up, declining nearly 80 percent to $635 billion in 1992 (24 percent of 1992 U.S. trading volume). Trading elsewhere in the world (outside of the United States and Japan), however, held its own. (Table 11-2).

In Europe.   The improvement in access to market-making for international shares is also very important. In London, increasing interest in continental European stocks on the part of British, American, and Japanese institutional investors has caused many London-based market-makers to offer French, German, Dutch, Italian, and Swiss shares through the LSE's Stock Exchange Automated Quotation (SEAQ) system. Many European shares are now listed in London, where reportedly 90 percent of all European cross-exchange share trading now occurs. SEAQ, which is similar to NASDAQ in the United States, claims to handle as much as three-quarters of all trading in blue-chip shares based in Holland, half those in France and Italy, and a quarter of those based in Germany, though these figures are subject to some double-counting due to interdealer purchases and sales.[4] Approximately half of the total trading volume in SEAQ, however, is now provided by trading in non-U.K. shares (see Figure 11-1).

The diversion of this business to London has encouraged continental

Table 11-2 Global Value of Shares Traded

	1987		1988		1989		1990		1991		1992		1993		1994	
	U.S. $ billions	%	U.S. $ billions	%	U.S. $ billions	%	U.S. $ billions	%	U.S. $ billions	%	U.S. $ billions	%	U.S. $ billions	%	U.S. $ billions	%
United States	2,423	41.4	1,720	28.7	2,016	27.0	1,815	32.5	2,255	44.3	2,679	49.8	3,507	47.8	3,593	37.3
Japan	2,047	35.0	2,598	43.3	2,801	37.5	1,602	28.7	996	19.6	635	11.8	954	13.0	1,121	11.7
Germany	373	6.4	350	5.8	629	8.4	502	9.0	379	7.4	446	8.3	303	4.1	461	4.8
United Kingdom	390	6.7	579	9.7	320	4.3	279	5.0	315	6.2	383	7.1	424	5.8	928	9.6
France	88	1.5	66	1.1	107	1.4	117	2.1	114	2.2	122	2.3	174	2.4	615	6.4
Hong Kong	48	0.8	23	0.4	35	0.5	35	0.6	39	0.8	79	1.5	132	1.8	147	1.5
Netherlands	40	0.7	35	0.6	90	1.2	40	0.7	39	0.8	46	0.9	67	0.9	171	1.8
Canada	75	1.3	67	1.1	90	1.2	71	1.3	78	1.5	83	1.5	142	1.9	161	1.7
Switzerland	N/A	N/A	N/A	N/A	N/A	N/A	N/A	N/A	69	1.4	75	1.4	168	2.3	227	2.4
Australia	59	1.0	37	0.6	45	0.6	39	0.7	47	0.9	45	0.8	68	0.9	95	1.0
Spain	36	0.6	26	0.4	38	0.5	41	0.7	41	0.8	40	0.7	47	0.6	N/A	N/A
Sweden	20	0.3	19	0.3	17	0.2	16	0.3	21	0.4	28	0.5	44	0.6	N/A	N/A
Italy	32	0.5	32	0.5	39	0.5	43	0.8	25	0.5	28	0.5	66	0.9	118	1.2
Denmark	2	0.0	5	0.1	14	0.2	11	0.2	9	0.2	16	0.3	21	0.3	N/A	N/A
Other developed markets	50	0.9	32	0.5	62	0.8	71	1.3	55	1.1	57	1.1	156	2.2	346	3.6
All emerging markets	165	2.8	409	6.8	1,166	15.6	895	16.0	606	11.9	613	11.4	1,069	14.6	1,640	17.0
World	5,848		5,998		7,469		5,577		5,088		5,375		7,342		9,622	

Source: International Finance Corp.

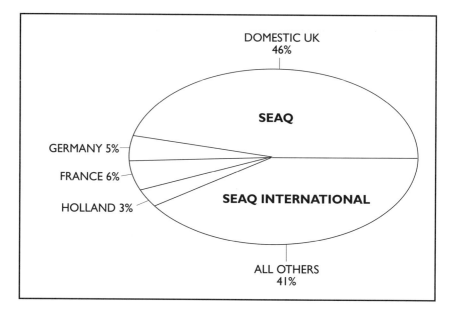

Figure 11-1. Trading on the London Stock Exchange, 1994. SEAQ = Stock Exchange Automated Quotation. Source: The London Stock Exchange.

European markets to accelerate internal reforms, which are long overdue; to consolidate local and regional exchanges into a single national market (this has recently been completed in Germany and Switzerland); to concentrate on market architecture to optimize efficiencies; and to encourage new innovations and increased competitive activity to recapture market share. Futures and options exchanges have also been opened in Paris, Frankfurt, and Zurich, and recently in Madrid and Milan, and equity-based derivatives are rapidly increasing in use. New market developments and innovations in New York or London are often copied quickly in these other markets, and trading volumes are rising.

The SEAQ system benefits from being the first European electronic trading system in place and from being located at the hub of European institutional trading activity, where the American presence is greatly felt. It has some disadvantages though: It must still depend on local market prices for its activities, it is subject to certain nontransparent LSE market-making practices for large blocks of securities that detract from market efficiency, and its settlement practices are considerably less modern than those of some of the newer continental exchanges.

Market capitalization of the various European stock markets has grown steadily since 1983, though most of this growth has been in London (Figure 11-2). It is not inconceivable that some trading in European stocks could migrate to other, more competitive marketplaces, but for the moment the massive English-speaking trading infrastructure, the regulatory environment, and the relative size of the London market compared with other European markets indicate a continuing advantage for market-makers to remain in London. While competition between London and the other markets continues, the ultimate EU goal is a single, integrated European market, at least for professional investors.

In Japan. A modern trading market exists in Japan, mainly through the Tokyo Stock Exchange on which approximately 1,600 companies are listed. During 1989, when the peak of market activity in Japan was reached, the market capitalization of the TSE was $4.4 trillion (compared with $3.5 trillion for all shares traded in the United States) and the value of shares traded was $2.8 trillion ($2.0 trillion in the United States). After 1989, however, the Japanese market fell steadily for the next two years as a result of financial crises and scandals, which brought to an end a period of great speculative activity. During 1993 the Japanese market began a cautious recovery and instituted a number of regulatory changes intended

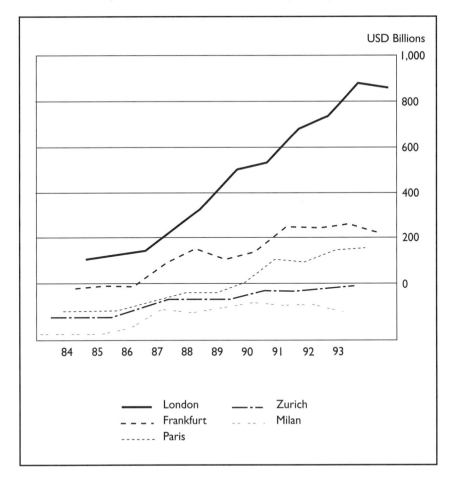

Figure 11-2. Market capitalization, European exchanges. Source: Datastream.

to curtail abuses in the future. Foreign investors, who became the most active buyers of Japanese stocks in 1992 (i.e., more active than Japanese investors), continued to purchase shares on the theory that the bottom had been reached and they had the liquidity to acquire low-priced shares that Japaneses institutions did not. Though licking their wounds, Japanese institutions were learning their lessons too: More professional standards of investment activity, such as those employed by major international institutions, would have to be used in the future, with greater reliance on research, trading, and portfolio diversification than had been applied in the past.

Changes in Investor Behavior

Participation in international equity investments is a comparatively new development for U.S. and Japanese investors—at least in the post–World War II period—but it is not for Europeans. For many years the most international of all investors were the Swiss banks, which had attracted foreign "safekeeping" funds. There was very little to invest in Switzerland, so the banks were always looking for suitable investment opportunities abroad. During the 1960s and 1970s Swiss banks were the principal foreign investors in U.S. stocks. Subsequently they became substantial investors in Japanese stocks as well. Similar to the Swiss banks were banks and investment companies in Holland, Belgium, and Luxembourg. In few of these countries did a sufficiency of good investment opportunities exist.

Just behind the Swiss as international investors were the British, who have had a long history of overseas portfolio investment. Until 1979, however, Britain had been subject to foreign exchange controls that required that a premium be paid for foreign currency to be used for investment outside the country. Most other countries in Europe had similar foreign exchange regulations, though these have now been abolished. Once the foreign exchange controls were lifted in the United Kingdom a substantial increase in overseas investment took place, into the United States and Japan mostly. Institutional investors in the United Kingdom have since greatly increased their activities abroad and now hold and trade substantial volumes of international securities of all types. More recently, U.S. and Japanese institutional investors also entered into active programs for investing in international equities. As a result the international pool of funds participating in equities has greatly increased. Indeed, the pool has now become "institutionalized" (much as the U.S. equity markets were in the 1960s), being managed by internationally sophisticated, professional money managers.

Moreover, as non-U.S. markets have become more active and attracted more attention from investors outside their own countries, they have grown in relative importance. Gradually, share prices in the countries with less developed markets have risen to international norms. In 1980, some

49 percent of world market capitalization was attributed to companies from the United States, 20 percent to companies from the EC, 17 percent to Japanese companies, and 14 percent to the rest of the world. By 1990 the U.S. share had declined to 35 percent, while the Japanese had increased to 33 percent, and that of the EC countries to 24 percent (Figure 11-3).

Growth of Pension Funds

Much of the new money flowing into the international equity market has been from pension funds. These have continued to enjoy a substantial inflow of funds each year, especially in Europe and Japan where the practice of providing for retirement benefits through market returns is more recent than in the United States. Not only have total pension assets grown, but (for reasons discussed below) there has also been a substantial increase in the percentage of total assets invested in foreign securities. This has been true for pension funds in countries all over the world, as Table 11-3 illustrates.

Japanese pension funds especially have been growing very rapidly as the country adjusts to an aging population that has not had sufficient pension programs in the past. An increasing amount of this money, which is managed by insurance companies and trust banks (and recently opened to foreign money managers) is invested in international equities. As the money managers become more familiar with international portfolio management practices (which vary considerably from portfolio management practices in Japan), the Japanese are expected to become increasingly important in the international investment field.

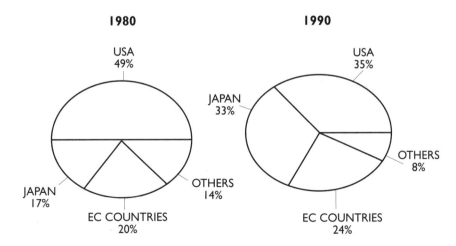

Figure 11-3. Market capitalization by country, 1980 and 1990. Source: *Financial Times—World Actuaries World Index*.

Table 11-3 Foreign Investment of Private-Sector Pension Assets ($ billions)

Country	1987	% of Total Investments	1992	% of Total Investments	1997[a]	% of Total Investments
United States	$44.0	3.9	$99.0	4.4	$264.0	9.0
Japan	20.6	9.8	58.0	16.0	117.0	20.0
United Kingdom	69.0	18.4	141.4	26.0	194.6	28.0
Netherlands	12.8	12.1	29.8	20.3	50.0	25.0
Canada	5.2	8.7	11.3	10.5	25.5	17.0
Switzerland	4.8	5.5	13.8	11.0	28.5	15.0
Germany	1.6	3.1	4.9	5.8	7.5	6.5
Australia	1.9	12.4	5.8	17.0	16.8	20.0
Denmark	—	—	1.1	5.0	2.9	9.0
France	—	—	0.7	3.0	1.6	5.0
Hong Kong	2.7	52.4	9.8	65.0	30.6	65.0
Ireland	1.5	21.0	3.3	30.0	5.1	30.0
Belgium	1.4	30.0	2.8	33.0	4.9	35.0
Rest of the world	3.8	7.5	10.6	10.0	32.3	14.7
Total	$169.3		$392.3		$781.3	

Source: InterSec Research Corp.
[a] Estimate.

International Application of Modern Portfolio Theory

Sometime during the 1980s, investors on the whole concluded that internationally diversified portfolios produced the best risk-adjusted returns, and that it was possible to identify and trade in a sufficient number of international stocks to make this conclusion a reality. Indeed, performance could also be enhanced by investing in a well-selected mix of stocks from other economies. Figure 11-4 illustrates that U.S. investors would have enjoyed a superior investment performance from the mid-1980s if they had invested in the Morgan Stanley Capital International world stock market index, compared with the Dow Jones industrial average. So a process of catching up ensued, in which portfolio managers began to accumulate the international shareholdings that were needed to bring about the appropriate mix of foreign and domestic investments.

Figure 11-5 shows the annualized returns on a range of different internationally diversified portfolios (ranging from 0 percent to 100 percent invested in Morgan Stanley's Europe, America, Far-East [EAFE] index) for the 10 years ended December 1994. These data indicate that a prudent pension fund manager, for example, might conclude that a balance of about 30 percent foreign shares (invested in the EAFE index) and 70 percent in the S&P 500 index would produce a safer and more profitable distribution of assets than if all were invested in the domestic market. It was not long before fund managers in Germany, Italy, Japan, and Singapore began to appreciate these considerations and commenced to rebalance their own portfolios with more international stocks. Because of the vast amounts involved and the as yet small amounts of foreign investments

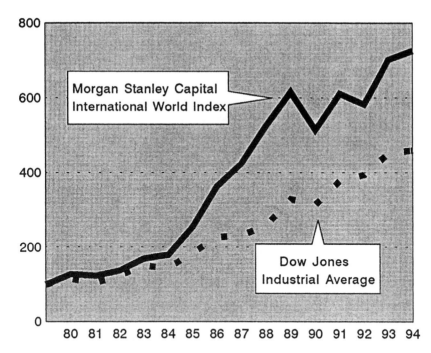

Figure 11-4. Equity index growth comparison, Morgan Stanley Capital International world stock market index versus the Dow Jones industrial average (end 1979 = 100). Sources: *Bloomberg Business News* and Morgan Stanley.

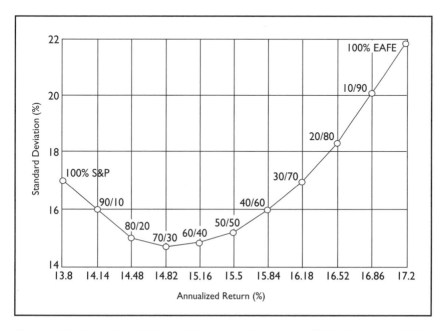

Figure 11-5. Portfolios of U.S. and foreign stocks, January 1973–December 1994.

as a percent of total investments (about 8 percent worldwide in 1992), and because of new market opportunities developing all the time to compete for the foreign allocation of investors' funds, we can expect the foreign investment surge to continue for some years.

The lasting benefit of all of this international investing, however, depended on a key tenant of modern portfolio theory—that overall portfolio risk was lowered through diversification into noncorrelated investments—which has been shown especially to apply to international investments. The key (to the theory) is the lack of correlation between most foreign markets and one's own. In a perfectly integrated market, on the other hand, the correlation between markets would be quite high and there could be no gain from diversification per se.

In the international markets for debt securities a high degree of correlation exists—the yields adjusted for currency, maturity, and ratings are about the same in the principal financial centers. The same is not true in equity securities, where correlation between the S&P 500 index and foreign market indices is low. There remain enough differences between individual equity markets, however, that integration and correlation have remained minimal, as shown in Figure 11-6. This is because stocks represent different economic values in different countries, and indeed are valued differently in terms of price earnings ratios and other common measures.

Differences in Valuation

The international markets are not all the same, which is part of their appeal. Differences exist in *risk exposure,* where, for example, volatility may be extremely high, information scarce, regulation inadequate, and market manipulation rife compared with the investor's home market. On the *return* side, differences can exist also in terms of the number of comparatively underpriced growth companies or privatization issues, or in the general economic outlook in countries undergoing major developmental changes, such as Korea or Mexico. Differences in the methods of securities valuation can also be significant.

While it may be true that each national market values its equity securities with similar views about how to determine the worth of a future stream of dividends when capitalized at a locally suitable discount rate, it is also true that very great differences can exist between markets that are not explained by factors in the formula.

In the United States, experienced financial institutions, employing what they consider the most sophisticated tools for valuing securities, tend to set prices. In Japan, fund managers with a large cash flow to invest and enthusiastic individual investors tend to follow the advice of stockbrokers. This can create a kind of herd instinct that can move the market more than careful attention to market valuation formulae. In Europe, local mar-

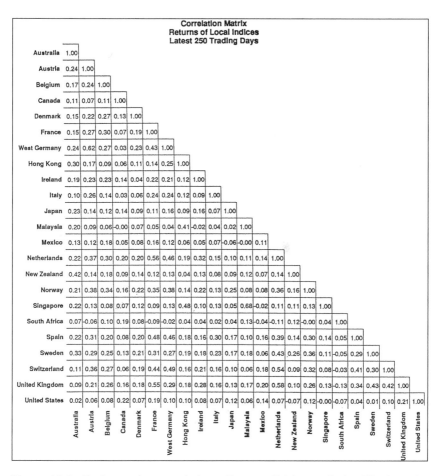

Figure 11-6. Equity market correlations. Source: Goldman, Sachs FT—Actuaries World Indices, February 1994.

kets may be so inactive in particular stocks that they appear undervalued by Americans looking for bargain investments they believe will reflect much higher "true" values in the long run. Many people believe they cannot apply their own valuation methods to equities that are mainly traded in another country. Instead one must understand the market as locals do and go with the flow. Why else would a foreigner buy a Japanese bank stock at 50 times earnings unless he had reason to believe he could sell it later to another buyer at 80 times earnings.

On the other hand, as the markets become more closely linked (and as foreign trading becomes as important as any other domestic source of trading), pricing mechanisms ought to converge. The circulation of high-quality securities research reports and the linking of trading mechanisms around the world indicate that in some respects the markets have already begun to do so.

New Issues and Distribution Methods

Shares offered to the market for the first time are called *new issues*. Generally the term refers to shares newly issued by a corporation that are sold to the public through an underwritten distribution and are subject to applicable disclosure, registration, and other regulations pertaining to "these securities." When these shares are sold they are said to constitute a *primary offering*, because they are being sold for the first time. Shares offered for sale by an existing shareholder are done so in the *secondary market*, which is where ordinary brokerage transactions occur. However, when a large existing shareholder sells shares through a public distribution (as in the case of a privatization issue by a government shareholder), the process is called a *secondary offering*, and it too is regarded as and usually subject to the same regulations as a new issue. International equity issues have been a growing and continually active part of international capital markets since the mid-1980s, as shown in Table 11-4.

Most distributions are insured by a group of *underwriters;* that is, the underwriters guarantee the sale of a specified number of shares at a specified price and commission. That is all underwriters do. The distribution (or sale) of the securities to investors is the responsibility of brokers, who may or may not be included among the underwriters. Some distributions, especially smaller *private placements,* which are usually exempt from national disclosure and registration requirements, are made directly with institutional investors on a "best efforts" basis and are not underwritten, although private placements may be, and often are, underwritten. Underwriting methods are discussed in the next section.

Table 11-4 International Equity New Issues[a]

Year	$ (millions)
1988	$ 6,982
1989	7,793
1990	7,400
1991	12,000
1992	17,800
1993	27,700
1994	32,400
1995	32,100
Compounded growth rate	24.3%

Source: IFR Equibase 1988–89, SDC 1990–95.

[a] Includes international distributions of national issues and Euroequity offerings of shares.

There are several methods for achieving international distribution of new issues of equity securities.

International Tranches. Issuers may tap equity markets in other countries through an *international tranche* to supplement domestic market liquidity. U.S. companies are common users of international tranches, in which the underwriters set aside 15 to 25 percent of the shares to be offered simultaneously with the U.S. distribution in the Euroequity market by a separate group of international underwriters. The international underwriters are usually led by the international affiliate of the lead U.S. underwriter to ensure tight control over the allocation of shares. Shares allocated to the international underwriters may not, by agreement, be sold in the United States, and vice versa. International underwriters (except for the U.S. lead manager(s)), are not included among the underwriters of the domestic U.S. offering. See Figure 11-7 for a "tombstone" advertisement of a recent issue with an international tranche.

Euro Equity Issues. There is an equity equivalent of the Eurobond market, called the "Euroequity" market, that can be used when an issuer wishes to tap a different and larger investor base because its domestic market is insufficient to meet the requirements of domestic participants, or as a way to avoid domestic market regulations and expenses. As in the case of the Eurobond market, the lack of regulation, the relatively low cost of issuance, and the presence of a large, highly diversified, and very liquid pool of international investment funds has attracted many issuers from all over the world.

The Euroequity market evolved to provide a source of equity finance for European issuers whose domestic market was too small or inactive to accommodate large institutionally oriented distributions. Equity issues (such as those recently issued by Fiat, Eurotunnel, The Wellcome Foundation, Euro Disney, Norsk Hydro, and Montedison) would be indigestible if offered only in the home country of the companies. Government privatization issues almost always fall into this category because of their large size and the need to attract institutional investors with an adequate trading market liquidity. Almost all of the countries in Western Europe have taken advantage of the opportunity to affect privatization issues of large industrial companies owned by the governments. Privatization issues by non-European governments, such as the recent sale of shares in the Argentine national oil company, YPF, or the Shanghai Petrochemical Company, rarely are attempted without heavy reliance on the Euroequity market.

Rule 144a Placements. In April 1990 the U.S. SEC approved its Rule 144a, through which it in effect permitted the sales to qualified institutional investors of securities not registered with the SEC in the United States. Such sales are made through private placements, which are exempt from registration with the SEC and therefore do not involve the full disclo-

This announcement is neither an offer to sell nor a solicitation of an offer to buy any of these Securities.
The offer is made only by the Prospectus.

7,187,500 Shares

GREENFIELD INDUSTRIES

Common Stock

Price $15½ a Share

Copies of the Prospectus may be obtained in any State from only such of the
undersigned as may legally offer these Securities in compliance
with the securities laws of such State.

5,937,500 Shares

This portion of the offering is being offered in the United States and Canada by the undersigned.

MORGAN STANLEY & CO.
Incorporated

THE FIRST BOSTON CORPORATION

WERTHEIM SCHRODER & CO.
Incorporated

DONALDSON, LUFKIN & JENRETTE Securities Corporation	A.G. EDWARDS & SONS, INC.	LEHMAN BROTHERS
OPPENHEIMER & CO., INC.		PAINEWEBBER INCORPORATED
PRUDENTIAL SECURITIES INCORPORATED		SMITH BARNEY SHEARSON INC.
DEAN WITTER REYNOLDS INC.		THE CHICAGO DEARBORN COMPANY
DAIN BOSWORTH Incorporated	KEMPER SECURITIES, INC.	McDONALD & COMPANY Securities, Inc.
THE ROBINSON-HUMPHREY COMPANY, INC.		WHEAT FIRST BUTCHER & SINGER Capital Markets
ROBERT W. BAIRD & CO. Incorporated		BREAN MURRAY, FOSTER SECURITIES INC.
FIRST ALBANY CORPORATION		INTERSTATE/JOHNSON LANE Corporation
JANNEY MONTGOMERY SCOTT INC.		RAGEN MacKENZIE Incorporated
STEPHENS INC.		STIFEL, NICOLAUS & COMPANY Incorporated

1,250,000 Shares

This portion of the offering is being offered outside the United States and Canada by the undersigned.

MORGAN STANLEY INTERNATIONAL

CREDIT SUISSE FIRST BOSTON LIMITED

WERTHEIM SCHRODER INTERNATIONAL LIMITED

ABN AMRO BANK N.V.	CREDIT LYONNAIS SECURITIES
DRESDNER BANK Aktiengesellschaft	NIKKO EUROPE PLC
N M ROTHSCHILD & SONS LIMITED	
SMITH NEW COURT SECURITIES LIMITED	UBS LIMITED
August 16, 1993	

Figure 11-7. Tombstone advertisement of international tranche issue.

sure requirements. This rule was developed on the theory that large, so-phisticated investors could look out for themselves and because the United States wanted to attract more international issuers to its capital markets. In practice the rule was helpful to non-U.S. governments and corporations that wanted to use the U.S. markets but did not want to incur the account-ing and legal expenses and to be committed to annual U.S. disclosure re-quirements. Now such issuers can arrange a private placement, often on an underwritten basis, to sell unregistered securities to U.S. institutions. These securities may then be traded in the market.

The rule applies to both debt and equity securities, though in the be-ginning very few 144a equity issuers appeared. For one reason, the Euro-equity market was an effective competitor for issuers seeking foreign in-vestors; for another, U.S. investors had not yet fully warmed up to interna-tional equities. As they did, however, they became especially interested in issuers from *emerging markets,* that is, third-world countries with promis-ing economic potential, the growth-stock markets of the future. Soon U.S. institutions were eager investors in equity (and debt) issues from Mexico, Chile, Argentina, and, in early 1993, Brazil and even Peru. Other countries of interest at this time included Indonesia, Philippines, Portugal, Greece, Turkey, and Poland. Few (if any) companies from these countries could meet U.S. SEC registration requirements. During 1994, more than $5.8 billion of 144a equity issues occurred, approximately 83 percent of which were international issues.[5] The 144a total was only a small percentage (6.2 percent) of total U.S. equity issues, but a somewhat more significant per-cent (14.9 percent) of total international equity new issues.

Global Issues. Some of the large Euroequity issues are in reality "global equity issues," because they involve a combination of a Euroequity offer-ing and additional offerings through separate but simultaneous tranches in other markets. For example, in July 1993 the Argentine YPF issue raised $2.76 billion for the government through coordinated offerings in the Euro-equity market, the U.S. market, and the domestic Argentine market (where only 25 percent of the issue was actually placed) (Figure 11-8). The YPF shares were in fact registered with the SEC, but often the U.S. tranche of global issues, especially for Latin American issuers, is handled according to Rule 144a. The "joint global coordinators" for the YPF issue were CS First Boston and Merrill Lynch, who also led each tranche except the do-mestic Argentine one.

Japanese Round Tripping. Despite the natural preeminence of Euro-pean companies in Europe and the importance of the Euroequity market in global placements, the most prolific users of the Euroequity market by far during the past 10 years have been Japanese corporations. Such heavy Japanese activity in the Euromarkets has pushed Japanese securities firms to the top of the underwriting league tables in Europe.

The Japanese issues actually are in the form of convertible debentures

YPF

$2,660,000,000

YPF Sociedad Anónima

140,000,000 Shares

Joint Global Coordinators

CS First Boston Group　　　　　　　　　　　**Merrill Lynch & Co.**

Banco General de Negocios S.A.
acted as advisor to the Joint Global Coordinators.

These securities were offered in Argentina, the United States and internationally.

International Offering

40,000,000 American Depositary Shares

35,000,000 American Depositary Shares
each representing one Class D Share were offered outside Argentina and the United States

Merrill Lynch International Limited			Credit Suisse First Boston Limited
Baring Brothers & Co., Limited		Cazenove & Co.	Deutsche Bank Aktiengesellschaft
Kleinwort Benson Limited		Nomura International	Paribas Capital Markets

ABN AMRO Bank N.V.	Banco Santander de Negocios	Banque Indosuez	Barclays de Zoete Wedd Limited	James Capel & Co.
Credit Lyonnais Securities	Dresdner Bank Aktiengesellschaft	N M Rothschild & Sons Limited	Swiss Bank Corporation　UBS Limited	S.G.Warburg Securities
		Smith New Court Securities Limited		
Yamaichi International (Europe) Limited		Argentaria Bolsa S.V.B.　BHF-BANK	BNP Capital Markets Limited	Daiwa Europe Limited
ING Bank	Jardine Fleming	Latinvest Securities Limited	Mediobanca-Banca di Credito Finanziario S.p.A.	J. Henry Schroder Wagg & Co. Limited

5,000,000 American Depositary Shares
each representing one Class D Share were offered elsewhere in North and South America

Merrill Lynch International Limited			Credit Suisse First Boston Limited
Citibank International plc			
	RBC Dominion Securities Inc.		
		Santander Investment Bank Limited	
		Scotia McLeod Inc.	
			Wood Gundy Inc.

Banco Alemán Paraguayo	Banco Comercial	Banco de Investimentos Garantia S.A.	Banco Itaú S.A.	Banco Pactual S.A.
Credit Lyonnais Securities (USA) Inc.	Filanbanco	Inverlat International, Inc.	Larrain Vial S.A.	Serfin Securities, Inc.

United States Offering

65,000,000 American Depositary Shares
each representing one Class D Share

The First Boston Corporation			Merrill Lynch & Co.
Goldman, Sachs & Co.			Salomon Brothers Inc
Bear, Stearns & Co. Inc.			J. P. Morgan Securities Inc.
		PaineWebber Incorporated	

Alex. Brown & Sons Incorporated	BT Securities Corporation	Dillon, Read & Co. Inc.	Donaldson, Lufkin & Jenrette Securities Corporation	A.G. Edwards & Sons, Inc.	Howard, Weil, Labouisse, Friedrichs Incorporated
Kidder, Peabody & Co. Incorporated	Lazard Frères & Co.	Lehman Brothers		Morgan Stanley & Co.	Oppenheimer & Co., Inc.
Prudential Securities Incorporated		Smith Barney, Harris Upham & Co.		Wertheim Schroder & Co. Incorporated	Dean Witter Reynolds Inc.
Baring Securities Inc.	Credit Lyonnais Securities (USA) Inc.	Deutsche Bank Capital Corporation		Kleinwort Benson North America Inc.	Nomura Securities International, Inc.
Paribas Capital Markets	Serfin Securities, Inc.	N M Rothschild and Smith New Court		S.G.Warburg Securities	Yamaichi International (America), Inc.
Advest, Inc.	Allen & Company Incorporated	Arnhold and S. Bleichroeder, Inc.	Robert W. Baird & Co.	Sanford C. Bernstein & Co., Inc.	William Blair & Company　J. C. Bradford & Co.　Cowen & Company
Dain Bosworth Incorporated	Fahnestock & Co. Inc.	First Albany Corporation	First of Michigan Corporation	Gruntal & Co., Incorporated	Interstate/Johnson Lane Corporation
Janney Montgomery Scott Inc.	Edward D. Jones & Co.	Kemper Securities, Inc.	Ladenburg, Thalmann & Co. Inc.	Legg Mason Wood Walker Incorporated	Mabon Securities Corp.
McDonald & Company Securities, Inc.	Morgan Keegan & Company, Inc.	Needham & Company, Inc.	Neuberger & Berman	Petrie Parkman & Co.	Piper Jaffray Inc.
The Principal/Eppler, Guerin & Turner, Inc.	Ragen MacKenzie Incorporated	Rauscher Pierce Refsnes, Inc.	Raymond James & Associates, Inc.		The Robinson-Humphrey Company, Inc.
Stephens Inc.	Stifel, Nicolaus & Company	Sutro & Co. Incorporated	Tucker Anthony Incorporated		Wheat First Butcher & Singer CAPITAL MARKETS
Baird, Patrick & Co., Inc.	The Chicago Corporation	Crowell, Weedon & Co.	Dominick & Dominick	Johnson Rice & Company	Johnston, Lemon & Co. Incorporated　Mesirow Financial, Inc.　The Ohio Company
Parker/Hunter Incorporated	Pennsylvania Merchant Group Ltd	Rodman & Renshaw, Inc.	Roney & Co.	Seidler Amdec Securities Inc.	Southcoast Capital Corporation　Utendahl Capital Partners, L.P.　Wedbush Morgan Securities

Argentine Offering

35,000,000 Class D Shares

Banco Rio de la Plata S.A.			Banco de Galicia y Buenos Aires S.A.
		Banco de Valores S.A.	
Banco Roberts S.A.		Banco Francés del Río de la Plata S.A.		Banco de Crédito Argentino S.A.
Banco General de Negocios S.A.		Banco Mercantil S.A.	Banco Quilmes S.A.	Banco del Sud S.A.

Figure 11-8. Tombstone advertisement of Argentine National Oil Company YPF issue.

or debt issues with detachable equity purchase warrants. Both are debt issues with "embedded" stock call options. If the options are exercised at the bond maturity date, as the issuer expects at the time of issuance, then the company is obliged to issue new shares of common stock at a price fixed at the time of the original offering.

More than $350 billion of these debt-based equity securities—over half the total amount of all Japanese equity securities issued—were sold by Japanese companies from 1984 through 1990.[6] This volume of new issues overwhelmed all other forms of Euroequities. They were the product of extraordinary times in Japan, in which markets were booming and corporations found it easier to make money through financial investments than through the manufacture of products. Japanese companies would borrow all they could to invest in the stock and real estate markets, a process the Japanese called *zaiteck*. Many companies found it much cheaper to borrow from the Euromarkets than from banks, and advantageous to issue new shares at p/e multiples above 75 in order to raise money for investments.

The Japanese Euroequity issues, which were offered as packages with extremely low coupon rates (sometimes as low as 1 percent), were stripped by investors into (1) the warrants, which were sold directly into Japan, and (2) deep discount bonds, which were bundled with an interest-rate swap and offered to other investors, mainly Japanese banks, as floating-rate notes on a LIBOR basis, which offered an attractive yield. Table 11-5 shows an example of the pricing mechanics of such issues.

In other words, the Japanese issuers were retaining Japanese underwriters to manage vast amounts of issues of Euromarket securities that were to be sold almost entirely to investors back in Japan! It is ironic that the country most celebrated in the world for its excess savings and huge balance-of-payments surplus should rely so heavily on capital markets outside its own borders for corporate financing. Why did they do this?

For two reasons. First, the companies wanted more money than they could take out of the Japanese domestic market through the issuance of straight equity shares. So they looked abroad for ideas, and settled on the debt with warrants approach because it was cheap. The shares would not be issued until the warrants expired, so they "didn't count" for earnings per share calculations and Japanese investors did not penalize the companies for the dilution. The only cost the companies did incur was the annual coupon, and at 4 percent or less this was almost negligible (especially when denominated in weakening U.S. dollars).

Second, even though the investors in both the bonds and the warrants would be Japanese, the scheme could not be done in Japan, because only a limited number of Japanese companies were qualified by local regulations to issue unsecured bonds. Also, the costs and regulatory delays in issuing bonds in Japan were well in excess of those in the Euromarkets.

Thus, a lower cost, more "user-friendly" financing opportunity was presented outside Japan, and Japanese companies moved quickly to take

Table 11-5 Japanese Warrant Bond Calculations

Issue: $100 million XYZ Corporation 1% 5-year notes with warrants attached for the purchase of 4.878 shares each of XYZ common stock at $20.50 per share.

At the time of issue, a $100 million 5-year dollar-denominated *straight* bond issued by XYZ would yield 8.5%. However, the bonds are offered as a package with the warrants to purchase common stock of XYZ, so the value of the package (sold at $1,000, or 100% per unit) is the sum of the value of the bond and the warrants. In other words, the bond is valued at a discount, and the warrants make up the difference.

The warrants may be exercised at a price per share of $20.50, a premium of only 2.5% over the last sale price, which was $20 per share. ($20 × 1.025 = $20.50). To exercise the warrant, an investor may exchange the bond, with the bond valued at par ($1,000). The warrant then becomes 48.78 common shares ($100 million/$20.50 per warrant per share = 4,878,000 new shares, which divided by 100,000 bonds of $1000 each = 48.78 shares/bond).

The bond part of the package is priced to yield 8.5%, the same as a straight bond. A bond at a discount of, say, 30% (a price of 70%) would yield 8.5% over 5 years if its coupon is 1%. The warrants then, by subtraction, must be worth the value of the discount, i.e., 30%.

But the warrants must also be valued correctly, according to the Black–Scholes method of valuing options or some other method. The warrrants have to be worth $3,200, which is the same as $6.15 per share ($300/48.78), or 30% of $20.50. If the warrant value is different, then the coupon of the notes should be adjusted.

When the bonds and the warrants are split after the offering, the bonds should trade at $700 and the warrants at $6.15 each ($20.50 × .3). Often, however, the parts trade at premiums above these prices.

---

advantage of it. This is yet another example of the change-inducing effects of the globalization of capital markets, in this case one that was beneficial to Japanese issuers. The Japanese Ministry of Finance (MOF) ultimately attempted to slow the migration to London by effecting certain overdue regulatory reforms to the Tokyo new-issue process (and by threatening to require overseas warrants sold into Japan to be registered with the MOF). Though the Japanese stock-market frenzy ended with the three-year market slump that began in late 1989, Japanese companies continue to use the Euromarket as a substitute for their own market. However, the greater portion of Japanese financing has returned to Tokyo. Thus a better market abroad triggered a deregulatory response in the home market, one that was not intended by regulatory officials, but one that nevertheless had to be implemented in the interest of preserving the order and effectiveness of their domestic markets.

Underwriting Methods

Underwriting is the process of assuring an issuer that an offering will occur for a specified number of shares at a specified price per share. It is in effect an insurance policy (hence the term "underwriter"). But what is being insured can vary greatly depending on which underwriting method is employed. The methods differ between the U.S. market, the Euroequity market, and the traditional British market. Virtually all national markets utilize one or the other (or a combination) of these methods.

Underwriting in the United States

In the United States, underwriting procedures are designed to obtain the highest price for the seller of the securities being offered. This is done by forming a syndicate of securities firms that will agree to purchase the shares from the seller and resell the shares immediately to investors. The price is not fixed until just before the offering is made to the public, after a period during which well-briefed salespeople from the underwriters have marketed the issue to their customers. The customers are not committed to purchase shares until they accept the final price, but sales personnel talk to them about probable price levels to make judgments as to where and how much they will buy. This process is called "building a book" and is essential to precise pricing efforts. A successfully priced issue is one in which the entire issue is sold out at the agreed offering price and the issue opens for trading at a premium of no more than about 10 percent. The underwriting syndicate in such an issue is exposed to only a minimal holding period between the purchase and the confirmation of sales with customers. Of course if the issue is mispriced, or if the market changes before the distribution is complete, underwriters can suffer losses.

To minimize these risks and to provide strong potential support in the aftermarket, underwriters generally overallot shares and companies usually agree to provide the underwriters with a "Green Shoe option." Under such an option (named for the company first employing it, the Green Shoe Company) the underwriters may call on the company to increase the size of the issue by an additional 10 or 15 percent or so. The lead underwriter will allocate to the selling brokers (on the basis of their reported orders for shares) a total of 10 to 15 percent more shares than are actually being issued. Thus the lead manager, on behalf of the underwriting syndicate, has gone "short" shares, having sold shares it did not own but is still required to deliver. Almost all underwritings involve some degree of short position that the lead manager covers by purchasing shares in the aftermarket to stabilize the offering price. If demand for the shares is weak, the lead manager will purchase unsold or unwanted shares in the market (from the other underwriters, or their customers) to support the offering at the original offering price. If the demand is strong, the underwriters will exercise the Green Shoe option to create the shares to cover the short position; otherwise they would have to buy them in the market at a premium price. Paying a premium for the shares substantially increases the cost to the underwriters of covering their short position. In exchange for granting the Green Shoe option the issuer expects tighter and more aggressive pricing for the issue.

From the issuer's point of view some negatives are associated with the

U.S. underwriting procedures. First, the market risk stays with the issuer while the issue is being prepared for the market—the seller must register the shares with the SEC and wait a few weeks for authorization to proceed with the offering. Nothing can be done about this delay, but under the U.S. underwriting method, any market decline during the SEC review period is the issuer's risk, not the underwriters. (It is possible to issue new equity securities under the shelf registration procedures established by SEC Rule 415, but very few companies wish to announce new share issues that might or might not occur over the next two years for fear of the effect of the "overhang" such an announcement might have on the market price.)

All the underwriter is insuring in a U.S. transaction is the price agreed with the seller the night before the offering is made—not a great risk under ordinary market conditions. The underwriter provides more useful service acting as a broker/distributor for the issue by providing the sales effort needed to achieve the highest possible price for the offering. Ideally this would be reflected by stimulating widespread interest in the offering, its purpose, and the company's future so as to generate a higher stock price than would have existed if no offering were made at all. In other words, the new issue would not result in a lowering of the share price to reflect the greater number of shares outstanding after the offering. When such is the case, the only cost to the seller is the gross spread (commission) paid to the underwriters and the out-of-pocket expenses associated with the issue. This result of an underwriting, however, is not insured: the seller must rely on the underwriter's best efforts in distributing the shares. These efforts may be frustrated by a variety of factors at the issuer's expense.

Underwriting Euroequities

The U.S. bookbuilding method of underwriting is used in the Euromarket, but there are several significant differences. Perhaps most important is the fact that the market does not require any waiting period while registration procedures are processed. Issuers (if they are able to do so, as most European and Japanese issuers are—U.S. issues must still be registered if the shares might be resold in the United States) may enter the market on virtually no notice; thus sellers need not be exposed to market risk while waiting for the offering to proceed. As a practical matter, however, for all but the best-known companies some sort of marketing period to generate demand is essential if a steep discount in the underwriting price is to be avoided.

Because most of the European underwriters on which the lead manager must rely are banks with a limited securities distribution capability (except when distributing to customer accounts within the bank) and an unwillingness to admit that they cannot place all the shares they have agreed to underwrite, the lead manager is unable to rely on the prepricing order book as much as in the United States. It may also be more difficult to maintain a fixed offering price during the underwriting period, as some underwriters will sell their unsold shares in the interdealer market, or back in the home country market. This significantly inhibits the stabilization efforts of the lead manager. Thus precise pricing is more difficult to achieve and stabilization is more erratic and unreliable than in the United States.

British Underwriting

In the United Kingdom, and in many other parts of Europe, an older system of underwriting is used, which many people refer to as the "British," or "front-end," underwriting method. In this system the announcement of the transaction, the offering price, and an agreement with a group of underwriters (usually merchant or investment bankers) to insure, or "backstop," the issue is made simultaneously, two or three weeks before the issue will be available for trading. That day the underwriters arrange a "subunderwriting group" to reinsure their commitment. Subunderwriters are usually institutional investors prepared to take down their share of any portion of the issue that should remain unsold after its completion. The bulk of the total commission paid by the issuer is made available to the subunderwriters as an insurance premium. Subunderwriters may reduce their risk to the extent that they subscribe to purchase shares in the offering. Most of the subunderwriters expect to be invited into all underwritings during the year, and therefore see the risks as being diversified against a pool of many underwritings, for which significant fees, in aggregate, can be earned.

British and many other European companies provide their shareholders with "preemptive rights," or the right to purchase new shares of the company before any nonshareholder. As an inducement to shareholders, the subscription rights are offered at a discount. This discount may vary from 5 percent to about 25 percent. The share price will be reduced by the market to reflect the dilution in the number of shares to be outstanding, and the rights will have value equal to the difference between the new share price and the subscription price. The rights can be sold if the shareholder decides not to subscribe.

Because it takes about two weeks to notify shareholders of the offer and to receive their subscriptions, there is a waiting risk for U.K. issues too. In the United Kingdom, however, this risk is assumed by the underwriters (and the subunderwriters). Their risk is tied to market movements as well as to mispricing by the underwriters. Until the subscription period ends it is impossible to know to what extent the issue has been "taken up" by shareholders or by purchasers of rights.

Apart from arranging the subunderwriting syndicate, brokers have little to do in the process. Nor do the underwriters, including the lead merchant bank handling the issue, have much to do with marketing. This system recognizes that the main institutional investors in the market will be the likely buyers. So they are used as subunderwriters, paid a fee for using their capital to prop up the issue while individual and other investors go through the subscription process. The definition of a successful issue is one that is fully subscribed, not fully priced; in fact, some believe the more oversubscribed the issue the more successful it is. Unfortunately, such oversubscription tends to result in a sharp rise in the stock price when it is free to trade (or put another way, the subscription price tends to be set sufficiently low to be sure that oversubscription occurs). On the other hand, if the issue is undersubscribed the subunderwriters can sustain substantial losses. Clearly in the U.K. system priority is given to getting the deal done (with existing shareholders if possible) without regard to price.

The British method was once used in the United States and in Japan, when preemptive rights were popular with many large companies and their principal investors. The last such "rights issue" for an industrial company occurred in the United States in the late 1960s and a bit later in Japan. They went out of style because companies wanted to broaden their shareholder bases to include new investors. They wanted more competition for their newly offered shares, more flexibility to take advantage of market opportunities abroad, and more opportunities to influence the market price by prepricing sales efforts. They also wanted to avoid reporting large dilution in the earnings and book value per share as a result of the discounts associated with rights issues. Investors were agreeable, so companies began to vote out their preemptive rights.

The British method is still in use in the United Kingdom, where the large institutional investors are unwilling to give up preemptive rights. Privatization and other secondary new issues, however, can be made directly to the market, as in the United States, though for the most part the British underwriting method continues to be used. Recent privatization issues have involved a considerable amount of prepricing sales and marketing efforts and other innovations so as to obtain the best from both the U.S. and the U.K. systems.

Combining the Systems

Global offerings that involve tranches from different parts of the world often find disadvantages in forcing all of the tranches to use the same underwriting method. It can be disadvantageous to U.K. or European underwriters without strong external securities distribution capability to have to compete with U.S. and Japanese firms for share allocations, especially when the these firms are free to sell in Europe through their formidable sales forces there. It can also be disadvantageous to U.S. firms to have to act as underwriters of U.K. issues during the subscription period, without access to subunderwriters.

The largest global share issue to take place was the sale of 2.2 billion shares of the British Petroleum Company in October 1987. This transaction, valued at $12 billion, which was underwritten according to the British method on October 15 for subscription before October 28, was divided about equally between the domestic U.K. market and markets outside the United Kingdom. The October 19 crash, which caused the BP share price to drop more than 30 percent, occurred during the subscription period. As a result the offering was almost completely unsubscribed, and the entire issue was left with the underwriters. Four U.S. underwriters had committed among them to underwrite $1 billion of the BP shares to be sold in the United States. These underwriters shared losses totaling more than $250 million. The issue was a disaster, but the international syndicate held and did its job, despite extreme duress.

More than five years later, however, U.K. privatization issues were still being done according to the British method. From the government's point of view, of course, the British method of underwriting proved itself far superior to the U.S. method during the BP share offering. Nonetheless, various steps have been taken in the United Kingdom to improve the effectiveness of global offerings by combining aspects of both systems.

One of the important ways to do this is to provide for a bookbuilding effort by requiring a "tender offer" to be made by investors to receive shares after the subscription period has ended. Under such an arrangement the issuer can reset (upward) the offering price on the basis of the tenders received, but only after the risk of underwriting has terminated. To support a tender offer approach, issuers have learned to circulate a preliminary prospectus (sometimes called a "pathfinder") to institutional investors to prepare them for analyzing the investment opportunities on offer. Brokers then follow up with them, American style, to urge them to tender for shares. Underwriters have also adopted other American practices such as Green Shoe overallotment options and using an institutional "pot" to set aside shares to be sold by the lead managers to large institutions. Though most large global offerings, over $500 million in value, have relied on regional syndication efforts coordinated by one or more lead managers, in 1993 a $7.5-billion privatization issue for British Telecom (its third) was distributed through a single global syndicate, with all members having unreserved access to all investors, wherever in the world they were. Further innovation and experimentation will surely continue.

Listing Shares on Foreign Exchanges

For the past 20 years companies have considered listing their shares on foreign exchanges to promote local investment in them, to provide a quotation in the shares for the benefit of local employees, and to gain appropriate recognition as a multinational firm. Frequently, however, such listings proved to be expensive, and very little trading on the local exchanges occurred. As foreign investors, especially in Europe, became more sophisticated, they preferred to trade in U.S. shares on U.S. markets, where they believed they could obtain better executions. The same came to be true for Japanese and American investors who found trading in overseas shares to be more efficiently done in the home country markets. These developments diminished to some extent the need on the part of American and Japanese companies to list their shares abroad.

In the United States, however, listings by foreign companies increased significantly during the late 1980s and early 1990s. (Figure 11-9). *Listings* in the United States is a term that includes all foreign companies that report annually to the SEC and therefore can be freely traded on stock exchanges or in over-the-counter markets. The companies listing in the United States want to tap the large equity markets in the country, especially at a time when U.S. investors are increasing investments abroad and purchasing new issues of foreign debt and stocks. In 1992 and 1993 the volume of such new issues was at record levels, as shown in Figure 11-10, and of course many foreign issuers wanted to be close to the action.

To qualify as a reporting company in the United States, a foreign corporation must provide most of the information required by the SEC of U.S. companies. It must, for example, supply financial statements prepared according to U.S. generally accepted accounting principles, or at least show and reconcile the differences between the company's home country accounts and generally accepted accounting principles (GAAP). This undertaking alone is expensive, time consuming, and more illuminating than most European and Japanese accounting standards require. Many prospective issuers balk at these requirements and forego the opportunity to be listed in the United States as a result.

However, in 1992 and 1993 market forces drew many foreign companies to the U.S. equity market for new issues. Some issued private place-

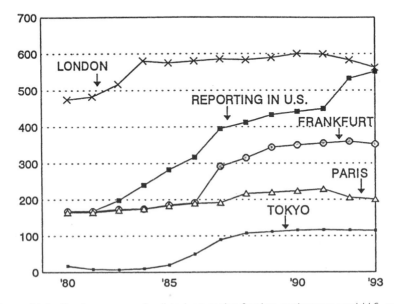

Figure 11-9. Foreign companies listed on major foreign exchanges and U.S. markets as of June 30, 1993. U.S. markets include all foreign-reporting companies.

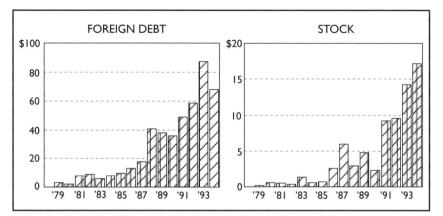

Figure 11-10. *The growing attraction of American money: public and private offerings of foreign debt and stock in the U.S. market 1979–1994 ($ billions). Data: Securities Data Corp.*

ments of equity securities under Rule 144a, but increasingly others preferred to undertake the burden of becoming a reporting company in order to have access to the broader market and listing on the NYSE. During 1992 16 foreign companies listed for the first time on the NYSE; during 1993 approximately twice that number listed, including about 17 from Latin America. One of those to list in 1993 was Daimler-Benz, the first German company to list equity securities on the NYSE.

Regulation of International Equity Markets

Vast amounts of cross-border capital flows have begun to integrate markets across the globe, influencing pricing, market behavior, and investor expectations, yet securities regulation is still a national concern, and varies enormously between countries. Investors, both local and international, increasingly demand that markets be fair and reasonably transparent, and that regulations be enforced. Yet the process of convergence toward an international regulatory norm has only just begun. Many questions are being raised by regulators around the world and by market practitioners, and efforts have begun to seek answers that are acceptable all around.

What Should Be Regulated?

As of the end of 1993 there appeared to be a consensus that three areas of activity should be regulated, as follows:

1. *Industry Structure and Competition.* The broadest forms of competition should be encouraged, consistent with providing for the capital adequacy and soundness of market-makers, underwriters, and brokers. EU rules are the most advanced in this area; in the United States and Japan

restrictions continue to exist that limit the securities activities of banks, though these are changing, slowly, in proportion to banking regulators' concerns about bank capital adequacy and competitive capability.

2. *Protection of Retail Investors.* Many countries provide "truth in investing" regulations that require minimum disclosure standards for new issues and annual reporting by companies whose shares are publicly traded. Though these standards vary greatly, efforts are under way at the EU level, and through an ad hoc effort by the United States, Canada, and Britain to establish common standards that each can use in the others' countries. Regulators are more relaxed about protecting institutional investors and other wholesale market players, thus the unregulated Euro-equity market and the various private placement markets for equity transactions, including Rule 144a transactions in the United States, remain undisturbed. The SEC, however, has been adamant about not changing its accounting standards for foreign companies becoming reporting, or publicly traded, companies.

3. *Protection against Securities Fraud.* Fraud can appear in a thousand forms, and many equity markets are not fully equipped to prevent it. Regulations against market rigging, insider trading, "stock parking," account churning, and "front-running" vary considerably between the major countries, and often do not even exist in emerging markets. But at least the countries are now aware that these problem areas exist, and some movement toward achieving an international standard can be expected over the next few years.

Some Governing Principles Emerge

In general, certain governing principles appear to have emerged as a result of the reforms of the 1970s and 1980s and the efforts by the BIS and the EU to provide a framework for increasing competition while still ensuring a stable global financial system. There is, however, considerable disagreement yet as to how these should be applied. A consensus has formed around the following points:

Regulation should be as light as possible, but not so light as to be ineffective. Too much regulation kills the competitiveness of a financial center; but so does regulation that is not supervisable or enforceable.

Minimum solvency standards for the securities industry must be established, and these must be consistent with standards applicable to the banking industry. The Basel accords on bank capital adequacy must be applied, one way or another, to the nonbank securities industry. The insolvency of a large investment bank could represent a threat to the global financial system, and therefore such firms need to be subject to minimum capitalization rules also. In reality such firms are already subject to minimum capitalization requirements of the various stock exchanges and market-making regulators; but these need to be applied on a consolidated basis to the entity as a whole.

A level playing field should be established for banks and investment banks. In Europe, "universal banking," which permits a full range of securities activities by banks, has become the model for the future. In the United States, deregulation has resulted in a de facto repeal of the 1933 Glass–Steagall Act, which separated banking and investment banking. Banks now can apply to the Federal Reserve Board for permission to set up securities subsidiaries under Section 20 of the Glass–Steagall Act as long as the total revenues, assets, and profits of the subsidiary do not constitute a significant (e.g., 10 percent) portion of the subsidiaries' total revenues, assets, and profits. In Japan, the MOF has provided a similar means for banks to engage in underwriting corporate securities through special-purpose subsidiaries. In the United States and Japan, the government approval process is slow, as protection of depositors' funds remains a primary goal, but those banks that are deemed to be well capitalized and competitively capable are expected to enter the full range of securities business activities in the near future.

Market surveillance is necessary, as are enforcement powers. Most countries agree that the SEC, as a regulatory body, works, but they question the cost and inefficiency of settling matters through the legal system. In Britain, the Securities and Investment Board oversees several self-regulating organizations, but it has resisted building up a large (and aggressive) market surveillance staff. In Japan, the MOF (in response to public pressure) has formed a securities "watchdog" unit, but it is considered toothless—a tiny staff and no enforcement powers make its role of questionable value. Though everywhere questions are raised about the unwanted aspects of an SEC-type of system, few alternatives that appear effective have been put forward.

Retail services need the most regulation. Many kinds of financial services are now sold directly to the public: discount brokerage, investment management services, mutual funds, pension investment programs, and life insurance with stock market returns, among others. These need to be regulated to ensure that unsophisticated investors are not taken advantage of. At the same time, however, sufficient regulation of market behavior or professionals needs to occur to ensure that the markets as a whole are fair and unmanipulated.

How Does All This Get Brought Together?

There are various "decision-makers" in the regulatory arena. Broadly these include the Bank for International Settlements (BIS), which acts as a neutral sounding board on regulatory matters concerning banks; the various national central banks (like the U.S. Federal Reserve and the Bank of England), which make up the ownership of the BIS; the EU Commission, which prepares the banking and securities industry "directives" that set EU policy under the Single Market Act; the various securities regulators; the stock exchanges; the law courts that increasingly (even in Europe) are relied on to resolve complex regulatory issues in dispute; and last (but not least), public opinion as reflected in the media.

Convergence of policy also occurs through market interaction and regulatory "competition," especially from the budding financial centers of tomorrow. Regulators consult with each other and argue over preferred methods. Growing familiarity with practices in well-regulated countries creates dissatisfaction in those countries that lack good regulation. The media publicize these matters, and gradually things change. Already, for example, new laws or regulations preventing insider trading and protecting minority shareholder rights are in the process of implementation in Germany, France, Japan, and other countries.

Competing in International Equities

The global market for equity securities is vast and involves many powerful competitors. No single firm will be successful in commanding a significant share of all the national markets for equities. However, the rapidly growing cross-border trading activity in international equities is heavily concentrated in a few countries, and participants in this market segment are capable of significant improvements in market share or of being displaced by more effective competitors.

Secondary market activity in international shares within one's own country is perhaps the place where competitors must begin to develop their strengths. U.S. brokerages must become proficient in offering U.S. shares to international investors and in offering international shares to U.S. investors, principally institutions. British firms must do the same in London, and Japanese in Tokyo. In each case a firm is competing not only with its traditional domestic competitors; it is also up against the biggest and best of the foreign firms. Once successful in dealing in international securities with one's own clients, an ambitious firm can attempt to compete abroad for the international business of nonclients.

Comparative Advantages

Firms have quite different comparative advantages in the international equities business. U.S. firms are especially keyed to institutional investors, including European institutional investors. Many U.S., U.K., and continental European banks or securities firms are also substantial money managers and know about the markets because of their experience as investors. There are a great many money managers in the international arena, however, and only a small percentage are able to use their in-house placing power and influence to attract lead managerships of international equity new issues.

Some firms will attempt to specialize in covering retail demand for international investments, including the demand for international or specific country mutual funds. Some firms prefer to be even more specialized, as for example concentrating only on banking or insurance. In all cases, however, to be a successful competitor a firm must be recognized as having broad "placing power." The more the better.

Those firms that can place international issues will be invited into or will be able to lead underwriting groups for new issues. They will also be able to profit from trading opportunities related to the issues they have underwritten.

Institutional Emphasis

Most firms agree that when operating abroad they must emphasize institutional business, because of the difficulty of creating a network of branch offices abroad and of luring loyal customers away from their traditional banks and brokers. Some, like Merrill Lynch, have tried overseas retail business with some success, but have also maintained a focus on the institutional side. Despite the lower commissions, institutional business is the only way to build up trading volume quickly. This provides the firm with customer activity and keeps it "in the market," knowing what is going on. Institutional business is, however, very competitive and hard to break into, though it can be done.

To succeed in institutional business, a firm must offer three basic services—sales coverage, research, and market-making. All of these can be expensive, yet if they are better than the competition's, business will soon follow. Generally, to win business from institutional customers a firm must offer services that are so good the customer wants to make room for them. Often this means starting small, with a major effort in a single specialized area, from which the firm can expand outward.

Traditionally firms would offer research and trading support to institutions from all over the world, but only in home country shares. Salomon Brothers would offer its research on General Motors to institutions in Europe and Japan as well as in the United States. But Japanese brokers did not sell Dutch stocks, U.S. firms did not promote German bank shares. Each participant stuck to what it knew best. Such tidiness is no longer in effect.

Research in International Equities

U.S. brokers, in an attempt to reclaim from U.S. investors a share of the commission volume on foreign stocks lost over the years to European and Japanese firms, first began to make trading markets in New York in a variety of popular international stocks. Then they began to promote the concept of global industries, in which they would attempt to recommend the best stocks in the world in, say, the auto industry. Research coverage was applied to BMW, Daimler Benz, Fiat, Toyota, and other companies, in addition to the big three from Detroit. Next, analysts began to focus on which countries and stocks their customers should be in to catch the next rising market, such as Mexico, Spain, or Taiwan. Before long the firms found themselves conducting macroeconomic research on several international economies and following dozens of large-capitalization non-U.S. companies. At first a firm's clients may doubt its ability to offer knowledgeable international advice, but if the quality of the firm's research is as good as the best domestic research it will soon gain a good reputation and will be sought out. Commission business and trading opportunities usually follow. This process is very expensive; good analysts are expensive, and often not productive for some time. It can take years to achieve a reputation for across-the-board excellence in research. When the process succeeds, however, it provides the firm with a strong international reputation for competence that enables it to attract a significant market share. The research capacity can also be useful in support of international corporate finance and merger and acquisition activities.

Trading and Market-Making

Researchers must trade in the securities they recommend, but traders do not have to offer research in the securities they trade. Some firms prefer to compete only as market-makers in international equity securities, that is, without offering research services. For years there has been an active over-the-counter market in New York in international stocks by firms that were specialists in trading, not research. This business has expanded greatly in recent years, especially as institutional investors have become more active in international shares and begun to look more closely for the best execution prices. Market-makers have expanded their activities too, often to include memberships on the London and the Tokyo Stock Exchanges. Also, more non-U.S. firms have become members of the New York Stock Exchange to improve their ability to execute U.S. orders for their non-U.S. clients.

Like large commitments to international research, these foreign exchange memberships, too, are expensive, not only due to the cost of the stock exchange seats, but also because a firm must become subject to capital and reporting regulations of the other exchanges and commit substantial resources to back-office operations. In addition, the management time involved in getting established and building up local trading connections can be considerable. A firm must have a fairly substantial volume in the shares traded on these exchanges to operate profitably. In New York and London commission rates are fully negotiable, and in Tokyo where they are not, institutional discounts are common. However, several firms have succeeded in recent years by developing opportunistic trading approaches such as arbitrage (program) trading and specialized focus on certain stocks. Again, the firms that successfully pursue concentrated strategies of international trading will end up with the strongest franchises and the largest market shares.

New Issues

Some firms have preferred to compete in the international equities business by emphasizing new issues and underwritings, rather than becoming quite so committed to the secondary markets. Firms with an effective corporate marketing capability, or with a special ability to place issues with funds under the firm's own management, have often succeeded in gaining mandates to lead manage public offerings of international equity issues. Such issues, however, do have to be priced competitively and distributed skillfully. Secondary market-making and research coverage has to be provided for, even if by different firms than the lead manager. It is possible, of course, by virtue of the relationship between banker and client, for firms without developed capabilities in research or trading, and without convincing placing power, to win mandates. But it is much more difficult to do so than in the past. Large international equity issues can be extremely profitable for lead managers, and as a result there is always keen competition for almost every management appointment. Most of the managerships are won by firms with the ability to demonstrate across-the-board qualifications. Co-managerships and other lesser positions, however, are still made available quite often to firms with fewer demonstrable qualifications but a longer and closer relationship with the issuer.

Mutual Funds

A number of firms have focused on the origination of specialized international mutual funds for which they can act as distributor, or as fund manager. Among the more popular funds are those restricted to investments from one or more countries only, such as the Germany Fund, or one restricted to investments in, say, Southeast Asia. Country funds have been a common means for individual investors to participate in international diversification. Such funds, usually closed-end investment companies, are distributed through global underwriting syndicates.

Country funds tend to be somewhat faddish, that is, they come out when new developments or a changed public attitude occurs. During 1992 and 1993, "emerging market" funds were extremely popular. Table 11-6 shows a 1995 listing of several funds specializing in international markets and their relative performance.

Equities as a Key Part of Total Capital Market Activity

Most firms provide both debt and equity services as part of their capital market activity. The two can be highly complementary, especially where such hybrid securities as convertible debentures and debt with warrants are concerned. A great deal of money has been earned by firms acting as market-makers in Japanese warrant bonds and the warrants attached to

Table 11-6 Performance Summary by Investment Objective

Number of Funds	Objective	Premium Discount % 12-31-95	NAV Total Return Percentage							Market Total Return Percentage						
			Year to Date 12-31-95	Through 12-31-95		1 Yr.	Annualized			Year to Date 12-31-95	Through 12-31-95		1 Yr.	Annualized		
				3 Mo.	6 Mo.		3 Yr.	5 Yr.	10 Yr.		3 Mo.	6 Mo.		3 Yr.	5 Yr.	10 Yr.
	Equity															
21	Europe Stock	−13.3	13.35	0.68	1.60	13.35	14.88	5.90	—	11.86	1.93	3.95	11.86	11.74	5.74	—
12	Latin America Stock	−6.5	−14.63	−4.05	−0.56	−14.63	8.44	20.77	24.89	−22.88	−5.46	−4.71	−22.88	6.92	21.68	29.05
35	Pacific/Asia Stock	−3.1	−8.77	−3.85	−4.50	−8.77	11.59	11.07	15.62	−3.14	−2.00	−2.26	−3.14	11.88	13.19	13.39
20	World Stock	−12.2	5.61	2.01	4.73	5.61	11.18	8.47	5.90	5.29	3.74	6.56	5.29	9.36	7.82	7.61
40	Domestic Stock	−9.3	33.32	2.97	13.48	33.32	12.83	17.09	10.21	37.66	6.86	17.81	37.66	12.65	18.33	11.76
	Hybrid															
17	Income	−3.5	24.34	4.71	9.36	24.34	10.56	13.27	12.53	25.18	3.60	6.74	25.18	6.62	13.26	11.26
11	Convertible	−6.8	22.15	2.08	8.10	22.15	11.21	15.50	9.01	26.25	4.61	11.20	26.25	11.91	18.82	9.03
27	Corporate Bond-High Yield	1.8	19.32	3.32	7.09	19.32	12.16	19.47	—	23.20	2.90	7.13	23.20	12.98	24.46	—
	Fixed-Income															
32	Corporate Bond-General	−8.3	21.03	4.44	7.15	21.03	9.57	11.66	10.18	21.54	3.67	6.64	21.54	6.05	11.35	9.34
29	Government Bond	−13.4	22.76	4.82	6.91	22.76	5.92	8.76	—	15.80	2.38	4.43	15.80	0.04	5.15	—
25	International Bond	−8.2	23.42	7.05	14.07	23.42	11.41	8.88	—	24.07	4.22	10.59	24.07	8.24	9.08	—
27	Multisector Bond	−11.1	22.35	5.29	8.98	22.35	10.02	12.54	—	17.77	2.15	5.27	17.77	6.43	11.20	—
97	Municipal-Bond-National	−8.7	21.20	5.55	8.57	21.20	8.69	8.90	—	22.07	4.52	6.29	22.07	6.02	8.12	—
105	Municipal Bond-Single State	−9.8	25.02	6.79	10.08	25.02	8.95	8.94	—	24.03	4.84	6.12	24.03	5.52	7.86	—
498	Total Fund Average	−8.4	19.36	4.11	7.78	19.36	10.06	12.04	10.69	19.46	3.50	6.44	19.46	7.46	12.21	10.68

Source: Morningstar Closed-End Funds

them. Arbitrage opportunities exist also in convertible debentures and preferred stock.

Continuing Trends and Issues for the Future

A great deal has happened in a very short time to the international equities market, and much is happening yet. International activity in equity markets gives every indication of being a permanent and growing feature of the investment business.

The world equity markets are not nearly so well integrated as the debt markets are. Debt issues are commodities defined by quality, maturity, and the yield curve. Swap markets permit arbitrage activity that eliminates price differences for the same commodity in other markets. Equities are different: Each stock is different, and markets have different methods of valuation, which though converging with one another are still fairly far apart. But other aspects of the international equity markets are integrating more rapidly: Regulation, competitive access, and the skills and services offered, and attitudes about international portfolio diversification, are some of these. Governments continue to want good markets to receive their large privatization issues, and countries that have been cut off from valuable capital market activity are now finding it possible to attract foreign capital seeking investments in emerging markets. However, these countries, now enlarged by the former Soviet bloc in Eastern Europe, are learning that to attract capital they have to compete for it by creating the most open and efficient marketplaces they can.

New methods of international distribution are also being tried. In a short period the world has gone from foreign issues sold in one market to Euroequity issues to globally coordinated, simultaneously offered, multiple-tranche issues. How else could an Argentine oil company raise nearly $3 billion in a single issue?

The demand for services to professional investors will rise to U.S. levels in the newly liberalized equity markets of Europe and Japan. New standards of investment performance are being adopted, which will create more competition and more services and result in better, more liquid markets for all equities interesting enough to attract international investors.

Summary

In equities, as in international bonds, issuers tap international markets to increase the pool of available funds, to lower costs of raising capital, to expand their investor base, and/or to avoid domestic regulatory complications. Investors move to international markets to improve portfolio performance and lower risks. Both groups' interests have been furthered by the erosion of regulatory barriers—exchange controls, limits on ownership, limits on participation in domestic markets, and obstructive listing and trading practices.

Particularly in Japan, which now boasts the second largest domestic equity capitalization in the world, deregulation has allowed an outflow of investing capital seeking diversification and higher returns. The institutional investors of the United States, home to the world's most sophisticated equity markets, have made their impact on developing Euroequity markets by demanding the same high standards of research, trading, and brokering as they enjoy at home.

While governments and stock-market regulatory agencies have made some progress in standardizing procedures, full integration is a long way off. Many non-U.S. issuers are discouraged from the otherwise attractive U.S. market by the stringent listing requirements of the SEC. Recent high volumes of new issues by Japanese issuers of Eurobonds with warrants—positioned to attract Japanese investors—clearly circumvent onerous regulatory requirements of the domestic market. Pricing conventions in the secondary market continue to exhibit national divergences, the most striking being the high Japanese p/e ratios that were so evident during the late 1980s.

But the emergence of a single world market is already discernible. The large investment houses, committed to supporting globalization of institutional investment, stand prepared to make markets 24 hours a day in selected stocks traded in New York, Tokyo, London, and elsewhere. That infrastructure, built during the bull market of the 1980s, is now being consolidated, sharpened, and challenged by new opportunities and competitive pressures.

Notes

1. Derived by the Federal Reserve Bank of Atlanta from U.S. Department of the Treasury, *U.S Treasury Bulletin,* Winter 1991, Table CM-V-5; Winter 1981, Table CM-VI-10.

2. *New York Stock Exchange Yearbook,* 1975, 1992.

3. ADRs are issued by a U.S. bank reflecting a deposit with the bank abroad of share of a foreign stock. The ADRs are quoted and traded in the United States, and transactions are settled and dividends paid in dollars as a convenience to U.S. investors. However, many institutions today prefer to won the underlying shares directly so as to have access to the home country trading markets.

4. "Too Many Trading Places," *The Economist,* June 19, 1993.

5. Securities Data Corporation, July 1993.

6. Nomura Securities Co, Ltd.

12

Mergers, Acquisitions, and International Advisory Services

In addition to raising capital for corporations through the issuance of new debt or equity securities or bank loans, capital market services include the giving of advice on a variety of complex matters that a corporation must deal with in order to evaluate or accomplish particular financial transactions. Such transactions are usually ones that require specialized knowledge of the markets involved, and often also require a network of contacts and extensive knowledge of local practices that a corporation itself is unlikely to possess to the degree necessary to ensure success. Advisory services are provided by both commercial banks and investment banks, although they have been a specialty of investment banks for a long time since they usually involve the valuation of new or unusual securities by the market.

Advisory services are provided on an agency basis for a fee that tends to reflect the value-added by the banker in the transaction. Typically a small retainer fee is agreed, which is payable regardless of the outcome of the transaction. The main part of the fee is dependent on the completion of the transaction and usually based on an agreed percentage of its value. Among such financial advisory services are those involving mergers, acquisitions and divestitures, recapitalizations, leveraged buyouts, creative "financial engineering" for new facilities or projects, real estate finance, and a variety of other transactions.

Advisory services follow the markets for the transactions they involve. International advisory services are simply advice on mergers, restructurings, and so on, applied to cross-border transactions or to transactions carried out in another country.

The Market for International Merger Advisory Services

The international dimension to the mergers and acquisition business is not at all confined to the growing number of important cross-border and non-U.S. transactions that occur every year. It also covers many transactions that are never completed or are completed differently. Hoffmann La Roche, the large Swiss pharmaceutical firm, did not succeed in acquiring the American Sterling Drug Co. in early 1988; Eastman Kodak did. But Hoffmann La Roche was a participant in the transaction anyway—as a potential buyer that in this case actually stepped forward to make an unsolicited bid. For every large transaction there are potential bidders beyond the border, whether they come forward or not. Those who advise in the business have to know their thinking and their telephone numbers. They have to be in touch. And being in touch, the advisers learn new things about the foreign companies and vice versa, and soon the advisers find themselves with a new client, and the circle expands.

The United States and the United Kingdom are the largest markets for financial advisory services, and their investment and merchant banks represent the greatest repository of financial advisory know-how. This is partly because of the large volume of merger and acquisition transactions that occur in these countries, but also because the underlying capital markets are active in many innovative ways that have not as yet caught on in the national capital markets of other countries. However, because of the effects of globalization in finance and changes in the underlying capital market structures in other countries, we can expect other financial centers in time to assimilate, in one form or another, the practices of corporate reorganizing and restructuring that are common in Britain and America.

The Intra-European Market

The market for M&A services within Europe differs considerably between the United Kingdom and continental Europe. Corporations in the United Kingdom have been able to benefit from a well-developed market for corporate control since the 1950s. A comparatively large number of publicly owned corporations exist in Britain and these have been, and continue to be, mainly owned by financial institutions. Share markets in Britain, compared with the rest of Europe, are active, investment information is plentiful, and prices of shares are held to be fair representations of the value of corporations. Takeover transactions are governed by the Takeover Panel, a self-regulatory organization, which is authorized to determine the rules of fair play. Next to the U.S. market, the British market is the largest in the world for M&A transactions.

Conditions are different on the continent. Many enterprises, including numerous very large ones, are not organized as publicly owned, limited-liability corporations like they are in the United States and Britain. A 1994 study by Pedersen and Thompson of ownership of the hundred largest corporations in each of six European nations showed 61 percent to be widely held by the public in Britain, 23 percent in the Netherlands, 16 percent in France, 10 percent in Denmark, 9 percent in Germany, and 4 percent in Sweden. In Sweden, Germany, and France, dominant ownership positions existed in nearly 30 percent of the largest hundred companies. These results are similar to a study published earlier by Booz Allen Acquisition Services for the EU, which also noted that in the three largest EU economies, only a relatively minor share of the GDP can actually be accessed through public takeovers. Nor do many of the continental European countries have a tradition of, or experience with, market-driven domestic M&A activity. As a result, only a comparatively small percentage of enterprises in continental European countries has so far participated in such transactions.

Accordingly, the environment on the continent for M&A transactions is quite different from that in the United Kingdom. Investment information is not as readily available, transactions tend to be negotiated face to face by controlling parties, stakeholdings and corporate alliances are common, hostile activity is limited, and sophisticated tactical and financial maneuvers are regarded with suspicion. Notwithstanding these traditions and attitudes, however, conditions are changing rapidly on the continent, and relatively larger numbers of transactions have been completed in recent years. Indeed, since the retrenchment of M&A activity in the United States and Britain after 1989, the most active area of M&A activity until 1994 was in continental Europe.

European Industrial Restructuring

One reason for the increase in continental M&A activity has been the growing recognition of the need for industrial restructuring in Europe following the adoption of the single European market concept by the EU countries. Originally announced in 1983, agreed on in 1987, and implemented at the end of 1992, the Single Market Act required the free movement of goods, capital, people, and ideas to enhance economic growth in the European Economic Community (now called the European Union) by moving toward free markets and more open competition. The private sector was not only to be invigorated by these steps, it was also to be enlarged by continued large-scale privatization programs that involved selling shares in government-owned industrial corporations to the public. Once in public hands, such companies would be run more efficiently, it was thought, and could participate in the growing "market for corporate control," which is what economists call the merger and acquisition market.

The emerging internal market of the late 1990s will require larger, more competitive enterprises able to reap significant economies of scale and economies of scope, particularly in such industries as transportation, information technology, telecommunications, financial services, food products, consumer electronics, and pharmaceuticals. As in the wave of mergers and acquisitions that have from time to time rolled over the United States, the current European restructuring is driven by underlying industry economics, global competitive shifts, and the perceived need to diversify.

Improved Financial Markets

These powerful economic drives have forced traditional concerns and practices to bend to market actions in a number of countries. The increasing liquidity of European capital markets has made nontraditional, market-oriented alternatives possible. No longer must entrepreneurs look for a friendly bank or competitor to buy all or part of their holdings on their retirement. They can now sell shares at a decent price in the open market (through an initial public offering), or hire an investment banker to find a suitable party—a fellow national or a foreigner—to buy the company. No longer must an industry suffering structural difficulties be forced to hold on to businesses that no longer fit. It can now dispose of them in the market. And of course, no longer must a healthy company seeking to expand across European borders build up new businesses in other countries step by step. It can now purchase a complete going concern at a market price.

Consequently, it is probable that industry and shareholders will both find incentives in effecting corporate restructuring though the financial markets, rather than through private transactions as in the past. Continental Europe has never had a merger boom, and very little industrial restructuring has taken place since the end of World War II. There is much to be done to streamline industry in Europe to keep pace with competition from the United States and Japan. Perhaps the fastest and most financially efficient way to do this is through the merger market. This being the case, it is likely that the market for corporate control and related M&A services will continue to grow rapidly throughout all of Europe, in both EU and non-EU countries.

For many, the conviction that their corporate objectives can be achieved in the short-run only through acquisition activity will be powerful. Consequently, as has been the case in the United States and the United Kingdom, a determination to pursue acquisitions despite objections of the target company will introduce, to a much greater extent than previously, predatory actions on the part of acquirers. Unless opposed by public policy—which, although much more relaxed on the matter of hostile offers than in the past, still differs considerably from country to country—the hostile takeover attempt can be expected to become much more common in Europe.

The growing concentration of shareholdings in institutional portfolios subject to a progressively higher performance orientation serves to increase the emphasis on realizing underlying equity values. More competition among investment managers, more liquidity, and greater room to maneuver will require all financial managers to become more performance oriented than they have been in the past. Thus, investment managers should be more inclined than in the past to favor takeovers and short-term returns in preference to maintaining long-term holdings out of loyalty or inertia. This change has already occurred to a significant degree in the United Kingdom. Such shifts in continental European investor behavior are likely—although perhaps not to the extent, for example, as has developed in the United States, where performance orientation appears to be at a maximum.

Ample financing continues to be available from banks anxious to earn large fees and spreads on M&A transactions. Under the BIS risk-based capital adequacy standards that lump all corporate lending into one category, M&A loans are advantageous for most banks, which can earn significantly increased spreads in takeover financings without any increased charge against capital than for a straight loan to an AAA corporation such as Unilever. In addition to the banks, liquidity is available for M&A financings from investment funds that purchase high-yield bonds and subordinated debt issues of acquiring corporations. Such funds have been widely sold to private, institutional, and corporate investors in the United States and Europe.

Merger Know-how

Finally, sufficient M&A "technology" is in place, both homegrown in Europe and that developed in the United States and adapted to European conditions, to facilitate a large increase in merger transactions. Because of national differences among the EU countries concerning the ways in which the market for corporate control is regulated, and the unpredictability of national or EU antitrust intervention, risk arbitrage markets in Europe have not fully developed. However, the increasing presence of international institutional investors in Europe (as well as stock market analysts that service them) has put pressure on companies to improve their performance relative to peer group companies and to avoid transactions that favor management or a small group of stockholders over public shareholders. Investors and combatants alike have grown accustomed to using the courts to resolve disputes over the rights of minority shareholders, something that would have been unthinkable a few years ago. Frequently, European companies employ U.S. or U.K. investment banks to represent their interests in local struggles over corporate control as well as for cross-border transactions. As a result of these factors, the M&A market in Europe has become considerably more efficient in the past ten years.

Other Financial Advisory Services

Most banks offer additional advisory services in addition to mergers and acquisitions such as:

1. *Hedging of financial risks.* Advice is given on how to manage liabilities and financial risk exposures for companies and other banks. This entails structuring of tailor-made derivative securities for which the bank will act as principal. These services are discussed in chapter 10.

2. *Share ownership.* More international companies are undertaking programs designed to promote ownership of their securities by investors in capital markets around the world. As a result, bankers arrange listings on international stock exchanges and issues of unregistered "private placements" of debt and equity securities of companies with institutional investors in the United States, Japan, and Europe. See chapter 11.

3. *Leveraged buyouts.* More international companies are showing interest in LBOs. So far this activity has been restricted mainly to management buyouts of subsidiaries that parent companies have agreed to sell. However, many observers believe a spreading of this activity will continue into continental Europe and elsewhere.

4. *Project finance and financial engineering.* Direct investments in factories and other facilities around the world can be financed in various creative ways, for example through the sale of adjustable-rate preferred stock, private placements, lease arrangements, commercial paper, and various forms of nonrecourse financing. Such transactions present opportunities for bankers to come up with and to communicate high value-added financing ideas. See chapter 3.

5. *Real estate.* Many corporations have real estate that can be refinanced or sold and leased back. Such transactions involve a highly specialized, increasingly global business. For those bankers active in real estate finance, many opportunities are created and many more are expected to be as real estate transactions of the sort conducted in the United States begin to appear in Europe and Japan.

The Structure of International M&A Deal-Flows

Between 1985 and 1995 the pattern of worldwide M&A activity—broadly defined to include mergers, acquisitions, tender offers, purchases of stakes, divestitures, and leveraged buyouts (LBOs)—has changed considerably, with transactions entirely in the United States having peaked in 1988 and then declined sharply to a level of one-third the peak volume just five years later. American cross-border transactions and transactions entirely outside the United States also declined after 1989 and 1990, respectively, but much less rapidly.

The Action Moves to Europe

Table 12-1 shows combined M&A activities on a worldwide basis for the eleven-year period 1985–1995, when approximately 46,000 transactions involving mergers, tender offers, purchases of stakes, divestitures, and leveraged buyouts with a market value of $4 trillion were completed. Another 49,000 transactions occurred for which no pricing information was reported. Of the valued transactions, approximately 50 percent were transactions between U.S. companies. Nearly $1.42 trillion, or 36 percent, were transactions entirely outside the United States, that is, in which only non-U.S. companies (or non-U.S. subsidiaries of American companies) were involved; and $616 billion, or 14 percent, were cross-border transactions in which U.S. parent companies acted as buyers and sellers with non-U.S. counterparts.

The predominance of U.S. to U.S. transactions obscures important changes that have been occurring abroad. Whereas the value of U.S. domestic transactions in 1988 was $293 billion, about one and a half times the volume of such transactions in 1985, U.S. cross-border transactions have grown much more rapidly. Transactions in which U.S. corporations were sellers to non-U.S. buyers were more than five times larger in 1989 than in 1985. U.S. buyer transactions in 1989 were six times what they were in 1985. Finally, deals completed outside the United States grew by a factor of 10 between 1985 and 1988. Similarly, these transactions declined less than domestic U.S. transactions during the period following 1989.

The completed acquisitions data have also been broken down by Standard Industrial Classification (SIC) codes identifying the primary business of firms on both sides of each transaction. Table 12-2 shows European M&A deals for 1985 through 1995 valued at $50 million or more by major industry category of the firm undertaking the transaction (a) and of the target (b). Industries most heavily involved as principals in European M&A transactions included food products, oil and gas, chemicals, banks, and electronics and electrical equipment, while those most heavily involved as targets comprised oil and gas, food products, chemicals, banks, and transportation equipment.

Table 12-2c shows that the industry segments so far subject to restructuring through M&A transactions in the EU correlate significantly with those subjected to M&A activity in the United States during the same period. This is not surprising, since the underlying economic forces affected these newly globalized industries in similar ways on both sides of the Atlantic.

Cross-Border Transactions

During the eleven-year period 1985–1995, cross-border transactions accounted for 23 percent (in value) of all M&A transactions involving United States corporations, and 73 percent of the value these deals were

Table 12-1 Volume of Completed International Merger and Corporate Transactions, 1985–1995

		Cross-Border									Global Total	
	Domestic U.S.		Buyer U.S.		Seller U.S.		Total Cross-Border		Outside U.S.			
Year	No.	U.S. $ million	No.	U.S. $ million	No.	U.S. $ million	No.	U.S. $ million	No.	U.S. $ million	No.	U.S. $ million
1985	815 (884)[a]	192,293.5	30 (79)	4,034.4	99 (122)	11,897.9	129 (201)	15,932.3	166 (124)	24,841.7	1,110 (1,209)	233,067.5
1986	1,205 (1,369)	200,913.2	46 (78)	2,672.3	212 (177)	36,658.3	258 (255)	39,330.6	347 (307)	54,597.1	1,810 (1,931)	294,840.9
1987	1,357 (1,409)	203,935.6	62 (142)	8,551.4	227 (173)	41,661.7	289 (315)	50,213.1	797 (560)	96,176.9	2,443 (2,284)	350,325.6
1988	1,642 (1,370)	293,194.1	91 (164)	7,038.5	324 (226)	70,817.2	415 (390)	77,855.7	1,664 (1,015)	140,331.1	3,721 (2,775)	511,380.9
1989	2,005 (1,969)	250,095.7	157 (250)	25,135.8	456 (293)	60,449.3	613 (543)	85,585.1	2,048 (1,817)	227,824.0	4,666 (4,329)	563,504.8
1990	1,741 (2,448)	124,874.3	154 (267)	16,604.0	453 (378)	56,349.9	607 (645)	72,953.9	2,218 (1,936)	236,187.4	4,566 (5,029)	434,015.6
1991	1,795 (2,050)	108,464.1	209 (327)	13,376.1	318 (266)	27,159.1	527 (593)	40,535.2	2,564 (3,894)	202,396.7	4,886 (6,537)	351,396.0
1992	2,173 (2,035)	119,264.4	249 (310)	14,991.4	263 (158)	18,513.4	512 (468)	33,504.8	2,348 (3,339)	163,769.4	5,033 (5,842)	316,538.6
1993	2,011 (1,855)	101,067.8	212 (366)	13,696.0	224 (134)	21,214.5	436 (500)	34,910.5	2,448 (2,989)	125,755.3	4,895 (5,344)	261,733.6
1994	2,898 (2,319)	199,783.7	284 (455)	19,089.1	319 (192)	39,299.1	603 (647)	58,388.2	2,867 (3,347)	148,737.8	6,368 (6,313)	406,909.7
1995	2,822 (3,002)	218,545	370 (578)	38,111	328 (223)	68,391	698 (801)	106,502	3,235 (4,054)	227,761	6,755 (7,857)	552,808
Totals	20,464 (20,710)	2,012,431	1,864 (3,016)	163,300	3,223 (2,342)	452,411	5,087 (5,358)	615,711	20,702 (23,382)	1,648,379	46,253 (49,450)	4,043,453

Source: Securities Data Company.
[a]Numbers in parentheses denote additional deals for which no values were available.

346

Table 12-2a Industry Group Rankings of M&A Buyer Companies, United States and Europe, 1985–1995 (U.S. $ millions)[a]

Description	U.S. Target			European Transactions		
	Rank	Value	Number	Rank	Value	Number
Investment & commodity firms/ dealers/exchanges	1	492,913	9759	1	216,666	7288
Commercial banks, bank holding companies	2	183,308	3557	2	119,555	1987
Telecommunications	3	145,591	908	16	20,633	210
Oil and gas; petroleum refining	4	118,418	1731	7	51,714	606
Drugs	5	81,967	694	5	62,903	514
Insurance	6	72,276	1322	4	91,615	1317
Chemicals and allied products	7	72,044	1117	6	61,009	1077
Food and kindred products	8	71,372	1159	3	95,306	1948
Radio and television broadcasting stations	9	66,148	898	44	3,940	216
Printing, publishing, and allied services	10	64,626	1256	8	46,421	1203
Health services	11	59,534	1605	45	3,831	108
Measuring, medical, photo equipment; clocks	12	55,595	1604	33	9,376	551
Electronic and electrical equipment	13	54,138	1319	11	31,040	1047
Business services	14	49,587	2870	19	19,349	1869
Tobacco products	15	46,090	50	48	2,658	47
Motion picture production and distribution	16	45,942	418	39	5,411	129
Electric, gas, and water distribution	17	44,104	547	9	36,471	479
Machinery	18	41,090	1153	23	15,681	1384
Computer and office equipment	19	38,766	912	43	4,238	226
Metal and metal products	20	38,623	1104	10	34,461	1488
Transportation equipment	21	37,442	490	13	27,764	593
Transportation and shipping (except air)	22	36,333	534	20	19,059	1143
Credit institutions	23	34,791	404	30	10,720	280
Retail trade—general merchandise and apparel	24	33,992	292	26	12,688	266
Paper and allied products	25	32,714	412	15	25,722	546
Aerospace and aircraft	26	29,352	197	47	3,065	128
Soaps, cosmetics, and personal-care products	27	29,066	253	35	7,347	208
Mining	28	26,008	432	17	19,548	222
Air transportation and shipping	29	20,386	207	41	5,052	196
Real estate; mortgage bankers and brokers	30	18,844	692	21	16,911	649
Prepackaged software	31	18,655	872	51	1,819	222
Stone, clay, glass, and concrete products	32	18,350	373	12	29,180	818
Savings and loans, mutual savings banks	33	18,019	1407	61	—	5
Retail trade—food stores	34	17,495	186	28	12,323	212
Wholesale trade—nondurable goods	35	15,837	826	24	15,543	868

continued

Table 12-2a (continued)

Description	U.S. Target Rank[b]	Number	Value	European Transactions Rank	Number	Value
Hotels and casinos	36	14,852	272	32	10,059	282
Textile and apparel products	37	14,358	476	31	10,398	781
Communications equipment	38	11,980	497	25	14,518	280
Miscellaneous retail trade	39	11,591	560	27	12,530	413
Wholesale trade-durable goods	40	11,546	911	29	10,863	1117
Wood products, furniture, and fixtures	41	10,182	286	36	7,171	367
Retail trade—eating and drinking places	42	9,791	328	34	8,267	192
Construction firms	43	9,699	323	18	19,365	935
Rubber and miscellaneous plastic products	44	9,374	419	22	16,200	565
Miscellaneous manufacturing	45	6,685	304	50	1,820	206
Sanitary services	46	5,723	452	54	780	117
Miscellaneous services	47	3,551	17	58	90	21
Repair services	48	2,802	111	49	2,224	100
Advertising services	49	2,704	325	38	6,234	349
Personal services	50	2,683	132	52	1,510	112
Leather and leather products	51	2,574	71	14	26,790	161
Agriculture, forestry, and fishing	52	2,477	174	37	6,782	187
Amusement and recreation services	53	2,431	157	40	5,210	131
Unknown	54	2,241	236	55	556	121
Public administration	55	1,106	47	42	4,960	98
Retail trade—home furnishings	56	1,101	121	53	1,484	101
Educational services	57	935	57	56	315	28
Social services	58	402	39	59	19	6
Other financial	59	175	49	46	3,350	27
Holding companies, except banks	60	67	7	57	125	11
Legal services	61	1	65	60	—	20
Nonclassifiable establishments	62	—	4	62	—	2

Source: Securities Data Company.

[a] Completed transactions include mergers, tender offers, tender mergers, purchase of stakes, divestitures, recapitalizations, exchange offers and LBOs. The volume data are classified according to the announcement date of a transaction—not taking into consideration when a transaction is completed. Million dollars of purchase price—excluding fees and expenses—at current exchange rates.

[b] Ranking is based on total dollar value of target industry.

Table 12-2b Industry Group Rankings of M&A Seller Companies, United States and Europe, 1985–1995 (U.S. $ millions)[a]

Description	U.S. Target			European Transactions		
	Rank[b]	Value	Number	Rank	Value	Number
Commercial banks, bank holding companies	1	154,005	2,715	1	115,674	1,344
Telecommunications	2	139,629	902	15	28,847	232
Oil and gas; petroleum refining	3	135,008	1,949	4	64,914	699
Food and kindred products	4	124,208	1,281	2	100,271	2,230
Radio and television broadcasting stations	5	116,191	1,184	32	10,987	432
Drugs	6	109,299	765	5	55,409	535
Insurance	7	106,229	1,360	3	77,080	1,053
Chemicals and allied products	8	99,955	1,146	12	35,105	1,110
Business services	9	83,099	3,948	14	30,483	2,717
Motion picture production and distribution	10	82,980	485	45	4,027	188
Health services	11	82,339	1,820	52	2,490	170
Electronic and electrical equipment	12	79,805	1,585	16	26,806	1,252
Measuring, medical, photo equipment; clocks	13	71,060	1,908	28	13,690	818
Printing, publishing, and allied services	14	68,889	1,386	8	40,930	1,436
Investment & commodity firms, dealers, exchanges	15	67,366	1,509	6	54,964	1,971
Retail trade—general merchandise and apparel	16	61,135	454	25	15,282	239
Metal and metal products	17	58,517	1,490	11	35,573	1,679
Electric, gas, and water distribution	18	52,984	532	7	54,888	442
Machinery	19	50,939	1,505	19	21,530	1,729
Computer and office equipment	20	50,704	930	42	5,602	288
Hotels and casinos	21	48,766	572	23	18,349	483
Transportation and shipping (except air)	22	48,609	742	17	23,682	1,536
Credit institutions	23	46,873	465	34	10,038	239
Real estate; mortgage bankers and brokers	24	45,607	1,285	13	32,001	1,064
Paper and allied products	25	44,481	424	10	36,347	685
Retail trade—food stores	26	43,312	341	26	14,340	301
Tobacco products	27	43,219	34	41	6,495	54
Savings and loans, mutual savings banks	28	42,406	2,327	61	—	6
Aerospace and aircraft	29	38,602	235	40	7,304	157
Stone, clay, glass, and concrete products	30	37,829	415	22	20,371	839
Mining	31	37,272	533	33	10,175	280
Textile and apparel products	32	35,638	735	27	14,065	1,037
Transportation equipment	33	33,689	543	9	36,746	855
Wholesale trade—nondurable goods	34	31,742	1,022	24	16,820	1,084
Air transportation and shipping	35	30,828	280	37	7,795	304
Retail trade—eating and drinking places	36	30,403	509	31	12,257	367

continued

Table 12-2b (continued)

Description	U.S. Target			European Transactions		
	Rank[b]	Number	Value	Rank	Number	Value
Soaps, cosmetics, and personal-care products	37	29,104	266	30	12,294	247
Miscellaneous retail trade	38	28,236	965	29	12,539	726
Prepackaged software	39	26,587	1,168	44	4,088	462
Rubber and miscellaneous plastic products	40	26,278	667	38	7,680	686
Communications equipment	41	18,093	617	21	20,427	389
Wholesale trade—durable goods	42	17,813	1,580	18	21,779	1,698
Wood products, furniture, and fixtures	43	14,982	445	39	7,307	565
Amusement and recreation services	44	13,510	364	36	7,828	239
Repair services	45	11,614	209	46	3,690	219
Miscellaneous manufacturing	46	11,407	433	49	3,412	365
Agriculture, forestry, and fishing	47	9,252	267	43	4,602	307
Construction firms	48	8,766	452	20	21,150	1,111
Advertising services	49	7,098	300	47	3,632	390
Retail trade—home furnishings	50	6,458	249	35	9,018	186
Sanitary services	51	6,130	453	50	3,102	196
Leather and leather products	52	4,415	106	53	2,382	155
Other financial	53	2,761	73	54	2,045	30
Miscellaneous services	54	2,700	26	57	168	24
Personal services	55	2,101	137	51	3,032	105
Educational services	56	1,083	75	56	225	47
Social services	57	649	59	59	140	17
Unknown	58	589	211	48	3,450	231
Public administration	59	71	18	55	467	34
Legal services	60	2	70	60	6	23
Holding companies, except banks	61	—	2	58	163	9

Table 12-2c Spearman Rank Correlation of U.S. and European Industries Participating in M&A Transactions, 1985–1995[a]

	Buyer's SIC	Seller's SIC
Number of deals		
r	0.6866	0.7024
N	(61)	(61)
p[b]	0.0000	0.0000
$ Volume		
r	0.5995	0.6345
N	(61)	(61)
p[b]	0.0000	0.0000

[a] Correlations are based on the number of transactions and the dollar volume of U.S. and European Industries (2-digit SIC codes).
[b] One-tailed significance.

inward investments, most of which involved European buyers. Clearly, European corporations were not interested only in the EU internal market. For many years they had recognized the importance of deploying more of their business activities into the United States, where the domestic economy had been expanding rapidly, the dollar had declined sharply after 1985, and fears of possible protectionism interrupting market access through imports were rising. During the 1980s, European and Japanese companies began to increase direct investment in the United States, which remains the world's largest market for just about all industrial and consumer products. In this respect, European corporations were acting similarly to American companies during the 1950s and 1960s, when a high level of de novo investment and acquisition took place in Europe to shore up U.S. market positions and competitive capabilities there. U.S. companies remain the largest direct investors in other countries today, and currently maintain about 25 percent of their manufacturing capability outside the United States.

Figure 12-1 shows the growth in foreign direct investment in the United States, and the national origin of the major investments. Total foreign direct investment includes not only mergers and acquisitions, but also direct investment in real estate, start-up operations, and additions to permanent and working capital of subsidiaries in the United States.

U.S. cross-border transactions have included numerous large transactions in which European corporations acquired the outstanding minority

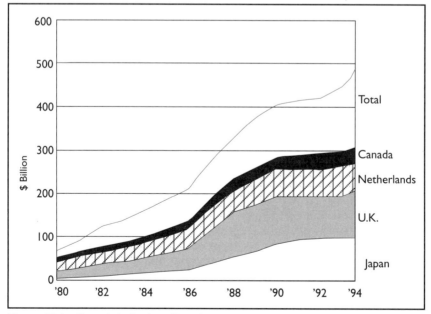

Figure 12-1. Growth in foreign direct investment in the United States, 1980–1994. Data from Bureau of Economic Analysis.

interests in their majority-owned U.S. subsidiaries. In 1970, British Petroleum exchanged certain Alaskan oil production interests for an increasing share interest in the Standard Oil Company (Sohio), which reached 53 percent in 1978. In 1987 BP decided to acquire the remaining 47 percent through a $7.9 billion tender offer to shareholders. Similar acquisitions of minority interests have been undertaken by Royal Dutch Shell; N.V. Philips Gloeilampenfabrieken, the large Dutch electronics concern; and the U.K.'s Midland Bank, which acquired the 43 percent interest in Crocker National Bank that it did not own preparatory to selling the whole of Crocker to Wells Fargo in 1986. In addition, of course, many smaller acquisition transactions took place, many of which involved U.S. companies that were for sale and looked with their advisers to international names among possible buyers.

Divestitures also took place of companies that no longer suited their foreign owners. BAT Industries, the large U.K.-based tobacco, and insurance concern, acquired Gimbels in 1973, sold it in 1986; Imperial Group, another U.K. tobacco company, acquired Howard Johnson's in 1980, sold it in 1985. The international aspects of the merger and acquisition business thus involve both the buying and the selling of companies, big and small.

Cross-border transactions have also involved a number of Japanese and other Asian corporations. Japanese corporations, on the whole, appear to have preferred making direct investments in the United States or in Europe through the construction of new facilities rather than through the purchase of businesses. Frequently such projects have involved imaginative low-cost leasing or other financing schemes that were arranged by U.S. financial advisers. Other transactions, however, have involved the purchase of facilities, or lines of business from U.S. companies, and converting them to Japanese manufacturing methods. On other occasions Japanese companies have purchased minority stakes in U.S. companies, particularly in the steel industry, as a basis for securing a source of production in the United States. Some Japanese companies, notably electronics giants Sony and Matsushita have made enormous investments in U.S. entertainment businesses. Japanese inestors in U.S. real estate were extremely active in the late 1980s. Banks and industrial and commercial companies were also active acquirers of U.S. corporations during this period. On one noteworthy occasion, a Japanese company, Dai Nippon Ink, acquired a U.S. company, Reichhold Chemicals Co., in 1987 through a hostile takeover bid.

Non-U.S. Transactions

Of the transactions entirely outside the United States between 1985 and 1995, approximately 56 percent have been intra-European deals, of which transactions entirely within the United Kingdom (the largest component of intra-European deals) accounted for about 36 percent. European corporations have been active on three fronts—domestic mergers and consolidations, intra-European cross-border transactions, and transactions in the United States. Table 12-3 shows the value of completed international merger and corporate transactions for Europe during 1985–1995. Table 12-4 shows the volume of completed intra-European M&A transactions by country. This table illustrates the concentration of activity within domestic markets in the United Kingdom, France, The Netherlands, Germany and Italy. It also shows the rising importance of European cross-border transactions.

The remainder of the non-US transactions have been, in descending order of transaction value, intra-Canadian, intra-Australian, and intra-Asian (including a comparatively small but growing activity in Japan). In aggregate, transactions not involving U.S. corporations grew to approxi-

Table 12-3 International Merger and Corporate Transactions, Europe, 1985–1995

			Cross-Border					
	Intra-Europe		European Buyer		European Seller		Total Cross-Border	
Year	No.	U.S. $ millions	No.	U.S. $ millions	No.	U.S. $ millions	No.	U.S. $ millions
1985	84 (62)[a]	11,508.4	51 (47)	6,335.3	32 (64)	2,511.3	83 (111)	8,846.6
1986	219 (184)	20,692.6	119 (85)	19,642.8	55 (58)	15,747.3	174 (143)	35,390.1
1987	581 (351)	54,852.0	142 (102)	28,123.6	81 (131)	13,259.0	223 (233)	41,382.6
1988	1,252 (728)	86,430.3	235 (164)	37,623.6	145 (174)	17,020.5	380 (338)	54,644.1
1989	1,507 (1,211)	130,115.7	316 (206)	39,120.7	225 (317)	35,150.8	541 (523)	74,271.5
1990	1,440 (1,191)	127,225.9	274 (219)	46,841.6	310 (361)	50,897.9	584 (580)	97,739.5
1991	1,430 (2,926)	117,248.5	220 (202)	21,445.8	316 (406)	32,346.5	536 (608)	53,792.3
1992	1,462 (2,667)	91,022.0	179 (116)	8,201.6	274 (328)	34,825.2	453 (444)	43,026.8
1993	1,290 (2,100)	59,946.1	183 (150)	12,519.1	247 (391)	20,446.7	430 (541)	32,965.8
1994	1,538 (2,335)	85,586.5	241 (163)	30,836.3	292 (445)	26,265.9	533 (608)	57,102.2
1995	1,686 (2,655)	151,763.3	302 (253)	41,195.0	296 467	31,165.0	598 214	72,360.0
Totals	12,489 (16,410)	936,391.0	2,262 (1,707)	291,885.0	2,273 (2,208)	279,636.0	4,535 (3,915)	571,522.0

Source: Securities Data Company.
[a]Numbers in parentheses denote additional deals for which no values were available.

Table 12-4 Intra-European M&A Transaction Volume by Country
(1985–1995 USD millions)

Country of Buyer	Year	U.K.	France	Italy	Germany	Other European	Totals Buyer
				Country of Seller Company			
U.K.	1985	9,186.2	0.0	0.0	0.0	12.2	9,198.4
	1986	12,806.4	23.8	0.0	1.0	80.4	12,911.6
	1987	33,500.1	302.6	125.9	341.4	576.3	34,846.3
	1988	42,890.3	1,213.5	409.1	369.7	1,158.4	46,041.0
	1989	55,799.6	1,221.8	305.7	344.6	3,289.9	60,961.6
	1990	27,549.1	2,597.4	115.1	1,245.9	4,054.5	35,562.0
	1991	30,689.0	624.4	39.5	316.5	1,526.7	33,196.1
	1992	17,250.8	1,141.8	402.4	796.4	10,558.6	30,150.0
	1993	20,536.1	5,318.2	46.4	516.1	1,219.0	27,635.8
	1994	22,127.0	4,508.0	83.0	542.0	3,723.0	30,983.0
	1995	68,943.2	1,924.6	433.3	2,995.3	3,417.9	77,714.3
France	1985	0.0	10.7	0.0	0.0	0.0	10.7
	1986	5.9	1,285.7	520.9	0.0	32.1	1,844.6
	1987	316.6	1,958.9	343.3	0.0	0.0	2,618.8
	1988	3,209.6	7,716.3	428.7	310.2	1,392.5	13,057.3
	1989	5,727.5	15,906.5	837.3	2,044.8	4,296.7	28,812.8
	1990	3,195.0	12,648.4	3,380.9	502.9	4,548.4	24,275.6
	1991	621.3	17,005.5	1,627.8	5,437.1	3,118.4	27,810.1
	1992	211.3	9,696.5	406.8	2,454.8	4,053.2	16,822.6
	1993	39.5	6,646.6	288.6	217.1	673.8	7,865.6
	1994	840.0	9,352.0	39.0	15.0	703.0	10,949.0
	1995	2,254.3	9,971.8	143.0	237.7	1,790.0	14,396.8
Italy	1985	16.8	0.0	165.0	0.0	0.0	181.8
	1986	0.0	0.0	1,199.4	129.0	0.0	1,328.4
	1987	0.0	20.4	8,039.9	0.0	1,050.8	9,111.1
	1988	0.0	504.9	1,509.6	429.3	887.7	3,331.5
	1989	7.9	294.4	8,523.6	180.6	0.0	9,006.5
	1990	68.6	602.8	15,752.9	772.3	518.8	17,715.4
	1991	71.9	335.1	4,415.4	356.1	536.9	5,715.4
	1992	10.6	2,279.3	4,589.9	747.6	308.2	7,935.6
	1993	0.0	156.5	2,535.8	2.3	102.9	2,797.5
	1994	0.0	281.0	7,542.0	54.0	1,475.0	9,352.0
	1995	189.4	103.5	4,972.0	299.1	575.1	6,139.1
Germany	1985	0.0	0.0	0.0	898.5	445.0	1,343.5
	1986	425.0	0.3	887.4	980.0	0.0	2,292.7
	1987	167.0	414.8	0.0	452.8	0.0	1,034.6
	1988	59.2	154.0	866.1	2,518.7	39.6	3,637.6
	1989	2,378.4	1,341.3	37.5	2,649.4	1,466.0	7,872.6
	1990	1,499.7	2.2	53.2	2,101.5	1,341.9	4,998.5
	1991	456.7	8.5	0.0	13,697.8	1,242.0	15,405.0
	1992	986.5	10.5	39.0	7,157.3	1,511.3	9,704.6
	1993	167.1	458.6	0.0	3,401.6	1,796.3	5,823.6
	1994	11.0	1,350.0	470.0	5,893.0	877.0	8,601.0
	1995	4,226.7	3.4	341.7	3,476.6	3,069.3	11,117.7
Other European	1985	268.5	0.0	0.0	0.0	505.5	774.0
	1986	828.6	0.0	0.0	0.0	1,486.7	2,315.3

Table 12-4 (continued)

| Country of Buyer | Year | Country of Seller Company | | | | | |
		U.K.	France	Italy	Germany	Other European	Totals Buyer
	1987	574.9	188.9	26.8	239.0	6,211.6	7,241.2
	1988	7,540.9	1,028.6	2,098.7	0.0	9,694.7	20,362.9
	1989	2,074.3	4,040.7	158.9	902.5	16,285.7	23,462.1
	1990	7,245.7	1,285.1	436.9	2,794.8	32,911.9	44,674.4
	1991	2,730.7	838.2	529.5	651.6	30,371.9	35,121.9
	1992	1,845.4	4,087.4	272.3	196.2	20,007.9	26,409.2
	1993	775.4	207.2	1,956.6	327.6	12,556.8	15,823.6
	1994	1,669.0	3,934.0	9.0	1,390.0	16,130.0	23,132.0
	1995	6,085.0	313.4	321.6	4,206.7	31,566.4	42,493.1
Totals seller	1985	9,471.5	10.7	165.0	898.5	962.7	11,508.4
	1986	14,065.9	1,309.8	2,607.7	1,110.0	1,599.2	20,692.6
	1987	34,558.6	2,885.6	8,535.9	1,033.2	7,838.7	54,852.0
	1988	53,700.0	10,617.3	5,312.2	3,627.9	13,172.9	86,430.3
	1989	65,987.7	22,804.7	9,863.0	6,121.9	25,338.3	130,115.6
	1990	39,558.1	17,135.9	19,739.0	7,417.4	43,375.5	127,225.9
	1991	34,569.6	18,811.7	6,612.2	20,459.1	36,795.9	117,248.5
	1992	20,304.6	17,215.5	5,710.4	11,352.3	36,439.2	91,022.0
	1993	21,518.1	12,787.1	4,827.4	4,464.7	16,348.8	59,946.1
	1994	24,647.0	19,425.0	8,143.0	7,894.0	22,908.0	83,017.0
	1995	81,698.6	12,316.7	6,211.6	11,215.4	40,418.7	151,861.0

Source: Securities Data Company.

mately 58 percent of the worldwide total in 1991, up from about 11 percent in 1985, before dropping back to 41 percent of the worldwide total in 1995. Non-U.S. and U.S. cross-border transactions, that is, international transactions from the point of view of U.S. investment bankers, have grown from 17 percent of worldwide transactions in 1985 to 69 percent in 1991 (60 percent in 1995), as shown in Table 12-1.

Mergers in Japan

Conventional opinion notwithstanding, a considerable volume of M&A transactions has occurred in Japan. With very few exceptions, however, these transactions have not been arranged through the market but instead have been negotiated in private between powerful principals involved, and then announced. Transactions have fallen into four basic types: strategic mergers to create large internationally competitive enterprises in particular industries (banking, steel, commercial trading); rescue mergers in which a distressed company is absorbed by a member of its *keiretsu* group or another company; consolidation mergers, mainly of smaller businesses seeking to band together to make a larger presence in a formative new industry such as retailing; and last, hostile takeover attempts, usually by sensational stock market operators of smaller, vulnerable companies. In Japan, corporate loyalty and identity are very strong among large, publicly traded companies, and mergers are socially very disruptive and therefore not to be undertaken unless necessary for the survival of the enterprise. As most public companies have approximately 30 percent to 50 percent of their share held by other companies or institutions in the *keiretsu*, or affinity group, it is quite difficult to obtain control of any company through market acquisitions or tender offers. However, following the collapse of the Japanese stock market in 1989, and many financial reforms introduced since then, the keiretsu groups and banks are beginning to dispose of shares held for relationship purposes. As in continental Europe, the lack of access to control through market transactions considerably limits activity in the M&A market. As in Europe, however, market and legal forces gradually work changes on old practices.

Special Characteristics of European M&A Transactions

European merger transactions have been propelled by several broad economic and political forces during the past decade. These forces include globalization effects on industrial competitive structure, integration of financial markets and the free flow of capital across borders, aggressive privatization policies, and the movement toward the single European market and ultimately a European economic and monetary union. More recently, the collapse of the communist powers in Eastern Europe and the effort to bring these countries into a general European capitalistic society, and an extended recessionary economic environment throughout Europe, have created great pressures for improved competitive performance and efficiency. Clearly these forces, in aggregate, have become extremely powerful, perhaps so powerful as to be irresistible even by the long entrenched practices and attitudes about corporate control and governance that have existed in Europe, especially on the continent, for generations. These practices and attitudes have centered on close control of corporations, nonmarket valuation of shares to be transferred, effecting control through minority positions in a large network of stakeholdings, and resistance to hostile takeovers, leveraged buyouts, and the advice of independent advisers. Now, after several years of observation, we can conclude that the market forces have driven changes into the European marketplace—changes that appear to be irreversible. These changes have been accompanied by a variety of regulatory reforms in national markets and at the EU level that will increase the efficiency of the marketplace. As this process continues, in 10 years or so it may not be possible to describe especially distinctive characteristics of the market for corporate control in continental Europe compared with the United States or Britain. As these characteristics exist, however, we shall examine them briefly.

Minority Stakeholdings

Table 12-5 compares partial ownership positions (stakes) as a percentage of all completed M&A transactions in the United States, the United Kingdom, and for the rest of Europe for the period 1985–1995. Compared with the United States, stakeholding transactions were approximately twice as prevalent in transactions involving non-U.K. European corporations, indicating a uniquely European modus operandi. European companies appear to favor stakes for several reasons, including the concept of forging a "strategic alliance" for a common purpose, offensive or defensive, without giving up their own independence; the idea that a gradual commitment to a final arrangement is wiser, cheaper, and reversible; and because in many situations a substantial minority stakeholding can assure de facto control of a company. In the United States, by comparison, acquirers are motivated by tax, accounting, and legal reasons to prefer 100 percent ownership. The American practice of minority shareholder litigation and class action suits makes the elimination of minority interests especially important to many companies, although these companies often rec-

Table 12-5 Partial Ownership Positions as a Percentage of All Completed U.S. and European M&A Transactions, 1985–1995[a]

Year	U.S. Seller[b]	European Seller[c]		Intra-European Deal[d]	
		U.K.	Rest of Europe	U.K.–U.K.	Europe–Europe
1985	6.30%	14.21%	25.13%	5.09%	25.59%
1986	17.12	7.15	38.14	6.51	39.05
1987	15.09	37.01	8.12	28.12	7.96
1988	11.77	24.03	42.25	12.58	42.72
1989	25.50	25.53	34.76	30.02	34.13
1990	13.82	22.20	20.74	20.91	17.57
1991	11.53	38.84	25.33	20.58	20.99
1992	7.62	41.42	31.98	41.97	29.17
1993	11.15	9.78	54.15	7.02	49.58
1994	14.33	24.92	48.84	24.33	54.97
1995	16.75	18.67	55.93	11.43	61.51
Average	13.73	23.98	35.03	18.96	34.84

Source: Securities Data Company.

[a] Partial ownership positions involve open or privately negotiated stake purchases of stock or assets. Data include only completed transactions. Data are classified according to announcement data of a transaction—not taking into consideration when a transaction is completed. Percentage values denote the fraction of total volume that involves partial stakes.

[b] Completed partial stakes as a percentage of total volume of completed transactions in which the seller was a U.S. company.

[c] Completed partial stakes as a percentage of total volume of completed transactions in which the seller was a company from the U.K. or the rest of Europe.

[d] Completed partial stakes as a percentage of total volume of completed intra-European transactions in which the seller was a company from the United Kingdom or the rest of Europe.

ognize that when in Rome, Brussels, Lyons, or Düsseldorf it may be acceptable to abide by local customs.

Some academic observers have suggested that lengthy European liaisons and courtships, or "trial marriages," may lead to full mergers that prove to be more lasting and beneficial than some of the more impulsive, opportunistic U.S. acquisitions that often appear to fail in delivering expected benefits. Minority investments, however, do not come without their problems. In many situations, for example, the seller of the stake wants above all to preserve a relationship, which is in fact economically inefficient. Strategic alliances, for example involving a 10 percent cross-shareholding between two competing companies from different countries, may appear shrewdly strategic when announced but not produce the intended synergies, and within a few years each company may find itself unable to influence policies in the company allied with it, and indeed in serious competition with it. Also, recently minority shareholder lawsuits, such as that by shareholders of the Belgian company Wagon-Lits against the French group Accord in 1992, blocked a below-market transfer of control. Increasing investment in companies like Wagon-Lits by powerful institutional investors from the United Kingdom or the United States makes these types of challenges more likely in the future.

Leveraged Buyouts

As recently as 1985, leveraged buyouts began to appear in Europe, especially in the United Kingdom, where they appeared in two forms: management buyouts (MBOs), in which existing management would receive financing sufficient to purchase the company from its owner, usually a large company no longer wanting the business; and management buy-ins (MBIs), in which new management and investors would take over a company on a highly leveraged basis. The inspiration for these transactions came from the United States where the LBO boom reached its peak in 1988 (the year of the RJR-Nabisco deal) and 25 percent of all completed U.S. transactions were LBOs. Table 12-6 compares LBO activity in the United States with that in the United Kingdom and the continent for 1985–1995; it clearly shows much more activity in the United States (where public financing of LBOs through the sale of junk bonds was available) than elsewhere. It also shows more than a trivial amount of LBO transactions occurring in Europe between 1987 and 1990, as divestitures increased and funds were made available to stake financial entrepreneurs. United Kingdom and continental LBOs valued at about £10 billion occurred in 1989, the peak year for such transactions. After 1989, LBO activity dropped sharply due to deteriorated market conditions for high-risk securities, though continental Europeans have continued to use MBOs and MBIs as a way to establish positions in the U.K. market since that time. As market conditions and the climate for LBOs improve in Europe, most observers believe that this method of financing acquisitions will again be-

Table 12-6 Leverage Buyouts as a Percentage of All Completed U.S. and European M&A Transactions, 1985–1995[a]

Year	U.S. Seller[b]	European Seller[c]		Intra-European Deal[d]	
		U.K.	Rest of Europe	U.K.	Rest of Europe
1985	13.43%	4.45%	0.00%	8.70%	0.00%
1986	16.45	1.67	0.85	3.83	0.00
1987	19.73	7.84	0.72	9.92	7.60
1988	31.10	8.00	3.67	12.09	4.29
1989	11.18	8.94	3.18	14.53	3.52
1990	6.60	4.64	2.21	11.05	2.33
1991	4.56	5.67	5.19	8.54	5.81
1992	6.60	6.78	1.91	14.96	2.15
1993	5.37	9.13	1.61	7.86	1.67
1994	2.97	8.69	0.83	9.99	0.83
1995	1.40	5.43	1.03	7.20	1.27

Source: Securities Data Company.

[a] Leverage buyout (LBO) is defined as a transaction in which an investor group, investor, or investor/LBO firm, acquires a company, taking on an extraordinary amount of debt, with plans to repay the debt with funds generated from the company or with revenue earned by selling off the newly acquired company's assets. Data include only completed transactions. Data are classified according to announcement date of a transaction—not taking into consideration when a transaction is completed. Percentage values denote the fraction of total volume that involves LBOs.

[b] Completed LBOs as a percentage of total volume of completed transactions in which the seller was a U.S. company.

[c] Completed LBOs as a percentage of total volume of completed transactions in which the seller was a company from the United Kingdom or the rest of Europe.

[d] Completed LBOs as a percentage of total volume of completed intra-European transactions in which the seller was a company from the United Kingdom or the rest of Europe.

come an important part of the acquisition scene, accounting perhaps for 10 percent to 15 percent of all transactions.

Hostile Takeovers

Takeover attempts made directly to shareholders that initially are opposed by management are called "hostile" offers. In the early 1980s, when hostile offers again became highly visible in the United States and Britain, there was little ambiguity as to whether an offer was hostile or not. Management usually criticized the offer as disruptive and undervalued; those on the other side pointed to management failures that had depressed the value of the company's shares. Both in the United States and Britain, hostile offers were fairly common—in a market dominated by independent financial institutions, such struggles for corporate control often are needed to decide conflicts that arise between a company's managers and its owners.

During the 1980s, however, defense measures evolved and various different ways to protect shareholders against undervalued offers emerged. It no longer was normal for management to complain about a bid it did not like. Instead management was sent looking for viable alternatives. One result was to obscure the difference between hostile and friendly offers. By the end of the 1980s it became clear that a friendly offer was one that was immediately declared such by the target company; all other offers were "unsolicited" or "nonfriendly" offers. Table 12-7 shows unsolicited or nonfriendly takeover offers as a percent of all completed offers in the United States, the United Kingdom, and the rest of Europe for 1985–1995. The table shows the extensive use of unsolicited offers in Britain, where permitted defensive maneuvers are much more limited than in the United States, and a significant incidence of unsolicited offers in the rest of Europe. Only completed deals are included—a number of unsuccessful unsolicited offers, such as the attempt on Navigation-Mixte by Paribas (France)

Table 12-7 Unsolicited or Nonfriendly Offers as a Percentage of All Completed U.S. and European M&A Transactions, 1985–1995 [a]

| | United States | | | United Kingdom | | | |
| | | Cross Border [c] | | | | Rest of Europe [e] | |
Year	Domestic [b]	U.S. Buyer	U.S. Seller	Domestic [d]	U.K. Buyer	U.K. Seller	Rest of Europe [f]
1985	22.3%	5.9%	11.2%	14.6%	14.3%	18.2%	12.1%
1986	17.7	7.8	10.6	11.1	12.5	13.0	6.7
1987	25.0	7.1	15.8	9.2	5.7	15.0	8.2
1988	19.8	8.5	8.0	8.1	2.6	17.1	10.4
1989	20.9	7.6	9.3	27.2	4.4	23.1	8.9
1990	24.0	4.3	6.1	20.5	2.8	15.3	7.9
1991	19.3	8.5	4.2	12.7	2.9	11.5	7.5
1992	14.1	7.3	7.0	8.0	2.2	10.4	8.0
1993	12.4	5.8	8.3	8.8	4.5	5.3	12.0
1994	14.4	6.9	10.1	8.0	3.6	6.3	13.2
1995	14.2	22.1	44.8	34.3	2.1	6.2	21.9
Average	20.4	9.2	13.5	16.2	5.8	14.1	11.7

Source: Securities Data Company.

[a] Hostile offers are defined as those transactions in which the acquiring company proceeds with its offer against the wishes of the target company's management. Data include only completed transactions. Data are classified according to announcement data of a transaction—not taking into consideration when a transaction is completed. Percentage values denote the fraction of total deals that involves partial stakes.

[b] Completed hostile deals as a percentage of total deals of completed transactions in which the buyer and seller was a U.S. company.

[c] Completed hostile deals as a percentage of total deals of completed transactions in which the buyer or seller was a U.S. company and the counterpart is a non-U.S. company.

[d] Completed hostile deals as a percentage of total deals of completed transactions in which the buyer or seller was a company from the United Kingdom.

[e] Completed hostile deals as a percentage of total deals of completed transactions in which the buyer or seller was a company from the United Kingdom and the counterpart is a continental European company.

[f] Completed hostile deals as a percentage of total deals of completed transactions in which the buyer or seller was a continental European company.

in 1989, Sandoz's effort to acquire Schering A.G. in 1990 (Switzerland and Germany, respectively), and Pirelli's celebrated effort to take over Continental A.G. (Italy and Germany, respectively) in 1991–1992, are not included.

Before the 1980s hostile offers were virtually unheard of in continental Europe, where markets were not dominated by institutions and concentrated holdings among insiders was the norm. This began to change during the 1980s as institutional holdings increased, markets improved and trading volume increased, and financial professionals from Britain and America became interested in the European scene. By the end of 1995, many highly visible hostile takeover attempts had been launched in France, Italy, Sweden, Germany, Denmark, Spain, Ireland, Portugal, and Switzerland. Such efforts included the attack on Société Generale de Belgique by the Italian industrialist Carlo de Benedetti in 1987, various struggles for control of Montedison in Italy, the takeover of Feldmuhle-Nobel by the Flick brothers in Germany in 1989, the Nestle and Indosuez's joint effort to take over Perrier, Krupp's acquisition of Hoesch Steel, and Swiss investor Martin Ebner's controversial challenge to the Union Bank of Switzerland. The effort by de Benedetti demonstrated that Belgium had far fewer legal barriers to takeover than had been assumed, and that the fact that the "right" people might own a corporation did not itself prevent takeovers. After this and some of the other early European hostile deals by well-established companies, attitudes began to change: Attention was paid to the actual performance of target companies and the management teams that led them, to the position of minority shareholders in change-of-control situations, to the rules affecting disclosure of share accumulations, and to restrictions on voting shares acquired by unwelcome holders. In 1991 the Amsterdam Stock Exchange limited the number of barriers to hostile takeovers that Dutch companies had relied on for years, and in 1992 it issued a warning to 20 listed companies that had not complied. Later in 1992, the chief of Germany's leading fund management company, a subsidiary of the Deutsche Bank, called for a code of practice to permit and regulate contested takeovers in Germany. Similar actions have occurred in other parts of Europe.

Since the Single Market Act and the various efforts at financial market reforms that have occurred in most of the principal European countries, attempts have been made by EU and member countries to devise a common set of takeover rules and procedures. These are discussed below. In general, there are two approaches to choose from, but as yet no EU directive on takeover policy has emerged, as the approaches are quite different. One approach—the British model—involves a set of rules designed to protect minority shareholders from unfair transactions. This system depends on full disclosure and proceeding according to established rules. The other system—sometimes called the German model, though many other countries follow similar practices—protects the rights of major shareholders, such as banks and insurance companies, to act paternalistically and responsibly, though not always visibly, in the interest of all shareholders. Market and legal forces are eroding the viability of the German model, and the Germans are still working toward a compromise between the two systems.

Converging Regulations

Regulations that affect takeovers are numerous. These include antitrust regulations and securities laws or regulations relating to fraudulent practice, for example, required disclosures, trading restrictions (such as insider trading), and prohibitions against making false markets. There are also rules, codes, and established procedures prescribed by stock exchanges or by self-regulatory bodies that may or may not be supported by enforcement powers. These various tiers of regulation can be imposed at national as well as at the EU level. Until a few years ago they were vastly different from one another, creating a confusing and often uneven playing field for participants. Efforts have been made to harmonize regulations, but progress through the end of 1995 was modest.

Regulation at the EU level has so far been confined to the antitrust sector. There are two governing principles in effect: (1) that of "subsidiarity" (a concept of EU governance that extends into all aspects of the common market), which provides that the EU will make no decision on issues that can equally well be decided nationally, and (2) that of "compatibility with the common market," which restricts EU actions to matters affecting the whole of the EU only. The EU regulations that were passed in 1990 provide:

1. that only deals involving combined worldwide sale of ECU 5 billion, or two or more companies with EU sales of ECU 250 million, will be reviewed by the EU's "merger task force."
2. that the merger task force must report within one month after announcement whether it believes the deal is compatible with the common market.
3. that if it reports doubts it has four months to resolve them and either approve the deal, block it, or insist on modifications.

After two years of operation, the 50-strong staff of the EU merger task force had reviewed more than 120 transactions, but had blocked only one.

At the national levels, regulatory bodies like Britain's Mergers and Monopolies Commission and Germany's Cartel Office rule on deals below ECU 5 billion in size, and are required by national regulations to consider mainly national competitive effects. These bodies usually decide within a few weeks of an announced transaction whether they see a competition problem. If so, a more extensive review, taking as long as six months, is undertaken before the deal can be completed. During this period the bid is usually withdrawn, to be reinstated after the review if the buyer decides to do so.

In terms of securities laws there are also considerable differences. Under the British system, all share accumulations above a threshold of 3 percent of outstanding shares have to be announced to the market; once a bidder accumulates 30 percent of the stock of the target he is obligated to make an offer to all the rest of the shareholders at the same price. Once a bid is announced, certain time schedules must be adhered to. The intent is to create a "level playing field" on which neither bidder nor defender would have any advantage over the other and the market could decide the outcome on a fair and unimpeded basis. To referee the conduct on the playing field, the British system relies on the Takeover Panel, a nongovernment body staffed by professionals seconded by their firms and a small permanent staff. The Panel has issued rules (the Takeover Code) that must be observed, previously only at penalty of sanction but now legally enforceable by the government. The Panel has the power to rule on disputes as they occur, and its decision is binding. Lawsuits are only rarely involved. The process is generally regarded as flexible, timely, fair, and efficient. Though different in many details from takeover procedures in the United States, which rely mainly on court actions in the state of incorporation of the defending company, the basic principles and objectives are very similar. Moves to accommodate the Anglo-Saxon model have been made in France and a few other countries, and are the basis of the draft European Takeover Directive, which requires a statutory body to regulate mergers.

A different system of corporate governance exists in Germany and several other European countries, which tends to minimize the frequency of takeovers. In these countries a two-tiered board system is used to govern corporate affairs. Companies are required to maintain a Supervisory Board, on which no members of management sit but representatives of labor unions, banks, local municipalities, and others do. Often the chairman of the Supervisory Board is a senior official of the company's main bank (*Hausbank*). This bank may own shares in the company itself, usually it will have debts outstanding to it, and it will also be given voting proxies by its customers who own shares in the bank. The bank will also maintain close contact with other financial shareholders and often act on their behalf. Accordingly the Hausbank will have considerable power to wield over the conduct of the company's affairs.

The main duty of the Supervisory Board is to appoint members of the Management Board, all of which are employees of the company. The Supervisory Board may also unilaterally decide to restrict voting rights of certain shareholders, subject only to challenge by 50 percent of all shareholders. If management should misbehave or the company run into difficulty or be in need of restructuring, the Supervisory Board, led by its chairman, is expected to step in and put things right. As the principal shareholders are mainly financial institutions or other corporations, the assumption is that if the Supervisory Board acts in accordance with the interests of this inside group of investors, then the interests of lesser shareholders will be taken care of, such investors being seen sometimes only as free riders. Thus, specific laws to protect minority shareholders are not needed and do not exist. Shareholdings need only be disclosed when they reach 25 percent of outstanding shares.

Various bodies in Germany, including the finance ministry, floated proposals early in 1992 for introducing a body of securities and takeover regulations, but these steps were resisted by traditional forces that opposed altering a system that had worked well for Germany for 40 years. However, some of the more international banks and corporations took up the cry for change, claiming that Germany's effort to create a competitive financial center, attract foreign equity investors, and fund more of its government deficit abroad would be frustrated by stubborn adherence to the old system. The Deutsche Bank actually imposed its own company regulations prohibiting insider trading. Also, in the spring of 1993 a member of the Supervisory Board of Daimler-Benz resigned after being associated with insider trading, and the public scandal and embarrassment that derived from the event accelerated the pace of reform. In July the finance ministry announced a draft law that would bring the regulatory environment for the German securities industry up to international standard. The law proposed the creation of a German Securities and Exchange Commission, similar to the SEC in the United States, the criminalization of insider trading, and disclosure of shareholdings when they reach 5 percent, among other provisions. The law was passed during 1994.

Merger and Acquisition Services

The basic distinction among merger and acquisition services is whether the service is offered to the buyer of a company or to a seller, and especially in the case of the latter, whether the sale is voluntary or involuntary. In each country local practices governing mergers and acquisitions differ considerably. For example, in the United States legal considerations and tactics are of paramount importance; there is a wide range of maneuver open to both sides and the pursuit and defense of companies can be quite aggressive. In most other countries aggressive legal actions are much less common, and the room for tactical maneuvering is less, but still the quality of the advice received by the company attempting to capture or escape the other will have much to do with the outcome.

Seller Representation

When advising a seller, whether a victim of a raid, a corporation seeking to divest a subsidiary, or a family hoping to sell the inherited business to "nice people," the role of the adviser starts with accepting the obligation to provide objective and experienced counsel and to assist the client in coping with the psychological trauma involved. There is almost always psychological trauma—buying and selling companies permits much room, which is almost always utilized, for emotional involvement and anxiety on the part of those directly affected by the outcome. Spending the time with a client to explain what lies ahead and what realistically can be expected often helps to lessen trauma that might otherwise be experienced later in the transaction.

A seller's adviser will perform the following tasks in the course of the assignment:

1. Value the company and advise the client what the probable selling price range is, based on a thorough understanding of the company's business, a review of current market data, and the banker's own experience.

2. Analyze a list of possible buyers, including all names of possible buyers furnished by the client, and LBO investors to determine the most likely buyers and the ability of each to obtain financing for the transaction.

3. Explain how these particular buyers would go about making an evaluation of the company and what the impact of the acquisition would be on the financial statements and stock price of each of them.

4. Prepare materials describing the company, on the basis of information supplied by it, that emphasizes the points of value to a buyer but is also in all respects fair and objective.

5. Contact potential buyers at decision-making levels and serve from then on as the exclusive contact person for buyers.

6. Control the process of distributing information to prospective buyers and providing opportunities for such buyers to ask questions about the business and meet with management, and so on.

7. Construct a bidding process so as to create an auctionlike situation aimed at getting the highest price for the seller (or to maximize any other factors that may be important to the seller).

8. Advise on the financing structure of the transaction so as to get the maximum advantage for both sides.

9. Ensure that all important nonfinancial terms are settled at an early stage, and see that post-agreement documentation flows smoothly.

This process is fairly straightforward. For larger-sized transactions, a number of international names will be included on the list of prospective buyers. It will be up to the banker to contact these at the appropriate level. In all transactions the banker's work is complemented by that of lawyers, accountants, tax experts, and other advisers selected by the seller.

Raid Defense

When defending a company against a raid, the banker, in addition to complying with all the regulatory and legal requirements of the country involved, must assist the client in evaluating quickly his or her own and the shareholders' alternatives. The principal lines of defense usually are that the raider has offered too low a price for the company, or that the take-over would violate antitrust regulations and should be prohibited by the government. In the former, the defender must convince institutional share-holders that they would be better off backing existing management; in the latter, the case has to be made to regulatory authorities and the politicians who control them. Neither is easy. Once an opposed takeover effort has begun it is very difficult to escape without either selling the company to someone (the raider, or a "white knight") or undergoing a substantial self-reorganization or recapitalization.

Over the years defenders have learned that they receive a higher net price for their shares by playing hard to get. No one accepts a first or even a second unsolicited offer. Tactics are employed to maximize the public visibility of the transaction with the hope of attracting additional suitors. To persuade prospective buyers that they must increase their bid, the de-fender must be credible, with respect to its wish not to be acquired and with respect to the viability of its alternatives. If the buyer senses a lack of credibility, it will not raise its bid further and indeed may even lower it.

Buyer Representation

Buyer assignments usually begin in one of three ways: (1) The buyer has already identified a target and wishes an investment banker to assist in executing the transaction, or in confirming the valuation placed on it; (2) the investment banker brings an acquisition idea to a buyer and is retained to pursue it; or (3) the buyer has only a general idea as to what is wanted and hires a banker to search for suitable targets and to pursue any that are accepted by the buyer. Many bankers are willing, even eager, to con-duct buyer searches for their clients as a way to develop relationships with prospective clients. Frequently, however, these searches do not result in a completed transaction and therefore are considered low probability assign-ments that well-established bankers may choose to reject.

Until recently, many international corporations did not fully under-stand how to use investment bankers and frequently did not act on their advice because they were not comfortable with it. Such corporations dis-liked the idea of a competitive auction process to acquire a particular tar-get. They preferred direct, off-market, one-on-one negotiations. But the seller and its banker knew that more aggressive bidding would result from an auction. The inexperienced international buyer would often balk at these procedures, or bid too low to win. Usually, however, when an inter-national company has been through the process unsuccessfully once, it adapts and does much better the next time.

When representing a buyer, a banker will perform the following tasks:

1. Conduct a thorough review of all publicly available information about the target and all of its subsidiaries. Advise as to the probable price range necessary to acquire the target, bearing in mind the advice that

would be given to the target if the target had asked the banker to sell the company.

2. Advise as to the likelihood of the target's receptiveness to an invitation to enter into discussions aimed at a merger and on how the target will react when apprised of client's interest, what it will consider to be its options, and what actions it is likely to take.

3. Prepare a list of probable white knights and an analysis of the pro forma effect on each of these companies of an acquisition of the target company, as well as an analysis of a self-tender or leveraged buyout transaction by the target.

4. Evaluate each of those options in detail. Play the role of the seller's adviser in the circumstances. Devise tactics accordingly.

5. Prepare recommendations on the financial structure of the transaction, and how the buyer should best proceed to arrange financing for the transaction. Advise also on the probable reaction of the stock market and rating agencies to the buyer's purchase of the target company.

6. Advise on the initial approach to the target, the value to be suggested, and steps for following up.

7. Function as a continuous liaison between client and target, or target's bankers, looking for and heading off problems all the way to the closing.

8. Advise on the changing tactical situation and responses to communications from the target or other bidders.

9. Arrange for the purchase of shares through a tender offer.

10. Assist in arranging long-term financing for the transaction and in selling assets that are not to be retained.

Other steps and functions occur within these categories. However, much of what goes on in an acquisition situation is in response to moves undertaken by the other side. It is essential that good communications and mutual understanding exist between banker and client to be able to respond to the changing circumstances in the most timely and effective way.

Even companies that know the buyer well and might like to be acquired will nowadays still impose an auction process on the sale of the company to protect shareholders' interests. In this context there are no longer many friendly, easy deals. European and Japanese buyers of U.S. companies have had to adapt to a tougher, more abrasive environment when seeking acquisitions. Many of course have already done so and perhaps will apply their newfound toughness to future transactions in their home areas.

It is perhaps predictable that, as merger and acquisition activity and tactics spread across the Atlantic and the English Channel, and perhaps someday across the Pacific, much of the rough and tumble of the U.S. market, with its heavy emphasis on aggressive legal maneuvering, will travel with it. The growing acceptability and effectiveness of hostile offers in Europe is an early indication that this is already happening.

Globalization of Financial Advisory Services

Few sources of revenue are more attractive to investment (and all other types of) bankers than merger and other high value-added fees. A loan involves a commitment of a bank's capital and offers the risk of nonrepayment. A bond or equity issue requires the bank's underwriting commitment and exposes it to market risk. A swap involves booking a contingent asset or liability. But advisory fees are earned exclusively as a result of putting the firm's skills and knowledge to work, not, as is increasingly the case in other parts of the international banking and securities business, as a result of committing the firm's capital. And the fees, commensurate with the value-added of the service, are considerable. On transactions of several hundred millions of dollars, fees average around 1 percent of the purchase price.

It is natural, of course, to expect leading financial firms to be in the business of providing advice and executing transactions in their own countries on behalf of foreign companies. They are selected because they have the knowledge of local markets, practices, and personalities that will be required to complete the transaction. The same is true when an American company wishes to obtain advice in a foreign market. In Germany, for example, a U.S. company might seek the advice of a German bank to complete a transaction. It might also, however, retain a U.S. banker whose investment banking skills and international knowledge it respects to help the company interpret the advice of the German banker. The reverse is perhaps also true: when German companies seek U.S. advice, they may also retain a German bank to help understand it.

What is new in recent years, as a result of the globalization of financial markets and the spreading worldwide presence of major financial services firms, is the movement of international firms into the business of providing indigenous financial advice. An example is the growing involvement of U.S. investment banks in the intra-U.K. merger and acquisition business, long the exclusive preserve of British merchant banks.

There are several reasons U.S. firms became involved in this activity. As their London operations and their senior British staff expanded, so did their knowledge of the U.K. merger market and the companies involved and the relationships they enjoyed with them. Many of these companies were ones that the U.S. firm had done business with in the United States. Also, many U.S. firms began to become familiar with U.K. merger transactions as a result of purchasing stocks of U.K. companies subject to takeover bids, that is, participating in risk, or merger, arbitrage, and in following such companies in their research departments for the benefit of U.S. investor clients.

Perhaps most important, however, was the fact that, like capital markets, the merger business had become globalized. Networks and procedures now exist to enable buyers and sellers of companies to participate in a single marketplace for corporate control. And the agents and brokers who are capable of providing advice and guidance to their clients seeking to use the marketplace are the bankers with the infrastructure, the trained personnel, and the contacts with the worldwide corporate community.

For some years U.S. companies looking to be sold sought to include international companies in the bidding. Now the same thing is happening in Europe. For example, if a U.K. company is to be sold voluntarily or is attempting to escape the unwelcome embrace of a U.K raider, a common practice is to look for alternatives in the United States and elsewhere in the world. These alternatives can include selling the company either to a white knight or to a group of investors seeking to buy the company as an LBO. To find an international LBO opportunity, or a white knight, one has to be able to access potential participants in the United States and the rest of the world quickly, efficiently, and confidentially. U.S. firms have this capability and, after a slow beginning, it has become fairly common to see U.S. investment banks working alongside, or in place of, British merchant banks in raid defenses in the United Kingdom and in seller representations in the rest of Europe.

Some U.S. firms have also become involved in giving advice to European companies acting as buyers of other European companies, so as better to be able to value companies for the global merger market and to respond to the evasive moves of their targets.

Tables 12-8 and 12-9 show two forms of league table rankings for international merger and acquisition activity for 1995. Table 12-8 is a ranking based on all international M&As, and Table 12-9 focuses on

Table 12-8 Completed Global M&A Deal Advisers, 1995

Rank	Adviser	Value ($ billions)
1	Morgan Stanley	$149.2
2	Goldman Sachs	112.4
3	Lazard Houses	80.1
4	CS First Boston/Crédit Suisse	79.9
5	Lehman Bros.	64.8
6	Salomon Bros.	61.7
7	J. P. Morgan	60.1
8	Merrill Lynch	48.3
9	Bear, Stearns	45.7
10	Baring Bros.	39.3
11	SBC Warburg	33.1
12	Smith Barney	26.5
13	Schroders	25.1
14	Rothschild Group	24.9
15	Donaldson, Lufkin & Jenrette	22.8
Top 15 Total		689.6

Data: Investment Dealers' Digest, January 15, 1996.

Table 12-9 Cross-Border European Deal Advisers, 1995

Rank	Adviser	No. of Deals	Value £m
1	Goldman Sachs (2*)	26	10,129
2	SBC Warburg (3~)	40	9,390
3	Morgan Stanley (1)	24	9,056
4	Schroders (17)	22	7,255
5	Credit Suisse First Boston (11)	25	7,102
6	Lazard Houses (5)	37	5,971
7	Rothschild Group (−)	25	5,969
8	Deutsche Morgan Grenfell (8)	34	5,456
9	Lehman Brothers (15)	15	5,381
10	Enskilda (−)	7	5,075
11	JP Morgan (16)	19	4,341
12	JO Hambro Magan (−)	8	4,053
13	Merrill Lynch (9)	14	3,142
14	Barclays de Zoete Wedd (−)	12	2,991
15	Hambros Bank (−)	8	2,472
16	Robert Fleming (−)	6	1,974
17	Kleinwort Benson (4)	10	1,749
18	UBS (6)	14	1,711
19	Baring Brothers (12)	10	1,636
20	Banque Indosuez (10)	9	1,587

Data: Acquisitions Monthly, February 1996.
* 1994 full-year ranking.
~ Based on SG Warburg's 1994 full-year ranking.
The above table includes only those advisers acting on two or more transactions.

cross-border European deals only. The high representation of U.S. firms, especially the investment banks, is evident from these tables.

The experience of a number of U.S. firms in Europe and elsewhere has encouraged many others to embark on efforts to enter the indigenous business for merger and other financial advice in other countries. It takes several years to develop a strong franchise in a particular market, but the rewards appear suitable to many to undertake the effort to build up local capabilities. Not all markets are equally penetrable by foreigners, nor do mergers and related transactions—or those involving a comparable degree of financial sophistication—represent equally attractive opportunities in all countries. However, many observers believe that as Europe and Latin America experience greater amounts of corporate restructuring, a new and broader market will develop for financial advisory services of virtually all types. Ultimately this phenomenon can be expected to spread to Japan, where it will undoubtedly change its shape somewhat to conform to unique Japanese cultural considerations that eschew outright takeover activity.

Thus, many new competitors have entered the field, including investment bankers that specialize in investing as principals in takeover or LBO situations, and small firms of specialized advisers. Commercial banks have also set up merger and acquisition departments and developed special capabilities in leveraged and related transactions. All participants in the mergers business now have to recognize the considerable strategic implications resulting from the globalization of mergers, restructuring, and financial advisory services.

Competing in International Financial Advisory Services

The market for international advisory services, because of its globalized characteristics, has been increasingly indistinguishable from financial advisory services conducted in the United States and the United Kingdom. Competing successfully in this market has more to do with basic competence in financial advisory work than it does with its international overlay, but at the same time, without international capabilities, even a firm with a strong reputation in the field may lose business to those operating on a global basis.

This would be the point of view of an American investment bank that is active in the merger and acquisition business. For such a firm, cross-border transactions are not separated from those that occur in the United States, and the distinction between "domestic" and "international" mergers has faded. The U.S. firm, however, would view the offering of merger advisory services to the indigenous market in, say, Australia as a separate international business.

A German bank, on the other hand, having had little opportunity to participate in the part of the worldwide merger and acquisition activity that involves German companies, might look at domestic and international mergers differently from the American firm. So would the Japanese banker, for whom international mergers are rare indeed but domestic ones even rarer.

This does not mean that only U.S. and British firms will be able to compete in the international merger advisory business of the future, but they do have the advantage of being firmly in place at the game's beginning. Some European banks, such as Paribas and Swiss Bank Corporation, have a long history of merger-related activity. Those other continental European and Japanese firms that want to become involved will find various ways to do so. They can acquire firms with an existing franchise in the merger field, as the Deutsche Bank did through the purchase of Morgan Grenfell & Co., a prominent U.K. merger house. Or they can create a jointly owned international firm, such as CS First Boston, that can operate independently from its parents in the more free-wheeling markets in London and New York. Or they can hire experienced professionals to conduct the mergers business for them. Perhaps renowned merger "stars," like those leaving investment banks in New York to set out on their own, will be induced to align themselves with Daiwa Securities, or Amro Bank, or Banco di Roma. Several have already lined up with other large international firms. European houses have set up shop in the United States before with their eyes on the high value-added investment banking business. Lazard Fréres formed an American partnership around 1900 that is today a small but extremely potent firm in the mergers and acquisitions business. The European Rothschild firms have a U.S. affiliate, Rothschild, Inc., that has been quite active in representing European firms seeking to buy companies in the United States

Developing a Strategy

To compete in the top bracket of the world mergers and acquisitions market, however, requires of every participant that it develop a strategy for the business that is consistent with the rest of the firm's business and is one that the firm can gain strong support for throughout its organization. A prospective entrant, be it a domestic commercial bank, a foreign bank, or an investment bank not in the business, must address three fundamental issues:

1. Mergers and acquisitions are essentially an aggressive and highly visible if not controversial activity. Can the rest of the firm's business, which may depend heavily on close, long-standing client relationships, survive the transition? Will clients draw back from the relationship if they fear that the firm might align itself with another client planning an unwelcome approach?

2. Costs, both out of pocket and contingent, are considerable. Is the firm prepared to pay the cost of fielding a world-class team of merger specialists, which not only requires highly paid executives but also a sizable support staff and, increasingly, expensive international facilities? Is it prepared for the next step too—to take equity and junk bond positions in client transactions for its own account? Is the firm prepared to accept the consequences of failure, and exposure to considerable litigation?

3. Is the firm prepared to grant the autonomy to the merger and acquisition team that it needs to act quickly and aggressively, and to allow it a kind of relationship priority with chief executives and other top executives of client companies?

Many players will feel the future rewards are worth the trouble and the money. Others will try to find a niche that does not require such a heavy commitment. Perhaps they can avoid unfriendly deals, or focus on helping clients with smaller, domestic transactions. Other banks will find the unexpected problems of the merger and acquisition business to be significant, and they may lose enthusiasm for being in the forefront of the business.

Commercial banking in most of the world is essentially a relationship business in which loyalty is expected and rewarded. Banks as lenders have loan portfolios to maintain, and to do so requires them to maintain credit information about their clients, some of which is highly confidential. Banks must guard carefully against breeches of the "Chinese Wall" that separates information retained in one part of the bank from being used by another, and from developing conflicts of interest, which can occur when one client wants to acquire another that does not wish to be acquired. Commercial banks, and perhaps some European universal banks, may also discover that their particular comparative advantages in the global competition for financial services, a large capital base and a large, client service organization, are not necessarily helpful in the area of merger-related services. Capital is not important in an advisory business, and their large calling organizations may not, in fact, have good access to chief executives.

Many banks will decide that they are better off in the business of lending to their clients, especially when they need acquisition financing, than in competing in a business they may not be especially good at or have the stomach for. Other banks will disagree, feeling that the future of wholesale banking is unattractive and that they must develop competence in the merger and acquisition field, with its many related transactions, in order to retain a prominent position in domestic and international financial services. Such banks obviously look at mergers and related services as part of a general restructuring of the banking industry.

Dangers and Pitfalls

A strategy that is well tailored to the bank's own circumstances, and effective and credible execution capability and a well-coordinated marketing effort, will surely produce results in time. Many things can go wrong, however, and many will. Top management must be prepared to stand by the commitment to be in the advisory business despite setbacks and occasional embarrassments. This is often easier said than done. Some of the difficulties that must be faced are the following:

Autonomy versus control. The firm must find the balance between freedom for well-informed professionals to peruse transactions aggressively and having reliable assurance that the system is under control—that the young tigers are not overlooking important legal, regulatory, and ethical issues in their quest for success.

Not controlling the client. Clients like things to be done their way, but often they are wrong or stubborn or misinformed. Under such circumstances they must be controllable, that is, the adviser must be able to get the client to sit down and understand the issues correctly, and at least to behave legally. An uncontrollable client at the very minimum can be embarrassing or can tie the firm to an unpromising player in the game, perhaps at the cost of having to refuse another. At worst such a client can get the firm involved in serious trouble or ugly litigation, and gravely risk its reputation.

Fee cutting. In a free market, fees are there to be cut. If cutting them makes it easier to land an assignment, then they tend to get cut. The newcomer, however, will realize that the reason that merger fees have remained where they are for so long is that they are, in the end, reflective of value (or the expectation of such value) created by the efforts of the adviser for the client. The major clients know this, or in due course are persuaded of it. Cut-rate surgeons, lawyers, or financial advisers are not always looked upon as the most valuable or reliable. Banks seeking to gain entry to the mergers business will invest heavily in the capability to participate in it. Markets of the future are not predictable; mergers activity may, as during the period 1989–1992, decline sharply. Fee cutting to get into the game may be difficult to reverse once established, and in any case may remove some of the economic incentive for entering the business in the first place.

Internal discord. There are many opportunities for internal discord within a firm active in providing merger and related high value-added services. Elite corps of young aggressive professionals with insufficient regard for their seniors are a constant problem, especially when they are earning salaries and bonuses that are multiples of the seniors'. The merger team's need for immediate (and often exclusive) access to client chief executives, and its need for restricting information to a need-to-know basis, can be highly irritating to conventional colleagues. Ordinary bankers too can become frustrated by their inability to reach members of the merger squad, or have them attend meetings with other clients. These complaints are balanced by the those of the advisory group that the ordinary bankers in the firm are excessively conventional, stodgy, bureaucratic, and overly conservative in terms of new clients to take on and transactions to do for them. The only resolution of difficulties like these is good leadership of the unit by experienced, mature professionals respected by both sides of the house, and a firmwide understanding and acceptance of what they are trying to do.

Summary

For U.S. and U.K. investment banks, providing international advisory services has been a natural extension of providing the same services domestically. Increasingly today, whether the client is a buyer, a reluctant seller, or a willing target, tapping the international market for better terms than can be accessed domestically is often advisable and sometimes imperative. Banks with a strong local M&A team and an international presence—primarily U.S. investment houses—have been well positioned to take advantage of this aspect of globalization.

To some extent the European and to a much greater extent the Japanese environments have lacked the freely accessed capital markets and strict legal framework that have fostered the U.S. (and to a much lesser extent the U.K.) M&A business. As globalization continues, however, a convergence of market conditions for M&As will occur. The evolving environment will have more of the transparent Anglo-Saxon characteristics than the continental European or Japanese.

As an activity generating substantial fees but requiring no direct commitment of the bank's capital, M&A and related advisory work has proved to be an irresistible attraction to many. Newcomers should be warned, however: M&A activities may not coexist easily with relationship banking in the same firm. Managing the M&A department is highly challenging. One must control the customer without alienating him and control the team without stifling it. One must maintain the delivery networks and the firm's image, knowing which deals to pursue and how to pursue them and which to decline. All demand skills specific to the M&A business increasingly projected into an international dimension.

13

International Investment Management

In the late nineteenth century, Great Britain had accumulated substantial excess savings as a result of its world preeminence as a manufacturer and an exporter. The United States was then, in the eyes of many British investors, an "emerging market," a land of the future. The United States had big plans—for railways that after 1869 connected the two sea coasts, for industry, and for farming and raw materials extraction. British capital poured into the United States to participate in these remarkable and comparatively inexpensive (in terms of the value of the pound) investment opportunities. The British were not alone—American opportunity was not a secret—French, German, Dutch, Swiss, and other Europeans also joined in, resulting in a substantial flow of investment capital from Europe to the United States. During the quarter century form about 1850 to 1875, one scholar estimates that approximately $2.7 billion of foreign capital was invested in U.S. railway securities, the bulk of which was from Great Britain, providing between 15 and 25 percent of the capital invested in American railroads.[1] The investments were made by wealthy individuals and families, and investment partnerships were made up of such persons. There were no institutional investors of note at the time, and corporations were not players as such, since business investments tended to be made by their owners directly as individuals.

Evolution of International Portfolio Management

European investors had investment advisers who assisted them in managing their money. These advisers were often bankers or lawyers of their acquaintance who knew their way around the City of London and the other European financial capitals. These advisors would be supplied with information about investment opportunities by brokers or promoters, whose job it was to place new issues of securities. Many European bankers and brokers had offices or affiliations in New York, Philadelphia, and Boston and were a steady source of new investment ideas.[2] Investment performance was difficult to measure—whether one made money or not and got in on the "really good" deals that one's friends were offered tended to be the crude yardstick by which success was measured.

America was a good speculation in the nineteenth century, but it was not really safe. One could not send one's "core capital" to New York to rest in an unregulated bank deposit or to invest in government securities of a country with such an unstable financial history. But money wasn't really safe in a lot of other places either. When political changes and upheavals came, as they did often in Europe during the latter part of the nineteenth century, especially in France, Germany, and Italy, families felt the need of a safe haven for their core capital that would be outside the political and fiscal reach of whatever new government they were then experiencing in their home countries. Some of this money migrated to London, then as now the financial capital of Europe, but some too found its way into neutral, stable, and remote Switzerland where for many years its thrifty and tidy inhabitants had offered safe, secure, and confidential banking services.

This periodic flow of private capital into the Alps continued as the reputation of the Swiss for competence and confidentially grew and spread. Latin Americans, Asians, Middle Easterners, middle Europeans, and investors from all over the rest of the world were attracted to Zurich or Geneva or Lugano, where their affairs would be handled reliably and graciously. During the 1920s and 1930s further political and economic upheavals sent additional funds to Switzerland, which, after Hitler's rise to power, found it expedient to offer secret bank accounts to Jewish and other clients. After the war the Swiss continued to attract funds from around the world, especially from those countries where political or economic instability was high, tax rates and social policies were seen to be confiscatory, or new wealth was accumulated without a commensurate structure for investing it, as in the Arab oil-producing countries.

The United States, after World War I, continued to grow and enjoy boom times, while most of the European economies were barely getting by. Spurred by its capital-raising experiences during the war and its lively economy, the New York securities markets bubbled with activity. More European funds flowed into the country for investment in the stock and bond markets, which were climbing to new heights. At the same time, U.S. funds were being invested in foreign securities, especially European bonds for the safety and security they provided their American investors.

A significant two-way traffic in capital had begun after the early years of the century when bonds were floated in New York for the first time by issuers from Britain, France, Germany, and Japan. World War I was substantially financed in New York, though the vast majority of the funds went to the Allied Powers. After the war, the bond-selling machinery was applied to issues from many other countries, including several European municipalities and government bodies, but also many countries of dubious (higher risk) creditworthiness, such as Russia, China, Colombia, the Philippines, and Brazil. The bonds were bought by U.S. individuals and by banks and other institutional investors who were just beginning to appear on the financial scene.[3] Most of these lower-rated bonds defaulted during the Great Depression.

After the stock-market crash of 1929, the depression, and World War II, U.S. institutions had lost much of their earlier interest in foreign securities, except for those of the highest quality. U.S. investors had little appetite for foreign securities—they had more than enough investment opportunities in the domestic market. During the 1960s, moreover, many insurance companies and pension funds began to invest heavily in U.S. common stocks.

Very little changed the institutional market for equities as much as the passage of the Employees' Retirement Income and Security Act of 1974, commonly called ERISA. This act required corporate contributions to pension funds to be fully paid, and trustees and investment managers to be governed by the "Prudent Man Rule," which held that fiduciaries would have to manage money entrusted to them with the same care and prudence that they would use in managing their own money. This caused a lot of new money to flow into common stocks, as underfunded conditions in pension funds were made up and large holdings of the employing company's common stock were liquidated to provide for prudent diversification. Another important change associated with ERISA was the provision for investment risk to be assessed at the portfolio level, as opposed to the individual security level. Thus a portfolio could prudently consist of a diversified holding of securities, some of which were riskier (or more exotic) than others. This enabled managers to look abroad for components of their portfolios, for which they were seeking an optimal balance between risk and return.

As the U.S. pension fund investor became an increasingly important, and then dominant, factor in U.S. securities markets, the professional standards of investment management began to rise. Prudence was of course essential, but one could be prudent and still provide exceptional performance if one's managers were trained in the most modern practices of investment management and motivated to perform well. The performance-oriented professional money manager appeared on the scene, and soon thereafter a market was found for the new "modern portfolio theory" of risk-adjusted returns and portfolio diversification that was developed by academic economists. Soon aggressive, hands-on, actively traded portfolio management practices became common and helped to stimulate the stock market, attracting to New York substantial additional portfolio investment from money managers in Europe, especially from Switzerland and the

United Kingdom, though the latter suffered the weight of exchange controls at the time.

Throughout much of the 1970s the U.S. markets struggled with high inflation and difficult securities markets. Europeans remained invested but dissatisfied because of the dollar's decline, the losses incurred in the bond market due to soaring interest rates, and a listless stock market—the Dow Jones Industrial Average had hardly increased at all during the 10-year interval ending in 1980. So they began to look elsewhere for investment opportunities. These were found in Japan.

Beginning in the early 1970s, Japan's stock market attracted huge investments from European portfolios, whose Swiss, British, Dutch, French, and German managers recognized it as the America of the future. They studied the Japanese economy and stock market well, though no doubt without really understanding it, and committed large amounts to Japanese stocks, which were almost immediately profitable. Some adventurous American investors joined the party, but most Americans did not fully appreciate the opportunities presented by the Japanese market, still believing that the greatest returns could be realized in the United States, especially while stock prices were low. By the time the main body of the U.S. portfolio managers had learned what they needed to know about Japan, the market there had already risen considerably. On the other hand, in the United States the Reagan-era bull market was about to take off and U.S. investors were well positioned to benefit.

Many European investors, especially the quick-acting British and Dutch fund managers, switched a large portion of their funds back into the United States to catch the market phenomenon, which was accompanied by the additional bonanza, from their point of view, of a soaring dollar. U.S. investments became irresistible to foreigners, at least until the dollar peaked in late 1985, after which it began a sharp decline. By this time, however, U.S. investors realized that nondollar investments could be very profitable for them, especially when they were made in local currency markets that were outperforming the U.S. market.

Thus U.S. investors began in the mid-1980s to look seriously again, for the first time since the 1920s, at foreign stocks and bonds, which then represented only a nominal portion of their investments. A few U.S. money managers had been significant investors in foreign securities for several years, but by 1989 it had become "professionally correct" for many others to join them. Money managers that were not involved in foreign securities looked old fashioned and behind the times. More important, though, their performance would suffer compared to those who were well invested in foreign securities. In the period from 1981 to 1989, for example, the Japanese stock market increased sixfold (and the American market threefold), offering a substantial performance advantage to a manager with a significant holding of Japanese stocks, what ever they were.

By the end of 1994 the overseas assets of U.S. private pension funds totaled about $300 billion, or about 8 percent of total, after a huge in-

crease of about $140 billion during 1993 and 1994, a year in which for-
eign market performance was very mixed. Of the $300 billion, about 75
percent was invested in international equities and 25 percent in debt. The
international investment patterns of U.S. private pension funds have been
consistent for several years as most have sought to reach a level of international investments equal to about 15 to 20 percent of total assets.

Also during the 1980s, mutual funds began to expand considerably.
Specialized funds of all types appeared in the market, including those to
be invested in international securities from particular countries or regions,
or in particular industries.

Whose Money Is Being Managed?

Pension Funds

Pension and retirement funds now represent a substantial portion of all
investment assets in the United States and other major developed countries. These are in the form of private pension funds (e.g., the U.S. Steel
Pension Fund) and public (sector) funds (e.g., the New York City Employees Retirement Fund). As of the end of 1992, the total of all the world's
pension assets was about $6 trillion, of which U.S. pension funds repre-
sented $3.3 trillion. World pension assets are estimated by InterSec Re-
search Group to grow by about $2.5 trillion, or more than 40 percent, by
the end of 1997, as indicated in Figure 13-1 During this period, the non-
domestic investments of the funds are expected to grow by about $500
billion, or approximately 25 percent of the total increase in pension funds
assets (see Figure 13-2 for comparative asset allocations).

Pension funds require investments of long duration to match their expected payout schedules, and seek growth in excess of the annual increase
in benefits in order to minimize cash payments by the employer to maintain a fully funded status. For both purposes substantial investments in
common stocks are appropriate. As employers (fund sponsors) are not necessarily equipped to manage investments in competition with the best professional managers, most funds retain professional money managers to do
this for them. These money managers consist of bank trust departments,
investment management units of insurance companies, and independent
advisers. They may specialize in certain investment areas or offer across-
the-board services. Because of the large amounts of pension fund assets
managed in this way, the fees received from managing sizable portfolios
for several pension funds can be considerable.

Such money managers, or investment advisers, are hired to manage, at
their full discretion, portions of the pension funds. Their performance is
reviewed periodically, and competition among managers is encouraged.
Managers considered to be performing less well than others are dropped,
and others may be added in their place. Common performance measures

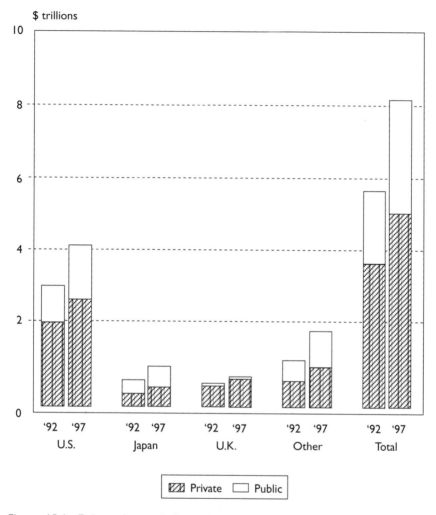

Figure 13-1. Estimated growth in world's pension assets, 1992–1997. Data: InterSetec Research Group.

compare managers' records with the market in which they have been chosen to operation (e.g., the U.S. stock market might be measured by the S&P 500 index).

In the United States.   The need to compete, and to exceed risk-adjusted performance measures established by fund sponsors, led to many changes in the investment management business in the United States. The number of money managers proliferated. Boutiques were formed by individuals with the hottest records. Traditional pension fund managers, insurance companies, and banks lost business, but then reorganized themselves and won some of it back. Money managers began to share the pressure

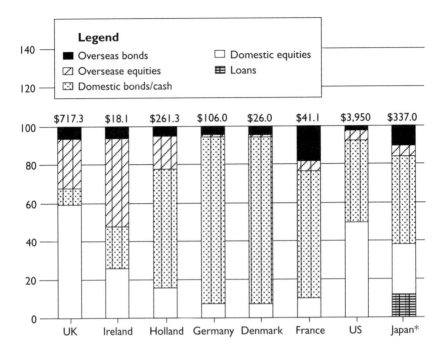

Figure 13-2. Pension funds' asset allocation, end = 1994 (approximate figures for selected countries). Data: Watson Wyatt Worldwide, InterSec Research Group, Employees Benefit Research Institute.

they were under with the brokers who supplied them with services. These services were extended to include high-quality securities research, including both idea generation (usually about specific stocks to buy or sell) and strategic advice on the overall shape of their portfolios. Block trading, and of course low-cost execution services, were also of great importance. Brokers, who compete vigorously with one another, responded to the pressure. They hired more research professionals so that the portfolio managers could keep their own staffs to a minimum. They cut commissions to the bone. They also offered up their best ideas and provided what clients wanted in the way of the latest investment theory, such as quantitative analysis and transactions involving options and futures, and ultimately program trading to support passive indexed investments and portfolio insurance.

Amid all this energy and effort to perfect investment management performance, investment in foreign securities was not overlooked, partly because the pension fund trustees had become believers in international diversification and were allocating portions of their funds to managers to invest in non-U.S. assets. Slowly at first, then with greater conviction, U.S. money managers began to make bold investments in stock markets in Europe, Asia, and Latin America. And they looked to their brokers to provide them with the same kind of back-up support and services for international investments that they provide for domestic investments.

Pension fund trustees realized there were several reasons for them to emphasize foreign investments. For over a decade it had been obvious that the fluctuating dollar and U.S. economic performance periodically created superior investment opportunities outside the United States. It would be prudent to invest a portion of the funds' assets in other markets to hedge against the underperformance of the U.S. market. (This also meant that, correctly done, U.S. money managers might be able to outperform U.S. indexes by spreading some of the investments in their care into other markets that would do better than the U.S. market). Public pension funds (for government employees), however, have approached international investing much more cautiously, because of political ramifications.

The trustees also knew that, with the boom in stock markets around the world, occasionally there were opportunities to invest in a totally new, emerging market that had room for enormous price appreciation—markets like Taiwan, Korea, and the newly interesting markets of Latin America.

Modern portfolio theory backs foreign investment as part of a well-diversified portfolio because other national markets are not (as yet) highly correlated with the U.S. market, and therefore a mixture of foreign and domestic investments will yield a higher return for the same amount of risk than would an all-domestic portfolio (see chapter 11, Figure 11-6).

In Europe. Pension funds are growing and changing rapidly, but in most countries the method is very different from U.S. and U.K. practice. Basically there are three rather incompatible systems, the fully funded, diversified investment system of the United Kingdom, the pay-as-you-go systems used in France and Italy in which annual pension disbursements become part of the national budget, and the German system in which the pension reserves are held on the books of the sponsoring companies. In the case of the latter two, pension funding is either nonexistent or not up to date, and investments in equities and other high-performance instruments is nominal. For example, in 1992, some 26 percent of the approximately $650 billion of U.K. pension fund assets were invested outside the country.[4] In the Netherlands, 14 percent of a $240 billion pension fund system was invested abroad. But in Germany ($114 billion in assets) and France ($23 billion), where funded pensions are scarce, foreign investment remains below 5 percent.

The European Single Market Act is expected to bring about many changes in the way European pension funds are operated. There are considerable differences in the way in which pension funds are structured, reserved, and accounted for between the respective EU countries, and approval of a draft pension fund directive has been late in coming. Negotiations, which were difficult, collapsed for a while in 1994. Among other considerations, the proposed directive had the potential to radically change things by forbidding countries from imposing low ceilings on investments in foreign and equity securities. Much of the debate has centered on competitive advantages that institutions from certain countries would receive, presumably at the expense of others.

Inevitably, however, the EU countries will have to sort out a system for funding retirement benefits for the aging populations. As they do so, they will be drawn to the Anglo-American system, which has been proven to work well. As this happens, fundamental changes will begin to affect European and global capital markets. Most of the European countries would have to set aside assets from other sources for funding pensions, and these would be invested in common stocks and other long-duration securities. According to scholars researching the subject, funds nearly equal in size to Britain's ($650 billion) would have to be created in Germany, France, and Italy. Such funds, however, could dwarf the markets of the countries concerned; for example, in 1994 the capitalization of the German stock market was $335 billion.[5]

In Japan.   Substantial pension reforms have been undertaken in Japan during the past 15 years. Before this Japanese workers faced a retirement age of 55, with a lump-sum retirement-severance payment based on the duration of employment. The payment was not nearly sufficient to purchase an annuity in an amount needed to support the worker's prospectively long retirement, so the worker was required to save for retirement and/or obtain postretirement employment or assistance from his family to make ends meet. Japan is a country in which the older portion of the population is increasing faster than all other portions, and retirement financial issues have received much attention. In the late 1970s the Japanese government and corporations adopted pension fund arrangements similar to those in the United States and these funds have grown extremely rapidly as a result of corporate contributions and the steep appreciation of the value of investments in the Japanese equity market. Total Japanese pension assets at the end of 1993 were approximately $1.5 trillion, of which about half were public pension funds, though by far the greatest growth in assets came from the private pension funds (Figure 13-3). Virtually all of these funds, beore to 1990 (and still today) were entrusted to Japanese life insurance companies and trust banks.

In 1990 the Ministry of Finance allowed some relaxation of the insurance and trust bank monopoly. Other qualified investment managers, including new foreign joint-venture investment advisory companies, were permitted to compete for funds management assignment, but only for (initially, the MOF says) a minor portion of the total asset pool, about $50 billion held in employee pension plans. Strict rules, however, govern which assets among these are eligible for management by the newcomers; at the end of 1993 only about $20 billion of these assets were available to the

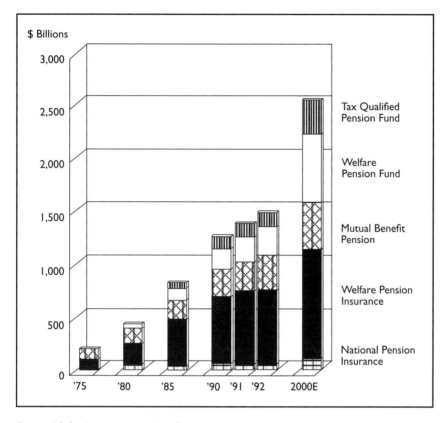

Figure 13-3. Japanese pension funds: high growth in a closed environment. Data: Wells Fargo Nikko Investment Advisors.

41 foreign and 100 Japanese investment management firms opened to compete with approximately 15 Japanese insurance companies and trust banks, opening up new market possibilities for non-Japanese banks and investment firms. In January 1995, in response to continuous pressure from the U.S. and European governments to open the market for pension funds to foreign competition, the Japanese agreed to increase the amount of the Japanese pension pool available for foreign management to about $500 billion.

By 1994, about 8 percent of Japanese private pension funds was invested abroad. Under present MOF regulations, pension funds must invest at least 50 percent of assets in fixed-income securities and may not invest more than 30 percent in stocks, 30 percent in foreign currency assets, or 20 percent in real estate. Recently new money going in to the non–fixed-income portion of the funds was free of such restrictions.[6] All expectations are for Japanese pension funds to increase considerably over the next few years. Increased amounts will be invested in equities and in foreign securities as Japan conforms to world portfolio management practices.

In Other Countries. Huge investment organizations designed to provide social security and/or other benefits for citizens have emerged in many countries. Especially active as international investors are such organizations from Singapore, Kuwait, Abu Dhabi, Saudi Arabia, and Venezuela.

Other Institutional Investors

Apart from pension fund managers and investment management companies, other institutional investors have become active participants in international securities markets. Such investors include insurance companies, savings institutions, central banks and monetary authorities, religious organizations, and a variety of not-for-profit institutions and foundations around the world. Many of these institutions manage their own international investments; others retain professional money managers to do it for them.

Corporations also are substantial investors in international securities. Apart from those engaging in merger and acquisitions activity during which shares are acquired (or sold), corporations periodically invest in foreign securities as a way of managing their own cash reserves, arbitrage between markets of various types, and hedging of foreign exchange, interest-rate, or other risks. In many countries corporations invest in securities as a way of improving corporate profits or to speculate on possible capital gains, especially in Japan where corporations during the latter 1980s were able to invest some of their large cash surpluses in tax-advantaged investment accounts called *tokkins*. Such modern, that is, "high tech," investment activity was called *zaitech* by the Japanese. Though it was extremely active during the 1980s, since the crash of the Japanese market beginning in December 1989 it is no longer so. A portion of the zaitech and tokkin investments found their way into international securities markets.

Individuals

Individuals have been substantial investors in overseas securities through accounts that are managed by professional investors. Such investments tend to be in the form of redeemable mutual funds (open end) or shares of investment companies (closed end), or through a personal account with a bank in which investment discretion is given to the bank or guidance is otherwise received from it along with a variety of other services aimed at wealthy customers.

Mutual funds and investment companies have existed for a long time, especially in the United States. Those specializing in general international investments have been common in Europe, especially in the United Kingdom (which offers various tax-advantaged funds based in the Channel islands), and Holland. In recent years they have also been widely offered in the United States, and in Japan through investment trust companies owned and operated by large Japanese securities firms. These funds are managed either by the investment management affiliates of banks or securities firms or by a designated foreign adviser, or by some combination of the two.

Also available are funds designed to appeal to particular areas of potential investor interest, such as North American growth companies; Japan, with or without the rest of the Pacific Rim; and high technology. Such funds are popular in the United States, where recently a rich array of different "country funds" have been sold to investors seeking new opportunities and emerging markets. Among these have been funds aimed at developed countries like Japan (though the first Japan fund was sold in the United States in 1962), Germany, France, and Spain and at developing countries such as Mexico, Argentina, Thailand, and Korea (see Table 11-6). Similar funds have also been sold in Europe and Japan. Bond funds and various money-market funds are also available for international investors.

Private banking accounts form the bulk of individual investments in foreign securities that emanate from Europe. Swiss banks are the best known among the continental banks offering private banking services (meaning dealing confidentially with private customers), featuring high degrees of confidentiality, a risk-averse investment bias, and individual client interaction with account managers. These services are also available in Luxembourg, Austria, and other countries. The three largest Swiss banks (which operate throughout the country) command about 50 percent of the $1.5 trillion of private banking assets estimated in 1994 to be under the control of banks in Switzerland. A number of smaller private banks exist in Geneva, Zurich, and Lugano where they manage a considerable amount of funds for their individual clients. Many of the clients of these private banks have been with the bank for more than one generation; continuity and consistency of service are very important to them. Many of the clients are secretive about the origins of their fortunes, especially those that have maintained the accounts for years without the knowledge of the tax authorities in their home countries. The investment strategy most often preferred by private banking clients is wealth preservation, not wealth enhancement. Such clients welcome numbered accounts and the old-fashioned, traditional ways of banks established as long ago as the eighteenth century. Among the traditional ways of such banks are the offering of unbankerlike services such as arranging transportation to ski resorts, purchasing opera tickets, and (as some wags put it) "walking the dog." Another tradition is for expensive charges for these services, usually running around 1 percent of assets under management plus all commissions and custodial fees. Some of the Swiss private banks are owned by non-Swiss concerns.

All of the universal banks on the European continent offer some form of private banking services to their clients, subject to local tax withholding and reporting requirements. Many of these are oriented to the domestic markets, but many also offer skilled international portfolio management.

In some countries, particularly the United Kingdom, Holland, Belgium, Germany, and France, merchant banks, banques d'affaires, and specialized investment advisers manage private wealth also.

International Investment Managers

By the end of the 1980s it had become clear that huge pools of investment funds had been accumulated around the world by pension funds, governments, investment companies and other institutional investors, and corporations and that an increasing proportion of these funds should be invested outside of the home countries of the funds. Equally, it was clear that different skills and capabilities, requiring different support services from brokers and dealers, were necessary to manage these internationally directed funds competitively. The funds' owners wanted superior investment performance, diversification, and safety in varying degrees. Few of these funds were fully capable of internally managing their international investments, so they turned to outside suppliers of international investment management services.

U.S. Investment Managers

In the United States there are approximately 200 to 300 institutional investors in international securities, and the number grows steadily. Not all of these investors have committed a substantial portion of the funds they manage to the international markets, however, and some have considerably more international investing experience than others. On the whole, the U.S. institutional investor is presently less internationally attuned than his or her European counterpart.

There are various types of international investment managers in the United States. Among the large investment institutions are the College Retirement Equity Fund (CREF); Prudential Insurance; several investment companies and mutual funds, such as Alliance Capital Management, Capital Guardian Trust, Templeton, and Fidelity International Funds; and banks like State Street Bank and Trust, J. P. Morgan Investment Management, and Bankers Trust. There are also specialized money managers such as Scudder Stevens and Clark, who advise on international investment funds. Finally there are investment bankers and brokers such as Morgan Stanley and Goldman Sachs, which manage funds for their clients.

These firms compete in the United States for contracts to manage international portions of pension funds and other assets with merchant banks from the United Kingdom, Swiss banks, Japanese investment managers, and others. There are perhaps a hundred or so non-U.S. investment managers operating in the United States to attract part of the lucrative pension fund business. All investment management business is highly competitive in the United States, and management fees are comparatively small (around 0.75 percent of assets actively managed in equity portfolios and considerably less for fixed-income assets or assets managed according to passive, i.e., indexed, programs).[7] For certain international equity investment programs, however, management fees can be higher than for domestic programs.

Competition in the investment management business in the United States has caused a number of significant changes in the last few years. The pressure on performance, and on fees, has caused several players long associated with the traditional money management business to leave the high-volume domestic equity and fixed-income management businesses behind in order to concentrate on the higher-margin businesses of international investment management and private banking. Early in 1988, for example, Citicorp announced that it was selling its $21 billion domestic pension management business, thereby joining Manufacturers Hanover and Bank of America, which had taken similar steps. Profitability and management compensation and integration issues were apparently at the root of the decisions to sell. At the same time, however, Chemical Bank (which later acquired Manufacturers Hanover) was reorganizing and reinforcing its investment management business, and others reaffirmed their commitment to remain in the game.[8]

In Europe

The scene is even more complicated in Europe by many more different types of competitors populating the landscape. In London, several fund managers affiliated with merchant banks and brokers, such as Mercury Asset Management, Kleinwort Benson, and Cazenove, manage funds that are to be invested abroad. There are also several independent investment management firms that serve pension funds and distribute their own mutual funds (called "unit trusts") in London, and others that are based in Edinburgh. Further, a number of insurance companies such as Prudential Assurance and banks like Barclays and National Westminster manage investments for pension funds for individual clients. Some have subsidiaries that specialize in private banking, like NatWest's Coutts & Co., often referred to as the "bankers to the Queen."

Well before Big Bang and the associated stock exchange reforms in late 1986, London had attracted financial firms from all over the world, each seeking to manage funds or execute transactions in all sorts of international securities. In London there is a steady procession of American, Japanese, Australian, Canadian, Singaporean, Indian, Hong Kong, and now Korean brokers and those from the emerging markets. These firms visit U.K. institutional investors, seeking to attract a portion of their assets to be managed in their home country securities. And there are various Swiss and other European institutions domiciled in London for the purpose of persuading investors to trust their long experience and global investment skills. London continues to be a bazaar of international financial services of all types. Other European cities, such as Paris, Frankfurt, Amsterdam, and Luxembourg, are also attracting visitors of this type.

In Japan

Investment trust management companies owned by the major securities firms in Japan are the principal managers of mutual fund assets, sometimes with the assistance of a designated adviser on whose name the fund was marketed to investors. In the 1980s, insurance companies and trust banks have become active investors in international securities, especially U.S. Treasury and other fixed-income securities. Insurance companies and trust banks are the principal managers of corporate pension fund assets (though, as indicated previously, new players have recently been authorized), which have been growing rapidly. Trust banks have also been active in managing corporate tokkin funds and fund trusts.

Foreign firms may now operate in the Japanese investment management market. They have been permitted, for example, to form joint ventures with Japanese banks or securities firms for the purpose of overseas investment management, and several have done so. They are also free to manage any accounts they may be able to attract without any partner. As in the other markets, competition for Japanese asset management is very keen. Non-Japanese managers were acting as advisers or themselves managing billions of dollars in Japanese institutional and individual assets as of the end of 1992. Among the top 10 of these foreign managers were three U.S. banks—Bankers Trust, Chemical Bank, and J. P. Morgan—which set up Japanese trust subsidiaries.[9]

Products and Services

Active Management

Investing in equity securities is an art more than a science, even when the task is not complicated by choices between currencies and markets. International investing is about as complex a task as can be set for any financial professional. One must weigh many factors in deciding how to allocate funds between different markets, while sticking to the basic investment approach that has sold the client on one's particular services.

Some managers believe that, as in domestic equity investing, patience on top of a solid and well-reasoned investment strategy is the best approach. Pick the main areas of concentration, by markets and by industry segment, and stick with them. Truly good investment selections do not have to be changed often. Many savvy portfolio managers invested in Japanese insurance companies and banks in the early 1970s and still hold their original investments, almost 20 years (and one major market crash) later, and their profits have been extraordinary. The investors selected the right market and country (Japan), the right segment of it (financial institutions then selling at very low price/book-value levels), and the right time (relatively early in the Japanese stock-market miracle).

Such investors often work against a main theme, such as a long-term confidence in European economic unification, faith in the Pacific Basin or technology, or changes in the way people live in Eastern Europe. In the international context, however, it is necessary to scan many horizons to find the next Japan. Could, for example, Hong Kong under Chinese rule after 1997 turn out to be the equity market that will reflect China's ultimate power and influence in the world economy—or will it not? The best managers of this type tend to get the answers right enough of the time to be able to reap gains large enough to cover a few mistakes and still look good on the performance charts.

Other investors prefer a more aggressive, trading-oriented approach. These investors look for the next market to experience substantial growth, or opportunistic situations wherever they appear. A number of such managers were first to discover the Korean, Spanish, and Thai markets, each of which appreciated considerably in the late 1980s. They might also invest in international merger arbitrage situations—for example, by purchasing shares in the Belgian company La Generale after the Italian entrepreneur Carlo de Benedetti had announced his position, or in international equity options and futures contracts to increase portfolio leverage. Or they might have invested in intermarket index arbitrage positions (for example, buying the Nikkei index on the Osaka Stock Exchange and selling it on the Singapore International Monetary Exchange), as Barings Securities was supposedly doing when the firm collapsed. Barings had shifted from a neutral position to one that bet heavily on the Japanese stock market just before the Kobe earthquake and subsequent market drop. Though breathtaking, these practices can be very rewarding to those who manage funds according to this approach, providing they do not lose control of their positions as Barings did.

Finally, some managers insist on formula guidelines that impose limitations and constraints on the overall balance of the portfolio. Within these guidelines portfolio managers may trade as they wish, but the principal investment and safety criteria will be preserved by the guidelines. Such guidelines, as practiced by one very large and successful Dutch funds group, the Robeco Group, include limitations on the maximum percentage of the shares outstanding in a single company, the market capitalization of the company and a maximum weighting that any single company investment or all investments in a single country may have in the portfolio as a whole. Even large funds find that such guidelines do not seriously restrict the ability of portfolio managers to turn in competitive performances.[10]

Two governing principles of international investment management that are reflected in these management practices are the freedom of the manager to find the best opportunities, even if these exist outside of his or her own country, and the idea that diversification of assets between countries does work. That the juiciest plums may fall in a neighbor's garden is no surprise. The principle of diversification was not so universally accepted; diversified assets may be impossible to repatriate in a hurry if one needs to, and diversification into markets that are less liquid than one's home market may seem to be a mistake when difficult times come.

The market crash of October 19, 1987, provided a test of the diversification principle, one it passed with honors. Perhaps, considering the extent to which communications and globalization of markets have developed, it was not much of a surprise to find all the world's principal stock markets participating, sympathetically and simultaneously, with the market collapse in New York. Markets crashed everywhere in tune with New York. But following the crash, markets recovered at different paces. By the end of October the Morgan Stanley Capital International's EAFE index fell by only 11 percent, compared with a 23 percent decline in the Standard & Poor's 500 index.[11] The EAFE is heavily weighted to Japan, which shrugged off the crash and soon exceeded precrash highs, but even with Japan weighted less, the diversified international portfolio outperformed a diversified U.S., U.K., German, or Swiss portfolio. Only the Japanese would have done better in 1987 in exclusively Japanese investments.

Such apparent strength in diversification encourages many active U.S. investment managers to believe that they can outperform the standard performance indices, such as the S&P 500, more easily both on the upside and on the downside by maintaining an internationally diversified portfolio.

The principle applies to other managers too. Swiss and German portfolios, for example, did not make such large gains on their investments in foreign stocks, but compared with losses that they incurred in their home markets in 1987 the foreign stocks were a help. Diversification has worked for them too. However, diversification cannot always be presumed just because a portfolio is invested in securities of many different countries. Following the collapse of the Mexican peso in December 1994, stock markets in emerging market countries around the world dropped almost simultaneously: markets which previously had not been correlated at all suddenly revealed that they were. Investors from wealthy countries, when rushing to get in on the latest investment idea (such as third-world emerging markets in 1992 and 1993), can oversupply the markets with more money than can be absorbed, creating a uniform price effect that has nothing to do with the investment merits of the securities purchased. These markets were very illiquid and could accommodate only a small amount of selling pressure without major price changes. When the Mexican events occurred, many U.S., European, and Japanese investors decided to sell their remaining emerging market holdings, to find there was no market for them.

Passive Management

Index funds have existed in the United States for a number of years. Most are based on the S&P 500, and many variations and reweightings of the 500 index have been introduced. A substantial amount of pension fund assets in the United States are now being indexed, on the grounds that most active managers fail to exceed the indexes, and passive management is much less expensive.

International indexes now exist and passive funds management based on them is being practiced, again, mainly by U.S. pension funds.

The leading indexes are the previously mentioned EAFE, the FT World Actuaries, WM-Goldman Sachs International, and the Frank Russell–Salomon Brothers index. All of these report on the major companies in the major markets around the world. Price data can be organized in many ways, and combined into other indexes to provide a tailormade product.

Indexing has not been confined to the United States, although it is still used there more than anywhere else. Barclays de Zoete Wedd Investment Management and Baring International Management, for example, have index funds that they offer to clients. The Baring approach is to use active management to select and weight countries, and to use indexing to invest in stocks from those countries.

As the technology of indexing improves and managers find more ways to tailor it to their purposes, and indeed as pension fund sponsors and others express frustration with the performance of funds under management, there is bound to be a substantial increase in the use of indexing for international investments. Such increases beg the questions of what impact on equity markets around the world such indexing and its companion program trading will have, what the regulatory responses in these markets will be, and what effect the regulatory responses themselves will have on the markets. Ultimately, if the markets cannot tolerate program trading they will have to reduce their reliance on indexing and revert to active management programs.

Competing in International Investment Management Services

Sorting Out the Segments

The market for international investment management services is extremely broad and diverse. It is made up of many segments and cells according to the type of client being served (institutional, individual), the type of product being offered (active/passive management, funds, private banking services), and the geographic market that is targeted (United States, Switzerland, Japan). No one firm can cover them all competitively, so each player has to choose which ones it believes it does best, which ones it wants to upgrade, and which to discard.

This process is essential if a coherent strategy for the business is to be achieved. The investment management business is such that without a coherent strategy, product and marketing focus and discipline can be lost, which greatly weakens competitiveness over time.

A large American bank, for example, may have been in the investment management business for many years, going back to the days when the bank's customers could be expected to use the bank for custodial, trust, and estate purposes and for assistance in managing the corporate pension fund. Wealthy individuals customers were offered personal attention together with a few additional services so they could spend all day on their sailboats without worrying about their money. Investment management services were usually offered in connection with other services, which were mainly aimed at keeping the customer's money in the bank in interest-free demand deposits.

Today things are different and the bank's need for and use of investment management services have changed, as has the basis for compensating the bank for the service. Many banks find that investment management has become just another commodity, that it is not sufficiently profitable to justify continuing in the business, and that it creates more than its share of management headaches because the key investment managers are not (and will never be) bankers. Several large banks have disposed of their *domestic* investment management business. Others, however, have taken advantage of the changes in the business to position themselves more favorably and aggressively.

This chapter concerns itself with *international* money management services, which may not be separable from the domestic variety. International investment management services consist of three basic groups of products and services: (1) managing international investments for domestic clients, (2) managing domestic investments for international clients, and (3) managing international and domestic investments for international clients. If, for example, a bank has developed a good business in the second category (as many U.S. banks did during the heyday of the petrodollar), it will have to have the product execution capability to manage U.S. investments competitively. If it has sold this "domestic" business, it may no longer have the capability to provide the service. As we know, to execute investment management services competitively in the United States a bank has to have many trained and talented specialists on hand with considerable back-office and supplementary support capabilities.

On the other hand, to offer international investment management services to domestic clients may be much more difficult without a domestic investment management client base to offer the services to and without the basic infrastructure of the domestic business which, with some modifications, can be used to support the comparatively lower-volume international business.

If the bank decides instead to go after the international business, it may have to do so without the benefit of a large client base or the international investment management infrastructure already in place. For some, this forced fresh start might be an advantage—the bank could invest in all the newest equipment and techniques, hire a prominent manager, and market the services on the strength of its existing franchise. But it takes time to build up enough assets under management to be profitable, particularly if the assets have to be weaned away from institutions where relationships and loyalty are very strong.

Also, when competing in the arena with other international investment managers, the bank will have to take account of (and be prepared to compete with) their different strengths and competitive characteristics. As U.S. institutional investors become more involved internationally, they will market their skills in indexing and quantitative analysis and their ability to attract and utilize first-rate investment research. U.K. money managers, being more internationally sophisticated, will continue to live on their wits and their ability to find the next rising market over the horizon, wherever it is, and to market their services on the basis of a truly global expertise. Swiss and other Europeans offer tempting confidential private banking services to rich Americans, Japanese, Arabs, and Brazilians, and emphasize their long-standing mastery of foreign exchange management. Japanese managers will claim a unique ability to understand the Japanese market and to explain the U.S. and other markets to Japanese investors. To compete with these players, the bank has to slot itself into the market in the most advantageous way possible.

Marketing

Many U.S. investment managers have been very successful in marketing their services abroad. For most of these, their capabilities in the United States have been their principal selling point. J. P. Morgan, Bankers Trust, and Chemical Bank have all been very successful in Japan, where they have subsidiaries specializing in investment management. They have attracted substantial sums from Japanese institutions and individuals for investment in the United States. These banks have marketed their U.S. expertise in Europe, the Middle East, and Latin America as well.

These banks and others, American and European, have attracted substantial U.S. funds for investment outside the United States. The competition is fierce, to be sure, but they appear to be maintaining their share. At the same time, other players are achieving success as well. In a field where so many look alike, even when differentiated by country, the ability to communicate one's own particular approach, record, and major selling points is crucial to success. Turned around, the point can be made equally well that, until a competitor has shaped exactly what its business is to be and what its own strengths are, its marketing message will be too vague to be effective.

J. P. Morgan can say to customers in Europe and Japan, "Look, we know the U.S. financial markets as well as anyone, and are a top money manager. We are also an old and reliable bank that your family has trusted for years, and we have people here in your own country to take care of any problems." Fidelity can explain its remarkable performance record, Morgan Stanley its unique structure, Prudential Insurance its stability, and so on. Each has something to say that can be said better or more convincingly through better marketing.

Investment Performance

In the end, the effectiveness of the services will be judged by the quality of the investment performance. For large institutions, with the ability to measure competitive performance against an index, providers of services will have to survive the gauntlet every year or so. For managers specializing in this business, special approaches to ensure a good performance will have to be undertaken. For those offering mutual funds or investment company shares, performance also has to be good, but by segmenting funds into special sectors the manager may escape some of the burden of comparison with the S&P 500 or other performance indices.

Investment performance in private banking services may be somewhat less important to customers who value other aspects of their banking relationships. But it is still important. Customers do not usually move some or all of their funds to other managers when they are happy with their performance, but they do when they are not. Customers are becoming more sophisticated, more demanding, and more inclined to take advantage of the large number of banks and brokers competing for their business. Also, private banking fees are high and subject to competition from rate cutters and unbundlers. Performance in private banking too is the glue that holds the clients.

Summary

Competitors in investment management must focus much of their attention on the quality of the performance they are able to offer clients. Much has changed in the art of investment management over the years, including the inclusion in portfolios of securities that would not have been there before—Korean stocks, German bonds, American options. Stock markets are linked globally as never before and are susceptible to synchronized rises and drops. Diversification across a global range of markets works— it can limit losses and improve performance against indexed measures. Other new investment management ideas and discoveries appear frequently; some work, some don't. The whole environment of international investing is undergoing major structural change, which creates opportunities for some and hazards for others. But to compete, players have to be able to function in the new environment and to deliver first-rate services.

Notes

1. D. C. M. Platt, *Foreign Finance in Continental Europe and the USA*. London: George Allen & Unwin, 1984; Appendix III.

2. D. C. M. Platt, *Foreign Finance in Continental Europe and the U.S., 1815–1870*. London: George Allen & Unwin, 1984, pp. 140–143.

3. Allin Dakin, "Foreign Securities in the American Money Market, 1914–1930," *Harvard Business Review*, January 1932.

4. Tim Dickson, "Cross-Border Barriers Remain in Force," *The Financial Times*, May 6, 1993.

5. Gillian Tett, "Pivotal Issue Is Pension Plans," *Financial Times*, November 8, 1994.

6. Michael Hirsh, "For Foreigners, Scraps from the Pension Feast," *Institutional Investor*, January 1994; *The Economist*, September 12, 1987.

7. Alliance Capital Management L.P., prospectus dated April 14, 1988.

8. Julie Rohrer, "Are Banks Calling It Quits on Money Management?," *Institutional Investor*, April 1988.

9. *Pension and Investment Age*, July 27, 1987.

10. Nicholas W. Veer, Robeco Group, "International Equity Funds," *Euromoney International Finance Yearbook*, 1987.

11. Margaret Elliot, "Beyond Diversification," *Institutional Investor*, April 1988.

III

COMPETITIVE STRATEGIES

14

Strategic Positioning and Competitive Performance

The previous chapters of this book have discussed the globalization of the financial services industry as well as describing and categorizing "products" of that industry in some detail. What emerges is a complex web of markets, services, and institutions that is not easily subjected to systematic analysis.

This chapter presents a coherent model of the international financial services industry that focuses on competitive market structure. It not only identifies markets capable of producing attractive profits, but also specifies the linkages among those markets that are the basis for economies of scale and economies of scope—critical performance dimensions in the global financial services industry. The model is then used to assess sources of national and institutional competitive advantage in banking and financial services, as well as the effects of competitive distortions.

The C-A-P Model

Three principal dimensions define the global market for financial services:

Client (C-dimension)
Arena (A-dimension)
Product (P-dimension)

Firms in the global financial services industry have an unusually broad range of choice with respect to each of these dimensions, and different combinations yield different strategic and competitive profiles. Figure 14-1 depicts these dimensions in the form of a matrix composed of C × A

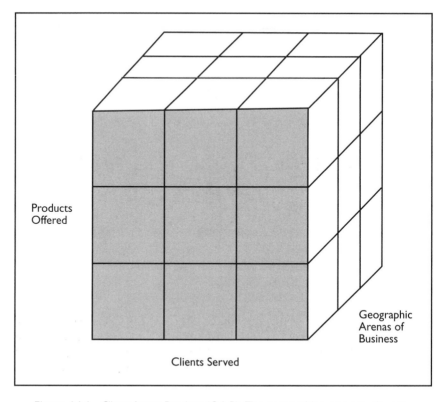

Products
Offered

Geographic
Arenas of
Business

Clients Served

Figure 14-1. Client-Arena-Product (C-A-P): The competitive opportunity set.

× P cells. Each cell has a distinctive competitive structure based on fundamental economic as well as public policy-related considerations. Largely
as a result of technological change and deregulation, financial institutions
confront increasing potential access to each of the dimensions in the global
C-A-P opportunity set. Financial deregulation in particular has had an important influence in terms of (1) accessibility of geographic arenas, (2) accessibility of individual client groups by players originating in different
parts of the financial services business, and (3) substitutability among financial products in meeting personal, corporate, and public sector financial needs.

Client

As conventionally used, the distinction between generic "wholesale" and
"retail" financial services is not particularly helpful in the context of the
C-A-P model, and the following categorization of the major client groups
may be more appropriate:

Sovereign: National states and their instrumentalities
Corporate: Nonfinancial corporations, regardless of industry classifi-

cation, ranging from multinational corporations and parastatals to middle-market and small, privately owned companies

Financial services: Other financial institutions in the same industry subcategory (e.g., correspondent banks) or in other segments of the financial services industry, such as brokerage or insurance

Private: High net worth and high net income individuals

Retail: Mass-market financial services, either sold cross-border or within domestic financial services markets, aimed at individuals and households

These client groups can be broken down into narrower segments, each differing with respect to product-related attributes such as currency requirements, liquidity and maturity needs, risk levels, industry categories, overall service-level requirements, price sensitivity, and timing aspects. Effective market definition and segmentation involve identifying coherent client clusters that embody relative uniformity with respect to each of these variables.

Arena

The international market for financial services can be divided into onshore and offshore arenas with respect to geographic location. The "arena" dimension is different from the standard definition of market "region" in that it encompasses the concepts of regulatory and monetary sovereignty, which are of critical importance in defining the geographic dimension in Figure 14-1. Each arena is characterized by different risk/return profiles, levels of financial efficiency, regulatory conditions, client needs, and other factors.

As discussed in chapter 1, geographic interpenetration on the part of commercial and investment banking institutions with respect to various domestic and offshore markets has become very significant indeed. The A-dimension in Figure 14-1 can be taken into the analysis at the global, regional, national, subregional, and location-specific levels, so that it is not purely country specific. However, the country level of analysis remains paramount due to the importance of national monetary policies, financial regulation, and competition policies, all of which are imposed at the country level. It is mainly in federal states that the rules of the game are sometimes importantly set at the subnational level.

Product

Financial services offered in the international market have undergone dramatic proliferation. With a clear requirement for product differentiation in the marketplace, firms in the industry have created new instruments and techniques tailored to the needs of their clients.

The range of financial services that can be supplied to the various client segments is evident from previous chapters. Table 14-1 combines

Table 14-1 Subclassification of International Financial Services

Product	Primary Classification[a]			
	1	2	3	4
Deposit taking				
Time deposits	L			
Demand deposits	L			
Other	L			
Trading and dealing	(X/L)			
Money Market				X
Securities				X
Foreign exchange				X
Swaps				X
Futures				X
Options				X
Bullion				X
Other				X
Sale of bank securities				
Certificates of deposit	L			
Ordinary shares	L			
Preferred shares	L			
Floating-rate notes	L			
Short- and long-term debt	L			
Lending (local or foreign currency)				
Sovereign	X	X		
Corporate				
Indigenous majors	X	X		
Multinational corporate affiliates	X	X		
Parastatals	X	X		
Indigenous middle market	X	X		
Foreign middle market	X	X		
Correspondent				
Indigenous banks	X	X		
Foreign banks	X	X		
Private				
High net worth	X	X		
High net income	X	X		
Retail	X	X		
Specialized financing activities				
Asset-based financing	X	X		
Equity financing	X	X		
Export financing	X	X		
Project financing	X	X		
Venture capital financing	X	X		
Real estate financing	X	X		
Mergers and acquisitions financing	X	X		
Leveraged buyout financing	X	X		
Securities underwiting				
Sovereign debt				
State debt, revenue, and agency bonds			X	X
Mortgage-backed securities			X	X
Insurance			X	X
Equities			X	X
Other			X	X

Table 14-1 (continued)

Product	Primary Classification[a]			
	1	2	3	4
Securities distribution				
Domestic				X
Fixed income				X
Equities				X
Other				X
International				X
Fixed income				X
Equities				X
Other				X
Advisory services				
Corporate cash management		X	X	X
Corporate fiscal (tax) planning		X	X	
General corporate financial services		X	X	X
Real estate advisory		X	X	X
Mergers and acquisitions		X	X	
Domestic		X	X	
International		X	X	
Risk management services		X	X	
Interest-rate risk		X	X	
Foreign exchange risk		X	X	
Country risk		X	X	
Other		X	X	
International trade advisory services		X	X	X
Trust and estate planning		X	X	
Legal and investment advisory services		X	X	
Tax advisory services		X	X	
General financial advice		X	X	
Consumer services				
Credit cards	X			X
Travelers' checks			X	X
Other consumer services	X		X	X
Asset management services				
Private/retail		X	X	
Fiduciary activities		X	X	
Safekeeping/lock-box services		X	X	
Mutual funds		X	X	
Corporate/correspondent		X	X	
Safekeeping/lock-box services		X	X	
Pension fund management		X	X	
Mutual fund management		X	X	
Brokerage				
Money market				X
Eurocurrencies/foreign exchange				X
Fixed income (government and corporate)				X
Equities				X
Financial futures				X
Options				X
Commodities				X
Gold				X
Insurance				X

continued

Table 14-1 (continued)

Product	Primary Classification[a]			
	1	2	3	4
Payments mechanism				
Domestic funds transfer				X
International funds transfer				X
Insurance-related services				
Standby letters of credit	X		X	
NIFs, RUFs, and MOFFs[b]	X		X	
Revolving credits	X			
C/P standby facilities	X		X	
Life insurance			X	
Property and casualty			X	
International trade services				
International collections			X	X
Letters of credit business		X	X	X
Bankers' acceptances	X		X	X
Countertrade		X		X
Market intelligence				X

[a]The classifications are as follows: 1. Credit products (L = credit extension by counterparties). 2. Financial engineering products. 3. Risk management products. 4. Market access products.

[b]NIF, note issuance facility; RUF, revolving underwriting facility; MOFF, multioption financing facility.

the "client" and "product" dimensions and links each combination to the underlying type of activities that is being undertaken by the institution concerned. It categorizes the activities of financial institutions into (1) liability-based activities, (2) asset-based activities, and (3) off-balance-sheet activities provided for clients. There is also a fourth category comprising activities in which the financial institution is acting for its own account on either the asset or the liability side of its balance sheet. This involves arbitrage and positioning, and to a large extent makes possible the other two types of activities. Financial institutions thus supply four more or less distinct primary products that are sold to clients. All products that appear in the market, including the most complex innovations, can be broken down into one or more of the following categories.

Credit Products. Although credit products have become a less significant source of returns for many international institutions, they remain the core of much of the business. Credit activities range from straightforward general-purpose term lending to sophisticated and specialized forms of lending such as project finance.

Financial Engineering Products. These comprise the design and delivery of financial services specifically structured to satisfy often complex client objectives at minimum cost. In a world where borrowers, issuers, savers, and investors often have distinctive and complex objectives, financial engineering is perhaps the ultimate form of product differentiation and accounts for a great deal of the value-added creation observed in the international capital markets. It can be either "disembodied" or "embodied," depending on whether the engineering components are part of specific financial transactions. Purely disembodied financial engineering may take the form of advisory functions that an American investment bank might undertake, on the basis of client-specific information, for a Japan-based multinational manufacturing firm seeking an acquisition in the same industry in the United States. Embodied financial engineering combines this with one or more financial transactions sold to the same client as part of a financing package. Other examples include structuring of project financings, leveraged buyouts, complex multicurrency financings, advice on appropriate capital structure, and so on.

Risk Management Products.   Risk bearing has long been recognized as one of the key functions of financial institutions, and one of the reasons they tend to be heavily regulated. The main forms of exposure include credit risk, interest-rate risk, liquidity risk, foreign exchange risk, country risk, project risk, commodity risk, and technical risk in areas such as cash transmission. Risk management activities can be broken down into (1) those in which financial institutions themselves assume all or part of the exposure and (2) those in which the institutions provide technology needed to achieve a shifting of risk or themselves take on exposure only on a contingent basis, that is, an off-balance-sheet commitment to buy or sell, borrow or lend. Effective risk reduction through diversification clearly depends on the independence of the various risks represented in the portfolio. Financial institutions provide risk management services that range from simple standby credit lines, swaps, and forward interest rate agreements to explicit tightly defined products addressed to a broad range of contingencies.

Arbitrage and Positioning.   Activities that financial institutions engage in for their own account facilitate and in many cases make possible the supply of the first four types of financial services to clients internationally. Arbitrage opportunities occur when the same asset is priced differently in different markets (or market segments), often because of information asymmetries. "Pure" arbitrage takes place when an asset is simultaneously bought and sold. By this definition, financial institutions rarely engage in pure arbitrage. Rather, they engage in "risk arbitrage"—buying an asset in a particular market, holding it for a time (however short), and reselling it in the same or different market. The institution is thus exposed to "differential risk," due to the possibility that the underlying price differential may evaporate or be reversed during the time needed to complete the transaction. Exposure to differential risk depends jointly on the time necessary to complete the transaction and the underlying volatility in the price of the specific asset and the markets in which it is traded. Positioning is a form of risk arbitrage that has become an integral part of managing international financial institutions during a time of significant exchange-rate and interest-rate volatility. Interest-rate-linked and foreign exchange-linked positioning drives securities, options, and futures trading and dealing.

Cell Characteristics and Competitive Dynamics

The competitive structure of each C-A-P cell in Figure 14-1 is an important determinant of the excess returns a financial institution may be able to obtain. Competitive structure is conventionally measured using concentration ratios based on the number of vendors, distribution of market share among vendors, and similar criteria. Cell characteristics can be analyzed in terms of conventional market-structure criteria, as summarized in Figure 14-2.

The inherent attractiveness of each cell clearly depends on the size of the prospective risk-adjusted returns associated with it. Entry into a new market (related either to a new product, client group, or arena), if initially successful, can be described in terms of a time path of subnormal, supernormal, and normal returns such as that depicted in Figure 14-3. This time path is important with respect to the entry and exit costs as well as size and durability of excess returns. Durability is described by the time path (decay) of excess returns that can be extracted from the new market in this context, and their discounted net present value can be compared with

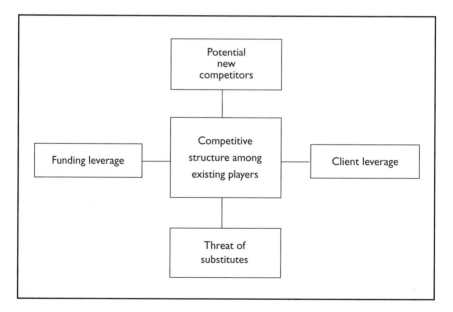

Figure 14-2. Application of a competitive analysis framework to financial services.

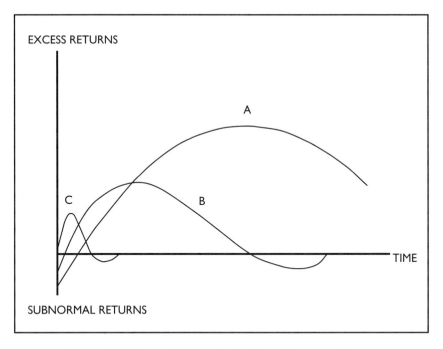

Figure 14-3. Time path (decay) of cell-specific excess returns.

those other market initiatives including transfers of financial innovations across clients, arenas, or products. For example, time path A in Figure 14-3 might be associated with a major retail banking or securities franchise, time path B with entry of foreign firms into a newly liberalized national financial market, and time path C with a new financial product such as a security design that can be reverse-engineered by competitors.

Normally the addition of vendors to a particular C-A-P cell would be expected to reduce market concentration, increase the degree of competition, lead to an erosion of margins, and trigger a more rapid pace of financial innovation. If a new vendor is from the same basic strategic group as existing players (e.g., one more commercial bank joining a number of others competing in a given cell), the expected outcome would be along conventional lines of intensified competition. But if the new player comes from a completely different strategic perspective (e.g., an industrial company offering banking services), the competitive outcome may be quite different. Cell penetration by a player from a *different* strategic group may lead to a greater increase in competition than that by an incremental player from the same strategic group. This is because of potential diversification benefits, scope for cross-subsidization and staying power, and incremental horizontal or vertical integration gains that the player from a "foreign" strategic group may be able to capture.

The higher the barriers to entry, the lower the threat of new entrants' reducing the level of returns available in each C-A-P cell. Natural barriers to entry include the need for capital investment, human resources, and technology and the importance of economies of scale. They also include the role of contracting costs avoided by a close relationship between the vendor and its client, which in turn is related to the avoidance of opportunistic behavior by either party.

Not least, the competitive structure of each cell depends on the degree of *potential* competition. This represents an application of the "contestable markets" concept, which suggests that the existence of potential entrants causes existing players to act *as if* those entrants were already active in the market. Consequently, pricing margins, product quality, and the degree of innovation in a given cell may exhibit characteristics of intense competition even though the degree of market concentration is in fact quite high.

In penetrating a particular cell or set of cells it may be to the advantage of a particular player to "buy into" a potential market by cross-subsidizing financial services supplied in that cell from returns derived in other cells. This may make sense if the assessed horizontal, vertical, or lateral linkages—either now or in the future—are sufficiently attractive to justify such pricing. It may also make sense if the cell characteristics are expected to change in future periods, so that an unprofitable presence today is expected to lead to a profitable presence tomorrow. And it may make sense if a player's behavior in buying market share has the potential to drive out competitors and fundamentally alter the structure of the cell in its favor.

The latter can be termed *predatory behavior,* and is no different from predation in the markets for goods. The institution "dumps" (or threatens to dump) financial services into the cell, forcing out competitors either as a result of the direct effects of the dumping in the face of more limited staying power or because of the indirect effects, working through expectations. Once competitors have been driven from the market, the institution takes advantage of the reduced degree of competition to widen margins and achieve excess returns. It is important to note, however, that the predatory behavior is not consistent with the view of market contestability. The greater the contestability and credibility of prospective market entry, the less will be the scope for price discrimination and predation.

Conversely, it may also be possible for an institution with significant market power to keep potential competitors out of attractive cells through explicit or implied threats of predatory behavior. It can make clear to new entrants that it will respond very aggressively to incursions, that they face a long and difficult road to profitability. In this way new competitors may be discouraged and the cell characteristics kept more monopolistic than would otherwise be the case.

Scale and Scope Linkages

Financial institutions clearly will want to allocate their available financial, human, and technological resources to those C-A-P cells in Figure 14-1 promising to throw off the highest risk-adjusted returns. To do this they will have to attribute costs, returns and risks appropriately across cells. But beyond this, the economics of supplying financial services internationally is jointly subject to *economies of scale* and *economies of scope*. The existence of both types of economies have strategic implications for players in the industry. Economies of scale suggest an emphasis on *deepening* activities within a cell or across cells in the P dimension.

Economies of scope suggest an emphasis on *broadening* activities across cells—that is, a player can produce a given level of output in a given cell more cheaply or effectively than institutions that are less active across multiple cells. This depends importantly on the benefits and costs of *linking* cells together in a coherent web of joint products.

The gains from linkages among C-A-P cells depend on the possibility that an institution competing in one cell can move into another cell and perform in that second cell more effectively than a competitor lacking a presence in the first cell. The existence of economies of scope and scale is a critical factor driving institutional strategy. Where scale economies dominate, the objective will be to maximize throughput of the product within a given C-A-P cell configuration, driving for market penetration. Where scope economies dominate, the drive will be toward aggressive cell proliferation.

Client-driven Linkages

Client linkages exist when a financial institution serving a particular client or client group can, as a result, supply financial services either to the same client or to another client in the same group more efficiently in the same or different arenas. With respect to a particular client, this linkage is part of the value of the "relationship." With respect to a particular client segment, it will clearly be easier for an institution to engage in business with a new client in the same segment than to move to another client segment. It is possible that client-driven linkages will decline as market segmentation in financial services becomes more intense.

Arena-driven Linkages

Arena-driven linkages are important when an institution can service a particular client or supply a particular service more efficiently in one arena as a result of having an active presence in another arena. The presence of multinational corporate clients in the same set of arenas as their financial institutions is one important form such linkages can take. By competing across a large number of arenas, a financial institution also has the possibility of decreasing the overall level of risk to which it is exposed and thereby increasing its overall risk-adjusted rate of return.

Product-driven Linkages

Product-driven linkages exist when an institution can supply a particular financial service in a more competitive manner because it is already producing the same or a similar financial service in different client or arena dimensions. Product specializations would appear to depend on the degree of uniformity of the resource inputs required, as well as on information and technology commonalities. Thus, certain types of skills embodied in key employees may be applied across different clients and arenas at relatively low marginal cost within a given product category, as may certain types of information about the environment, markets, or client needs.

If scale-related linkages are important, then the size rankings presented in Table 14-2, which lists the top 20 banks in the world in terms of asset footings and capital in 1974, 1984, and 1994, respectively, may have significant competitive implications on the cost side. If scope-related linkages are important, then the permissible range of financial services activities in various countries is important as well. The allowable range of financial services in major countries is presented in the appendix to this chapter.

Figure 14-4 depicts the potential scope-related linkages across retail and wholesale commercial and investment banking, insurance, and investment management. Table 14-3 shows a number of U.S.-based financial services firms in terms of the various types of activities they supply to their clients.

To summarize, the C-A-P model discussed here can be applied in both a descriptive and a strategic positioning context in several ways:

- It can be used to analyze the size and durability of excess returns associated with individual segments of domestic and international financial markets by applying conventional market-structure analysis. In the case of imperfect competition, it can be used to identify the importance of scale economies in the financial services industry.
- It can clarify the linkages that exist between different types of financial services and the importance of economies of scope in this industry.
- It can be used to explain industry internationalization both through the value coefficients embedded in individual C-A-P cells and by superimposing on the basic structure economies of both scale and scope.
- It can be used to identify appropriate public policies toward the financial services industry in a competitive structure-conduct-performance context.
- It can serve a normative function by identifying coherent firm strategies that combine correctly identified market characteristics and firm-specific advantages.

Table 14-2 The 20 Largest Banks in the World (in millions of U.S. dollars)

	June 1974			June 1984			June 1994	
Bank	Total Assets	Capital and Reserves	Bank	Total Assets	Capital and Reserves	Bank	Total Assets	Capital and Reserves
1 BankAmerica Corp.	48,772	1,550	1 Citicorp	125,974	1,606	1 Fuji Bank	538,243.2	19,545.5
2 Citicorp	44,018	1,770	2 BankAmerica Corp.	115,442	6,505	2 Dai-Ichi Kangyo Bank	535,356.5	19,399.7
3 Chase Manhattan Corp.	36,790	1,348	3 Dai-Ichi Kangyo Bank	110,333	466	3 Sumitomo Bank	531,835.3	21,931.4
4 Banque Nationale de Paris	30,142	251	4 Fuji Bank	103,524	644	4 Sanwa Bank	525,126.8	19,813.9
5 Dai-Ichi Kangyo Bank	28,467	845	5 Sumitomo Bank	101,147	752	5 Sakura Bank	523,730.6	17,842.9
6 Barclays Bank	28,304	1,586	6 Banque Nationale de Paris	101,019	334	6 Mitsubishi Bank	487,547.2	17,887.3
7 National Westminster Bank	27,555	2,095	7 Mitsubishi Bank	98,062	451	7 Norinchukin Bank	435,599.1	3,391.9
8 Fuji Bank	24,418	1,083	8 Barclays Group	94,146	808	8 Industrial Bank of Japan	414,925.5	13,659.0
9 Deutsche Bank	24,389	836	9 Sanwa Bank	91,257	462	9 Crédit Lyonnais	337,503.0	10,839.0
10 Sumitomo Bank	23,905	879	10 Crédit Agricole	90,211	514	10 Bank of China	334,752.7	12,871.6
11 Crédit Lyonnais	23,450	221	11 Crédit Lyonnais	88,123	na	11 Mitsubishi Trust & Banking	330,478.7	7,960.4
12 Mitsubishi Bank	23,433	958	12 National Westminster Bank	87,057	730	12 Tokai Bank	328,685.4	10,982.5
13 Société Générale	22,821	187	13 Société Générale	86,346	209	13 Deutsche Bank	319,997.7	11,321.6
14 Banca Nazionale del Lavoro	22,651	402	14 Deutsche Bank	76,793	695	14 Long-Term Credit Bank of Japan	315,026.1	10,949.7
15 Sanwa Bank	22,373	728	15 Midland Bank	76,317	326	15 Sumitomo Trust & Banking	305,347.4	7,708.7
16 Dresdner Bank	20,667	556	16 Chase Manhattan Corp.	75,350	703	16 HSBC Holdings	304,521.3	13,791.4
17 J. P. Morgan & Co.	19,905	957	17 Norinchukin Bank	75,235	109	17 Mitsui Trust & Banking	296,910.5	6,330.4
18 Manufacturers Hanover	19,540	895	18 Industrial Bank of Japan	71,720	435	18 Crédit Agricole	281,787.3	18,415.3
19 Banco di Roma	19,395	150	19 Mitsui Bank	67,162	318	19 Asahi Bank	277,688.1	10,468.6
20 Westdeutsche Landesbank	19,366	605	20 Royal Bank of Canada	65,654	729	20 Bank of Tokyo	273,884.3	10,238.2

Data: *New York Times,* July 15, 1995.

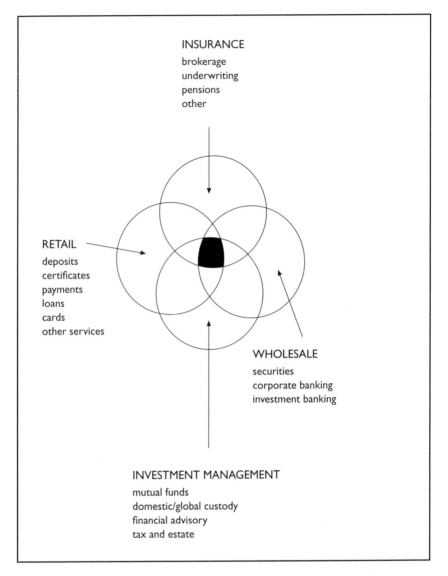

Figure 14-4. Scope-related linkages across commercial and investment banking, in-surance, and investment management.

The Role of Competitive Distortions

Using the C-A-P model in Figure 14-1 we can now describe how competitive distortions affect the accessibility and profitability associated with the individual cells in the matrix and therefore the formulation and execution of institutional strategies and the competitive performance of financial services firms. This can be discussed in terms of entry barriers, operating

Table 14-3 Range of Financial Services Provided by Selected Firms

Firm	FDIC-Insured Depository	Consumer Loans	Credit Cards	Mortgage Banking	Commercial Lending	Mutual Funds	Securities	Insurance
American Express	●	●	●			●	●	●
AT&T	●		●		●			●
Bankers Trust	●	—[a]			●	●	●	●
Citicorp	●	●	●	●	●	●	●	●
Ford	●	●		●	●			●
General Motors	●	●	●	●	●			●
General Electric	●	●			●	●	●	●
ITT	●	●		●	●	●	●	●
John Hancock	●	●		●		●	●	
J. P. Morgan	●	—[a]			●	●	●	
Merrill Lynch		●	●	●	●	●	●	
Primerica		●	●	●		●	●	●
Prudential	●	●	●		●	●	●	●
Sears, Roebuck	●	●	●	●		●		●
Transamerica		●	●		●	●		●

Data: National Journal, the American Financial Services Association, and annual reports.
[a] Minor involvement.

restrictions that affect access to client groups, and operating restrictions affecting the ability to supply the market with specific products.

First, and most obvious, entry barriers restrict the movement of financial services firms in the *arena* dimension of the matrix. A firm that is excluded from a particular national market faces a restricted lateral opportunity set that excludes the relevant tranche of *client* and *product* cells. To the extent that it is the outcome of protectionist political activity, the entry barrier will itself create supernormal returns in some or all of the cells in the tranche. It may, of course, have this effect even if there is no protectionist intent. Institutions already in a particular market will, as noted earlier, tend to have a vested interest in keeping others out. Windows of opportunity, created by relaxing of entry barriers, will be taken advantage of by institutions envisioning potential supernormal returns in some of the previously inaccessible cells.

Second, firms that are allowed into a particular market only through representative or sales offices may nevertheless be able to access particular *client/product* cells in that tranche, securing business and returns by transferring the actual transaction to a different *arena*, for example, to one of the Euromarket functional or booking centers. This option applies primarily to the wholesale and private banking components of the *client* and *product* dimensions. Correspondent relationships with local banks or strategic alliances among financial services firms are probably the only alternatives for sharing in the returns associated with the blocked cells in *product* dimensions having to do with international trade, foreign exchange, syndications, and other wholesale transactions.

The story becomes more complicated in the case of operating restrictions. The firm now has access, in one form or another, to the *arena* tranche, but is constrained either in the depth of service it can supply to a particular cell (e.g., lending limits, staffing limits, restrictions on physical location) or in the feasible set of cells within the tranche (e.g., limits on services foreign banks are allowed to supply and the client groups they are allowed to serve). These limits may severely reduce profitability associated with the arena concerned.

To the extent that horizontal integration is important in the international financial services industry, despite the presence of barriers and other competitive distortions affecting a given arena, supernormal returns may still be obtained in unaffected cells. Even a limited scope for transactions with the local affiliate of a multinational enterprise may generate business with that company elsewhere in the world, for example. The value of a physical presence of any sort in an otherwise restricted market may thus support competitive positioning elsewhere in the institution's international structure. Obviously, the value of these linkages is very difficult to assess.

Clearly, regulatory issues have an important bearing in terms of accessibility of geographic cells in the matrix. Besides applying entry and operating restrictions to foreign-based players or firms in other industries, regulators may tolerate a certain amount of anticompetitive, cartel-like behavior on the part of domestic institutions. Economies of scope and scale may be significantly constrained by entry and operating restrictions in a particular market, indicating the importance of the impact of competitive distortions on horizontal integration. These will surely affect the static and dynamic efficiency properties of the national financial system. Indeed, if they are considered sufficiently costly to users, the users will turn to foreign or offshore financial systems where they face better conditions in the form of more cost-effective funding, improved portfolio performance, or lower transactions costs.

Competitive and Cooperative Behavior

Whether within cells or across as depicted in Figure 14-1, one complication in analyzing the competitive behavior of firms in the financial services industry that does not arise to as great an extent in other industries is the need to *cooperate* closely with rivals on individual transactions while at the same time *competing* intensively with them. Examples include securities underwriting and distribution, loan syndication, project finance, and credit card networks.

When does it make sense for an institution to compete and when to cooperate in order to extract maximum returns from the individual cells in the C-A-P matrix? The diagram in Figure 14-5 can be used to model an institution's behavior with respect to a particular cell or a transaction within that cell.

The vertical axis measures the degree of *assertiveness* the institution will tend to bring to bear vis-à-vis the competition. This is a joint product of the perceived *stakes* the organization has in the game and its competitive *power*. The higher the stakes and the greater its power to ride over the competition, the more assertive the institution will want to be. Both stakes *and* power have to be high for the assertive mode to make sense.

The horizontal axis measures the extent to which the game is perceived as being *zero sum* (what one gains the other loses) or *positive sum* (both can gain), and the quality of the *relationship* with other players— usually a cumulative product of past experience. The more the game is viewed as being positive sum and the better the relationship, the more likely it is that the institution will want to *cooperate* with others.

The grid in Figure 14-5 can be divided into five "zones" on the basis of how these four underlying variables appear in a particular case—compete, collaborate, comply, avoid, and compromise. It is thus likely that one institution will be seen to work closely with another in a given project in a particular cell even while it is competing vigorously elsewhere, submitting to the dominance of the other institution, or avoiding involvement on the same kind of project in a different cell or a different project in the same cell. A large number of combinations are clearly possible in imposing this behavioral grid onto the underlying market matrix in Figure 14-1.

The evolution of international correspondent banking relationships provides an interesting example of cooperative behavior in a fundamentally competitive market structure. Correspondent banking activities include management of local currency accounts, effecting of payments, provision of access to the local clearing system, opening and confirming of documentary credits arising from international trade transactions, participation in loans and syndicated credits, and custody services in securities business—traditionally paid for largely through correspondent balances. Banks that do not pose a direct threat to their correspondents in their own home markets, either because of their strategic positioning or because of government restrictions, have been in an ideal position to develop correspondent relationships—a classic case of "collaboration" in terms of the diagram in Figure 14-5.

Things have changed, however. Improvements in communications and automation have provided direct access for banks to services previously accessible only through correspondents. Disintermediation has altered the

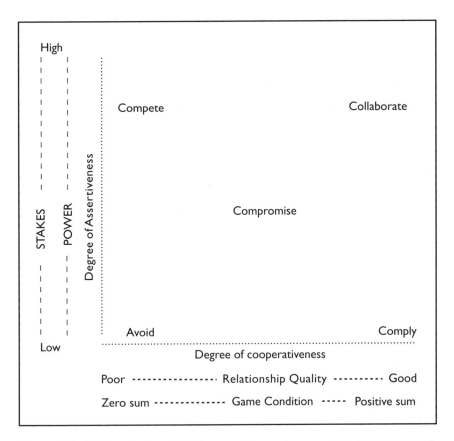

Figure 14-5. A behavioral model of competition and cooperation in international financial services.

value of correspondent banking on the lending side, and high real interest rates have raised the cost of correspondent balances. The result has been a significant "unbundling" of the previously stable correspondent relationship into a less stable and more price-sensitive one centered around a specific set of services that one bank sells to another. Like international finance generally, the drift has been from a relationship-driven to a transactions-driven business. In terms of Figure 14-5, the correspondent banking business has drifted laterally from "collaboration" in the direction of "competition."

In loan syndication and securities underwriting the same phenomenon can be observed. Although large banks and securities firms are bitter rivals in battling for syndication and underwriting mandates from issuers, they also need to work closely together in providing for effective distribution and market support. Firms will therefore invite each other into syndicates along reciprocity patterns that develop over time, taking into account relative strengths and weaknesses in distribution to different bank selldown and investor groups.

It is thus important to remember that the conflict management grid in Figure 14-5 applies only to a single institution evaluating its own situation against a protagonist and using it to derive a normative conflict management strategy. Whether these relationships are stable over time, or whether the outcome will drift into the tension-filled "compete" zone, the "avoid" zone (with a joint venture being taken over by one of the partners), or the "submit" zone (with one partner being taken over by the other) usually is not clear at the outset.

Sources of Competitive Advantage

The ability of financial institutions to exploit opportunities within the C-A-P framework depicted in Figure 14-1 depends on a number of key firm-specific attributes. These include the adequacy of the institution's capital base and its institutional risk base, its access to human resources, its access to information and markets, its technology base and managerial culture, and the entrepreneurial qualities of its people.

Adequacy of the Capital Base

In recent years, financial institutions and their regulators have started to pay increasing attention to the issue of capital as a source of competitive power as well as prudential control. This has always been true with respect to activities appearing on the balance sheet. But with increasing concentration of domestic and international finance in the securities markets, the role of capital has become important as the principal determinant of risk-bearing ability in securities underwriting and dealing as well as in off-balance-sheet activities. One step removed, a large capital base that allows an institution to be a successful player in securities underwriting and dealing also may enable it to undertake mergers and acquisitions activities, private placements, and other value-added services for its clients. Capital adequacy thus conveys a decided competitive advantage in bringing specific products to specific international markets, in maximizing firepower and reducing costs in funding operations, in being able to stick with particular clients in good times and bad—thus being considered a reliable financial partner, and in achieving compliance with capital requirements mandated by the regulators.

The Institutional Risk Base

Financial institutions fund themselves by creating financial assets held by others. In a deregulated environment where financial institutions are forced to bid for funds, the perceived quality of an institution is an important determinant of its ability to fund itself at the lowest possible cost. The level of embedded exposure to institutional risk has become particularly significant in the interbank market and the securities industry, leading to a substantial spread in funding costs between institutions and in erosions of funding availability from time to time, particularly in crisis situations. Institutions of lesser perceived quality can be caught in a difficult position in terms of liquidity or if they are forced to pay a premium over the other institutions to fund themselves. A high credit rating thus assures a financial institution substantial advantages on the funding side. This is also true in dealings with corporate and other institutional clients that are often highly sensitive to the perceived quality of suppliers of financial services.

Quality of Human Resources

While it has long been recognized that financial services are basically a "people business," it is only recently that the importance of having truly superior human resources has become apparent to all of the major players. Human capital can be viewed as a financial institution's most important asset, and many of the critical opportunities to exploit individual C-A-P cells, or clusters of them, are dependent directly on the quality of human resources encompassed within the organization. Both credit and risk evaluation depend on the intellectual caliber, experience, and training of the decision-maker—qualities that are no less important in the securities business than they are in the more traditional dimensions of banking. Due to the increase in the role of transactions-driven financial services, individuals are increasingly having to make decisions of a highly complex nature very quickly or lose deals. The need for rapid and accurate decision-making is particularly evident in the trading function, but is no less important in maintaining relationships with clients, specifically to anticipate client financial requirements and respond to them in ways that add value.

Growing competition and increased complexity has placed a premium on human resource-based advantages, reflected in severe rivalry to attract top-quality people in the labor markets of various financial centers, with compensation levels bid up at an extraordinary rate.

Information Advantages

The drive by financial institutions to move beyond commodity-type activities into higher value-added services is augmenting the importance of information-intensive products, both quantitatively and qualitatively. Indeed, *asymmetries* of information among various competitors and their clients contribute a great deal toward explaining differentials in competitive performance. Information is embedded in specific financial services sold in various arenas to various clients, and all forms of lending and credit-related activities depend on the collection, processing, and evaluation of large amounts of information. Similarly, the assimilation of information about the needs of clients is critical in the development of services addressed to their needs. There are three special factors regarding information as a determinant of competitive performance.

First, information is the only resource that can be used simultaneously in the production of any number of services, and this gives it some unique characteristics. For example, information generated to build an international cash management system for a multinational corporate client can also be used to develop a long-term financial strategy for the same company, or perhaps to develop a slightly different international cash management system for another multinational firm.

Second, the half-life of information as a source of competitive advantage has been decreasing. Due to a great deal of financial market volatility, important types of financial information decay at a rapid rate, and actions that may have been warranted at one moment may no longer be appropriate shortly thereafter. It is an environment consisting of many small windows of opportunity.

Third, the growing complexity of the international financial environment and the wide variety of services offered has made it increasingly difficult for companies and individuals to plan in a straightforward manner. In effect, what clients often need is a means to evaluate the information that is available and some way of distinguishing relevant information from irrelevant. Financial institutions can provide information-related services that help accomplish this, and they in turn are increasingly served by vendors of sophisticated research and analytics (e.g., Reuters, Extel, Bloomberg).

Financial Technology and Innovation

Financial innovation depends heavily on information incorporated in value-added services sold to clients. The parts of the international financial services industry that have seen the most far-reaching structural changes are those that appear to be the most knowledge intensive. Information technologies allow financial institutions to have at their disposal increasing amounts of data, and reduce the time necessary to transfer data across arenas, client segments, and product applications. With information increasing at a rapid pace, internal decision and filter systems of financial institutions have come under pressure and new ones have had to be built, as have transaction-driven "back office" systems. Along with management and marketing know-how, these technologies are principally *process related*.

There is an equally important set of *product-related* financial technologies, which to a significant degree are made possible by information- and transactions-oriented advances in financial processes. Technology-intensive financial services may be either embodied or disembodied. The former incorporate technology in a financial transaction, and differentiate that transaction from others available in the market. Disembodied technology is provided to clients independent of a specific financial transaction (e.g., in the form of financial advice), although it may subsequently lead to transactions. Returns on financial technology may come through positioning (trading) profits, fees, or enhanced returns associated with financial product differentiation.

Whether process or product related, financial technology permits the innovating firm to open up an "intertemporal gap" between itself and its competitors, reflected either in the cost of delivering financial services or in product differentiation. That gap has both *size* and *durability* implications, and may also be more or less cell specific within the C-A-P model. In general there appears to be a strong positive relationship between innovation and client specificity in the international financial services industry. There also seems to be a positive relationship between the complexity of the innovation and the imitation lag, perhaps partly offset by a negative relationship between product complexity and success of the innovation—with some innovations being too complex to be put to effective use. In the absence of anything like patent or copyright protection, the imitation lag for financial innovations tends to be relatively short. It is therefore important for an institution to maintain a continuous stream of innovations.

Innovation in this industry can thus be looked on as the introduction of a new process or technique—new in terms of a particular cell—that provides durable returns and adds significant value to the client. The spread of an innovation through the matrix allows the firm to take advantage of its inherent profit potential across the cells.

Innovative capabilities—the continuous application of new product and process technologies—are very much a function of the quality of human capital and of investments in the financial equivalent of research and development, which is usually much more market driven, informal, and inductive than industrial R&D. They are also highly sensitive to the "culture" of an organization, its management (see following), the incentives associated with successful innovations versus the penalties of unsuccessful innovations, and the amount of horizontal communication and information transfer that takes place within the organization. Financial institutions compete in the same capital and labor markets, and people move from one institution to another with growing frequency. Yet some institutions appear to be consistently more innovative than others.

Franchise

A financial institution's "franchise" is probably its most important asset. While it is also the most intangible of assets, it clearly distinguishes the more successful competitors in the financial services industry from the rest. A franchise can arise from a number of different sources. It is generally related to a specific expertise, expertise valued by the market, that an institution has developed over time. It results from the institution's "standing" in the market, a synergistic combination of all competitive attributes in which the whole is greater than the sum of the parts. Franchise is a function of past performance projected over future transactions. Especially in commodity-type activities there is little to differentiate one institution from another, and franchise becomes an all-important performance variable. A firm's franchise can be either product specific or industry specific, an important consideration with respect to the strategy that the bank should follow.

Franchise value is thus reflected in the market, driven by the perceived quality of its services but also by the quality and quantity of its public relations and advertising activities. Some banking services are more dependent on advertising than others. For many institutions, advertising and public relations are relatively new activities and, in keeping with market orientation, are becoming increasingly important, as reflected in growing advertising expenditures. Still, some banking services are quite independent of promotional outlays and driven largely by past performance. In such cases—securities underwriting for example—one failure is worth more than many successes, and a single bad deal can cause a bank to lose an enormous amount of face in markets that have very long memories.

An institution's franchise is thus its most intangible asset, yet one that clearly distinguishes ex post facto the most successful competitors in the international financial services industry from the rest. It can be used to explain a variety of competitive phenomena.

The Importance of Corporate Culture

Culture is something every bank and securities firm has, even if it is weak. In one important sense, corporate culture can be boiled down to the institutional environment in which people have to work. If a firm wants to get a lot out of people, the first thing management has to give them is a highly desirable environment in the workplace, where they spend more of their time than anywhere else. Some key ingredients are:

- High-quality peers from whom to learn, and with whom to compete
- A sufficiently loose organizational structure to permits ideas to rise, be taken seriously, considered carefully on the basis of merit, and acted on quickly—a structure that protects high-potential individuals from bureaucratic stifling
- An esprit de corps that thrives on measurable competitive success, such as significantly increasing market share or profit margins, in a business where winners and losers are not difficult to distinguish and where valuable franchises are difficult to build but easy to lose
- A performance-based compensation and advancement system that is generally respected as being fair and right not less than about 80 percent of the time, a system that is a benign form of ruthless Darwinism, including a reasonably high level of involuntary turnover and in which only the best survive and progress

In short, the climate has to be in which bright people, if they are found suitable, will *want* to spend their careers. This climate requires a sense of continuity, admired and respected seniors, and a serious, consistent commitment to careful recruitment, management development, and training. Especially in times of growing international activity, those who are not from the institution's home country cannot be deemed unworthy of high office.

Corporate culture in a highly competitive industry such as global financial services increasingly has to be regarded as an important competitive weapon, centered on grasping and preserving the qualities of winning. This includes:

- Sound strategic direction and leadership from the top—knowing the right thing to do, then getting it done by providing sufficient resources
- An overriding attention to teamwork, the avoidance of "stars" and stamping out of arrogance (many so-called "strong" cultures are really not much more than institutionalized arrogance)
- The selection of hundreds of loyal and efficient "squad and platoon leaders" to carry out day-to-day activities at high levels of quality and professionalism, to include a fine, ingrained sense of what is unacceptable conduct—including conduct that does not violate law or regulation but nevertheless could impair the franchise of the firm and compromise its responsibility to clients
- A high level of adaptability by the whole organization in an industry subject to rapid change

The last is what the cultures of investment banks like Goldman Sachs do so well. It is why they continue to rank as top market players year after year. Nevertheless, *sic transit gloria*. Senior management must be keenly aware of the need for adaptability, and communicate it effectively by word and deed. A certain amount of corporate *angst* keeps people on their toes.

To become a market-share and profitability winner overall, a firm must be positioned and structured to deliver the best possible products to the greatest number of clients in the shortest period of time. It must also learn to take and manage large trading risks quickly. When failures occur, replacements must be available to step forward until the right people are in the right jobs. If the front-line people are well selected and trained, nurtured and coached, the number of failures will be minimized.

Today, however, to *become* a winner is not enough. To *stay* a winner, a firm must be able to adapt to wrenching industry change, intense margin competition, and the management of vastly complicated technology and risk issues. Few people can do all of this without becoming obsolete after a while. Then they need to be moved out of the way, with dignity and grace if possible, to make room for more up-to-date replacements. This implies that such a culture—not unlike that of professional athletics or an effective military—needs to have young people on the front lines and plenty of senior coaching backing them up. The young don't know everything, and a good institutional memory is an invaluable asset.

In view of its importance as a determinant of competitive performance, corporate culture has disproportionate importance in the banking and securities sector because of a number of more or less unique industry characteristics, among which are the following:

- As a service industry, banking and securities activities frequently involve close personal contact with clients. Consequently, the morale of the banker is more directly identified with the quality of the service than in other industries.
- Clients tend to associate their own prestige with the prestige of the firm under the rubric, "First-class clients are served by first-class institution." The franchise of the firm therefore has direct marketing implications.
- Banking involves longer-lasting client relationships than many other industries, both wholesale and retail, sometimes extending over decades. Setbacks suffered by a bank are sometimes felt as setbacks by clients.
- By definition, banking involves a fiduciary relationship with clients, who expect the culture of the bank to validate that relationship. However, a strong fiduciary culture may not be one that welcomes innovation.
- Financial services require trust in institutional stability and bureaucratic procedures, which may promote a culture that resists change and innovative thinking.
- Banking and securities activities are and will continue to be highly regulated due to their "special" role in the economy, and regulated firms with "utility" characteristics may develop cultural attributes that are not ideal for the more dynamic parts of the industry.
- Nonprice competition in banking and securities services may be more

important than in other industries where price and cost differences are relatively greater, especially in lines of activity whose competitive structure is oligopolistic.

- Product differentiation in commercial and investment banking is often unusually difficult to achieve—given the lack of copyright or patent protection, ease of entry and exit, and short imitation cycles that exist in the industry—so that the *mode* of delivery becomes extraordinarily important.
- Cross-selling of products and economies of scope may be more important in banking, particularly among universal banks, than in some other industries, so that a cooperative culture that maximizes lateral communication and internal referrals may be of unusual significance.

Each of these aspects, and perhaps others as well, may make competitive performance in banking and financial services particularly "culture sensitive," which means that firms with superior cultural attributes outperform others that otherwise may have substantially the same resources.

One question that constantly arises is whether a single culture is appropriate for an organization that covers a very broad range of activities, extending from foreign exchange dealing to mass-market retail banking and to M&A transactions in investment banking. On the other hand, there are often some overarching cultural attributes (a superculture) that can be an effective "umbrella" covering widely different business cultures and national cultures within an organization. If this is considered impossible to achieve, it is likely that a holding company form of organization— where unit cultures are closely aligned to the respective businesses—is superior to more integrated structural forms among banks, as discussed in the next section. However, cultural fragmentation in such a structure has potential drawbacks, including the fragmentation of market delivery and quality control, that are not to be taken lightly.

Banking Structure and Industry Linkages

One determinant of competitive performance in global financial services may be how the banking system is structured, in particular the degree of *universality* it incorporates, as well as the role of banks in the ownership and control of nonfinancial enterprises, in particular their own clients.

Universal banking can be defined as the conduct of an array of financial services comprising credit, trading of financial instruments and foreign exchange (and their derivatives), underwriting of new debt and equity issues, brokerage, corporate advisory services (including mergers and acquisitions advice), investment management, and insurance. Clearly, the more important are economies of scale and scope, the more competitive should universal financial institutions be as against smaller and more narrowly focused financial institutions. Universal banking can take the basic forms depicted in Figure 14-6.

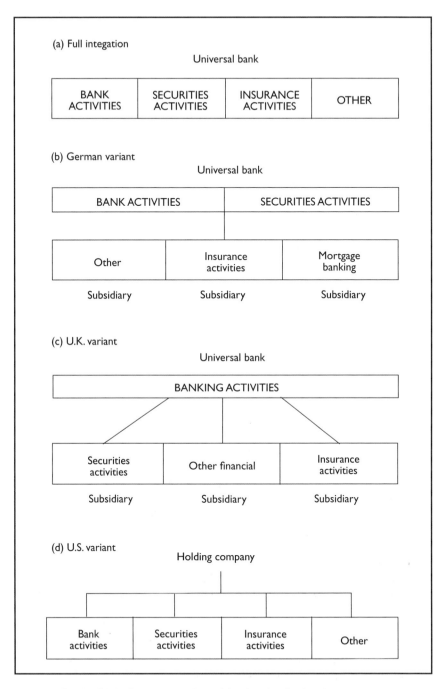

Figure 14-6. Prototype universal bank organizational structures.

- The *fully integrated universal bank,* capable of supplying the complete range of financial services from one institutional entity.
- The *partially integrated financial conglomerate,* capable of supplying substantially the same set of services but with several (such as mortgage banking, leasing, and insurance) provided through wholly owned or partially owned subsidiaries.
- The *bank-subsidiary structure,* under which the bank focuses essentially on commercial banking and all other services, including investment banking and insurance, are carried out through legally separate subsidiaries of the bank.
- The *holding company structure,* where a holding company owns both banking and nonbanking subsidiaries that are legally separate and individually capitalized, insofar as financial activities other than "banking" are permitted by law. These may be separated by *Chinese walls* and *firewalls* if there are internal or regulatory concerns about institutional safety and soundness or conflicts of interest. The holding company may also be allowed to own industrial firms (see below). Or the holding company may itself be an industrial company. Both cases raise the issue of central bank bailouts of industrial companies.
- The *separated* system, in which banks are not allowed to engage in securities or insurance activities, as has been true in the United States and Japan until relatively recently.

Recent studies have suggested that the separated system, as has existed in the United States and Japan, incorporates a number of competitive disadvantages against various forms of universal banking as practiced in most of the rest of the world. In particular, the holding company form and the bank-subsidiary form of universal banking appear to offer many of the scale and scope advantages of fully integrated universal banking without necessarily encountering some of the disadvantages that accompany bureaucracy and inflexibility in fast-moving financial markets. This does not suggest that smaller, leaner, faster specialist firms, such as investment banks focusing on corporate finance, will be driven from the market by universals. Problems of potential conflicts of interest, cost structures, and agility virtually ensure such firms a viable role in the financial system. It does suggest, however, that competitive conditions in the open market should drive the structural forms that financial institutions decide to adopt.

A related issue concerns the linkages between financial institutions and industry. Investment banks have always taken large equity positions in nonfinancial firms in the process of taking them public, restructuring them, or engaging in leveraged buyouts. The principal objective, however, has been to profit from the difference between the acquisition price of shares and the price received from an industrial acquirer or from the general public, not to hold permanent control positions and play a major role in management (except in severe problem situations). Under some forms of universal banking, however, banks have acquired and held permanent equity positions in nonfinancial companies, taken positions on boards of directors, and played an important role in corporate governance. In the process, such banks have simultaneously served as owners, advisers, lenders, and underwriters for a given company, with virtually all of its business going to that bank.

Three stylized models for bank–industry linkages can be described in terms such as Figure 14-7. All assign central but quite distinct roles to financial institutions.

The equity-market system. Shares of corporations are held by the public, either directly or through institutional investment vehicles such as mutual funds and pension funds, and are actively traded. Corporate restructuring is triggered by exploitation of a *control premium* between the existing market capitalization of a firm and that which an unaffiliated acquirer (whether an industrial company or an active financial investor) perceives and acts upon by initiating a takeover effort designed to unlock shareholder value through management changes. There is a high level of transparency and reliance on public information, with systematic surveillance by equity investors and research analysts. Concerns about unwanted takeover efforts prompt management to act consistently in the interests of shareholders, many of whom tend to view their shares as put options—options to sell. The role of credit institutions in the control structure of this *outsider* system is mainly confined to arm's-length financing, including takeovers and internal corporate restructuring, although investment banks may be active in giving strategic and financial advice and sometimes taking equity positions in (and occasionally control of) firms for their own account.

The bank-based system. Major equity stakes in corporations are held by banks, which act as both commercial and investment bankers to their clients. With substantial equity as well as debt exposures, banks exert a significant monitoring role in the management of corporations, including active board room participation and guidance with the benefit of nonpublic *(inside)* information. The public holds shares in both banks and corporations, either directly or through mutual funds usually managed by banks and whose shares are voted by banks. Markets for corporate equity and debt tend to be poorly developed, with relatively large investor holdings of public sector bonds as opposed to corporate bonds or stocks. Financial transparency tends to be relatively low, as does the free float of shares. External efforts to gain control of corporations against the wishes of management are virtually unknown.

The bank-industrial crossholding system. Nonfinancial corporations hold significant stakes in each other and hold reciprocal seats on boards of directors. Both linkages may complement close supplier-

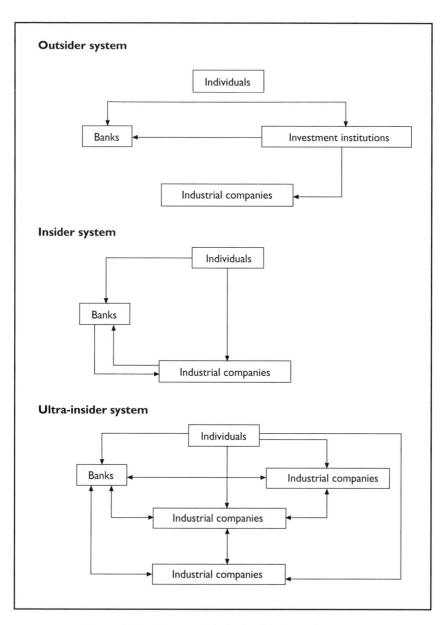

Figure 14-7. Three models for bank-industry linkages.

customer relationships, with dependability and cooperation often dominating price as transactions criteria. Banks hold shares in industrial companies and play a significant role at the board level, and at the center of equity crossholding structures. The public holds shares in both industrial companies and banks. There is significant free float of shares and relatively well-developed corporate equity and debt markets. Managements of companies connected through crossholding structures are generally felt to be acting in the interests of public shareholders, and the structures themselves may be viewed in the market as redefinitions of the boundaries of a "firm" using *ultra-inside* information, both among clustered industrial firms and between firms and banks. Unwanted corporate control change by active investors in this system is virtually unknown.

Under the first (Anglo-American) system, the typical industrial firm is "semidetached" from banks and maintains an arm's-length relationship with government. Financing is done to a significant degree through the capital markets, with short-term needs satisfied through commercial paper programs, longer-term debt through straight or structured bond issues and medium-term note programs, and equity through public issues or private placements. Bank relationships continue to exist and can be very important indeed, often through backstop credit lines, but the relationship is between arm's-length buyer and seller, with closer monitoring and control coming into play only in cases of difficulty. Corporate control is exercised through the takeover market on the basis of outside information, with bank roles limited to financing bids or defensive restructurings. The government role is normally even more arm's length, with a focus on setting ground rules considered to be in the public interest, and relations between government, banks, and industry are sometimes antagonistic.

At the other extreme is the crossholding system (typified by the Japanese *keiretsu*), in which interfirm boundaries themselves become blurred through equity crossholdings and long-term supplier-customer relationships. Banks have traditionally played a central role and provided guidance and coordination, as well as financing, although in recent years the financing role has been somewhat diminished with the development of active capital markets access for Japanese companies domestically and internationally. Strong formal and informal links run from the government through the Ministry of Finance and the Ministry of International Trade and Industry to both the financial and real sectors. Restructuring tends to be done on the basis of inside information by drawing on these business-banking-government ties, and the open market for corporate control is virtually nonexistent.

The classic interpretation of the insider (Germanic) approach centers on close bank-industry relationships, with financing needs met by retained earnings and bank financing and bank roles extending beyond credit to stock ownership, share voting, and board memberships. Capital allocation and restructuring of enterprises is undertaken significantly on the basis of inside information, and unwanted takeovers are rare. Mergers and acquisitions tend to be undertaken by *Hausbanken,* whose importance is amplified by the large role played by *Mittelstand* firms in the German economy. Capital markets are relatively poorly developed with respect to both corporate debt and equity. Although state *(Länder)* governments play an important role in bank ownership and control, the relations between the federal government and both industrial firms and banks are mainly arm's length in nature, with some exceptions involving public-sector shareholdings and sectoral restructurings.

The French version of this approach has traditionally needed a strong role by government through national ownership of major banks and corporations, as well as government central savings institutions. Financing of enterprises represents a mixture of bank credits and capital markets issues, domestic as well as international, on the part of both private and public-sector firms. Formal channels of government influence exercised through the Ministry of Finance are supplemented by informal channels centered on the Grandes Ecoles, and government generally appoints the heads of state-owned companies. The market for corporate control operates on the basis of both public and private information. There have been a number of takeover battles in France, but the Ministry of Finance has often played a determining role in the outcomes. Privately owned investment banks *(Banques d'Affaires)* are engaged in ownership of enterprise and corporate restructuring, although the state actively seeks to shape French industrial structure through patterns of public ownership and influence.

Like the distinctions among various degrees of universality in banking, international differences in bank-industry linkages can have a significant effect on the evolution of financial systems as well as the competitive positioning of individual financial institutions.

Strategic Targeting

To maximize performance in the international financial services industry a firm clearly has to go through some sort of strategic process to seek an optimal expansion path within the C-A-P matrix. This may involve deepening penetration of individual cells or incursions into new cells. Decisions in this regard obviously depend on the perceived cost and risk versus benefits of opportunities that present themselves or that are sought out. The process itself (see Figure 14-8), in stylized form, may look something like this:

- Development of a consensus on the future macroenvironment (e.g., interest-rate and exchange-rate stability, disequilibria, real-sector shocks, etc.) that could affect markets and products globally or represent sources of covariance in returns and hence systematic risk
- Surveying of existing cell-based activities in terms of market structure, risk and return, linkage effects, and impact on overall competitive performance and identification of each in terms of its product-, client-, or arena-driven characteristics
- Assessment of the feasibility set of additional cell-based activities in terms of market structure, risk and return, linkage effects, and prospec-

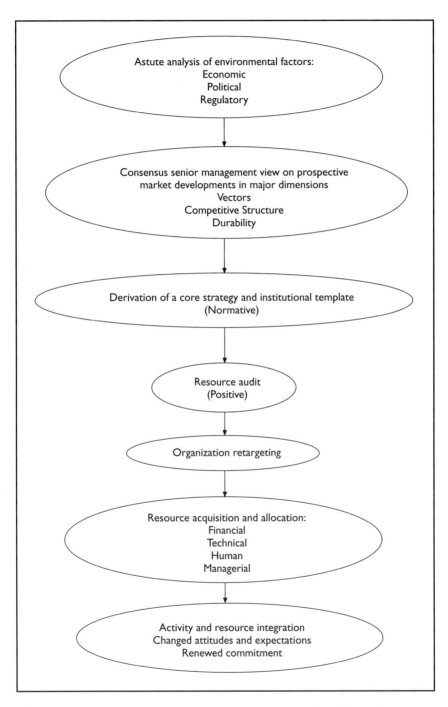

Figure 14-8. Strategy development in international financial services.

tive impact on overall competitive performance, as well as product-, client-, or arena-driven characteristics

- Breakdown of the relevant product, client, and arena variables into components that identify key competitive factors
- Development of an inventory of organizational resources and prospective access to incremental resources
- Identification of strategic options involving possible deepening or broadening of cell activities, acquisitions, or divestitures and their impact on economies of scale and scope as well as actuarial risk base
- Identification of resistance lines, cost, and risk dimensions associated with each strategic option
- Selection of optimum strategic path consistent with prospective returns/cost/risk profiles and institutional resource constraints

Some institutions will be able to react more rapidly than others to competitive opportunities and therefore may have a key advantage over their rivals. This ability to react will tend to depend jointly on an organization's inherent flexibility and its organizational structure.

Finally, it is important that some sort of coherent competitive positioning emerge from the strategic process. In taxonomy of possible strategies for international financial institutions, at the product level the strategy can be defined as niche, diversified, or supermarket; at the arena level it can be defined as national, international, or global; and at the client level it can be defined as focused, segmented, or nonsegmented. Segmentation in this context does not necessarily mean that a financial institution has actively segmented the market, but rather that it supplies products to some client groups but not all. Across this taxonomy, an institution's strategic positioning and clarity are invariably projected to clients, regulators, and competitors alike. It becomes a significant competitive advantage or disadvantage for the financial institution in the marketplace.

Competitive Restructuring in Global Banking

A firm in the financial services industry faces a given C-A-P cell configuration and linkages at any point in time, alongside a particular institutional capability profile. Some of the cells have already been accessed, and some form a feasibility set for possible further development. The firm's expansion path—and the desired cell configuration of its business—depends on the level of perceived risk-adjusted economic returns associated with the feasibility set of cells, resistance lines impeding access to those cells, and the assessed value of intercell linkages. Successful players must therefore identify the specific sources of their competitive advantage; those cells where this competitive advantage can be applied, adds value, and is sustainable; and the competitive potential inherent in the cell linkages. Application of a competitive-structure framework, such as the one presented here, will help identify the cells and cell clusters where significant returns based on market power are likely to exist, and (equally important) where they are likely to be durable.

Given the potential size of the C-A-P matrix and the complexity of the linkages that exist among the individual cells, it becomes clear how wide is the range of strategic options that faces a financial institution in the global environment. Consequently, it is not surprising that an individual organizations' international structures and their development through time often appear somewhat haphazard, lacking in consistency or coherence. This is the result of management actions under conditions of *bounded rationality* when faced with the task of determining expansion paths. In effect, management confronts an enormous opportunity set, of which it is usually familiar with only a small part. Therefore it appears to operate much of the time by a process of trial and error—trying various options under best available information, assessing results to the extent this is possible, and trying again. It is thus not surprising that many institutions appear ex post facto to have a relatively ambiguous strategic positioning in the global market for financial services.

To perform well in working through the strategic process, institutions must first develop the ability to scan the environment and to identify potential changes in that environment, including strategic moves by competitors and changes in the regulatory setting. Moreover, some institutions will be able to react more quickly than others to changes in the competitive environment and therefore may have a key advantage over their rivals.

In the pervasive economic restructuring that goes on in response to changing consumer and demand patterns, resource costs, international competition, and perceived economies of scale and scope, individual industrial firms in search of maximum shareholder value constantly reassess the activity span of their businesses. Vertical integration to secure sources of supply or downstream distribution may serve this purpose. Horizontal and geographic expansion to acquire market share, complementary product lines, or risk spreading may be attempted for the same reason.

When management appears to be on the wrong track, the financial markets provide appropriate signals leading to further restructuring or retrenchment. When the firm's objectives collide with the public interest in keeping markets functioning efficiently or in achieving noneconomic objectives—even at a cost to the economy—regulatory constraints are imposed in the form of antitrust, environmental, employment, consumer protection, or other types of legislation, along with appropriate enforcement measures. These involve a delicate balancing act to ensure that the *social benefits* of regulation more than justify any *social costs* (which come in the form of less efficient use of resources and possibly slower growth). Within the bounds of such necessary regulatory constraints, industrial restructuring and shifting forms of business organization in the banking and financial services sector should be driven mainly by the economic fundamentals.

Indeed, competitive restructuring in the financial services sector is conceptually no different from restructuring in the industrial sector. Market forces may dictate vertical positioning somewhere on the spectrum from the ultimate consumer to the wholesale financial markets, or horizontal positioning ranging in breadth from the financial specialist to *Allfinanz* or *bankassurance*—the respective German and French terms for providing the full range of financial services under one roof. As in other industries, the functions to be performed and the underlying demand and supply characteristics in a highly competitive market tend to dictate the sizes and forms of the organizations that compete in the marketplace. The penalties for having suboptimum organizational structures may be very severe indeed.

Summary

To assess the competitive structure of the international financial services industry, we have introduced a model that permits identification of sources of potential supernormal returns as a product of the competitive structure of markets. The concepts of strategic groups, contestable markets, and predatory behavior were introduced in this context as having an important bearing on market structure. Intermarket linkages were discussed in terms of their contribution to global economies of scale and economies of scope, as were patterns of collaborative and competitive behavior in those markets.

The analysis in this chapter also suggests that an institution's competitive performance in the international financial services industry is a function of (1) the competitive power the organization is able to bring to bear, based on its institutional resource profile; (2) the structural characteristics of the various cells in which it chooses to compete; (3) the lateral, horizontal, and vertical integration gains associated with cell linkages; and (4) economies of scale and economies of scope potentially available from transactions within cells and across cells. These dimensions jointly determine the returns that can be extracted from each cell and from the market as a whole. The goals of strategic positioning in this industry involve each of these dimensions, including the institution's relative strengths and weaknesses, and then creating and projecting an unambiguous strategic profile.

Appendix: Permissible Activities for Banking Organizations in Various Financial Centers

	Securities [a]	Insurance [b]	Real Estate [c]	Bank Investments in Industrial Firms [d]	Industrial Firm Investments in Banks
Argentina	Unlimited, certain activities through subsidiaries	Permitted through subsidiaries	Limited based on bank capital and investment objective	Limited	Permitted but subject to prior approval of authorities
Australia	Unlimited, but in practice through a subsidiary	Permitted through subsidiaries, subject to controls of insurance legislation	Limited by prudential guidelines	Limited by prudential guidelines	Acquisition of more than 10% of a bank's voting stock requires regulatory approval
Austria [e]	Unlimited	Unlimited through subsidiaries	Unlimited	Permitted but subject to limits based on the bank's capital	Permitted but subject to notification and prohibition under certain circumstances
Bahrain	Limited by terms of license and supervisory guidelines	Not permitted	Generally limited to holding bank premises	Not permitted	No legal restriction, but subject to approval of banking authorities
Belgium	Unlimited, some activities through subsidiaries	Unlimited through subsidiaries	Generally limited to holding bank premises	Single shareholding may not exceed 10% of bank's own funds and such shareholdings on an aggregate basis may not exceed 35% of own funds	Unlimited, but subject to prior approval of authorities
Bolivia	Unlimited through subsidiaries	Permitted through subsidiaries	Not permitted	Not permitted	No legal restriction, but subject to approval of banking authorities

(continued)

Appendix: Permissible Activities for Banking Organizations in Various Financial Centers (continued)

Brazil	Unlimited through subsidiaries	Unlimited through subsidiaries	Unlimited through subsidiaries	Generally limited to holding bank premises	Limited to suppliers to the bank	Permitted
Canada	Unlimited through subsidiaries	Unlimited through subsidiaries	Unlimited through subsidiaries	Unlimited through subsidiaries	Permitted to hold up to 10% interests, with aggregate shareholdings not to exceed 70% of bank capital	Permitted to hold up to 10% interests
Cayman Islands	Unlimited	Permitted upon issuance of a license	Unlimited	Unlimited	Not restricted by law	Permitted, but subject to consultations with authorities
Chile	Limited, certain activities through subsidiaries	Not permitted	Not permitted	Not permitted	Not permitted	Unlimited
China	Permitted through subsidiaries	Permitted through subsidiaries	Permitted through subsidiaries	Not permitted	Not permitted	Not permitted
Colombia	Unlimited through subsidiaries	Unlimited through subsidiaries	Generally limited to holding bank premises	Unlimited through subsidiaries	Unlimited through subsidiaries	Permitted, but investments over 10% subject to prior approval of banking authorities
Denmark	Unlimited	Unlimited through subsidiaries	Limited to 20% of capital	Unlimited	Permitted with restrictions; permanent controlling holdings in industrial companies are prohibited	Not prohibited, but such investments are generally not made

(continued)

European Community[b]	Not applicable; permissibility is subject to home country and host country regulation	Not applicable; permissibility is subject to home country and host country regulation	Not applicable; permissibility is subject to home country and host country regulation	Each 10% or more shareholding may not exceed 15% of the bank's own funds and such shareholdings on an aggregate basis may not exceed 60% of own funds	No general restriction; does not allow investments of 10% or more if home country supervisor is not satisfied with the suitability of the shareholder
Finland	Unlimited	Only selling of insurance policies as an agent is permitted	Permitted to hold real estate and shares in real estate companies up to 13% of total assets	Permitted to hold directly up to 10% of shares of nonfinancial companies, and up to 20% on an aggregate basis through subsidiaries	Not prohibited, but such investments are generally not made
France	Unlimited	Unlimited, usually through subsidiaries	Unlimited	Permitted with regulatory approval of interests in excess of 10%	Not prohibited, but such investments are generally not made
Germany	Unlimited	Unlimited, but only through insurance subsidiaries	Permitted, subject to limits based on bank's capital; unlimited through subsidiaries	Limited to 15% of the bank's capital, in the aggregate limited to 60% of the bank's capital	Permitted (subject to regulatory consent based on suitability of the shareholder)

Greece	Underwriting permitted by certain credit institutions; brokerage and dealing permitted through subsidiaries	Permitted to hold shares in insurance companies subject to limits based on the bank's capital and the insurance company's capital	Generally permitted	Permitted, subject to the EC directive on qualified holdings	Permitted, subject to the EC directive on qualified holdings
Hong Kong	Permitted (except for limitation on shareholding in certain listed companies and subject to limits based on the capital of the bank)	Permitted (subject to limits based on the capital of the bank and approval from Insurance Authority for 15% or more shareholding)	Permitted (subject to limits based on the capital of the bank)	Permitted (subject to limits based on the capital of the bank)	Permitted (subject to regulatory consent based on suitability of the shareholder)
India	Permitted, some activities through subsidiaries	Not permitted	Generally limited to holding bank premises	Limited to 30% of the share capital and reserves of the company or the bank, whichever is less	Permitted subject to acknowledgement of Reserve Bank of India to transfer 1% or more of the capital of the bank
Ireland	Unlimited, usually through a subsidiary	Unlimited agency, certain life assurance activities through subsidiary which must be separate and independent	Unlimited	Unlimited	Permitted subject to Central Bank prior approval for acquisition of more than 10% of total bank shares

Italy	Unlimited, but not permitted to operate directly on the Stock Exchange	Limited to 10% of own funds for each insurance company and 20% aggregate investment in insurance companies	Generally limited to holding bank premises	Not permitted	Permitted up to 15% of shares of the bank, subject to approval of the Bank of Italy
Japan	Permitted through subsidiaries, except for equity brokerage for the time being; banks are allowed to own more than 50% of a securities subsidiary	Not permitted	Generally limited to holding bank premises	Limited to holding 5% interests	Permitted, provided total investment does not exceed investing firm's capital or net assets
Korea	Permitted through affiliates	Not permitted	Limited to banking activities and to 40% of bank capital	Subject to prior approval for investments in excess of 10%	Permitted up to 8% of the bank's shares
Luxembourg	Unlimited	Unlimited through subsidiaries	Limited to the amount of the bank's own funds	Strictly limited	Investment may not exceed 50% of banking capital
Mexico	Securities trading permitted; options and futures trading permitted	Permitted through affiliates	Not permitted	Not permitted	Not permitted
The Netherlands	Unlimited	Unlimited through subsidiaries	Unlimited	Subject to regulatory approval for voting shares in excess of 10%	Subject to regulatory approval for voting shares in excess of 5%

(continued)

Appendix: Permissible Activities for Banking Organizations in Various Financial Centers (continued)

Country					
New Zealand	Unlimited, but in practice through a subsidiary	Permitted through subsidiaries	Unlimited through subsidiaries	Permitted	Permitted, but subject to approval of authorities
Norway	Generally permitted through subsidiaries	Unlimited through subsidiaries	Permitted subject to restrictions based on total assets of the bank	Investments of up to 49% in single companies permitted; only 4% of total bank assets permitted to be invested in shares	Generally, maximum ownership of 10% for any single owner of financial institution; some exemptions, the most important relating to subsidiaries of foreign institutions
Pakistan	Mostly government securities	Not permitted	Generally limited to holding bank premises	Permitted	Permitted
Panama	Unlimited	Not permitted	Generally limited to holding bank premises	Permitted up to 2.5% of the bank's capital	Not prohibited, but such investments would require approval by the National Banking Commission
Peru	Permitted through subsidiaries	Not permitted	Generally limited to holding bank premises	Generally not permitted	Permitted subject to approval of Superintendent of Banks if investments exceed 15% of bank's capital
Poland	Permitted	Unlimited	Unlimited	Permitted up to 2.5% of the bank's capital	Unlimited

	Securities	Insurance	Real estate	Equity investments in commercial firms	
Portugal	Generally permitted; mutual funds only through subsidiaries	Unlimited through subsidiaries	Generally limited to holding bank premises	Permitted up to 15% of bank's own funds (but not to exceed 25% of the voting rights of the company) and such investments may not in the aggregate exceed 60% of the bank's funds	Subject to regulatory approval for acquisitions of voting shares in excess of 20, 33, and 50%
Singapore	Banks may hold equity participants in stockbrokering firms with Monetary Authority of Singapore approval	Locally incorporated banks may own insurance companies with Monetary Authority of Singapore approval	Limited in the aggregate to 40% of bank's capital	Limited in the aggregate to 40% of bank's capital	Acquisition of 5% or more requires regulatory approval
Spain	Unlimited; banks are permitted to own up to 100% of stock exchange members	Unlimited through subsidiaries	Unlimited	Permitted, subject to capital-based limits	Need authorization from Bank of Spain for equity investments of 15% or more; notification to Bank of Spain required for all purchases and sales of 5%
Sweden	Unlimited	Unlimited	Generally limited to holding bank premises	Limited	Not prohibited, but such investments are generally not made

(continued)

Appendix: Permissible Activities for Banking Organizations in Various Financial Centers (continued)

Switzerland	Unlimited	Unlimited through subsidiaries	Unlimited	Unlimited	Not prohibited, but such investments are generally not made
Thailand	Unlimited through subsidiaries	Unlimited through subsidiaries	Generally limited to holding bank premises	Permitted to hold up to 10% interest	Maximum equity interest limited to 5%
Ukraine	Not permitted	Not permitted	Permitted up to 10% of the bank's authorized capital	Permitted up to lesser of 10% of the bank's authorized capital or 15% of other firm's authorized capital	Commercial state enterprises are prohibited from such investment
United Kingdom	Unlimited, usually through subsidiaries	Unlimited through subsidiaries	Unlimited	Permitted subject to consultations with the Bank of England	No prohibitions contained in the Banking Act of 1987[g]
United States[h]	Limited, through affiliates	Generally not permitted	Generally limited to holding bank premises	Permitted to hold up to 5% of the voting shares through a holding company	Permitted to make noncontrolling investments up to 25% of the voting shares
Uruguay	Unlimited underwriting authority; dealing limited to public debt; brokerage and mutual funds not permitted	Not permitted	Not permitted	Not permitted	Not permitted

Source: Institute of International Bankers, *Global Survey*, 1994.

[a] Underwriting, dealing, and brokering all kinds of securities and all aspects of the mutual fund business.

[b] Underwriting and selling insurance as principal and as agent.

[c] Real estate investment, development, and management.

[d] Including investments through holding company structures.

[e] This information is effective January 1, 1994, the scheduled date for effectiveness of the Banking Act of 1993.

[f] The Second Banking Directive contains a broad list of securities and commercial banking activities that EC "credit institutions" (i.e., entities engaged in deposit-taking and lending) may conduct directly or through branches throughout the EC so long as their home countries authorize the activities. Subsidiaries of credit institutions governed by the law of the same member state may also conduct activities on the list throughout the EC, subject to conditions that include 90% ownership and a guarantee of commitments by the parent credit institutions. Insurance and real estate activities are not on the list and are therefore determined by home country and host country regulations.

[g] No statutory prohibition, but the Bank of England has indicated it would not favor controlling investments by industrial firms in major banks.

[h] In 1991 and 1992, the U.S. Department of Treasury proposed legislation to modernize the U.S. financial services industry. The proposal would have permitted banks to affiliate with securities firms and insurance companies within a financial services holding company, subject to restrictions on financial transactions among the affiliates. Commercial firms could also have invested in financial services holding companies subject to more stringent "firewalls" on transactions between commercial and financial companies.

15

Competitive Execution, Organization, and Management

In 1975 Alfred Brittain III became chairman and chief executive of Bankers Trust New York Corporation, then the seventh largest bank in the United States and the fifth largest in New York City. The bank was engaged at the time in trying to cope with serious loan delinquency problems, many related to real estate loans made in the early seventies that went wrong after the oil price rise in 1973, which sharply increased inflation and interest rates. Brittain and his colleagues continued to fight fires all the way through the seventies.

"There's got to be a better way," he must have said to himself one day. "The oil shock was bad enough, but it really destabilized our financial economy. It's true that Regulation Q has now come off, which has freed up interest-rate ceilings, but now we've got to pay for our deposits, which really eats into our lending profits. And not only that, we're now facing a technological revolution in retail banking with automatic teller machines, new consumer services, and enormously greater and more complex data-processing requirements."

So Brittain commissioned a strategic review.

In 1979 Bankers Trust was a 200-branch bank with total assets of $31 billion and capital of less than $1 billion. Like most banks at the time, loans accounted for 52 percent of assets, and deposits were 75 percent of liabilities. More than a third of the bank's deposits were noninterest bearing. Net interest income after loan loss provisions was about $500 million, more than twice noninterest income. The bank earned $114 million after taxes, a 12.6 percent return on capital.

Goals Come First

In the strategic review that followed, the Bankers Trust executives were asked to assess what they were good at and what they were not, and where they thought they wanted to be in the future. They concluded that they had good relationships with large corporate clients in the United States and abroad, a well-regarded portfolio management and securities custody group, and a state-of-the-art trading capability in government and municipal securities. They also concluded that the expected capital investment necessary to maintain even their fifth ranking position in New York retail banking was high, and the returns low. They were doubtful that even with appropriate levels of investment they would be able to increase their market share at the expense of their larger competitors.

"We're fifth now, but in a few years we may get pushed lower," one of the reviewers said. "Why not specialize instead in something we're good at: wholesale banking and securities trading."

"You mean get out of retail banking entirely, sell off our branches and everything, and put the money into wholesale?"

"Right, it's a radical idea—something nobody else has done, but it could work for us."

"Hang on a minute," Brittain himself interjected, "we can't go off half cocked on this. Before we try to decide whether or not to chop the business in half, we'd better be clear on what it is we are going to achieve by doing so. We need to define where it is we want to go—in economic and market share terms—and then see whether or not we can get there from here.

"But whatever we do it's got to make sense to the stockholders. If we are going to change, it ought to result in an increase in our return on investment, and ultimately our stock price."

The executives involved decided that a risk-adjusted return on investment of 20 percent would be possible in an all-wholesale regime, so that became one key goal. The key to achieving this goal was the risk adjustment and measuring systems, which had to be installed throughout the bank. There was no point in setting goals that couldn't be monitored closely.

Another goal, they decided, was to redeploy capital from weakening areas of the bank's business to stronger areas to avoid a deterioration in the bank's return on investment. A third was to gain the benefits of specialization, focus, and competitive intensity needed to become one of the top three New York City wholesale banks. The plan was presented as such to the board and approved. The details were sparse, but the move was made.

Understanding Comparative Advantage

Mr. Brittain and his colleagues understood that, in competitive terms, they suffered a probable comparative disadvantage in retail banking that it would be wise to avoid, and enjoyed some comparative advantages in foreign exchange and government bond trading, investing and processing, that should be exploited. Some areas, such as corporate finance, were competitively neutral, and these in time would have to be reinforced. By shedding the weak and emphasizing the strong points in the bank's competitive makeup, the bank was increasing its competitive leverage.

So Bankers Trust decided that it would redirect its business thrust to large corporations and governments, financial institutions, and wealthy individuals. The services it would offer were bank loans (which the bank would attempt to originate but not keep; it would sell participations in the loans to other banks), corporate financial advice and deal structuring, trading in securities and foreign exchange, and investment management and custodial services.

New capital was invested into the trading areas, then headed by Charles S. Sanford, Jr., who became president of the bank in 1983 and succeeded Brittain as chief executive in 1987. Among the initiatives the bank supported in this area was the handling of corporate commercial paper, which after a prolonged legal struggle was opened up to commercial banks in 1984. Later, when the Federal Reserve first entertained the possibility of Section 20 securities affiliates for banks, Bankers Trust was one of the first to apply for permission to create one.

Once committed to the change, the momentum built and various organizational changes were introduced to ensure that necessary internal infrastructure would be present to sustain an all-wholesale environment in which, increasingly, Bankers Trust's chief competitors would be J. P. Morgan and New York's largest and toughest investment banks. Decentralization and profit orientation came first. Titles were changed to deemphasize hierarchy, and a loose, partnership-type of management style was introduced. The duties of the former lending officers were changed—they became sales personnel for the bank's full range of products and services, for many of which substantial retraining was required. New investment bankinglike incentive compensation schemes were introduced to encourage individuals to generate profits that corresponded with corporate and departmental goals. All-around efforts were made to establish a more entrepreneurial spirit inside the bank to replace the somewhat stuffy and old-fashioned banking culture of the past. Existing employees were encouraged to accept the changes enthusiastically. Those who would not or could not do so were let go. New people, some with investment banking backgrounds, were brought in to shore up areas in which the bank was lacking skills. A major bankwide reorganization and management acclimation effort was put into effect to accompany the strategy shift. Inside the bank, the objective of the changes was understood to be "do it better, and smarter, with fewer but better-paid people."

But it still took about 10 years to effectuate the change.

The retail branches were not all sold until 1984. By this time the risk-adjusted return on investment had risen to over 16 percent, higher than any other major money center bank, but well short of the goal. However, in 1984 noninterest income had tripled since 1979 and was now equal to net interest income after loan loss provisions. Bank loans still accounted for about 50 percent of total assets, which were now over $45 billion, reflecting very little success in distributing rather than holding loans. Deposits, of which now only 18 percent were noninterest bearing, dropped to 58 percent of total liabilities. Without the branches, Bankers Trust had to purchase most of its lendable funds in the market.

In 1984, Alfred Brittain commented on the changes that were still occurring

> Bankers Trust will combine the on-balance-sheet capability and service breadth of a commercial bank with the intermediary skills and entrepreneurial spirit of an investment bank. We call that worldwide "merchant banking" . . . .[1]

During the eighties, Bankers Trust had to face several market-related problems: reserving more for third-world debt, most of which had been a legacy of the past; getting its fast-growing commitment to sophisticated trading activities under control (a substantial loss in trading foreign exchange options occurred in 1990); and coming to terms with financing LBOs and hostile takeovers, a field in which Bankers Trust became a market leader. The bank also needed to upgrade its technology systems to produce effective controls and efficient back-office operations, and to support fully competitive trading and corporate finance activities. Bankers Trust installed a highly cost-efficient, all-purpose, bankwide system than would not have been possible at a large multiple-purpose universal bank.

By the end of 1990, Charlie Sanford, the first major U.S. bank CEO to come from the trading end of the business, could safely say that at last the strategic conversion was complete. Total assets reached $63.6 billion, of which loans (after credit provisions) were just over 30 percent, an amount well less than the 45 percent of assets than were devoted to securities and trading inventories. Total deposits had dropped to less than half of all liabilities. Borrowing against trading inventories rose to $25 billion, more than 40 percent of liabilities. Total capital exceeded $3 billion, providing a tier 1 ratio of 5.4 percent and a total capital ratio of 10 percent. Net income was $665 million, and the banks return on capital was over 22 percent. At year end, its stock price was 141 percent of book value, a rare situation in American banking at the time when the average money center stock price to book value ratio was 83 percent. Like J. P. Morgan, Bankers Trust had emerged as a different kind of bank from the rest, specialists in wholesale banking.

Noninterest revenues for 1990 were $2.3 billion (75 percent of total revenue), about half of which was from trading securities and foreign exchange. Fees and commissions were $559 million (down from over $700 million the year before, in which Bankers Trust assisted in the RJR-Nabisco LBO financing), and fiduciary services and funds management revenues were $468 million. These amounts were comparable to the revenue components of many investment banks.

A Strategic Checklist

For most banks, strategy changes are small and infrequent. If a franchise is operating at nearly optimal value, radical changes are counterproductive. If, on the other hand, a franchise is operating way below optimal value, radical changes may be necessary to restore the franchise value or to prevent further deterioration. The banking industry, however, is regulated, conservative, and for the most part resistant to radical changes, even when these are necessary.

Bankers Trust's conversion was no doubt far more extensive than Mr. Brittain and his colleagues had in mind when the decision to give up retail banking was made. Bankers Trust's decision differs from some of the other major strategic adjustments that have occurred in the banking field in that it was entirely voluntary. What all banks that have been through such changes, voluntarily or otherwise, have learned is that a lot of organizational change is necessary to effect even modest strategic changes. This is no doubt why so few strategic changes are attempted. Everyone knows that large organizational changes are difficult to go through and often don't seem to work. A strategy change requires a top-to-bottom shake-up that must be applied over a sustained period before it can work. During this period, which may stretch out for years, there will be numerous opportunities for backsliding—times when leaders are tempted to take the heat off in exchange for a little peace and quiet—but there can be no backsliding if the transformation is to "take."

Bankers Trust started in the right place, with a review of its goals. It thought about a lot of things, and applied reality checks to its thinking on several occasions, but only one explicit goal was changed, the level of return on investment. To achieve the higher return, however, the bank would have to increase profitability at a time of high competitiveness and market changes in its basic business that appeared to reduce profits, not increase them. To meet the goal, something different would have to be done. That something different would have to emphasize Bankers Trust's comparative advantages (of which there were then only a few), and avoid its disadvantages. The bank would need new skills too, and a climate would have to be established in which new talent could be attracted and retained. New, implicit goals would develop once the new direction had been chosen, such as to increase trading and market-making, to be innovative in corporate finance, and to learn how to market ideas better—to become "real" investment bankers.

At this stage, Bankers Trust had to make another choice. What sort of role did it want to play in the market? It is very difficult to fix a strategy until the role that goes with it is clarified. For example, did Bankers Trust aspire to be a *world-class player* in global financial circles? Or was it content to be only a *major national player,* that is, a prominent U.S. financial services firm like the larger regional banks, or maybe an investment bank like Dillon Read? Other alternatives included seeking out a highly profitable *niche player* position, like Brown Brothers Harriman or maybe KKR. Failing all of these, the bank might consider becoming a merger candidate. Each of these roles was a viable one that Bankers Trust could have selected. As it was, it chose to be a major national player with substantial world-class ambitions.

Having addressed these issues, the toughest one must be faced. Do we have the money, the time, and the grit to implement the strategy changes we are contemplating in such a way that we can be sure of producing something better at the end of the process than that which we are giving up? Reorganizations are expensive: new investments have to be made, job termination settlement payments paid, and new talent acquired. Some mistakes might have to be paid for too.

Strategy changes also take time. Even a patently successful transformation, such as Bankers Trust's, took 10 years. Perhaps no changes of comparable magnitude can be completed in less time—the organization has to be remolded and then hardened. Compensation and promotion policies have to be established, sometimes on a trial-and-error basis; new people have to be hired and trained; new leaders selected; and role models have to emerge. These things take a while when you are rebuilding a business. If the time factor is difficult to meet, then maybe you are better off selling the business to another compatible firm.

These are all issues of implementation. The best of strategies will fail if the implementation is not effective.

Doing It Right

During the summer of 1989, the management board of a large continental European universal bank met to consider the bank's future in the light of new regulatory and competitive conditions that were being introduced around the world. The bank was very secure in its home country, where banking spreads were high, competition light, and the bank's market share large. The home country market was not growing, however, and as competition from foreign banks and nonbanks increased, the board expected a gradual decline in domestic profits, which comprised considerably more than 50 percent of the bank's consolidated net income.

The profitability of the bank's international business was much lower than for the domestic business, and in recent years it had deteriorated to practically nothing after all additions to loan loss reserves had been accounted for. The bank operated wholesale and securities businesses in New York, London, and Tokyo and a very successful private banking business in these and several other cities around the world. In New York the bank had a grandfathered license to participate in investment banking that pre-dated the International Banking Act of 1978. In London it was active in the Euromarkets and had acquired a small brokerage firm in the run up before Big Bang. This firm had nearly failed, and had to be assisted with a substantial capital infusion soon after negotiated commissions came into effect. In Tokyo the bank controlled a Hong Kong-based joint venture that had acquired a seat on the Tokyo Stock Exchange, though it did not yet make any money.

The chairman was concerned about the changing environment. "At present, we are one of the 20 or so top banks in the world," he said to the others, "but this may not be so in 10 or 20 years. Our domestic growth opportunities are limited, overseas competitors are being introduced to all of our clients because of the new deregulation, but (except for private banking) we are not making comparable progress abroad where we are neither growing nor advancing strongly anywhere. We need to redefine our corporate mission, our goals, and our strategy."

The group studied these matters and restated the bank's mission, its goals, and its objectives. It was no longer to be mainly a prominent na-tional entity, its mission was now defined in global terms. Its goals were to maintain its status as one of the world's most prestigious and profitable banks. Its objectives were to shore up its international operations over the next 10 years so these too would be among the world's most prestigious and profitable when the year 2000 was reached. The plan was to treat Europe with the highest priority, the United States, next, and only then to deal with Japan and the rest of the Far East.

Problems of Implementation

The word went out. Build up the international business, especially the in-vestment banking part. In Europe there were only a few acquisition possi-bilities, mostly second-tier English merchant banks, and the bank was leery of these after its experience with the English broker. There were some stra-tegic alliances with other European banks to consider also, but these mainly offered linkages to some other large, domestic-oriented retail bank and were not of much use in developing investment banking. There was also the possibility of hiring stars away from some of the Anglo-Saxon firms, but the bank had never done this before and feared that language and cultural difficulties would negate much of the value in hiring leaders from outside.

Meanwhile, some of the senior wholesale lending officers were getting into the act. One wanted to buy a medium-sized commercial bank in Bel-gium, another to lead a large underwriting for a questionable client in France. Disputes were carried to the top, where the chairman felt it was better to get everybody into the act with as much enthusiasm as possible, so all these proposals were approved, though few were successful. The idea seemed to be forming that it was too difficult to achieve rapid growth

through internal expansion because of overlapping and conflicting authority and a traditional aversion to risky transactions, so expansion would
have to depend on business brought in through acquisitions.

Large acquisitions, however, were not likely to be approved, regardless
of the changed mission of the bank, because they involved too great a risk
of losing control of operations to executives from the acquired entity, and
because if anything ever went wrong in a large acquisition it could affect
the bank's high-grade bond rating and its stock price.

"Look what happened to Credit Suisse when First Boston got in trouble, or to Midland Bank when it acquired Crocker National Bank in the
early eighties," some of the board members could be counted on to say.
"The results were disastrous—large acquisitions are out, but you can
probably get small to medium-sized deals through the board without too
much trouble."

Meanwhile, in the United States, a young American MBA working for
the grandfathered investment banking arm of the bank had an idea that
could really put the bank on the map in the states and would make a lot
of money too. The idea was for the bank to specialize in raising equity
capital for American (and other) banks. Most banks needed new equity,
and would for years. Raising bank equity capital clearly was a growth
industry. It could be raised by selling new common stock or various kinds
of ingenious convertible securities or subordinated debt that counted as
tier-2 equity capital under the Basel accords. It could also be raised
through mergers or by selling assets in various ways to capture unrealized
gains, and retiring debt with the proceeds. A full menu of highly profitable
investment banking activities, in the United States and overseas, could be
devoted just to raising equity for banks.

"The problem is," said a colleague, "we don't know much about bank
equities, and many of them are pretty sick. We don't trade them or have
any capability to distribute them (especially in the United States). Nor are
we particularly competent in mergers or real estate deals or securitization."

"True," the MBA replied, "but those are things we can learn or hire
people to do for us. But we've got three things going for us that the big
American investment banks don't. First, we have terrific access to the top
level of these banks, thanks to years of dealing with them as correspondents and in the interbank market. Second, we know banks and bank credits; we ought to be able to spot the sick ones early and avoid them. Third,
we've got the bank's securities portfolios in Europe."

"They'll never let you within 10 miles of those portfolios, they're not
about to let them become dumping grounds for American mistakes."

"Look," continued the MBA. "I know the portfolios are sacred, but
they have made risky investments before. If the top guys over there say
'this is something we're going to do,' then the rest will do it.

"Say we set it up as a big in-house mutual fund to invest only in bank
stocks. Only banks that had been prescreened would be accepted. The

portfolio managers could invest their clients' money in a well-diversified single-industry play at a time when bank stocks are cheap. It would be voluntary, of course, and ultimately make a lot of money for them.

"Then we go around to the top people at Citibank, Chase, whatever. Those on our list. And we tell them what we trying to do. 'We want to buy a lot of your stock,' we say, 'in order to sell it in Europe.' We tell them that we are prepared to underwrite up to, say, $100 million of a domestic U.S. equity issue for them, providing that we get to be a lead manager of the deal. A few deals like that, and the phone will be jumping off the wall, we'll shoot up in the league tables, and people will start to take us seriously. Of course, we don't have to take down the full $100 million each time, we can either distribute it ourselves (in the United States and Europe), pass it on to the syndicate, or just sit on it for a while, if we have to. We'll only have to worry about it though the first few deals."

"Man, that's pretty wild. Have you talked to London about it?" London was the headquarters for the bank's international investment banking activity; the MBA's unit reported to London.

"They were pretty cool toward the idea. They said they didn't have much distribution capability either, and that they doubted the head office would go for it and weren't sure they wanted to push it. Also, they pointed out that at present they are invited into the international tranche of most U.S. bank deals, which are modestly profitable. The idea might irritate the American syndicate managers, they said, and cause them to cut us off. They worry about losing some piddly little syndicate business, even though over here we would be working on large, very profitable deals. And, they told me I had to see what the branch thinks." This was the New York branch of the commercial banking arm, which has a large lending portfolio in the United States, and is responsible for most of the relationships with the major banks.

"Did you talk to the branch?"

"Yeah, but they have a real not-invented-here problem. No idea of ours for how we can make a lot of money off their clients is going to appeal to them very much. They want to make absolutely sure we can deliver before we can even talk to any of 'their' banks, and their people always have to be present whenever there is to be a discussion with one of them.

"Unless I can get all this worked out, London won't raise the issue with the head office. However, London did say that the head office might buy it if we said we would restrict ourselves to banks with double-A bond ratings; but there are only a handful of them and they're the ones that don't need new equity."

"A nonstarter, heh?"

"No wonder none of the big European banks, despite their exemption from Glass–Steagall, has ever amounted to anything in the U.S. investment banking market!"

How Bankers Trust Would Have Done It

The European bank did not realize it was instituting a major strategy change when it "clarified its mission and objectives," and it made very few organizational changes to accompany it. If few changes are made, nothing really changes—it's the people involved and their motivation to take on a new task that drives change inside an institution.

Put in C-A-P matrix terms (chapter 13), the plan to focus on bank equities meant moving along all three axes. A new emphasis on marketing to banking clients would be needed; the targets initially would be U.S. banks, but plenty of other banks needed equity too. Ultimately the capability to handle a new product, equities, would have to be developed, probably in cooperation with the head office portfolio managers. Like most new capital market products, it would extend globally. Many new responsibilities would be involved with so many changes in the matrix; leadership and authority questions would clearly arise and need to be resolved before internal warfare broke out that would certainly kill the idea.

The bank did not recognize that the new product idea was being developed right on the seam between the wholesale banking and capital markets businesses—between the old-style relationship-oriented banking business, and the new style of capital market innovation backed up by aggressive pricing and position taking. One of these must have the final responsibility to lead the effort to develop the new activity.

Bankers Trust, already oriented toward the new style of capital market activity, would have previously appointed a head of Capital Market Services and let this person confirm or replace subordinate heads of corporate finance and trading as necessary. There would also be a head of American Capital Markets, who would report to the Capital Markets head. The young MBA's new idea would have to be championed first by the capital markets units, whose leaders would understand and share the importance of the bank's overall strategic goals and the urgency for realizing them. These leaders would be compensated on the basis of goal realization and they would evaluate, promote, and compensate their subordinates accordingly. Those who didn't like the new system would be gracefully retired. Investment banking in Europe would be centralized, and regional and national marketing and the capability to handle indigenous deals in particular countries would be developed. Under such an arrangement, disagreement over issues is not eliminated, but it is reduced and settled among like-minded executives.

In the case involving the bank equities proposal, Bankers Trust would have congratulated the young MBA on his idea and helped him explore it at all the right levels. When the heads of American and European Capital Markets got wind of it, they would see whether it fit in with other plans then in the works, and if it did, they would get hold of the heads of the private banking and portfolio management units and work it out together. If they couldn't do so, the matter would be referred to the bank's chief executive, who would decide the issue, and, if it was approved, would make someone accountable for the results.

Bankers Trust would have known that major strategy changes are fairly uncommon. They may happen only once or twice over an employee's whole career. So they are important when they do happen, and require commitment to the changes at all levels to make them work. Sometimes the only way this can be done is to replace executives who do not exhibit the commitment expected of them. Bankers Trust's attitude toward management changes is no doubt much more freewheeling and opportunistic than that of most European banks.

Bankers Trust would also have savored the opportunity to create a specialization in a potentially profitable sector of the capital markets where, if it moved swiftly and aggressively, the bank might secure a significant market share. If it worked, great. If it didn't, the idea could be abandoned with relatively little damage—at minimum, the bank would have learned something.

The Bankers Trust of old would not have acted like this. Bankers Trust has changed, it is an entirely different organization from the one Mr. Brittain was elected to head. But the changes did not result from access to great supplies of capital, or from new customers and markets acquired through acquisitions, or from some technological innovation. They occurred because the bank wanted to change itself, and before that could happen the people who worked there had to be changed: They had to be inspired, retrained, motivated, and compensated differently, and in some cases, replaced. But if the people are not changed not much else will be.

Measuring Success

Bankers Trust almost unquestionably has been successful in changing its strategy and in forming the culture needed to implement the new strategy effectively. Relative to other U.S. money-center banks, Bankers Trust has excelled in terms of profitability, creditworthiness, and stock price appreciation. Relative to these other banks, Bankers Trust has increased its standing, reputation, and influence. By the reckoning of most knowledgeable observers, as of the end of 1991, more than a decade after the strategy shift was adopted, Bankers Trust was the third most important wholesale banking organization in the United States, behind J. P. Morgan and Citibank.

The sea-change at Bankers Trust and its implementation over a period of perhaps a decade and a half, based on what top management considered to be fundamental shifts in global financial market realities, certainly had large embedded risks. Probably the most important of these involved the possibility of periodic tough times in highly volatile financial markets—an issue that Bankers Trust expected to address for itself and for its clients by means of superior approaches to financial risk management. But management itself incorporates "model risk," that is, quantitative trading and hedging approaches built on historical data might be difficult to implement, to understand on the part of senior management, and to explain fully to clients. It also required enormous trading activities in far-flung financial centers that could go wrong in difficult markets, the most sophisticated risk management techniques notwithstanding. The quality of earnings, in other words, could well deteriorate as volatile earnings streams replaced more stable ones, and this could be penalized by financial markets in terms of the firm's debt ratings and in terms of its stock price—both representing penalties with respect to its cost of capital.

The Bankers Trust share price during it strategic repositioning and implementation (1979–94) is depicted in Figure 15-1, along with those of J. P. Morgan (with a roughly similar strategy) and Citicorp (with a very different strategy), as well as the indexes for all U.S. banks and the Standard & Poor's 500 stock price index. Figure 15-2 shows how both Bankers Trust and J. P. Morgan performed against cohort banks during the more recent 1988–94 period. Note that both Bankers Trust and Morgan outperformed Citicorp and all other U.S. bank shares during the second half of the period, but this was reversed in the difficult trading conditions of 1994. Meanwhile, Citicorp seriously underperformed until 1991, while

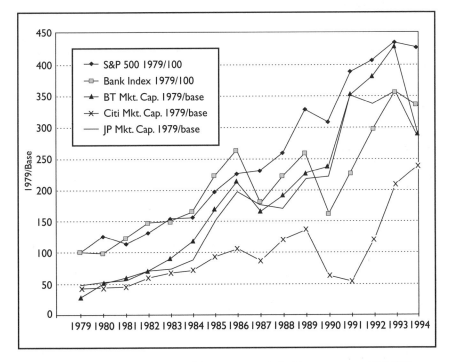

Figure 15-1. Bankers Trust versus Citicorp versus J. P. Morgan versus S&P 500 versus Bank index.

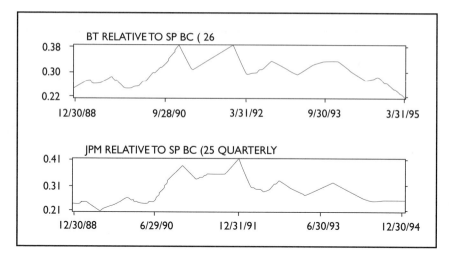

Figure 15-2. Performance of Bankers Trust Company and J. P. Morgan against the Standard & Poor's wholesale banking industry average. Data: Goldman Sachs & Co., Research Portable.

it was digesting loan losses that nearly proved fatal, but it surged once the crisis was over and the 1994 market difficulties were masked by its heavy retain emphasis. Against cohort, both Morgan and Bankers Trust performed well during most of 1988–94, but both were back where they started at the end of the period. Note also that a buy-and-hold investor would have done best of all by simply buying the S&P 500 index.

But is that the right measure to apply?

Size and the League Tables

For years, the publication of annual rankings of commercial banks by size (total assets, profits, etc.) has been an important ritual, even though not many changes were reported on a year-to-year basis within any single banking market. However, when the rankings were compiled on a global basis, the annual rankings changed considerably. The principal reason for this change was different exchange rates, rates at which bank assets from other countries were converted into dollars. As the dollar weakened after 1985, U.S. banks slid down the list. Another reason for change was the rise of Japanese banks during the eighties, when their total assets increased at double-digit rates of growth for several years. Thus by the end of 1990, 7 of the 10 largest banks in the world, ranked by assets, were Japanese.

As we have seen, not all of the asset increases of banks were to support wholesale transactions: many went to finance consumer borrowing and stock-market and real estate purchases. Assets size also says nothing about the profitability or soundness of a bank, other than reminding us that the bank may enjoy some economies of scale and be considered too big to fail by regulators at home. By itself, asset size is more a measure of stability and customer relationships than of competitiveness, particularly on an international scale.

In the early days of the Eurobond market, bankers soon found that their deals were being watched closely and reported on by an eager financial press. The press, in the form of weekly newsletters and magazines devoted to the international financial community (e.g., *Euromoney*), began to keep score of who did the most deals and then to publish the results for all to see. One banker compared the process with the weekly publication in the London newspapers of the standings of various teams in the U.K. professional soccer league. These tables, which now cover many categories of financial market activity, are referred to everywhere as "the league tables." Most bankers hate them; they reveal the strengths of a few and the weaknesses of hundreds of others.

In the beginning, the tables showed only the rankings in Eurobond new issues. They were similar to tables published by *Investment Dealers Digest* in New York, but they included only Eurobonds. Even though a firm might be making millions in secondary market trading, brokerage of U.S. shares to European investors, arranging of cross-border mergers, or stock issues, it would get credit in the tables only for Eurobonds. Later, foreign bonds were added; together these two make up "international bonds." Most professionals knew the tables were not useful predictors of a firm's overall profitability or success in penetrating foreign markets, or in developing future business potential, but those who read them (clients and head office superiors) believed that they were good indications of international market prowess and influence.

Because so many people believed this, the tables were the reason for many otherwise foolish competitive moves taken by firms trying to increase their ranking. In the Euromarkets, there are moments from time to time when a bank will decide to increase its market share and visibility by moving up in the Eurobond tables. Such occasions are usually marked by a flurry of mispriced deals that the ambitious bank has bought from issuers on a basis in which it must subsidize the mispricing in order to accumulate market share. After a few issues, internal accountants tally up the losses and stop the process. Euromarket observers also have come to understand that league tables are not especially meaningful during times when great distortions exist, such as when the Japanese issue corporate bonds in the Euromarket to avoid restrictions in the Japanese bond market and then sell the bonds back to Japanese institutional investors. Such round-tripping can hardly be viewed as a measure of international competitiveness on the part of the Japanese underwriters that lead these issues, but nonetheless the league tables display Nomura and the others very prominently.

In time, the tables were broadened to include ranks in more categories—international equities, mergers and acquisitions, medium-tern notes, and bank loans arranged. Shifting positions over a period of time give indications of changing competitive capabilities.

The various league table rankings, together with the data describing the volume of financing in each category, have enabled the competitive dynamics of the world's first totally unregulated, wholesale financial marketplace to be analyzed scrupulously by academics, journalists, and market competitors alike. Academics have pointed out that statistical measures of change among market leaders show the Euromarket environment to be about twice as volatile for participating firms as the domestic U.S. capital market. Journalists make headlines out of changes in market positions and glamorize some of the leading figures behind the changes. The firms themselves are constantly in the process of rearranging the data so as to show themselves in the best light possible when marketing their services to prospective clients.

If what we are looking for, however, is a rough measure of market influence and competitive ability of firms across a range of related wholesale services, we need to consider rankings in several different events. For example, by adding together the total volume of reported transactions led by different banks for comparable clients during the same time period it is possible to judge the relative order of market penetration that each firm has developed, both in its home market and in the international market, and the competitive distance that exists between players. In this sense, a consolidated approach to league table measures, that is, one involving several different categories for which tables exist, may actually give a better idea of the aggregate competitive power that firms, and types of firms, have put together over the years.

This approach seeks to assess the extent of penetration of the market for wholesale financial services of a variety of banks and investment banks. For this purpose we can assume that other services offered to different customers, for example retail banking services and asset management, can be set aside. The same sort of analysis, however, also could be performed for these service sectors, which no doubt would also show a significant degree of market penetration by nonbanking competitors.

Indeed, to focus the analysis we can revert to the C-A-P model and identify a common set of clients (governments and corporations), a common set of products (capital raising and corporate finance), and a common arena (by country, or by global data). This process can be limited by the need to select the most actively utilized wholesale services where individual bank participation can be clearly seen. League tables, for example, are not published for the annual volume of government securities or commercial paper distributed by individual firms (most issuers select several dealers to whom they auction off their securities at regular intervals). Equally, rankings are not prepared for domestic securities markets in all countries. The rankings, too, are not reliable predictors of profitability, since different profit margins apply to different services. Accordingly, not all firms seek to maximize their activity in certain services, and in effect, drop out of some.

Rankings do not exist for the volume of secondary market trading in various different securities markets. At a time when trading has become an extremely important segment for all banks and investment banks it is perhaps regrettable to be without reliable league tables for trading activity. However, trading is essentially an underlying activity that permits firms to become competitive in the primary markets (i.e., for new issues). Success in primary markets now has to presume success in secondary markets, where if carried out well, such success will also contribute significantly to a firm's overall profitability. In the long run, market leaders tend to be involved in most services that are important to their clients and develop what capabilities are necessary to be effective in offering these services. Also, they are usually among the most profitable firms in the industry. The consolidated approach is a search for market leaders and world-class players with the greatest impact on the market. Multiple indexing efforts using the best data available, give better information about competitive capabilities than do single indexed data.

Scoring in the Consolidated League Table Competition

Wholesale banking is no longer defined as the business commercial banks do with corporations and governments. It has become integrated with investment banking as large segments of once-captive banking business has migrated through securitization processes into the securities market, a market controlled by investment banks, not commercial banks. How, therefore, does Bankers Trust look when compared with its new competitors?

Table 15-1 presents league-table data for 1995 for several wholesale and investment banking services, which record on a "full credit to lead manager" basis whenever possible.[2] J. P. Morgan, was responsible for about $259 billion in transactions, Chemical Bank and Chase Manhattan combined had $284 billion, and Citicorp $138 billion. Bank loans accounted for most of the volume for both Chemical Bank and Citicorp.

Merrill Lynch, however, with $173 billion in U.S. and international underwriting in 1995, $209 billion of medium-term notes underwritten, and $35 billion in global M&A transactions, led a total of $419 billion of global wholesale financing transactions. Bankers Trust did not appear on the top 20 list in 1995 or in 1994.

On this basis, U.S. investment banks captured six of the top 20 firms rankings—and in turn represented approximately 39 percent of total market volume. Five U.S. commercial banks were included among the top 20 firms accounting for a total of 21 percent of the top 20 volume.

If the rankings are recast to include totals for all global suppliers of wholesale financing services, CS/First Boston would appear in second place with $291 billion, followed by SBC Warburg (eleventh) with $80 billion,

Table 15-1 Global Wholesale Banking and Investment Banking 1995, Full Credit to Lead Managers Only ($ billions)

Firm	Global Debt & Equity Securities Underwriting & Placement[a]	Global M&A Advisory[b]	Int'l Loans Arranged[c]	Medium Term Notes Lead Managed[d]	Total	% of Industry Total
Merrill Lynch	173.43	34.76	2.00	208.80	418.99	10.8
CS/First Boston	109.58	66.22	45.90	69.00	290.70	7.5
Chemical/Chase	11.30	—	272.40	—	283.70	7.3
JP Morgan	76.32	53.72	128.60	—	258.64	6.7
Morgan Stanley	104.52	113.77	—	18.00	236.29	6.1
Goldman Sachs	96.44	83.64	2.00	39.06	221.14	5.7
Lehman Brothers	91.15	46.17	—	55.00	192.32	5.0
Salomon Brothers	82.28	39.34	—	21.40	143.91	3.7
Citicorp	10.70	—	116.50	10.30	137.50	3.6
Bear Stearns	38.31	47.81	—	31.50	117.62	3.0
SBC Warburg	36.75	31.50	11.30	—	79.55	2.1
Deutsche MG	23.87	21.35	20.40	12.50	78.12	2.0
UBS	30.06	15.81	31.10	—	76.97	2.0
Lazard Houses	—	75.45	—	—	75.45	2.0
NationsBank	18.40	—	38.90	13.00	70.30	1.8
Smith Barney	29.33	25.75	—	5.96	61.04	1.6
ABN/Amro	20.94	—	23.10	7.50	51.54	1.3
Bank of America	7.00	—	42.20	—	49.20	1.3
Nomura	48.32	—	—	—	48.32	1.2
DLJ	32.26	14.83	—	—	47.09	1.2
Total Industry	1535.1	575.80	1098.40	656.70	3866.00	100.0
Top 10% as % of Total	51.72%	84.31%	51.66%	68.99%	59.49%	59.49
Top 20 as % of Total	67.81%	116.38%	66.86%	74.92%	75.98%	75.98

[a] Global rankings, top 25, completed deals only, including all U.S. private placements. Securities Data Corp.
[b] By market value of completed global transactions, full credit to both advisors, top 25 advisors; Securities Data Corp.
[c] Full credit to book manager, top 25 managers as reported, *IFR International Financing Review*, Jan. 20, 1996.
[d] Global MTNs, top 25 managers, Securities Data Corp.

Deutsche Bank (twelfth place) with $78 billion, UBS (thirteenth place) with $77 billion, and ABN/Amro (seventeenth place) with $52 billion. In other recent years, non-U.S. firms have enjoyed somewhat higher standing in the tables. Of the global top 20 in 1995, 14 (excluding CS First Boston, now owned by Crédit Suisse) were American (of which 9 were investment banks), 5 were European universal banks, and 1 was Japanese.

The top 10 firms, as they have since 1990, comprised over 50 percent of the total composite volume. The top 20 composite volume of transactions in 1990 was 14 times greater than what it was in 1980, reflecting an exceptionally high annual compound growth rate of 30 percent. The volume in 1994 was twice that of 1990. During this period, underwriting of international bonds and equities, medium-term notes, and mergers and acquistions all developed considerably, and bank loans became less important. Also during the period, CS First Boston and First Boston Corporation became subsidiaries of Crédit Suisse, Deutsche Bank acquired Morgan Grenfell and moved its capital market headquarters to London, Barclays Bank acquired Barclays deZoute Wedd, Kidder Peabody was substantially acquired by PaineWebber, Bankers Trust and J. P. Morgan transformed themselves into investment banking-type organizations, and Nomura and Daiwa Securities appeared as a financial powerhouse in Europe as a result of Japanese round-trip issues.

The composite international table shows that a bank's asset size is not essential to effective competition. Some sort of minimum size is understood, of course, but otherwise there is no correlation between the largest banks in the world and competitive performance. None of the seven banks with total assets greater than those of the Deutsche Bank was included among the top 20. Only 5 of the world's 30 largest banks by assets at the end of 1994 were included in the top 20 composite rankings.

They also show that as a bank moves across its domestic borders into the international world beyond, it lays down the power it has that is based entirely on its domestic relationships. Across borders, banking business is done very differently, especially for large European universal banks. It is more competitive; good prices and new ideas matter. In this kind of environment, the Anglo-Saxon investment banking firms seem to have had an advantage over their larger, more traditional, slower-moving rivals. Among these several, including Merrill Lynch, Goldman Sachs, CS First Boston, J. P. Morgan, and Salomon Brothers, have made significant penetration into foreign markets for wholesale banking services, especially in the areas of mergers and acquisitions and Eurobonds and equity securities.

But so far, none of the investment banks or the large European universals has yet carved out a share of market outside its own country that it enjoys within it. And even such modest shares as these tend to be are only obtained at great expense and effort over many years. Accordingly, many potential competitors prefer to stay at home, or to reduce their commitments abroad. Only those with the strongest domestic positions, who are also bold and confident, make big plans for international business. Today these firms make up a small cohort indeed. Ten or so American firms, two or three British, three Swiss, two or three French, one German universal bank, and one or two Japanese.

An Era of Great Changes

The major changes in the financial marketplaces, and in the competitive dynamics of banking that began in the eighties, are continuing. The economic philosophy of the governments of the OECD (and many other) countries are committed to securing the blessings of economic growth that can only come from the maximum sensible exposure to free-market capitalism. No one is forecasting any significant degree of backsliding on this commitment, though European and Japanese governments have a history of weighing in on competitive issues so as to support their own teams. Deregulation and integration have been allowed to progress and have released and focused powerful market forces that have improved capital market efficiency all around the world. The deregulation has fostered a convergence of financial regulatory practices around the world, which has resulted in greater market access by nonbanking and foreign firms in the United States, Europe, and Japan. This has increased competition for market share, both because fixed commissions and distribution structures have been eliminated and because new players have been allowed into formerly restricted national markets. The basis of competition in many parts of the world has moved away from historical, single relationships toward multiple relationships based on performance. Thus the markets have been full of innovation, and aggressive market-making on the part of those seeking to improve their position or to protect existing relationships. One of these innovations, which has been extremely successful in the United States over a period of less than a decade, is securitization of assets formerly held on the balance sheets of banks and insurance companies. Thus, in the United States at least, a large part of traditional wholesale banking activity is moving off of the balance sheets of large commercial banks into securities markets.

This movement is partly the result of a widening gap between bank lending rates and the market rates for these assets that are otherwise available. Though market rates are often competitive with the rates quoted by the banks with the best credit ratings, many American banks have so deteriorated in terms of credit quality that their own cost of funds has become too high to offer competitive rates on high-grade assets. American banks have suffered considerable credit quality erosion from losses on loans to third-world borrowers, real estate developers, and highly leveraged corporations. The American and European banks suffered their wave of credit losses early in the cycle; Japanese banks are now beginning to catch up with them in terms of credit exposure problems.

It is likely that these conditions will continue for several years in Eu-

rope and Japan, and the pressure provided by attractive market alternatives to bank lending will accelerate during the nineties. Events such as the
completion of the single-market efforts in Europe, the integration of Eastern Europe with the West, and the reconstitution of the Japanese markets
after its Big Bang sometime during the nineties, will assist the process.
These are all big events and they will make big differences to the players.
Strategies will be revised, new approaches taken, mergers made, and firms
restructured. Many firms will feel that it is too difficult and costly to attempt to become a fully equipped world-class player. A large number of
firms from around the world will review the pros and cons of settling
instead for a major national leaguer position, and be happy with it. Others
may decide to become a specialized entity of some other world-class player
by selling out. Some, of course, will stick it out, seeking to become one of
a dozen or so global banking champions.

Adapting to Change

Adaptation is the key to survival. It is the essential requirement for all of
the players who aspire to world-class roles in the year 2000 and beyond.
Adaptation presumes that there is a prototype firm that is ideal for the
wholesale financial markets of the future and that most of the players are
not yet there. Such a prototype would be a relatively lean, tightly managed
but nonhierarchical securities- and trading-oriented entity, with global relationships and marketing capabilities, adequate capital, and large numbers of talented, specialized personnel in place who are capable of making
attractive profits as a result of both innovation and quick reaction, and
who can train and develop others in their place. Such firms will have to
be able to develop a high tolerance for risk (and ability to manage it), but
also a deep commitment to serving clients before they serve themselves.

All firms will have to adapt, though some more than others. Some will
benefit from starting positions that are advantageous, that is, being "almost there" (CS First Boston, Goldman Sachs, SBC Warburg), or possessing an existing market franchise that is almost as difficult to destroy as
it is to duplicate (Deutsche Bank, J. P. Morgan, IBJ). Management, cultural, and financial bottlenecks will confront many firms, and their adaptations will be slowed or in some cases prevented by them.

It is arguable that those adapting first will have a comparative advantage over the others. These firms will be able to offer the most up-to-date,
responsive, comprehensible, and useful (i.e., the most competitive) services, engaging capital markets from all over the world. These firms will
have the latest ideas for sale and will benefit the users of their services the
most. Such firms should attract more clients and business than the others.
The difference may be between getting in to the highly concentrated, top-
20 elite circle of competitors or in being outside the circle. The top 20
firms account for more than 70 percent of the total revenues for global
wholesale banking services. Within the circle itself, the top five firms in

1995 accounted for market shares six times greater than the shares of the bottom five firms. Those outside the circle end up with very small market shares.

Adapting to such an ideal firm prototype becomes a function of how far where you want to go is from where you start, and how rapidly you want to make the trip. Generally how fast you want to change is related to how much change you have to make and the quality of the leadership on hand to manage the change.

Those with the greatest changes to make may be the Japanese banks. Little in their backgrounds have prepared them for the securities business or for open, performance-oriented relationships. Their home markets have not imparted much competitive strength to them that is useful abroad. They suffer from language and cultural problems more than similar European banks. Their experience as lenders may cause them to overprice financings to obtain business, but then lose money on it. Senior management in Tokyo, distracted by a rapidly changing, almost dangerous domestic banking environment, and many important regulatory changes on the way, may be unable or unwilling to learn the new requirements for international wholesale success, and therefore block or interfere with it. Any major deal failures during the transition period, if combined with other unhappy news at the time, may result in the de facto closing down of their wholesale business abroad, which in turn may adversely affect the banks' relationships with their major domestic wholesale clients. The merger of Bank of Tokyo and Mitsubishi Bank in 1995 to form the world's largest commercial bank may be indicative of Japanese thinking as to what drives domestic competition but is unlikely to accomplish much in the highly performance-oriented global capital markets.

Japanese securities firms should have a somewhat easier time than the banks, because after all they understand the securities market environment, if not always markets abroad. However, since they share most of the other characteristics applicable to Japanese banks, they too will find it difficult to make such a large adaptation, not to mention making it quickly.

Large European universal banks are next on the list of decreasing levels of difficulty in adapting to the new prototype required for the future. The universals have several advantages as global competitors—they already know the securities business, especially the trading end; they manage money themselves and therefore have substantial placing power at their disposal; and being European, they have become comfortable with the language and cultural differences in at least two of the three global markets. The universal banks, however, are stable, relationship-oriented, loan-making organizations with a majority of their earnings coming from domestic business. Such a structure is quite different from the structure to which it must adapt. The banks' boards of directors, mainly populated with people who are from the old structure, not the new, are very likely to see no need for change at all. But already, these directors, many of whom are involved with domestic business and do not themselves have much familiarity with the changing international environment, are finding it difficult to understand or approve risk exposures, reaction times, and profitability consequences of decisions that it must make to be competitive in the investment banking aspects. Indeed, many have had disastrous experiences from investing too aggressively abroad. The boards of universal banks are not the most eager to see changes made that involve heavy exposure to unfamiliar risks or radically different operating methods from what they are used to. In some cases, however, this has changed drastically.

The German universal banks, with the important exception of Deutsche Bank, which acquired Morgan Grenfell to help with international acquisitions and money management, have not yet adapted very much. The Germans have been especially focused on bringing the Eastern part of the country under control and in sorting out their ongoing problems in Poland, Hungary, the former Czechoslovakia, and the former Soviet Union. The Germans also feel that their traditional wholesale business in Germany may be changing. It is not changing very quickly, however, and therefore the bank has time to watch how things develop before adjusting its internal structure.

Most other European universal banks have comparatively little securities market expertise, a full panoply of structural obstacles to adaptation, and in many cases industrial portfolios of their own which they manage. Some banques d'affaires, like Paribas, have already adopted an investment banking-type of culture, and are quite adaptable. But most of the others do not appear willing or capable of undergoing any sort of drastic change unless such should be seen to be vitally necessary. Many of these sorts of banks prefer instead to replace adaptation with some kind of strategic alliance with similar types of banks in other countries. Exceptions include the Crédit Suisse Group, which is already a major global player, and SBC Warburg, which has achieved that status in derivatives and fund management. Union Bank of Switzerland, Internationale Niederlanden Grop, and Santander of Spain are among those not far behind.

The preceding also applies to British banks, which have already adapted considerably to the new requirements for successful wholesale banking in Europe. National Westminster, through its subsidiary NatWest Markets, is endeavoring to keep up with Barclays, but it has not been easy. Other large British banks, like Lloyds and Midland, have either abandoned their intentions to compete in the international wholesale banking business or have yet to take it seriously. Most of the merchant banks appear content to make their living inside the United Kingdom and selective overseas markets and have essentially opted for a niche-playing role.

This leaves the Americans, which have been prominent in their presence in the top 20 composite rankings since 1990. The large commercial banks, though somewhat active on the international scene, are fading and being replaced by investment banks and rebuilt commercial banks like J. P. Morgan. The most internationally active American banks in the past,

Citicorp and Chase, both deeply weakened by their poor domestic performances over the past several years, have withdrawn from attempting major advances in the investment banking sector, though neither has indicated a permanent departure from the field. Either or both, may come back into the game in the future.

The large American investment banks have the least amount of adapting to do to fit the new firm prototype for a global wholesale banker of the future. They have the least distance to travel, and the greatest ability to adapt quickly, based on a lifetime of adapting to changing market and competitive conditions. Firms like Goldman Sachs, Merrill Lynch, and Morgan Stanley have sailed through the tumultuous eighties virtually unscathed, largely because management adapted to constantly changing circumstances and was successful in controlling the firms under difficult conditions. High profitability during this period has enabled the firms to attract excellent staff, to put them to good use, and to retain them. They were also able to attract all the capital they needed and to invest a lot of it in information technology and other programs that would enable them to lower costs and manage the risks of the business better in the future.

Other top firms like First Boston, Lehman Brothers, and Salomon Brothers all experienced troubles in the 1989–1995 period, which resulted in substantial losses, a complete replacement of top management, and a large number of defections from key employees. Yet these firms all adapted to their changed circumstances quickly and bounced back from their ordeals, regained profitability, and began again to increase their market shares.

The group of firms best able to adapt to these conditions are the ones that specialize in adapting, firms that have already tuned their organizations to globally competitive conditions. In that sense, despite the tough times many U.S. banks and some investment banks have been through during the last several years, American financial preeminence in wholesale banking services is likely to continue. The firms are stronger for having survived their difficulties, and find great opportunity in the fact that the market for their services has spread widely in Europe and to some extent in Japan. All expectations are for the spreading to continue further. Meanwhile, banks from Europe and Japan will continue to suffer from problems in their own regions that may hamper their ability to adapt themselves to world competitive conditions, at least for a few years. These various factors point to increasing competitive strength among 10 or so American firms.

Losing National Identity

However, increasingly these firms are losing their American identity. J. P. Morgan now claims that about a third of its professional employees are non-Americans, including several of its top officers. CS First Boston is increasingly hard to label as American. Though its U.S. subsidiary, First Boston, is as American as Merrill Lynch, the rest of the bank is not, nor is its parent or many of its board members. Morgan Stanley and Goldman Sachs each now say that about a third of their firm's employees, capital, and profits are non-American. Merrill Lynch hires hundreds of foreign nationals around the world. These firms are far more international in their make-up, their offices and representations, their clients and revenues, and their outlook than many of the most "international" of banks in Europe or Japan, such as Deutsche Bank, BNP, or Industrial Bank of Japan.

American-style wholesale banking and ultimately, no doubt, technology-driven American-style retail banking will become the models for the rest of the world, as long as competitive conditions are maintained and free markets are allowed to send capital to where it is appreciated the most. Universal banks are solid but less competitive. If competitiveness over time is allowed to be the principal factor separating those who are successful from those who are less so, the American-style bankers should predominate and become the champions. But if so, it is unlikely that they will be Americans anymore. The firms will be groups of ten thousand or fewer employees, made up of professionals, managers, officers, and management committee members from all over the world.

Summary

The coming years will represent great challenges to most of the world's large financial service organizations. These firms will have to rethink their basic business strategies and attempt to reposition themselves so as to maximize their comparative advantages and minimize their weaknesses. Strategic repositioning, however, can be very difficult to execute, because the magnitude of internal change is so great. However, the key to succeeding in the new world financial order is adaptability.

Notes

This chapter is adapted from Roy C. Smith, *Comeback: The Restoration of American Banking Power in the New World Economy.* Cambridge, Mass.: Harvard Business School Press, 1993.

1. Harvard Business School, "Bankers Trust New York Corporation," Case No. 0-286-005, Cambridge, Mass. 1985.

2. The sources used were Securities Data Corporation, Investment Dealers Digest, and Euromoney Bondware and Noteware.

Index